NETWORK + FUNDAMENTALS and CERTIFICATION

CISCO Learning Institute

Russell Hillpot and Michael Ivy

Taken from:
Network + Fundamentals and Certification
by Russell Hillpot and Michael Ivy

Taken from:

Network + Fundamentals and Certification
by Russell Hillpot and Michael Ivy
Copyright © 2005 by Cisco Learning Institute
Published by Prentice-Hall, A Pearson Education Company
Upper Saddle River, New Jersey 07458

This special edition published in cooperation with Pearson Custom Publishing.

Printed in the United States of America

10 9 8 7 6 5 4 3 2 1

ISBN 0-536-91854-6

2005200086

EM

Please visit our web site at *www.pearsoncustom.com*

PEARSON CUSTOM PUBLISHING
75 Arlington Street, Suite 300, Boston, MA 02116
A Pearson Education Company

In our lives many people shape our character and help us become better individuals, both personally and professionally. I give great credit and respect to my wife as my primary friend and mentor. My daily thoughts revolve around her. Of course, my daughter has been a treasure that I am highly grateful for. Watching her grow from an infant to a young lady has been wonderful. She has brought a lot of joy to my life. Without a doubt my parents and other family members also have helped make me who I am. They continue to do so.

With all that said, I have been blessed with many friends along the way who have been the seasoning of my life. They have been a source of greater pleasure than I could ever explain, and I care deeply for them.

But there is one individual in particular that I would like to dedicate this book to: my high school printing instructor. He was one of those instructors that taught not only content, but also character. He stressed quality in everything that we did together. I often think of him when I am doing projects. He helped enforce a positive work ethic, and his mentorship has helped me be successful in many of my endeavors. He knows who he is and knows of my respect for him. To him I dedicate this book.

Russell Hillpot

Contents

CHAPTER 5. TOKEN RING, FDDI, AND OTHER LAN TECHNOLOGIES 84

CHAPTER 6. NETWORK DESIGN AND TROUBLESHOOTING SCENARIOS 96

PART IV: NETWORK OPERATING SYSTEMS

CHAPTER 16.   AN INTRODUCTION TO NETWORKING WITH WINDOWS   342

CHAPTER 17.   WINDOWS NT/2000 DOMAINS   360

Preface

Computer networks are everywhere. They span the globe, interconnecting with each other, weaving a web of communication that extends outward to the domain of satellites orbiting above the earth. They fail, they heal themselves, and they move staggering amounts of information between distant locations. They are in our schools, our businesses, and even our homes.

The purpose of this textbook is to prepare the reader to successfully prepare for the latest CompTIA Network+ Certification Exam. The attainment of Network+ certification requires that the person seeking certification possess a working knowledge of Network Media and Topologies, Protocols and Standards, Network Implementation, and Network Support. This book is suitable for readers and students in computer engineering technology, electrical engineering technology, networking technology, and telecommunications technology programs, as well as corporations and government agencies.

Concepts and techniques are presented through real-world examples (such as examining all the packets captured while loading a Web page or sending e-mail). Where appropriate, the Internet is used to explain a new network service or mechanism. This includes heavy use of various sites located on the World Wide Web. In Part III, we demonstrate the use of many of the networking concepts covered in Part II in several network client-server applications, Java applets, and CGI programming examples.

■ ORGANIZATION OF THE TEXT

This text is divided into four parts.

Part I: Network Hardware

The basics of computer networking are presented, with a quick overview of network protocols and history. Networking hardware, topology, and technology (particularly Ethernet) are covered in detail.

Part II: Network Protocols

Wide coverage is provided on many topics relevant to the typical hardware and software protocols employed in computer networks. These topics include the popular TCP/IP suite of protocols, the mechanics of switching and routing, network management and security, and the IEEE 802 standards.

Part III: Network Applications

The principles of operation behind many everyday networking applications are presented in this part, including e-mail, FTP, streaming audio and video, and the Internet browser.

Part IV: Network Operating Systems

This part covers the networking components of several network operating systems (particularly NT/2000 Server, NetWare, and Mac OS X). The operation of a network domain is examined, as are the details of file and printer sharing, dial-up networking, and setting up a network server.

The chapters in each part all have the same format. Each chapter begins with a list of the **Network+ objectives** that are covered in the chapter. Look for objective icons in the text to indicate where specific Network+ objectives are presented.

Also included at the beginning of each chapter are **performance objectives,** which indicate what new skills and knowledge will be learned in the course of completing the chapter. The instructor will usually administer the requirements of the performance objectives. The text section of each chapter, the heart of the chapter, presents all the information needed to perform the exercises and pass the review quiz. The next section of each chapter contains a **troubleshooting** area. Tips, techniques, and real-world problems and their solutions are presented. Last is the **self-test** section to help the student verify understanding of the material. The self-test is divided into two types of test questions: true/false and multiple choice. Answers to self-test questions are given at the end of the book.

Labs are provided for each chapter in the companion laboratory manual. These labs give the Network+ student an opportunity to practice the concepts taught in the chapter.

Industry tips are provided throughout the book. These tips are written by various network professionals and provide insight into how networks are connected and administered. Many different types of troubleshooting tips and helpful facts are also sprinkled throughout the text. Look for the following icons in the margin to find these hints for quick reference:

A rich set of appendices provides details on numerous network-related topics, including telecommunications technology, Web links, the Ethereal protocol analyzer, Windows NT/2000 fault tolerance, setting up a network repair shop, modems, and the process of becoming network certified.

■ SUPPLEMENTS

Network+ Fundamentals and Certification is supported by the following materials:

- ReviewMaster Tutorial on CD packaged with this text, provides review questions designed to prepare the reader for the Network+ examination.
- Another CD-ROM contains useful example programs and files designed to aid the student in developing and understanding the concepts presented in each part. View the README document (text, Microsoft Word, and HTML formats) to get a detailed description of the companion CD-ROM.
- The laboratory manual accompanying the text provides hands-on experiments for each chapter.
- An instructor's manual is available, which contains teaching suggestions, sample syllabi and tests, and other helpful items.

■ ACKNOWLEDGMENTS

We would like to thank our editor, Charles Stewart, and his assistant, Maria Rego, for their encouragement and assistance during the development of this project. Thanks also go to our production editor, Alex Wolf, our development editor, Susan Hobbs, and our copyeditor, Bret Workman.

Many individuals and companies have provided permission for their hardware and/or software products, and we appreciate their support:

- Sue Runfola, for screen shot(s) reprinted by permission from Apple Computer, Inc.
- Mariana Mihaylova of Ipswitch, Inc., for screen shots of WS_FTP.
- Christine Kizer of Quantum Corporation, for permission to use photographs of Quantum's Snap Server line of storage solutions, and for her donation of a 40 GB Snap Server 1100 for educational experimentation.
- Sue Goodwill of Novell, Inc.
- Victor Kunkel of TrueTime, Inc., for screen shots of WinSync.
- Corel Corporation for screen shots of HoTMetaL.

State of the Information Technology (IT) Field

Just about all organizations today rely on computers and information technology to streamline business processes and boost productivity and efficiency. Evolving technology further changes how companies do business. The widespread availability of the Internet provides the opportunity for a business to extend its reach around the globe, interacting with customers and suppliers that they were unable to reach before. This fundamental change in business practices has increased the need for skilled and certified IT workers across industries. This shift moves many IT workers out of traditional IT business settings and into many IT-reliant industries such as government, healthcare, insurance, and banking.

According to the U.S. Department of Labor's Bureau of Labor Statistics, in 2000 there were 2.1 million computer and data processing services jobs within organizations and an additional 164,000 self-employed workers. This huge growth in jobs over the last decade has made IT-related jobs one of the largest sectors in the economy. Even in more challenging economic times the job opportunities for skilled and certified IT professionals remain fairly strong.

As with any industry, the workforce is essential in moving business forward. Thanks to evolving technologies, businesses are constantly challenged to keep the IT skills of their workers current. It has been estimated that technologies change approximately every 2 years. With such a short product life cycle employees must strive to keep up with these changes to continually bring value to their employers.

■ CERTIFICATIONS

Many jobs in the IT industry require different levels of education. The level of education and type of training required vary from employer to employer, but the need for qualified workers with verifiable technology skills is a constant. As technology evolves and the number of devices and systems continues to grow, many employers look for employees who possess the skills necessary to implement the latest technology solutions in their companies. One dilemma faced by employers is that traditional degrees and diplomas alone do not identify the precise skills that an applicant possesses. As the IT industry has grown, it has increasingly relied on technical certifications to identify the skills of a particular job applicant. Technical certifications provide an excellent method for employers to ensure the quality and skill qualifications of their computer professionals and can offer job seekers a competitive edge. According to Thomas Regional Industrial Market Trends, one of the 15 trends that will transform the workplace over the next decade is a severe labor and skill shortage, specifically in technical fields, which are struggling to locate skilled and educated workers.

Certifications can be divided into two categories, vendor-neutral and vendor-specific. Vendor-neutral certifications are those that do not subscribe to the technology solutions of a specific vendor, but rather measure the skills and knowledge required in specific industry job roles. Vendor-neutral certifications include all of the Computing Technology Industry Association's (CompTIA) certifications, Project Management Institute's certifications, and Security Certified Program certifications.

Vendor-specific certifications validate the skills and knowledge necessary to be successful utilizing the technology solution of a specific vendor. Some examples of vendor-specific certifications include those offered by Microsoft, IBM, Novell, and Cisco.

In many careers, compensation is determined not only by experience and education, but also by the number and type of certifications earned. As employers grapple to fill open IT positions with qualified candidates, certifications provide a means for employers to validate the skill sets necessary to be successful within their organizations. According to the Department of Labor's Bureau of Labor Statistics, the computer and data processing industry has grown at a dramatic rate from 1990 to 2000 and is anticipated to grow an additional 86% in wages and salaries by the year 2010. Robert Half International reported that starting salaries for help-desk support staff in 2001 ranged from $30,500 to $56,000 and more senior technical support salaries ranged from $48,000 to $61,000 in the United States.

Certification credentials can benefit individuals with more than just a competitive edge over non-certified individuals applying for the IT positions. Some institutions of higher education grant college credit to students who have successfully passed certification exams. Certified individuals are able to move through their degree programs more quickly and they also save money that would have been spent on tuition and books. Many technology certifications give individuals the ability to advance more quickly within the U.S. military. Finally, several advanced certification programs require or accept many certifications as part of their exams. For example, Cisco and Microsoft accept some CompTIA certifications as electives for their certification programs.

■ CAREER PLANNING

Finding a career that fits your personality, skill set, and lifestyle is challenging, fulfilling, and often difficult. What are the steps you should take to find that dream career? First, you wouldn't be reading this unless you had already expressed an interest in IT. The world of work within the IT industry is vast. Are you a person who likes to work alone or do you need to have people around you? Do you like speaking directly with customers or prefer to stay behind the scenes? Does your lifestyle embrace a lot of travel or do you prefer to stay in one location? All of these factors influence an individual's decision when faced with choosing the right job. A first step to learning more about yourself, your interests, work values, and abilities can be obtained by inventory assessments. There are a variety of Web sites that offer assistance with career planning and offer assessments.

The Computing Technology Industry Association (CompTIA) hosts an informational Web site outlining careers in the IT industry called the TechCareer Compass™ (TCC). The TCC is located at http://tcc.comptia.org. This Web site was created by the industry and contains a wealth of information about IT industry jobs. Each job listing includes a description, alternate job titles, critical work functions, activities and performance indicators, and skills and knowledge required by the job. In other words, it shows exactly what the job functions are so that you can find a job that best fits your interests and abilities. Additionally, the TCC maps the objectives of over 700 technical certifications to the skills required by each specific job, allowing individuals to research their job interest, then plan their certification training. Within this Web site is a regularly updated resource section with articles and links to many other career Web sites, which gives an individual a one-stop location for all their IT career information.

In addition to CompTIA's TechCareer Compass, there are many other Web sites that cover components of IT careers and career planning. Many of these sites are listed on the TCC Web site in the Resources section under Career Links. Some of these include YourIT-Future.com, ITCompass.net, and About.com.

As you begin your studies in this text, keep in mind the various resources that are available to you to help plan your career. Your instructor may be able to provide guidance and advice about careers in your local area. Arrange visits with companies. Periodically revisit those that interest you to learn more about potential careers. If possible, arrange an internship to acquire practical skills and experience. Finally, periodically revisit the

TechCareer Compass site to verify that you are on course and moving toward the goals you have set for yourself.

Good luck in this course and in your career.

■ REFERENCES

Bureau of Labor Statistics, U.S. Department of Labor, Career Guide to Industries, 2002–03 Edition, Computer and Data Processing Services, at http://www.bls.gov/oco/cg/cgs033.htm (visited August 14, 2003).

Bureau of Labor Statistics, U.S. Department of Labor, Occupational Outlook Handbook, 2002–03 Edition, Computer Support Specialists and System Administrators, at http://www.bls.gov/oco/home.htm (visited August 14, 2003).

Thomas Regional Industrial Market Trends, July 8, 2003 Newsletter, *15 Trends That Will Transform the Workforce*, at http://www.thomasregional.com/newsarchive2.html?us= 3f61ed4162269&to=5&from=0&id=1057266649 (visited September 10, 2003).

Network+
Fundamentals
and Certification

What Is a Computer Network?

PERFORMANCE OBJECTIVES

Upon completion of this chapter, you will be able to:

■ Sketch and discuss the different types of network topologies and their advantages and disadvantages.

■ Sketch and explain examples of digital data encoding.

■ Discuss the OSI reference model.

■ Explain the basic operation of Ethernet and token-ring networks.

NETWORK+ OBJECTIVES

This chapter provides information for the following Network+ objectives:

1.1 Recognize the following logical or physical network topologies given a schematic diagram or description:

■ Star/hierarchical

■ Bus

■ Mesh

■ Ring

■ Wireless

1.2 Specify the main features of 802.2 (LLC), 802.3 (Ethernet), 802.5 (token ring), 802.11b (wireless), and FDDI networking technologies, including

■ Speed

■ Access

■ Method

■ Topology

■ Media

2.2 Identify the seven layers of the OSI model and their functions.

3.1 Identify the basic capabilities (such as client support, interoperability, authentication, file and print services, application support, security, and so on) of the following server operating systems:

■ UNIX/Linux

■ NetWare

■ Windows

■ Macintosh

4.9 Given a network problem scenario, select an appropriate course of action based on a general troubleshooting strategy. This strategy includes the following steps:

1. Establish the symptoms.
2. Identify the affected area.
3. Establish what has changed.
4. Select the most probable cause.
5. Implement a solution.
6. Test the result.
7. Recognize the potential effects of the solution.
8. Document the solution.

■ INTRODUCTION

LANs
WANs

Internet

A computer network is a collection of computers and devices connected so that they can share information. Such networks are called local area networks or **LANs** (networks in office buildings or on college campuses) and wide area networks or **WANs** (networks for very large geographical areas). Computer networks are becoming increasingly popular. With the **Internet** spanning the globe, and the advent of the *information superhighway* (also called the National Information Infrastructure), the exchange of information among computer users is increasing every day. In this chapter we will examine the basic operation of a computer network, how it is connected, how it transmits information, and what is required to connect a computer to a network. This chapter lays the foundation for the remaining chapters in the book.

■ IEEE 802 STANDARDS

Objective 1-3

The Institute of Electrical and Electronic Engineers (IEEE) has, over the years, established several committees dedicated to defining standards for computer networking. These standards are listed in Table 1–1. Any company entering the networking marketplace must manufacture networking hardware that complies with the published standards. For example, a new Ethernet network interface card (NIC) must operate according to the standards presented in IEEE 802.2 and IEEE 802.3. You will encounter the IEEE standards many times in the remaining chapters.

TABLE 1–1
IEEE 802 Standard.

Standard	Purpose
802.1	Internetworking
802.2	Logical Link Control
802.3	Ethernet LAN (CSMA/CD)
802.4	Token-Bus LAN
802.5	Token-Ring LAN
802.6	Metropolitan Area Network (MAN)
802.7	Broadband Technical Advisory Group
802.8	Fiber-Optic Technical Advisory Group
802.9	Integrated Voice/Data Network
802.10	Network Security
802.11	Wireless Networks
802.12	Demand Priority Access LAN (100 VG-AnyLAN)

■ COMPUTER NETWORK TOPOLOGY

Hosts

Mesh

Objective 1-1

Topology has to do with the way components are connected. The topology of a computer network is the way the individual computers or devices (called **hosts** in a TCP/IP environment) are connected. Figure 1–1 shows some common topologies.

Figure 1–1(a) illustrates a **mesh** topology. A mesh topology is characterized by the fact that every host on a network is directly connected to every other host on the network, thereby creating no single point of failure. The primary advantage of a mesh topology is the fault tolerance gained from redundant links. Another advantage of a mesh topology is that data need only traverse a single link to get from any host to any other host on the network. The primary disadvantage of this topology is the expense involved in establishing all the

FIGURE 1–1
Topologies in a five-node
network.

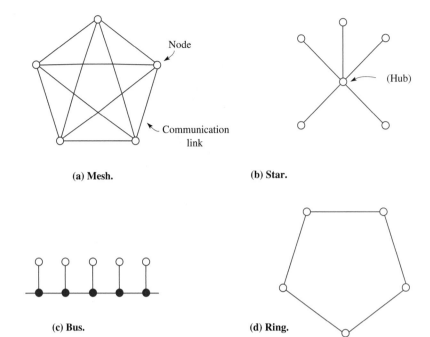

Node

(Hub)

Communication
link

(a) Mesh.

(b) Star.

(c) Bus.

(d) Ring.

links between hosts. The five-host network pictured in Figure 1–1(a) requires 10 links. A 20-host network would require 190 links. The large volume of links makes this type of topology very expensive. The formula used for determining the amount of links required is $n(n-1)/2$ where n is the number of hosts on the network. A mesh topology is normally used only when fault tolerance is a critical design factor of a network.

Star

Figure 1–1(b) shows a *star* topology. A star topology is characterized by the fact that all connections to hosts radiate outward from a central connection device such as a hub or switch (giving it the appearance of a star). Centralized connection points make the star the favored topology of network administrators. When one host on a star topology fails, no other hosts on the network are affected. Centralized connection points also make network monitoring and management easy. A star network is also very cost efficient since a network administrator only needs to install cabling for current needs. This provides a great deal of scalability for modern networks that need to adjust to dynamic business environments. Depending on the availability of an open port on the central connection device (a hub or switch), adding an additional host to the network may be as easy as installing a new cable between the central connection device and the new host. The primary disadvantage of a star topology is the single point of failure that could render the network unusable. This type of topology is also referred to as a hub and spoke topology, mirroring the concept that the spokes (links) radiate out from a central connection point (a hub or switch).

Bus topology
Ethernet

The **bus topology** is shown in Figure 1–1(c). All hosts in the bus topology are connected to a single physical link. One popular bus network is **Ethernet**, which will be covered more completely in Chapter 4. The physical link in an Ethernet network is normally a coaxial cable connected to each host through a T-connector. The bus topology is inexpensive to build, and it is easy to add a new host to the network just by tapping into the physical link. When using coaxial cabling it is essential that all cable ends be terminated. Cable ends that are not terminated allow electronic signals to "bounce back" into the data stream. Effectively a terminator (a network interface card or a special termination device designed for this purpose) acts like an electronic sponge absorbing all stray communication signals. This is necessary because there can be only one communication signal on the cable at any given time. Stray signals that are allowed to remain on the cable would prevent hosts from transmitting any further data onto the cable. This issue makes troubleshooting a bus topology very difficult and is the major disadvantage of a bus topology. Another disadvantage of a bus topology is its limited capability to scale to changing network requirements. If you

Ring topology

physically change the makeup of your network, you may also have to change the physical link (bus) that is used for the network. This type of topology is normally used in 10BASE2 and 10BASE5 Ethernet networks.

The last topology is the ***ring topology***, shown in Figure 1–1(d). In this type of topology there is no single cable or central connection point that is common to every host on the network. When one host wants to transmit data to another, the data is passed on to the adjacent host for use by the adjacent host, or for retransmission by multiple hosts until the data finally arrives at the intended destination. Each host has equal access to the transmission media (cable). Depending on how the network is implemented, multiple hosts may be permitted to transmit data at the same time. This is a major advantage to a ring topology. Another benefit of this topology is the lower signal generation between hosts that are not physically close to each other. In a bus topology a signal that travels from a host on one end of the network to a host on the other end of the network would degrade as it traveled across a long stretch of cable. In a ring topology, the signal is regenerated as it is retransmitted by each host. A primary disadvantage of this topology is the fact that if one host on the network fails, the entire network may fail (a break in the ring). Similarly, installing a new host into the ring means that there will be a period of time that the network will be disabled due to a break in the ring.

■ WIRED NETWORKS VERSUS WIRELESS NETWORKS

Wireless networking

Objective 1-1

Pulling copper wire, or even fiber, throughout a building may be unsafe or prohibitively expensive. One solution involves the use of ***wireless networking*** equipment. In this topology, a base station connected to the network broadcasts data into the air in the form of a high-frequency RF signal (or through a line-of-sight infrared laser). Remote, or mobile, stations must stay within the range of the base station for reliable communication but are allowed to move about. Figure 1–2 shows several wireless clients communicating with a base station. Using wireless technologies is a good alternative to installing cable in hard-to-reach areas as well as in buildings that have restrictions to installing wire, such as in historical buildings. Wireless technologies are also gaining popularity in businesses that have workers that need to use their laptop computers while moving around the workplace. Examples of this include managers that need to use their computers during staff meetings, employees that need to conduct inventories, and so on. Wireless Ethernet is examined in more detail in Chapter 4.

FIGURE 1–2
Example of a wireless network.

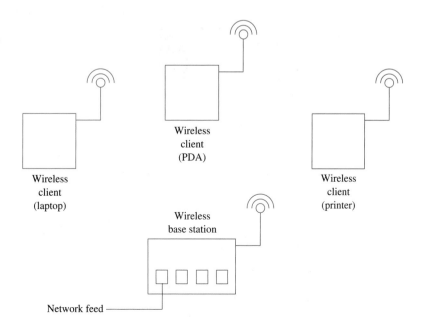

■ REPRESENTING DIGITAL DATA

Encoding

Computers represent data in the form of zeros and ones, which originates from the concept that an electrical current exists (a one) or doesn't exist (a zero). When a computer transmits information on a network it must represent the zeros and ones in a manner compatible with the network equipment in use. If data is transmitted over fiber-optic cable, typically the presence of light indicates a 1 and the absence of light represents a 0. When transmitting data over copper media, information can be represented in a variety of methods using electronic signals. The process of representing data in a specific format for transmission is called ***encoding***. When a computer converts data into a form that can be transmitted over a specific media the computer is said to be encoding the data for transmission.

Electrical engineers have designed a variety of ways to use electronic signals to represent data. Electronic signals have properties that we collectively refer to as a wave form (sine wave). Data can be represented by manipulating the properties of the wave form. Analog signals commonly manipulate the amplitude of a wave form (modify the amount of deviation from the common null reference point of the carrier wave) to represent information. This is called amplitude modulation (AM). Analog information can also be represented by varying the frequency of the wave (total number of complete wave forms transmitted during a given time period). This is called frequency modulation (FM). Both of these types of modulation can be seen in Figure 1–3.

Computers use a form of communication referred to as digital (Figure 1–3). There are only two values of information that need to be represented: a 1 or a 0. Conceptually a 1 is normally represented by the presence of a signal and a 0 is represented by the absence of a signal (especially when using media such as fiber-optic cabling). In digital networks 1s and 0s are often represented by a shift from one phase of a wave form to another phase. In a process called Non-Return to Zero (NRZ), a 1 may be represented by a positive frequency value and a zero may be represented by a negative frequency value. Another popular

Manchester encoding

method of representing data is called ***Manchester encoding***. In Manchester encoding the computer uses a shift from one phase of the wave form to another phase to represent a 1 or a 0. An example would be a signal that shifts from the top of a wave form to the bottom of the wave form, representing a 1, and shifts from the bottom of a wave form to the top of a wave form, representing a 0. There are many varieties of the Manchester encoding process. Manchester encoding is the encoding method used by modern Ethernet networks.

FIGURE 1–3
Methods of representing digital data.

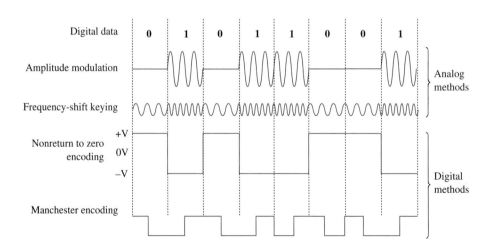

■ WORKING WITH DIGITAL DATA

Some uses for digital data transmitted over a network include:

• Sharing files
• Printing to a network printer

- Loading a Web page
- Sending e-mail
- Listening to music (via streaming audio)
- Watching an MP3-encoded MPEG video
- Studying an e-learning course
- Making a phone call
- Chatting
- Making a purchase
- Searching the World Wide Web
- Playing a network game
- Studying an electronic course

Many of these applications require large amounts of data to be exchanged. Some even require a secure connection. So, in addition to representing the digital data electronically (or physically), you also must represent it logically. Video files, for example, are compressed to reduce their storage requirements and downloading time. The information exchanged during a credit card purchase is typically encrypted to provide a measure of security. Compression and encryption are handled by software and are also supported by the use of communication protocols. The following sections examine the need for these protocols.

■ THE OSI REFERENCE MODEL

Layer	Function
7	Application
6	Presentation
5	Session
4	Transport
3	Network
2	Data-Link
1	Physical

FIGURE I–4
OSI reference model.

Just throwing 1s and 0s onto a communication link is not enough to establish coherent communication between two hosts in a network. The computing industry uses various networking models to identify all the processes that must take place in order for effective networking communications to occur. The Open Systems Interconnection (OSI) reference model (Figure 1–4) was created by the International Organization for Standardization and is the most common network model used by today's network professionals.

The OSI reference model divides the required network processes into seven different layers. The benefits of using a layered approach to network models include:

Reducing complexity

Standardizing the interfaces between the various processes

Ensuring interoperability between vendors

Facilitating modular engineering

Accelerating the evolution of the processes, technologies, and products at each layer

Simplifying teaching and the learning process

An additional benefit of using the OSI model is that it makes an excellent tool for troubleshooting network problems. After you become comfortable with this model, you will find it much easier to mentally isolate the processes taking place on the network, thereby making it easier to isolate the cause of a malfunctioning network.

The OSI model consists of seven layers including Application (layer 7), Presentation (layer 6), Session (layer 5), Transport (layer 4), Network (layer 3), Data-Link (layer 2), and Physical (layer 1). Two mnemonic phrases that are commonly used to remember the different layers are "Please Do Not Throw Sausage Pizza Away" (in the order of layers 1 to 7) and "All People Seem To Need Data Processing" (in the order of layers 7 to 1). The Data-Link layer (layer 2) is actually subdivided into two distinct sublayers consisting of the Logical Link Control (LLC) and the Media Access Control (MAC).

During the discussion of the OSI model this book will list common networking protocols that operate at the various layers of the OSI model. Most of the protocols listed are actually components of other common networking protocol suites such as the TCP/IP suite.

An example of this is the fact that HTTP works at layer 7 (the Application layer) of the OSI model, but is actually a protocol defined in the TCP/IP suite of protocols. It is important to understand that the OSI model is a common networking model that can be used to organize and group network functions even when a single network uses multiple protocol suites (such as the TCP/IP and IPX/SPX suites). Chapter 8 will compare the various layers and protocols of the TCP/IP suite and demonstrate how that protocol suite correlates to the OSI model.

The Application Layer

The Application layer (layer 7) provides network services to application processes such as e-mail, terminal emulation software, file transfer processes, and so on. The Application layer interacts and supports the network needs of various software applications. Note that this layer supports non-network–related applications such as word processing, but those types of applications do not natively work at any of the OSI layers; that is, Microsoft Word is not a network process or protocol. For example, you do not need to be on a network to use Word, but if you want to support Word's need for network services (such as when you click on a hyperlink in a Word document) the support for that network service (HTTP in this case) would start at the Application layer.

Many network protocols and services do work at the Application layer including HTTP, HTTPS, FTP, Telnet, POP3, DNS, SMTP, DHCP, and TFTP (more on these protocols in Chapter 2). Depending on the protocol being used or the software application that is being supported, the Application layer is one of three layers that can provide for error correction (resend data that was corrupted or lost during the communication process).

Redirectors also work at this layer. A redirector is a process that intercepts requests for services on remote computers and tries to provide those services. It is a common practice for system administrators to provide some file storage space to employees on the organization file servers. There are multiple organizational benefits to doing this. A system administrator

Share

will create what is called a *share,* which is simply a folder on a file server's hard drive that a particular user can use to store files. Typically the system administrator will go to the employee's computer and map a lettered drive (create a logical link) to the share created on the file server. Basically the system administrator is tricking the user's computer into thinking that it has another hard drive when the particular mapped drive is actually a share on another computer (file server). Suppose that a system administrator mapped the local "S" drive to the remote share. When a user tries to access their local S drive, the redirector will intercept the request for access to the S drive and initiate communications across the network to access the share that contains the user's files. This is just one example of using a redirector.

The Presentation Layer

The Presentation layer (layer 6) deals with how data is represented from one host to another. Processes that take place at this layer include encryption, compression, and file format issues. Note that all of these processes deal with the issue of ***data representation*** (how

Data representation

one network host presents data to another host). When humans communicate with each other, both individuals must use a common language. For example, if a grandparent writes a letter in cursive writing to a grandson who is in the second grade (and hasn't yet learned cursive writing), the grandson will not be able to understand the letter; thus, effective communications do not take place. The same is true for computers. Both hosts must represent the data in a common format for effective communications to take place. Note that this is the only layer that can change the format of the actual data.

In addition to knowing that data encryption and compression take place at this layer, it is important to be familiar with common file formats used in computer communications (again, data representation or format). Some common formats include:

ASCII (American Standard Code for Information Interchange): The predominant character set encoding for present-day computers

EBCDIC (Extended Binary Coded Decimal Interchange Code): A binary code for alphabetic and numeric characters developed by IBM for use on mainframe systems

PICT: Used by Macintosh operating systems for QuickDraw graphics

TIFF (Tagged Image File Format): High-resolution bit-mapped images

JPEG (Joint Photographic Experts Group): Compressed still images

MIDI (Musical Instrument Digital Interface): A standard for digitized music

MPEG (Motion Picture Experts Group): A standard for compression and encoding of motion video for digital storage

Although you may be confused by the fact that many non-network software applications perform the conversion between data formats, a network model still needs to address the fact that data must be understandable by both communication partners (hosts). The network model is not concerned with which software/process formats the data, it is only concerned that the correct formatting is done.

As you progress in the networking career field, you will discover that there are encryption processes that function at other layers of the OSI model. For purposes of a generic discussion of the OSI model, encryption is associated with the Presentation layer.

The Session Layer

The Session layer (layer 5) "*establishes, manages, and terminates sessions between applications*." (Note that this is a process between applications that runs on different hosts and is not the actual management of the flow of electrons between hosts. That happens at other layers.) An example of this is a spreadsheet program on a client host querying a database server for information. This layer controls the dialog between the applications. It establishes the specific communications process between the applications, it manages the communications process, and then it terminates the specific communication session between those two applications. This is somewhat similar to a project manager for a conversation between two applications. The project manager defines what needs to take place for two applications to exchange information. The project manager keeps track of what information has been sent and determines whether both applications can talk, and at the same time or not (simplex, half-duplex, or full-duplex conversation). Finally, the project manager terminates the session when all the information has been exchanged. Do not confuse this activity with the actual shipment of the information (the groups of zeros and ones traveling across the physical media). This is just the control of the actual information exchange between the two applications. Every conversation between applications is treated as a separate session (even if multiple applications on one host are exchanging information with multiple applications on another host). An example of a session would be when you want to check your e-mail service for new messages. You open your e-mail application and instruct it to check for new mail. If there is new mail your application works with the e-mail server application to successfully retrieve the new e-mail. This is an example of two applications communicating with each other. Your e-mail application establishes a session with the e-mail server application, the information is exchanged (your new e-mail is retrieved), and your e-mail application disconnects from the e-mail server (session termination). Common protocols that function at the Session layer include:

NFS (Network File System)

SQL (Structured Query Language)

RPC (Remote Procedure Call)

ASP (AppleTalk Session Protocol)

DNA SCP (Digital Network Architecture Session Control Protocol)

X Window System

The Transport Layer

The Transport layer (layer 4) is concerned with end-to-end connections (virtual circuits) between hosts. Depending on the protocol in use, other activities that occur at this layer include data segmentation, sequencing, flow control, and ensuring reliability of data transfer. When you want to send a file over a network it is rare that the file is small enough to be sent as a single data packet. Usually data files are broken into manageable sizes called **segments**. The Transport layer breaks files into segments and numbers each segment so the file can be correctly reassembled at the receiving host (every segment placed in its proper order). Within the TCP/IP protocol suite there are two primary protocols that operate at this layer: Transmission Control Protocol (TCP) and User Datagram Protocol (UDP).

Segments

The TCP protocol is categorized as connection-oriented, meaning that it uses processes that establish, maintain, and terminate virtual circuits between hosts. Take note that these processes could easily be confused with the similar sounding processes at the Session layer. Again, the Session layer is concerned with establishing, managing, and terminating sessions between applications, not host-to-host (computer to computer) connectivity. An analogy to represent these concepts is a corporate executive that uses an office assistant to manage her communications. The office assistant manages the flow of communications between the executive and executives from other corporations. This would be an example of the activities that take place at the Session layer. When the office assistant starts to process the correspondence for mailing, that assistant may also use features of the mailing system to track the correspondence (i.e., give the letter a tracking number and ask for a receipt of delivery). These mailing and tracking processes are similar to what happens at the Transport layer, and more specifically using the TCP protocol. TCP is categorized as connection-oriented because it uses tracking processes (similar to those used by the office assistant) to number and verify receipt of each data packet that is sent. The tracking process is referred to as **windowing**. When a host A wants to establish a flow of data packets with host B, host A will send a request for communication to host B. The two hosts will carry on a dialog and agree on various items such as sequence numbers (tracking numbers) and the size of the window that will be used. The window size refers to how many data packets can be sent before the receiving host has to acknowledge receipt of those packets. If any packet gets lost along the way the sending host will have to resend that packet, as well as any packet that was transmitted after that packet. If the two hosts are communicating over a reliable network connection the window size will often be larger. This means that more packets can be sent before the receiving host has to acknowledge receipt of the packets, thereby reducing the overall overhead traffic on the network. If the network is not reliable, and a lot of packets get corrupted or lost, a large window size would cause too many packets to be re-sent every time one packet is lost (taking up limited network resources retransmitting all the good packets that were sent after the lost packet); therefore, a smaller window size would be used. This is the primary way that the Transport layer handles the flow control part of the services offered at this layer. The Transport layer is the second of three layers that can handle error correction (resend the packets that get lost or corrupted).

Windowing

TCP supports many of the upper layer protocols such as HTTP, HTTPS, FTP, TELNET, POP3, SMTP, and so on. UDP is the other primary TCP/IP protocol that operates at the Transport layer. UDP is categorized as a connectionless protocol because it does not employ the packet arrival verification procedures that TCP does. If the office assistant in the example above did not ask for a delivery receipt then you could say that the office assistant was mimicking the UDP process used on a network. TCP is similar to a return receipt process, and UDP is similar to dropping a letter in the post office and hoping the letter arrives. The latter is often called a "best effort" process. There are many situations in which it would be undesirable to have the additional verification overhead that TCP employs and the delivery of every packet is not critical. This is where UDP is used. If a packet is lost or corrupted during the communication process, an upper layer protocol may still handle the request for retransmission. UDP supports many of the upper layer protocols such as TFTP and DNS name resolution requests. (More on this later in the book.)

Multiplex

Port number

Another concept to understand at the Transport layer is the fact that this layer can *multiplex* (combine) many Session layer conversations into a single data stream. For example, a computer user can check e-mail while downloading a file from an organization's server. The e-mail server and file server can be the same computer. The user can start a file download using an FTP application (this is one layer 4 session taking place) and then check their e-mail using their e-mail application (this is another layer 4 session taking place). The Transport layer would mix the packets of both sessions into one single data stream and keep track of which packets belong to which services (file download or e-mail services) based on a *port number* assigned to each service. The port number is a Transport layer addressing scheme used to identify different services that are functioning on a host. (More on this in Chapter 8.)

The Network Layer

The Network layer (layer 3) is concerned with logical addressing of hosts as well as routing packets between networks. The logical address of a host is based on which network the host is a member of and is changeable by the network administrator. Routers are the network devices that work at this layer. Each interface has a different network assigned to it. When a host wants to send data to a host that is on a different network, the host sends the data to the router to be routed out the appropriate interface. The two most common logical addressing protocols that operate at this layer are the Internet Protocol (IP) and the Internetwork Packet Exchange (IPX) protocols. These are also classified as connectionless protocols. These protocols have their own addressing schemes and they are not interchangeable. The most common of the layer 3 addressing schemes is IP version 4. IP is the protocol used for routing packets through the Internet. (More on this in Chapter 8.)

Some other common protocols also work at this layer. They include Address Resolution Protocol (ARP) and Internet Control Message Protocol. These will be discussed in Chapter 8.

The Data-Link Layer

The Data-Link layer (layer 2) is concerned with issues such as physical addressing of NICs, media access techniques, framing packets received from the Network layer protocols, error checking, and error correction (depending on the technology in use). Note that this is one of the three layers that can perform error recovery (resend data that is corrupted or lost in transit), depending on the technology used. As noted before, the Data-Link layer is divided into two sublayers called the LLC and the MAC.

Frames

The LLC sublayer provides the logical link between upper layer media-independent protocols and the technologies used on a local network. Network layer protocols do not care about what technologies are in use on the local network. For example, IP will work on Ethernet networks as well as token-ring networks. The LLC sublayer encapsulates the various upper layer protocols into *frames* for transmission onto the local network media. When the LLC sublayer creates frames out of upper layer packets it includes addressing components known as Destination Service Access Points (DSAP) and Source Service Access Points (SSAP). These are layer 2 service designators that identify which Network layer protocol is being used by the encapsulated data.

Burned-in addresses

The MAC sublayer is concerned with physical addresses of the NIC and the processes used to gain access to the physical media. When you are using a shared physical media, such as Ethernet, two hosts cannot transmit frames on the same wire at the same time. If this happened the transmissions (electronic signals) from one host would be corrupted by the transmissions of the other host. Different network technologies use different media access methods, and the most common ones are discussed later in the book. The addresses used at this layer are normally preset on the NIC when it is manufactured. They are commonly called *burned-in addresses* because they are usually burned into the read-only memory (ROM) of the NIC by the manufacturer. Other common names for these addresses are MAC addresses, physical addresses, hardware addresses, and Ethernet addresses (on an Ethernet network). All of these names refer to the same thing. Common network devices that work at this layer of the OSI model include bridges and switches.

The Physical Layer

The Physical layer (layer 1) is concerned with various physical characteristics of the transmission process. Some of the issues addressed at this layer include length and thickness of the media, signal strength, the data rate, the encoding process, and the type of connector used. The primary responsibility of this layer is to transmit and receive bits onto and from the media.

Common network devices that work at this layer of the OSI model include repeaters and hubs.

Protocol Data Units

Protocol data unit

Data

Segment

Packet

Frame

One of the general concepts to grasp about the different layers is that each layer (except for the Application layer) receives data from the layer above it and acts upon that data as is appropriate to that layer. As each layer takes the appropriate action on data received from the layers above it, it creates an entity called a *protocol data unit* (PDU). (Refer to Figure 1–4.) Layers 5, 6, and 7 all deal with specific aspects of the actual data. The PDU generated by each of these layers is called *Data*. Layers 1 to 4 each add additional information to the data received from the layer above it. When layer 4 (the Transport layer) receives data from layer 5 (the Session layer), it segments and encapsulates (wraps) that data and adds various other pieces of control data (such as sequencing numbers, port numbers, etc.). The PDU generated by this layer is called a *Segment*. The Segment (which now contains the data from layer 5 as well as the added control information from layer 4) is passed down to layer 3 (the Network layer). Layer 3 treats everything contained in the Segment as data (the payload for that layer) and adds additional control data, including information such as logical source and destination addresses. The PDU generated after layer 3 encapsulates the layer 4 data with its additional control information and is called a *Packet*. The Packet now contains the layer 4 Segment as well as the layer 3 information. The Packet is then passed on to layer 2 (the Data-Link layer), and this layer encapsulates it with information appropriate to the needs of layer 2 (such as source and destination physical addresses). The PDU generated by layer 2 is called a *Frame.* The Frame is now passed on to layer 1, where it is placed onto the physical media in the form of Bits (the PDU at this layer).

A person new to networking can easily become confused by the use of terms such as data, packets, frames, segments, and so on. Many of these words have different meanings depending on how they are being used. It is common to use the term "packets" when referring to any group of bits that make up a complete logical transmission. Of course, a packet is also the PDU that specifically refers to the unit of information created at layer 3. The term "segment" likewise may refer to a specific portion of a network as well as to the PDU at layer 3. The term "data" is used in a wide variety of ways. What you will come to realize is that the networking profession has a lot of terms that were created and used by many different individuals and organizations, and those terms have many different common uses. When referring to the PDUs created by the various layers of the OSI model, you must know which one is which. There is no compromise on that fact. Other than that, become as knowledgeable as you can about the terms used by the industry, and use them as correctly as you can.

■ ETHERNET LANS

Objective 1-2

Baseband system
Broadband system

One of the most popular communication networks in use is Ethernet (IEEE 802.3). Ethernet was originally developed jointly by Digital Equipment Corporation, Intel, and Xerox (commonly referred to as DIX). Including that first version, four primary versions of this common protocol have been developed. Though Ethernet actually refers to the original version created by DIX, the term "Ethernet" has been retained as a common word to refer to all versions of this technology. Ethernet is referred to as a *baseband system*, which means that a single digital signal is transmitted. Contrast this with a *broadband system* (such as cable television), which uses multiple channels of data.

Ethernet transmits data at the rate of 10 million bits per second (which translates to 1.25 million bytes per second). This corresponds to a bit time of 100 nanoseconds. Manchester encoding is used for the digital data. New 100 Mbps and 1000 Mbps Ethernet is already being used. Note that Ethernet refers to the 10 Mbps implementations of this technology. You can recognize them by designations such as 10BASE2, 10BASE5, and 10BASE-T.

Transceivers
Tap

Earlier implementations of Ethernet used coaxial cable as the media type. The coaxial cable used a physical bus topology in which a single cable was run through the areas where hosts were located to access the network segment. *Transceivers* were used to connect the NIC to a length of cable that would connect to the main bus cable using a device called a *tap*. This type of physical network was used in 10BASE2 and 10BASE5 Ethernet networks. Though some of those coaxial based networks are still in existence, common implementations of Ethernet use a physical star topology and comply with the 10BASE-T standards.

Collision

Each Ethernet device has its own unique binary address. The Ethernet card in each device waits to see its own MAC address on the media before actually paying attention to the data being transmitted. Thus, when one host transmits data to another, every host listens to every transmission but only reacts to transmissions addressed to that specific host. Ethernet NICs contain special hardware that detects when two or more devices attempt to transmit data at the same time (called a *collision*). When a collision occurs, all devices that are transmitting stop, broadcast a short jamming signal (so all devices on the network segment have an opportunity to detect the collision), and wait a random period of time before transmitting the same data again. The random waiting period is designed to help reduce multiple collisions. This procedure represents a protocol called *Carrier Sense Multiple Access with Collision Detection* (*CSMA/CD*). Carrier Sense means that each device listens to the media to see if any other host is transmitting. This is much like an old Western movie where someone listened for vibrations on a railroad track to hear if a train was coming. If there are no other hosts transmitting, that host may transmit its message on the media. Multiple Access simply means that multiple devices share the same media segment. This is also referred to as a logical bus topology (versus a physical bus topology). Collision Detection is the process that the hosts use to detect the presence of two transmissions on the media at the same time and take the appropriate actions as outlined above.

Carrier Sense Multiple Access with Collision Detection

Frame

The format in which Ethernet transmits data onto the media is called a *frame* (layer 2 of the OSI model). Figure 1–5 details the individual components of the Ethernet II frame. The Ethernet II frame format is the most common version of Ethernet frame in use today.

To comply with networking requirements the data field should be a minimum of 46 bytes and a maximum of 1500 bytes. The frame should be a total minimum of 64 bytes and a maximum of 1518 bytes. The frame consists of the fields from the destination address to the frame check sequence. Those fields make up an Ethernet frame. The preamble and start-of-frame delimiter are used for Physical layer control issues and are not passed up to the Data-Link layer of the receiving host; therefore they are not part of the frame. When the preamble and start-of-frame delimiter are added to the frame, the entity is referred to as a packet. Again, do not confuse this packet with the PDU at layer 3 of the OSI model.

■ TOKEN-RING LANS

Token-ring

Token-ring networks (IEEE 802.5) are not as popular as Ethernet but have their own advantages. The high collision rate of an Ethernet system is eliminated in a token-ring network.

FIGURE 1–5
Ethernet frame format.

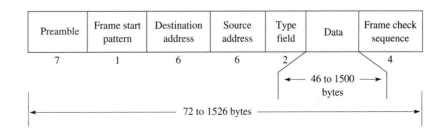

The basic operation of a token-ring network involves the use of a special token (just another binary pattern) that circulates between hosts in the ring. Even when no data is being transmitted between hosts, the token is still circulated. When a host receives the token, it simply transmits it to the next host if there is nothing else to transmit. If a host has its own frame of data to transmit, it holds on to the token and transmits the frame instead. Token-ring frames are similar to Ethernet frames in that both contain source and destination addresses. Each host that receives the frame checks the frame's destination address with its own address. If the addresses match, the host captures the frame data, changes one bit of the frame to indicate that it received the frame, and then retransmits the frame to the next host. If the addresses do not match, the frame is simply retransmitted.

When the host that originated the frame receives its own frame again, it verifies that the intended destination received the frame. If the frame was not received by the intended destination, the host retransmits the frame. If the frame was received by the intended destination, it places the token back onto the network so other hosts may transmit frames as needed.

Unfortunately, only one node's frame can circulate at any one time. Other nodes waiting to send their own frames must wait until they receive the token, which tends to reduce the amount of data that can be transmitted over a period of time. However, this is a small price to pay for the elimination of collisions. Token-ring is sometimes used in production environments because of other features, such as its ability to set priorities so that hosts with higher priorities can gain control of the token over hosts with lower priorities. For example, if you have a machine receiving computerized instructions on how to cut expensive parts, that machine should have priority over a machine cutting a less expensive **Talking stick** part. The concept of a token-ring network comes from cultures that used a ***talking stick*** to determine who was allowed to talk. The community elders would pass around a token. The individual that had possession of the token was allowed to talk and all others would be silent. This is also similar to parliamentary procedures where you may address the group if you "have the floor."

Although you should understand the basic concepts just mentioned, there are implementations of token-ring networks that allow for early release of a token so that more than one station may transmit at the same time. This will still be controlled so that there will not be any collisions on a token-ring network.

■ NETWORK OPERATING SYSTEMS

Objective 3-1

In addition to the communication protocols that enable reliable communication across a LAN or WAN, a computer network also requires software to control the communication protocols used between the clients (such as PCs) and the servers. Desktop operating systems such as Windows, UNIX, Linux, and Mac OS all provide native support for the common client/server protocols. Servers are the computer devices that provide services to the desktop clients. The operating systems that run on servers are designed to be more efficient at supporting the services that they offer. These operating systems are called Network Operating Systems (NOS). They are specialized operating systems designed to support a large number of network clients and are rarely used to perform normal desktop functions. A short list of services typically provided by a network operating system is as follows:

- DHCP (assign IP address to client at boot time)
- E-mail
- Authentication (verify username and password)
- Web services
- FTP services (for transferring files)
- Telnet services (for remote connections)

More information on NOSs is provided later in this book.

■ TROUBLESHOOTING TECHNIQUES

Troubleshooting a network problem can take many forms. Before the network is even installed, decisions must be made that will affect the way it is maintained in the future. For example, Ethernet and token-ring networks use different data encoding schemes and connections, as well as different support software. Each has its own set of peculiar problems and solutions.

Objective 4-9

Troubleshooting a network may take you down a hardware path (e.g., bad crimps on the cable connectors causing intermittent errors), a software path (e.g., the machine does not have its network addresses set up correctly), or both. There even may be nothing wrong with the network if the failure comes from the application using the network. In the remaining chapters, many of these troubleshooting scenarios will be discussed.

For now, one important thing to remember about any troubleshooting scenario is that you must be organized. A systematic approach to determining the cause of a problem and its solution will yield better results than a haphazard, random approach. One approach to troubleshooting, which you will use in this textbook, consists of these eight steps:

1. Establish the symptoms.
2. Identify the affected area.
3. Establish what has changed.
4. Select the most probable cause.
5. Implement a solution.
6. Test the result.
7. Recognize the potential effects of the solution.
8. Document the solution.

For each step, it's necessary to develop a set of procedures to aid in the troubleshooting process. For example, how is the affected area identified, or how do you test the result? The answer may be different for each problem encountered. Experience will help answer these questions.

INDUSTRY TIP

Using the trial-and-error method of troubleshooting network problems needlessly consumes time and money. Experienced network professionals develop techniques for isolating problems. One of the most proven methods for troubleshooting network problems is to use the OSI model to mentally isolate the various tasks performed during network communications. Understanding the various functions that take place during network communications will make you a better network troubleshooter. There will be times when it is fairly obvious what a problem is and you can save time by going directly to where you think the problem is being caused and fixing the problem without going through a checklist. Much of the time you will not be so lucky and you will need to use proven techniques to solve a complex problem. Using the OSI model you would normally start at layer 1 (the physical layer) and go from there. Many network problems are caused by the physical portion of the network, so starting your troubleshooting at this layer may save you a lot of time and effort. A good network troubleshooter is invaluable to an employer. Using the OSI model as a trouble isolating tool is a great way to become an accomplished network troubleshooter.

Russ Hillpot, CCNP, CCDP, CCAI, Security+, Network+, HTI+, Instructor/Consultant.

■ SELF-TEST

1. The topology that doesn't have a central connection point or single cable common to every host on the network is _____.
   a. bus
   b. star
   c. ring
   d. mesh

2. What is the primary disadvantage of networks that utilize a star topology?
   a. Single point of failure
   b. Difficult to troubleshoot
   c. Token passing delays
   d. Most expensive topology to implement

3. Segments are the PDU of what OSI model layer?
   a. Physical
   b. Application
   c. Session
   d. Transport

4. Network layer PDUs are called _____.
   a. bits
   b. frames
   c. packets
   d. segments

5. How are addresses applied to Data-Link layer devices?
   a. Network neighborhood, properties, address
   b. Burned in
   c. Statically
   d. Logically

6. Which sublayer of the Data-Link layer is responsible for creating frames out of upper layer packets?
   a. MAC
   b. LEC
   c. LLC
   d. LMI

7. True or False: The network protocols IP and IPX have addressing schemes that are interchangeable.

8. Which Transport layer protocol depends on upper layer protocols for retransmission?
   a. TCP
   b. UDP
   c. IPX
   d. UPX

9. The TCP protocol uses processes that establish, maintain, and terminate _____ between hosts.
   a. virtual sessions
   b. virtual circuits
   c. virtual LANs
   d. data streams

10. What layer of the OSI model controls the dialog between applications?
    a. Network
    b. Transport
    c. Session
    d. Presentation

11. What two devices work at the Physical layer of the OSI model?
    a. Hubs
    b. Switches
    c. Routers
    d. Repeaters

12. What are the **three** layers of the OSI model that might provide error correction?
    a. Application
    b. Presentation
    c. Transport
    d. Data-Link

13. What is the process called whereby the local computer lists an available drive that does not exist locally but on a remote server?
    a. Spoofing
    b. Mapping a drive
    c. Data mining
    d. DNS

14. Which of the following acronyms refers to a network confined to an office building or school campus?
    a. LAN
    b. MAN
    c. WAN
    d. SAN

15. How many separate links are required for a full mesh topology among 9 hosts?
    a. 81
    b. 1
    c. 36
    d. 16

16. Arrange the layers of the OSI model in order from top to bottom.
    a. Presentation, Physical, Application, Data-Link, Transport, Session, Network
    b. Application, Presentation, Session, Transport, Network, Data-Link, Physical
    c. Application, Data-Link, Network, Transport, Session, Presentation, Physical
    d. Data-Link, Transport, Session, Network, Presentation, Physical, Application

17. Which of the following is not an Ethernet designation?
    a. 10BASE2
    b. 10BASE5
    c. 10BASE-T
    d. 10BASE-FX

18. Routers operate at the _____ layer of the OSI model.
    a. Physical
    b. Logical
    c. Data-Link
    d. Network

19. What type of addressing is used by the Network layer of the OSI model?
    a. MAC
    b. Logical
    c. Physical
    d. Port

20. Which OSI layer is responsible for data encryption and compression?
    a. Physical
    b. Session
    c. Application
    d. Presentation

21. Which layers of the OSI model deal with specific aspects of the actual data?
    a. Physical, Data Link, Network
    b. Network, Transport, Session
    c. Session, Presentation, Application
    d. Application, Data Link

22. A Transport layer protocol that is connection oriented is:
    a. UDP
    b. SAP
    c. TCP
    d. IPX

23. What is the formula for determining the number of links required to connect hosts in a mesh topology?
    a. $N(N-1)$
    b. $N(N)$
    c. $N+N/2$
    d. $N(N-1)/2$

24. Which of the following topologies provides a great deal of scalability?
    a. Ring
    b. Bus
    c. Star
    d. Mesh

25. What topology type is characterized as inexpensive to build?
    a. Ring
    b. Bus
    c. Star
    d. Mesh

Network Topology

PERFORMANCE OBJECTIVES

Upon completion of this chapter, you will be able to:

- Describe the difference between physical topology and logical topology.
- Sketch the physical topologies of bus, star, ring, and fully connected networks.
- Explain what is meant by network hierarchy.

 ## NETWORK+ OBJECTIVES

This chapter provides information for the following Network+ objectives:

1.1 Recognize the following logical or physical network topologies given a schematic diagram or description:

- Star/hierarchical
- Bus
- Mesh
- Ring
- Wireless

1.6 Identify the purpose, features, and functions of the following network components:

- Hubs
- Switches
- Bridges
- Routers
- Gateways
- CSU/DSU
- Network Interface Cards/ISDN adapters/system area network cards
- Wireless access points
- Modems

2.10 Identify the differences between public vs. private networks.

4.5 Given a wiring task, select the appropriate tool (such as wire crimper, media tester/certifier, punch-down tool, tone generator, optical tester, and so on).

4.10 Given a troubleshooting scenario involving a network with a particular physical topology (such as bus, star/hierarchical, mesh, ring, wireless) and including a network diagram, identify the network area affected and the cause of the problem.

4.12 Given a network troubleshooting scenario involving a wiring/infrastructure problem, identify the cause of the problem (such as bad media, interference, network hardware).

■ INTRODUCTION

Cloud

Topology concerns the structure of the connections between computers in a network. Figure 2–1 shows three computers (A, B, and C) and a network *cloud*, a graphic symbol used to describe a network without specifying the nature of the connections.

The network cloud may comprise only the network found in a small laboratory, or it may represent a wide area network (WAN) such as the Internet. Using a cloud to represent a specific portion of a network provides the ability to hide the specifics of those connections and still accept the fact that those connections exist. Normally our discussions allow us to treat a cloud as a layer 1 and layer 2 issue, permitting us to ignore more advanced concepts that exist within a cloud and concentrate on our immediate portion of the network. For example, if I were talking with you about how to configure a router to connect to a Frame Relay connection provided by the telecommunications carrier, I would not want to talk about how the carrier set up their entire system. We would just assume that it existed (and worked) and focus our attention on our router configuration.

This chapter starts with a discussion of the common topologies. The chapter then discusses the difference between physical and logical topologies. The chapter ends with an introduction to the public network.

FIGURE 2–1
Network cloud connecting three machines.

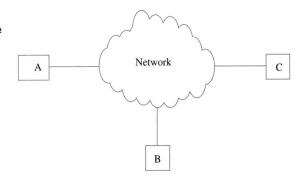

■ MESH TOPOLOGY

N	L
2	1
3	3
4	6
5	10
6	15
10	45
100	4950

TABLE 2–1
Number of links in a fully connected network.

Networks have many different types of topologies, or structures. Figure 2–2 shows the four basic types of network typologies.

The mesh topology in Figure 2–2(a) is the most expensive to build because each host has a link (communication channel) to every other host. Just adding one more host (for a total of six hosts) brings the number of links to 15. Seven fully connected hosts require 21 links. In general, the number of links (L) required in a fully connected network of N hosts is

$$L = (N(N - 1))/2$$

Refer to Figure 2–2(a). To calculate the links required for that network we will use the formula and use 5 (the number of hosts on the network) as the value of N. The formula would be $5(5 - 1)/2$. The result is 10 links needed for that network. Table 2–1 shows the number of links for several values of N.

It is easy to see that the number of links required in a mesh network quickly becomes unmanageable. Even so, mesh networks provide quick communication between hosts, because there is a one-link path between every two hosts in the network. Even if a link fails, the worst-case path only becomes two links long. So, mesh networks are very reliable and somewhat secure, since many links have to fail for two hosts to lose contact. Due to the expense involved, fully meshed topologies are rarely implemented; however, if your organization has a critical need for redundancy, and cost is not a primary factor, a mesh topology might be the answer to your needs. Another answer is a partially meshed network. You can

FIGURE 2–2
Network topologies.

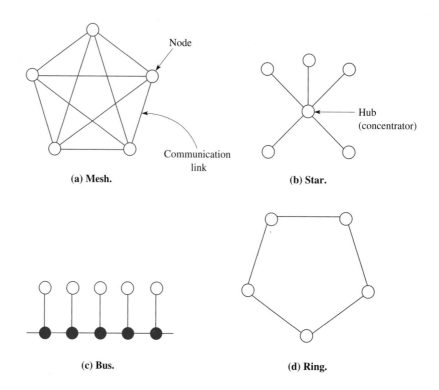

(a) Mesh.

(b) Star.

(c) Bus.

(d) Ring.

build several redundant links into your network design (thereby increasing network reliability) and still not incur the major expense of a fully meshed network. Many organizations build redundancy into their network design. The Internet is a good example of a large network that has many redundant links. Although each host on the Internet is not connected to every other host, many redundant links (a partial mesh topology) are used at critical points of the network.

■ STAR TOPOLOGY

Hub

Objective 1-1

Objective 1-6

Figure 2–2(b) shows a star topology. All hosts connect to a central **hub** (sometimes called a *concentrator*). For small networks, only a single hub is required. Four, eight, and even sixteen or more connections are available on a single hub. One advantage to a star topology is that if a host on the network fails, the hub will isolate it so that the other hosts are not affected. Star topologies also provide a lot of flexibility for network designers. A hub can be placed in a central location (such as a wiring closet) and cables can be run to locations where you want to place hosts. When you want to move the hosts to a new location, you only need to run a cable to the new location, which can be done without rebuilding the entire network. Star topologies are the most popular physical topology in use on modern networks.

■ BUS TOPOLOGY

Objective 1-1

Collision

A bus network uses a single common communication link that all hosts tap into. Figure 2–2(c) shows the bus topology connection; 10BASE2 and 10BASE5 Ethernet use coaxial cable as the common media for the bus topology. All hosts on the common bus compete with each other for access to the transmission media, broadcasting their data when they detect that the bus is idle (free of other transmissions). If two or more hosts transmit data at the same time, a *collision* occurs, requiring each host to stop and wait before retransmitting. As mentioned in Chapter 1 this technique of sharing a common bus is known as Carrier Sense Multiple Access with Collision Detection (CSMA/CD), and is the basis of the Ethernet communication system.

Objective 4-5

Segment

Objective 4-12

Time domain reflectometer

Wiring a bus network is not too difficult. Suitable lengths of coaxial cable, properly terminated with BNC connectors on each end, are daisy-chained via T-connectors into one long physical *segment* of hosts. Each T-connector plugs into a network interface card. The problem with the daisy-chain bus connection is that bad crimps on the BNC connectors, poor connections in the T-connectors, or just an improperly terminated cable (no 50-ohm terminating resistor) can cause intermittent or excessive collisions; these problems can be difficult to find as well. A special piece of equipment called a *time domain reflectometer* (TDR) can be used to send a pulse down the coaxial cable and determine where the fault is by displaying a response curve for the cable.

In terms of convenience, the bus network is relatively easy to set up, with no significant hardware costs (no hubs are required). With 185 meters of cable possible in a segment (for 10BASE2 Ethernet), a large number of hosts can be wired together. Individual segments can be connected together with *repeaters* (more on this in Chapter 3). The major drawbacks to this type of network are the many errors associated with improper wiring terminations and the lack of flexibility in physically locating the cabling where the hosts will be in a room or building. Using a bus topology, you will often have to change the physical bus cabling when you want to rearrange a room or building. Using a star topology provides a much greater degree of physical flexibility in physically locating the hosts in a building. Although the cabling used in a 10BASE2 or 10BASE5 network allows for greater segment lengths over the later Ethernet implementations of 10BASE-T, other networking techniques, such as using switches, have made the benefits of extended coaxial cable lengths virtually irrelevant. The physical bus topology is decreasing in popularity and has already been largely replaced by the star topology.

■ RING NETWORKS

Objective 1-1

The last major network topology is the ring. As Figure 2–2(d) shows, each host in a ring is connected to exactly two other hosts. Data circulates in the ring, traveling through many intermediate hosts if necessary to get to its destination. Similar to the star connection, the number of links in a ring is the same as the number of hosts. The difference is that there is no central hub connecting the hosts. Data sent between hosts will typically require paths of at least two links. If a link fails, the worst-case scenario requires a message to travel completely around the ring (in the opposite direction), through every link (except the one that failed). The increase in time required to relay messages around the bad link may be intolerable for some applications. The star network does not have this problem. If a link fails, only the host on that link is out of service.

MAUs or MSAUs

Token-ring networks, although logically viewed as rings, are connected using central multistation access units (***MAUs or MSAUs***). The MAU provides a physical star connection. Actual implementations of ring networks typically use a dual ring configuration, which provides redundancy and the ability to route traffic around bad physical segments. These are typically seen in fiber-distributed data interface networks (FDDI). FDDI will be covered in later in Chapter 5.

■ HYBRID NETWORKS

There are very few instances where one topology will solve all the needs of an organization. A hybrid network simply combines the components of two or more network topologies (or variations of a single topology) as needed to fulfill all the various design requirements of an organization. One of the most common hybrid topologies in use today is the extended star topology as shown in Figure 2–3.

Notice that one of the links of one of the stars extends out to become the core of another star. This is a common way to extend a network to connect different groups of users in different physical locations of an organization. Network designers also gain more control of the traffic flow depending on what network equipment they use as the center of the star (hubs, switches, routers, etc.).

FIGURE 2–3
Extended star.

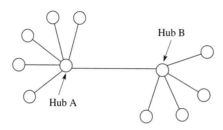

Another common hybrid network is illustrated in Figure 2–4.

It's common for organizations to have specific needs for the different technologies (such as Ethernet versus token ring) within their organization. A manufacturer may want to use a token ring technology (which uses the ring topology) on their shop floor, but Ethernet (which typically uses a bus star topology) in their office areas. These different technologies use different frame formats (layer 2, the Data-Link layer), and a device such as a translational bridge, switch, or router will be used to combine these different technologies on the same organizational network. (More on networking devices in Chapter 3.)

There isn't any secret to understanding what a hybrid network is. It is purely a matter of understanding that you can mix and match various forms of the standard topologies and that you need to use whatever network devices are appropriate to translate between the various technologies in use.

FIGURE 2–4
Hybrid network with different topologies.

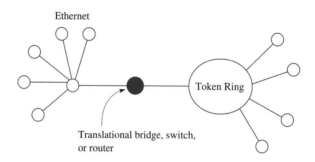

■ NETWORK HIERARCHY

Hierarchy

Objective 1-6

The machines networked together in Figure 2–3 are not organized into a *hierarchy* (a layered organization). Data transmitted by any machine is broadcast through both hubs. Everyone connected to the network sees the same data and competes with everyone else for bandwidth (access to transmit data onto the media).

If we were to replace both hubs with switches, which act much like hubs except that they forward data to other segments of the network only when needed, we could segment our network and isolate which network machines see what data. For example, any machine in group A can send data to any other machine in group A through the switch, without the data being broadcast onto the link going to the group B machines. The same is true for machines in group B. Their traffic is isolated from the traffic of the group A machines. If any machine wants to transmit data to a machine in the other group, the switches will forward

Keeping local traffic local

that data across the common link. This concept is known as *keeping local traffic local*. A common guideline is that 80 percent of your network traffic should be local traffic and only 20 percent of your traffic should travel across links between different network segments (also called the backbone). As you progress into more complex switched networks you will find that this ratio almost reverses itself; but for now you can see that keeping local traffic local has many benefits, especially with networks that have large amounts of hosts on them. (Switches will be covered later in the book.)

■ PHYSICAL TOPOLOGY VERSUS LOGICAL TOPOLOGY

Objective 1-1

Another important concept to understand is the difference between the physical and the logical topology of a network. The physical topology is how the network devices and cables are physically arranged. The devices may be arranged in a bus topology or in a star topology. The logical topology is determined by the way traffic behaves on the network given the technology in use (such as Ethernet versus token ring). Ethernet commonly uses a physical star topology, but since every station on a network (when a hub is used) sees all the traffic of every other device, it logically uses a bus topology (all hosts compete for access to the media like a bus topology).

Token-ring networks use an MAU as their central connection point. (Refer to Figure 2–5.) This device acts like a hub, and all hosts connect to the MAU via cables called lobe cables. Because all cables radiate from the central MAU, the physical topology is a star topology. Because token ring requires each packet to travel through all machines in the proper order, the MAU must route the packet out one port to a host, wait for the host to receive the packet and return it to the MAU, and then route the packet to the next host. The MAU keeps track of who is to receive the packet next and routes the packet to only one host at a time. This creates a logical ring topology even though the hosts are all connected to the MAU in a physical star topology.

FIGURE 2–5
Token-ring network.

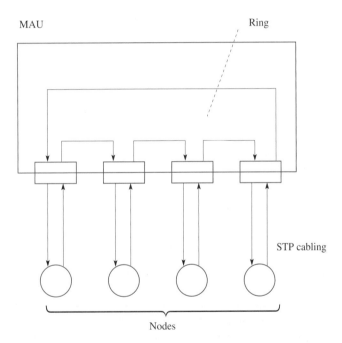

■ PUBLIC NETWORKS VERSUS PRIVATE NETWORKS

Objective 2-10

One common way that telecommunications networks are categorized is according to whether they are public or private networks. It is very common for organizations to have public and private portions of their networks. Many homes have private computer networks set up and also access the Internet via their Internet Service Provider (ISP). When the home network is not connected to the Internet, users are using their computers in a private network. When they connect to the ISP, the computer that connected to the ISP is now joined to a public network (with access to the Internet).

Public networks are characterized by direct access to the commercial telecommunications network. When you pick up your telephone and dial someone in another part of the city you are using a public telecommunications system. Because you are using a public network, you must follow the operating rules associated with that network. Your telephone has to meet certain frequency requirements. It also must conform to other requirements such as the power it consumes to operate the ringer, and the phone number it uses to be uniquely identified on the telephone network. If everyone on the public telephone network didn't follow these rules, the network would not function efficiently.

These same concepts apply to operations on the Internet. The Internet is a portion of the public telecommunications system that is dedicated to data traffic (the voice and data systems are rapidly merging their technologies, but that is beyond the scope of this book). When you are connected to the public Internet your computer is directly accessible to all those on the Internet. Just as you need a specific telephone number to be accessible on the public telephone network, so you need a specific Internet Protocol (IP) address for your computer to be accessible on the Internet. The computer network addressing system is controlled by the Internet Assigned Numbers Authority (IANA). The IANA assigns IP address blocks (groups of IP addresses) to the various ISPs. When you connect to your ISP you are assigned one of those IP addresses for your use while you are connected to the Internet. That IP address uniquely identifies your computer on the Internet, just as your telephone number uniquely identifies your individual telephone on the telephone network. If you are connected to the public Internet, you must have an IP address that was ultimately (directly or indirectly) assigned by the IANA.

Private networks provide a lot of flexibility and privacy that public networks do not. Many individuals and organizations have computers that they do not want to be directly accessible from the Internet. When a private network is used, you have more control over the IP addressing scheme used on your network. The IANA has set aside blocks of IP addresses that can be used on private networks. These private IP address blocks are not used on the Internet, so the same IP address block can be used by any private network since the computers on one private network will never directly communicate with computers on another private network.

Organizations often have private networks that need to connect to the public network. There are a few methods that these organizations can use to allow their private networked computers to access the public Internet. One method is to use a ***proxy server***.

Proxy server

When used as a gateway between the private and public networks, the proxy server will intercept requests from a computer on the private network for information from the public network and use its own public IP address to access the public information. The computer on the private network will contact the proxy server and ask for information that is available on a computer with a public IP address. On behalf of the private network computer, the proxy server will contact the publicly addressed computer (using a public IP address assigned to the proxy server) and retrieve the information requested by the private network computer. When the proxy server retrieves the requested information, it will relay the information back to the private network computer. In this situation the only computer that the public network knows about is the proxy server. The computer on the private portion of the network is never directly accessible to the public network.

Another method of indirectly joining private networks to public networks is Network Address Translation (NAT). This method uses a device, typically a router or firewall, to translate private addresses to public addresses at the boundary between the private and public portions of the network. NAT will be covered later in the book. It is important to remember that computers on a private network do not have direct access to the public network and are not seen by the public network. Computers that are directly connected to the public network must have an IP address that was ultimately (directly or indirectly via an ISP) assigned by the IANA.

■ TROUBLESHOOTING TECHNIQUES

Partition

It is a fact of life that we must worry about potential harm being done to our network by inside and outside parties. In terms of security and reliability, we must concern ourselves with what is required to *partition* our network, breaking it up into at least two pieces that may have restrictions on the communications allowed between each other. Figure 2–6 shows how bus, star, ring, and meshed networks are partitioned. Note that the star

FIGURE 2–6
Partitioning a network.

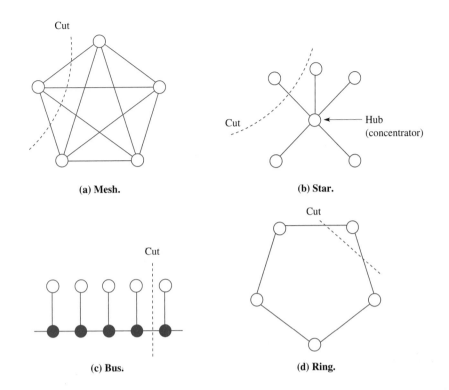

(a) Mesh.

(b) Star.

(c) Bus.

(d) Ring.

Objective 4-10

network is completely partitioned (all hosts isolated) if the central hub fails or is disconnected.

When troubleshooting a network, knowledge of its topology, both physical and logical, is essential to proper partitioning so that testing and repairing can proceed smoothly.

INDUSTRY TIP

Topologies originally designed for data transmission can also be used for a variety of other applications. One such application is home technology integration. As integrators design home automation systems they employ a variety of data topologies to control home devices. Phone line systems and power line carrier systems are used in conjuction with star topologies to control lights and security systems in homes. Ethernet is also used extensively in homes to connect residential networks as well as for control systems in home video and audio systems.

■ SELF-TEST

1. True or False: The network cloud symbol is only used to depict a WAN.
2. The network cloud symbol typically represents the _____ and _____ layers of the OSI model to the network professional. (Choose two.)
   a. Physical
   b. Data-Link
   c. Network
   d. Transport

3. What does the *N* represent in the formula for determining how many links are required for a mesh network topology?
   a. Number of links
   b. Number of hosts
   c. Network number
   d. Network topology

4. If redundancy is necessary and cost is not a primary factor, a _____ network topology could be implemented.
   a. bus
   b. star
   c. ring
   d. mesh

5. How many links are required to provide a star topology to 50 hosts?
   a. 50
   b. 500
   c. 1225
   d. 2500

6. Which device is used to describe the central component used in a star topology?
   a. Spoke
   b. Hub
   c. Transceiver
   d. Repeater

7. Where should a hub/concentrator be placed in a star topology?
   a. Network gateway
   b. Network layer
   c. Central location
   d. Network edge

8. The technique of sharing a common medium is known as CSMA/CD, which means _____.
   a. Carrier Sense Media Access with Collision Detection
   b. Carrier Sense Multiple Access with Collision Detection
   c. Carrier Sense Media Aware with Collision Detection
   d. Cable Star Media Access with Collision Detection

9. What is the longest possible single Ethernet segment length using coaxial cabling?
   a. 85 meters
   b. 100 meters
   c. 185 meters
   d. 500 meters

10. Suitable lengths of coaxial cable can be _____ together with T-connectors into one physical segment of hosts forming a bus network topology.
    a. concatenated
    b. looped
    c. daisy-chained
    d. meshed

11. True or False: 10BASE-T networks have the capacity to carry data over longer cable segments than 10BASE2 and 10BASE5 networks.

12. What is a special piece of equipment that can send a pulse down a cable and determine the location of a fault?
    a. Multimeter
    b. TDR
    c. Breakout box
    d. Loopback cable

13. What must be placed at the end of a bus topology cable run in order to properly terminate the run?
    a. T-connector
    b. 50-ohm resistor
    c. Ground wire
    d. Hardware loop

14. How many hosts are logically connected to each host in a ring topology?
    a. 1
    b. 2
    c. 4
    d. 6

15. The MAU acronym relates to the ring network term _____.
    a. Media Access Unit
    b. Multistation Access Unit
    c. Multiple Auxiliary Unit
    d. Multi Access Unit

16. What implementation of a ring network provides redundancy and the ability to route traffic around bad physical segments?
    a. Dual-ring
    b. Ability to reverse traffic ring pattern
    c. Extended ring
    d. Physical star

17. What is one of the most common hybrid topologies used today?
    a. Star/bus
    b. Star/ring
    c. Extended bus
    d. Extended star

18. What device could be used to combine different technologies in the same organizational network?
    a. Hub
    b. Repeater
    c. Translational bridge
    d. Protocol

19. Which of the following differentiates token-ring from Ethernet at layer 2?
    a. Media
    b. Frame format
    c. Logical address
    d. Encoding

20. Which of the following layer 1 devices will ensure that every machine connected to the network sees the same data and competes for bandwidth?
    a. Gateway
    b. Hub
    c. Bridge
    d. Switch

21. What is the term used to define traffic links between different network segments?
    a. Backbone
    b. Highway
    c. Cloud
    d. Bus

22. What does the term "hierarchy" mean in relation to networks?
    a. One device holds priority.
    b. A layered model

    c. Devices assigned hierarchical code

    d. Flat network configuration

23. According to a common guideline, how much of your network traffic should travel outside your local segment?

    a. 20%

    b. 50%

    c. 80%

    d. 90%

24. Which term is used to describe how devices are physically arranged?

    a. Physical hierarchy

    b. Physical topology

    c. Logical structure

    d. Logical topology

25. What type of logical topology is used in a token-passing network?

    a. Ring

    b. Star

    c. Extended star

    d. Bus

Networking Hardware

CHAPTER **3**

PERFORMANCE OBJECTIVES

Upon completion of this chapter, you will be able to:

■ List and describe the basic networking hardware components.

■ Explain the differences in 10BASE2 Ethernet and 10BASE-T Ethernet.

■ Compare the advantages of fiber over copper wire.

NETWORK+ OBJECTIVES

This chapter provides information for the following Network+ objectives:

1.2 Specify the main features of 802.2 (LLC), 802.3 (Ethernet), 802.5 (token ring), 802.11b (wireless), and FDDI networking technologies, including:
- ■ Speed
- ■ Access
- ■ Method
- ■ Topology
- ■ Media

1.3 Specify the characteristics (e.g., speed, length, topology, cable type, etc.) of the following:
- ■ 802.3 (Ethernet) standards
- ■ 10BASE-T
- ■ 100BASE-TX
- ■ 10BASE2
- ■ 10BASE5
- ■ 100BASE-FX
- ■ Gigabit Ethernet

1.4 Recognize the following media connectors and/or describe their uses:
- ■ RJ-11
- ■ RJ-45
- ■ AUI
- ■ BNC
- ■ ST
- ■ SC

1.5 Choose the appropriate media type and connectors to add a client to an existing network.

1.6 Identify the purpose, features, and functions of the following network components:
- ■ Hubs
- ■ Switches
- ■ Bridges
- ■ Routers
- ■ Gateways
- ■ CSU/DSU
- ■ Network Interface Cards/ISDN adapters/system area network cards

- ■ Wireless access points
- ■ Modems

2.1 Given an example, identify a MAC address.

2.2 Identify the seven layers of the OSI model and their functions.

2.3 Differentiate between the following network protocols in terms of routing, addressing schemes, interoperability, and naming conventions:
- ■ TCP/IP
- ■ IPX/SPX
- ■ NetBEUI
- ■ AppleTalk

2.4 Identify the OSI layers at which the following network components operate:
- ■ Hubs
- ■ Switches
- ■ Network Interface Cards
- ■ Bridges
- ■ Routers

4.1 Given a troubleshooting scenario, select the appropriate TCP/IP utility from among the following:
- ■ TRACERT
- ■ PING
- ■ ARP
- ■ NETSTAT
- ■ NBTSTAT
- ■ IPCONFIG/IFCONFIG
- ■ WINIPCFG
- ■ NSLOOKUP

4.5 Given a wiring task, select the appropriate tool (e.g., wire crimper, media tester/certifier, punch-down tool, tone generator, optical tester, etc.).

4.6 Given a network scenario, interpret visual indicators (e.g., link lights, collision lights, etc.) to determine the nature of the problem.

■ INTRODUCTION

This chapter examines many of the different hardware components involved in networking. You are encouraged to look at the network interface card inside your personal computer, around your lab to locate hubs and cables, and around your campus (especially the computer center) to see what other networking hardware you can find. If you are part of an organization that has a complex network established, you should be able to observe many different components used by your organization. In an office area you should be able to spot patch cables used to connect the PCs and printers to the network infrastructure. Depending on how your network is designed, you may be able to spot hubs or switches into which the PCs and printers are plugged. If your PCs and printers are plugged into a wall

Horizontal cables

Distribution facility

jack, there are cables (called ***horizontal cables***) that go from the wall jacks back to a patch panel located in another room of your building. In that room (commonly called a ***distribution facility***) there will be a variety of devices such as repeaters, hubs, bridges, switches, and routers, depending on the design of your network.

■ ETHERNET CABLING

Objective 1-3

This hardware presentation begins with Ethernet cabling. Ethernet cables come in three main varieties. These are:

Thinnet

RG-58 coaxial cable, used for 10BASE2 operation (also called ***thinnet***)

Thicknet

RG-11 coaxial cable, used for 10BASE5 operation (also called ***thicknet***)

Twisted pair (UTP - Unshielded Twisted Pair), used for 10BASE-T and 100BASE-T operation

There are other, specialized cables, including fiber (10BASE-FL), that are used as well. The 10 in 10BASE-T stands for 10 Mbps, the speed at which the bits travel, or the bit rate of the system. BASE stands for baseband, a signaling method that uses a single carrier for data. The T stands for twisted pair. In a similar fashion, 100BASE-TX stands for 100 Mbps baseband twisted pair.

RG-58 Cable

RG-58 cable is typically used for wiring laboratories and offices, or other small groups of computers. This cable is called ***thinnet*** because the outside diameter is only .35 cm. Figure 3–1 shows the construction of a coaxial cable.

Thinnet

FIGURE 3–1
Coaxial cable construction.

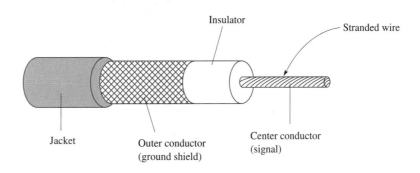

Objective 1-4

The maximum length of a thinnet Ethernet segment is 185 meters. This limitation is due to the nature of the Carrier Sense Multiple Access/Collision Detect (CSMA/CD) method of operation, the cable ***attenuation*** (loss or weakening of the signal strength over

Attenuation

distance), and the speed at which signals propagate inside the coax. The cable length is limited to guarantee that collisions are detected when machines that are far apart transmit at the same time. BNC connectors are used to terminate each end of the cable. Figure 3–2 shows several different cables and connectors, including BNC-T connectors (one containing a terminating resistor).

FIGURE 3–2
Ethernet cabling.

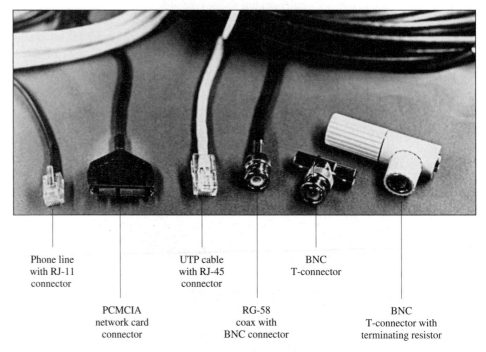

Phone line
with RJ-11
connector

PCMCIA
network card
connector

UTP cable
with RJ-45
connector

RG-58
coax with
BNC connector

BNC
T-connector

BNC
T-connector with
terminating resistor

(a) Assorted connectors and cables (photograph by John T. Butchko).

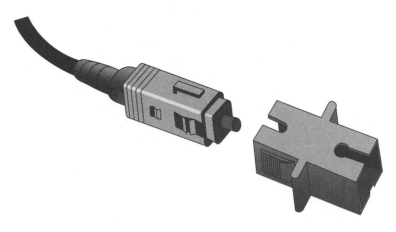

(b) Fiber-optic cable with ST connectors.

(c) Fiber-optic cable with SC connector and SC-to-SC optical coupler.

Objective 1-5

Figure 3–3 shows 10BASE2 Ethernet wiring. When many hosts are connected to the same Ethernet segment, a daisy-chain approach is used, as shown in Figure 3–3(a). The BNC T-connector allows the network interface card (NIC) to tap into the coaxial cable and the coax to pass through the machine to the next machine. The last machines on each end of the cable (or simply the cable ends themselves) must use a terminating resistor (50 ohms) to eliminate collision-causing reflections in the cable. This connection is illustrated in Figure 3–3(b).

FIGURE 3–3
10BASE2 Ethernet wiring.

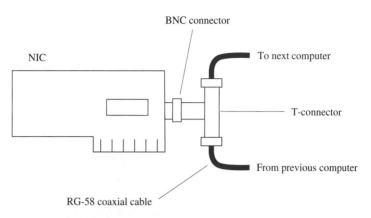

BNC connector

NIC

To next computer

T-connector

From previous computer

RG-58 coaxial cable

(a) Daisy-chain connection.

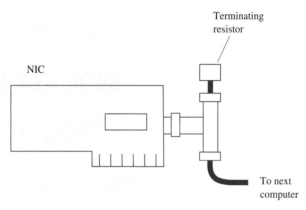

Terminating resistor

NIC

To next computer

(b) Terminating connection (required at each end of the cable).

RG-11 Cable

Backbone cable
Thicknet

RG-11 coaxial cable is used as a ***backbone cable***, distributing Ethernet signals throughout a building, an office complex, or other large installation. RG-11 is called ***thicknet*** because it is thicker (an outside diameter of approximately .5 inches) and sturdier than RG-58 coax. Thicknet Ethernet segments may be up to 500 meters long. RG-11 cable is typically orange, with black rings around the cable every 2.5 meters to allow taps into the cable. The taps, called *vampire taps,* are used by transceivers that transfer Ethernet data to and from the cable.

Unshielded Twisted Pair Cable

Modern networks rarely implement Ethernet networks using coaxial cable. Most modern networks use UTP cabling. UTP cable, used with hubs and other 10/100BASE-T equipment, uses twisted pairs of wires to reduce noise and crosstalk and allow higher-speed data rates. The twists cause the small magnetic fields generated by currents in the wires to cancel each other out, thereby reducing signal noise (crosstalk) on the wires. UTP cable length is limited to 100 meters and RJ-45 connectors are used for termination. The network diameter (the total allowable length of a network segment using a hub or repeater) for UTP-based 10BASE-T networks is 500 meters. To meet all of the standards set for 10BASE-T Ethernet networks there is a rule of thumb called the ***5-4-3 rule***. This rule states that for 10BASE-T networks you can only have a maximum of five segments (a maximum of 100 meters each), using four repeaters, with only three of the segments populated (populated means that hosts reside on those segments). Remember, the 5-4-3 rule only applies to 10BASE-T networks. For 100BASE-TX the diameter drops to 200 meters (or 205 meters using a special class of repeater). The structure of the 8-pin RJ-45 connector is shown in Figure 3–4. Its modular

5-4-3 rule

Objective 1-5

format is similar to the telephone companies' 6-pin RJ-11 connector. Figure 3–4(c) shows the crimping tool used to attach the RJ-45 connector to the end of a UTP cable.

FIGURE 3–4
RJ-45 (10BASE-T) connector.

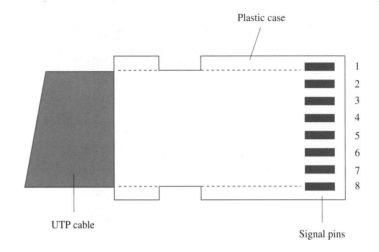

(a) Top view.

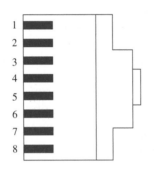

(b) Side view.

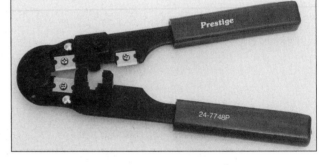

(c) RJ-45 cable crimper.

 Objective 4-5

Table 3–1 shows the wire color combinations used in UTP cabling. Note that only two pairs are required for 10BASE-T operation, one pair for transmit and the other for receive.

TABLE 3–1
RJ-45 pin assignments (568B standard).

Pin	Color	Function	Used for 10BASE-T
1	White/Orange	T2	✔
2	Orange/White	R2	✔
3	White/Green	T3	✔
4	Blue/White	R1	
5	White/Blue	T1	
6	Green/White	R3	✔
7	White/Brown	T4	
8	Brown/White	R4	

UTP cables are wired as straight-through or crossover cables. Figure 3–5 shows the wiring diagrams for each type of cable.

Straight-through cables typically connect the computer's network interface card to a port on the hub. Crossover cables are used for NIC-to-NIC communication and for hub-to-hub connections when no crossover port is available. To mount an RJ-45 connector

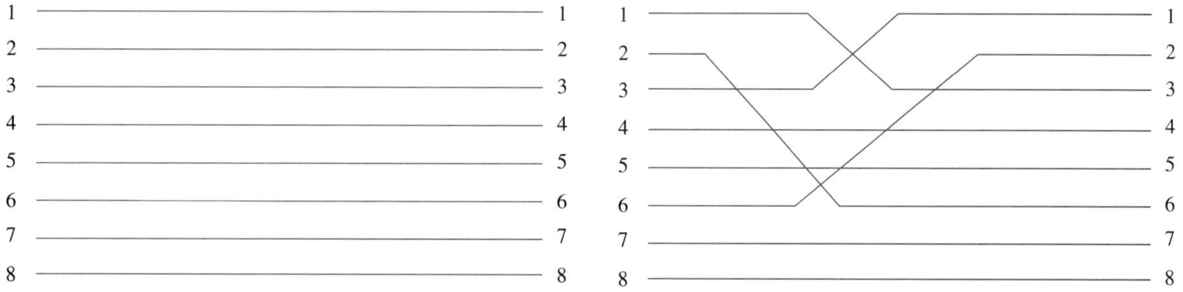

(a) Straight-through.

(b) Crossover.

FIGURE 3–5
RJ-45 cabling.

PC – Hub or Switch (handwritten)

on the end of a UTP cable, follow these steps:

1. Cut the tip off the end of a UTP cable.
2. One inch from the end, carefully cut into the cable jacket with wire strippers. Go fully around the cable. Do not cut too deep, or you might damage the internal wire pairs.
3. Remove the piece of cable jacket.
4. Untwist the four wire pairs and straighten out the wires as much as possible.
5. Hold the end of the cable side by side with an RJ-45 connector so that the end of the cable jacket has enough length to extend into the bottom of the connector approximately 5/16". After you insert the wires into the RJ-45 connector, it is important that the cable jacket extend into the connector approximately 5/16". This ensures that the cable jacket is crimped during the crimping process, allowing the jacket to provide strain relief for the internal wires. It is very common among novice installers to not crimp the cable jacket during the crimping process, which leaves all the strain of the wire on the individual twisted wires.
6. Trim off the excess length of the wires so that the ends align with the ends of the metal pins in the RJ-45 connector.
7. Arrange the wires according to the 568B standard color patterns shown in Table 3–1. Refer to Figure 3–5(b) for crossover cable wiring. Hold all the wires close together and parallel between your thumb and index finger.
8. Carefully slide the wires into the end of the RJ-45 connector. The wires should all slide into small plastic grooves in the connector. Push the wires into the connector until they reach the end of the metal pins. A small amount of the outer jacket should end up inside the RJ-45 connector. There should not be any untwisted wire coming out of the connector.
9. Insert the RJ-45 connector into a crimping tool and squeeze the crimper handles strongly to firmly attach the connector to the cable. Release the handles and pull the connector out of the crimping tool.
10. With a small amount of force, try to pull the cable out of the connector. It should not budge.
11. Repeat steps 1 through 10 to terminate the other end of the UTP cable.
12. Test the new cable with a cable tester before using it within any networking equipment.
13. Label each end of the cable with identical letters, numbers, or names so that it may be easily identified in a mass of cables.

Sample wiring configurations are shown in Figure 3–6.

Fiber-Optic Cable

Fiber

Fiber-optic cable relies on pulses of light to carry information. Figure 3–7(a) shows the basic construction of an optical *fiber*. Two types of plastic or glass, with different physical properties, are used (the inner *core* and the outer *cladding*) to allow a beam of light to reflect off the boundary between the core and the cladding. This is illustrated in Figure 3–7(b).

FIGURE 3–6
10BASE-T Ethernet wiring.

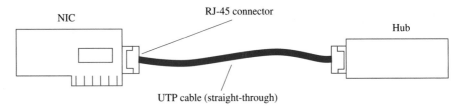

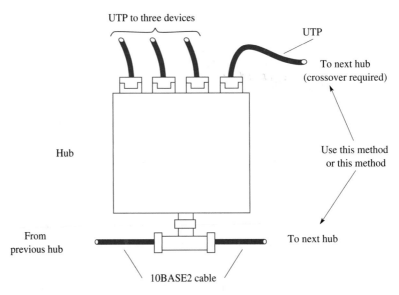

(a) Individual machine connection.

(b) Connecting the hub.

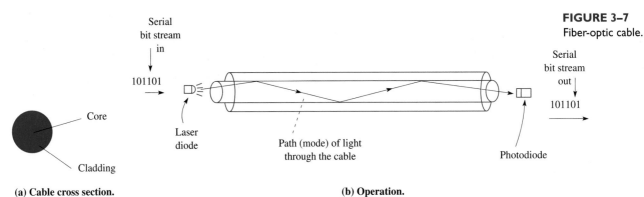

FIGURE 3–7
Fiber-optic cable.

(a) Cable cross section.

(b) Operation.

Modes

    Some fiber-optic cables allow many different paths (or ***modes***), others allow for one single mode. These are called multimode and single-mode fibers, respectively. A popular multimode fiber has core/cladding dimensions of 62.5/125 nanometers.

    High-speed laser diodes generate short bursts of light of a particular wavelength (typically 850 nanometers). These bursts travel down the fiber and affect a photodiode on the receiving end of the fiber. Because this light-based communication is one-way, two fibers are used to make a two-way connection.

    Fiber does not suffer from the problems found in copper wires such as sensitivity to electromagnetic interference (EMI), high signal loss, and bandwidth limitations. The original 10BASE-FL fiber standard specifies a cable length of 2000 meters, significantly longer than the 10BASE-5 segment length of 500 meters. In addition, fiber supports data rates in the gigabit range, providing the fastest communication method available for networking.

    Table 3–2 compares each cabling system.

TABLE 3–2
Comparing cabling systems.

	10BASE5	10BASE2	10BASE-T	10BASE-FL
Cable Type	RG-11	RG-58	UTP	Fiber
Maximum Segment Length	500 m (1640 ft)	185 m (606 ft)	100 m (328 ft)	2000 m (6560 ft)
Max Nodes	100	30	2	2

■ THE NIC

Network interface card

Objective 1-6

Combo card

The **network interface card** (NIC) is the interface between the PC (or other networked device) and the physical network connection. In Ethernet systems, the NIC connects to a segment of coaxial or UTP cable (fiber NICs are available but not very common). As with any other type of adapter card, NICs come in ISA, PCMCIA, USB, and PCI bus varieties. Figure 3–8(a) shows a typical Ethernet NIC. Since the NIC contains both BNC and RJ-45 connectors, it is called a **combo card**. The NE2000 Compatible stamp indicates that the NIC supports a widely accepted group of protocols.

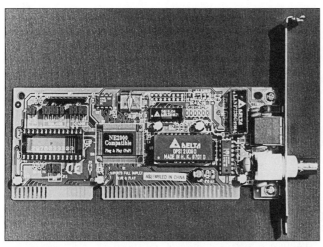

(a) Network interface card (Ethernet) (photograph by John T. Butchko).

(b) 100BASE-FX Fiber NIC

FIGURE 3–8
Two types of NICs.

The NIC in Figure 3–8(a) is a 10/100 PCI NIC adapter card. Figure 3–8(b) shows a 100BASE-FX fiber NIC PCI card. Figure 3–9 shows a PCMCIA Ethernet NIC and cable.

The NIC is responsible for operations that take place in the Physical and Data-Link layers of the OSI network model as well as providing the MAC address (a layer 2 function). It is only concerned with sending and receiving 0s and 1s, using the IEEE 802.3 Ethernet standard (or IEEE 802.5 token ring).

Figure 3–10 shows the Network and Dial-up Connections dialog box and the current network connections on a Windows 2000 PC. Note that there are two NICs installed.

As the dialog box indicates, the second NIC is currently unplugged. The Network and Dial-up Connections dialog box displays the model of each NIC installed. In the case of the Local Area Connection 2 entry, the NIC is a 3Com Ethernet XL 10/100 TX NIC, model 3C905B-TX. The 10/100 portion of the NIC classification means that the NIC can support either a 10BASE-T network or a 100BASE-TX network. This particular NIC has

FIGURE 3–9
PCMCIA Ethernet card with
cable (photograph by John T.
Butchko).

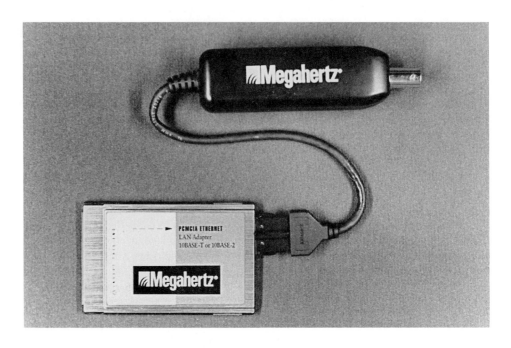

FIGURE 3–10
Network and Dial-up
Connections dialog box.

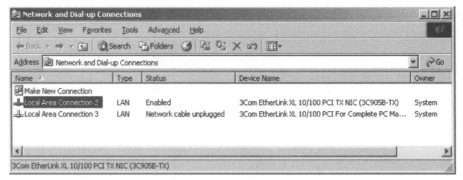

Autosense

the capability to *autosense* what speed of network it is working on and adjust its transmissions accordingly. If this PC had a modem installed it would be noted here as well. Double-clicking on the Local Area Connection 2 entry (shown in Figure 3-10) brings up the Local Area Connection 2 Properties dialog box (Figure 3–11) that provides more information about the properties associated with that NIC.

You can see in Figure 3–11 that some services and protocols are bound (associated) with that particular NIC. The first two entries show the Client and File and Printer services that are bound to the NIC. The third entry shows that the NetBEUI protocol is installed on the PC but is not bound to this particular NIC. The fourth entry shows that the TCP/IP protocol suite is bound to this NIC. If other protocols, such as Novell's IPX/SPX protocol suite, were bound to this NIC they would also be listed here. This is a good place to note that each NIC can have different (and multiple) protocols and services bound to it, a technique used on proxy servers. One portion of a network can be plugged into one NIC on a server and supply services appropriate to the needs of that network segment. Another network segment can be plugged into another NIC on the server and provide services appropriate to that network segment. The server could then be the proxy between the two network segments, providing whatever services are needed on each network segment. Refer again to Figure 3–11. If you select the Internet Protocol (TCP/IP) entry and then click on the Properties button you will see the Internet Protocol (TCP/IP) Properties dialog box shown in Figure 3–12. This is the dialog box that allows us to configure the TCP/IP properties associated with that particular NIC.

The top set of numbers in the dialog box represents the IP address (layer 3 address or logical address) associated with that specific NIC. The other numbers are discussed in Chapter 8.

Objective 2-3

FIGURE 3–11
Local Area Connection 2 Properties dialog box.

FIGURE 3–12
Internet Protocol (TCP/IP) Properties dialog box.

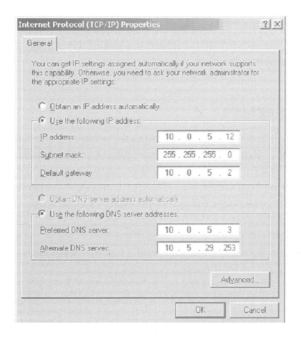

It is important to mention that all NICs are manufactured with a unique 48-bit MAC address. Refer to Figure 3–13 to see the output of the *ipconfig /all* command entered at a command prompt. This output demonstrates that the MAC address (physical address) of this NIC is 00-50-04-9B-37-1B.

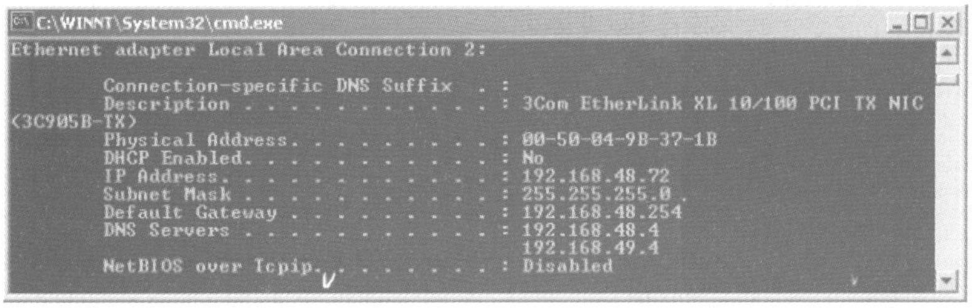

FIGURE 3–13
ipconfig /all output.

Objective 2-1

MAC addresses are represented in hexadecimal (or hex) format. Because each hex number represents 4 bits, you can see that the 12 hex numbers relate to a 48-bit address (12 hex numbers × 4 bits each = 48 bits). This address might also be written using colons to separate the digits, 00:50:04:9B:37:1B. This is the layer 2 address that we talked about in the discussion of the OSI model in Chapter 1. This address uniquely identifies the individual NIC on the local network segment. Remember that several names are associated with this address including MAC address, physical address, hardware address, adapter address, and Ethernet address. They all mean the same thing. The first six hex digits (00-50-04) indicate the manufacturer (3Com in this example). These numbers are assigned to each manufacturer by the IEEE and are formally called an Organizationally Unique Identifier (OUI). The remaining six hex digits (9B-37-1B) are used by the manufacturer to individually identify each specific NIC with what they produce. This process should generally ensure that no two NICs have the same MAC address (there are a few exceptions in specific situations). In our example the last six digits, 9B-37-1B represent the specific numbers assigned to our NIC by the manufacturer. As noted earlier in this chapter, you can view your NIC's MAC address using the *ipconfig /all* command at a command prompt in Windows 2000 and XP. (If you are using a command prompt on a Windows 9x PC you need to use the *winipcfg /all* command.)

There are actually many layer 2 addresses to which a NIC might listen. Another address that NICs listen to is called a ***broadcast address***. Many common protocols need to send traffic to all hosts on the network. To ensure that the message is looked at by all hosts connected to the media these protocols broadcast the message with a destination address of all Fs (such as FF-FF-FF-FF-FF-FF). In a binary format this address equates to all 48 bits being turned on (all 1s). There is a similar layer 3 broadcast address, which we will talk about later in the book.

Broadcast address

Objective 4-1

■ TOKEN RING COMPONENTS

Objective 1-2

The IEEE 802.5 standard describes the token ring networking standards. IBM developed the initial 4 Mbps standard in the mid-1980s. A 16 Mbps standard became available at a later date.

Token-ring networks use a multistation access unit (MAU), which establishes a logical ring connection even though the physical connections to the MAU resemble a star. Figure 3–14 shows the basic operation of the MAU.

FIGURE 3–14
Token-ring network.

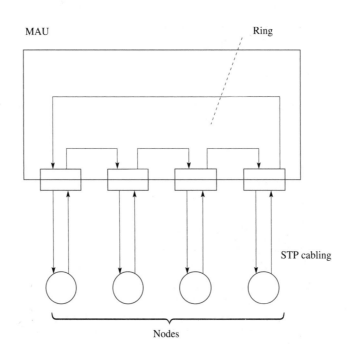

Token

Active monitor

Computers in the ring circulate a software *token*. The machine holding the token is allowed to transmit data to the next machine on the ring, even if the data is not meant for that machine. One machine (typically the first to boot and connect) is identified as the ***active monitor*** and keeps track of all token-ring operations. If the active monitor detects that a machine has gone down (or has been shut off), the connection to that machine is bypassed. If the active monitor itself goes down, the other machines vote to elect a new active monitor. Token-ring networks are *self-healing,* unlike Ethernet, which is only capable of resolving collisions.

Token-ring connections are made using shielded twisted pair (STP) cable. STP cable contains a metal shield around the twisted pairs that provides isolation from external crosstalk and noise. In general, do not substitute STP for UTP.

■ REPEATERS

Repeater

A ***repeater*** connects two network segments and broadcasts packets between them. As signals travel down a wire they lose strength and shape, causing attenuation. This is one of the reasons that we have maximum lengths of cable that can be used on a network segment (such as the aforementioned 100 meter maximum length for 10BASE-T networks). To extend network segments beyond these limitations, a repeater is used to amplify the signal (effectively repeating the signal). Repeaters also retime and reshape the signals on the network. Discussions about retiming and reshaping the signal are beyond the scope of this book; but basically it means to clean up and retransmit the signal out another port of the repeater in as good a shape as it was when it was originally transmitted by the PC. At this point you might think that you could just continue to use repeaters and extend your local Ethernet network around the world. You may recall the discussion about the 5-4-3 rule for 10BASE-T networks. There are timing issues with the overall diameter (length from end to end) of the local network when we are dealing with collision detection. If you extend the length of a 10BASE-T network beyond the five-segment rule, one machine on one end of the network might not detect a transmission from a machine on the other end of the network soon enough to properly react to collisions on the network (when two machines try to transmit at the same time). This is why there is a maximum of five segments in a 10BASE-T network. Although not specifically designed for this purpose, a repeater can also connect two separate network segments together. Traditionally, repeaters have only two ports. The signal comes in on one side of the repeater and goes out the other side retimed and reshaped. Both network segments are now joined into a common collision domain (they all share access to transmit on the media). Repeaters are not as common as they used to be. Most modern networks use hubs instead of repeaters. Repeaters operate at layer 1 (the Physical layer) of the OSI model.

■ TRANSCEIVERS

A *transceiver* converts from one media type to another. For example, a 10BASE2-to-fiber transceiver acts like a repeater, except that it also interfaces 10BASE2 coaxial cable with a fiber-optic cable. It is common to use more than one media type in an installation, so many different kinds of transceivers are available. Figure 3–15 shows three examples of Ethernet transceivers. Transceivers operate at layer 1 of the OSI model.

■ HUBS

Concentrators

Objective 1-6

Hubs, called ***concentrators*** in some applications, are used to join multiple network devices or segments in a logical bus network. For example, a four-port hub connects up to four machines (or other network devices) via UTP cables. The hub provides a physical star connection for devices connected to the four ports.

A hub can also be uplinked (daisy chained) to another hub via one of its ports. Typically one port is designed to operate in either straight-through or crossover mode, selected

(a) Thinwire coax to fiber.   (b) UTP to AUI.   (c) 100BASE-T to 100BASE-FX transceiver

FIGURE 3–15
Transceivers.

Stackable

by a switch on the hub. Hubs that can connect in this fashion are called *stackable* hubs. Figures 3–16(a) and (b) show an eight-port stackable Ethernet hub. Port 8 is switch selectable for use as either a straight-through or crossover (cascade) port. Figure 3–16(c) shows the front of an eight-port 10/100 Ethernet switch.

FIGURE 3–16
Ethernet hub and switch.

(a) Front view.

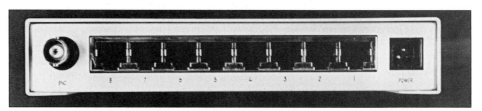

(b) Rear view.

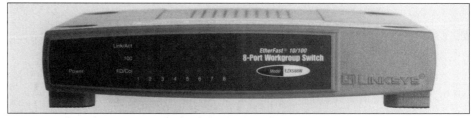

(c) Eight-port 10/100 switch.

A hub is similar to a repeater, except that a repeater traditionally has only two ports (in and out) and a hub normally has multiple ports, typically sized in groups of four. This is why a hub is often referred to as a multiport repeater. Most hubs contain a small amount of intelligence as well, examining received packets and checking them for integrity. If a bad packet arrives or the hub determines that a port is unreliable, the hub will shut down the line until the error condition disappears. All signals coming into any port on a hub are transmitted out all other ports on the hub. Because hubs connect multiple network segments and devices together, when one PC transmits a message onto the media, all devices connected to the joined segment will see every transmission (just like what takes place when a repeater is used to join two network segments).

Collision domain

The concept of sharing a common media is called a ***collision domain***, meaning that all devices connected to the common collision domain (shared media) are subject to collisions from transmissions from all other connected devices. It is easy to understand that the more devices you connect together via hubs, the more problems you are likely to have with collisions. Every PC connected to the network segment increases the probability of a collision. There is a practical limit to how many devices you can connect on a shared media (collision domain). At some point, you will have so many collisions that the network will cease to function. Some designers use a practical limit of 200 PCs per collision domain (in a 10BASE-T network), but the practical limit is actually dictated by the type and quantity of traffic on the network. Some protocols, such as Microsoft's NetBEUI, are very chatty (broadcast a lot) on the network and take up a lot of bandwidth with network overhead. Some users, such as engineers sharing large design files between each other, place heavier demands on the network than others, such as a typical office user. If you use chatty protocols or support heavy users of bandwidth, you will need to take that into account during the design process.

Objective 2-4

Similar to repeaters, active hubs retime and reshape signals when they are retransmitted out of the ports. Also similar to repeaters, hubs operate at layer 1 (the Physical layer) of the OSI model.

Figure 3–17 shows how several hubs are used to connect five Ethernet segments, within the accepted limits (the 5-4-3 rule).

FIGURE 3–17
Connecting five segments with hubs.

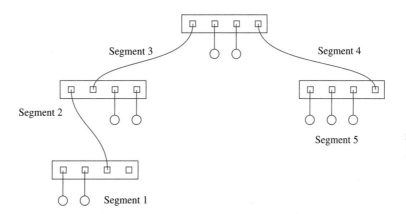

Because each UTP cable may be as long as 100 meters, the maximum distance between nodes is 500 meters (the network diameter). One interesting thing to note is that repeaters and hubs do not contain any RAM (Random Access Memory) useable for storing incoming data streams. When a data stream enters one port on a repeater or hub, it must be immediately processed and sent out to all the other ports of the device. This is why all segments connected via a repeater or hub belong to the same collision domain. When we start using layer 2 and layer 3 devices we are using equipment that contains some internal RAM that can temporarily store data streams for later retransmission. These devices have the capability to accept and store a packet, listen to the media on the intended outgoing ports, and wait until there are no transmissions on the outgoing media before they retransmit the data stream. Not only does this allow those devices to reduce the size of collision domains (by increasing the total quantity of collision domains because of segmentation of larger collision domains into smaller pieces), but it also helps us deal with the total diameter of the domain. Remember the 5-4-3 rule for 10BASE-T segments. You can replace layer 1 devices with layer 2 or layer 3 devices in your network design and extend your network diameter beyond the aforementioned limits. You can do this because you create new collision domains every time you use a layer 2 or layer 3 device to physically segment your network.

■ BRIDGES/SWITCHES

Bridges
Switches

When a network grows in size, it is often necessary to partition it into smaller groups of hosts to help isolate traffic and improve performance. Devices such as ***bridges*** and ***switches*** can be used to accomplish this. As mentioned earlier, layer 2 and layer 3 devices can break large collision domains into multiple (but smaller) collision domains. Bridges and switches also filter traffic based on layer 2 addresses. They examine traffic that passes through their ports and build a table of which MAC addresses are associated with which ports. When traffic is sent by one device to another device, the bridge or switch will only send the traffic out of the port that the destination device is connected to. If a NIC has a MAC address of 00-50-04-9B-37-1B, and a PC is plugged into port A of a bridge or switch, the MAC address of 00-50-04-9B-37-1B will be associated with port A and any traffic destined for the MAC address will be sent out of port A. If a bridge or switch has traffic destined for devices that it does not yet know about, it will transmit the information out of all ports except the port that the transmission was received on. When the destination device responds to the transmission (carrying on a conversation with the original sending host), the bridge or switch will now know what port the destination device resides on and will subsequently only transmit traffic destined for that device out of the port that the device resides on. When a device transmits a broadcast message (a message sent to a layer 2 address of FF-FF-FF-FF-FF-FF), the transmission is sent out every port except for the port that the message was received from.

Objective 1-6

Bridges traditionally have only two ports and divide up one previously larger segment (or connect two previously unjoined segments together), filtering traffic between those two segments. Figure 3–18 illustrates a bridge used to filter traffic between two network segments.

FIGURE 3–18
Operation of a bridge.

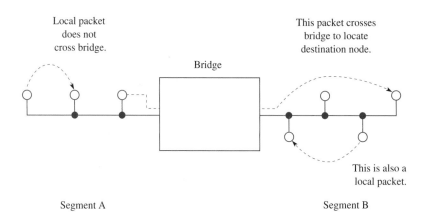

The bridge keeps segment A traffic on the A side and segment B traffic on the B side of the bridge. Packets from segment A that are meant for a host in segment B will cross the bridge (the bridge will permit the packet to cross). The same is true for packets going from B to A. Figure 3–18 shows a logical bus topology on each side of the bridge. Physically, modern implementations of an Ethernet network would use a hub to connect the devices on each side of the bridge, and a single cable would connect the hub to a bridge (on each side of the bridge). In this situation the bridge would associate multiple layer 2 addresses with each of the ports. All the layer 2 addresses of the hosts on segment A would be associated with the port connecting segment A to the bridge. The same would apply for the hosts located out of port B of the bridge. A special type of bridge called a ***translational bridge*** is used when you need to connect networks that use dissimilar technologies such as Ethernet and token ring. While these are not very common in modern networks, they do still exist in some legacy (older technology) networks. Bridges are being replaced with switches in modern networks.

Translational bridge

Switch

A ***switch*** is similar to a bridge, with some important enhancements. A switch typically contains multiple ports, thus directing packets to several different segments, further partitioning and isolating network traffic. Figure 3–19 shows an eight-port N-way switch, which can route packets from any incoming port to any outgoing port.

FIGURE 3–19
One configuration in an eight-port N-way switch.

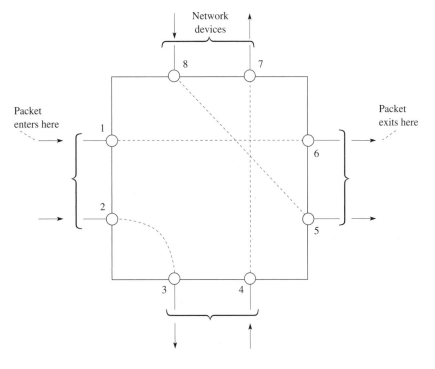

Store-and-forward

Some or all of an incoming packet is examined to make the routing decision, depending on the switching method that is used. One common method is called ***store-and-forward***, which stores the received packet and examines it for errors before retransmitting the packet out the appropriate port. Bad packets, packets with errors, are not forwarded.

In addition, a switch may have auto-sensing 10/100 Mbps ports, which allow it to adjust the speed of each port accordingly. Furthermore, a *managed* switch supports Simple Network Management Protocol (SNMP) for further control over network traffic.

As mentioned earlier in this chapter, switches have internal RAM, which can be used to temporarily store data streams. That is why they have the ability to reduce the overall size of a collision domain. Switches also provide additional security features for a network. Because data coming into a switch only goes out the port associated with a particular host (based on layer 2 addresses already learned by the switch), not every host on the network will see all the traffic that travels across the various segments of the network. This reduces the capability of any single individual to eavesdrop on all conversations taking place on the network. When we get further into the book we will also talk about segmenting the network with virtual local area networks (VLANs). Switches are used to control VLANs.

Switches and bridges operate at layer 2 (the Data-Link layer) of the OSI model.

■ ROUTERS

A router is a networking device that works at layer 3 (the Network layer) of the OSI model. Layer 3 addresses are referred to as Network layer addresses. Examples of these include IP and Novell's IPX addresses. Routers have multiple interfaces (ports), which are used to connect multiple networks together. When we talk about multiple networks at layer 3 we are referring to portions of our network that use the same layer 3 network address for all hosts associated with a particular interface (port) of a router. IP addresses are explained in Chapter 8.

Routers provide a lot of functionality for modern networks and are the basis for the orderly flow of information on a large network, such as a corporate network or the Internet. The two primary functions of a router are path selection and packet switching. Path selection refs to determining which interface to send data out of, and packet switching means to physically take a packet received on one interface and transfer it (switch it) out another interface. Path selection and packet switching together make up the basic routing process. When hosts on a network need to send data to destinations outside their own logical network (meaning that the network portion of the layer 3 address of the sending host and the receiving host are not the same), they will send the data to their *default gateway* (the router in this case). The router becomes the exit point for all traffic destined for other networks. This is like the gate around a home that you use to exit your property (your local network), which is why it is called a default gateway (the gate, or exit point, out to the rest of the world). Routers route traffic between different networks. To do this, routers keep track of the various networks so they can determine how to route data that is destined for other networks. The list of networks, and the interfaces that must be used to send data to those networks, is called a routing table.

Routing protocols

Routers use ***routing protocols*** to talk with each other so they can find out about other networks that are available. Routing protocols will be discussed later in the book.

In addition to performing the functions that make up the routing process (path selection and packet switching), routers can connect networks that use different technologies such as Ethernet and token ring as shown in Figure 3–20(a), addressing methods such as IP versus IPX, media types such as fiber versus UTP, frame formats such as Ethernet versus token ring layer 2 frames, and speeds such as 10 Mbps versus 100 Mbps. Routers can also perform other functions such as prioritizing traffic for transmission over slow WAN links (time-sensitive data should be transmitted before e-mail) and filtering traffic for traffic control and security reasons.

Figures 3–20(b) and 3–20(c) show the top and rear views of the Cisco 1600 router. This router connects two Ethernet networks and has an expansion slot for a wide area network (WAN) connection. Figure 3–20(d) shows the Linksys cable modem/DSL router.

This device, which also contains four 10/100 Mbps switch ports, allows up to 254 devices to share Internet access through a single connection. Figure 3–21 illustrates how two routers can be used to connect three different networks.

Objective 2-4

Figure 3–22 illustrates the typical flow of data as it passes from the source computer, through the intermediate router, to the final destination. Note that within the router the data only has to go through the bottom three layers of the OSI model. That is because a router routes traffic using layer 3 (logical) addresses and does not typically process the data at any higher layers of the OSI model. When you get into more advanced networking topics such as security access control lists, you will find out that a router can process packets based on information at the higher layers of the OSI model, but that information is beyond the scope of this book. Remember that routers primarily function at layer 3 of the OSI model.

FIGURE 3–20
Router views.

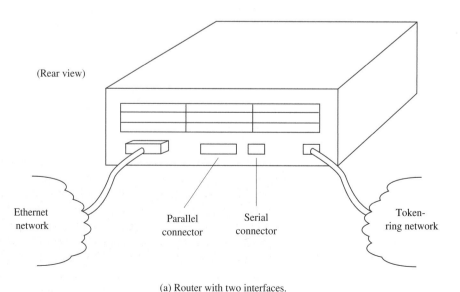

(a) Router with two interfaces.

FIGURE 3–20
(continued)

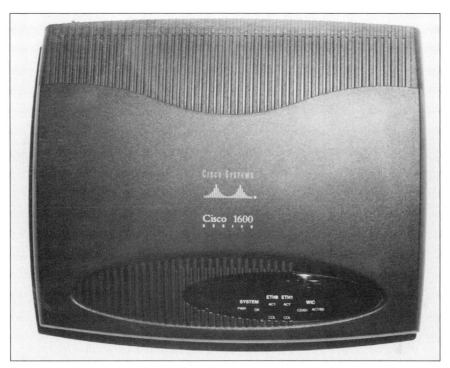

(b) Top view of Cisco 1600 router.

(c) Rear view of Cisco 1600 router.

(d) Cable modem/DSL router.

FIGURE 3–21
Two routers connecting three networks.

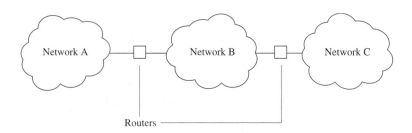

FIGURE 3–22
Intermediate host routes packet.

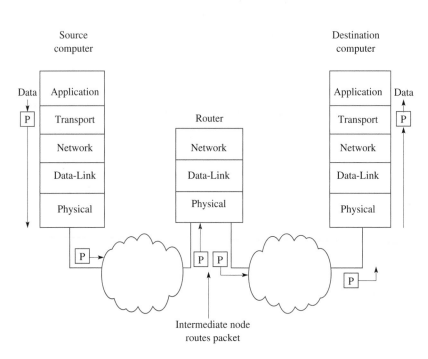

■ MODEMS

The word *modulate* means to change the properties of a carrier wave; therefore, an electronic circuit that changes digital data into analog data can be called a *modulator.* The word *demodulate* can be thought of as meaning "unchange," or restore to an original condition. Any electronic circuit that converts the analog signal used to represent the digital signals back to the ONs and OFFs (0's and 1's) understood by a computer can, therefore, be called a *demodulator.* If a computer needs to send its digital signals over an analog circuit (such as a standard telephone line) it must be capable of both transmission and reception, and it must contain an electrical circuit that can modulate as well as demodulate. Such a circuit is commonly called a *mo*dulator/*dem*odulator, or **modem**.

Modem

A typical use for a modem is in a home PC that needs to connect to an ISP. The modem is used to convert the PC's digital signals into analog signals (the type of signal that the analog telephone is designed to transmit and receive). Those analog signals will travel across the plain old telephone system (POTS) to the ISP, where the modem will convert the analog signals back into digital signals that the computer will understand. These modems may be installed in one of the internal slots on a motherboard or may be connected externally via a serial cable between the modem and a serial port on a PC. The modem is connected to the POTS via a standard telephone jack and telephone line (an RJ-ll type plug).

Objective 2-2

Objective 1-5

Objective 1-6

There are some other devices that connect computers to services provided by commercial telecommunications carriers. These carriers provide services such as digital subscriber lines (DSL), cable services, and so on. Many of these services are already in digital form, so there is no need to convert digital signals into analog signals and back again. Nonetheless, these devices are commonly called modems even though there is no digital-to-analog conversion taking place. In human terms it is easy to accept these devices as modems, so that has become common practice.

DSL is a common technology in a lot of areas of the United States and some other countries. Frequently DSL is noted as xDSL, with x standing for the many possible varieties of DSL technologies. For simplicity's sake this chapter refers to the generic technology as DSL. When connecting DSL technologies to a small office or home office (SOHO), the telecommunications carrier connects their incoming line to the DSL modem. There will be an RJ-45 jack on the DSL modem. That is the data jack that is used to connect a PC or other networking device (such as a hub). Typically a straight-through cable will be used to make that connection. Appendix E lists other modem technologies that are in common use.

■ SATELLITE NETWORK SYSTEM

The Hughes Corporation offered one of the first solutions to low-speed Internet connections. For a few hundred dollars, you can buy their DirecPC Internet satellite networking system. Figure 3–23 shows its basic operation.

FIGURE 3–23
Internet connection via satellite communications.

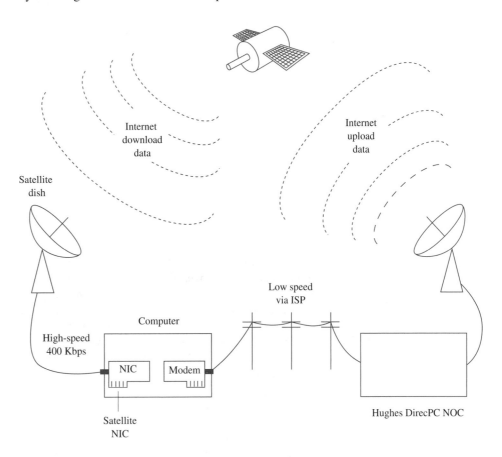

Internet data comes to your PC via satellite at 400 kbps. Through your modem and ISP, data goes back to Hughes's network operations center (NOC), where it is uploaded to the Internet. This is an ideal situation for browsing, when you need to receive information fast (if a Web page contains many images) but only occasionally send information out (clicking on a new URL to load a new page). A low-speed line for transmitted packets is acceptable, unless you are uploading large files to an FTP site or sending e-mail with large attachments. If there is no cable modem capability where you live or work, DirecPC may be the answer for you.

Other satellite services have emerged that offer both downlink and uplink capabilities. This means that you are no longer required to use a telephone line to send your outbound information to the ISP. These services are often joined with television services and offer a great alternative for individuals living in rural communities.

■ OTHER HARDWARE AND SOFTWARE TECHNOLOGIES

This chapter has examined only the basic types of networking hardware. Many more specialized (and expensive) networking components are available. For example, instead of multiple 16-port switches, a single industrial switch with 64 ports or more, including port management, may be used. IP addresses can be assigned to specific ports, ports can be activated/deactivated with software, and the port speed can be controlled.

For networks that must be distributed over a large geographic area such as a college or industrial campus, line-of-sight infrared lasers can be used to link separate networks together. If fiber is used instead, fiber repeaters may be necessary to obtain the required distance for a link.

Objective 1-6

Computer users can now walk around with their laptops, relying on wireless Ethernet technology to maintain the connection with the mobile machine. Figure 3–24 shows some typical wireless Ethernet hardware.

FIGURE 3–24
Wireless Ethernet components.

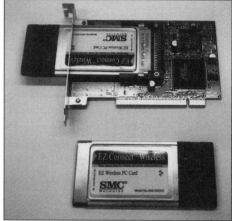

(a) Base station (wireless access point).   (b) Wireless NICs.

Figure 3–24(a) shows the base station or wireless access point that plugs into a port on a hub or switch as if it were an ordinary device such as a PC. The base station communicates with one or more wireless NICs that may be located up to several hundred feet away, depending on the environment. Each NIC is allocated a 1 Mbps bandwidth. Figure 3–24(b) shows two typical wireless NICs, one mounted on a PCI card and the other a standard PCMCIA card variety for laptop use. The wireless access point will be plugged into a network device such as a hub or switch. The signals from the wireless NIC are transferred back and forth to the wireless access point. The media used for communications between the wireless NIC and the wireless access point is radio information sent through the atmosphere (radio or IR signals). As noted in Chapter 1, wireless technologies are becoming very popular as solutions to retrofitting old buildings or in situations where users need mobile access to the network. Before you rush out and convert your network to all wireless, realize that network communications are transmitted through the air to anyone who is within transmission range. This may create significant security issues that must be addressed.

Figure 3–25 shows a line-of-sight RF-based Ethernet transceiver, which provides an 11 Mbps full-duplex link to a second transceiver that may be located up to 3 miles away.

FIGURE 3–25
Line-of-sight Ethernet
transceiver.

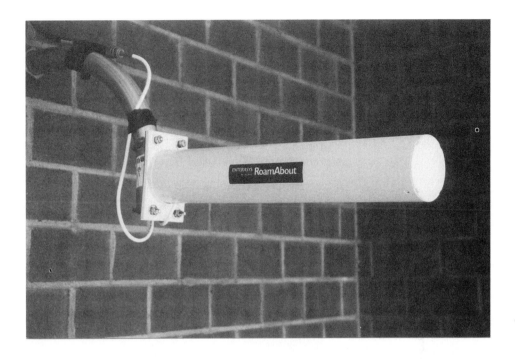

For security purposes, many companies now utilize network-ready cameras to view sensitive areas. Figure 3–26 shows two views of the Axis 2100 network camera (www.axis.com). This camera plugs directly into a 10/100 port on a hub or switch and can be programmed to output image snapshots (via a built-in FTP server) or live video. Up to 10 clients may access the camera at one time. A modem connector is also provided for low-speed access.

FIGURE 3–26
Axis 2100 network camera.

(a) Front view.   (b) Rear view.

Network software has also evolved. Network management software will display a graphic diagram of your network, with pertinent information (IP/MAC addresses, link speed, activity, and status). Most systems provide a method for the network technician to be paged when a problem occurs.

■ TROUBLESHOOTING TECHNIQUES

Objective 4-5

Cable tester

Most of the problems that occur with networks happen at the lower levels of the OSI model (especially layer 1). Correct physical wiring cannot be overemphasized. One of the most important phases of a network installation is making the cables required for all the nodes. It is often less expensive to buy UTP cable and RJ-45 ends and make custom-length cables than it is to buy finished cables.

A valuable tool to have at your disposal when preparing or checking cables is a *cable tester*. Figure 3–27 shows an electronic cable tester, capable of performing these (and many other) tests on UTP cable:

- Passive and active profiles
- Continuity
- Cable length
- NEXT (near-end crosstalk)
- Attenuation
- Noise

FIGURE 3–27
Electronic cable analyzer
(photograph by John T. Butchko).

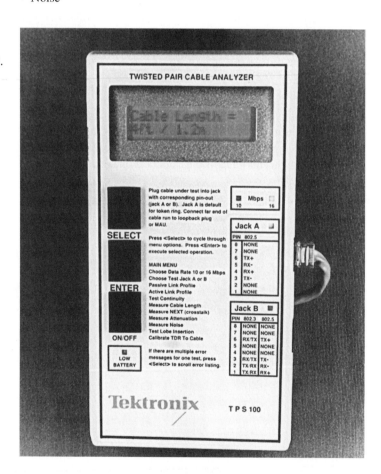

Other, more sophisticated network test equipment, such as the Fluke LANmeter, capture and diagnose network packets of many different protocols, gather statistics (collisions, packets sent), perform standard network operations such as PING and TRACERT, and can transmit packets for troubleshooting purposes. The power of this type of network analyzer is well worth the cost.

Objective 4-6

It pays to have a fresh mind when approaching a troubleshooting problem. For example, always look at the indicator lights provided by the network components. Cable modems, NICs, external modems, hubs and switches, routers, and CSU/DSUs all typically contain one or more indicator lights that show the current operational status (Link status, transmit information, receive information, collisions, etc.). Look at the lights to make sure the correct ones are lit.

Troubleshooting Problem

One user had difficulty accessing the Internet through his cable modem. He looked at the lights on the cable modem and saw that the cable light was not on. He turned on his television to see if the cable was working and was able to view all the stations, with a clear picture on each channel. He checked the coaxial connectors on all of the cables running from the two-way splitter that feeds the cable modem. All connectors were firmly connected. As a last resort, the user swapped out the two-way splitter and connected the incoming cable directly to the cable modem. The cable light came on and he was able to access the Internet. Instead of waiting three days for his local cable provider to fix the problem, he purchased a new splitter and reconnected the modem, with no further trouble.

INDUSTRY TIP

The networking field moves very quickly and companies rise and fall on the success of their products. As a networking professional you will need to keep up to date with as many product announcements and innovations as possible. Your job will often rely on your ability to implement the best technology has to offer.

Nearly every company has a website that includes product information and network applications for their products. Cisco has a general site (www.cisco.com). Another site worth checking out is http://www.cisco.com/univercd/home/home.htm

■ SELF-TEST

1. What type of network uses RG-11 cabling?
   a. 10BASE2
   b. 10BASE5
   c. 10BASE10
   d. 10BASE-T

2. Which of the following refers to an Ethernet cable capable of a single 500-meter segment?
   a. 10BASE2
   b. 10BASE5
   c. 10BASE-T
   d. 100BASE-T

3. What term is commonly used to refer to 10BASE5 cabling?
   a. Thinnet
   b. Thicknet
   c. Airnet
   d. Cablenet

4. What Ethernet cabling standard requires the use of BNC connectors?
   a. 10BASE2
   b. 10BASE5
   c. 10BASE-T
   d. 10BASE-B

5. Modern networks rarely implement Ethernet networks using _____ cable.
   a. UTP
   b. coaxial
   c. fiber
   d. CAT 5

6. What type of cable is used to connect a computer to a hub?
   a. Straight-through
   b. Crossover
   c. Rollover
   d. Loopback

7. The customer has specified that a single unrepeated segment be run end to end between two hosts. The problem is that the computers are 650 meters apart. The maximum network speed is stated as 10 Mbps. What cable can be used to meet these requirements?
   a. No single segment can meet this requirement.
   b. 10BASE5
   c. 10BASE-T
   d. 10BASE-FL

8. The 5-4-3 rule regarding 10BASE-T Ethernet states that you can have a maximum of five _____, using four _____ , with only three _____. (Select the three correct answers.)
   a. receivers
   b. segments
   c. routers
   d. populated segments
   e. repeaters

9. What is the maximum diameter of a 100BASE-TX network using a class 2 repeater?
   a. 100 meters
   b. 185 meters
   c. 205 meters
   d. 400 meters

10. Where can we view the services that are bound to a network interface card on a PC with a Windows 2000 operating system?
    a. Netstat –a command at the DOS prompt
    b. My Computer>Properties
    c. Network and Dial-up Connections dialog box
    d. Winipcfg

11. The last six hexadecimal numbers of a MAC address refer to what?
    a. OUI
    b. Vendor identity
    c. Specific NIC identity
    d. Logical address

12. Which command can be used to view the MAC address on a PC running Windows 98?
    a. Ipconfig /all
    b. Winipcfg /all
    c. Wipconfig /all
    d. Show MAC

13. What is the destination MAC address used to send network traffic to all hosts on a network?
    a. 11-11-11-11
    b. 00-00-00-FF-FF-FF
    c. FF-FF-FF-FF-FF-FF
    d. FF-FF-FF-00-00-00

14. How many ports does a repeater typically have?
    a. 1
    b. 2
    c. 4
    d. 8

15. True or False: Each hub that is added to a network segment increases the size of the collision domain.

16. What is the concept of several devices sharing a common media called?
    a. Workgroup
    b. Multipoint connection
    c. Collision domain
    d. Collision group

17. True or False: Hubs, repeaters, and transceivers can be used to create new collision domains on a network segment.

18. What ports will a switch use to forward traffic for a device it knows nothing about?
    a. All ports
    b. All ports except trunk
    c. Trunk ports
    d. All ports except the port it received traffic from

19. True or False: A bridge differs from a switch in that a bridge can provide numerous ports for connecting multiple networks.

20. How many ports do bridges traditionally have?
    a. 1
    b. 2
    c. 4
    d. 8

21. True or False: Routers can be used to connect networks that use different technologies to communicate.

22. True or False: The word "demodulate" means to restore to an original condition.

23. What type of connector is used to connect a modem to a telephone line?
    a. RJ-31X
    b. RJ-45
    c. MAU
    d. RJ-11

24. True or False: When using DSL services to connect to the Internet, the digital signal must be modulated to an analog signal by using a DSL modem.

25. True or False: Present satellite technologies only permit the ability to download information through the dish. The upload process must still be done via POTS.

26. What is the media used for wireless networking?
    a. CAT 5
    b. CAT 3
    c. Air
    d. STP

27. Which of the following devices is used for security purposes to view sensitive areas?
    a. Network-ready camera
    b. Scanner
    c. WAP
    d. Port scanner

28. Which of the following is **NOT** discerned through the use of a common cable tester?
    a. Continuity
    b. NEXT
    c. Attenuation
    d. Packet capture

Ethernet Technology

PERFORMANCE OBJECTIVES

Upon completion of this chapter, you will be able to:

- Describe the format of an Ethernet frame.
- Explain the basic operation of collision detection.
- Compare and contrast the features of the different 10 Mbps Ethernet, Fast Ethernet, and Gigabit Ethernet technologies.
- Discuss the principles of wireless Ethernet.

NETWORK+ OBJECTIVES

This chapter provides information for the following Network+ objectives:

1.1 Recognize the following logical or physical network topologies given a schematic diagram or description:
  - Star/hierarchical
  - Ring
  - Bus
  - Wireless
  - Mesh

1.2 Specify the main features of 802.2 (LLC), 802.3 (Ethernet), 802.5 (token ring), 802.11b (wireless), and FDDI networking technologies, including
  - Speed
  - Topology
  - Access
  - Media
  - Method

1.3 Specify the characteristics (e.g., speed, length, topology, cable type, etc.) of the following:
  - 802.3 (Ethernet) standards
  - 10BASE-T
  - 100BASE-TX
  - 10BASE2
  - 10BASE5
  - 100BASE-FX
  - Gigabit Ethernet

1.4 Recognize the following media connectors and/or describe their uses:
  - RJ-11
  - RJ-45
  - AUI
  - BNC
  - ST
  - SC

1.5 Choose the appropriate media type and connectors to add a client to an existing network.

1.6 Identify the purpose, features, and functions of the following network components:
  - Hubs
  - Switches
  - Bridges
  - Routers
  - Gateways
  - CSU/DSU
  - Network Interface Cards/ISDN adapters/system area network cards
  - Wireless access points
  - Modems

2.1 Given an example, identify a MAC address.

4.6 Given a network scenario, interpret visual indicators (e.g., link lights, collision lights, etc.) to determine the nature of the problem.

4.12 Given a network troubleshooting scenario involving a wiring/infrastructure problem, identify the cause of the problem (e.g., bad media, interference, network hardware).

■ INTRODUCTION

Objective 1-3

This chapter examines the details and operation of the popular LAN technology called Ethernet, as well as some of the encoding processes used for data transmissions. The term Ethernet is often used as a generic term to refer to a group of past, current, and emerging technologies that have a common design and characteristic base. If you engage in a conversation with someone talking about Ethernet technologies, expect to discuss a variety of general concepts. Officially, Ethernet refers to the 10 Mbps variety of this group of technologies. If you are talking about Ethernet, you are talking about 10 Mbps transmissions and the standards that go with them. Examples of some other names of the Ethernet family are Fast Ethernet (100 Mbps transmissions) and Gigabit Ethernet (1000 Mbps transmissions). Ethernet is primarily concerned with layers 1 and 2 (the Physical and Data-Link layers) of the OSI model.

■ UNDERSTANDING ETHERNET

Ethernet has its initial roots in a technology called X-Wire, which was a 3 Mbps specification developed by Xerox's Palo Alto Research Center in 1973. As noted in Chapter 1, in 1980 DIX (Digital Equipment Corporation, Intel, and Xerox) created the first formal version of Ethernet using a 10 Mbps data rate. The Ethernet family now includes a variety of versions with various standards.

Very few information technologies have lasted as long as the Ethernet technology. Design concepts such as low overhead, flexibility, adaptability, and ease of use have contributed to the extensive life cycle of the Ethernet technology. Unlike some other technologies such as token ring, Ethernet does not support reliable delivery of data, meaning there is no acknowledgement of receipt of the packet sent nor any indication of transmission. The discussion of the OSI model in Chapter 1 noted that layer 2 of the OSI model is one of three layers that may provide error correction (versus error detection). Ethernet has the capability to discard a bad frame (using the Frame Check Sequence (FCS) field discussed later in this chapter), but does not possess the capability to ask the sending host to resend the bad frame. Thus, Ethernet can detect an error (FCS) but not correct the error. If the data gets corrupted during the transmission process, an upper layer protocol would be responsible for the retransmission of the data. Reducing the overhead of error correction makes Ethernet a more efficient technology. The improvement of this efficiency is yet another reason Ethernet has grown as a popular technology. If your network operations require reliable delivery of data at the Data-Link layer, you will need to use a different technology.

Another issue to be concerned with on a network is clocking of the transmission signal. When you are using signals on a wire to represent data you must contend with how a receiving NIC can tell what the starting and ending points of a bit are. Some technologies use a network device to induce a clocking signal on the wire. Every device can then use that clocking signal and "get in step" with every other device on the network so that all devices know when the beginning and ending of a bit is taking place. (Music teachers use a similar device called a metronome to help students "clock" their rhythm.) Of course, a clocking signal takes up overhead on the wire, and requires more expensive equipment.

This chapter uses some common terms, so this is a good place to cover terminology. Remember that at layer 2 the protocol data unit (PDU) is called a frame. When you pass the frame down to layer 1 you encapsulate it with some physical layer signals, which are called bits (the layer 1 PDU). When you transmit those series of bits onto the wire as a logically complete transmission you refer to them collectively as a packet.

Ethernet packets are placed onto the physical wire starting with an enforced idle (quiet) time of 96 bit times followed by a 64-bit preamble (more on this later), which serves as a recognizable warning to the receiving NIC that it needs to synchronize with this particular transmission and prepare for a valid transmission of a frame (the layer 2 data after the physical clocking signal is used and discarded). This means that devices on an Ethernet segment only have to stay synchronized for the length of time it takes to transmit a single frame versus staying synchronized for weeks, months, years, and so on. This makes Ethernet circuitry cheaper to design and purchase, thereby making it more affordable to individuals and organizations.

Another positive characteristic of the Ethernet design is its capability to adjust to different size transmission needs. Many network transmissions are very small; others are much larger. Though there are exceptions, the standard design size of an Ethernet frame is 46 to 1500 octets (bytes). This allows for transmission of small messages from only 40 octets in size up to a sizeable but still manageable frame of 1500 octets. Transmitting a larger frame for small amounts of data (with padding to fill up the empty bytes) would be wasteful. Transmitting large amounts of data using smaller frame sizes (thereby adding extra overhead at the layer 1 level) would also be wasteful. Having the capability to adjust the size of the frame creates a lot of efficiency on the network.

The predominant properties, procedures, and definitions associated with Ethernet are contained in the IEEE Standard 802.3. This document contains over 1,200 pages and includes such information as:

- Flowcharts for transmitting and receiving a bit
- Signal speed, noise, and other parameters for various media
- Data encoding methods (Manchester, 4B5B, etc.) used by each technology
- The method for computing the frame check sequence
- Detailed discussion of collision detection
- Autonegotiation using fast link pulses
- Repeater operation

Standard	Technology
802.3	10BASE5
802.3a	10BASE2
802.3i	10BASE-T
802.3j	10BASE-FL
802.3u	100BASE-T
802.3z	1000BASE-X

TABLE 4–1
Selected IEEE 802.3 standards.

As noted earlier in Chapter 1, these standards outline the tasks needed to fulfill the functions at layers 1 and 2 (the Physical and Data-Link layers) of the OSI model.

Table 4–1 shows some of the different Ethernet technologies covered by the IEEE 802.3 Standard. The most common of these technologies are discussed in this chapter, beginning with the 10 Mbps systems.

■ MEDIA AND MULTILAYER SIGNALING/ENCODING

When you are new to the networking field it is easy to become overwhelmed by the avalanche of technical details—and it's often difficult to see the big picture. To help you absorb some of the concepts we will pause to grasp some of those "big picture" ideas with some common-sense discussion. A note of caution: Most workers in this career field are purists at heart (after all, their career deals with a lot of necessary details). Most of the discussion in the next few paragraphs is designed to look at simple concepts, and may occasionally drift from specific details to focus on general concepts.

Media

The Ethernet standards include specifics about the type of media used on the network (layer 1 of the OSI model). One of the benefits of Ethernet is its capability to adapt to the changing needs of the industry, while still maintaining the flexibility to be used in a wide variety of environments. Three types of media are commonly used for the various implementations of the family of Ethernet standards: copper cable, fiber-optic cables, and the air. The various versions of the Ethernet standards define what type of media is needed for that standard. When Ethernet (the 10 Mbps version) was developed, the primary media available was copper wire, primarily in the form of coaxial cable. This proved to be reasonably reliable for the needs of the time and is reflected in the standards for 10BASE2 and 10BASE5. As our technology developed we were able to improve on how we used the network and migrated to using copper wire in the form of twisted-pair wire. Twisted-pair wire comes in many forms, but during the evolution of the Ethernet standard, wire called Category 3 (CAT 3) was the common wire available. Implementations of Ethernet started using this wire, which is reflected in the 10BASE-T standard. Using twisted-pair wiring allows you to move from the physical bus topology (used by 10BASE2 and 10BASE5 standards) to the physical star topology. Network design and implementation became much easier.

As the use of computer networks expanded, users realized that they needed to extend the distances that the data traveled, as well as deal with other issues such as running wires in areas of high electrical interference (such as around fluorescent light fixtures in office buildings). To this end standards were developed that use fiber-optic cabling. This allowed the data to travel longer distances than the 100 meter limitation of copper cable as well as installation of networks in areas of high electronic noise (the light signals in fiber are not affected by stray electronic signals). This brought about standards such as 10BASE-FX. Now a single transmission segment can be up to 2,000 meters (2 km).

This is a good time to discuss single-mode versus multimode fiber transmissions. Simplistically speaking, single-mode fiber transmissions use a stronger light-emitting device and transmit only a single signal straight down the center of the core of the fiber cable. This feature allows single-mode transmissions to travel longer distances than multimode. Multimode transmissions use a different light-emitting device, which is capable of bouncing multiple light signals through the core of the fiber cable at different angles. While you can get multiple light signals through the core at the same time in multimode, the distance that you can carry these transmissions is less than what you can obtain with single-mode transmissions. In the course of designing a network you have to weigh the advantages and disadvantages of each technology and implement the type that is best for your network environment.

Wireless Media Technologies

Wireless technologies are relatively new and were developed to fulfill needs that couldn't easily be met by other physical media. Wireless technologies are useful in applications in which you need mobility for networked devices, such as a manager's laptop that has to travel between various meetings throughout a building, and in instances where installing physical media is not a good option, such as retrofitting a historic building. Of course wireless also offers welcome convenience for a wide variety of other individuals. Many home owners are migrating from the stationary home networked PC to the more mobile laptop. Wireless allows them to use the laptop anywhere in the house while still maintaining home network connectivity. Wireless is starting to become a benefit to individuals such as computer science instructors who need to use their laptop in the office, but also need it in the classroom.

Multilevel Signaling/Encoding

As our appetite for bandwidth increases we need to develop new ways to increase our transmissions greater than the 10 Mbps limit imposed by Ethernet standards. To solve this problem we can improve the physical characteristics of the media, improve the abilities of the transmitting and receiving devices, change how we use the physical media (use more wire pairs to simultaneously transmit more data at the same time), and change how we represent the data during transmission. Typically we use these options in concert with each other to increase our network throughput. Physical standards for wire performance are reflected in more modern versions of twisted-pair wire such as those in Categories 5, 5e, 6, and 7 wiring. Of course, we have also improved the transmitting and receiving devices, such as NICs. In addition to all of these changes we have also changed how we represent data (encoding schemes) on the wire. Two examples of this include 8B6T and 4B5B, which are covered later in this chapter.

Here's an analogy of encoding using the human voice for transmissions, with the vocal cords being the transmitter and the ear being the receiver, and the air as the physical media. (Purists beware: This analogy is conceptual in nature and is not intended to produce exact comparisons.) For this analogy we'll refer to a military cargo helicopter commonly called the Chinook. The formal designation of this helicopter is Cargo Helicopter, series 47, model D. Now you can clearly see that in routine conversations (transmissions), referring to this aircraft in this manner would become cumbersome (15 syllables). In good military fashion the military also uses an abbreviated reference to this aircraft and calls it a CH-47D. In daily conversations this more efficient form of reference (seven syllables with the word "dash" not spoken) is much preferred. We can use this abbreviated reference and reduce our vocal transmission time by almost half and still represent the same information to the receiver. In keeping with their tradition the military came up with yet another reference for this aircraft and called it a Chinook. This form is even more efficient requiring only two syllables of speech to represent the same aircraft (further reducing the transmission time). The "informationdata" represented by these various voice encoding schemes is the specific helicopter. The informationdata never changed, only the transmission representation of the informationdata changed. The transmission time is now reduced from 15 syllables to 2 syllables. This analogy represents some simple concepts with data transmission. When we used simple encoding schemes on Ethernet networks our transmission speeds were limited. There are only so many actions you can perform with physical media to improve its performance (basic physics do not change, only how we apply them); so other techniques are needed to increase the resultant transmission speed of modern networks. You could compare the original Ethernet encoding to the original form of Cargo Helicopter, series 47, model D. It was accurate and worked but was not as efficient. You might compare the more abbreviated form of reference of CH-47D to Fast Ethernet, which transmits data at 100 Mbps. Lastly, you might compare the Chinook form of reference to the Gigabit Ethernet with transmission speeds of 1000 Mbps. The concept you need to understand is that we can change the physical forms of the data stream as long as both the transmitter and receiver use the same techniques. All this is being done at layer 1 and does not affect how the data looks at layer 2 or above. The transmission techniques at layer 1 can transmit data streams in the form of electrical, light, or radio signals, and the encoding techniques used at layer 1 do not alter the resultant layer 2 data (frames) in any manner.

■ THE ETHERNET FRAME FORMAT

Figure 4–1 shows the format of an Ethernet 802.3 frame. A separate and practically identical frame format called Ethernet II has an 8-byte preamble of identical 10101010 patterns (no 10101011 SFD) and a 2-byte Type field in place of the Length field. Because the Data field of an 802.3 Ethernet frame is limited to 1500 bytes, a value larger than 1500 in the Type/Length field indicates an Ethernet II frame. The Type field is used to identify the upper layer protocol supported in that frame, such as IP. Most modern implementations of Ethernet actually use the Ethernet II frame format, which uses the Type field.

FIGURE 4–1
IEEE 802.3 Ethernet frame.

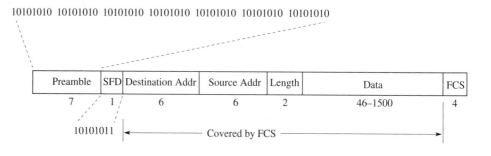

SFD: Start frame delimiter
FCS: Frame check sequence (32-bit CRC value)

All data is packaged into one or more frames for transmission over an Ethernet LAN. Take a look at each portion of the Ethernet frame:

• **Preamble (7 bytes):**   The Preamble contains 7 bytes with the identical pattern 10101010. This alternating sequence of 1s and 0s are the first bytes transmitted. They are provided to help listening stations synchronize quickly on the new data stream.

- **SFD (1 byte):** The SFD (Start Frame Delimiter) is the 1-byte pattern 10101011. Note that the least significant bit (LSB, the last bit in the byte) is high (a "0"), whereas all the bytes of the Preamble had their LSB low (a "1"). With the LSB being a 0 the receiving NIC can determine that the physical clocking signal is ending and the actual data frame is about to start, hence the name Start Frame Delimiter. During discussions such as this you will also see a reference to the most significant bit (MSB), which refers to the first bit in the byte.

MAC address

- **Destination Address (6 bytes):** This is the destination *MAC address* of the station that is to receive the frame.
- **Source Address (6 bytes):** This is the MAC address of the source station transmitting the frame.
- **Length (2 bytes):** This field indicates the number of bytes in the Data field. In an Ethernet II frame this would be the previously discussed Type field.
- **Data (46 to 1500 bytes):** The Data area is where all data from the upper networking layers is carried. In Chapters 7 through 10 we will see how upper layer protocols are encapsulated and stored in the Data area.
- **FCS (4 bytes):** The FCS (frame check sequence) is a 32-bit CRC (cyclic redundancy check) value used to determine the validity of the received Ethernet frame. The FCS is found using a generator polynomial defined mathematically as:

$$G(x) = x^{32} + x^{26} + x^{23} + x^{22} + x^{16} + x^{12} + x^{11} + x^{10} + x^8 + x^7 + x^5$$
$$+ x^4 + x^2 + x + 1$$

which is equivalent to the binary value 100000100110000010001110110110111. The 1s in the pattern indicate where exclusive OR gates are used in a recirculating shift register circuit that is able to generate/check a valid stream of data of variable length. If even a single bit in the frame is received in error, the shift register will not generate the proper output and the error will be discovered.

All bits in the frame except those in the FCS are transmitted from LSB to MSB.

From the numbers provided in Figure 4–1, the minimum and maximum sizes of an Ethernet frame are 72 bytes and 1526 bytes, respectively. Many individuals refer to the smallest Ethernet frame as 64 bytes, by not including the 8 bytes of Preamble and SFD. The largest frame would then be 1518 bytes. For the purposes of the discussion in this chapter, the Preamble and SFD are included in the length of the frame.

So, how is this information used? The sending host performs a mathematical calculation of the content of the layer 2 frame and appends this to the end of the frame. The receiving NIC performs the same calculation when the frame arrives and compares that result with the one appended to the end of the frame by the transmitting NIC. If they match, the frame is assumed to have arrived without any errors being induced during the transmission process. If the two values are different, the frame is discarded as a bad frame. This is called error detection, not error correction (no request from any layer 2 process to retransmit the bad frame).

■ THE INTERFRAME GAP

Interframe gap

The *interframe gap* is a self-imposed quiet time appended to the end of every frame. This idle time gives the network media a chance to stabilize, and other network components time to process the frame. Figure 4–2 shows a sequence of frames separated by the fixed-size

FIGURE 4–2
Interframe gap separates
each Ethernet frame.

9.6 μs @ 10 Mbps = 96 bit times
0.96 μs @ 100 Mbps = 96 bit times
0.096 μs @ 1000 Mbps = 96 bit times

interframe gap. For 10 Mbps Ethernet, the interframe gap is 9.6 microseconds. This corresponds to 96 bit times (divide 9.6 microseconds by 100 nanoseconds/bit). Thus, the 576 bits of a minimum-length Ethernet frame are followed by 96 bit times of silence.

■ CSMA/CD

CSMA/CD

Objective 1-2

As mentioned in Chapter 1, *CSMA/CD* (Carrier Sense Multiple Access with Collision Detection) is part of the 802.3 specification, and is the technique used to share access to the available bandwidth. Ethernet was designed to operate in an environment where all hosts have equal access to the media for transmission. This means that all hosts connected to the media are peers. Some network standards, such as token ring, provide a network administrator the ability to set different transmission priorities for different hosts. Other standards use a polling method and ask a host if it has any data to send. In these standards, each host may not have equal access to the media. Ethernet uses a standard that allows every host on the network segment to have equal access to the media. These hosts function in an environment referred to as a collision domain. *Collision domains* exist when two or more hosts must share transmission access to the media. Recall that a repeater or hub receives a signal in one port and must immediately retransmit the signal out all other ports. These devices do not have circuitry that permits them to store information and delay the transmission out the other ports. When a signal comes in one port, it is retransmitted out all other ports even if a signal already exists on the media connected to the outgoing port. Of course, this results in what is called a *collision*, or two transmissions on the same media at the same time.

Collision domains

Collision

To access the media for transmission purposes, a NIC must listen to see if there are any transmissions on the wire. The previous section mentioned the interframe gap, which is the quiet time that a NIC must observe before it can start transmitting on the media. The NIC must see a quiet time of at least the 96 bit times (in a 10 Mbps network) before it can transmit on the media. When a NIC starts transmitting on the media it uses circuitry to monitor electrical activity on the media. It also uses internal loopback circuitry to monitor its own transmissions and compares them with what it sees on the media. If the NIC detects signals other than its own on the media, it will determine that a collision has occurred. When a collision occurs the host will transmit a jamming signal for a period long enough to alert everyone on the network to stop transmitting. The hosts that were transmitting signals on the media will stop their transmissions, then start an internal timer and wait for the timer to time out before they try to transmit again. The NICs will attempt to transmit up to 16 times. If collisions occur 16 times, the NIC will notify the upper layers that it was unable to complete the transmission.

If you stop and think about network congestion, you will easily realize that on a segment with a lot of hosts each additional host that is added exponentially increases the chances for collisions and failure of a network segment. If you take two disconnected network segments and join them with a hub or repeater, you decrease the quantity of collision domains (there used to be two separate collision domains), but you also increase the size of the collision domain (the hosts from both segments are now sharing the same media access). Bridges, switches, and routers contain RAM that can buffer (store in memory) packets for transmission. These devices also possess circuitry that can listen for transmissions on the wire just like the NIC on a PC. This means that when a transmission comes in one port of one of these devices and is destined to be retransmitted out another port of the device, that device can wait for the media to become clear before it transmits the message via the outgoing port. If you have one large collision domain and divide it with a bridge, switch, or router, you increase the quantity of collision domains (divide a single domain into two domains) and decrease the overall size of the collision domain (each collision domain connected to a port on a bridge, switch, or router is now in a separate domain).

■ ETHERNET CONTROLLERS

Objective 1-6

The complex digital operations required by a NIC to transmit and receive Ethernet frames are performed by a single dedicated ASIC (Application Specific Integrated Circuit) Ethernet controller. In addition to handling all the Ethernet chores, the ASIC also typically contains bus interface logic to connect directly to PCI or other standard PC bus architectures.

One such ASIC is the Realtek RTL8130, which comes in 160-pin QFP (Quad Flat Pack) or 100-pin PQFP (Plastic QFP) packages. Some of the many built-in features of the RTL8130 include:

- Ethernet MAC, Physical layer, and transceiver all on-chip
- 10 Mbps and 100 Mbps operation, with autonegotiation and full duplex flow control
- UTP + MII or UTP + AUI interface support for fault-tolerant applications
- Wake-On-LAN capability, including remote wakeup
- PCI bus mastering with ACPI and PCI power management
- Major network operating systems compatibility

The RTL8130 is but one example of a controller. There are many popular brands of controllers, and new enhancements to these devices are always in development.

■ 10 Mbps ETHERNET

Objective 1-3

The first three widely used Ethernet technologies were 10BASE5, 10BASE2, and 10BASE-T. Figure 4–3 shows the general 10 Mbps architecture of the Data-Link and Physical layers.

FIGURE 4–3
10 Mbps architecture.

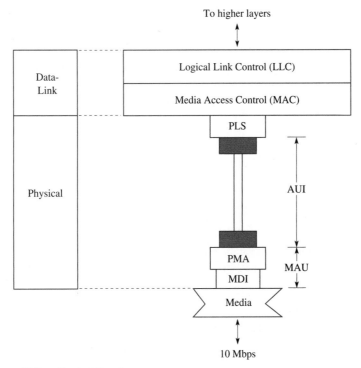

Beginning with the media (coax and UTP) we first encounter the MDI (medium dependent interface). The MDI is essentially the connection method used with the media, such as a vampire tap or an RJ-45 connector.

The PMA (physical medium attachment) provides the functions necessary for transmission, reception, and collision detection. Together, the MDI and PMA make up the MAU (medium attachment unit). Don't confuse this with the token ring MAU.

FIGURE 4–4
Pin numbering on the AUI
connector.

TABLE 4–2
AUI connector signal
descriptions.

Pin	Signal
1	Ground
2	CI+, Collision in circuit A
3	TX+, Data out circuit A
4	Ground
5	RX+, Data in circuit A
6	Ground
7	N/C
8	Ground
9	CI-, Collision in circuit B
10	TX-, Data out circuit B
11	Ground
12	RX-, Data in circuit B
13	+12 Volts
14	Ground
15	N/C

The AUI (attachment unit interface) may be a transceiver cable up to 50 meters in length, connected via a 15-pin AUI connector. Figure 4–4 shows the pin numbering of the AUI connector.

Objective 1-4

Table 4–2 lists the signals on each pin of the AUI connector. The AUI cable may be used, for example, to connect a thickwire vampire-tap transceiver to the upstream AUI port of a hub or switch. The PLS (physical signaling) is where Manchester encoding is applied to the bit stream.

The properties of each 10 Mbps technology are as follows.

10BASE5

- Media: RG-11 coaxial cable
- Propagation velocity: 0.77 c
- Impedance: 50 ohms
- Connector: Vampire tap
- Segment length: 500 meters
- Maximum nodes/segment: 100
- Node spacing: 2.5 meters
- Topology: Bus

The 2.5-meter spacing requirement is designed to prevent signal distortions from each station from adding together in phase. The number of nodes allowed on a segment is limited by the electrical properties of the cable. Don't forget that all wires must be properly terminated. 10BASE5 networks are not common anymore and are usually seen only in legacy networks.

10BASE2

- Media: RG-58 coaxial cable
- Propagation velocity: 0.65 c
- Impedance: 50 ohms
- Connector: BNC T
- Segment length: 185 meters

- Maximum nodes/segment: 30
- Node spacing: 0.5 meters
- Topology: Bus

Here you can see that the type of coaxial cable affects the allowable cable length as well as the number of nodes/segment. Don't forget that all wires must be properly terminated. 10BASE2 networks are not very common anymore and are usually seen only in legacy networks.

10BASE-T

- Media: Category 3, 4, or 5 UTP
- Propagation velocity: 0.585 c
- Impedance: 100 ohms
- Connector: RJ-45
- Segment length: 100 meters
- Maximum nodes/segment: 2
- Topology: Star

The number of nodes/segment is misleading because the UTP cable requires a point-to-point connection, typically a NIC to a port on a hub, or a hub-to-hub connection.

All three technologies have some common properties. These include:

- 10 Mbps data rate
- Manchester encoding
- Maximum of 1024 stations in a single collision domain (repeaters do not count toward this maximum limit)
- Maximum of four repeaters in longest path through the network

Figure 4–5 shows an example of how a digital signal is Manchester encoded. A logic zero is encoded as a falling edge in the middle of a bit time. A logic one is encoded as a rising edge. This guarantees an edge during every bit time, making the signal easier to synchronize with and decode.

FIGURE 4–5
Manchester encoding.

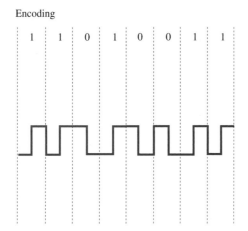

Encoding

| 1 | 1 | 0 | 1 | 0 | 0 | 1 | 1 |

5-4-3 rule

The four-repeater limit, chosen to maintain CSMA/CD operation, is part of a larger set of restrictions, commonly referred to as the **5-4-3 rule**, which has the following properties:

- 5 segments in the longest path
- 4 repeaters in the longest path
- 3 segments with nodes

Again, these rules apply to a single collision domain.

Objective 1-1

Figure 4–6 shows two ways of applying the 5-4-3 rule. In Figure 4–6(a) a 10BASE5/10BASE2 system is illustrated. Three of the five segments contain nodes. The longest path between stations (A and Z) is five segments, with four repeaters in between. Figure 4–6(b) shows a 10BASE-T network. The A and Z stations are separated by five UTP segments with four hubs in between. Each UTP cable from a station to a hub, or from a hub to another hub, is considered a segment and may be up to 100 meters in length.

FIGURE 4–6
Utilizing the 5-4-3 rule.

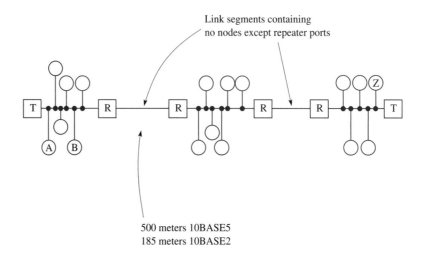

Link segments containing no nodes except repeater ports

500 meters 10BASE5
185 meters 10BASE2

(a) 10BASE5/10BASE2 network.

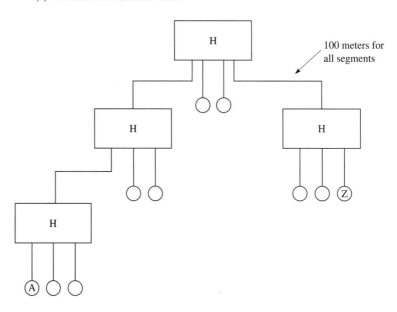

100 meters for all segments

(b) 10BASE-T network.

Collisions are detected in the 10BASE-T network whenever the transmit and receive pairs in a single UTP cable are active at the same time. For example, a frame transmitted from port 3 on a hub collides with a frame coming into port 3. Even though the transmit and receive wire pairs are different, and there is no electrical collision (as seen on coaxial cable), the two stations attempt to use the network simultaneously, which results in a collision. This indicates half-duplex operation because any station may send or receive, but not at the same time. New autonegotiating Ethernet transceivers are capable of operating in full-duplex, sending and receiving frames simultaneously.

10BASE-FX

FOIRL

Originally, the ***FOIRL*** (fiber-optic inter-repeater link) specification was used to standardize Ethernet communication over fiber. It allowed for a 1000-meter fiber between repeaters.

Eventually, the demand for fiber to the PC exceeded the FOIRL specifications, and a new set of fiber specifications was designed. Called 10BASE-FX, it contains three categories: 10BASE-FL, 10BASE-FB, and 10BASE-FP. (The "X" in 10BASE-FX generically represents all three technologies.)

10BASE-FL

- Fiber link specification
- Station-to-station, station-to-hub, and hub-to-hub connection
- 2000-meter segment length
- Manchester encoding
- Replaces FOIRL, works with existing FOIRL hardware
- Connector: ST

Objective 1-5

This specification is the most widely used. Figure 4–7 shows a portion of a 10BASE-FL network. Before fiber NICs became available, a 10BASE-FL to 10BASE-T (or 10BASE2) transceiver was used to interface fiber with the PC.

FIGURE 4–7
10BASE-FL wiring.

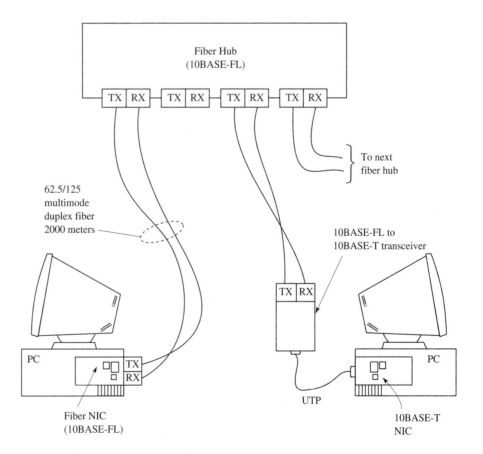

10BASE-FB

- Fiber backbone specification
- Hub-to-hub connection
- Synchronous operation
- 2000-meter segment length

The synchronous operation on the 10BASE-FB link is used to reduce the delays normally associated with Ethernet repeaters that cause the interframe gap to shrink as it propagates through multiple repeaters. This allows the segment distance to be extended without compromising the collision detection mechanism.

10BASE-FP

- Fiber passive specification
- Station-to-hub, hub-to-hub connection
- Hubs link up to 33 stations
- 500-meter segment length

This specification allows groups of 10BASE-FP computers to be passively connected via a hub that optically shares signals transmitted from any station. This technology is well suited for low-power environments.

■ 100 Mbps ETHERNET (FAST ETHERNET)

Objective 1-3

Fast Ethernet

Demand for bandwidth quickly exceeded the capacity of 10 Mbps Ethernet. Even moving from hub-based 10BASE-T networks to switch-based networks only provided temporary relief. Increasing the data rate by a factor of 10 over 10 Mbps Ethernet, 100 Mbps Ethernet, or *Fast Ethernet* as it is officially called, is implemented in several different ways, all collectively referred to as 100BASE-T technology. One disadvantage of Fast Ethernet is its smaller network diameter of around 200 meters. This reduction in network diameter is necessary to maintain the parameters of CSMA/CD at the faster data rate, since the signals still move at the same speed in the cable, but the frame times are shorter by a factor of 10.

Figure 4–8 shows the 100 Mbps Ethernet interface definition. Several new sublayers have been added, due to the requirements of 100 Mbps transmission. For example, the Manchester encoding used in 10 Mbps Ethernet is not well suited to high-frequency operation. Other data encoding and signaling techniques are used instead, using special bit patterns and multilevel signaling to transfer data in 4-bit chunks instead of one bit at a time (as in 10 Mbps Ethernet).

Take a look at each 100 Mbps technology.

100BASE-T4

- Data is exchanged over 3 pairs of Category 3 (or higher) UTP
- Data rate is 33.3 Mbps (25 M baud, 12.5 MHz) on each pair (total of 100 Mbps)
- 8B6T encoding is used
- Fourth pair is used for collision detection
- Half duplex only
- Maximum segment length: 100 meters
- Maximum network diameter: 205 meters
- Maximum number of repeaters: 2
- Connector: RJ-45

8B6T coding replaces 8-bit data values with 6 ternary codes that may have the values −, +, or 0. Table 4–3 shows a small sample of the 256 code patterns used in 8B6T encoding. The patterns are chosen to provide good DC characteristics, error detection, and reduced high-frequency effects. Special patterns can also be used as markers or control codes.

A multilevel signaling scheme is used, which allows more than one bit of data to be encoded into a signal transition. This is why a 12.5 MHz frequency carries a 33.3 Mbps stream. Think about it this way: Each cycle of the 12.5 MHz carrier contains two levels. This gives 25 million level changes per second on a single UTP pair. The signals on each of the three UTP pairs change a total of 75 million times each second. Dividing 75 million levels per second by 6 levels per 8B6T symbol gives 12.5 million symbols/second. Each symbol is equivalent to a unique 8-bit pattern, so multiplying 12.5 million symbols/second

FIGURE 4–8
100BASE-T architecture.

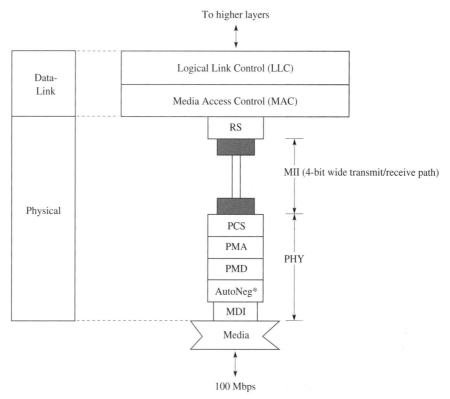

RS   Reconciliation Sublayer
PCS   Physical Coding Sublayer
PMA   Physical Medium Attachment
PHY   Physical Layer Device
PMD   Physical Medium Dependent
MII   Media Independent Interface
MDI   Medium Dependent Interface

* Optional.

TABLE 4–3
Selected 8B6T codes.

Hex Value	6T Code Group					
00	+	−	0	0	+	−
01	0	+	−	+	−	0
02	+	−	0	+	−	0
03	−	0	+	+	−	0
04	−	0	+	0	+	−
05	0	+	−	−	0	+
06	+	−	0	−	0	+
07	−	0	+	−	0	+
08	−	+	0	0	+	−
10	+	0	+	−	−	0
3F	+	0	−	+	0	−
5E	−	−	+	+	+	0
7F	0	0	+	−	−	+
80	+	−	+	0	0	−
C0	+	−	+	0	+	−
FF	+	0	−	+	0	0

Original
data

0101 1110

8B6T
encoding

−−+++0

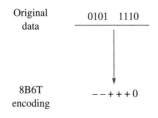

FIGURE 4–9
8B6T encoding.

4-bit Data	5-bit Code
0000	11110
0001	01001
0010	10100
0011	10101
0100	01010
0101	01011
0110	01110
0111	01111
1000	10010
1001	10011
1010	10110
1011	10111
1100	11010
1101	11011
1110	11100
1111	11101

TABLE 4–4
4B5B coding.

by 8 bits per symbol gives 100 million bits/second, the required data rate. Figure 4–9 shows a sample 8B6T encoded waveform. Note that the 12.5 MHz signaling frequency is within the 16 MHz limit of Category 3 cable.

100BASE-TX

- Data is exchanged over 2 pairs of Category 5 UTP
- Data rate is 125 Mbps on each pair (at 31.25 MHz)
- 4B5B encoding is used
- Half- and full-duplex operation
- Maximum segment length: 100 meters
- Maximum network diameter: 205 meters
- Maximum number of repeaters: 2
- Connector: RJ-45

Table 4–4 shows the 4B5B coding for all 16 4-bit data patterns. Notice that there is always a mixture of 0s and 1s in each 5-bit pattern. This is done to prevent long strings of 0s or 1s from being encoded, which contributes to loss of synchronization on the signal.

Figure 4–10 shows how a three-level signal called MLT-3 (multiple level transition) is used to represent the 4B5B bitstream. Each 4-bit data value is replaced by its 5-bit 4B5B counterpart. Thus, the 100 Mbps data stream becomes a 125 Mbps 4B5B encoded data stream. Using MLT-3 allows the 125 Mbps 4B5B data stream to be carried using a signal rate of 31.25 MHz (31.25 MHz times 4 bits/cycle equals 125 Mbps).

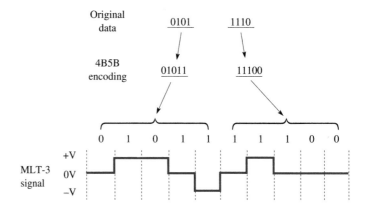

FIGURE 4–10
MLT-3 signaling for 4B5B encoded data.

Because the signaling frequency of 31.25 MHz is greater than the 16 MHz limit of Category 3 cable, a better cable, Category 5, is required. Category 5 cable has a frequency limit of 100 MHz.

100BASE-FX

- Single-mode fiber limit: 3000 meters
- Multimode fiber limit: 2000 meters (412 meters half duplex)
- 4B5B encoding is used
- Connector: duplex SC, ST, and FDDI MIC allowed

In this technology, the 4B5B encoded data is transmitted using NRZI (nonreturn to zero, invert on one). A 4B5B data rate of 125 Mbps is obtained using a 62.5 MHz carrier. Figure 4–11 illustrates a sample encoding and waveform. NRZI is well suited for fiber, due to its bi-level nature.

FIGURE 4–11
NRZI signaling for 4B5B encoded data.

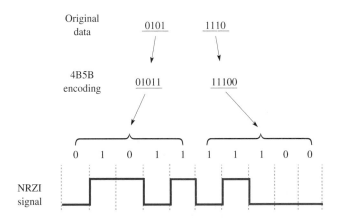

Fast Link Pulses

Fast link pulses

Along with 100BASE-T technology came the capability to perform autonegotiation between each end of a 100BASE-T connection. When the connection is established (plugging both ends of the UTP cable into their respective ports), a series of ***fast link pulses*** (FLP) is exchanged between the ports. The 33 pulses contain 17 clock pulses and 16 data pulses. The 16 data pulses form a 16-bit code indicating the capabilities of the port, such as communication mode (half duplex, full duplex) and speed (10, 100, 10/100). Originally, 10BASE-T NICs used a single normal link pulse (NLP) to perform a link integrity test. An indicator LED on the NIC shows the status of the link. If the link LED is off, there is a problem with the link (bad connection, wrong cable type, faulty NIC). Other LEDs may be used to indicate half- or full-duplex operation, as well as network activity. It is a good idea to check the LEDs whenever there is a problem. NLP pulses are typically generated every 16 milliseconds when the transmitter is idle, as indicated in Figure 4–12(a). NICs that support fast link pulses send an FLP burst containing 2 milliseconds of pulses, as illustrated in Figure 4–12(b). Note that the even pulses are the data pulses (a 1 when a pulse is present 62.5 microseconds after a clock pulse, a 0 if there is no data pulse). The 125-microsecond spacing between the clock pulses allows the entire burst to complete in 2 milliseconds.

FIGURE 4–12
Fast link pulse details.

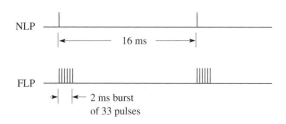

(a) General timing.

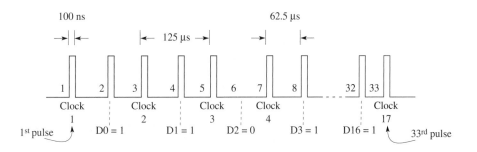

(b) FLP burst organization.

After the FLP bursts are exchanged, the ports decide on the best capabilities for the link according to the priority shown in Table 4–5. This happens as soon as you plug a live UTP cable into a port.

TABLE 4–5
Autonegotiation priorities.

Priority	Link Choice
1 (Highest)	100BASE-T2 (full duplex)
2	100BASE-TX (full duplex)
3	100BASE-T2 (half duplex)
4	100BASE-T4
5	100BASE-TX (half duplex)
6	10BASE-T (full duplex)
7 (Lowest)	10BASE-T (half duplex)

Two Repeater Types

The original 10 Mbps Ethernet specified a single repeater type to propagate frames between segments. Fast Ethernet contains specifications for two types of repeaters: Class I and Class II. Class I repeaters are slower (140 bit times for its round-trip delay) than Class II repeaters (92 bit times or less), but provide functions such as translation between the many different 100BASE-T technologies. Class II repeaters, although faster, only support a single technology.
Standard topologies for 100BASE-T networks include:

- One Class I repeater: provides a network diameter of 200 meters using copper cable. Stations may be 100 meters from the repeater.
- Two Class II repeaters: connected via a 5-meter cable. This provides a diameter of 205 meters. Stations may be 100 meters from each repeater.

100VG-AnyLAN

Domain-based priority access

Developed by Hewlett-Packard, the IEEE 802.12 standard 100VG-AnyLAN technology is a 100 Mbps LAN technology capable of handling both Ethernet and token-ring frames. 100VG-AnyLAN uses *domain-based priority access,* an access method whereby stations are polled in a round-robin fashion. Each polled station may make a normal-priority or high-priority request, which is processed by a higher-level 100VG-AnyLAN hub (not the same as an Ethernet hub). This access method eliminates collisions, allowing 100VG-Any-LAN networks to have a larger diameter than a 100BASE-T network. The high-priority requests are intended to support real-time multimedia applications such as voice and video.

■ 1000 Mbps ETHERNET (GIGABIT ETHERNET)

Objective 1-3

When the demand for bandwidth exceeded 100 Mbps Ethernet, it was natural to think about extending Ethernet to 1000 Mbps, rather than use some other, noncompatible technology such as ATM (asynchronous transfer mode) or FDDI (fiber distributed data interface). Extending the data rate, however, leads to a decrease in the network diameter (so that CSMA/CD is maintained). You might agree that a network diameter of 25 meters or less is not practical. Two techniques used to increase the data rate from 100 Mbps to 1000 Mbps but still maintain a reasonable network diameter are carrier extension and frame bursting.

Carrier Extension

Carrier extension

Figure 4–13 shows an Ethernet frame with a 0- to 448-byte carrier extension field. The *carrier extension* is used to maintain a minimum 512-byte Ethernet frame (not including the Preamble and SFD). So, a 10/100 Mbps Ethernet frame containing only 100 bytes would require a carrier extension field of 412 bytes to be used over Gigabit Ethernet.

FIGURE 4–13
100VG-AnyLAN network.

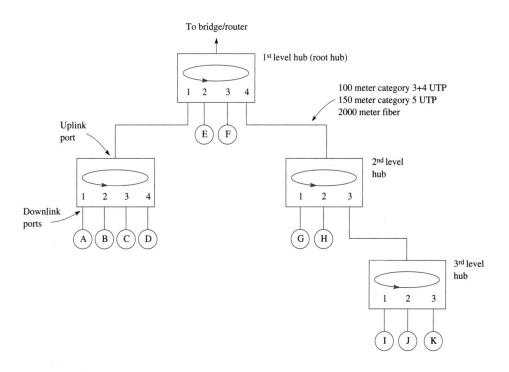

Frame Bursting

Frame bursting

Frame bursting involves sending multiple frames in a burst of transmission. The first frame in the burst must be carrier extended if its length is less than 512 bytes. Additional frames in the burst do not require carrier extensions, but an interframe gap of 0.096 microseconds (96 bit times) is needed between frames. The transmitter continues transmitting during the interframe gap to maintain its hold on the network media. A burst timer, started when the first frame is transmitted, limits the length of the burst to a maximum of 65,536 bits.

Single Repeater Type

Gigabit Ethernet

Unlike Fast Ethernet, *Gigabit Ethernet* goes back to a single repeater type. A Gigabit Ethernet repeater must support all 1000 Mbps technologies and operate at a fixed speed of 1000 Mbps. No 10/100/1000 or 100/1000 capabilities are defined, although multispeed Gigabit switches are available on the market.

Gigabit Ethernet Architecture

Figure 4–14 shows the multilayer architectural model for Gigabit Ethernet. You may notice the similarities to 10 Mbps and 100 Mbps Ethernet. One notable difference is the new 8-bit-wide transmit and receive paths.

In addition, notice that full-duplex operation is available in every Gigabit technology, which was not the case for 10 Mbps Ethernet and Fast Ethernet. The MAC layer, described in IEEE 802.3z, deals with issues such as half/full-duplex operation, carrier extension, and frame bursting.

The following examines the different Gigabit Ethernet technologies.

1000BASE-T
- IEEE standard 802.3ab
- Cable type: 4 pairs of Category 5 (or higher) UTP
- Maximum cable length: 100 meters
- Data rate: 1000 Mbps (2000 Mbps full duplex)

FIGURE 4–14
Gigabit Ethernet architecture.

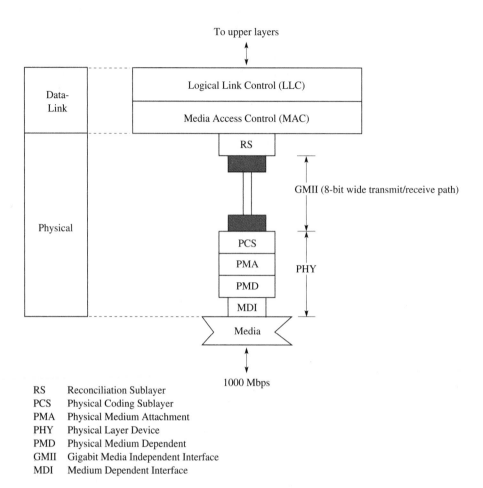

RS   Reconciliation Sublayer
PCS   Physical Coding Sublayer
PMA   Physical Medium Attachment
PHY   Physical Layer Device
PMD   Physical Medium Dependent
GMII   Gigabit Media Independent Interface
MDI   Medium Dependent Interface

- PAM5 × 5 encoding
- Connector: RJ-45

The two-dimensional PAM5 × 5 encoding introduced in 100BASE-T2 is extended here to a four-dimensional PAM5 × 5 system.

1000BASE-CX
- Short haul copper
- Cable: shielded, balanced copper (twinax)
- Maximum cable length: 25 meters
- Data rate: 1000 Mbps (2000 Mbps full duplex)
- 8B10B encoding
- Connector: 9-pin D or 8-pin Fiber Channel Type 2 (HSSC)

Transferring 8 bits of data reliably at gigabit speeds requires another change in the method used to encode the data. The 8B10B coding method (originally developed for Fiber Channel) replaces 8-bit data values with 10-bit code words. The code words are chosen from groups such that the number of 0s and 1s transmitted is kept in balance. A signaling rate of 1.25 Gbps is required to encode the 1 Gbps data stream.

1000BASE-SX
- Short-wavelength laser
- Wavelength: 770–860 nanometers
- Data rate: 1000 Mbps (2000 Mbps full duplex)
- 8B10B encoding

- 62.5/125 multimode fiber length limit: 275 meters (half and full duplex)
- 50/125 multimode fiber length limit: 550 meters (full duplex), 316 meters (half duplex)
- Connector: SC

1000BASE-LX
- Long-wavelength laser
- Wavelength: 1270–1355 nanometers
- Data rate: 1000 Mbps (2000 Mbps full duplex)
- 8B10B encoding
- Single-mode fiber length limit: 5000 meters (full duplex), 316 meters (half duplex)
- Multimode fiber length limit: 550 meters (full duplex), 316 meters (half duplex)
- Connector: SC

Table 4–6 summarizes the 10, 100, and 1000 Mbps Ethernet copper and fiber technologies.

TABLE 4–6
Comparison of Ethernet technologies.

Technology	Max Segment Length	Encoding Method	Topology	Media	Bit Rate (bits/sec)
10BASE5	500 meters	Manchester	Bus	50-ohm coax	10 M
10BASE2	185 meters	Manchester	Bus	50-ohm coax	10 M
10BASE-T	100 meters	Manchester	Star	2 pairs UTP Cat. 3, 4, 5	10 M
10BASE-FL	2000 meters	Manchester	Star	multimode fiber*	10 M
100BASE-T2	100 meters	PAM 5X5	Star	2 pairs UTP Cat. 3, 4, 5	100 M
100BASE-T4	100 meters	8B/6T	Star	4 pairs UTP Cat. 3,4,5	100 M
100BASE-TX	100 meters	4B/5B with MLT-3	Star	2 pairs UTP Cat. 5	100 M
100BASE-FX	412 meters/ 2000 meters	4B/5B with NRZI	Star	multimode* fiber	100 M
1000BASE-T	100 meters	PAM 5X5	Star	4 pairs UTP Cat. 5	1000 M
1000BASE-SX	275 meters	8B/10B	Star	multimode fiber+	1000 M
1000BASE-LX	316 meters/ 550 meters	8B/10B	Star	multimode fiber†	1000 M
1000BASE-CX	25 meters	8B/10B	Star	twinax	1000 M

* Fiber is duplex 62.5/125 μm mulitmode fiber.

\+ Maximum segment length is 316 meters/550 meters with 50/125 μm multimode fiber.

† Maximum segment length is 316 meters/550 meters with 50/125 μm multimode fiber or 316 meters/5000 meters with 10/125 μm single-mode fiber.

Even with this wide selection of technologies, there is still one more to examine: wireless Ethernet.

■ WIRELESS ETHERNET

Wireless Ethernet, the use of Ethernet over radio frequency (RF) or infrared (IR), is covered by the IEEE 802.11 Wireless LAN Standard. A wireless Ethernet network consists of

Objective 1-2

one or more fixed stations (base stations) that service multiple mobile stations. Some implementation details include:

- Frame formats for IEEE 802.3 (Ethernet) and IEEE 802.5 (token ring) remain the same
- CSMA/CA utilized
- 1 Mbps, 2 Mbps, 11 Mbps, and 54 Mbps operations

This method differs from CSMA/CD in that the wireless transceiver cannot listen to the network for other transmissions while it is transmitting. Its transmitter simply drowns out any other signal that may be present. Instead, stations attempt to avoid collisions by using random backoff delays to delay transmission when the network is busy (when some other station is transmitting). A handshaking sequence is used between communicating stations (ready and acknowledge packets) to help maintain reliable delivery of messages over the air.

Types of Wireless LANs

There are two primary types of Wireless Ethernet LANs: RF-based and IR-based, as described below.

RF-based: RF signals can propagate through objects, such as walls, reducing security. The ISM band (industrial, scientific, medical) is used for transmission at the following frequencies:

Industrial: 902 to 928 MHz

Scientific: 2.40 GHz to 2.4835 GHz

Medical: 5.725 GHz to 5.850 GHz

Frequency hopping
Direct sequence

Data is transmitted using the spread spectrum technologies *frequency hopping* and *direct sequence*. In frequency hopping, the transmitter hops from frequency to frequency, seemingly at random, transmitting a portion of each frame at each frequency. The receiver hops to the same frequencies, using the same pseudorandom sequence as the transmitter. A measure of security is added to the data because it's difficult to eavesdrop on all the associated frequencies and reassemble the frame fragments.

The direct sequence method involves exclusive-ORing a pseudorandom bitstream with the data before transmission. The same pseudorandom bit sequence is used in the receiver to get the original data back.

Multipath effect

IR-based: Two types of IR wireless Ethernet are used—diffused IR and point-to-point IR. Diffused IR bounces signals off walls, ceilings, and floors. The data rate is limited by the *multipath effect*, whereby multiple signals radiate from a single transmission, each taking a different path to the receiving stations. This is illustrated in Figure 4–15.

FIGURE 4–15
The multipath effect in diffused IR wireless Ethernet.

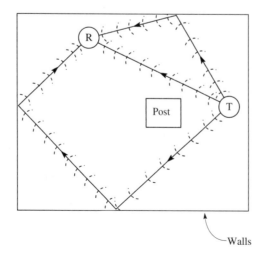

Point-to-point IR uses line-of-sight IR lasers and provides a faster data rate than diffused IR. It also works over larger distances—up to 1 mile.

■ TROUBLESHOOTING TECHNIQUES

When working with Ethernet systems, it is useful to be familiar with some common problems encountered in actual networks.

MTU Affects Available Bandwidth

MTU

The *MTU* (maximum transmission unit) is the maximum frame size allowed on the network. For Ethernet, the MTU may range from 68 to 1500, with many Internet service providers setting their lines to an MTU of 576. If the MTU is too small, large frames will be fragmented into two or more smaller frames, contributing to excess utilization of the bandwidth and increased collisions. Windows users may adjust their MTU by modifying the Registry.

Jabber

Jabbering

An out-of-control Ethernet transmitter may generate a frame that is longer than 1526 bytes. Other conditions on the network, such as bad terminations or a failing power supply in a hub or switch, may cause distortions that resemble a *jabbering* device. Repeaters are designed to prohibit retransmission of any frames for a short period of time when jabbering is detected, to prevent the network from being saturated with meaningless signals.

Runts

Runt

A *runt* is any transmitted frame whose length is less than the minimum frame size, even a short frame with a valid FCS.

Alignment Error

When all the bits of a frame have been received, it is possible that the last bit received is not the last bit of the final byte in the frame. In other words, the number of bits in the frame is not a multiple of eight. This is called an *alignment error.* This will most likely cause the FCS to be invalid and the frame will be discarded. Intermittent connections contribute to this type of error, as do collisions (which terminate with an unknown number of bits transmitted followed by the jam sequence).

Packet sniffers keep track of many different Ethernet errors. Figure 4–16 shows a sample error display. The errors were created by pulling the RJ-45 connector out of its port on a hub while a large file download was in progress.

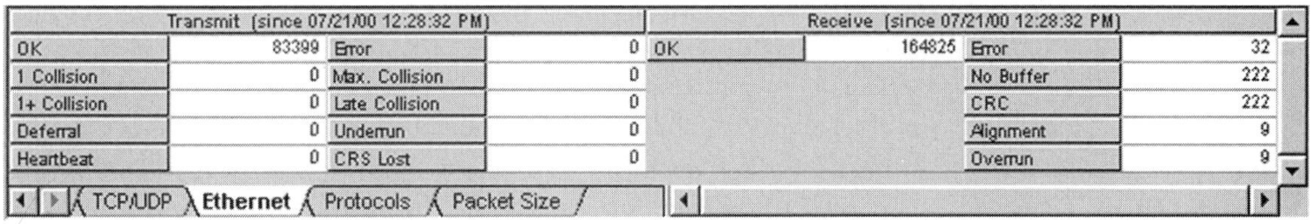

Transmit (since 07/21/00 12:28:32 PM)				Receive (since 07/21/00 12:28:32 PM)			
OK	83399	Error	0	OK	164825	Error	32
1 Collision	0	Max. Collision	0			No Buffer	222
1+ Collision	0	Late Collision	0			CRC	222
Deferral	0	Underrun	0			Alignment	9
Heartbeat	0	CRS Lost	0			Overrun	9

TCP/UDP \ **Ethernet** \ Protocols \ Packet Size /

FIGURE 4–16
Packet sniffer Ethernet error display.

Cabling

Cabling errors are typically one of the following:

Coax
- Bad BNC connector crimp
- Improperly installed vampire tap
- Dirty (oxidized) connector
- Loose or missing terminator

UTP
- Wrong category cable
- Bad cable (open pair)
- Wrong cable type (crossover instead of straight-through)

Lost Termination

Removing the 50-ohm terminating resistor from the end of a 10BASE2 or 10BASE5 cable causes distorted signals to reflect off the end instead of being absorbed by the terminating resistor (due to high-frequency properties of transmission lines). The signal reflections cause repeated collisions, effectively shutting down the entire cable segment.

Excess Utilization

Ethernet exhibits poor performance when its utilization is approximately 60% or more. Excess utilization (including plenty of lost bandwidth due to collisions) is typically the result of too many stations operating in the same collision domain. Replacing hubs with switches or routers will partition the network into multiple collision domains, each containing a smaller number of stations. The improvement in performance will be very noticeable.

INDUSTRY TIP

According to a recent survey conducted by Belden, industry contractors who use Bonded-Pair cables experience fewer performance failures, resulting in less time spent troubleshooting and less re-work. The result is an efficient, cost-effective installation.

Cable can kink as it comes off the reel, plus it can be pulled and bent around corners and tight spaces in the pathway between the telecommunications closet and the workstation. These stresses significantly impact the cable's performance, even when the installation is relatively simple.

Additional stress is put on the cable during termination. After the cable has been routed through the pathway to the various termination points, more stresses are applied when removing the other jacket, separating the twisted pairs, and terminating the individual conductors on a connector's ICCs.

All of these installation factors can change the physical properties of the cable, which in turn can degrade the cable's electrical performance. To ensure that the cable performs not only on the reel but, more importantly, after installation, it is critical to maintain the physical integrity of the cable throughout the installation. Cable performance, in turn, can affect profitability on the job. Cable that fails performance tests must be fixed or replaced, which costs contractors both time and money.

Reprinted from a Technical Bulletin from Belden Inc.

CAREER DEVELOPMENT

Home Technology Integration is a new discipline offering new opportunities. This field covers the installation and integration of home security, low-voltage lighting, home entertainment, HVAC and plumbing control, as well as home networking. The technician that gets the appropriate training and certification can build a business of their own as a technology integrator.

CompTIA has a vendor-neutral certification called HTI+. This certification requires the successful completion of two exams that cover all of the subsystems as well as integration techniques and structured cabling. In addition to the CompTIA certification a technician can also gain certification from CEDIA and other industry organizations. Check out the certifications and job opportunities at www.comptia.org or www.cedia.org.

■ SELF-TEST

1. True or False: Ethernet supports reliable delivery of data.

2. The PDU of layer 2 is called a _____.
   a. bit
   b. frame
   c. packet
   d. segment

3. True or False: Ethernet transmission rules specify a fixed frame size of 1500 octets.

4. Which of the following is **not** a common media type according to Ethernet standards?
   a. Copper cable
   b. Fiber optic
   c. Air
   d. Aluminum cable

5. Multimode fiber transmissions use a(n) _____ capable of bouncing multiple light signals through the core of a fiber cable at different angles.
   a. laser
   b. SED
   c. LED
   d. LLC

6. True or False: Multimode fiber is capable of longer segment lengths than single-mode fiber.

7. Which bit is referred to as the MSB of the start frame delimiter byte?
   a. Last bit in the byte
   b. First bit in the byte
   c. First bit that is a 1
   d. Last bit that is a 1

8. True or False: MSB refers to the term Most Significant Bit.

9. If an Ethernet frame contains the same FCS represented on the sending and receiving NICs, the frame _____.
   a. is discarded
   b. has no errors
   c. is re-sent
   d. sends acknowledgement

10. True or False: CSMA/CA is an integral part of the 802.3 Ethernet standard.

11. Hosts in an Ethernet environment function in a _____.
    a. ring
    b. collision domain
    c. polling domain
    d. logical star

12. Which of the following devices **do not** contain circuitry that would permit temporary storage of Ethernet frames until the media is clear for transmission?
    a. Hubs
    b. Switches
    c. Bridges
    d. Repeaters

13. True or False: When a signal is received on a hub port, it must be immediately retransmitted out all other ports.

14. The NIC must see a quiet time of _____ bit times before it can transmit on the media.
    a. 32
    b. 64
    c. 96
    d. 128

15. NICs will attempt to transmit up to _____ times if a collision is experienced.
    a. 4
    b. 8
    c. 16
    d. 24

16. Adding a hub to connect two network segments _____ the quantity of collision domains.
    a. increases
    b. decreases
    c. does not change
    d. regulates

17. True or False: Bridges can buffer frames because they contain RAM.

18. The MDI is essentially the _____ used with the media.
    a. signaling mode
    b. connection method
    c. bit stream
    d. Manchester data interpreter

19. The Attachment Unit Interface may be a transceiver cable up to 50 meters in length connected with a(n) _____ connector.
    a. BNC
    b. NIC
    c. AUI
    d. T

20. True or False: A network segment that allows a host to send and receive at the same time is known as half-duplex.

21. What was the original standard for Ethernet communication over fiber called that allowed 1000-meter fiber segments between repeaters?
    a. 10BASE-FX
    b. 10BASE-FL
    c. 10BASE-FP
    d. FOIRL

22. What is the CSMA/CD network called that operates at speeds of 100 Mbps?
    a. Ethernet
    b. Fast Ethernet

    c. Token ring

    d. Gigabit Ethernet

23. What type of cabling is specified as the minimum for a 100BASE-T4 network?

    a. CAT 3

    b. CAT 5

    c. CAT 6

    d. RG-11

24. Why is a better cable required for 100BASE-TX networks versus the cable required for a 10BASE-T network?

    a. Higher signaling frequency

    b. Greater distance

    c. Repeater limitation

    d. Synchronization limits

25. True or False: 100BASE-FX multimode fiber is limited to 5000 meters.

26. What is a feature of most NICs that provides an indication of a problem or connection speed?

    a. LCDs

    b. LEDs

    c. Autonegotiation

    d. NRZ

27. Which repeater type used in 100BASE-T networks provides a larger network diameter?

    a. Class I

    b. Class II

    c. Class III

    d. Class IV

28. How are stations polled in 100VG-AnyLAN networks?

    a. First come, first served

    b. Round-robin fashion

    c. Central server

    d. Token passing

Token Ring, FDDI, and Other LAN Technologies

Limita 256 Hosts

PERFORMANCE OBJECTIVES

Upon completion of this chapter, you will be able to:

- Discuss the features and topology of a token-ring LAN.

- Describe the features and topology of FDDI.

- List some key features of token-bus and broadband LANs.

NETWORK+ OBJECTIVES

This chapter provides information for the following Network+ objectives:

1.1 Recognize the following logical or physical network topologies given a schematic diagram or description:
- Star/hierarchical
- Bus
- Mesh
- Ring
- Wireless

1.2 Specify the main features of 802.2 (LLC), 802.3 (Ethernet), 802.5 (token ring), 802.11b (wireless), and FDDI networking technologies, including
- Speed
- Access
- Method
- Topology
- Media

2.11 Identify the basic characteristics (e.g., speed, capacity, media) of the

following WAN technologies:
- Packet switching vs. circuit switching
- ISDN
- FDDI
- ATM
- Frame Relay
- Sonet/SDH
- T1/E1
- T3/E3
- Ocx

4.10 Given a troubleshooting scenario involving a network with a particular physical topology (i.e., bus, star/ hierarchical, mesh, ring, wireless) and including a network diagram, identify the network area affected and the cause of the problem.

4.12 Given a network troubleshooting scenario involving a wiring/ infrastructure problem, identify the cause of the problem (e.g., bad media, interference, network hardware).

■ INTRODUCTION

This chapter explores token ring, token bus, and fiber-distributed data interface (FDDI) networking technologies. Even though Ethernet is by far the most popular, each of the other LAN technologies examined in this chapter currently have, or have had, their own particular advantages and uses. In order, this chapter looks at the following types of networks:

- Token ring
- Token bus
- FDDI

Token

These three technologies have a common concept in that they use an electronic packet, called a *token*, to control the conversations on the network. As noted in Chapter 1, the token has its conceptual origins in a device referred to as a talking stick. A talking stick was a physical item that members of a society used to designate which individual was allowed to speak at any given time. Elders would convene meetings and during these meetings the individual allowed to speak was the one holding the talking stick. This is somewhat similar to our current parliamentary equivalent of "having the floor." In a network that uses the token concept, only the station possessing the electronic token may transmit data onto the media. Typically the first device active on the network generates a token, which is then passed around among the other stations in a prescribed manner. Depending on the design of the technology, there are many control mechanisms that can be implemented.

Finally, broadband LANs are discussed. These are new but growing in their implementation.

■ TOKEN RING

Objective 1-2

Currently, token ring is the second most popular networking technology after Ethernet. A token-ring network, specified by the IEEE 802.5 standard, uses a token passing mechanism to regulate data flow in a logical ring-based topology. In a token-ring network, a *token* is a three-byte packet containing a starting delimiter, frame control, and ending delimiter fields. When a station wants to transmit data it rebuilds the token with additional fields such as source and destination address, data, FCS, and so on. The token then becomes a normal data frame. The station will transmit the data frame onto the ring. The frame circulates from one station to the next as it travels to the destination station. When a data frame makes a complete trip around the ring, the originating station checks the frame to make sure the data was received by the destination, and then rebuilds the token frame and releases the token back onto the network. The token will then travel the network, waiting for the next station that needs to transmit data.

Unlike Ethernet, token ring contains support for prioritized transmissions. In addition, there are no collisions in a token-ring network caused by multiple stations transmitting at the same time. Thus, token ring performs better under heavy traffic loads than Ethernet does.

IEEE 802.5 specifies 4 Mbps and 16 Mbps speeds. Data is transmitted using *differential* Manchester encoding. Figure 5–1 illustrates the difference between Manchester encoding and differential Manchester encoding.

In Manchester encoding, a 0 is encoded as a falling edge in the middle of the bit time. A 1 is encoded as a rising edge in the middle of the bit time. In *differential* Manchester encoding, there is always a transition in the middle of the bit time. A transition at the beginning of a bit interval indicates a 0. No transition indicates a 1. An advantage of *differential* Manchester encoding is that the polarity of the signal is independent of the bit stream. In other words, inverting a differential Manchester signal will result in the same received data, whereas inverting an ordinary Manchester encoded signal will invert all the data bits.

FIGURE 5–1
Comparing Manchester and differential Manchester encoding.

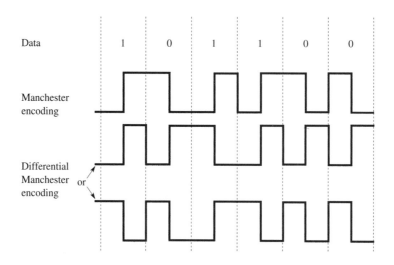

Token-Ring Topology

Objective 1-1

Though the logical topology of a token-ring network is a ring, the physical topology is a combination of star and ring. As shown in Figure 5–2, stations (or *lobes*) in a token-ring network connect to an MAU (multistation access unit) using lobe cables. Multiple MAUs are connected serially, using patch cables, to form a ring. Shielded twisted pair (STP) is typically used for wiring, although UTP and fiber are also supported. The number of MAUs in the ring affects the maximum distance between MAUs. IEEE 802.5 limits the number of stations on any ring to 250 and the number of MAUs to 33. Stations can be added or removed without major disruption to the ring.

FIGURE 5–2
Token-ring topology.

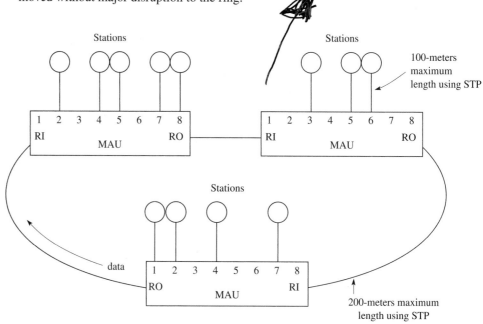

Token-Ring Frame Formats

Priority

Reservation

Figures 5–3 and 5–4 illustrate the formats of the Token and Information frames used by token ring. The token format in Figure 5–3 is a 24-bit frame generated by the active monitor (described in the following section). Notice that the Access Control field contains ***Priority*** and ***Reservation*** bits. The *Priority* bits indicate the current priority of the token and any associated information frames. The *Reservation* bits are used to reserve the next token at a specific priority. The Token bit is used to differentiate between Token frames and Information frames.

FIGURE 5–3
Token-ring token format.

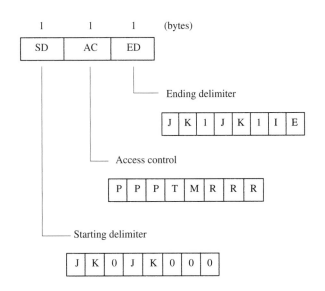

Key:

J—Nondata J symbol
K—Nondata K symbol
P—Priority bits (111 highest)
T—Token bit (0 = token, 1 = frame)
M—Monitor bit
R—Reservation bits
I—Intermediate frame bit
E—Error-detected bit

The Monitor bit helps identify a frame that is stuck circulating on the ring.

The J and K symbols are illegal differential Manchester codes (no transition in the middle of the bit time) used to identify the Starting and Ending delimiters.

The Information frame diagrammed in Figure 5–4 contains many of the same fields as the Ethernet frame covered in Chapter 4. One significant difference is the length of the INFO field, which may be 4550 bytes in length in 4 Mbps token ring, or 18,200 bytes for 16 Mbps token ring. Compare this with Ethernet's 1500-byte limit (for all Ethernet speeds).

FIGURE 5–4
Token-ring frame format.

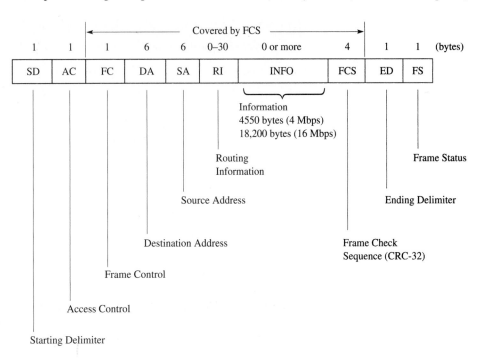

Ring Management

One station on the ring acts as the *active monitor* and is responsible for ensuring that valid tokens circulate on the ring. The active monitor also controls the timing of the tokens on the ring and initiates a *ring purge* operation to recover from errors, such as lost or corrupted tokens or timeouts during transmission of a frame. Stations on the network can also fail after transmitting an information frame, which means that there would be no rebuilding of the token, thereby preventing other stations from ever transmitting. The active monitor can clean the network of bad tokens and generate a new token to get the ring operating properly again. This is known as the ring purging operation of a network.

All other stations on the ring act as standby monitors. If the active monitor fails, a standby monitor will initiate a "Claim Token" process to choose the new active monitor.

Catastrophic errors on the ring, such as a broken ring or an error during the "Claim Token" process, initiate the *beaconing procedure.* Beacon frames are then circulated to determine the nature of the fault (the *fault domain*) and possibly isolate the cause of the failure. This beaconing procedure is used to identify any break in the network (i.e., a PC failure) and make adjustments to isolate and work around this break in the logical ring. This is part of the self-healing quality of token-ring networks.

Comparing Token Ring and Ethernet

Token-ring networks control access to the network media using a token. Ethernet networks use CSMA/CD techniques to control access to the transmission media. Token-ring networks can use reservation and priority fields to give some stations higher access to the transmission media than others. Ethernet is a peer network providing equal access to all stations. Since token-ring networks can control access you can actually determine how much time it will take for controlled transmission to take place on a network. If you want to give priority to a specific station you can mathematically determine how long it will take to communicate with a particular station. Ethernet has no control over the timing of transmissions, so there is no ability to predict how soon a station can respond to a specific transmission (e.g., if the media is busy when the station wants to respond to a transmission). Table 5–1 shows a comparison between token ring and Ethernet characteristics. Take a few minutes to look at some of the differences such as maximum frame size, transmission speeds, and so on.

TABLE 5–1
Comparing token ring and Ethernet.

Item	Token Ring	Ethernet
Standard	IEEE 802.5	IEEE 802.3
Speed	4, 16 Mbps*	10, 100, 1000 Mbps
Max Nodes	250	1023
Self-healing	Yes	No
Max. Frame Size**	4550 bytes (4 Mbps) 18,200 bytes (16 Mbps)	1500 bytes
Encoding	Differential Manchester	Manchester, 4B/5B, 8B/6T, 8B/10B, PAM 5x5
Prioritized Access	Yes	No
Routing Information in Frame	Yes	No
Access Method	Token Passing	CSMA/CD
Physical Topology	Ring, Star	Bus, Star

* 100 Mbps and 1000 Mbps specifications exist but are not widely used.
** Amount of data in one packet

■ TOKEN BUS

Objective 1-1

The IEEE 802.4 token-bus standard describes the mechanism by which multiple stations share access to a common bus. Figure 5–5 shows a sample token-bus network.

FIGURE 5–5
Token-bus operation.

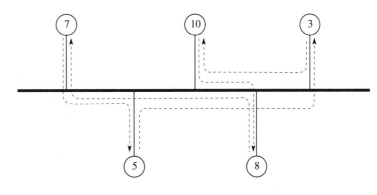

------► Path of token

Each station knows the addresses of the previous and next stations in the sequence of stations. Tokens are circulated in a logical ring, from station 10, to stations 8, 7, 5, and finally 3. Station 3 transmits back to station 10 to complete the logical ring. Note that the physical location of the station on the bus does not affect the sequence.

If a station fails, a special "who follows" frame is transmitted to determine the next station in sequence following the failed station. Some additional details are as follows:

- Token bus is available in speeds of 1, 5, 10, and 20 Mbps
- Data frames may contain over 8000 bytes of information
- Four levels of priority are available
- Operates over coax and fiber

Note that the token-bus standards have been formally withdrawn by IEEE. This technology is all but nonexistent, but since it is still occasionally referred to, it was included in this book.

■ FDDI

FDDI

Objective 1-2

Objective 2-11

FDDI (fiber-distributed data interface) is a self-healing baseband network technology similar to token ring. As indicated in Figure 5–6, an FDDI network consists of nodes connected together with dual fiber rings. Both rings, called primary and secondary (or backup), operate at 100 Mbps using 4B/5B encoding. An error detected with the primary ring will cause an instant changeover to the secondary ring to prevent loss of communication.

Using 4B/5B encoding, 4 bits of data are encoded as a 5-bit symbol. Bits are transmitted over the fiber as transitions of light (off-to-on or on-to-off). LEDs operating at 1300 nanometers provide the light source for the fiber. 62.5/125 micrometer multimode fiber is typically used.

The large circumference of an FDDI ring (100 kilometers for dual ring, 200 kilometers for single ring) makes it ideal for use over a large geographical area.

FDDI nodes come in two types:

- **Single Attached Station (SAS):** Attaches to the primary ring only
- **Dual Attached Station (DAS):** Attaches to both rings

Note that an SAS may not be directly connected to the primary ring because the entire ring would fail if the SAS failed. Instead, the SAS is connected via a modified DAS called a *wiring concentrator.* Wiring concentrators are also used to connect individual rings together.

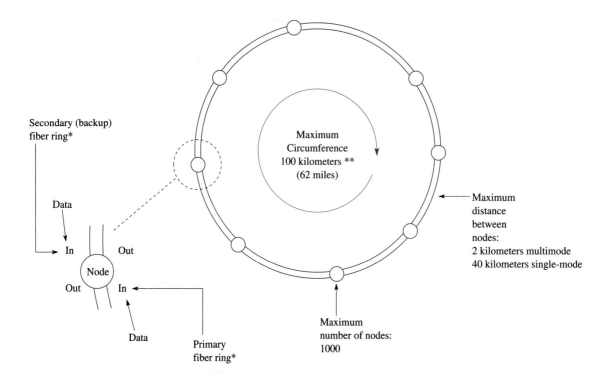

* Each ring operates at 100 Mbps.
** Maximum circumference is 200 kilometers (124 miles) if only primary ring is used.

FIGURE 5–6
FDDI topology.

Figure 5–7 shows the details of the token and information frames used over the FDDI ring.

FIGURE 5–7
FDDI token format.

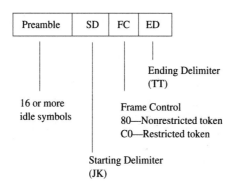

Figure 5–8 shows the details of the FDDI information frame format.

4B/5B symbols are used in both examples. Note the large size of the FDDI information frame (up to 4500 bytes). This helps reduce overhead when transmitting a large block of data that must be broken into multiple frames. The 4500-byte limit is a function of the maximum circumference of the ring, the data rate, and the allowable variation in clock speeds between nodes.

A newer variation of FDDI called FDDI-II (or *hybrid ring control*) contains support for voice, video, and other multimedia applications. This is accomplished through the addition of circuit-switching capability to the original packet-switching technique.

You can view an excellent tutorial on FDDI at http://www.iol.unh.edu/training/fddi/htmls/index.html.

FIGURE 5–8
FDDI information frame format.

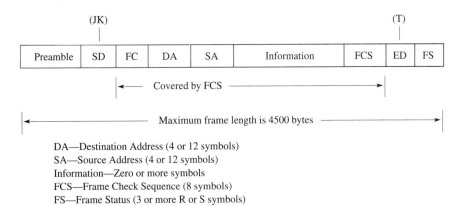

DA—Destination Address (4 or 12 symbols)
SA—Source Address (4 or 12 symbols)
Information—Zero or more symbols
FCS—Frame Check Sequence (8 symbols)
FS—Frame Status (3 or more R or S symbols)

■ BROADBAND LANS

Broadband LANs, in contrast to baseband LANs, use multiple carriers to exchange information. Just as your cable television allows you to select one of many different channels, broadband LAN technology divides the available bandwidth of the cable system into multiple channels (frequency division multiplexing). A *head-end* is used to maintain communication with each node on the broadband network. The broadband information signal is varied in both amplitude and phase to encode the digital data. One 6 MHz channel is capable of providing 27 Mbps using an encoding technique called *64 QAM* (quadrature amplitude modulation).

As a homeowner you would contact your local ISP (Internet service provider), in this discussion our cable service provider, and contract for Internet services to be delivered along with your normal cable TV service. The broadband signals come into your home via the cable TV cabling. The signals are channeled through a cable modem and then into your data network. The signals from the cable TV provider to your cable modem are broadband signals capable of carrying the data channels as well as the cable TV channels. The connection on the back of the cable modem is an RJ-45 style connector that uses UTP wiring to connect to your data network. As technology progresses, we continue to increase our use of networking within our homes. The advent of high-speed broadband access to the home is fueling a booming market for home network equipment. The IEEE 802.7 standard describes broadband LAN operations.

■ TROUBLESHOOTING TECHNIQUES

Diagnosing problems with any of the LAN technologies covered in this chapter requires the following:

• Detailed knowledge of the LAN technology and its operation
• Diagnostic software
• Diagnostic hardware

Objective 4-12

Time domain reflectometers (TDR) and spectrum analyzers are two pieces of diagnostic hardware that might be required to diagnose errors. TDRs can be used to determine the distance to a fault in a cable. Spectrum analyzers can be used to examine the range of frequency bands that exist on the media. In a fiber-based LAN, an optical TDR (OTDR), a fiber-optic power meter, and even a fusion splicer may be needed.

Detailed knowledge of the LAN technology, and a little common sense are also helpful. For example, never assume anything about the network before analyzing it. If you are working on a 16 Mbps token-ring LAN, make sure all the components are operating at 16 Mbps. It only takes one NIC running at 4 Mbps to keep the network from working properly. Also, token-ring MAC addresses may be locally administered (assigned by the network administrator), overriding the MAC address programmed into the NIC at the factory. Care must be taken to guarantee that no duplicate MAC addresses exist.

If the network is coax based, make sure the impedance of the cable is correct (and matches the impedance of the NICs). Also, make sure the terminators are attached.

Network Troubleshooting Example

Objective 4-10

Although we have not yet covered the details of network design and troubleshooting, an example is presented here to show why it is good to be familiar with many different network technologies.

Examine Figure 5–9, which shows a bus/token-ring hybrid network.

FIGURE 5–9
Example of a network diagram for troubleshooting.

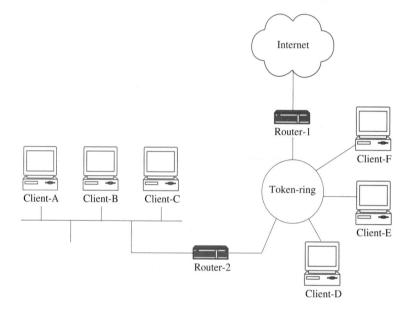

PING

Clients A, B, and C can access the Internet and *PING* each other.

Clients D, E, and F can *PING* each other but not access the Internet.

Clients D, E, and F can *PING* clients A, B, and C.

What is the most likely cause?

a. Router-2 is not configured correctly.
b. Router-1 is not configured correctly.
c. The bus workstations do not have their default gateways set correctly.
d. The ring clients do not have their default gateways set correctly.

Analysis and Solution

How does one begin analyzing this problem? First, look at the choices that are given. None of the four possible causes is a hardware problem. That immediately allows you to concentrate on what software requirements must be met for correct operation. Beginning with answer (a), let us compare the network behavior against the possible problem and see if they go together.

a. If Router-2 was not configured correctly, clients A, B, and C could not access the Internet. This is not the problem.
b. If Router-1 was not configured correctly, clients A, B, and C would also be prevented from accessing the Internet. So, both routers must be configured correctly.
c. Since bus clients A, B, and C can all access the Internet, they must have their default gateways configured correctly.

By elimination, the correct answer must be (d). The ring clients need to have two gateway addresses set up, one for Router-1 and one for Router-2. The gateway for Router-2 is set correctly, since clients D, E, and F can PING clients A, B, and C. The gateway address for Router-1 must be missing or incorrect, since clients D, E, and F cannot access the Internet.

■ SELF-TEST

1. What is the electronic packet called that is used to control conversations on ring networks?
   a. Token
   b. Delimiter
   c. Active monitor
   d. Designated monitor

2. IEEE 802.5 networks are called _____ networks.
   a. Ethernet
   b. FDDI
   c. frame-relay
   d. token-ring

3. Which of the following networks perform better under heavy network loads?
   a. IEEE 802.2
   b. IEEE 802.3
   c. IEEE 802.5
   d. IEEE 802.5a

4. Token-ring networks are specified to operate at _____.
   a. 2 Mbps
   b. 6 Mbps
   c. 10 Mbps
   d. 16 Mbps

5. Which of the following factors affects the maximum distance between MAUs on an IEEE 802.5 network?
   a. Number of MAUs in ring
   b. Number of hosts per MAU
   c. Number of tokens on network
   d. Frame size on the ring

6. True or False: Stations on a ring cannot be removed from the topology without a major disruption to the ring.

7. What generates a frame in a token-ring network?
   a. Active station
   b. Active monitor
   c. MAU
   d. Station

8. The Token bit is used to differentiate Token frames and _____ frames.
   a. Monitor
   b. Reservation
   c. Information
   d. Priority

9. The _____ is used to differentiate between Token frames and Information frames.
   a. Access bit
   b. Token bit
   c. active monitor
   d. polarity of the signal

10. 4 Mbps token-ring networks can carry a _____ -byte load in the INFO field.
    a. 1500
    b. 3000
    c. 4550
    d. 18,200

11. Which of the following is **not** a function of the active monitor in a token-ring network?
    a. Traffic routing to remote LANs
    b. Ensures that valid tokens circulate the ring
    c. Controls token timing
    d. Initiates ring purge

12. True or False: Beaconing is used to identify breaks in the token-ring network.

13. True or False: Token-ring networks use CSMA/CD methods to avoid collisions.

14. Which addresses of other network stations are known by each token-bus station?
    a. Previous and next stations in sequence
    b. Each station on the bus
    c. Only the active monitor station
    d. Designated station

15. True or False: Token bus operates with four levels of priority.

16. Which two of the following physical media are used in a token-bus network?
    a. UTP
    b. Coaxial
    c. Fiber
    d. STP

17. True or False: FDDI is a broadband technology similar to token ring.

18. What type of media is used in an FDDI network?
    a. UTP
    b. STP
    c. Coaxial
    d. Fiber

19. True or False: An FDDI ring using multimode fiber and a single ring can have a circumference of 200 meters.

20. What are the two types of FDDI nodes?
    a. MIDI, MPEG
    b. SAS, DAS
    c. MAU, MSAU
    d. Primary, secondary

21. The large FDDI frame size reduces _____ when transmitting large blocks of data.
    a. network size
    b. network overhead
    c. encryption
    d. compression

22. One 6 MHz channel of a broadband LAN is capable of providing _____ of bandwidth.
    a. 1.5 Mbps
    b. 2.7 Mbps
    c. 10 Mbps
    d. 27 Mbps

23. What encoding technique provides 27 Mbps over a broadband LAN?
    a. Time division multiplexing
    b. Frequency division multiplexing
    c. Quadrature amplitude modification
    d. Time domain reflectometry

24. Signals from your cable TV provider are capable of carrying _____ channels as well as TV channels.
    a. data
    b. baseband
    c. narrowband
    d. wireless

25. True or False: The speed of a token-ring NIC is irrelevant to the proper operation of the ring.

26. Make sure that all NICs are operating _____ in a token-ring network.
    a. at the same speed
    b. at different speeds
    c. at 10 Mbps
    d. at 20 Mbps

Network Design and Troubleshooting Scenarios

CHAPTER **6**

PERFORMANCE OBJECTIVES

Upon completion of this chapter, you will be able to:

- Discuss several considerations that must be made when networking computers together.

- Estimate the hardware components needed for a specific network.
- Discuss some initial steps to take when troubleshooting a network.

 ## NETWORK+ OBJECTIVES

This chapter provides information for the following Network+ objectives:

1.1 Recognize the following logical or physical network topologies given a schematic diagram or description:
- Star/hierarchical
- Bus
- Ring
- Mesh
- Wireless

1.5 Choose the appropriate media type and connectors to add a client to an existing network.

1.6 Identify the purpose, features, and functions of the following network components:
- Hubs
- Bridges
- Gateways
- Switches
- Routers
- CSU/DSU
- Network Interface Cards/ISDN adapters/system area network cards
- Wireless access points
- Modems

2.11 Identify the basic characteristics (e.g., speed, capacity, media) of the following WAN technologies:
- Packet switching vs. circuit switching
- ISDN
- ATM
- Sonet/SDH
- T3/E3
- FDDI
- Frame Relay
- T1/E1
- Ocx

4.1 Given a troubleshooting scenario, select the appropriate TCP/IP utility from among the following:
- TRACERT
- ARP
- NBTSTAT
- IPCONFIG/IFCONFIG
- WINIPCFG
- PING
- NETSTAT
- NSLOOKUP

4.2 Given a troubleshooting scenario involving a small office/home office network failure (e.g., xDSL, cable, home satellite, wireless, POTS), identify the cause of the failure.

4.7 Given output from a diagnostic utility (e.g., TRACERT, PING, IPCONFIG, etc.), identify the utility and interpret the output.

4.8 Given a scenario, predict the impact of modifying, adding, or removing network services (e.g., DHCP, DNS, WINS, etc.) on network resources and users.

4.9 Given a network problem scenario, select an appropriate course of action based on a general troubleshooting strategy. This strategy includes the following steps:
1. Establish the symptoms
2. Identify the affected area
3. Establish what has changed
4. Select the most probable cause
5. Implement a solution
6. Test the result
7. Recognize the potential effects of the solution
8. Document the solution

4.10 Given a troubleshooting scenario involving a network with a particular physical topology (i.e., bus, star/hierarchical, mesh, ring, wireless) and including a network diagram, identify the network area affected and the cause of the problem.

4.12 Given a network troubleshooting scenario involving a wiring/infrastructure problem, identify the cause of the problem (e.g., bad media, interference, network hardware).

■ INTRODUCTION

This chapter takes a look at several different network scenarios, each more complex than the last. The goal is to provide you with ideas to begin designing your own network. Several network troubleshooting examples are also examined.

One of the key issues in designing a network is selecting the technologies that best meet the goals of the project. It is common for new network technicians to want to use their knowledge and select the most advanced technologies for their network design. Although it would be great to run high-speed fiber to all desktops, the expense would not be realistic for most budgets. When we design networks for our employers we must remember that we need to design the network to meet the needs of the organization while still protecting the bottom line of the organization's budget. There will be times when it is wise to spend a few extra dollars to *future proof* our network. This means that we typically look at possible future expansion over a three- to five-year growth period. Looking much past the five-year time frame is hard to do, given the fast advances in technologies. What looks like advanced technologies now may be replaced by new technologies (perhaps even less expensive) in four years. There are some common-sense things that are good to consider. The difference in price between implementing 10 Mbps and 100 Mbps technologies is small. You may want to spend a few extra dollars to future proof your network at the 100 Mbps level. Conversely, you may determine that it isn't worth the few extra dollars to do so. Most individuals have more bandwidth at the 10 Mbps level than they need. A typical office user that primarily uses e-mail and the Internet may not need more than 10 Mbps. A typical school or small organization uses only a T1 line for their Internet connection. The speed of a T1 line is 1.544 Mbps. All employees share the 1.544 Mbps connection, making that the speed bottleneck on the network. Internal speeds greater than 10 Mbps may be a waste of money. If the employees of an organization transfer large files internally, or use internal multimedia delivery systems, 100 Mbps or greater technologies may make sense.

Another point to consider is the choice between technologies such as 10BASE2, Ethernet, Fast Ethernet, Gigabit Ethernet, token ring, and so on. Technologies such as 10BASE2 and 10BASE5 offer an advantage of longer runs for a single physical segment but have problems that include difficulty of installation and use. The advantages of distance of 10BASE2 and 10BASE5 installations pale in comparison to the disadvantages and are rarely used for modern installations.

Token ring has some advantages of priority control (who has higher transmission priority) and collision-free environments, but the added expense of the equipment and complexity of setup make it a less popular technology in the normal office environment.

Ethernet and Fast Ethernet are common choices for routine office environments. The use of hubs and switches overcomes most distance and collision domain issues, and the ease of installation makes Ethernet a very popular technology. On the backbone segments (the segments that carry a lot of traffic between switches and floors of a building) it is common to use Fast Ethernet or Gigabit Ethernet. Backbone segments normally use a minimum of CAT 5 wiring or fiber cables. When practical, UTP wiring is easier to install and maintain. Fiber cable offers longer runs between network devices and more future-proof properties, and is less susceptible to electronic interference from power supply lines, fluorescent lights, and electronic machinery. The use of fiber cables over UTP cables also makes it harder to eavesdrop on an organization's electronic communications and is a better security choice in areas of high communications sensitivity.

The examples in this chapter normally use Ethernet and Fast Ethernet technologies and use a combination of UTP and fiber cables as appropriate.

■ NETWORKING TWO COMPUTERS

Objective 1-6

Connecting just two computers, such as in a home or small office, can be done using either a direct cable connection or through NICs. These methods are illustrated in Figure 6–1.

The least expensive route is the direct cable connection. The connection may be through a serial cable or a parallel cable. There are various steps to go through to set up this

FIGURE 6–1
Connecting two computers.

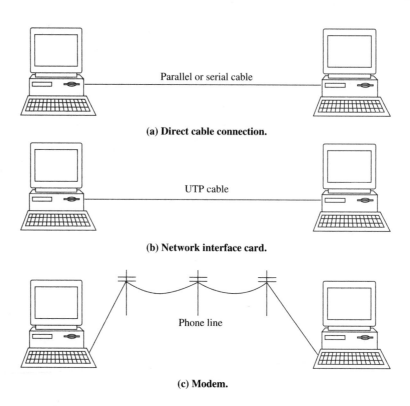

(a) **Direct cable connection.**

(b) **Network interface card.**

(c) **Modem.**

type of connection depending on which operating system you are using. On a Windows 2000 operating system, follow these steps:

1. Go to Start, Settings, Control Panel, Network and Dial-up Connections, and select the Make New Connection option. That will open up the Network Connection Wizard shown in Figure 6–2.

FIGURE 6–2
Network Connection Wizard.

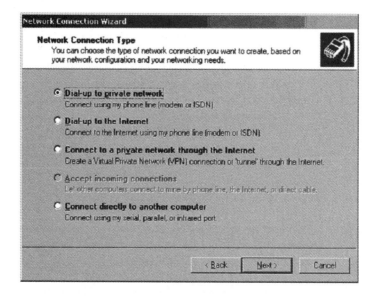

You can use this wizard to set up many types of network connections, such as a dial-up connection, a VPN connection, and a direct connection to another computer.

2. For this example, select the Connect directly to another computer option.

Instead of using a serial or parallel cable, you could opt to use NICs and a crossover cable. Because you are connecting only two computers, you could save the added expense of a hub, which is why you are using a crossover cable instead of a straight cable. An added benefit of using NICs instead of a serial or parallel cable is that your computers are ready to accept links to additional computers just by adding a hub and switching from a crossover cable to straight cables between the computers and the hub. This is how most modern connections are made.

■ NETWORKING A SMALL LAB

Objective 1-1

The last few years have seen a tremendous increase in the number of schools connected to the Internet. On college campuses, many departments use networking laboratories to share resources, save money on equipment, and provide Internet access to their students and faculty.

What is required to network a small laboratory? Figure 6–3(a) shows an overhead diagram of the laboratory indicating the positions of computers, printers, and other devices.

FIGURE 6–3
A small laboratory.

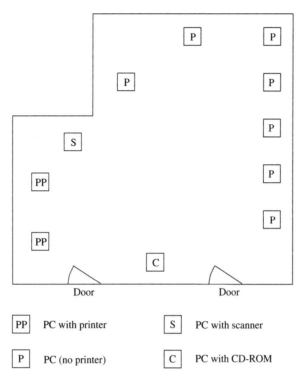

PP	PC with printer		S	PC with scanner
P	PC (no printer)		C	PC with CD-ROM

(a) Overhead diagram.

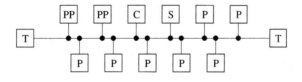

(b) Bus network topology.

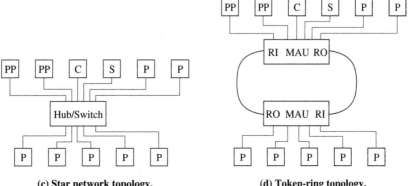

(c) Star network topology.   **(d) Token-ring topology.**

There are 11 PCs to be networked. For your benefit we have included three options to allow you to visually compare the basics of using various technologies. Those options are depicted in Figures 6–3(b), (c), and (d). In keeping with modern practices we will use the star topology using Ethernet standards. In the star topology we can use either a hub or a switch to make the connection. We can save money here by using a hub. As long as we do not have troubles with bandwidth and collisions on the network this would be a good choice. Unless the PC users are heavy users of the network this is a good option for this situation. If we want to spend some extra money we can build a hierarchical element into our network and use a switch instead of a hub. This might be a good option if we anticipate connecting this network segment with another network segment in the near future.

After the network is physically set up you will need to select a networking protocol such as NetBEUI for Windows machines or TCP/IP (which works on any modern operating system). The protocol of choice for modern networks is TCP/IP. If you are connecting to some older Windows operating systems you may have to also use NetBEUI; but this is a very chatty protocol (using a lot of bandwidth for network overhead communications) and should only be used to support legacy network communications that cannot be migrated to full TCP/IP communications. Part of the logical setup of a TCP/IP network is assigning an IP address to each machine. You will obtain these addresses from your organization's network administrator. Depending on how your organization's network is designed you may use all public IP addresses, or you may use IP addresses from the private addresses set aside for this purpose. Typically, organizations use addresses in the private address range of 192.168.xxx.xxx. Address ranges will be explained later in the book.

■ NETWORKING A SMALL BUSINESS

Objective 1-5

For the sake of this discussion, consider a small business with 80 employees. These employees are spread out over several floors of a small office building. In addition to one PC per employee, there are 15 additional PCs in various locations, mostly performing special duties as file servers or network print servers. Figure 6–4 shows the distribution of machines throughout the office building.

FIGURE 6–4
A small business.

	Employee PCs	Network printer PCs	File servers
Third floor	11	2	1
Second floor	31	3	2
First floor	38	4	3
Totals	80	9	6

A network of this size (both the number of machines and the physical size of the office building) is well suited to use a hybrid topology such as the extended star, with hubs or switches used to group clusters of PCs together, and UTP or fiber-optic cable to connect the hubs or switches together. If hubs are used, whenever anyone sends a job to one of the network printers or requests a file from a file server, everyone (all 95 machines) must contend with the traffic. If switches are used, a network hierarchy can be established that isolates switched groups of users to their own local network printer; thus, only members within the group contend with the printer traffic, not the entire network. File servers should be isolated in the same way. Using switches instead of hubs also allows the network to be repartitioned at a later time, to tweak performance or add new machines. A combination of switches and hubs may also be used, with switches isolating each floor of the building and hubs connecting all the users on a single floor.

Figure 6–5(a) and Figure 6–5(b) show two switch-based topologies that could be used to guarantee 10/100 Mbps to each machine.

FIGURE 6–5
Sample network topologies for office building.

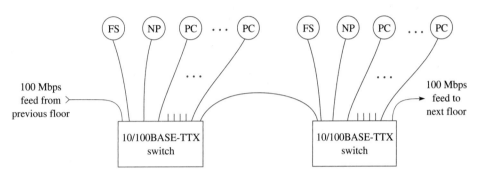

(a) Daisy-chained UTP.

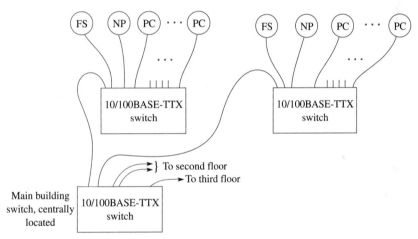

(b) Star of switches.

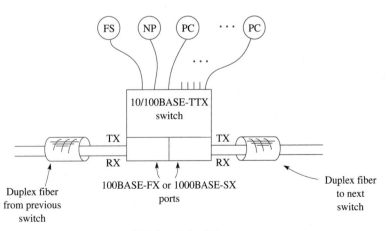

(c) Daisy-chained fiber.

Key:
FS: File server
NP: Network printer
PC: Machine

If the nature of the business is heavily data dependent (multimedia presentations, streaming audio/video), it may be necessary to connect each floor via fiber and utilize Fast or Gigabit Ethernet technology. This can be done using a fiber switch topology. The high-speed fiber backbone between floors guarantees that floor-to-floor bandwidth is available for all applications. Figure 6–5(c) shows how duplex fiber is used to daisy-chain the fiber-10/100BASE-T switches. An extended star topology with a central fiber-only switch would be a good option, though at the cost of an extra switch.

■ NETWORKING A COLLEGE CAMPUS

Objective 2-11

A typical community college may employ several hundred faculty and staff, and host several thousand students. Computers for student use are grouped into laboratories, with several laboratories in each building on campus. Our sample college in Figure 6–6 has a total of 14 laboratories, each containing 16 machines and a network printer (stand-alone, no PC required). The number of labs in each building is circled in the figure.

FIGURE 6–6
A college campus.

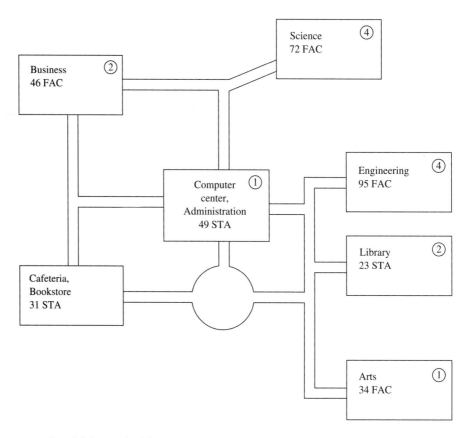

In addition to the lab computers, there are 350 faculty and staff wired to the network. Their numbers are indicated by the FAC and STA terms.

Figure 6–7 illustrates the network diagram of the campus. Each building connects to a central communications rack in the Computer Center. A pair of fiber cables (duplex cables) run from each building to the Computer Center, where they all plug into a 100 Mbps fiber switch.

Fiber was used instead of UTP because of environmental concerns, as the college's geographical area is prone to thunderstorms. Each floor has its own switch to isolate traffic. Figure 6–8 shows the layout of a typical campus building.

In the Computer Center, two mainframes connect to the central communications switch. One mainframe is for administrative use, the other for faculty/student use. The switch provides the necessary hierarchy separating the mainframes and their associated users. In addition, a router connected to the switch performs gateway duties, connecting the college to the Internet through a leased T1 (1.544 Mbps) line. Last, the switch also connects to a modem bank, where eight dial-up POTS lines can be used for remote access.

FIGURE 6–7
Computer Center network diagram.

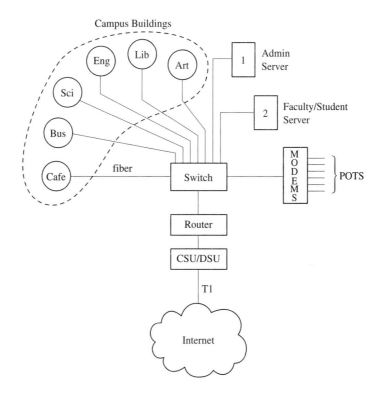

FIGURE 6–8
Network structure of a typical campus building.

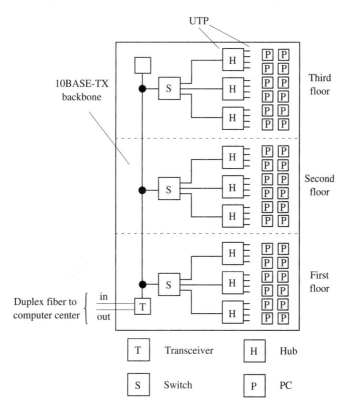

Because of the large number of machines (close to 240 in the labs plus 350 for the faculty/staff), the college uses three class C address blocks. With a number of IP addresses from each subnet reserved by the Computer Center, there are still over 700 IP addresses available for campus use. Taking away the lab and employee computers leaves 110 IP addresses, all available for future expansion.

■ REMOTE ACCESS METHODS

Remote access capability is an increasingly important component of a network. Individuals working at home, distance learning and on-line courses, eBay and stock traders, and many other people and devices are using remote access technology to gain access to public and private networks and the Internet. There are many ways to accomplish remote networking. Table 6–1 lists several ways a residential user may connect to the Internet and the characteristics of each type of connection.

TABLE 6–1
Remote access connection methods.

Connection	Cost	Speed	Availability	Restrictions	Maintenance
Telephone modem	Low	Low (56 Kbps)	Dial-up connection required	None	None
DSL modem	Low	Medium (1.5 Mbps)	Always on	Not available everywhere, limitations on distance from CO	None
ISDN modem	Medium	Low (128 Kbps)	Connection on demand	Not available everywhere	None
Cable modem	Low	High (10 Mbps)	Always on	Not available everywhere	None
Satellite	Medium	Medium (400 Kbps)	Always on	Geographic, line-of-sight	Periodic mechanical alignment
Wireless	Low to medium	High (11 Mbps)	Always on	Limited range	None
Dedicated	Highest	Highest (T3, OCx)	Always on	None	None

DSL (Digital Subscriber Line) is becoming an increasingly popular choice for individuals. DSL provides the "always on" feature of a dedicated connection at a fraction of the cost and at a reasonable speed. ADSL (Asynchronous DSL) is a version of DSL where the upstream bandwidth is lower than the downstream bandwidth, hence the term asynchronous. For example, you may be able to download at a rate of 8.448 Mbps, but only upload at a rate of 640 Kbps. One of the limitations of DSL is the drop in capability as you move further from the Central Office (CO) equipment. As an example, ADSL promises to provide up to 8.448 Mbps upstream capability if you are using 24 AWG wiring and are within 9,000 feet of the CO equipment. Move to a distance of 12,000 feet from the CO and your upstream capability drops to 6.1 Mbps. Move out to a distance of 18,000 feet from the CO and your upstream drops to 1.5 to 2.048 Mbps. ADSL services beyond the distance of 18,000 feet are generally not available in the average customer market. This service is constantly being perfected, and new ways of providing this service, such as using fiber cabling to extend the service range, are being developed. Other types of DSL services are available that provide various rates and characteristics, but ADSL is the common service provided to the average home owner and many small businesses. One of the primary reasons that ADSL is popular is that it can use existing telephone wiring to deliver both data and normal telephone services over the same wiring. Figure 6–9 shows a typical DSL network connection through the telephone company CO.

The key component in the Central Office is the DSLAM (DSL Access Multiplexer), which manages voice and data traffic between the residential user, public switched telephone network (PSTN) switch, and ISP.

Integrated Services Digital Network (ISDN) can provide an alternate service to the typical dial-up POTS connections. A Basic Rate Interface (BRI) service can provide a bandwidth of 128 Kbps, well over twice the speed of a 56 Kbps POTS connection. Normally

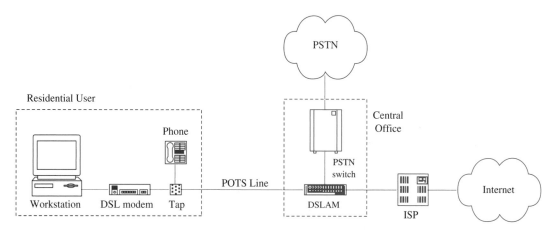

FIGURE 6–9
DSL architecture from home to Central Office.

your local telecommunications company sends you a bill for the basic service, which will include a specific amount of cumulative time that you can maintain a connection without additional fees. If you maintain connections beyond that time you will pay for the additional connection time at a previously stated access rate. This is much like typical cell phone service where your basic service includes a predetermined amount of free time and you pay for any additional use of their services past that amount of time. Some individuals have subscribed to unlimited ISDN access time, but that is not the typical subscriber agreement.

Objective 4-2

Wireless networking is also becoming more popular as the technology improves. Figure 6–10 illustrates a wireless networking setup where four wireless laptop computers are spread out among two rooms and a hallway. The wireless access point (WAP) in the

FIGURE 6–10
Overhead view of wireless network.

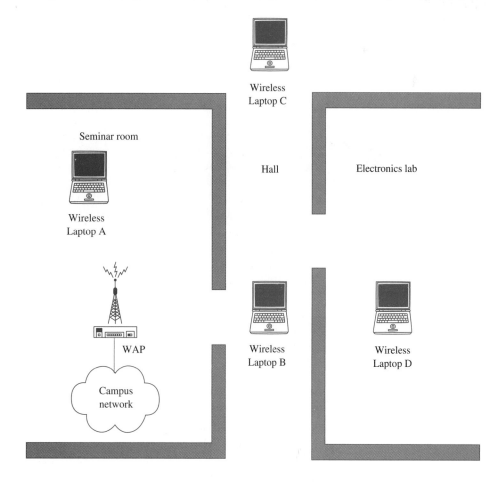

Seminar room is connected to the campus network and provides up to 10 simultaneous wireless connections. The indoor range is listed as 150 feet (with 400 feet for the outdoor range).

Each room is 30 feet wide. The hallway is 10 feet wide. All four laptops are configured the same way. Even so, wireless laptops C and D are not able to establish a connection to the WAP. This is due to the nature of the environment where the wireless equipment is operating. The walls of the campus building contain enough metal conduit and other construction materials that the signal from the WAP is severely degraded just by traveling the short distance between the rooms. These same laptops experience no connection problems when they are moved closer to the WAP.

Outdoors, the WAP performs better, easily connecting with laptops hundreds of feet away. It is therefore important to consider the location when planning a wireless network since the local environment will affect its range. Wireless technologies are being implemented by ISPs, allowing their customers the ability to establish a line-of-sight connection to their services without needing the services of the local telecommunications company. Obvious line-of-sight limitations exist in congested areas, but this service offers a lot of benefits for less populated areas and in areas where the ISP can establish an access point on taller structures such as a tall office building or an antenna.

Cable modem service is rapidly becoming a popular service for cable service subscribers. While the cable modem promises high-speed access it must be understood that this advertised bandwidth is shared by others in your neighborhood. This is a shared media much like the concepts discussed in the Ethernet section of the book. Many other subscribers share your media access and have direct LAN-type access to your connection. As in all connections to the public information network, access security procedures should be a consideration for this type of Internet access.

Satellite access is becoming a popular choice for those who live in rural areas of the country and do not have local access to other technologies such as DSL or cable services. The cost is moderate but still within the reach of most home owners. Satellite access can be interrupted by the occasional storm. To use this type of access you would typically be a subscriber to satellite television services and include this as an additional subscriber service.

■ TROUBLESHOOTING TECHNIQUES

This section presents a number of troubleshooting tips as well as a few case studies involving actual networking problems and their solutions. Bear in mind that troubleshooting network problems requires time, patience, and logical thinking. This is a good opportunity to correlate your knowledge of the OSI model with the troubleshooting tips offered. As a general rule, when you use the OSI model as your mental troubleshooting checklist, you should examine the processes that start at layer 1 and work up the model from there. Having an understanding of the issues that are addressed at each layer of the model may allow you to skip some of the layers as you progress through the troubleshooting process. The tips presented here offer a place to begin troubleshooting a network problem.

Checking the Hardware

Objective 4-2

On a Windows 2000 or XP operating system right-click the My Computer icon and select Properties to open the System Properties window. Select the Hardware tab; then click the Device Manager button to examine the list of installed hardware. If a small exclamation mark is present on the Network adapters device, there is a problem with the NIC or its driver. It is not uncommon for an interrupt conflict to arise when a device wants to use the same interrupt as the network adapter. Sometimes you can successfully change the interrupt of one of the devices. You may also be able to find and install a newer driver for the network card on the World Wide Web. Current Windows operating systems do a good job at handling hardware conflicts and so the need for manual intervention in this process is becoming less common. It pays to check the physical hardware as well (layer 1 of the OSI model for physical characteristics and layer 2 for drivers). Never assume that everything is still connected properly, plugged in, turned on, and so on. For example, refer back to Figure 6–9. The residential user is able to connect to the Internet through the computer, but cannot make any calls with the telephone. A different phone plugged into the same tap does not work either, although both phones work fine when plugged into other phone lines in the same residence. Do you think the problem is with the DSL modem, the tap, or the DSLAM?

If the DSL modem was malfunctioning, Internet access would not be possible. If the DSLAM was malfunctioning, other phones in the residence would not work (and there may not be Internet access, either). With nothing else to blame except the tap, we now have our culprit.

Using Test Equipment

For some hardware problems, such as intermittent connections, it may be necessary to use sophisticated test equipment, such as a cable tester, a time domain reflectometer (TDR), an optical TDR (for fiber), or a network analyzer.

What's My IP?

Objective 4-1

Objective 4-7

It is a good idea to run *winipcfg/ipconfig* and view the network information (addresses, mask, lease details, etc.). Recall that the *winipcfg* utility is used for older home Windows operating systems such as Windows 95 and Windows 98. *Ipconfig/all* is used on more recent Windows operating systems such as Windows 2000 and XP (and Windows NT). Figure 6–11 shows an abbreviated output of the *ipconfig/all* command given on a Windows 2000 PC. Looking through the entries you can select relevant items such as the IP address 192.168.48.72, the subnet mask of 255.255.255.0, the default gateway of 192.168.48.254, and two addresses for the DNS servers. Also notice that DHCP is not enabled, which means that we are using static IP addresses.

FIGURE 6–11
ipconfig/all output.

```
C:\WINNT\System32\cmd.exe                                          _ □ X
Ethernet adapter Local Area Connection 2:

        Connection-specific DNS Suffix  . :
        Description . . . . . . . . . . . : 3Com EtherLink XL 10/100 PCI TX NIC
(3C905B-TX)
        Physical Address. . . . . . . . . : 00-50-04-9B-37-1B
        DHCP Enabled. . . . . . . . . . . : No
        IP Address. . . . . . . . . . . . : 192.168.48.72
        Subnet Mask . . . . . . . . . . . : 255.255.255.0
        Default Gateway . . . . . . . . . : 192.168.48.254
        DNS Servers . . . . . . . . . . . : 192.168.48.4
                                            192.168.49.4

        NetBIOS over Tcpip. . . . . . . . : Disabled
```

Figure 6–12 shows a winipcfg display for a machine that is using DHCP and was not able to communicate with its network.

Notice that the DNS Server and Default Gateway fields are blank and that the DHCP Server address is 255.255.255.255. Compare this display with the one shown in Figure 6–13.

In addition to different addresses in each field, the Lease Expires field is now filled in, and the Host Name has changed (indicating that the machine WAVEGUIDE is now part of the stny.rr.com domain). Note that when we check the IP addresses of the settings we are checking layer 3 information of the OSI model (logical addresses). These are addresses that identify specific networks and the individual device addresses that are part of those specific logical networks.

FIGURE 6–12
winipcfg display. Invalid network information.

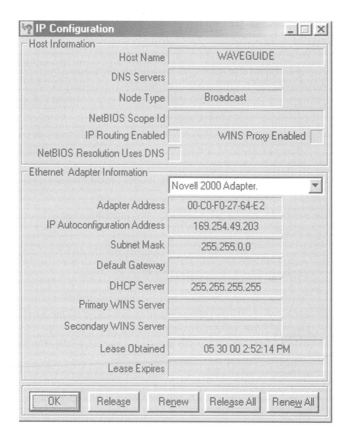

FIGURE 6–13
winipcfg display. Valid network information.

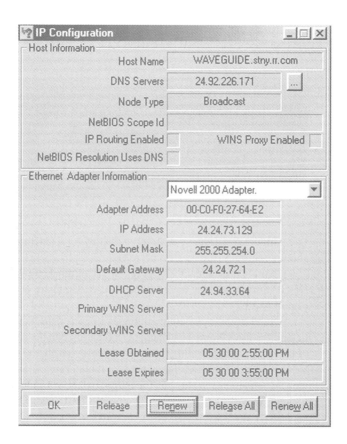

Objective 4-1

Objective 4-7

Can You PING?

Just being able to PING another network host (or not being able to) is valuable information. By successfully PINGing the other host, we have proof that the network hardware and software are operating correctly. A sample PING report looks similar to the following:

```
C> ping www.sunybroome.edu

Pinging sbccab.cc.sunybroome.edu [192.203.130.2] with 32 bytes of data:

Reply from 192.203.130.2: bytes=32 time=66ms TTL=245
Reply from 192.203.130.2: bytes=32 time=82ms TTL=245
Reply from 192.203.130.2: bytes=32 time=92ms TTL=245
Reply from 192.203.130.2: bytes=32 time=122ms TTL=245

Ping statistics for 192.203.130.2:
    Packets: Sent = 4, Received = 4, Lost = 0 (0% loss),
Approximate round trip times in milliseconds:
    Minimum = 66ms, Maximum = 122ms, Average = 90ms
```

Notice that PING used DNS to look up the IP address for www.sunybroome.edu. If you can PING a host by using its IP address but not its domain name, there could be a problem with your DNS server. If you are successful with the PING command, you have layer 3 connectivity.

CASE STUDY #1: RJ-45 Connector Partially Inserted

Objective 4-12

One user was confused when her machine would not connect to the network, even though the light on her hub was lit and the machine had been working on the network the previous evening. After spending a good deal of time on the phone with a technician and checking all hardware and software properties, she was about to give up. She began recalling her steps, thinking about everything she had done or seen since the computer last worked. She remembered that she had pulled the mini-tower case to the front of her computer desk to adjust the volume control on her sound card. She carefully pulled the computer across the desk again, and saw that the RJ-45 connector was partially pulled out of its socket on the NIC. When she pushed on it she heard a snap as it clicked into place. After rebooting, her machine worked fine again.

CASE STUDY #2: Missing Terminator

After rearranging the old networking hardware in a closet, a technician discovered that the entire 10BASE2 network was not functioning. Not a single machine worked on the network. Careful inspection of the rearranged equipment revealed that the technician forgot to reconnect the terminating resistor on the end of the coax.

CASE STUDY #3: Wrong UTP Cable Type

Objective 4-12

Of the eight machines connected to a hub in a new networking lab, only seven can connect to the network. When the UTP cables are swapped between the bad machine and a good one, the problem moves to the good machine and the bad machine is able to connect to the network. When the two cables are swapped into different ports on the hub, the problem also moves. Examining the ends of the original cable, it was discovered that the cable was a crossover cable, not a straight-through cable, which normally connects a NIC to a hub or a switch port.

CASE STUDY #4: Broadcast Storm

Broadcast storms

One business suffered frequent ***broadcast storms***, a flooding of its network with so many packets that its switches were forced to drop the excess packets that it was not able to process. Eventually, by capturing network traffic with a protocol analyzer and examining it, the network technicians found a network packet used as a trigger for the broadcast storm, a message sent to a broadcast address on the business's subnet. Someone was PINGing their broadcast address!

After more digging, the technicians learned that a software engineer at the company was experimenting with a network application he had downloaded from a hacker Web site. The application, whether intentionally or not, was responsible for the broadcast storms.

CASE STUDY #5: DHCP Not Working

Objective 4-8

On a particular college campus, a DHCP server is used to dynamically assign IP addresses to machines when they boot. One day the entire system stopped working, and no one could obtain an IP address. After isolating the portion of the network that was causing the DHCP server (in the computer center) to fail, the campus network technician went from lab to lab in the affected portion of the network. He finally found the problem: A Linux machine set up by a student as a DHCP server for a project was accidentally connected to the college network. After the machine was disconnected, the normal DHCP service resumed. The Linux machine was giving out IP addresses that were inconsistent with the addresses used for the college network, causing errors in the normal layer 3 routing processes.

CASE STUDY #6: Mystery Traffic on the Network

Objective 4-9

Problems that occur on a computer network are often very challenging to solve, even for experienced network technicians. Is the problem caused by hardware, software, or both? Even after the problem has been discovered and a solution devised, new problems may occur when the solution is applied. Thus, the effects of a proposed solution should be considered as well. The entire process must also be well documented to keep track of the steps taken during the troubleshooting process, and to benefit those who may encounter the problem again in the future.

One way to approach the solution to a problem consists of the following steps:

1. Establish the symptoms.
2. Identify the affected area.
3. Establish what has changed.
4. Select the most probable cause.
5. Implement a solution.
6. Test the result.
7. Recognize the potential effects of the solution.
8. Document the solution.

Now apply this method to an actual network problem.

1. Establish the symptoms. A network technician at a small university noticed from a network traffic chart that there is an average of 10 percent more broadcast traffic than usual. After reviewing the history charts for the network, he discovered that the increased traffic has existed for five days.

2. Identify the affected area. The technician ran a packet sniffer program and captured network traffic for 10 minutes. While examining the captured data, he noticed frequent bursts of packets from a device having an IP address that does not match the address class of the university network. The packets are also broadcast packets, which account for the 10 percent increase discovered by the technician. He recorded the IP and MAC addresses of the broadcasting device.

3. Establish what has changed. The technician wondered if new hardware had recently been added to the network that he was unaware of. He also wondered if a hacker had targeted his network for some mischief or if a computer with a virus could be generating the traffic.

4. Select the most probable cause. Based on the IP address being used by the broadcasting network device, the network technician concluded that the device generating the traffic was located on campus and not off campus. The technician did not think the campus router would let the traffic through if the traffic had originated from outside of the network.

5. Implement a solution. The information captured by the packet sniffer identified the MAC address of the broadcasting device, but did not provide any additional information that would help isolate where the device was located. The technician then decided to disconnect one campus building at a time from the central network switch while PINGing the broadcasting device. When the PING failed to get a reply, this would isolate the broadcasting device to a specific building. Refer to Figure 6–14 for a diagram of the campus network.

FIGURE 6–14
Simplified diagram of a university network.

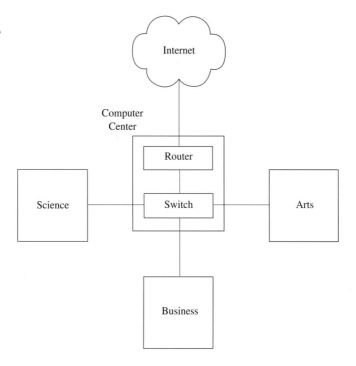

The Science building was disconnected first. The broadcasting device in the Science building responded to a PING and thus could not be the source of the problem. The same was true for the Business building. When the Arts building was disconnected, there was no reply to the PING. Thus, the problem broadcasting device was located in the Arts building.

6. Test the result. After the problem device was isolated to the Arts building, the network technician went to the network closet in the Arts building and examined both 48-port Ethernet switches mounted on a 19-inch rack. The manufacturer's label on each switch listed its MAC address, and one switch matched the MAC address captured by the packet sniffer. The technician unplugged the switch and reconnected the power.

Back in the network technician's office, the packet sniffer no longer saw any broadcast traffic from the switch. The problem went away after the switch was reset.

7. Recognize the potential effects of the solution. When each of the buildings was disconnected one at a time, everyone in an affected building would lose their campus network and Internet connection. This would affect individuals sharing printers or files, especially if they were in the middle of a transaction. Anyone busy with an Internet connection would be required to reload a Web page or resend an e-mail once the building came back on line. Anyone watching a streaming video or listening to Internet-based streaming audio would be interrupted and lose their connection. No permanent damage would be caused; however, it is normally unwise to disconnect major portions of your network if other troubleshooting methods are available. Routinely disconnecting major portions of your network in a business environment is not optimal and may not be an option.

8. Document the solution. The network technician recorded the problem symptoms, the investigative techniques used, and the solution in his journal. A work study student located the manufacturer's instruction manual on the switch and discovered that, if the switch loses its configuration information, it engages in the same kind of broadcast activities witnessed on the campus network while trying to locate the configuration file on a file server. No one had ever set up the switch with the correct server address.

The importance of a methodical approach to troubleshooting network problems will become clear when you begin solving your first problem on your own. It is important to acquire the habit of applying these steps to each problem you encounter.

CASE STUDY #7: Intermittent Access

Objective 4-10

Examine Figure 6–15, the network diagram of a small business with an on-site Web server. Off-site users are experiencing intermittent access to the Web server. Workstation-A has no trouble accessing the Web server. Workstation-B has no trouble accessing the Web server. Both workstations experience intermittent access to the Internet.

FIGURE 6–15
Network diagram for
Case Study #7.

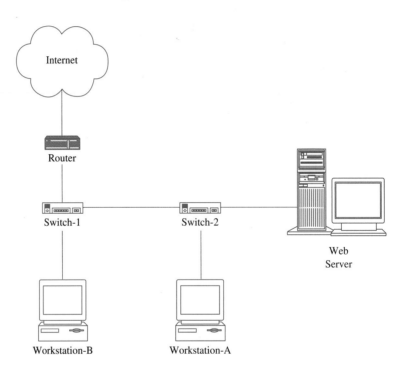

What is the most likely cause?

a. Switch-1 is going bad.
b. Switch-2 is going bad.
c. The NIC in the Web server is going bad.
d. The router is very busy and periodically loses packets due to overflowing buffers.

Analysis and Solution   If Switch-1 is going bad, that would explain why Workstation-B has intermittent access to the Internet, but it cannot be the cause of the problem because Workstation-B has no trouble accessing the Web server. The same reasoning applies to Switch-2 and Workstation-A.

Because both workstations can access the Web server, this means that both switches, four network cables, and the NIC in the Web server are all working. Note that the router is not used when either workstation accesses the Web server.

The router is used when information must pass from Switch-1 to the Internet (leaving the small business network) or from the Internet into the small business network (through Switch-1). Because packet loss is intermittent in both directions, answer (d) is the most likely cause.

CASE STUDY #8: Where's the Problem?

Objective 4-10

Examine the network diagram shown in Figure 6–16.

Clients A, B, and C can PING each other but cannot PING stations D, E, or F. None of them can print to the laser printer or access the server. Clients D, E, and F have no problems; they can access the printer and server.

FIGURE 6–16
Network diagram for Case Study #8.

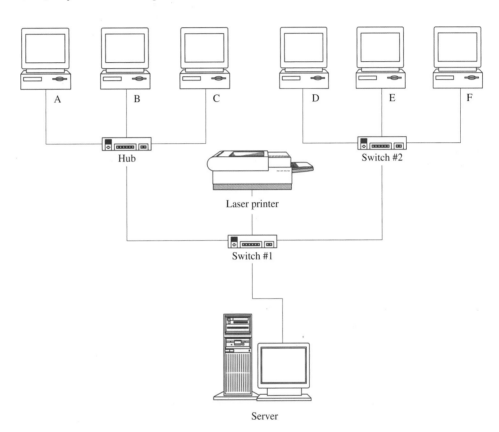

Based on your reasoning, which is the most likely cause of the problem?

a. The hub
b. Switch #1
c. Switch #2
d. Cabling

Explain how you determined which components are working properly and why the correct answer is most likely (d).

Baseband Versus Broadband

All of the networks discussed in the preceding exercises were *baseband* communication networks. A baseband network has a single information carrier that is modulated with the digital network data. *Broadband* communication networks, like the cable television system, use many different carriers and thus support multiple channels of data. Broadband communication systems require more expensive hardware than baseband systems and are typically used for high-bandwidth applications, such as broadcast video and FM audio.

INDUSTRY TIP

Case Study #6 reviewed the eight basic steps used for routine troubleshooting procedures. You will be expected to know this material for the Network+ exam as well as its practical application in daily troubleshooting scenarios. Step 8 notes that you should document the solution. This is often an item overlooked by technicians. In general we focus on the immediate problem and don't realize the value of documentation.

I once worked in an area that had a digital classroom in one section of the building and all the UTP cable runs went to another room in the building. The installers made the classic mistake of not labeling all wire runs at both ends of the cable. The installation had been accomplished a few years before I took responsibility for that network. For a few years, every time that a problem was encountered with the network multiple individuals would create a verbal relay chain with one individual located in the room with the computers, one located in the room where the cable runs were terminated into a switch, and one or two individuals standing in the hall yelling information back and forth between the technicians. When I took over I asked them why they did not go back and document the cable runs at both ends and they told me that there was just never enough time to take on that project. I estimated the average man-hours spent on relaying the information back and forth and realized that they were wasting thousands of man-hour dollars over the course of those few years. We set aside one morning, did our last event of yelling down the hall to trace which wire went to which computer and switch port, and labeled each end of a cable run and documented those runs on a schematic sheet. After that, network troubleshooting was usually accomplished by one individual and only took minutes instead of hours of yelling information down the hall. The lesson learned is that proper documentation can save time and money and is well worth the initial effort to do it right the first time.

CAREER DEVELOPMENT

You may notice the need for advanced project management skills when undertaking an IT project of any significant size. Even small IT projects require some minimal project management skills. Project management covers many critical topics such as defining the overall goals of the project, deciding who officially represents the organization and possesses the ability to make official decisions, determining what the scope of the project is, change management, acceptance of the end product, and so on. Anyone who has ever managed a project of any significant size can attest to the fact that these are significant issues that need to be handled by someone with strong management skills.

Another new specialty in the technology field is the Home Technology Integrator (HTI). The increasing availability of high-speed broadband Internet connections has sparked a strong demand for advanced networking within the home. Home owners are starting to demand the benefits of a networked home that can provide remote access to their home system controls. Many corporations are requiring that their home system installers become certified in home system integration. The current industry certification for this discipline is CompTIA's HTI+ certification. HTI+ certified individuals are expected to understand the basics of integrating multiple home systems, such as HVAC, computers, security systems, watering systems, and others. The real estate industry is starting to realize the benefits of building and selling homes that are integrated and ready for advanced network communications. One of the other aspects of an HTI+ certified individual's job is to manage the home integration project. This will require an understanding of the various technologies that the home owner wants to integrate as well as an ability to coordinate the work flow of the various technicians that specialize in the individual technologies.

As your technological skills advance you may want to consider a career track that specializes in project management, which has traditionally been a well-paying specialty. One of the CompTIA certifications, IT Project+, focuses on the basic industry tasks that are expected of the average project manager. Looking through the list of objectives for this certification will give you an idea of the tasks that a project manager is expected to perform. You can find more information about this certification at www.comptia.com/certification/itproject/default.asp.

■ SELF-TEST

1. What is a typical time frame useful in evaluating future expansion of a network?
   a. 1 year
   b. 2–3 years
   c. 3–5 years
   d. 5–10 years

2. Which of the following is an advantage of using 10BASE2 technologies for a network?
   a. Speed
   b. Distance
   c. Bandwidth
   d. Duplex

3. True or False: 10BASE5 network segments provide the ability to traverse longer distances than 10BASE-T network segments without using a repeater.

4. What network type might be required if large files are transferred internally or use multimedia delivery systems?
   a. 10BASE5
   b. 10BASE-T
   c. 100BASE-T
   d. 16 Mb token ring

5. A school or small organization typically uses a(n) _____ line for their Internet connection.
   a. 56k
   b. E-3
   c. T-1
   d. T-3

6. _____ networks have the advantage of priority control.
   a. Ethernet
   b. Fast Ethernet
   c. CSMA/CD
   d. Token-ring

7. The _____ and _____ generally make token ring less popular than Ethernet as a network implementation choice. (Choose two.)
   a. high cost of equipment
   b. large frame size
   c. complexity of setup
   d. collision-free segments

8. _____ and _____ are common choices for backbone Ethernet segments. (Choose two.)
   a. Fast Ethernet
   b. Token-ring
   c. Fiber-Net
   d. Gigabit Ethernet

9. Which cable type provides longer runs, has more future-proof properties, and resists interference from RFI and EMI?
   a. UTP
   b. Coaxial
   c. Fiber
   d. CAT 3

10. _____ cable is considered more secure because eavesdropping is more difficult.
    a. STP
    b. UTP
    c. Coaxial
    d. Fiber

11. True or False: Computers can be directly connected using a serial or a parallel cable.

12. What network and dial-up option should be chosen first in order to connect two computers together with a serial cable?
    a. VPN
    b. Connect directly to another computer
    c. Make new connection
    d. Dial-up connection

13. What device must be installed on a computer to permit connection to another computer with a crossover cable?
    a. UPC
    b. NIC
    c. AUI
    d. UTP

14. What physical topology is defined by using a hub to connect computers?
    a. Bus
    b. Star
    c. Ring
    d. FDDI

15. Which of the following network troubles can be solved by using a switch instead of a hub?
    a. Speed
    b. Public addressing
    c. Cost
    d. Bandwidth

16. PC users that are heavy users of the network require the use of a _____ instead of a _____.
    a. switch, hub
    b. hub, switch
    c. gateway, hub
    d. NIC, hub

17. What chatty protocol should only be used to support legacy network communications over networks that cannot take advantage of TCP/IP?
    a. OSPF
    b. NetBEUI
    c. IPX
    d. RIP version 2

18. True or False: ADSL requires that additional wiring be constructed from the CO to the home.

19. The billing process for _____ is similar to cell phone service, which provides basic service with a specific amount of connection time and costs extra for additional minutes.
    a. T-1
    b. DSL

    c. ISDN

    d. ISL

20. True or False: Wireless Access Points perform better outdoors than they do indoors.

21. Which of the following services are used to complete the command "ping www.partlowuniv.edu"?

    a. Trace

    b. DNS

    c. DHCP

    d. FTP

22. Network analysis revealed a problem on a campus network. The possible solution was implemented successfully and tested, and the potential effects of the solution were examined. What is the last step in the troubleshooting process?

    a. Establish the symptoms

    b. Select the cause

    c. Implement additional changes

    d. Document the solution

23. What is the most overlooked step in the troubleshooting model that involves reporting the changes made to the network?

    a. Document the solution

    b. Implement the action plan

    c. Establish what has changed

    d. Gather the facts

24. Users on a SOHO network cannot access printer services on the local network. What is the first step toward repairing the problem?

    a. Implement an action plan

    b. Test the result

    c. Establish the symptoms

    d. Identify the affected area

25. _____ communications are typically used for high-bandwidth applications.

    a. Baseband

    b. Narrowband

    c. Broadband

    d. Time division

Serial Protocols, 802.2 (LLC), NetBIOS, and NetBEUI

PERFORMANCE OBJECTIVES

Upon completion of this chapter, you will be able to:

- Describe the format of a serial data transmission.
- List the differences between SLIP and PPP.

- Explain the operation of the Logical Link Control sublayer.
- Discuss the role of NetBEUI and NetBIOS in a Windows network environment.

 ## NETWORK+ OBJECTIVES

This chapter provides information for the following Network+ objectives:

1.2 Specify the main features of 802.2 (LLC), 802.3 (Ethernet), 802.5 (token ring), 802.11b (wireless), and FDDI networking technologies, including:
- Speed
- Access
- Method
- Topology
- Media

2.2 Identify the seven layers of the OSI model and their functions.

2.3 Differentiate between the following network protocols in terms of routing, addressing schemes, interoperability, and naming conventions:
- TCP/IP
- IPX/SPX
- NetBEUI
- AppleTalk

2.7 Identify the purpose of the following network services:
- DHCP/BOOTP
- DNS
- NAT/ICS
- WINS
- SNMP

2.12 Define the function of the following remote access protocols and services:
- RAS
- PPP
- PPTP
- ICA

3.7 Given a remote connectivity scenario (e.g., IP, IPX, dial-up, PPPoE, authentication, physical connectivity, etc.), configure the connection.

4.11 Given a network troubleshooting scenario involving a client connectivity problem (e.g., incorrect protocol/client software/authentication configuration, insufficient rights/permission), identify the cause of the problem.

■ INTRODUCTION

This chapter is the first of four chapters designed to provide coverage of the wide number of hardware and software protocols used in modern network communications. It examines the protocols used to establish serial communication, exchange data over different hardware technologies, and provide peer-to-peer communication.

■ SERIAL DATA COMMUNICATION

Serial data communication takes place one bit at a time over a single communication line. For example, an 8-bit binary number is transmitted one bit at a time. Examples of devices that use serial data communication are the keyboard, mouse, COM ports on a PC, modems, and Ethernet NICs.

ASCII

One popular standard for transmitting *ASCII* characters uses the 11-bit transmission waveform shown in Figure 7–1. Here the ASCII character being transmitted is a lowercase i. Its ASCII code is 69 hexadecimal, or 1101001 binary. The first bit in the waveform is the start bit, which is always low. This identifies the beginning of a new transmission, since the normal inactive state of the line is high. The next 7 bits are the ASCII code, beginning with the least significant (the right-most bit) bit. Do you see the 1001011 levels in the waveform?

FIGURE 7–1
11-bit transmission code.

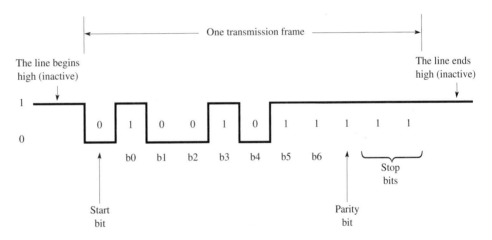

Following the last data bit is a parity bit. Parity bits are used to help determine if there is an error in the received character. Count the number of 1s in the data. There are four. If we include the 1 in the parity bit we have five 1s. This is an odd number, so the waveform has odd *parity*.

Parity

Suppose that the waveform in Figure 7–1 is transmitted correctly, but during transmission the 1 in b_5 is changed to a 0 by noise. The received waveform will then have even parity. If we expect received waveforms to have odd parity, an even parity waveform must contain an error.

The last two bits in the transmission frame are the stop bits, which are always high. This gets the transmission line back to its normal inactive state, and also provides some time for processing the received waveform. Note that one, one and one-half, or two stop bits may be used.

Each bit of the waveform takes the same amount of time. This time is related to the *baud rate* of the serial transmission (it is the inverse). Baud rate is generally regarded to be the number of bits per second in a transmission, but is actually the number of transitions per second. For instance, a 9600 bits/second modem may require only 2400 baud (when each signal transition represents 4 bits). For simplicity's sake, we will use bits/second here. As an example, if the time of one bit is 833.3 microseconds, the baud rate is 1 divided by 833.3 microseconds, or 1200 bits/second.

An advantage of serial data transmission is its simple connection requirements: a single transmit wire and a single receive wire (plus a ground wire). With only one transmit wire, it is not possible to send a clock signal with the waveform. This is referred to as *asynchronous communication.* To compensate, the start and stop bits are used to synchronize the transmitter and receiver.

Serial data transmission is handled by a digital device called a UART (universal asynchronous receiver transmitter). Figure 7–2 shows the basic operation of a UART. Parallel input data is converted to serial output data and serial input data is converted into parallel output data. In a modem, the UART interfaces with analog circuitry that converts bits to varying frequencies within the bandwidth of the telephone connection.

FIGURE 7–2
The UART.

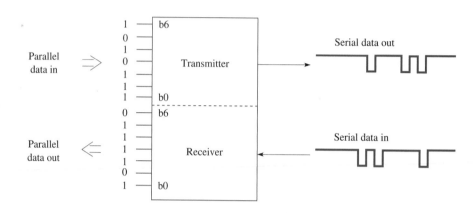

■ SLIP

SLIP
TCP/IP

IP

Objective 2-2

SLIP (Serial Line Internet Protocol) was the first protocol used to transmit ***TCP/IP*** (Transmission Control Protocol/Internet Protocol) over dial-up phone lines. SLIP provides a basic method to encapsulate the TCP/IP data but does not provide support for error detection, ***IP*** (Internet Protocol) address assignments, link testing, synchronous communication (clock included with data), or any layer 3 protocols other than IP to be transmitted. Compressed SLIP (CSLIP) is also available to increase the amount of data that can be transmitted; however, due to its many limitations SLIP has been replaced by PPP, the Point-to-Point Protocol. SLIP primarily performs layer 1 signal encapsulation and operates at layer 1 (the Physical layer) of the OSI model.

■ PPP

PPP

Objective 2-2

Objective 2-12

PPP (Point-to-Point Protocol) provides the capability to encapsulate many different protocols over a serial connection. In fact, PPP supports TCP/IP, IPX, NetBEUI, AppleTalk, and other protocols. The format of a PPP frame is shown in Figure 7–3. In addition, unlike SLIP, PPP provides for error detection, the capability to dynamically assign IP addresses

FIGURE 7–3
PPP frame format.

7E	FF	03			CRC–16	7E
Flag	Addr.	Control	Protocol	Data	Frame check sequence	Flag
1	1	1	2	0–1506	2	1

Protocol data unit
(payload)

to hosts, link testing, both synchronous and asynchronous communication modes, security (user name and password authentication), and compression.

Error detection over PPP uses a checksum value to test for data validity. The capability for dynamic address assignment in PPP allows an address to be assigned to a host during the communications establishment phase of a connection. Link testing provides a mechanism to periodically test the status of the PPP link operation.

Security is available in PPP using either the Password Authentication Protocol (PAP) or the Challenge Handshake Authentication Protocol (CHAP). Due to these additional features, PPP is widely used. Table 7–1 summarizes the differences between SLIP and PPP. Additional coverage of communication via PPP is provided in Chapters 17 and 18. PPP operates on layers 1 (Physical) and 2 (Data-Link) of the OSI model.

TABLE 7–1
Comparing SLIP to PPP.

SLIP	PPP
Static IP addresses	Dynamic IP addresses
Supports TCP/IP only	Supports TCP/IP, IPX, NetBEUI, AppleTalk, and others
Asynchronous	Asynchronous and synchronous
No compression	Compression supported
No security	Security supported
56 Kbps maximum	No speed limit
No link testing	Link testing supported
Layer 1 operation	Layers 1 and 2 operation

■ PPPoE

PPPoE

Objective 3-7

PPPoE (PPP over Ethernet) provides a way for multiple users on a LAN to share a single Internet connection (DSL line, cable modem, wireless device) by encapsulating PPP within an Ethernet frame. Instead of a single user using PPP over a modem, multiple users on the LAN can each establish a PPPoE session through the single Internet connection provided by the ISP. Each PPPoE user session can be monitored for billing purposes.

Figure 7–4 shows a diagram of the PPPoE header and frame. The Code field indicates the type of PPPoE frame (discovery, session). The Session ID, along with the Ethernet frame's source and destination MAC addresses, uniquely identify the PPPoE session. The Length field indicates the size, in bytes, of the payload. The payload is limited to 1494 bytes because an Ethernet frame has a maximum data field length of 1500 bytes. More information on PPPoE is provided in Chapter 8.

FIGURE 7–4
PPPoE frame format.

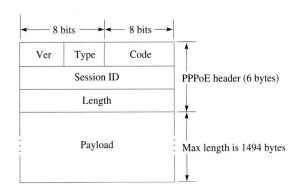

■ IEEE 802.2 LOGICAL LINK CONTROL

Objective 1-2

As previously noted, the Data-Link layer of the OSI model contains the LLC (Logical Link Control) and MAC (Media Access Control) sublayers. Figure 7–5 lists several of the functions that take place at each of these sublayers. The MAC sublayer handles topology-specific details, hardware addresses (MAC address, etc.), source and destination MAC addresses, media access issues, and so on. The LLC sublayer handles issues such as providing the interface between the specific characteristics of the chosen topology and the various upper layer protocols, the Source Service Access Point (SSAP), the Destination Service Access Point (DSAP), a portion of the total layer 2 frame creation, flow control, and error recovery (depending on the underlying topology). The SSAP and DSAP refer to the type codes in the frame that identify which upper layer protocol is being serviced by that particular frame. The LLC is the interface between the specific NIC (which is dependent on the topology being used) and the upper layer functions of the OSI model. Take note that Ethernet II includes the LLC issues (such as the type field).

FIGURE 7–5
Data-Link layer details.

			802.2 LLC	FDDI (ISO 9314)	802.3 CSMA/CD (Ethernet family)	802.4 Token Bus	802.5 Token Ring	Ethernet II (Includes 802.2 issues)
Data Link (Layer 2)	LLC	• Setup/teardown link • Frame data • Detect/correct errors • Control traffic flow • SSAP/DSAP (Type codes) • Multiplexes multiple layer 3 protocols • NIC drivers						
	MAC	• Topology specific (i.e., 802.3, 802.5, etc.) • Hardware addressing • Interfaces with NIC drivers in LLC • Additional framing (i.e., Source and Destination MAC addresses) • Media access controls						
Physical (Layer 1)		• Physical layer framing • Encoding the signal						

(Layers 3 to 7 of the OSI model were omitted for brevity)

LLC

The IEEE 802.2 standard describes the operating characteristics of ***LLC*** (Logical Link Control), which provides three types of service:

• Type 1: Connectionless communication
• Type 2: Connection-oriented communication
• Type 3: Acknowledged connectionless communication

Connectionless communication is unreliable. The sending station makes a *best effort* to deliver its information. Connection-oriented communication is reliable, with the sending and receiving stations exchanging acknowledgement messages to guarantee error-free delivery. Connectionless communication relies on upper layer protocols to provide reliability.

How is reliable communication established? The sender and the receiver must send messages back and forth, according to an established protocol. For example, the sender sends four messages of information, and the receiver acknowledges getting four. If an error occurs, and the receiver acknowledges getting only two messages, the sender knows to resend the missing messages.

HDLC

The LLC protocol is based on a popular protocol called **_HDLC_** (High-Level Data-Link Control), which provides a mechanism for sending commands and responses over a communication link. The format of an LLC protocol data unit is shown in Figure 7–6.

FIGURE 7–6
Logical Link Control PDU.

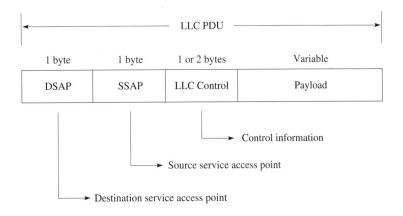

■ NETBIOS

NetBIOS

Objective 2-3

NetBIOS (Network Basic Input/Output System) provides all the functionality needed to share resources between networked computers, such as files and printers. Originally developed by IBM and Sytek, NetBIOS defines an interface to the network service protocols, acting as an API (application programming interface) for clients accessing LAN resources. NetBIOS was not designed to comply with the OSI model and mirrors functionality at layers 2, 5, 6, and 7 of the OSI model. It was not designed to be a routable network protocol and therefore does not need to address all the issues associated with a modern network. One note—even among the experts you will find a lot of discussion about which OSI layers relate to this protocol. This is due, again, to the fact that NetBIOS doesn't directly correlate to the OSI model.

NetBIOS utilizes three types of services: name, session, and datagram. The features of each service are as follows:

- Name: Finding and naming machines
- Session: Connection-oriented reliable transfer of messages
- Datagram: Connectionless non-reliable datagram transfer

SMB

The main component of a NetBIOS message is the **_SMB_** (server message block) it carries. SMBs provide all of the functionality possible under NetBIOS. Table 7–2 shows a sample of some of the many operations possible under NetBIOS. These are commands executed by the NetBIOS code (not by the user).

TABLE 7–2
Sample NetBIOS commands.

Command	Description
Bad command	Invalid SMB command
Change/check dir	Change to directory or check path
Change password	Change password of user
Copy file	Copy file to specified path
Delete file	Delete the specified file
Find unique	Search directory for specified file
Get resources	Get availability of server resources
Mailslot message	Mail slot transaction message
Named pipe call	Open, write, read, or close named pipe
Rename file	Rename the specified file to a new name
Reserve resources	Reserve resources on the server
Session setup	Log-in with consumer-based authentication

A sample SMB message, decoded for readability, looks like the following:

```
Destination    Source        Protocol                       Summary  Size  Time Tick
------------------------------------------------------------------------------------------
030000000001   00C0F02764E2  NetBIOS SMB C Transaction      LLC UI   193   12/06/99 14:15:48


Addr.   Hex. Data                                              ASCII
0000:   03 00 00 00 00 01 00 C0 F0 27 64 E2 00 B3 F0 F0        .........'d.....
0010:   03 2C 00 FF EF 08 00 00 00 00 00 00 00 52 41 59        .,...........RAY
0020:   43 41 53 54 20 20 20 20 20 20 20 20 1E 57 41 56        CAST        .WAV
0030:   45 47 55 49 44 45 20 20 20 20 20 20 00 FF 53 4D        EGUIDE      ..SM
0040:   42 25 00 00 00 00 00 00 00 00 00 00 00 00 00 00        B%..............
0050:   00 00 00 00 00 00 00 00 00 00 00 00 00 11 00 00        ...............
0060:   2E 00 00 00 00 00 00 00 00 00 00 00 00 00 00 00        ...............
0070:   00 00 00 00 2E 00 56 00 03 00 01 00 01 00 02 00        ......V.........
0080:   3F 00 5C 4D 41 49 4C 53 4C 4F 54 5C 42 52 4F 57        ?.\MAILSLOT\BROW
0090:   53 45 00 0F 08 C0 27 09 00 57 41 56 45 47 55 49        SE....'..WAVEGUI
00A0:   44 45 00 00 00 00 00 00 00 04 00 03 22 45 00 15        DE.........."E..
00B0:   04 55 AA 6A 6C 61 27 73 20 6D 61 63 68 69 6E 65        .U.jla's machine
00C0:   00                                                     .
```

```
802.3 [0000:000D]
  0000:0005   Destination Address: 030000000001 (NetBEUI Multicast)
  0006:000B   Source Address: 00C0F02764E2 (Kingston2764E2)
  000C:000D   Ethernet Length: 179
LLC [000E:0010]
  000E:000E   Destination SAP: NETBIOS
  000F:000F   Source SAP: NETBIOS (Command)
  0010:0010 LLC Control: UI (Unnumbered Information) frame
NETBIOS [0011:003C]
  0011:0012   Header Length: 44
  0013:0014   Delimiter: 0xEFFF
  0015:0015   Command: Datagram
  0016:0016   Data1: Reserved
  0017:0018   Data2: Reserved
  0019:001A   Transmit Correlator: Reserved
  001B:001C   Response Correlator: Reserved
  001D:002C   Destination Name: RAYCAST       (name of receiver)
  002D:003C   Source Name: WAVEGUIDE          (name of sender)
SMB [003D:005C]
  003D:0040   ID: 0xFF, 'SMB'
  0041:0041   Command Code: Transaction (Client Command)
  0042:0042   Error Class: Success
  0043:0043   Reserved: 0
  0044:0045   Error Code: Success
  0046:0046   Flag: 0x00
  0047:0048   Flag2: 0x0000
  0049:0054   Reserved: Not Used
  0055:0056   Tree ID: 0x0000
  0057:0058   Process ID: 0x0000
  0059:005A   User ID: 0x0000
  005B:005C   Multiplex ID: 0x0000
```

Notice that the source and destination addresses are 6-byte MAC addresses, and not 4-byte IP addresses. The SMB is being transmitted from the machine named WAVEGUIDE.

Machine names are the NetBIOS names that identify each machine on a Windows network. To view or alter your machine name, right-click on the Network Neighborhood icon and select Properties to bring up the Network properties display. Left-click the Identification tab to see the machine name. Figure 7–7 shows the Identification display for the WAVEGUIDE machine.

FIGURE 7–7
Network Identification display.

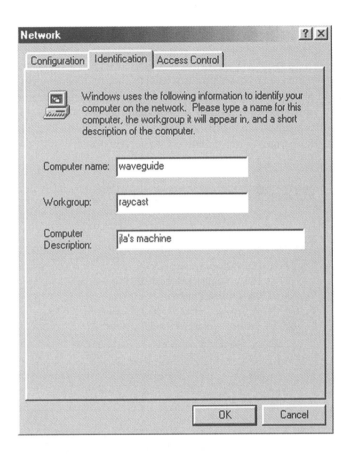

NetBIOS names may be up to 15 characters including letters, numbers, and a limited set of symbols. Figure 7–8 shows the error display resulting from entering an invalid machine name.

FIGURE 7–8
Invalid NetBIOS computer name error message.

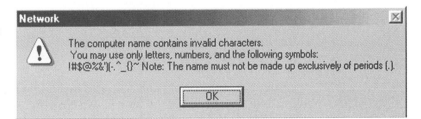

Windows uses the machine name to identify a computer so that it can share resources and engage in other network activities, such as locating other machines in the network neighborhood.

■ NETBEUI

NetBEUI

Objective 2-3

Objective 2-7

NetBEUI (NetBIOS Extended User Interface) provides a transport mechanism to deliver NetBIOS messages over a LAN. Like NetBIOS, NetBEUI does not directly conform to the OSI model but mirrors functionality at layers 2, 4, and 5 (the Data-Link, Transport, and Session layers). NetBEUI is not a routable protocol because it uses MAC addresses to specify source and destination computers and is thus only used on small networks (up to 254 machines). A special dynamic database called WINS (Windows Internet Name Service) maps NetBIOS names to IP addresses when larger networks are needed. Clearly, it is easier for a human to remember the name of a machine than its IP address, so the WINS database provides an important function.

TCP

NetBIOS over TCP/IP allows NetBIOS messages to be transported using *TCP*, which is a routable protocol used to connect computers in different networks (such as computers on the Internet). NetBIOS over TCP/IP can therefore be used to share resources over a WAN, instead of just a LAN environment. This is supported by a look at the Network properties window shown in Figure 7–9 (right-click on Network Neighborhood and choose Properties, or left-double-click the Network icon in Control Panel).

FIGURE 7–9
Network properties showing protocol bindings.

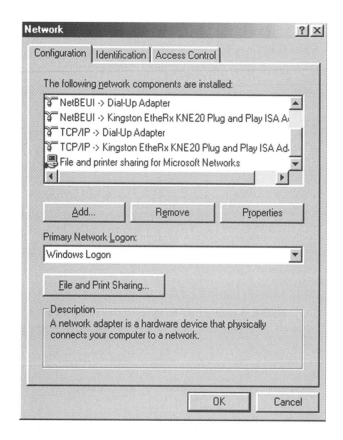

Although NetBEUI was originally used by IBM for its LAN Manager network, it has been adapted by Microsoft for use in Windows for Workgroups 3.11 and Windows 95/98/Me/NT. Figure 7–10(a) and 7–10(b) show the NetBEUI Properties dialog boxes. These are displayed by selecting one of the bound protocols from the Network properties window and examining its properties. It is normally not necessary to adjust any of the NetBEUI parameters.

With the delivery of Windows 2000, Microsoft is moving away from using the NetBEUI protocol. Microsoft, along with other major software companies, now designs their operating system to use the Internet standard, TCP/IP, as the default protocol suite. Some legacy networks and software packages still use the NetBEUI protocol, but that will change as individuals and organizations migrate to more current software.

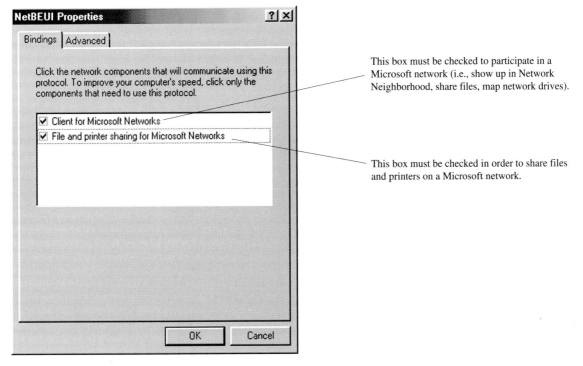

This box must be checked to participate in a Microsoft network (i.e., show up in Network Neighborhood, share files, map network drives).

This box must be checked in order to share files and printers on a Microsoft network.

(a) Bindings.

(b) Advanced.

This field limits the maximum number of concurrent sessions that may be active at the same time.

Network Control Blocks. NCBs contain information such as NetBIOS names, pointers, and command codes.

Check this box to make NetBEUI the default protocol in a multi-protocol environment.

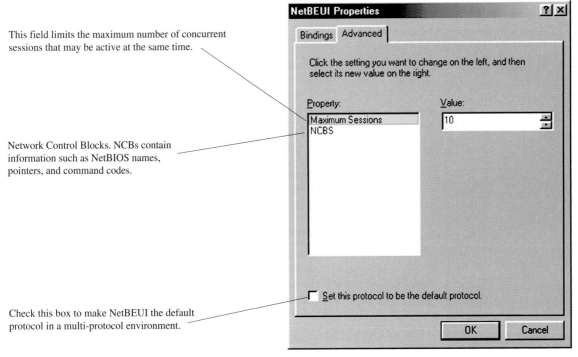

FIGURE 7–10
NetBEUI Properties dialog boxes.

■ TROUBLESHOOTING TECHNIQUES

To troubleshoot effectively, it is often necessary to dig deeper into the specifics of a protocol. An excellent source of protocol information can be found on the Web at www.protocols.com. Just click the Search icon and enter the name of the protocol you are looking to research for.

Another good site is www.whatis.com, which provides short descriptions of the items being searched for, with links to additional information provided. Use both sites to supplement your study of the protocols covered in this chapter and those you will be exposed to in Chapters 8 through 10.

Remote Access Trouble

Objective 4-11

A forest ranger completed his two-mile hike up the side of a mountain, stopping at a remote weather station. Every three months he made the two-mile hike to the station to upload his sensor data to a National Weather Service computer. The equipment was old: a 2400-baud external modem connected to a 25 MHz, 386 personal computer running Windows for Workgroups. The weather software established a SLIP connection to upload the data. Today, however, the weather software was not able to establish the connection. The forest ranger listened to the phone line and it did not sound noisy. He tried connecting again, with no luck. The ranger dialed the support number for the weather service and reported the problem.

The service technician discovered that, sometime during the last three months, the weather service's ISP changed their access method, switching over to PPP from SLIP. The old 386 PC was replaced by a 200 MHz Pentium laptop, using PPP with dial-up networking to upload data.

INDUSTRY TIP

Protocols are the languages of a computer network. They define rules of how information is to be organized (which bit represents what piece of information), how information is to be presented (light signals, electronic signals, etc.), what actions are taken when a specific event occurs, and so forth. The protocols that are with us today are the product of approximately 30 years of various organizations and companies designing their protocols to accomplish various tasks on a network. These protocols have been developed in response to changing developments in technology. The increase of the popularity of the Internet has driven the need for standardization of which protocol to use on a network. Until the last five to seven years major corporations implemented their own sets of protocol suites. These organizations included giants such as Microsoft, Novell, and IBM. Over the last five to seven years these major vendors have migrated to using the TCP/IP protocol suite as their native protocol of choice. In the past a network engineer would have to design very complex networks to accommodate all the various protocols that would be needed on a corporation's infrastructure. While there is still a common need to support many legacy (and current) protocols on a modern network, many of the diverse protocols are fading out of existence and soon network engineers will need to select fewer common protocol suites to use on their infrastructure. The benefits of fewer protocols on a network are many and include reduced training requirements for the network technicians, a better understanding of the specific protocols in use (with fewer protocols you can better learn the ones that you are using), less bandwidth used (especially when we can do away with the more chatty protocols), lower cost of network equipment, and greater security (the more complex a network, the more security holes exist). As you progress through your career, read industry journals and Web sites and note what is happening to the development of common protocol usage. The continuing migration toward IPv6 is a good example of what is happening to the industry.

CAREER DEVELOPMENT: NETWORK+

The Network+ certification focuses on professionals with at least nine months experience in network support or administration. The certification demonstrates a professional's technical ability in networking administration and support, and validates their knowledge of media and topologies, protocols and standards, network implementation, and network support. For more information on the Network+ certification visit www.comptia.org.

■ SELF-TEST

1. Which of the following is not a PC device that uses serial communication?
   a. Keyboard
   b. Mouse
   c. COM1 port
   d. Printer

2. True or False: Each bit of the waveform used in serial transmission takes the same amount of time.

3. The clock signal is sent with the _____ when using synchronous transmission methods.
   a. data
   b. link delimiter
   c. network address
   d. application

4. Asynchronous transmission is synchronized through the use of _____.
   a. clock regeneration
   b. start frame synchronization
   c. start and stop bits
   d. async bit set to 0

5. SLIP provides an encapsulation method for layer 3 _____ data.
   a. IPX
   b. BGP
   c. Appletalk
   d. IP

6. True or False: SLIP provides error correction for IP transmissions.

7. What kind of test for data validity is used by PPP to facilitate error detection?
   a. Parity
   b. Upper layer protocols only
   c. Checksum value
   d. Mirroring

8. SSAP codes in an 802.2 frame identify the _____ serviced by that frame.
   a. upper layer protocol
   b. line transmission method
   c. source and destination MAC addresses
   d. wireless transmission method

9. Connectionless communication is characterized as _____.
   a. asynchronous
   b. synchronous
   c. reliable
   d. unreliable

10. The sending and receiving stations exchange acknowledgements regarding a message to guarantee delivery. What type of communication does this describe?
    a. Connection-oriented
    b. Connectionless
    c. Unreliable
    d. Synchronous

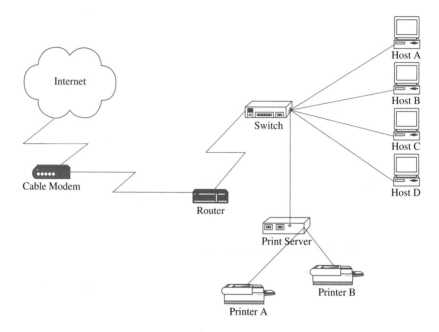

The network diagram shown above will be used to answer the following two questions.

11. The router in the diagram above is connected via remote access to another SOHO network with the same design as this one. Our network uses PPP on the WAN link connection to the other network. The remote link uses SLIP on their WAN link. What is the result of this configuration?
    a. It will work properly.
    b. No connection
    c. Connection, but no authentication
    d. Connection from SLIP link only

12. Hosts on the network pictured above are able to obtain services on any VLAN in the network. However, they are unable to access the Internet? Which of the following is the most likely problem device?
    a. Router
    b. Switch
    c. Printer server
    d. Modem

13. Which protocol is 802.2 based upon?
    a. PPP
    b. SHLC
    c. LAPB
    d. HDLC

14. True or False: NetBIOS was designed to comply with the OSI model and functions at layer 3 of the OSI model.

15. Which of the following is not a service provided by NetBIOS?
    a. Name
    b. Session
    c. Clocking
    d. Datagram

16. Which of the following represents a NetBIOS source or destination address?
    a. 030000000001
    b. 03000001
    c. 0G0FF010222
    d. 1HFC0003201

17. What icon on the desktop should you right-click to start the process of displaying the NetBIOS name on your computer?
    a. My Computer
    b. My Documents
    c. Internet Explorer
    d. Network Neighborhood

18. Windows identifies a computer by name to _____.
    a. record software installed
    b. provide Internet connectivity
    c. allow software installation
    d. share resources

19. What protocol provides the transport mechanism needed to deliver NetBIOS messages over a LAN?
    a. PPP trunking
    b. NetBEUI
    c. PPP ANYLAN
    d. NBTSTAT

20. What command must be issued to see the output listed in the figure above?
    a. Network ?
    b. NetBios ?
    c. Netstat -a
    d. NetBstat -a

21. What is the meaning of the word "established" in the output of the MS-DOS prompt listed in the figure above?
    a. A session is established between two computers.
    b. The correct password has been provided.
    c. The first step in IP address configuration is complete.
    d. The computer has sent a dialing packet.

22. What utility is used to troubleshoot NetBIOS over TCP/IP on a Windows network?
    a. Netstat
    b. Nbtstat
    c. Ping
    d. Ipconfig/all

23. Which of the following is not a routable protocol?
    a. IP
    b. IPX
    c. NetBEUI
    d. NetBIOS over TCP

24. True or False: NetBIOS over TCP/IP allows NetBIOS messages to be transported using UDP.

25. True or False: Protocols are used to define how information is organized and presented on computer networks.

The TCP/IP Protocols

CHAPTER **8**

PERFORMANCE OBJECTIVES

Upon completion of this chapter, you will be able to:

- Describe how the TCP/IP protocol stack is organized compared to the ISO/OSI protocol stack.
- Discuss the different protocols that make up the TCP/IP suite.
- Show how TCP/IP data is encapsulated inside a hardware frame for transmission.
- Describe the relationship between IP addresses and MAC addresses.
- Discuss the role of the PING and TRACERT applications.

 ## NETWORK+ OBJECTIVES

This chapter provides information for the following Network+ objectives:

1.6 Identify the purpose, features, and functions of the following network components:
  - Hubs
  - Switches
  - Bridges
  - Routers
  - Gateways
  - CSU/DSU
  - Network Interface Cards/ISDN adapters/system area network cards
  - Wireless access points
  - Modems

2.2 Identify the seven layers of the OSI model and their functions.

2.5 Define the purpose, function, and/or use of the following protocols within TCP/IP:
  - IP
  - TCP
  - UDP
  - FTP
  - TFTP
  - SMTP
  - HTTP
  - HTTPS
  - POP3/IMAP4
  - TELNET
  - ICMP
  - ARP
  - NTP

2.6 Define the function of TCP/UDP ports. Identify well-known ports.

2.7 Identify the purpose of the following network services (e.g., DHCP/ BOOTP, DNS, NAT/ICS, WINS, and SNMP).

2.8 Identify IP addresses (Ipv4, Ipv6) and their default subnet masks.

2.9 Identify the purpose of subnetting and default gateways.

2.13 Identify the following security proto- cols and describe their purpose and function:
  - IPsec
  - L2TP
  - SSL
  - Kerberos

4.1 Given a troubleshooting scenario, se- lect the appropriate TCP/IP utility from among the following:
  - TRACERT
  - PING
  - ARP
  - IPCONFIG/IFCONFIG
  - WINIPCFG
  - NSLOOKUP
  - NETSTAT
  - NBTSTAT

4.7 Given output from a diagnostic utility (e.g., TRACERT, PING, IPCONFIG, etc.), identify the utility, and interpret the output.

■ INTRODUCTION

Objective 2-2

This chapter examines the features of the TCP/IP (Transmission Control Protocol/Internet Protocol) suite. Similar to most protocol suites, the TCP/IP protocol suite is named after the primary protocols within the suite; in this case, the TCP and IP protocols. The TCP/IP protocol suite is unquestionably one of the most popular networking protocol suites ever developed. TCP/IP has been used since the 1960s as a method to connect large mainframe computers together to share information among the research community and the Department of Defense (DOD). TCP/IP is now used to support the largest computer network, the Internet. Most manufacturers incorporate TCP/IP into their operating systems, allowing all types of computers to communicate with each other. The TCP/IP protocol suite and model was developed prior to the OSI model. The developers of the TCP/IP model took a different approach in a few areas. They did not directly concern themselves with the underlying transmission technologies and therefore rely on other standards bodies to define these issues. They also were not concerned with dealing with the other issues of separating the specifics of the items addressed by layers 5 to 7 of the OSI model. Their approach was to develop the actual applications and let the model support it at a later date; hence the fact that layer 5 to 7 (OSI model) issues are all grouped into the single Application layer of the TCP/IP model. Other than that, the protocols within the TCP/IP protocol suite can be closely associated with the layers of the OSI model. The TCP/IP protocol suite (also called a protocol stack) is contained and organized in the TCP/IP model. You will also hear the TCP/IP model referred to as the DOD model since the U.S. Department of Defense is the originator of this model. This is a good place to note that the OSI model also possesses its own set of protocols; but, though all the protocols within the OSI suite are not as widely used, the model itself is the industry standard reference for organizing networking concepts.

The OSI model breaks network communication down into seven layers. In contrast, the TCP/IP network model contains only four layers. Figure 8–1 shows the relationship between the OSI network model and the TCP/IP network model.

OSI Model		TCP/IP Model		
Layer	**OSI layers**	**TCP/IP layers**	**Sample Common Protocols**	
7	Application	Application	HTTP, HTTPS, FTP, TELNET, SMTP, POP3, IMAP4, DNS	SNMP, DHCP, TFTP, DNS, NTP
6	Presentation			
5	Session		LDAP	
4	Transport	Transport	↑ TCP	↑ UDP
3	Network	Internet	IP, IPv6, ARP, RARP, ICMP, IGMP	
2	Data Link — LLC / MAC	Network Access	PPTP, L2TP (Traditional layer 1 and 2 technology standards not defined by the TCP/IP model. Relies on other standards bodies.)	
1	Physical			

FIGURE 8–1
OSI versus TCP/IP model.

The bottom layer of the TCP/IP model is called the Network Access layer and does not directly address the characteristics of the underlying technology. The original name for this layer was the Network Interface layer, but through time it became known as the Network Access layer. You will likely see a few other names for it, such as the Host-to-Network layer. Over time, additional functionality was added to network communications, and the Network Access layer does address some modern protocols such as Layer 2 Tunneling Protocol (L2TP).

The next layer up, called the Internet layer, performs the same function as the Network layer (layer 3) in the OSI model. The Internet layer uses the Internet Protocol (IP) as its logical addressing protocol. IP version 4 (IPv4) is the current protocol of choice but IP version 6 (IPv6) is already being implemented in parts of the world and will eventually overtake IPv4 as the standard. Other protocols that work at this layer are the Address Resolution Protocol (ARP), Reverse Address Resolution Protocol (RARP), Internet Control Message Protocol (ICMP), and Internet Group Management Protocol (IGMP). The Transport layer is the same in both the OSI and TCP/IP network stacks. There are two primary Transport-layer protocols in TCP/IP, the Transmission Control Protocol (TCP) and the User Datagram Protocol (UDP). TCP provides for *connection-oriented* reliable transport and UDP provides for *connectionless* unreliable transport.

The TCP/IP Application layer provides the same functionality as the Session, Presentation, and Application layers in the OSI network model. The Application layer is where the communicating application programs running on the source computer and the destination computer reside. The packet of data that is transmitted from the source computer contains an informational header for each layer in the protocol stack (except layer 1). This concept is shown in Figure 8–2.

FIGURE 8–2
TCP/IP stack layering.

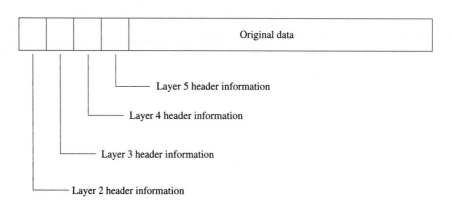

When a hardware frame is sent out onto the network, it contains all of the information necessary to be forwarded to and received properly by the destination computer without errors. At the destination host, as the received message moves up the stack toward the application, identical copies of the packaged information are available at each layer, just as they were on the source host. This is illustrated in Figure 8–3. TCP/IP uses this layering technique to transmit all data between the applications running on the communicating computers.

Look again at Figure 8–1 and you can see which of the various common protocols work at the various layers. The protocols listed at the Application layer are divided into two groups (look at the row equal to the OSI layer 7 but under the TCP/IP model columns). Those that are listed above the TCP section (Transport layer) of Figure 8–1 are connection-oriented protocols. They include common protocols such as HTTP, FTP, and so on. Remember that connection-oriented protocols use the underlying TCP processes and require acknowledgement of packets received. This is much like a return receipt request for a mailed letter or package. The Application layer protocols that are listed in the section above the UDP layer 3 protocol are connectionless protocols and do not require any acknowledgement of delivery of packets. These include common protocols such as TFTP and SNMP.

You may notice that the DNS (Domain Naming System) protocol is listed in both columns. This is not a mistake. The DNS process that resolves an Internet name, such as www.prenhall.com, to an IP address, such as 165.193.123.253, uses the UDP version of DNS. The DNS processes that make zone transfers of DNS information between DNS servers use the TCP version of DNS.

Each of the protocols in the TCP/IP protocol stack is described in detail by an RFC.

FIGURE 8–3
TCP/IP message layering.

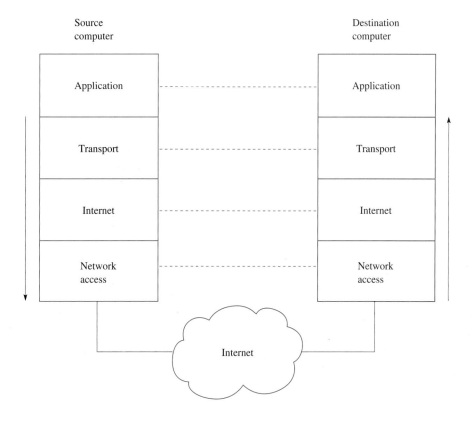

■ RFCs

RFCs

Official standards for the Internet are published as electronic documents called Requests for Comments, or *RFCs*. The RFC series of documents on networking began in 1969 as part of the original Advanced Research Projects Agency wide-area networking project called ARPAnet. RFCs cover a wide range of topics in addition to Internet standards, from early discussion of new research concepts to status memos about the current state of the Internet.

Refer to Table 8–1 for a list of RFCs associated with some of the most popular protocols in TCP/IP. The Internet Engineering Task Force (IETF) Web site located at www.ietf.org/rfc.html provides quick access to all of the RFC documents. Appendix D

TABLE 8–1
Several important TCP/IP RFCs.

Protocol	RFC	Name
Telnet	854	Remote Terminal Protocol
FTP	959	File Transfer Protocol
SMTP	821	Simple Mail Transfer Protocol
SNMP	1098	Simple Network Management Protocol
DNS	1034	Domain Name System
TCP	793	Transport Control Protocol
UDP	768	User Datagram Protocol
ARP	826	Address Resolution Protocol
RARP	903	Reverse Address Resolution Protocol
ICMP	792	Internet Control Message Protocol
BOOTP	951	Bootstrap Protocol
IP	791	Internet Protocol
IMAP4	1730	Internet Message Access version 4

contains a list of RFC numbers and their titles. The RFC number is used (entered into an HTML form) on the IETF Web site to examine the individual RFCs. You are encouraged to review the RFC documents, as they provide much insight into how TCP/IP and the Internet work.

Internet Protocol (IP)

Objective 2-5

The Internet Protocol (IP) is the protocol used to provide the logical addressing scheme used on the Internet. IP uses a hierarchical addressing scheme, which contains a network and a host portion in the address. This design enables packets to be routed between multiple networks, classifying it as a *routed* protocol. It also provides a unique address that identifies your computer on a specific network. It is much like the street address for your house. IP is considered to be an unreliable protocol since it provides no acknowledgement services for packets sent. There are various ways to refer to packets generated at this layer. Though many individuals refer to these packets as datagrams, the term "datagram" actually refers to packets that use the UDP layer 4 protocol. In keeping with standard industry practices we will refer to these as packets (the layer 4 PDU of the OSI model).

The IP packet is transmitted on a local network to a special-purpose device called a *router* whose job is to forward the packet onto another router or possibly deliver the packet to the LAN where the destination host is located. Routers divide the network into logical portions that contain different IP address networks. You will understand this more when we discuss IP addresses later in this chapter.

There is no direct link between the source and destination computers on the Internet. The source computer system sends packets out onto the local LAN network where they are then forwarded on to their destination. When an IP packet is sent, it is treated as an independent entity on the network, with no relationship to any other packet. Packets sent to the same location may take different routes as network conditions change. This may cause the destination computer to receive the packets in a different order than the order in which they were sent due to the various delays.

As noted previously in this chapter, the Internet Protocol is considered to be unreliable due to the fact that there is no guarantee the packet will reach its destination. IP provides what is called *best effort* delivery. For example, a common reason for packet loss is network congestion. Figure 8–4 shows a reason why congestion might occur.

Consider the situation in which computers connected to network C are trying to communicate with computers in the E and F networks that are connected to network D. The link between networks C and D may not be able to handle all of the traffic, creating network *congestion*. On a congested network, some network traffic may simply be discarded to eliminate the congestion. Usually, when an IP packet runs into trouble on the network, it is simply discarded. An error contained in an **ICMP** (Internet Control Message Protocol) message may or may not be returned to the sender. Figure 8–5 illustrates an example of how an ICMP message is encapsulated in an IP datagram. Additional information about ICMP will be provided later in this chapter. If a packet is lost during the routing process it will be the responsibility of an upper layer protocol to request a retransmission. Remember that error correction can take place at layers 2, 4, and 7 depending on the technologies and protocols in use.

The IP packet header and data field containing the ICMP message is shown in Figure 8–6. An IP packet has a maximum size of 64K, or 65536 bytes. This total includes the header and the data area. Table 8–2 shows the size and purpose of each of the fields in the IP packet header. Basically, the IP packet header contains data fields to identify the version of IP, the length of the IP header (usually 20 bytes), the type of service, the total length of the packet, and other fields that are used to identify the source and destination addresses and various error detection, reassembly, and delivery options.

When an IP packet is encapsulated in a hardware frame, it is done so according to the local network maximum transmission unit, or MTU. A typical value for an MTU is 1500 bytes. This MTU value specifies the maximum size of an IP packet that may be transmitted on that particular network. Some networks may set the MTU to a larger or smaller value. During transit, a packet generated with an MTU value of 1500 might encounter a network where the MTU is smaller. This is illustrated in Figure 8–7.

ICMP

FIGURE 8–4
A source of network congestion.

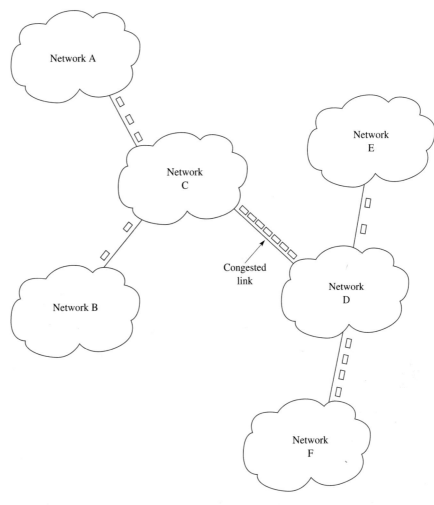

FIGURE 8–5
ICMP encapsulated in an IP datagram.

IP Datagram header	IP data

ICMP header	ICMP data

FIGURE 8–6
IP encapsulated message.

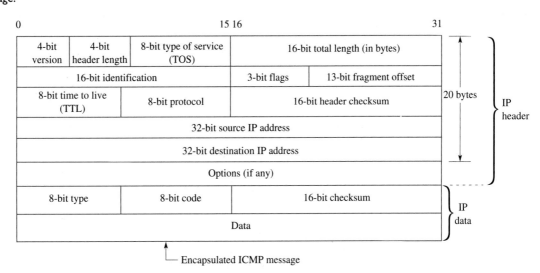

TABLE 8–2
IP header field information.

Header Field	Size	Meaning
Version	4 bits	Indicates the IP version number.
Hlen	4 bits	Length of the header in 32-bit words. The minimum value is 5 (20 bytes).
Service Type	8 bits	Specifies various parameters for throughput, reliability, precedence, and delay.
Total Length	16 bits	Specifies the total datagram length in bytes.
Identification	16 bits	Used to uniquely identify a datagram.
Flags	3 bits	Parameters used to specify information about fragmentation. Only two of these bits are defined.
Fragment Offset	13 bits	Indicates where in the original datagram the fragment belongs.
Time to Live (TTL)	8 bits	Used to specify how many hops a datagram can travel on the network.
Protocol	8 bits	Specifies the next higher level protocol to receive the data.
Header Checksum	16 bits	Used to detect errors in the header field only. This value is recomputed at each router since some of the header fields such as TTL are changed.
Source Address	32 bits	Sender IP address.
Destination Address	32 bits	Destination IP address.
Options and Padding	32 bits	User requested options.
Data	Variable	The data field is an integer multiple of 8 bits. The maximum size of the IP datagram is 64K bytes.

When this situation occurs, it is necessary to fragment the IP datagram to comply with the network's lower MTU value, as shown in Figure 8–8.

When a packet is fragmented, additional information is coded in the fragment offset field in the IP header to allow the receiving computer to correctly reassemble the data segments back into their original state.

To understand how an IP packet is forwarded to the destination, it is necessary to understand how the IP packets are addressed.

■ IP ADDRESSES

IP packets are routed on the network using an IP address. The IP address consists of a 32-bit number, divided into four sections, each containing 8 bits. These four sections are called *octets* (they contain 8 bits) and may contain an equivalent decimal value in the range 0 to 255. The four values from these sections are separated by periods in the IP address. This is called **dotted decimal notation** because the binary value of the octet is noted in decimal format (to make it easier on humans since we normally work in decimal values) and the octets are visually separated by dots. An example of dotted decimal notation is shown in Figure 8–9.

Dotted decimal notation

Objective 2-8

The IP address is assigned to a host either dynamically, via *Dynamic Host Configuration Protocol* (DHCP), or statically (manually entered by an individual) and must be a unique address on the network.

Address Classes

The Internet addresses are grouped into five address classes labeled from A to E. These addresses are shown in Figure 8–10. Each address class consists of a network ID and a host ID.

Before we start looking at the specifics of the classes there are a few rules that should be stated. These rules identify IP addresses that have special purposes and are not assignable to hosts on a network. You cannot assign an IP address to a host if the address has all zeros in the network portion of the IP address nor can you use an address that has all zeros

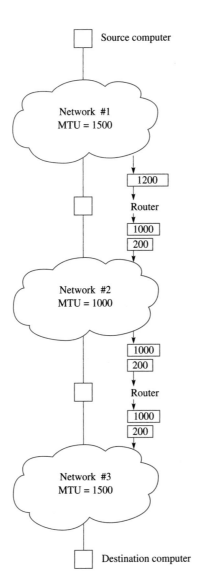

FIGURE 8–7
Networks with different MTUs.

FIGURE 8–8
IP datagram fragmentation.

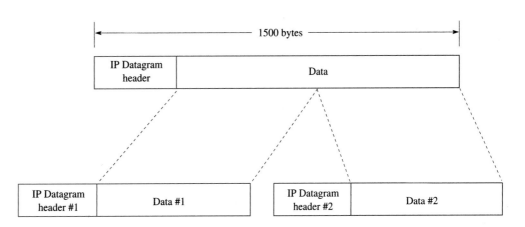

FIGURE 8–9
Class C network IP address.

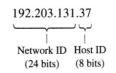

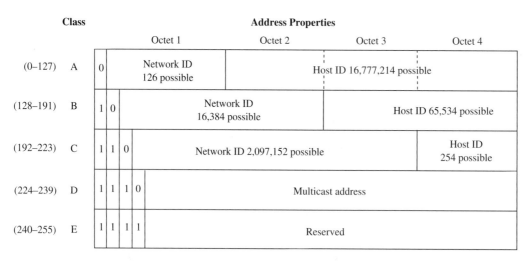

FIGURE 8–10

IP address classes.

in the host portion of the address. All zeros in the network portion of the address represent a *null network ID*. An example of this would be 0.0.0.0. All zeros in the host portion of the address are used when we want to identify a specific network (making that the network ID). An example would be 10.0.0.0. This would designate the 10.x.x.x network ID, allowing us to discuss the entire 10 network without talking about a specific host (e.g., a computer with an address of 10.0.3.1).

All ones in the network portion of an IP address are not allowed. All ones are used as a *broadcast address*. All ones in the host portion of the address are not allowed. All ones in the host portion of an IP address are used to send a layer 3 broadcast to every host on that specific network. This is what is called a *directed broadcast*.

For example, to send a message to all hosts in the 10.x.x.x network, you would send a message to 10.255.255.255. This is done by a host on one network who wants to send a message to all hosts on another network. All ones in both the network and host portions of an IP address are used as a layer 3 *local broadcast* address. This is like the layer 2 broadcast address of FF-FF-FF-FF-FF-FF. An example of this use is when a host is booting up and is configured to use DHCP to obtain an IP address. It will broadcast a DHCP request to all hosts on the local network (255.255.255.255) and any DHCP server that is available will try to service the request. The host must use the broadcast address because it doesn't know the address of the DHCP server.

The final rule for now: the Class A 127.x.x.x network is set aside for loopback testing of the TCP/IP protocol stack (pinging your computer for testing purposes). Formally the specific IP address of 127.0.0.1 is designated as the loopback address, but usually you can use any 127.x.x.x address for testing (stick to using 127.0.0.1 and you will do better on those certification tests). This address is actually used for testing proper installation of the TCP/IP protocol stack. This tests the stack all the way down to the LLC layer of the OSI model. Normally you can use this address even if you do not have a NIC installed (remember that the TCP/IP model does not care about the underlying technology in use) but your operating system may require that you install a null (generic) NIC driver before this works. Armed with the preceding rules we will now review the various classes.

Class A networks were designed for large networks and use the first octet for the network portion of the IP address, and the remaining three octets (24 bits) for the host portion of the address. The design rules also call for the first bit of the first octet to be a "0". If the first bit is always a "0" for class A networks then mathematically we can have network IDs of 0 to 127. If you recall the above rules you will remember that we cannot have all "0"s in the network portion of the address and the 127.x.x.x network is reserved for loopback testing purposes. This means that our useable class A networks for assigning IP addresses to a host must remain within the 1 to 126 range of network IDs, even though mathematically a class A includes 0 to 127 networks or 128 total. Examples of a valid class A network ID include 1.x.x.x, 10.x.x.x, 52.x.x.x, all the way up to 126.x.x.x. Looking at the host portion of the class A address you will note that there are 24 bits available for assigning addresses to hosts. If you do the math you will note that 2^{24} (there are 24 binary bits in the host portion of the class A address) equals a total of 16,777,216 addresses. In Figure 8–10 note that only 16,777,214 are listed as useable (assignable to a host). That is because of the rules that there cannot be all "0"s in the host portion of the address (which designates the network ID) and there cannot be all "1"s in the host portion of the address (which designates the directed broadcast address for the network). If you take these two available addresses out of the number 16,777,216 you will have 16,777,214 assignable addresses for each class A network.

Class A, B, and C networks have one address block reserved for use on private networks. The class A address block for private networks is the 10.x.x.x network.

Class B networks were designed for medium to large networks and use the first and second octets for the network portion of the IP address and the remaining two octets (16 bits) for the host portion of the address. The design rules also call for the first bit in the first octet to be a "1" and the second bit to be a "0". This means that the possible range of decimal values for the first octet of a class B network is from 128 to 191. Since the first two bits of a class B network are dictated by the designers of the addressing scheme we have a total of only 14 bits left to use to create class B network IDs. This means that we have 16,384 possible class B networks ($2^{14} = 16,384$). Note that we did not have to deal with any of the rules about all "1"s or "0"s in the network portion of the address because the first two bits contain a "1" and a "0". The host portion of a class B address includes 16 bits, which equates to a decimal number of 65,536 (2^{16}). Since we still have to follow the rules of not using all "0"s (the network ID for the specific network) or all "1"s (the directed broadcast address for the specific network) we must reduce the assignable address space from 65,536 to 65,534.

The class B address block reserved for private networks is from 172.16.0.0 to 172.31.255.255. There was not a demonstrated need to reserve an entire class B address block of 172.16.x.x for private addresses, so only half of that particular network was set aside for private networks.

Class C networks were designed for use by smaller networks and use the first, second, and third octets for the network portion of the address, and the last octet for the host portion of the address. The design rules also call for the first and second bits in the first octet to be a "1" and the third bit to be a "0". This means that the possible range of decimal values for the first octet of a class C network is from 192 to 223. Since the first three bits of a class C network are dictated by the designers of the addressing scheme we have a total of only 21 bits left to use to create class C network IDs. This means that we have 2,097,152 possible class C networks ($2^{21} = 2,097,152$). Note that we did not have to deal with any of the rules about all "1"s or "0"s in the network portion of the address because the first three bits contain a combination of "1"s and "0"s. The host portion of a class C address includes 16 bits, which equates to a decimal number of 256 (2^{8}). Since we still have to follow the rules of not using all "0"s (the network ID for the specific network) or all "1"s (the directed broadcast address for the specific network) we must reduce the assignable address space from 256 to 254.

The class C address block reserved for private networks is 192.168.x.x. Note that this private address space leaves the third octet available for your use, meaning that 256 class C address blocks are useable for private networks.

Class D addresses were set aside for use as *multicast* addresses. These are special addresses used when transmitting data to multiple hosts at the same time. An example is streaming audio and video. The design rules call for the first three bits of the first octet to be all "1"s and the fourth bit to be a "0". Mathematically this means that multicast addresses will have a decimal value between 224 and 239 in the first octet. As a network administrator you will never assign any IP addresses from this range to a host on a network.

Class E addresses were set aside for experimental purposes and you will never assign these addresses to a host on a network. The design rules call for the first four bits to be all

"1"s in the first octet, which means these addresses will have a first octet value between 240 and 255.

One of the shortcomings in the design of IP version 4 is in the addressing scheme. Class A networks, while able to support more than 16 million hosts, rarely contain that many hosts. The same is true for class B addresses (though there are not as many wasted addresses, since class B networks have a limit of 65,534 hosts). The popular class C networks have had such a high demand that there is now a shortage of these addresses. A solution to this problem was established by introducing a classless IP address that can take advantage of the unused addresses. This addressing is accomplished using *CIDR* (Classless Inter-Domain Routing) as discussed in Chapter 10.

CIDR

An additional item that is usually entered when configuring a host with an IP address is a similar looking item called a *subnet mask*. One of the pieces of information that a computer needs to know is how many of the 32 bits belong to the network portion of the address and how many of them are host bits.

While the previous sections about address classes might lead you to believe that a computer would know this, modern IP addressing methods allow us to ignore the address class boundaries; therefore we must be able to tell the computer how many bits of the address belong to what part of the address (network or host bits). We use a dotted decimal form of the 32 bits and designate how many bits of the address belong to the network portion of the address. The remaining bits then belong to the host portion of the address. A subnet mask for a standard class C network would be 255.255.255.0. This means that the first 24 bits (3 octets) are *turned on* (are all "1"s) so the computer now knows that those bits belong to the network portion of the address. The remaining bits (all "0"s) are host bits.

With an understanding of addressing and how messages are transmitted using IP, let us now examine the transport protocols that are used to get the data from an application running on a source computer to the application running on a destination computer.

■ TCP

The Transmission Control Protocol defines a standard way that two hosts can reliably communicate together over interconnected networks. Applications using TCP establish *connections* with each other, through the use of predefined *ports* or *sockets.* A TCP connection is reliable, with error checking, acknowledgment for received packets, and packet sequencing provided to guarantee the data arrives properly at its destination. Telnet and FTP are examples of applications that use TCP.

Ports
Sockets

The TCP provides the communication link between the application program and IP. A set of function calls provides an application process a number of different options. For example, there are calls to open and close connections and to send and receive data on previously established connections. These functions will be discussed in detail in Chapter 16.

Objective 2-5
Objective 2-6

The TCP header format is illustrated in Figure 8–11. The TCP header and associated data are encapsulated into a hardware frame, such as Ethernet.

A brief description of the purpose of each field in the header is provided in Table 8–3.

The primary purpose of the TCP is to provide reliable communication between applications running on a source host and a destination host. To provide guaranteed delivery on top of IP requires attention to the following areas:

- Data transfer
- Reliability
- Flow control
- Multiplexing
- Connections
- Message precedence and security

Take a look at each of these areas.

FIGURE 8–11
TCP header format.

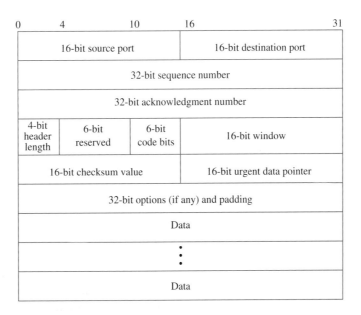

TABLE 8–3
TCP header field information.

Header Field	Size	Meaning
Source Port	16 bits	Source port service access point
Destination Port	16 bits	Destination port service access point
Sequence Number	32 bits	Sequence number of the current data segment
Acknowledgment Number	32 bits	The acknowledgment number contains the sequence number of the next data byte that TCP expects to receive
Header Length	4 bits	Number of 32-bit words in the TCP header
Reserved	6 bits	Flags reserved for future use
Code Bits	6 bits	Flags used to control the Urgent pointer, Acknowledgment field, Push function, Reset function, Sequence number synchronization, and final data indication
Window	16 bits	Contains the number of data bytes starting with the one in the acknowledgment field
Checksum	16 bits	The checksum value of the entire data segment to be transmitted
Urgent Pointer	16 bits	Indicates the amount of urgent data in the segment
Options and Padding	32 bits	One option currently defined that specifies the maximum data segment size that will be accepted

TCP is used to transfer a stream of data in each direction between the applications by packaging data into segments for transmission through the network.

To provide *reliability*, the TCP must be able to recover from data that is lost, damaged, delivered out of order, or duplicated by the network. This reliability is accomplished by assigning sequence numbers to the data as it is transmitted and requiring a positive acknowledgment (ACK) from the destination computer after the data has been received without error. If the ACK is not received within a certain timeout interval, the data is automatically retransmitted by the source computer. The timeout interval is based on an estimate of the time it takes for a packet to be sent to the destination computer and then acknowledged. This value is also called the *round trip estimation* time. A good estimated value for the round trip time allows for the highest level of network utilization.

At the destination computer, the sequence numbers are used to correctly reassemble the data segments. Duplicate packets that may be received are discarded. To ensure that a complete data segment has not been damaged, a checksum value is assigned to each segment that is transmitted. The destination computer checks the checksum value and discards any damaged segments. The TCP checksum field is based on a pseudo TCP header that contains only the source address, the destination address, the protocol, and the TCP segment length. In addition to error checking, the checksum field gives protection against misrouted packets.

TCP *flow control* provides a means for the receiver to govern the amount of data sent by the sender. This is achieved by returning a "window" with every ACK indicating a range of acceptable sequence numbers beyond the last segment successfully received. The window indicates an allowed number of octets that the sender may transmit before receiving further permission to send more. As the data is acknowledged, the window can be slid over the data that must still be transmitted. This is known as *sliding window* flow control. Figure 8–12 shows a simplistic example of two flow control methods. In Figure 8–12 on the left, the stop-and-go flow control requires that an acknowledgment be received before the next packet can be sent. The stop-and-go flow control method turns out to be extremely inefficient when compared to the sliding window flow control, as shown in Figure 8–12 on the right.

FIGURE 8–12

Stop-and-go (left) versus sliding window flow control (right).

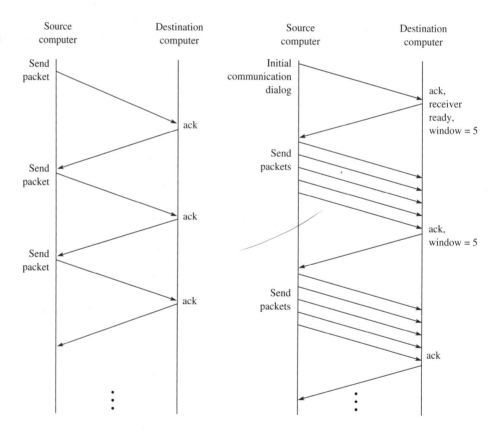

Using a sample window size of five, the source computer sends the first five packets and then waits for an acknowledgment from the receiver. Additional packets are sent as the receiver indicates it is ready to receive them. Figure 8–13 shows a sliding window in the process of sending 15 data packets.

In practice, window sizes are much larger and can accommodate large transfers of data very efficiently. One of the problems associated with the sliding window is called the *silly window syndrome*. The silly window syndrome occurs when the receiver repeatedly advertises a small window size due to what began as a temporary situation. The sender then

FIGURE 8–13
Sliding window flow control in operation.

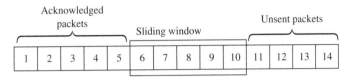

(a) Beginning of transmission.

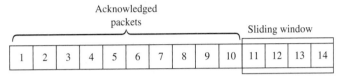

(b) After one acknowledgment.

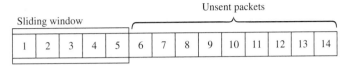

(c) After two acknowledgments.

transmits small segments to fit the small window size. Because less information is transmitted, some of the network bandwidth is unused and therefore wasted. When examining TCP packets using a protocol analyzer, pay attention to the window size field. Try to determine how often the window size changes, if at all.

Port Numbers

Objective 2-6

All data communication between two TCP applications takes place through specific *ports*. A port is associated with the network *socket* created and used by the application. A pair of sockets uniquely identifies a *connection*.

A single computer may receive several TCP packets, with the port number associated with the TCP application stored in each packet. The port number is used to demultiplex the packet stream and forward the correct TCP packet to each application's input buffer. The binding of port numbers to application programs is handled independently by each operating system. However, commonly used network applications are assigned to fixed port numbers that are publicly known. The services then can be accessed through the well-known port numbers. Port numbers between 0 and 1,023 are referred to as Well-Known Ports and are assigned by the Internet Assigned Numbers Authority (IANA). Ports 1,024 through 49,151 are referred to as Registered Ports. These are additional ports that organizations have registered and the IANA registers these ports as a convenience to the community. Ports from 49,152 through 65,535 are categorized as Dynamic and/or Private Ports. Table 8–4 lists several popular well-known TCP and UDP ports. You can find port number information at www.iana.org/assignments/port-numbers.

When two applications want to communicate, the TCP is used to establish a connection. After the connection has been established, data can be exchanged as necessary. After the communication is complete, the connection will be closed. Because these connections are established between hosts using the unreliable Internet Protocol, a *three-way handshake* (accomplished by TCP) is used to avoid the error condition that occurs when a connection is closed before all of the data has been transmitted. Essentially, this handshaking consists of three messages sent back and forth between the hosts, with each successive message containing information based on the previously received message.

The precedence and security of TCP communication may be specified. The TCP may have a requirement to indicate the security and precedence of the data or it may use default values when these special features are not needed.

TABLE 8–4
Selected well-known port numbers.

Port	TCP	UDP	Protocol
7	✔	✔	Echo
13	✔	✔	Daytime
20	✔		FTP Data
21	✔		FTP Control
23	✔		Telnet
25	✔		SMTP
53	✔	✔	DNS
67		✔	BOOTP/DHCP Server
68		✔	BOOTP/DHCP Client
69		✔	TFTP
70	✔		Gopher
79	✔		Finger
80	✔		HTTP
88	✔		Kerberos
110	✔		POP3
111	✔	✔	SUN RPC
119	✔		NNTP
123	✔	✔	NTP
137	✔	✔	NetBIOS Name
138	✔	✔	NetBIOS Datagram
139	✔	✔	NetBIOS Session
143	✔		IMAP v2
161		✔	SNMP
179	✔		BGP
194		✔	IRC
220	✔		IMAP v3

See how much of this information you can extract from a decoded packet that shows a portion of a file transfer that uses the TCP:

```
Capture 1:Packet 61

Destination    Source      Protocol      Summary      Size  Time Tick
----------------------------------------------------------------------------
24.24.78.84  192.203.130.2             File Transfer Protocol [Default Data]  TCP
                                        (ACK,PSH)     60    07/15/00 12:37:57.477

Addr.  Hex. Data                                          ASCII
0000:  00 60 97 9E EA D5 08 00 3E 02 07 8D 08 00 45 00    .'......>.....E.
0010:  00 2E 90 A6 00 00 75 06 0B EA C0 CB 82 02 18 18    ......u.........
0020:  4E 54 00 14 04 19 54 1C 3A 01 00 15 32 6A 50 18    NT....T.:...2jP.
0030:  24 00 28 DF 00 00 74 65 73 74 0D 0A                $.(...test..

802.3 [0000:000D]
   0000:0005  Destination Address: 0060979EEAD5 (3Com9EEAD5)
```

```
  0006:000B   Source Address: 08003E02078D (Motorola02078D)
  000C:000D   Ethernet Type: DOD Internet Protocol (IP)
IP [000E:0021]
  000E:000E   Version: 4; Header Length: 20
  000F:000F   TOS, Precedence: Routine; Delay: Normal; Throughput: Normal;
Reliability:   Normal
  0010:0011   Packet Length: 46
  0012:0013   Identification: 0x90A6
  0014:0014   DF: May Fragment; MF: Last Fragment
  0014:0015   Fragment Offset: 0
  0016:0016   Time to Live: 117
  0017:0017   Transport: Transmission Control
  0018:0019   Header Checksum: 0x0BEA (correct)
  001A:001D   Source Address: 192.203.130.2
  001E:0021   Destination Address: 24.24.78.84
TCP [0022:0035]
  0022:0023   Source Port: File Transfer Protocol [Default Data]
  0024:0025   Destination Port: 1049
  0026:0029   Sequence Number: 1411136001
  002A:002D   Acknowledgment Number: 1389162
  002E:002E   Header Length (bit 7..4): 20
  002F:002F   Control Bit - ACK; PSH;
  0030:0031   Window Size: 9216
  0032:0033   Checksum: 0x28DF (correct)
  0034:0035   Urgent Pointer: 0x0000
```

Compare each of the protocols (IP and TCP) shown in the Ethernet frame to their respective headers to determine what value each header field contains.

Next, we will examine the User Datagram Protocol that you use when guaranteed reliable data transfer is deemed unnecessary.

■ USER DATAGRAM PROTOCOL

User Datagram Protocol (UDP)

Objective 2-5

The *User Datagram Protocol (UDP)* is similar to TCP except it is *connectionless* and *unreliable*. Data is transmitted with no acknowledgment of whether it is received or not, thus UDP is not as reliable as TCP. Many applications do not require the additional overhead and complexity of TCP handshaking, such as the Domain Name Service (DNS), the Dynamic Host Configuration Protocol (DHCP), and network games. For example, a DNS or DHCP request will use UDP and will retransmit the request if a response is not obtained in a timely fashion. A multiplayer network game might use UDP because it is simple to implement, requires less overhead to manage than TCP, and also because the game may not be severely affected if a few packets are lost now and then.

The format of a UDP header is shown in Figure 8–14, and a description of the data fields inside the header is provided in Table 8–5. The UDP header format is quite a bit simpler than TCP, with fields used to identify the port number on the source computer, the port

FIGURE 8–14
UDP datagram format.

0	16	31
16-bit UDP source port		16-bit UDP destination port
16-bit message length		16-bit UDP checksum
Data		
⋮		
Data		

TABLE 8–5
UDP header field information.

Header Field	Size	Meaning
Source Port	16 bits	Source port service access point
Destination Port	16 bits	Destination port service access point
Length	16 bits	Contains the length of the segment including the header field and the data
Checksum	16 bits	The checksum value of the complete data segment

number on the destination computer, the length of the message in bytes, and a checksum value used to ensure that the data was received properly. The port numbers in UDP are used to identify the specific application running on the source computer and the destination computer. Similar to TCP, the UDP port numbers between 0 and 1,023 are referred to as Well-Known Ports and are assigned by the Internet Assigned Numbers Authority (IANA). Ports 1,024 through 49,151 are referred to as Registered Ports, and ports from 49,152 through 65,535 are categorized as Dynamic and/or Private Ports.

The UDP checksum field is based on a pseudo header that will work under any conditions. The pseudo header contains the source address, the destination address, the protocol, and the UDP segment length. The use of the UDP checksum field is optional. It must contain zeros to indicate that no checksum is supplied. A good reason to use the checksum field is that it gives protection against misrouted datagrams.

A decoded packet provides a good look at UDP in action while it is performing a DNS request:

```
Capture 1:Packet 6


Destination    Source      Protocol      Summary        Size  Time Tick
-----------------------------------------------------------------------------
24.92.226.171   24.24.78.84  Domain Name Server  Query    78    07/15/00
                                                              12:37:28.351


Addr.  Hex. Data                                      ASCII
0000:  08 00 3E 02 07 8D 00 60 97 9E EA D5 08 00 45 00   ..>....'......E.
0010:  00 40 11 01 00 00 80 11 C8 38 18 18 4E 54 18 5C   .@.......8..NT.\
0020:  E2 AB 04 16 00 35 00 2C 06 74 00 01 01 00 00 01   .....5.,.t......
0030:  00 00 00 00 00 00 03 66 74 70 0A 73 75 6E 79 62   .......ftp.sunyb
0040:  72 6F 6F 6D 65 03 65 64 75 00 00 01 00 01         roome.edu.....

802.3 [0000:000D]
  0000:0005   Destination Address: 08003E02078D (Motorola02078D)
  0006:000B   Source Address: 0060979EEAD5 (3Com9EEAD5)
  000C:000D   Ethernet Type: DOD Internet Protocol (IP)
IP [000E:0021]
  000E:000E   Version: 4; Header Length: 20
  000F:000F   TOS, Precedence: Routine; Delay: Normal; Throughput: Normal; Reliability:
Normal
  0010:0011   Packet Length: 64
  0012:0013   Identification: 0x1101
  0014:0014   DF: May Fragment; MF: Last Fragment
  0014:0015   Fragment Offset: 0
  0016:0016   Time to Live: 128
  0017:0017   Transport: User Datagram
  0018:0019   Header Checksum: 0xC838 (correct)
  001A:001D   Source Address: 24.24.78.84
  001E:0021   Destination Address: 24.92.226.171
```

```
UDP [0022:0029]
  0022:0023  Source Port: 1046
  0024:0025  Destination Port: Domain Name Server
  0026:0027  Packet Length: 44
  0028:0029  Checksum: 0x0674 (correct)
DNS [002A:004D]
  002A:002B  ID: 0x0001
  002C:002C  QR: Query, Opcode: Standard Query, AA: No, TC: No, RD: Yes
  002D:002D  RA: No, Reserved: 0, Response Code: No Error
  002E:002F  Question Count: 1
  0030:0031  Answer Count: 0
  0032:0033  Authority Count: 0
  0034:0035  Additional Count: 0
  0036:0049  Question Name: ftp.sunybroome.edu
  004A:004B  Question Type: host address
  004C:004D  Question Class: Internet
```

■ ARP AND RARP

Objective 2-5

Before any packet can be transmitted from one networked computer to another, the hardware address of the destination computer must be known. This address is called a *MAC* (media access control) *address*. It is a 48-bit binary number that uniquely distinguishes one machine from every other. Every network interface card manufactured has a preassigned MAC address.

Address Resolution Protocol (ARP)

The *Address Resolution Protocol (ARP)* uses a broadcast message to obtain the MAC address for a given IP address. For example, an ARP request may say, "What is the MAC address for 204.210.133.51?" The ARP reply may be, "The MAC address is 00-60-97-2B-E6-0F."

Once the ARP reply has been received, it is possible for the source computer and destination computer to communicate directly. Figure 8–15 shows the format of the ARP message. Notice that there is a place to hold the hardware address (MAC) and software address (IP) for both the source and destination computer systems. The purpose of each of these data fields is shown in Table 8–6.

Examine a packet decode of an ARP request and the subsequent reply message. First, the ARP request:

```
Capture 3:Packet 18

Destination   Source        Protocol        Summary  Size Time Tick
-----------------------------------------------------------------------------
24.24.78.1    24.24.78.84    ARP   Request      60   07/17/00  17:37:55.279

Addr.  Hex. Data                                         ASCII
0000:  FF FF FF FF FF FF 00 60 97 9E EA D5 08 06 00 01   .......'........
0010:  08 00 06 04 00 01 00 60 97 9E EA D5 18 18 4E 54   .......'......NT
0020:  00 00 00 00 00 00 18 18 4E 01                     ........N.

802.3 [0000:000D]
  0000:0005  Destination Address: FFFFFFFFFFFF (Broadcast)
  0006:000B  Source Address: 0060979EEAD5 (3Com9EEAD5)
  000C:000D  Ethernet Type: Address Resolution Protocol (ARP)
ARP [000E:0029]
  000E:000F  Hardware Type: Ethernet (10Mbps)
  0010:0011  Protocol Type: DOD Internet Protocol (IP)
  0012:0012  Hardware Address Length: 6
  0013:0013  Protocol Address Length: 4
```

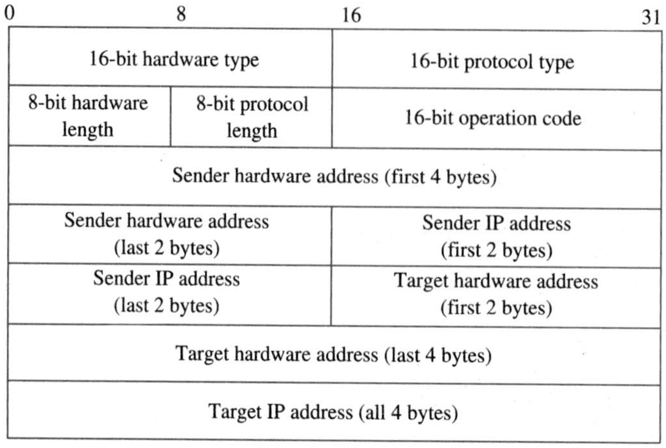

FIGURE 8–15
ARP/RARP message format.

TABLE 8–6
ARP/RARP header field information.

Header Field	Size	Meaning
Hardware Type	16 bits	Specifies the type of hardware interface
Protocol Type	16 bits	Specifies the type of high-level protocol to get
Hardware Length	16 bits	Indicates the length of the hardware address
Protocol Length	16 bits	Indicates the length of the protocol address
Operation Code	16 bits	Specifies the ARP/RARP operation (request or reply) to perform
Sender Hardware Address	48 bits	Identifies the sender's hardware address
Sender Protocol Address	32 bits	Identifies the sender's IP address
Target Hardware Address	48 bits	Place for the target hardware address to be stored (contains zeros in ARP request)
Target Protocol Address	32 bits	Identifies the target computer IP address

```
0014:0015   Opcode: Request
0016:001B   Source HW Address: 0060979EEAD5
001C:001F   Source IP Address: 24.24.78.84
0020:0025   Destination HW Address: 000000000000
0026:0029   Destination IP Address: 24.24.78.1
```

Notice that the destination hardware address contains all zeros. The ARP request is transmitted to the destination network in the form of a directed broadcast, asking which machine in that network has the IP address 24.24.78.1. The machine with that particular address responds with the ARP reply message as shown below:

```
Capture 3:Packet 19

Destination   Source      Protocol     Summary         Size  Time Tick
-----------------------------------------------------------------------------
24.24.78.84   24.24.78.1  ARP  Reply   60              07/17/00 17:37:55.324

Addr.   Hex. Data                                      ASCII
0000:   00 60 97 9E EA D5 08 00 3E 02 07 8D 08 06 00 01  .'......>.......
0010:   08 00 06 04 00 02 08 00 3E 02 07 8D 18 18 4E 01  ........>.....N.
0020:   00 60 97 9E EA D5 18 18 4E 54 8F 1E 76 01 00 00  .'......NT..v...
0030:   00 00 00 00 00 00 18 5E 3E 8A 60 51              .......[*]>.'Q

802.3 [0000:000D]
  0000:0005   Destination Address: 0060979EEAD5 (3Com9EEAD5)
  0006:000B   Source Address: 08003E02078D (Motorola02078D)
```

```
000C:000D  Ethernet Type: Address Resolution Protocol (ARP)
ARP [000E:0029]
  000E:000F  Hardware Type: Ethernet (10Mbps)
  0010:0011  Protocol Type: DOD Internet Protocol (IP)
  0012:0012  Hardware Address Length: 6
  0013:0013  Protocol Address Length: 4
  0014:0015  Opcode: Reply
  0016:001B  Source HW Address: 08003E02078D
  001C:001F  Source IP Address: 24.24.78.1
  0020:0025  Destination HW Address: 0060979EEAD5
  0026:0029  Destination IP Address: 24.24.78.84
```

Reverse Address Resolution Protocol (RARP)

The ***Reverse Address Resolution Protocol (RARP)*** performs the opposite of ARP, providing the IP address for a specific MAC address. The message format for RARP is the same as the ARP message shown in Figure 8–15. RARP is usually performed on diskless computer workstations that do not have any other way of obtaining an IP address. A RARP server is used to perform the required translations. Figure 8–16 gives an example of both protocols at work.

FIGURE 8–16
Using ARP and RARP.

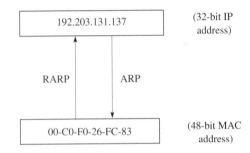

ARP is also the name of an application program that can be run from the DOS prompt. ARP is used to display/manage a table of IP/MAC addresses for all machines on the local network that have been communicated with recently. A router is not required for two machines on a local network to communicate, so the ARP table stores the associated MAC address for each local IP address. When multiple messages must be sent between two local machines, the ARP table allows reuse of the IP/MAC addresses. By reusing the table entries, additional ARP traffic is reduced or eliminated. See Chapter 10 for more information on ARP and routing. Online help for ARP appears as follows:

Objective 4-1

```
C:\>arp

Displays and modifies the IP-to-Physical address translation tables used by
address resolution protocol (ARP).

ARP -s inet_addr eth_addr [if_addr]
ARP -d inet_addr [if_addr]
ARP -a [inet_addr] [-N if_addr]

  -a          Displays current ARP entries by interrogating the current
              protocol data.  If inet_addr is specified, the IP and Physical
              addresses for only the specified computer are displayed.  If
              more than one network interface uses ARP, entries for each ARP
              table are displayed.
  -g          Same as -a.
  inet_addr   Specifies an Internet address.
  -N if_addr  Displays the ARP entries for the network interface specified
              by if_addr.
```

```
-d              Deletes the host specified by inet_addr.
-s              Adds the host and associates the Internet address inet_addr
                with the Physical address eth_addr.  The Physical address is
                given as 6 hexadecimal bytes separated by hyphens. The entry
                is permanent.
eth_addr        Specifies a physical address.
if_addr         If present, this specifies the Internet address of the
                interface whose address translation table should be modified.
                If not present, the first applicable interface will be used.
```

```
Example:
  > arp -s 157.55.85.212 00-aa-00-62-c6-09  .... Adds a static entry.
  > arp -a                                  .... Displays the arp table.
```

A display of the ARP table on a typical computer may reveal the IP and physical addresses of the default router or gateway on the network, as well as the physical addresses of all stations that the host computer has recently communicated with. For example, note the IP addresses in the following ARP output:

```
C:\WINDOWS>arp -a

Interface: 24.24.78.84 on Interface 0x1000002
  Internet Address        Physical Address        Type
  24.24.78.1              08-00-3e-02-07-8d        dynamic
```

The IP address of the host is 24.24.78.84. The station having the IP address 24.24.78.1 might be the gateway for the LAN or simply another computer. The ARP table may contain several entries, as in:

```
Interface: 192.168.1.112 on Interface 0x2000003
  Internet Address        Physical Address        Type
  192.168.1.1             00-20-78-c6-78-14        dynamic
  192.168.1.101           00-03-47-8f-15-f5        dynamic
  192.168.1.102           00-03-47-8f-05-7a        dynamic
  192.168.1.103           00-d0-b7-b5-12-24        dynamic
```

In this example, the default gateway is 192.168.1.1 and the other three IP addresses are for clients recently PINGed by the host (192.168.1.112). PINGing another station on the network is an easy way to add an entry to the ARP table. You could also open a Web page to an off-site location, or perform any kind of network operation that involves contacting another station, in order to add an entry.

Another possible output from ARP is:

```
C:\WINDOWS\arp -a
No ARP Entries Found
```

What does this mean? Windows is telling us that there are no entries in the ARP table. This is due to the dynamic nature of the ARP table, which will *discard* entries after a period of non-use (typically several minutes). You can use the -s option to add a static entry to the ARP table that will not be discarded. In fact, this is a popular way to configure a network device such as a network video camera (see the Axis network camera in Chapter 3), which requires an IP address during its initial configuration. ARP is used to associate an IP address with the MAC address of the camera, so that a PING to the camera's new IP address will be successful. The camera is configured by the destination IP address contained in the PING ICMP message. For example, the two commands

```
C:\WINDOWS\arp -s 192.168.1.210 08-00-2B-3C-9E-AA
C:\WINDOWS\ping 192.168.1.210
```

will cause the IP address of the camera to be initialized to 192.168.1.210. The MAC address required by the ARP command is printed on a label attached to the camera. Try running ARP on your computer to see what the ARP table contains.

■ TCP/IP SUPPORT PROTOCOLS

Objective 2-7

The TCP/IP protocol suite includes a variety of protocols that are used to transfer data, manage network devices, and provide messaging services that help with the effective flow of data on a modern network. Explanations of the protocols most commonly follow.

DNS

DNS

Every machine on a network must be uniquely identified. On the Internet, this identification takes the form of what is called an *IP address*. The IP address consists of a 32-bit number, commonly represented in dotted decimal notation. For example, 204.210.133.51 specifies the IP address of some machine on some network somewhere in the world. To make it easier to remember an address, a *host* name can be associated with an IP address. The Domain Name Service (**DNS**) provides the means to convert from a host name to an IP address and vice versa. Instead of using the IP address 204.210.133.51, we may instead enter "raycast.rwa.com" as the host name. Typically a DNS server application running on the local network has the responsibility of converting host names to IP addresses.

When the DNS server on the local network is not able to resolve the host name to an IP address, it contacts its own DNS server higher up in the DNS hierarchy. Eventually, a DNS query may make its way all the way up to a *root* DNS server.

Figure 8–17 shows the format of the DNS header. The Resource Records used by the DNS contain information about the host names being resolved.

FIGURE 8–17
DNS header format.

0	1	4	5	6	7	8	9	10	11	12	15
Identification											
QR	Opcode		AA	TC	RD	RA	Z	AD	CD	Rcode	
Total Questions											
Total Answer RRs											
Total Authority RRs											
Total Additional RRs											
Questions											
Answer RRs											
Authority RRs											
Additional RRs											

QR – Query/Response	Z – Reserved
AA – Authoritative Answer	AD – Authentic Data
TC – Truncated	CD – Checking Disabled
RD – Recursion Desired	Rcode – Return code
RA – Recursion Available	RR – Resource Record

DNS can be transported using TCP or UDP (over port 53) depending on the specific process involved.

BOOTP

BOOTP (Bootstrap Protocol) is a routable UDP protocol that allows a diskless workstation to:

- discover its own IP address.
- discover the IP address of a BOOTP server.
- specify a file to be downloaded (via TFTP) and executed.

Figure 8–18 shows the format of the BOOTP header. The *Options* field identifies the type of BOOTP message contained within the header. There are two types: bootrequests and bootreplies. The hardware address supplied by the BOOTP client in a bootrequest message is used by a BOOTP server to look up the client IP address. This IP address is returned to the client in the *Your IP Address* field of a bootreply message. The *Number of Seconds* field indicates the number of seconds since the initial bootrequest from the client. If no bootreply is received, a timeout will cause the client to resend the bootrequest until a reply is received. To locate a BOOTP server, the client uses the broadcast IP address 255.255.255.255. If the client needs to boot from a specific server, the server address must be specified in the *Server IP Address* or *Gateway IP Address* fields.

FIGURE 8–18
BOOTP header organization.

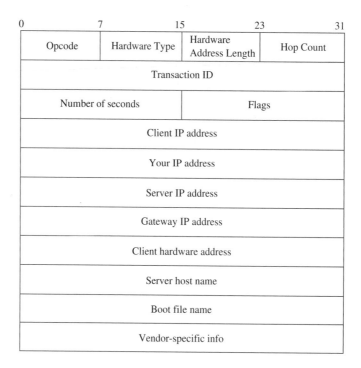

BOOTP clients use port 68, while BOOTP servers communicate through port 67. The BOOTP server IP-to-hardware address mapping table is managed by a network administrator. BOOTP was first proposed in RFC 951.

The role of IP address assignment has been largely replaced by the DHCP protocol, covered in a later section. One significant difference is that DHCP *leases* IP addresses, whereas BOOTP does not.

Trivial FTP

The *Trivial FTP* (TFTP) protocol is a simple file transfer protocol (compared to FTP) that is used when it is not necessary to authenticate the user information or view the directory structure. TFTP is used to send files from a server (UDP Port 69) to diskless workstations, communication servers, and other network devices on a network that uses TFTP. TFTP uses the UDP as the transport protocol, and each fixed 512-byte block of data is acknowledged separately. This acknowledgement must be received before the next packet can be transmitted. A TFTP packet consists of a 16-bit opcode followed by the 512-byte block of data as shown in Figure 8–19.

FIGURE 8–19
TFTP header format.

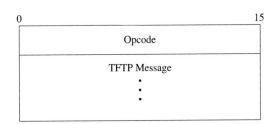

A TFTP data block that contains less than 512 bytes indicates the end of transmission. The opcode field specifies one of the following message formats:

- Read request (RRQ)
- Write request (WRQ)
- Data (used for both Read and Write modes)
- Acknowledgement (ACK)
- Error message (ERROR)
- Option Acknowledgement (OACK)

The current version of TFTP is version 2, which is defined by RFC 1350. In addition, TFTP read requests and options are defined by RFC 2090 and 2347, respectively. Table 8–7 gives a breakdown of error codes and descriptions.

TABLE 8–7
TFTP error codes.

Error Code	Description
0	No error
1	File not found
2	Access violation
3	Disk full or allocation exceeded
4	Illegal TFTP operation
5	Unknown transfer ID
6	File already exists
7	No such user
8	Terminate transfer due to option negotiation

TFTP supports three modes of data transfer: netascii, octet, and mail. Netascii mode is defined in the "USA Standard Code for Information Interchange." Octet mode is typically used to exchange binary information consisting of raw 8-bit bytes of data. Mail mode is obsolete. It was used to send data to a user rather than a file. For security considerations, because no authentication is performed, it is necessary to limit the TFTP server process to be able to access files in read-only mode with no ability to write files.

DHCP

DHCP

Objective 2-7

DHCP (Dynamic Host Configuration Protocol) is a protocol for dynamically assigning IP addresses to devices on a network during the bootstrap process. Using DHCP, a device may be assigned a different IP address every time it connects to the network. Sometimes a computer's IP address can change even while it is still connected to the network.

IP addresses are *leased* to a computer for a period of time set by the network administrator. Before the lease expires, the network software will request a renewal of the lease.

DHCP addressing simplifies network administration because the software keeps track of IP addresses rather than requiring an administrator to manage the task. This means that a new computer can be added to a network without the hassle of manually assigning it a unique IP address. Many Internet service providers use dynamic IP addressing for dial-up users.

The basic operation of DHCP is outlined by the mnemonic Discover, Offer, Request, and Acknowledge (DORA), and the steps are:

1. The DHCP client sends a DHCPDISCOVER broadcast message at boot time.
2. The DHCP server offers an IP address to the client (DHCPOFFER).
3. The client notifies the server of its request to use the offered address (DHCPRE-QUEST).
4. The server acknowledges the client's request (DHCPACK).

Some additional properties of DHCP are as follows:

- Carried by UDP datagrams
- Based on earlier BOOTP protocol
- Found in RFCs 1533, 1534, 1541, and 1542
- DHCP client support is built into most operating systems including Windows, UNIX/Linux, and many others.
- DHCP server support is provided by Windows NT Server, UNIX/Linux, and other mainframe operating systems. Refer to Chapter 18 for additional information about running a DHCP server on Windows NT.

ICMP

Objective 2-5

ICMP (Internet Control Message Protocol)

Usually, when an IP packet runs into trouble on the network, an error message is generated (which is sent back to the source computer) and then it is simply discarded. An error contained in an *ICMP (Internet Control Message Protocol)* message may or may not be returned to the sender due to use of UDP as the transport protocol. If an ICMP message must be discarded, no ICMP error message is generated. This is because of a specific rule in the implementation that prohibits error messages being generated about other error messages.

The format of the ICMP header is shown in Figure 8–20.

FIGURE 8–20
ICMP message format.

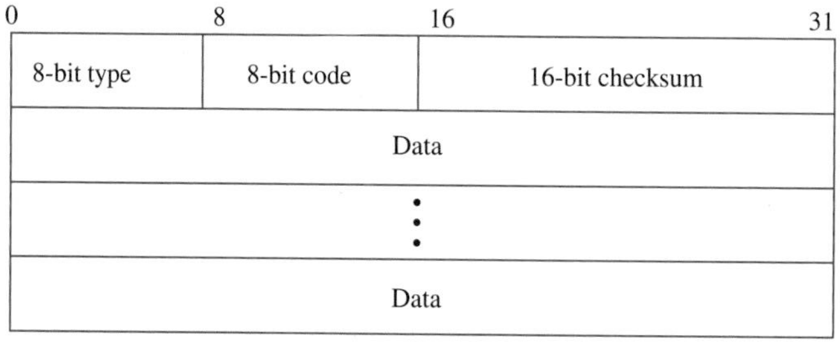

The entire message header contains only three fields. These fields and their descriptions are shown in Table 8–8. Depending on the value of the Type and Data fields, one or more additional descriptive data messages will follow. These messages will provide the necessary details to determine what happened when the message was generated.

TABLE 8–8
ICMP header field information.

Header Field	Size	Meaning
Type	8 bits	Identifies the message type
Code	8 bits	Additional information based on the Type field
Checksum	16 bits	Checksum value computed using the ICMP message

Table 8–9 shows a list of the different ICMP messages. Notice that there are many other ICMP message types than error messages. One example is the echo-request and echo-reply messages that are used with the ping command.

TABLE 8–9
ICMP messages.

Type	Code	Description	Query	Error
0	0	Echo reply	✔	
3		Destination unreachable		
	0	network unreachable		✔
	1	host unreachable		✔
	2	protocol unreachable		✔
	3	port unreachable		✔
	4	fragmentation needed but don't fragment bit set		✔
	5	source route failed		✔
	6	destination network unknown		✔
	7	destination host unknown		✔
	8	source host isolated (obsolete)		✔
	9	destination network administratively prohibited		✔
	10	destination host administratively prohibited		✔
	11	network unreachable for TOS		✔
	12	host unreachable for TOS		✔
	13	communication administratively prohibited by filtering		✔
	14	host precedence violation		✔
	15	precedence cutoff in effect		✔
4	0	Source quench (elementary flow control)		✔
5		Redirect		
	0	redirect for network		✔
	1	redirect for host		✔
	2	redirect for type-of-service and network		✔
	3	redirect for type-of-service and host		✔
8	0	Echo request	✔	
9	0	Router advertisement	✔	
10	0	Router solicitation	✔	
11		Time exceeded		
	0	time to live equals 0 during transit (trace route)		✔
	1	time to live equals 0 during assembly		✔
12		Parameter problem		
	0	IP header bad (catchall error)		✔
	1	required option missing		✔
13		Timestamp request	✔	
14		Timestamp reply	✔	
15		Information request (obsolete)	✔	
16		Information reply (obsolete)	✔	
17		Address mask request	✔	
18		Address mask reply	✔	

SMTP

Simple Mail Transport Protocol (SMTP)

Objective 2-5

The ***Simple Mail Transport Protocol (SMTP)*** is responsible for routing electronic mail on the Internet using TCP and IP. The process usually requires connecting to a remote computer and transferring the e-mail message, but due to problems with the network or a remote computer, messages can be temporarily undeliverable. The electronic mail server will try to deliver any messages by periodically trying to contact the remote destination. When the remote computer becomes available, the message is delivered using SMTP. Refer to Chapter 12 for more information on SMTP.

Objective 2-7

SNMP

Simple Network Management Protocol (SNMP)

Network managers responsible for monitoring and controlling the network hardware and software use the ***Simple Network Management Protocol (SNMP)***. This defines the format and meaning of messages exchanged by the manager and agents. The network manager

(*manager*) uses SNMP to interrogate network devices (*agents*) such as routers, switches, and bridges in order to determine their status and also retrieve statistical information. Chapter 11 contains additional details about SNMP.

HTTP

**HyperText Transport
Protocol (HTTP)** Objective 2-5

The ***HyperText Transport Protocol (HTTP)*** is used to transfer multimedia information over the Internet, such as Web pages, images, audio, and video. An HTTP client, such as a browser, sends a request to an HTTP server (also called an HTTP *daemon*), which services the request.

Figure 8–21 shows a portion of the sequence of HTTP messages exchanged between client and server while a Web page is being loaded. It is important to note that HTTP is carried via TCP and not UDP. There is a great deal of back and forth between the client and server, with many acknowledgment messages ensuring reliable communication.

FIGURE 8–21
A sequence of HTTP messages to display a Web page.

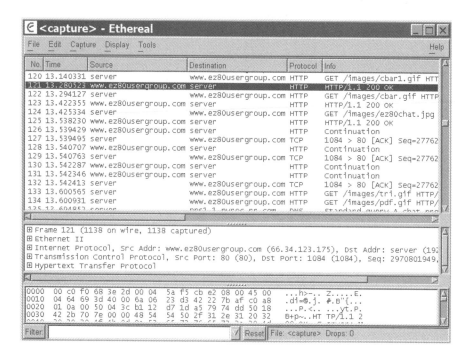

A packet containing an HTTP GET request is decoded for you to examine:

```
Capture 1:Packet 7

Destination Source     Protocol   Summary    Size    Time Tick
---------------------------------------------------------------------------
63.236.73.230    192.168.1.105   World Wide Web HTTP   343   07/21/00
                                 TCP (ACK,PSH)       00:25:16.384

Addr.  Hex. Data                                        ASCII
0000:  00 20 78 C6 78 14 00 C0 F0 27 64 E2 08 00 45 00  . x.x....'d...E.
0010:  01 49 1F 07 40 00 40 06 CE C4 C0 A8 01 69 3F EC  .I..@.@......i?.
0020:  49 E6 05 0B 00 50 00 F6 E6 00 21 60 F5 5E 50 18  I....P....!'.^P.
0030:  FF FF 19 86 00 00 47 45 54 20 2F 54 45 52 4D 2F  ......GET /TERM/
0040:  73 2F 73 77 69 74 63 68 2E 68 74 6D 6C 20 48 54  s/switch.html HT
0050:  54 50 2F 31 2E 30 0D 0A 43 6F 6E 6E 65 63 74 69  TP/1.0..Connecti
0060:  6F 6E 3A 20 4B 65 65 70 2D 41 6C 69 76 65 0D 0A  on: Keep-Alive..
0070:  55 73 65 72 2D 41 67 65 6E 74 3A 20 4D 6F 7A 69  User-Agent: Mozi
0080:  6C 6C 61 2F 34 2E 35 31 20 5B 65 6E 5D 20 28 57  lla/4.51 [en] (W
```

```
0090:   69 6E 39 38 3B 20 49 29 0D 0A 48 6F 73 74 3A 20   in98; I)..Host:
00A0:   77 65 62 6F 70 65 64 69 61 2E 69 6E 74 65 72 6E   webopedia.intern
00B0:   65 74 2E 63 6F 6D 0D 0A 41 63 63 65 70 74 3A 20   et.com..Accept:
00C0:   69 6D 61 67 65 2F 67 69 66 2C 20 69 6D 61 67 65   image/gif, image
00D0:   2F 78 2D 78 62 69 74 6D 61 70 2C 20 69 6D 61 67   /x-xbitmap, imag
00E0:   65 2F 6A 70 65 67 2C 20 69 6D 61 67 65 2F 70 6A   e/jpeg, image/pj
00F0:   70 65 67 2C 20 69 6D 61 67 65 2F 70 6E 67 2C 20   peg, image/png,
0100:   2A 2F 2A 0D 0A 41 63 63 65 70 74 2D 45 6E 63 6F   */*..Accept-Enco
0110:   64 69 6E 67 3A 20 67 7A 69 70 0D 0A 41 63 63 65   ding: gzip..Acce
0120:   70 74 2D 4C 61 6E 67 75 61 67 65 3A 20 65 6E 0D   pt-Language: en.
0130:   0A 41 63 63 65 70 74 2D 43 68 61 72 73 65 74 3A   .Accept-Charset:
0140:   20 69 73 6F 2D 38 38 35 39 2D 31 2C 2A 2C 75 74   iso-8859-1,*,ut
0150:   66 2D 38 0D 0A 0D 0A                              f-8....
```

```
802.3 [0000:000D]
  0000:0005   Destination Address: 002078C67814 (RuntopC67814)
  0006:000B   Source Address: 00C0F02764E2 (Kingston2764E2)
  000C:000D   Ethernet Type: DOD Internet Protocol (IP)
IP [000E:0021]
  000E:000E   Version: 4, Header Length: 20
  000F:000F   TOS, Precedence: Routine, Delay: Normal, Throughput: Normal,
Reliability: Normal
  0010:0011   Packet Length: 329
  0012:0013   Identification: 0x1F07
  0014:0014   Fragment Flag (bit 6..5): Don't Fragment
  0014:0015   Fragment Offset: 0x0000
  0016:0016   Time to Live: 64
  0017:0017   Transport: Transmission Control
  0018:0019   Header Checksum: 0xCEC4
  001A:001D   Source Address: 192.168.1.105
  001E:0021   Destination Address: 63.236.73.230
TCP [0022:0035]
  0022:0023   Source Port: 1291
  0024:0025   Destination Port: World Wide Web HTTP
  0026:0029   Sequence Number: 16180736
  002A:002D   Acknowledgment Number: 560002398
  002E:002E   Header Length (bit 7..4): 20
  002F:002F   Control Bit - ACK; PSH;
  0030:0031   Window Size: 65535
  0032:0033   Checksum: 0x1986
  0034:0035   Urgent Pointer: 0x0000
```

The GET request is contained within the data area of the TCP message.
Some additional HTTP details are:

- Version 1.1 is defined in RFC 2616.

- Well-known port number is 80.

- Methods are operations performed on HTTP objects. Some methods are GET, PUT, POST, DELETE, LINK, and TEXTSEARCH.

- It supports MIME.

- It supports compression on certain data types (HTML pages, for example).

- It utilizes a *persistent connection* to enable multiple requests and responses to use the same connection, eliminating the overhead of opening and closing a session for each item transferred.

HTTPS

HTTPS

Objective 2-5

Objective 2-13

The *HyperText Transfer Protocol over Secure Socket Layer* (HTTP over SSL) is used to exchange encrypted Web pages between a client/server connection. Originally developed by Netscape, **HTTPS** is now included in Microsoft and most other Web server products. HTTPS uses port TCP 443; HTTP uses TCP port 80. The default secure socket layer uses a 40-bit key, but a higher-strength 128-bit key version is available in the U.S. and other areas.

HTTPS interacts with the TCP/IP protocol stack between the HTTP application layer and TCP layer. HTTPS uses the RSA (Rivest, Shamir, and Adleman) Security encryption/decryption technique, which is used under license. The mathematical strategy used to perform the encryption and decryption involves a public key and a private key (based on very large prime numbers). The public key, which is available to everyone on the network, is used to encrypt the data to be sent, and the private key, which is kept secret, is used to decrypt the data. HTTPS can also use **digital certificates** that contain the certificate holder's public key and digital signature.

Digital certificates

SSL provides a secure method to exchange private information over the network. Typically, HTTPS is used during the checkout process when ordering products online. SSL has recently been superceded by a new protocol called **Transport Layer Security (TLS)** that is based on SSL.

Transport Layer Security (TLS)

NTP

Objective 2-5

Accurate, synchronized time is a necessity for many important network operations, particularly those involving distributed databases such as airline reservation systems, where the time of a transaction is important for correct updates to the database. The Novell NetWare operating system *Network Directory Service* (NDS) uses four types of time servers to help process file operations across multiple computers.

Network Time Protocol (NTP)

The **Network Time Protocol (NTP)**, developed by David Mills of the University of Delaware, provides a simple way to synchronize the time of multiple computers on a network (even across the Internet). The cornerstone of NTP is the reliance on a stratum-0 timing source, such as an Atomic Radio Clock (ARC) or Global Positioning System (GPS) Satellite Clock, that receives and decodes timing information transmitted from the atomic clock maintained by NIST (National Institute of Standards and Technology). Figure 8–22 shows the various stratum levels in the NTP timing hierarchy.

A stratum-1 server, also called a *primary* time server, connects directly to a stratum-0 time source or even includes the stratum-0 source within itself. Many companies already manufacture stratum-0 and stratum-1 time sources. As shown in Figure 8–22, a stratum-2 time client (or time server) gets its time over a network connection. The Internet contains many public stratum-1 and stratum-2 (*secondary*) time servers.

NTP uses UDP port 123 to perform updates. This may seem strange, considering UDP is an unreliable protocol. How can a reliable timing sequence be established using an unreliable protocol? The answer involves timeouts, multiple transmissions, and a timing algorithm that provides accuracy to the millisecond or faster. The NTP header contains a 64-bit timestamp that represents the number of seconds elapsed since January 1, 1900. The time is based on Coordinated Universal Time (UTC).

NTP clients may obtain their time from a public stratum-1 or stratum-2 server or even a private server. An NTP client application, such as TrueTime's WinSync shown in Figure 8–23, connects to the NTP server to update the host computer's clock. NTP typically requires six messages over a 5–10 minute period to initially synchronize the computer clock and then one message every 10 minutes to update the time. Note the 100 percent success rate for each of the public servers contacted by WinSync. 100 percent success with UDP is pretty impressive.

NTP was originally proposed in RFC 958. Visit www.ntp.org for more information on NTP or www.truetime.com for details of their NTP hardware and software products.

FIGURE 8–22
NTP timing hierarchy.

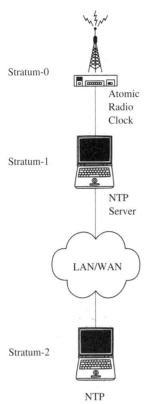

Stratum-0

Atomic
Radio
Clock

Stratum-1

NTP
Server

LAN/WAN

Stratum-2

NTP
Client

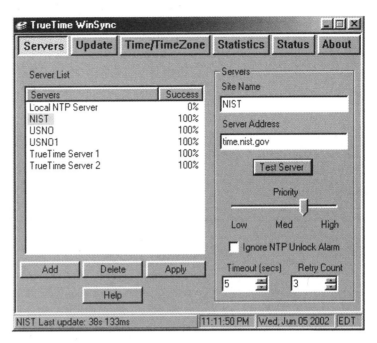

FIGURE 8–23
WinSync NTP client display showing list of public NTP servers (screen shot copyright 2002, TrueTime, Inc.).

PING

PING (Packet InterNet Grouper) is a TCP/IP application that sends multiple transmissions, typically once every second, in the hope of receiving an echo response from the machine being PINGed. If the machine is connected and running a TCP/IP protocol stack, it should respond to the PING packet with a packet of its own. If PING encounters an error condition, an ICMP message is returned. PING displays the time of the return response in milliseconds or one of several error messages (request timed out, destination host unreachable, etc.).

PING can be used to simply determine the IP address of a www site if you know its URL. For example, the IP address for www.yahoo.com is 204.71.200.75, which can be found with PING by opening a DOS window and entering

```
C> ping www.yahoo.com
```

You should see something similar to this:

```
Pinging www.yahoo.com [204.71.200.75] with 32 bytes of data:

Reply from 204.71.200.75: bytes=32 time=180ms TTL=245
Reply from 204.71.200.75: bytes=32 time=127ms TTL=245
Reply from 204.71.200.75: bytes=32 time=145ms TTL=245
Reply from 204.71.200.75: bytes=32 time=146ms TTL=245
```

So PING performed DNS on the URL to find out the IP address and then sent packets to Yahoo's host machine and displayed the responses. If you know the IP address you can enter it directly and PING will skip the DNS phase.

To get a list of PING's features, enter PING with no parameters. You should see something similar to this:

```
Usage: ping [-t] [-a] [-n count] [-l size] [-f] [-i TTL] [-v TOS]
            [-r count] [-s count] [[-j host-list] | [-k host-
            list]]
            [-w timeout] destination-list
```

```
Options:
    -t                Ping the specified host until interrupted.
    -a                Resolve addresses to hostnames.
    -n count          Number of echo requests to send.
    -l size           Send buffer size.
    -f Set            Don't Fragment flag in packet.
    -i TTL            Time To Live.
    -v TOS            Type Of Service.
    -r count          Record route for count hops.
    -s count          Timestamp for count hops.
    -j host-list      Loose source route along host-list.
    -k host-list      Strict source route along host-list.
    -w timeout        Timeout in milliseconds to wait for each reply.
```

PING can also be used to determine the MTU value between two networks. Normally, packet fragmentation automatically occurs without the knowledge of the source computer. PING can determine the MTU value between a source and a destination computer by specifying that no fragmentation is allowed and choosing a custom message length to send. PING will display an ICMP error message if fragmentation is required to send the data but it is not allowed to do so. For example, setting the do not fragment flag (-f) and sending a buffer size of 1472 bytes (-l 1472) of data is permitted when sending to www.yahoo.com as shown in the following:

```
C:\> ping -f -l 1472 www.yahoo.com

Pinging www.yahoo.akadns.net [204.71.200.75] with 1472 bytes of data:

Reply from 204.71.200.75: bytes=1472 time=140ms TTL=241
Reply from 204.71.200.75: bytes=1472 time=146ms TTL=241
Reply from 204.71.200.75: bytes=1472 time=145ms TTL=241
Reply from 204.71.200.75: bytes=1472 time=161ms TTL=241

Ping statistics for 204.71.200.75:
    Packets: Sent = 4, Received = 4, Lost = 0 (0% loss),
Approximate round trip times in milli-seconds:
    Minimum = 140ms, Maximum =  161ms, Average =  148ms
```

A packet decode of a successful PING exchange looks like the following:

```
Capture 1:Packet 24

Destination  Source      Protocol    Summary Size     Time  Tick
-----------------------------------------------------------------------------
204.71.200.67  24.24.78.84  ICMP  Echo  ID=0001  Seq=0020  1514  07/17/00
10:33:55.754

Addr.  Hex. Data                                       ASCII
0000:  08 00 3E 02 07 8D 00 60 97 9E EA D5 08 00 45 00  ..>....'......E.
0010:  05 DC 4C 02 40 00 20 01 0E 28 18 18 4E 54 CC 47  ..L.@. ..(..NT.G
0020:  C8 43 08 00 1F 48 01 00 20 00 61 62 63 64 65 66  .C...H.. .abcdef
0030:  67 68 69 6A 6B 6C 6D 6E 6F 70 71 72 73 74 75 76  ghijklmnopqrstuv
0040:  77 61 62 63 64 65 66 67 68 69 6A 6B 6C 6D 6E 6F  wabcdefghijklmno
.
.
                    (1500 bytes of data)

0590:  63 64 65 66 67 68 69 6A 6B 6C 6D 6E 6F 70 71 72  cdefghijklmnopqr
05A0:  73 74 75 76 77 61 62 63 64 65 66 67 68 69 6A 6B  stuvwabcdefghijk
```

```
05B0:   6C 6D 6E 6F 70 71 72 73 74 75 76 77 61 62 63 64   lmnopqrstuvwabcd
05C0:   65 66 67 68 69 6A 6B 6C 6D 6E 6F 70 71 72 73 74   efghijklmnopqrst
05D0:   75 76 77 61 62 63 64 65 66 67 68 69 6A 6B 6C 6D   uvwabcdefghijklm
05E0:   6E 6F 70 71 72 73 74 75 76 77                     nopqrstuvw


802.3 [0000:000D]
   0000:0005   Destination Address: 08003E02078D (Motorola02078D)
   0006:000B   Source Address: 0060979EEAD5 (3Com9EEAD5)
   000C:000D   Ethernet Type: DOD Internet Protocol (IP)
IP [000E:0021]
   000E:000E   Version: 4; Header Length: 20
   000F:000F   TOS, Precedence: Routine; Delay: Normal; Throughput: Normal;
Reliability: Normal
   0010:0011   Packet Length: 1500
   0012:0013   Identification: 0x4C02
   0014:0014   DF: Don't Fragment; MF: Last Fragment
   0014:0015   Fragment Offset: 0
   0016:0016   Time to Live: 32
   0017:0017   Transport: Internet Control Message
   0018:0019   Header Checksum: 0x0E28 (correct)
   001A:001D   Source Address: 24.24.78.84
   001E:0021   Destination Address: 204.71.200.67
ICMP [0022:0029]
   0022:0022   Type: Echo
   0023:0023   Code: 0x00
   0024:0025   Checksum: 0x1F48
   0026:0027   Identifier: 0x0001
   0028:0029   Sequence Number: 32
```

Again, notice how the ICMP data is encapsulated inside an IP packet, which is further encapsulated into an Ethernet frame.

During the experiment to determine the MTU value, what happens if one additional byte is added to the PING packet size? The PING operation fails and an ICMP error is returned as the following shows:

```
C:\>ping -f -l 1473 www.yahoo.com


Pinging www.yahoo.akadns.net [204.71.200.67] with 1473 bytes of data:


Packet needs to be fragmented but DF set.
Packet needs to be fragmented but DF set.
Packet needs to be fragmented but DF set.
Packet needs to be fragmented but DF set.


Ping statistics for 204.71.200.67:
    Packets: Sent = 4, Received = 0, Lost = 4 (100% loss),
Approximate round trip times in milli-seconds:
    Minimum = 0ms, Maximum =  0ms, Average =  0ms
```

It may seem strange to pick a PING buffer size value such as 1472 when checking the MTU value, but the buffer size specifies only the data portion of the IP packet. When the size of the IP header (20 bytes) is added to the size of the ICMP header (8 bytes) for a total header size of 28 bytes, the 1500-byte MTU is determined. So the 1473-byte message that was attempted is one byte too many. You are encouraged to experiment further with all of the PING parameters.

Tracert

Objective 4-1

TRACERT (trace route) is a TCP/IP application that determines the path through the network to a destination entered by the user. Creative use of ICMP messages is the basis for the trace route application.

For example, running

```
C> tracert www.yahoo.com
```

generates the following output:

```
Tracing route to www7.yahoo.com [204.71.200.72]
over a maximum of 30 hops:

  1    20 ms    19 ms    19 ms  bing100b.stny.lrun.com [204.210.132.1]
  2    10 ms    14 ms     9 ms  m2.stny.lrun.com [204.210.159.17]
  3    12 ms    24 ms    10 ms  ext_router.stny.lrun.com [204.210.155.18]
  4    46 ms    40 ms    44 ms  border3-serial4-0-6.Greensboro.mci.net [204.70.83.85]
  5    42 ms    53 ms    46 ms  core1-fddi-0.Greensboro.mci.net [204.70.80.17]
  6   109 ms   160 ms   122 ms  bordercore2.Bloomington.mci.net [166.48.176.1]
  7   123 ms   126 ms   113 ms  hssi1-0.br2.NUQ.globalcenter.net [166.48.177.254]
  8   125 ms   117 ms   115 ms  fe5-1.cr1.NUQ.globalcenter.net [206.251.1.33]
  9   114 ms   125 ms   113 ms  pos0-0.wr1.NUQ.globalcenter.net [206.251.0.122]
 10   125 ms   124 ms   121 ms  pos1-0-OC12.wr1.SNV.globalcenter.net [206.251.0.74]
 11   122 ms   139 ms   115 ms  pos5-0.cr1.SNV.globalcenter.net [206.251.0.105]
 12   128 ms   129 ms   138 ms  www7.yahoo.com [204.71.200.72]

Trace complete.
```

The trace indicates that it took twelve *hops* to get to Yahoo. Every hop is a connection between two routers on the network. Each router guides the test packet from TRACERT one step closer to the destination. TRACERT specifically manipulates the TTL (time to live) parameter of the packet, adding 1 to it each time it rebroadcasts the test packet. Initially the TTL count is 1. This causes the very first router in the path to send back an ICMP time-exceeded message, which TRACERT uses to identify the router and display path information. When the TTL is increased to 2, the second router sends back the ICMP message, and so on, until the destination is reached (if it ever is).

It is fascinating to examine TRACERT's output. Notice that hop 5 contains a reference to *FDDI,* which means that the packet spent some time traveling around a fiber-distributed data interface network.

Online help for the TRACERT program is available by simply entering TRACERT at the DOS prompt as shown:

```
C:\tracert

Usage: tracert [-d] [-h maximum_hops] [-j host-list] [-w timeout] target_name

Options:
    -d                 Do not resolve addresses to hostnames.
    -h maximum_hops    Maximum number of hops to search for target.
    -j host-list       Loose source route along host-list.
    -w timeout         Wait timeout milliseconds for each reply
```

You are encouraged to experiment with the TRACERT program.

Objective 4-1

NBTSTAT

NBTSTAT

Objective 4-7

NBTSTAT provides information on the state of NetBIOS-over-TCP/IP connections that exist within a Windows computer. These connections are used for various activities, such as file transfers between mapped drives and Network Neighborhood. Command-line options for NBTSTAT are as follows:

```
NBTSTAT [ [-a RemoteName] [-A IP address] [-c] [-n]
        [-r] [-R] [-RR] [-s] [-S] [interval] ]

  -a   (adapter status) Lists the remote machine's name table given its name.
  -A   (Adapter status) Lists the remote machine's name table given its IP address.
  -c   (cache)         Lists NBT's cache of remote [machine] names and their
                       IP addresses.
  -n   (names)         Lists local NetBIOS names.
  -r   (resolved)      Lists names resolved by broadcast and via WINS.
  -R   (Reload)        Purges and reloads the remote cache name table.
  -S   (Sessions)      Lists sessions table with the destination IP addresses.
  -s   (sessions)      Lists sessions table converting destination IP addresses
                       to computer NETBIOS names.
  -RR  (ReleaseRefresh) Sends Name Release packets to WINS and then starts Refresh.


  RemoteName  Remote host machine name.
  IP address  Dotted decimal representation of the IP address.
  interval    Redisplays selected statistics, pausing interval seconds
              between each display. Press Ctrl+C to stop redisplaying
              statistics.
```

The -a option produces the following sample output:

```
        NetBIOS Remote Machine Name Table
        ------------------------------------------

        Name                 Type       Status

        WAVEGUIDE     <00>   UNIQUE     Registered
        RAYCAST       <00>   GROUP      Registered
        WAVEGUIDE     <03>   UNIQUE     Registered
        WAVEGUIDE     <20>   UNIQUE     Registered
        RAYCAST       <1E>   GROUP      Registered
        SMITH_J       <03>   UNIQUE     Registered
        RAYCAST       <10>   UNIQUE     Registered
        ..__MSBROWSE__.<01>  GROUP      Registered


        MAC Address = 00-C0-F0-27-64-E2
```

From this output, you can see that the machine name is WAVEGUIDE and the workgroup the machine belongs to is RAYCAST.

Current sessions that the computer is participating in are shown with the -s option:

```
C> nbtstat -s


            NetBIOS Connection Table

Local Name          State    In/Out  Remote Host          Input    Output
---------------------------------------------------------------------------
WAVEGUIDE    <03>   Listening
WAVEGUIDE           Listening
SMITH_J      <03>   Listening
```

Here we discover the user SMITH_J logged onto the computer named WAVEGUIDE.

Objective 4-1

Objective 4-7

NETSTAT

NETSTAT (network statistics) displays protocol statistics and current TCP/IP network connections. NETSTAT command-line options are as follows:

```
NETSTAT [-a] [-e] [-n] [-o] [-s] [-p proto] [-r] [interval]
```

-a	Displays all connections and listening ports.
-e	Displays Ethernet statistics. This may be combined with the -s option.
-n	Displays addresses and port numbers in numerical form.
-o	Displays the owning process ID associated with each connection.
-p proto	Shows connections for the protocol specified by proto; proto may be any of: TCP, UDP, TCPv6, or UDPv6. If used with the -s option to display per-protocol statistics, proto may be any of: IP, IPv6, ICMP, ICMPv6, TCP, TCPv6, UDP, or UDPv6.
-r	Displays the routing table.
-s	Displays per-protocol statistics. By default, statistics are shown for IP, IPv6, ICMP, ICMPv6, TCP, TCPv6, UDP, and UDPv6; the -p option may be used to specify a subset of the default.
interval	Redisplays selected statistics, pausing interval seconds between each display. Press CTRL+C to stop redisplaying statistics. If omitted, netstat will print the current configuration information once.

A sample execution of NETSTAT using the -a option gives the following results:

```
C> netstat -a

Active Connections

     Proto      Local Address        Foreign Address      State
     TCP        waveguide:1247       WAVEGUIDE:0          LISTENING
     TCP        waveguide:137        WAVEGUIDE:0          LISTENING
     TCP        waveguide:138        WAVEGUIDE:0          LISTENING
     TCP        waveguide:139        WAVEGUIDE:0          LISTENING
     UDP        waveguide:1247       *:*
     UDP        waveguide:137        *:*
     UDP        waveguide:138        *:*
```

Here the machine WAVEGUIDE is utilizing several TCP and UDP ports.

NETSTAT also reports the number of bytes associated with each type of network
transmission. This is accomplished with the -e option:

```
C> netstat -e

Interface Statistics

                                        Received            Sent

     Bytes                              3068531             460078
     Unicast packets                    4198                3873
     Non-unicast packets                106                 94
     Discards                           0                   0
     Errors                             0                   0
     Unknown protocols                  0
```

NETSTAT is a useful utility for examining a computer's protocol traffic.

Table 8-10 summarizes all of the useful networking utilities that may be used on
many network operating systems.

TABLE 8–10
Comparison of different network utilities.

Application	Purpose	Command Line Examples	When to Use
TRACERT	Trace the network route from a source station to a destination station.	TRACERT www.yahoo.com	When routing information is required.
PING	Send and receive a test message to a destination station.	PING www.yahoo.com	To test network connectivity and verify TCP/IP is running.
ARP	Examine and configure the local ARP table.	ARP –A	To examine the contents of the static and dynamic ARP table.
NETSTAT	Shows the protocol statistics and status of TCP/IP network connections.	NETSTAT -r	To examine the status of current network connections and routing table contents.
NBTSTAT	Displays NetBIOS over TCP/IP (NetBT) protocol statistics, including name tables and name cache.	NBTSTAT -c	To examine and refresh the NetBIOS names and cache registered with WINS.
IPCONFIG	Examine host IP configuration, release or renew IP address.	IPCONFIG /ALL	To discover or verify IP addressing information on Windows NT/ 2000/XP computers.
IFCONFIG	Examine host IP configuration, release or renew IP address.	IFCONFIG	To discover or verify IP addressing information on Linux/UNIX computers.
WINIPCFG	Examine host IP configuration, release or renew IP address.	Start WINIPCFG from the Run menu or from a command prompt. Click More Info to expand the WINIPCFG display window and examine DHCP and other details.	To discover or verify IP addressing information on Windows 9x/Me computers.
NSLOOKUP	Test DNS operation.	NSLOOKUP	To verify proper operation of a DNS server.

FTP

Objective 2-5

The *File Transfer Protocol* (FTP) allows a user to log in to a remote computer and transfer files back and forth through simple commands. Many FTP sites allow you to log in as an anonymous user, an open account with limited privileges, but still capable of file transfers. A typical FTP application might look similar to the one shown in Figure 8–24. Files may be transferred in either direction. Refer to Chapter 13 for more information about FTP.

Telnet

Objective 2-5

A Telnet session allows a user to establish a terminal emulation connection on a remote computer. For example, an instructor may Telnet into his or her college's mainframe to do some work. Figure 8–25 shows how the Telnet connection is set up.

After the connection has been made, Telnet begins emulating the terminal selected in the Connection Dialog window. Figure 8–26 shows this mode of operation. Refer to Chapter 13 for additional information about Telnet.

■ IP VERSION 6 (IPv6)

Objective 2-8

One of the problems with the current version of the Internet is the lack of adequate addresses. Basically, there are no more conventional addresses available. Thanks to classless addressing techniques, however, some address space has been freed up and is still available.

FIGURE 8–24
FTP application.

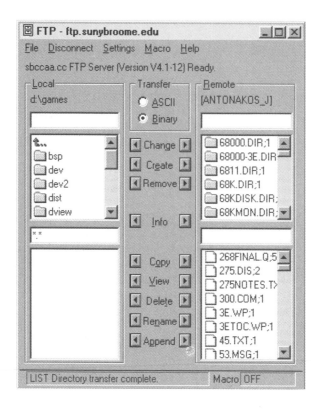

FIGURE 8–24
FTP application.

FIGURE 8–25
Establishing the Telnet
connection.

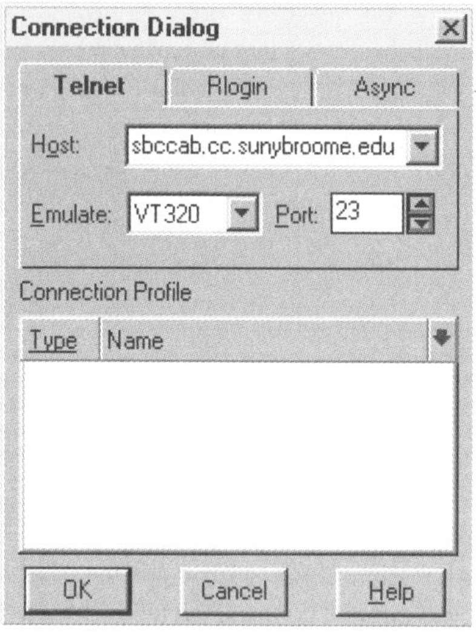

A new version of the Internet, sometimes called the "next generation Internet," has resolved many of the problems experienced by its predecessor.

For example, the address for the next generation Internet is 128 bits as opposed to 32 bits. This additional address space is large enough to accommodate network growth for the foreseeable future. Addresses are grouped into three different categories, *unicast* (single computer), *multicast* (a set of computers with the same address), and *cluster* (a set of computers that share a common address prefix), routed to one computer closest to the sender.

Other changes include different header formats, new extension headers, and support for audio and video. Unlike IP version 4, IP version 6 does not specify all of the possible

FIGURE 8–26

Sample Telnet session.

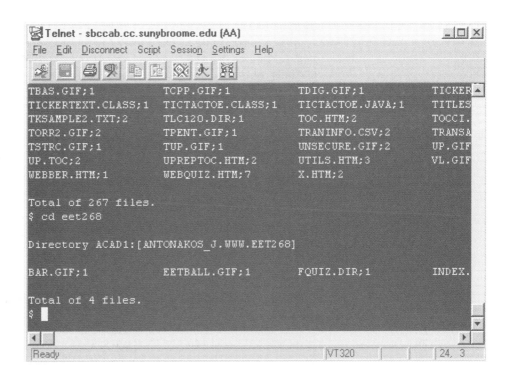

protocol features. This allows new features to be added without the need to update the protocol.

A review of all of the changes that IP version 6 introduces would actually require a complete reexamination of the same material that we have examined looking at version 4. Your best source about the next generation Internet is available to you on the Web at www.ipv6.org. Compare IPv4 addresses with IPv6 addresses. In IPv4, the IP address is 32 bits wide and written as a dotted-decimal group of four integers between 0 and 255, such as 192.204.65.8. In contrast, an IPv6 address is 128 bits long and written using colons (:) and 4-digit groups of hexadecimal numbers instead of periods and decimal numbers. An example IPv6 address is

```
F300:2AC9:0000:0000:0000:00C0:F027:64E2
```

where each 4-digit hexadecimal group represents 16 bits of binary addressing information. Note that a shorthand technique is allowed to eliminate groups of 0000 patterns by using a double-colon (::), as in

```
F300:2AC9::00C0:F027:64E2
```

This abbreviated IPv6 address is equivalent to the original 8-group address.

As with IPv4 addresses, IPv6 addresses are composed of network addressing bits and host addressing bits. A subnet mask is used to determine the network associated with a specific IP address. In IPv4 addressing, we may have an IP address of 204.210.131.60 and a subnet mask of 255.255.255.0. The 255 values in the subnet mask represent three groups of eight 1s in the subnet mask or a total of 24 1s for the network portion. An alternate way of writing the subnet mask is to attach it to the IP address, as in 204.210.131.60/24, where the /24 indicates there are 24 bits allocated for the network portion of the IP address. A similar method is used in IPv6 addresses. For example, the address

```
F300:0000:0000:0000:00C0:F0FF:FE27:64E2/48
(or F300::00C0:F0FF:FE27:64E2/48)
```

indicates that 48 bits are used for the network address (leaving 64 bits for the host address and 16 bits for additional subnetting). A standard way of assigning the 64 host bits is to use the 48-bit MAC address of the host together with a fixed 16-bit FFFE code. In the previous example, the MAC address 00C0:F027:64E2 becomes 00C0:F0FF:FE27:64E2 in the IPv6 address. This type of address is called an EUI64 address. EUI stands for Extended Unique Identifier, an IEEE standard method for host address representation.

■ PROTOCOL ANALYZERS

Protocol analyzers (or *sniffers*) are hardware or software devices that listen to the traffic on a network and capture various packets for examination. Hardware analyzers also double as cable testers.

Figure 8–27 shows the Ethereal protocol analyzer at work. Ethereal displays an ongoing update of network traffic statistics; allows packets to be captured, disassembled, and saved; and can also transmit packets to facilitate testing and troubleshooting.

FIGURE 8–27
Ethereal packet capture window showing decoded packet.

No.	Time	Source	Destination	Protocol	Info
180	52.859892	192.168.1.1	SERVER	HTTP	Continu
181	52.860003	SERVER	192.168.1.1	TCP	1047 >
182	52.860940	SERVER	192.168.1.1	TCP	1046 >
183	52.862637	192.168.1.1	SERVER	HTTP	Continu
184	52.865854	192.168.1.1	SERVER	HTTP	Continu
185	52.865979	SERVER	192.168.1.1	TCP	1047 >
186	52.868539	192.168.1.1	SERVER	HTTP	Continu
187	52.868638	SERVER	192.168.1.1	TCP	1047 >
188	52.871924	192.168.1.1	SERVER	HTTP	Continu
189	52.874522	192.168.1.1	SERVER	HTTP	Continu
190	52.874623	SERVER	192.168.1.1	TCP	1047 >
191	52.875775	192.168.1.1	SERVER	HTTP	Continu
192	52.876317	192.168.1.1	SERVER	TCP	80 > 1(

```
⊞ Frame 188 (1200 on wire, 1200 captured)
⊞ Ethernet II
⊞ Internet Protocol, Src Addr: 192.168.1.1 (192.168.1.1), Dst Addr: SERVE
⊞ Transmission Control Protocol, Src Port: 80 (80), Dst Port: 1047 (1047)
```

```
0000   00 c0 f0 68 3e 2d 00 20   78 c6 47 c4 08 00 45 00   ...h>-. x.G..
0010   04 a2 00 06 00 00 40 06   f2 99 c0 a8 01 01 c0 a8   ......@. ....
```

Filter: _____ Reset File: <capture> Drops: 0

■ TROUBLESHOOTING TECHNIQUES

Objective 4-1

Objective 4-1

Objective 4-7

Windows provides a useful utility called IPCONFIG (Windows 2000/XP)/WINIPCFG (Windows 9x), which you can run from the Run command prompt menu. Because the network software used by the system receives an IP address *on the fly,* via DHCP, the IP address of the DHCP server (24.94.33.64) is known to the system. DHCP is not used when your system has been allocated a static IP address by your network administrator.

If you have difficulty with your network connection, the information displayed by WINIPCFG will be valuable to the individual troubleshooting the connection. Note that a similar application program is available on other operating systems as well.

Network utilities come in handy for a variety of reasons, some of which are invented on the spot. For example, a group of students was asked to determine the effective distance of operation for a wireless laptop using a particular wireless base station. The students used the -t option of PING to establish a repetitive communication exchange between the laptop and the campus network. They watched the PING replies as they walked away from the base station, noting the distance whenever PING began indicating timeouts.

A sample output of PING using the -t option is:

```
C:\WINDOWS>ping -t www.ez80usergroup.com
Pinging www.ez80usergroup.com [66.34.123.175] with 32 bytes of data:

Reply from 66.34.123.175: bytes=32 time=77ms TTL=109
Reply from 66.34.123.175: bytes=32 time=94ms TTL=109
Reply from 66.34.123.175: bytes=32 time=96ms TTL=109
Reply from 66.34.123.175: bytes=32 time=284ms TTL=109
Reply from 66.34.123.175: bytes=32 time=94ms TTL=109
Reply from 66.34.123.175: bytes=32 time=151ms TTL=109
Reply from 66.34.123.175: bytes=32 time=87ms TTL=109
Reply from 66.34.123.175: bytes=32 time=91ms TTL=109


Ping statistics for 66.34.123.175:
    Packets: Sent = 8, Received = 8, Lost = 0 (0% loss),
Approximate round trip times in milli-seconds:
    Minimum = 77ms, Maximum =  284ms, Average =  121ms
```

The user must press Ctrl-C to stop the program. The results indicate a good connection (0% loss) and a reasonably fast route (77 milliseconds for the quickest round-trip time to the server hosting www.ez80usergroup.com).

Examine the route a little more carefully using TRACERT. Tracing the route to www.ez80usergroup.com gives the following results:

```
Tracing route to www.ez80usergroup.com [66.34.123.175]
over a maximum of 30 hops:

  1     19 ms     16 ms     16 ms  bgm-24-95-135-1.stny.rr.com [24.95.135.1]
  2     21 ms     20 ms     13 ms  24.94.33.2
  3     19 ms     15 ms     11 ms  24.94.32.161
  4     43 ms     17 ms     14 ms  syr-spp-gsr-plz-gsr.nyroc.rr.com [24.92.224.17]
  5     60 ms     34 ms     35 ms  pop2-alb-P3-1.atdn.net [66.185.148.141]
  6     42 ms     23 ms     38 ms  bb2-alb-P0-1.atdn.net [66.185.148.130]
  7     39 ms     30 ms     26 ms  bb2-new-P6-0.atdn.net [66.185.153.106]
  8     38 ms     35 ms     32 ms  pop1-new-P1-0.atdn.net [66.185.137.6]
  9     35 ms     29 ms     49 ms  ewr-edge-06.inet.qwest.net [65.115.225.165]
 10     44 ms     41 ms     53 ms  ewr-core-01.inet.qwest.net [205.171.17.29]
 11     68 ms    104 ms     60 ms  kcm-core-03.inet.qwest.net [205.171.8.185]
 12     85 ms     79 ms     95 ms  dal-core-02.inet.qwest.net [205.171.5.201]
 13     90 ms     78 ms     77 ms  dal-edge-11.inet.qwest.net [205.171.25.150]
 14     86 ms     76 ms     78 ms  ci-dfw-OC12.cust.qwest.net [65.118.50.2]
 15    105 ms    116 ms     83 ms  gige1.fire1.propagation.net [66.34.255.3]
 16     89 ms     93 ms     78 ms  66.34.255.78
 17     85 ms     95 ms     82 ms  www.ez80usergroup.com [66.34.123.175]

Trace complete.
```

The 17 routers between the source computer running TRACERT and the destination computer hosting www.ez80usergroup.com make an interesting trip across a wide number of networks. In particular, note the "core" and "edge" routers, as well as one apparently using an OC12 fiber connection.

Combining the TRACERT results with the PING results, we have a 121-millisecond average round-trip time through 17 routers, giving an average one-way hop time of 121 milliseconds divided by 34, or 3.56 milliseconds. This 3.56-millisecond time includes the router latency and the time for the TRACERT message to traverse the physical media between each router. For information that may be traveling hundreds or even thousands of miles, 3.56 milliseconds on average seems fairly quick.

CAREER DEVELOPMENT

As you progress throughout your networking career, you will likely want to gain new skills, obtain multiple certifications, and advance in the positions that you are assigned. Many certifications exist in the networking field. In addition to the Network+ certification, Cisco corporation controls the most widely obtained and valued network-specific certifications in the industry. The entry level certification offered by Cisco is the Cisco Certified Network Associate and it tests much of the same knowledge covered by the Network+ certification. Additionally it tests more advanced computer math skills, including your ability to work with the IP addressing process. If you are going to make computer networks your career you will need to learn to comfortably use computer math skills including conversion between the binary, decimal, hexadecimal, and octal numbering formats. When you first study these skills it may seem a bit overwhelming, but once you do learn them you will find out that it is not very difficult at all. In additional to learning the computer math skills, you will want to become very comfortable with the TCP/IP protocol suite, including the network troubleshooting tools available as part of the protocol suite.

■ SELF-TEST

1. Which of the following is the most popular protocol ever developed?
   a. UDP
   b. TCP/IP
   c. RTP
   d. NTP

2. Which layers of the OSI model are combined in the Application layer of the TCP/IP model?
   a. Network, Transport
   b. Session, Application
   c. Session, Presentation, Application
   d. Network, Transport, Session

3. IP provides a _____ that identifies your computer on a specific network.
   a. network ID
   b. packet flag
   c. unique address
   d. physical address

4. What network device is used to forward a packet to a remote LAN where a destination computer resides?
   a. Hub
   b. Transceiver
   c. Bridge
   d. Router

5. Which of the following layers of the OSI model do not provide error correction depending on the technologies and protocols in use?
   a. Data-Link
   b. Transport
   c. Application
   d. Presentation

6. IPv4 addresses are _____ numbers divided into four sections called _____.
   a. 48-bit, nodes
   b. 32-bit, octets
   c. 128-bit, zones
   d. 16-bit, quartets

7. Class A networks are designated by _____ octet(s) of an IP address.
   a. 1
   b. 2
   c. 3
   d. 4

8. Class B network numbers range from _____.
   a. 128 to 191
   b. 128 to 192
   c. 192 to 223
   d. 127 to 224

9. Class __ network addresses are special addresses used for transmitting data to multiple hosts at the same time.
   a. A
   b. B
   c. C
   d. D

10. What is entered when entering the IP address to specify how many bits of the 32 bits belong to the network portion of the address?
    a. Wildcard mask
    b. Subnet mask
    c. Default gateway
    d. DNS server

11. Applications using TCP establish connections with each other through the use of _____ or _____. (Choose two.)
    a. sockets
    b. ports
    c. nodes
    d. link states

12. What TCP mechanism provides a means for the receiving device to govern the amount of data sent by the sending device?
    a. BECN
    b. FECN
    c. Positive Asyn
    d. Flow control

13. _____ are used between two TCP applications to forward the correct TCP packet to the proper input buffer.
    a. Packet sniffers
    b. Connection sequence numbers
    c. Port numbers
    d. UDP ports

14. Which of the following transport protocols is regarded as unreliable?
    a. TCP
    b. RTP
    c. UDP
    d. TFTP

15. _____ uses a broadcast message to obtain the MAC address for a known IP address.
    a. RARP
    b. IARP
    c. UART
    d. ARP

16. What type of service is used to resolve a host name to an IP address?
    a. DHCP
    b. DNS

    c. BOOTP

    d. NAT

17. BOOTP servers communicate through port number _____ and BOOTP clients communicate through port number _____.

    a. 67, 68

    b. 53, 54

    c. 20, 21

    d. 137, 138

18. _____ is a simple file transfer protocol that is used when authentication of the user is not necessary.

    a. FTP

    b. TFTP

    c. ICMP

    d. LMI

19. The protocol that notifies the sender with an error message if a sent IP packet has trouble on its way to the destination is _____.

    a. IGMP

    b. DHCP

    c. IARP

    d. ICMP

20. _____ is responsible for routing electronic mail on the Internet using TCP and UDP.

    a. SMTP

    b. POP3

    c. FTP

    d. DNS

21. The protocol that provides the ability to monitor and control network devices is _____.

    a. SMTP

    b. SNMP

    c. TFTP

    d. POP3

22. What protocol is used to encrypt Web pages in a connection between a client and a server, providing the ability to buy products online?

    a. HTTP

    b. HTTPS

    c. SSLTP

    d. DES

23. What UDP port number is used by NTP to perform updates?

    a. 23

    b. 53

    c. 123

    d. 443

24. What protocol can be used to find the IP address of a Web site?

    a. PING

    b. ARP

    c. HTTP

    d. IGMP

25. IPv6 addresses are _____ bits long.

    a. 32

    b. 64

    c. 128

    d. 256

IPX/SPX, AppleTalk, and SNA Protocols

PERFORMANCE OBJECTIVES

Upon completion of this chapter, you will be able to:

■ Discuss the features of the IPX/SPX, AppleTalk, and SNA protocols.

■ Describe how IPX/SPX is similar to TCP/IP.

 ## NETWORK+ OBJECTIVES

This chapter provides information for the following Network+ objectives:

2.3 Differentiate between the following network protocols in terms of routing, addressing schemes, interoperability, and naming conventions:

■ TCP/IP
■ IPX/SPX
■ NetBEUI
■ AppleTalk

3.1 Identify the basic capabilities (i.e., client support, interoperability, authentication, file and print services, application support, security) of the following server operating systems:

■ UNIX/Linux
■ NetWare
■ Windows
■ Macintosh

■ INTRODUCTION

This chapter continues an examination of networking protocols. In order, this chapter looks at

- IPX/SPX (from Novell)
- AppleTalk (from Apple Computer)
- SNA (from IBM)

As you read about each new suite of protocols, try to find similarities and differences between them.

■ IPX/SPX

Objective 2-3

Objective 3-1

The IPX/SPX protocol suite, developed by Novell for its NetWare network operating system, is based on the Xerox Network System (XNS), which was developed in the 1970s. It is similar to the TCP/IP protocol suite, offering connectionless and connection-oriented delivery. Figure 9–1 shows the IPX/SPX protocols and their relationship to the OSI networking model. Similar to TCP/IP, the IPX/SPX protocol is a routable protocol containing both a network and a host portion of the address.

FIGURE 9–1
NetWare protocol suite.

ISO/OSI Layer	IPX/SPX Protocols	
7 = Application	NCP	SAP
6 = Presentation	NCP	SAP
5 = Session		SAP
4 = Transport	SPX	SAP
3 = Network	IPX	
2 = Data-Link		
1 = Physical		

IPX

The Internet Packet Exchange (IPX) protocol is similar to UDP under TCP/IP, providing connectionless (unreliable) network communication. IPX packets are used to carry higher-level protocols such as SPX, RIP, NCP, and SAP.

Figure 9–2 shows the 30-byte IPX header format. The Checksum field is normally set to FFFF hexadecimal and is typically not used for error detection. The Length field indicates the number of bytes in the IPX packet, including the 30-byte header. The maximum size of an IPX packet is 576 bytes, providing 546 bytes of data.

The Transport Control field is initially set to 0 by the transmitting station (the source node) and is incremented each time the IPX packet passes through a router. Thus, it indicates the number of hops the packet has encountered on the way to its destination. Using RIP, this field may not exceed 16 (the maximum hop count), or the packet is discarded.

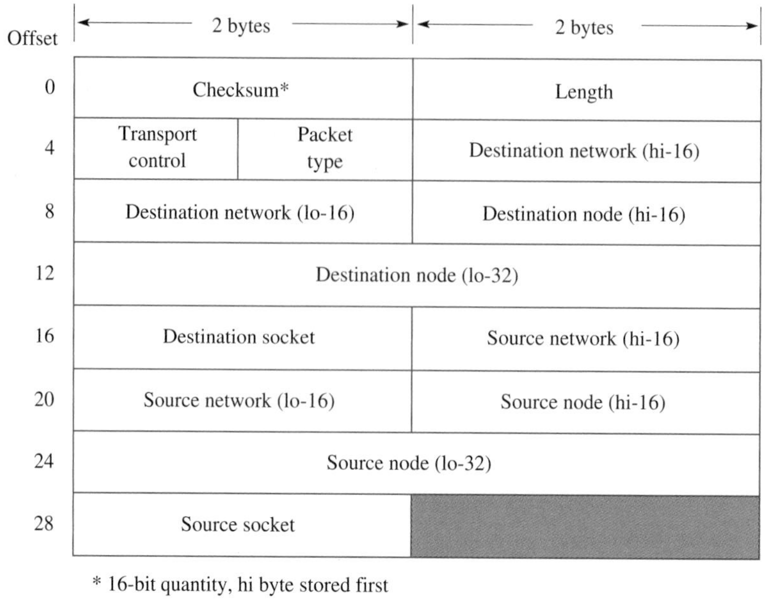

FIGURE 9–2
30-byte IPX header.

Offset	← 2 bytes →	← 2 bytes →
0	Checksum*	Length
4	Transport control / Packet type	Destination network (hi-16)
8	Destination network (lo-16)	Destination node (hi-16)
12	Destination node (lo-32)	
16	Destination socket	Source network (hi-16)
20	Source network (lo-16)	Source node (hi-16)
24	Source node (lo-32)	
28	Source socket	

* 16-bit quantity, hi byte stored first

The Packet Type field indicates the higher-level protocol encapsulated in the IPX packet. Table 9–1 lists the values associated with each higher-level protocol.

TABLE 9–1
IPX packet types.

Packet Type Value	Protocol
0	Unknown
1	RIP
2	Echo packet
3	Error packet
4	PEP
5	SPX
17	NCP

The remainder of the IPX header is dedicated to storing the Destination and Source Network, Node, and Socket addresses. The 32-bit Network address is similar to, but not the same as, an IP address. The IPX network addressing space is flat, meaning there is no subnetting allowed. An address of 00000000H indicates that the Source and Destination nodes are on the same network and no routing is required.

The Node portion of an IPX address uses the 48-bit MAC address of the NIC. Broadcasting is accomplished by using FFFFFFFFFFFFH for the Destination node.

The Socket number is similar to the port number used in TCP/IP. Table 9–2 lists some well-known IPX Socket numbers.

TABLE 9–2
Well-known IPX Socket numbers.

Socket	Function
451H	NCP Server
452H	SAP
453H	RIP
455H	NetBIOS

NCP

The NetWare Core Protocol (NCP) is the workhorse of NetWare, responsible for the majority of traffic on a NetWare network. Spanning three layers of the OSI protocol stack (Session, Presentation, and Application), NCP carries all file system traffic in addition to numerous other functions, including printing, name management, and establishing connection-oriented sessions between servers and workstations. NCP provides connection-oriented packet transmission, allowing for positive acknowledgment of each packet. A more efficient implementation called NCPB (NetWare Core Protocol Burst) was added to reduce the amount of control traffic necessary when using NCP.

SPX

The Sequenced Packet Exchange (SPX) protocol is similar to the TCP portion of the TCP/IP suite, providing connection-oriented communication that is reliable (lost packets are retransmitted). SPX packets contain a sequence number that allows packets received out of order to be reassembled correctly. Flow control is used to synchronize both ends of the connection to achieve maximum throughput.

Figure 9–3 compares an ordinary IPX packet and one encapsulating the SPX protocol. Because the overall IPX packet length is limited to 576 bytes, the size of the Data portion must shrink by 12 bytes to accommodate the SPX header.

FIGURE 9–3
Different types of IPX packets.

IPX header	Data
30 bytes	0–546 bytes

(a) IPX packet transporting some data.

IPX header	SPX header	Data
30 bytes	12 bytes	0–534 bytes

(b) IPX packet transporting the SPX protocol.

The 12 bytes are allocated as indicated in Figure 9–4.

FIGURE 9–4
SPX header.

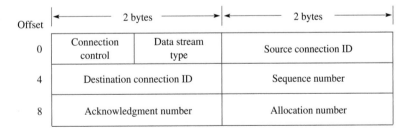

Offset	2 bytes		2 bytes
0	Connection control	Data stream type	Source connection ID
4	Destination connection ID		Sequence number
8	Acknowledgment number		Allocation number

The meaning and purpose of each portion of the SPX header is as follows:

- Connection Control: A set of four flags that are used to help control the connection. Table 9–3 lists the flags' values and their meanings. Note that only the upper 4 bits of the 8-bit Connection Control number are used.

- Data Stream Type: This number provides information on the type of data included in the SPX packet. As indicated in Table 9–4, values between 0 and 253 are ignored by SPX (and can be used by applications for identification). The values 254 and 255 are used when a connection terminates.

- Source Connection ID and Destination Connection ID: Used to identify the connection associated with the packet.

TABLE 9–3
Connection Control flag values.

Connection Control Flag	Meaning
10H (bit 4)	Last packet in message
20H (bit 5)	Attention
40H (bit 6)	Acknowledgment
80H (bit 7)	System packet

TABLE 9–4
Data Stream Type values.

Data Stream Type	Meaning
0–253	Ignored by SPX
254	End of connection
255	End of connection Ack

The reliability of SPX is a function of the Sequence and Acknowledgment numbers. Every SPX packet in a stream of packets making up a large message contains a unique Sequence number. The Acknowledgment number indicates which Sequence number the receiving application expects next and also serves to acknowledge reception of all previous (lower) Sequence numbers. For example, an Acknowledgment number of 100 acknowledges that packets numbered up to 99 have already been received.

The number of receive buffers available to be managed by flow control are indicated by the Allocation number.

SAP

The Service Advertising Protocol (SAP) is a broadcast protocol that is used to maintain a database of servers and routers connected to the NetWare network.

RIP

RIP

Like SAP, the Routing Information Protocol (*RIP*) is also a broadcast protocol. RIP is used by routers to exchange their routing tables. Multiple routers on the same network discover each other (during a RIP broadcast) and build entries for all networks that can be reached through each other. When conditions on the network change (a link goes down or is added), the change will be propagated from router to router (using RIP packets).

MLID

The Multiple Link Interface Driver (*MLID*) provides the interface between the network hardware and the network software. A specification called Open Data-Link Interface (*ODI*) is supported by MLID. ODI allows NetWare clients to use multiple protocols over the same network interface card. The LSL (Link Support Layer) provides the ODI facilities.

Similar to many other companies Novell has migrated their network operating system to support TCP/IP as their native protocol stack. While many networks still use the IPX/SPX suite in all or portions of their network, you should not expect to see that remain that way for very long.

■ APPLETALK

Objective 2-3

Objective 3-1

The AppleTalk suite of protocols was developed in the 1980s for use in networks of Macintosh computers. The two versions of AppleTalk are called Phase 1 and Phase 2. AppleTalk Phase 1, the initial version, limited networks to 127 workstations and 127 servers. This limited network is called a *nonextended* network. AppleTalk Phase 2 breaks the restriction and allows workstation/server numbers to be anything between 1 and 253. Larger networks are made possible by assigning multiple network numbers to a network. AppleTalk Phase 2 networks are called *extended* networks.

As indicated in Figure 9–5, AppleTalk contains a rich set of protocols. A brief description of each protocol is shown in Table 9–5.

FIGURE 9–5
AppleTalk protocol suite.

ISO/OSI Layer	AppleTalk Protocols				
7 Application				AFP	Postscript
6 Presentation					
5 Session	ZIP	ASP	PAP	ADSP	
4 Transport	AEP	ATP	NBP	RTMP	AURP
3 Network	AARP	DDP			
2 Data-Link	ELAP	TLAP	FLAP	LLAP	ARAP
1 Physical	Ethernet 802.3	Token ring 802.5	FDDI	Local talk	Serial (RS–422)

TABLE 9–5
AppleTalk protocols.

Protocol	Name	Function
AFP	AppleTalk Filing Protocol	Allows applications to communicate with network
ZIP	Zone Information Protocol	Maintains zone information
ASP	AppleTalk Session Protocol	Start-up/tear-down session
PAP	Printer Access Protocol	Provides network printing service
ADSP	AppleTalk Data Stream Protocol	Reliable packet delivery
AEP	AppleTalk Echo Protocol	Echoes packet from receiver back to sender
ATP	AppleTalk Transaction Protocol	Reliable packet delivery
NBP	Name Binding Protocol	Associates device names with network addresses
RTMP	Routing Table Maintenance Protocol	Discovers routing information
AURP	AppleTalk Update Routing Protocol	Updates routing tables only during changes to network
AARP	AppleTalk Address Resolution Protocol	Maps AppleTalk address to physical addresses
DDP	Datagram Delivery Protocol	Unreliable packet delivery
ELAP	EtherTalk Link Access Protocol	IEEE 802.3 Ethernet
TLAP	TokenTalk Link Access Protocol	IEEE 802.5 Token Ring
FLAP	FDDITalk Link Access Protocol	100 Mbps FDDI
LLAP	LocalTalk Link Access Protocol	230 Kbps RS-422 Serial
ARAP	AppleTalk Remote Access Protocol	Network access using serial line

There is wide support for AppleTalk in the Data-Link and Physical layers, with several different Link Access Protocol drivers available (such as EtherTalk for Ethernet and TokenTalk for token ring).

Once again, connectionless (DDP) and connection-oriented (ADSP) packet delivery are provided. Note that reliable ADSP messages are carried by unreliable DDP packets. In fact, every protocol above the Network layer is carried by a DDP packet.

File sharing is accomplished using AFP, which relies on a session controlled by ATP and ASP.

ZIP is used to help manage the *zones* used in an AppleTalk extended network. A zone is a logical group of computers that may belong to different networks. Every computer on an extended network belongs to a single zone, or to no zone at all.

AppleTalk network addresses are composed of three parts:

- 16-bit Network number
- 8-bit Node number
- 8-bit Socket number

For example, in the network address 50.66.100, the Network number is 50, the Node number is 66, and the Socket number is 100. Phase 1 Node numbers are assigned as indicated in Table 9–6. AppleTalk network components, such as clients, servers, and printers, are all AppleTalk *objects*. For convenience, objects can be given descriptive names and their names bound to their actual AppleTalk addresses, similar to the way a domain name is bound to its IP address. The Name Binding Protocol (NBP) associates AppleTalk names with AppleTalk addresses. An example of an AppleTalk name is JLA:HPlaserjet@Engineering where JLA is the object name, HPlaserjet is the object type, and Engineering is the zone name. Up to 32 characters may be used for the object name, type, and zone fields. AppleTalk names are not case-sensitive.

TABLE 9–6
Network Node number assignments.

Network Node Number	Assignment
0	Reserved
1–127	Workstation
128–254	Server
255	Reserved

Figure 9–6 illustrates the different fields of the DDP header. Most of the header is devoted to storing the Source and Destination network addresses.

* Type

1 RTMP response
2 NBP
3 ATP
4 AEP
5 RTMP response
6 ZIP
7 ADSP

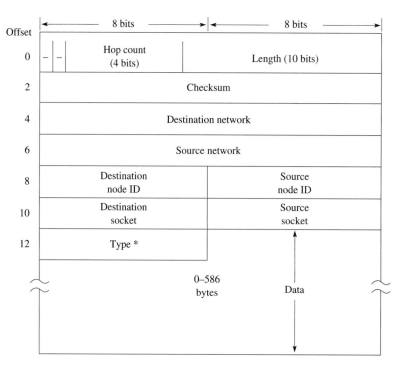

FIGURE 9–6
DDP header fields.

The Hop Count is used by RIP to control the lifetime of the packet during routing. There are many excellent Web sites containing detailed discussions of AppleTalk networking. Visit http://www.ieng.com/univercd/cc/td/doc/cisintwk/ito_doc/applet.htm for additional information.

Take a moment to examine Table 9–7, which compares the features of the major protocol families discussed so far in this book.

TABLE 9–7
Comparison of four major networking protocol families.

Protocol Family	Routable Across LAN	Routable Across WAN	Addressing	Unreliable Service	Reliable Service	Used on the Internet	Operating System
TCP/IP	Yes	Yes	32 bits for Network and Host (IP)	Yes, UDP	Yes, TCP	Yes	Windows, Macintosh, NetWare, UNIX, Linux
IPX/SPX	Yes	Yes	32-bit Network, 48-bit Node (MAC)	Yes, IPX	Yes, SPX	No	Windows, Macintosh, NetWare, Linux
AppleTalk	Yes	No	16-bit Network, 8-bit Node	Yes, DDP	Yes, ADSP	No	Windows, Macintosh
NetBEUI	No	No	Up to 15-character alphanumeric	Yes, Datagram	Yes, Session	No	Windows

■ SNA

The SNA (Systems Network Architecture) protocol was designed by IBM to allow communication between IBM mainframe computers and any other types of computers that support SNA. In the early days of SNA, all traffic on the network required processing by a centralized mainframe computer.

The architecture of the SNA protocols contains seven layers, the same as in the OSI model although the names of the layers are different, as shown in Figure 9–7.

FIGURE 9–7
SNA protocol stack.

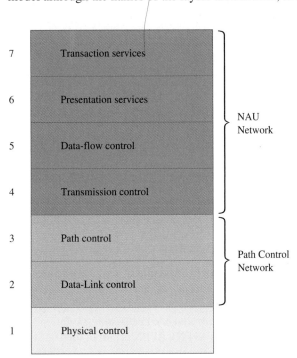

The SNA protocol stack is further divided into two segments called the Path Control network and the NAU network. The Path Control network portion is responsible for the delivery of network information. The Advanced Communications Function/Network Control Program (ACF/NCP) is used to manage the Path Control network.

The NAU layers of the network are responsible for controlling the process to move the data between the source and the destination. An NAU is any entity on the network that can be assigned a network address. These entities are grouped into three categories called a host, a communications controller, and a peripheral. The communication between two NAUs is called a session.

SNA categorizes the network entities into physical units and logical units. A physical unit contains all of the hardware and software needed to control a logical unit. A logical unit is used to access the programs run by the end-user. A physical unit is designed to manage many logical units. To connect the logical units together, IBM developed several systems to offer different types of network application services. These application services are:

- CICS (Customer Information Control System)
- CMS (Conversational Monitor System)
- IMS (Information Management System)
- TSO (Time Sharing Option)

In general, these services are provided by system applications that are bundled inside the operating system and that are able to take full advantage of all network resources. You are encouraged to learn more about each of these network services.

When the capabilities of the personal computer were added to SNA in the 1980s, a new feature called Advanced Program-to-Program Communication (APPC) was developed. This allowed for communication directly between two PCs. To accommodate the additional network communication requirements, a physical unit and a logical unit were added to the SNA protocol. APPC allows two programs on the same computer to communicate, as well as client-server applications. Table 9–8 lists the physical unit types and Table 9–9 lists the logical unit types within an SNA network.

TABLE 9–8
SNA physical unit types.

Physical Unit Types	Description
1	Low-end peripheral node (obsolete)
2.0	Peripheral node
2.1	APPC peripheral node
4	Sub-area node
5	Host processor

The System Service Control Point (SSCP) services are used to manage all (or part) of the sessions on the physical and logical units within a network, which collectively make up a domain. An SNA network session can take on many different forms. For example, a session can be established between any of the following entities:

- Logical unit to logical unit
- Physical unit to physical unit
- SSCP to logical unit
- SSCP to physical unit

Two additional types of communication are also provided. SSCP to SSCP is used to enable communication between two host computers, and control point to control point is used to provide communication between two APPN applications.

An even more advanced networking solution from IBM is called Advanced Peer-to-Peer Networking (APPN). APPN is part of the IBM Systems Applications Architecture and offers more flexibility than SNA with the added benefits of dynamic routing.

TABLE 9–9
SNA logical unit types.

Logical Unit Types	Description
0	User-defined logical unit
1	Printer supporting SCS (SNA character strings)
2	Terminal device
3	Printer that does not support SCS
4	Peer-to-peer communication using SCS
6.0	Program-to-program communication using CICS
6.1	Program-to-program communication using CICS or IMS
6.2	General-purpose program-to-program communication not requiring the service of a host computer (APPC)
7	Communication between a host and terminal supporting SCS or stream data

In summary, each of the protocols introduced in this chapter provides a unique solution to solve the problems of networked communications. Although most of these protocols have been replaced by TCP/IP, you will continue to find them in use today in networking environments.

■ TROUBLESHOOTING TECHNIQUES

The large number of protocols in use on today's networks requires a good understanding of their basic principles of operation. There are many excellent online references that provide valuable protocol information. Some places to examine can be found at:

- http://www.protocols.com
- http://www.techfest.com/networking/prot.htm

In addition, many companies will send you a free networking poster, such as one showing several protocols and their OSI model layers, or another detailing Voice over IP protocols. Try searching the Web for "networking poster" or something similar. You will have to navigate through the search results carefully. Some sites make it easy to find their free poster; others will require you to dig through them. It took one student only five minutes to order posters from three different companies, so spending a few minutes doing this research on the Web may be very rewarding.

INDUSTRY TIP

Supporting multiple protocols on a network becomes very expensive in terms of technician training, equipment expense, bandwidth expense, and so on. Large networks supporting multiple protocol suites become very expensive in terms of bandwidth and man-hours to troubleshoot and maintain. Often there is great debate over the expense of upgrading to a single system that uses only one protocol suite versus maintaining the current (and operational) system. One of the ways to help determine when it is cost effective to migrate to a new single protocol suite is to review network documentation. Records of network usage rates (especially bandwidth usage), trouble tickets, man-hours spent on maintenance of the network, and training dollars spent on technicians can often provide enough evidence to justify the initial expense of upgrading a network to a modern single protocol suite. There may still be business processes and applications that require some minimal use of legacy protocol suites on a small portion of the network, but these are usually isolated to a specific group of users who need to work with legacy systems. Isolating the use of legacy protocol suites to small portions of the network can often save a lot of expense for an organization.

■ SELF-TEST

1. Which of the following protocols is routable?
   a. IPX
   b. IPTV
   c. SMTP
   d. NTP

2. On which network system is the IPX/SPX protocol suite based?
   a. SLIP
   b. XEOn
   c. XNS
   d. TCP/IP

3. How many bytes are in an IPX header?
   a. 12
   b. 24
   c. 30
   d. 36

4. How many subnet bits are allowed in an IPX node address?
   a. 0
   b. 8
   c. 16
   d. 24

5. What is meant by the statement that IPX addressing is flat?
   a. No errors
   b. No static entries
   c. No subnetting
   d. Address represented in hex

6. Which of the following is an IPX socket number for RIP?
   a. 451H
   b. 452H
   c. 453H
   d. 455H

7. Which of the following is a NetWare protocol that spans the Session, Presentation, and Application layers of the OSI model?
   a. NTP
   b. NCP
   c. FTP
   d. RIP

8. Which of the following NetWare protocols carries the most data per packet?
   a. IPX
   b. SPX
   c. IP
   d. TCP

9. Every SPX packet in a stream of packets associated with a large message contains a unique _____ in the SPX packet header.
   a. Source connection ID
   b. Data Stream type
   c. Sequence number
   d. Acknowledgement number

10. What part of the SPX packet header indicates the number of receive buffers available to be managed by flow control?
    a. Sequence number
    b. Acknowledgement number

    c. Allocation number

    d. Connection control

11. Which of the following is a characteristic of the SAP protocol?

    a. Unicast

    b. Multicast

    c. Simulcast

    d. Broadcast

12. What NetWare protocol is used by routers to exchange their routing tables?

    a. EIGRP

    b. RIP

    c. OSPF

    d. IPX

13. What NetWare driver provides the interface between the network hardware and software?

    a. MLID

    b. NLID

    c. NLSP

    d. NCP

14. What protocol is now supported as Novell's native protocol stack?

    a. IPX

    b. SPX

    c. OSPF

    d. TCP/IP

15. What is the maximum number of workstations and servers allowed in an AppleTalk Phase 1 network?

    a. 100

    b. 127

    c. 156

    d. 253

16. DDP is considered to be a _____ protocol.

    a. reliable

    b. connection-oriented

    c. connectionless

    d. management

17. What protocol is responsible for file sharing in an AppleTalk network?

    a. FTP

    b. TFTP

    c. ATP

    d. AFP

18. Given the AppleTalk network address 51.62.100, what is the node number?

    a. 51

    b. 62

    c. 100

    d. Not given

19. What AppleTalk protocol associates AppleTalk names with AppleTalk addresses?

    a. NTP

    b. NCP

    c. NBP

    d. ATP

20. What node numbers can be assigned to servers in an AppleTalk network?

    a. 1–64

    b. 1–127

c. 128–254

d. 1–254

21. AppleTalk network components such as clients, servers, and printers are all AppleTalk _____.

a. objects

b. hosts

c. ApplePeers

d. zones

22. True or False: The names of the seven layers of the SNA model map closely to the OSI model.

23. _____was designed to process mainframe computer traffic.

a. DEC

b. SNA

c. SNAP

d. NTP

24. APPC was developed by IBM to allow direct communication between _____.

a. two PCs

b. two servers

c. two separate networks

d. applications

25. True or False: Isolating the use of legacy protocol suites to small portions of the network can save money.

Switching and Routing

CHAPTER **10**

PERFORMANCE OBJECTIVES

Upon completion of this chapter, you will be able to:

■ Explain the basic differences between hubs and switches.

■ Discuss the difference between store-and-forward switching and cut-through switching.

■ Describe the operation of a router.

■ Explain the differences between distance-vector and link-state routing protocols and give examples of each.

■ Illustrate the differences between interior and exterior routing protocols.

NETWORK+ OBJECTIVES

This chapter provides information for the following Network+ objectives:

1.6 Identify the purpose, features, and functions of the following network components:

■ Hubs   ■ Switches

■ Bridges   ■ Routers

■ Gateways   ■ CSU/DSU

■ Network Interface Cards/ISDN adapters/system area network cards

■ Wireless access points

■ Modems

2.1 Given an example, identify a MAC address.

2.3 Differentiate between the following network protocols in terms of routing, addressing schemes, interoperability, and naming conventions:

■ TCP/IP   ■ IPX/SPX

■ NetBEUI   ■ AppleTalk

2.4 Identify the OSI layers at which the following network components operate:

■ Hubs   ■ Switches

■ Bridges   ■ Routers

■ Network Interface Cards

2.8 Identify IP addresses (IPv4, IPv6) and their default subnet masks.

2.9 Identify the purpose of subnetting and default gateways.

2.10 Identify the differences between public vs. private networks.

2.11 Identify the basic characteristics (e.g., speed, capacity, media) of the following WAN technologies:

■ Packet switching vs. circuit switching

■ ISDN   ■ FDDI

■ ATM   ■ Frame Relay

■ Sonet/SDH   ■ T1/E1

■ T3/E3   ■ Ocx

3.8 Identify the purpose, benefits, and characteristics of using a firewall.

3.10 Given a scenario, predict the impact of a particular security implementation on network functionality (e.g., blocking port numbers, encryption, etc.).

4.1 Given a troubleshooting scenario, select the appropriate TCP/IP utility from among the following:

■ TRACERT   ■ PING

■ ARP   ■ NETSTAT

■ NBTSTAT

■ IPCONFIG/IFCONFIG

■ WINIPCFG

■ NSLOOKUP

4.3 Given a troubleshooting scenario involving a remote connectivity problem (e.g., authentication failure, protocol configuration, physical connectivity), identify the cause of the problem.

4.8 Given a scenario, predict the impact of modifying, adding, or removing network services (e.g., DHCP, DNS, WINS, etc.) on network resources and users.

4.10 Given a troubleshooting scenario involving a network with a particular physical topology (i.e., bus, star/hierarchical, mesh, ring, wireless) and including a network diagram, identify the network area affected and the cause of the problem.

■ INTRODUCTION

Chapter 8 examined the many different TCP/IP protocols and their use. Several higher-layer protocols provide the methods required for two stations to communicate, reliably or unreliably. This chapter takes a look at the routing protocols used by routers to communicate network information between themselves. It also explores the details of switching and makes comparisons between hubs, switches, and routers.

■ HUBS VERSUS SWITCHES

Objective 1-6

The essential difference between hubs and switches is that hubs retransmit frames received on one port to all other ports, whereas a switch will forward a received frame to a specific port (except for broadcast messages, which will be retransmitted out every port except the one that it was received on). This is illustrated in Figure 10–1, in which a small network of six stations (A through F) are connected two different ways.

FIGURE 10–1
Comparing a hub and a switch.

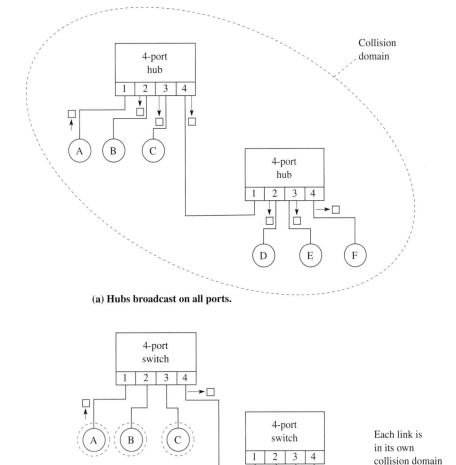

(a) Hubs broadcast on all ports.

(b) Switches forward frames to specific ports.

In Figure 10–1(a), station A transmits a frame whose destination is station F. This does not matter to the 4-port hubs that simply retransmit copies of the frame from station A to the other five stations. This amounts to a good deal of wasted bandwidth. Furthermore, all six stations operate in the same collision domain, making them compete for bandwidth.

Figure 10–1(b) shows the same network with the 4-port hubs replaced by 4-port switches. A frame transmitted from station A with a destination of station F is forwarded between the switches and sent directly to station F on port 4. Stations B, C, D, and E do not receive copies of the frame as they do in Figure 10–1(a); therefore, network traffic has been reduced.

The switches also partition the network into seven separate collision domains (including the link between the switches). Each station now has unrestricted access to its own dedicated bandwidth (the speed of the switch port).

The switch is capable of specific forwarding because it learns which MAC addresses are associated with each port. Recall that every Ethernet frame contains a source MAC address and a destination MAC address. When a frame is received by a port on a switch, the switch will save a copy of the source MAC address and its associated port number in a special internal lookup table. Though we are storing the source MAC address, it is a destination MAC address to every other station in the network. Now, when a frame requires forwarding, the switch examines the destination MAC address stored in the frame, and looks for it in the lookup table. If the destination MAC address is found in the table, the frame is forwarded to the associated port. If the destination MAC address is not found, the frame is broadcast to all ports. Eventually the destination station will most likely respond with its own frame, and its port will be identified. Further broadcasts for that station will not be required.

Figure 10–2 shows the results obtained when a hub and switch are used together. Stations A, B, and C are in one collision domain and are competing for bandwidth. Stations D, E, and F are in their own collision domains, each having full access to the available bandwidth. In Figure 10–2(a), station A transmits a frame destined for station F. The frame is retransmitted out all ports except the port the frame was received on by the hub and forwarded by the switch. Stations B and C must contend with the retransmitted frame, waiting their turn for access. Neither station is allowed to transmit while the hub is retransmitting the frame, otherwise a collision will result. So, even though station A is sending a frame to station F, stations B and C are affected.

Figure 10–2(b) shows station A sending a frame to station C. The hub still retransmits the frame out all other ports, which affects station B but not stations D, E, or F.

In Figure 10–2(c), station F sends a frame to station A. The frame is forwarded by the switch and retransmitted out all other ports by the hub. Stations B and C are affected by F's frame; stations D and E are not.

Figure 10–2(d) shows station F sending a frame to station D. Station E is unaffected and may transmit a frame to stations A, B, or C without affecting the F-to-D transmission.

FIGURE 10–2
Mixing hubs and switches.

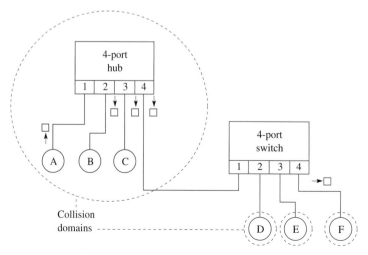

(a) A sending to F.

FIGURE 10–2
(continued)

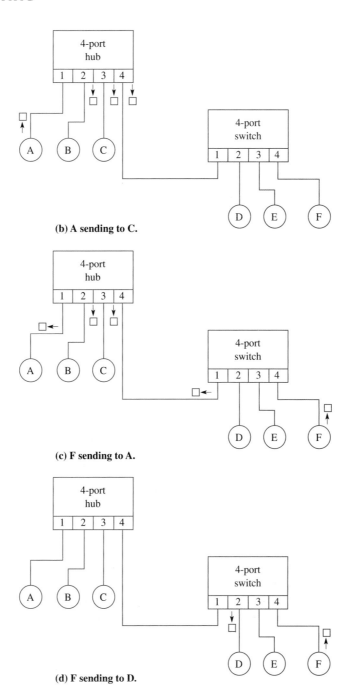

(b) A sending to C.

(c) F sending to A.

(d) F sending to D.

■ INSIDE A SWITCH

If you wanted to start your own networking company and begin designing and manufacturing switches, where would you begin? Let us examine the block diagram of a simple switch, shown in Figure 10–3.

As illustrated, the switch contains the following components:

- Input port logic
- Output port logic
- Switching fabric
- Control logic

What would be required of each component?

FIGURE 10-3
Block diagram of a switch.

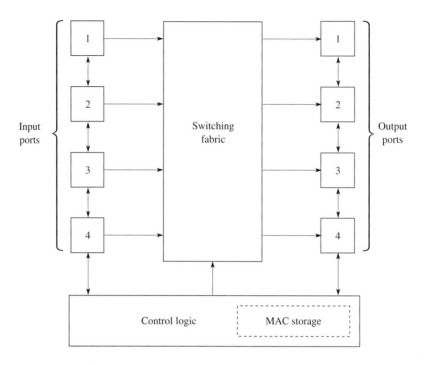

Input Port Logic

This section contains the receiving logic and buffers for received frames. Buffering received frames lowers the rate of collisions and allows the switching fabric to be busy for short periods of time without losing data. If the frame buffer fills up, any new frame received by the port will trigger a collision. The random delay of CSMA/CD will then give the switch time to empty a portion of the input buffer before the station attempts retransmission.

Output Port Logic

Each output port contains a transmitter and output frame buffer. Again, the buffer allows the switch fabric to service multiple output ports on a demand basis. For example, several frames may arrive simultaneously, with each frame directed to the same output port. The buffer is required to prevent the switching fabric from stalling. In addition, the input and output frame buffers allow different speeds between ports (e.g., port 1 operating at 10 Mbps and port 3 operating at 100 Mbps). The buffers may be filled at one speed and emptied at another speed.

Switching Fabric

The switching fabric is responsible for directing the received frames from each input port to the appropriate output port. In addition, the switching fabric must also be able to handle a broadcast to all output ports. In general, there are two ways to build the switching fabric: crossbar switch and high-speed multiplexed bus. Both methods are shown in Figure 10–4.

The crossbar switch in Figure 10–4(a) is a two-dimensional set of data buses. Any combination of input-to-output connections is possible, even broadcasting. Each intersection of input wires and output wires in the crossbar switch contains an electronic switch that is either open or closed. A small amount of control information is required to configure the crossbar switch. Changing the control information changes the input-to-output connections.

The multiplexed bus in Figure 10–4(b) effectively makes one input-output connection at a time, with each input port getting its turn at using the bus. When many signals are

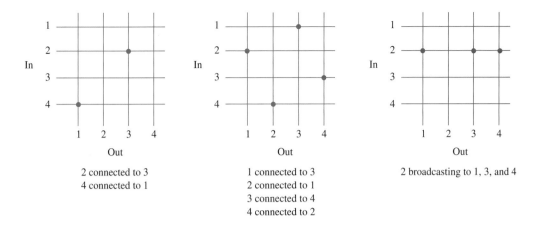

2 connected to 3
4 connected to 1

1 connected to 3
2 connected to 1
3 connected to 4
4 connected to 2

2 broadcasting to 1, 3, and 4

(a) Crossbar switch.

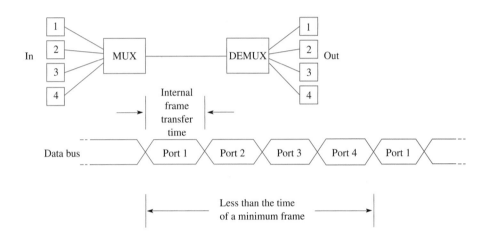

(b) Multiplexed bus (round-robin TDM).

FIGURE 10–4
Switching fabrics.

multiplexed in this fashion, the data rate on the multiplexed bus must be much faster than the individual speeds of each port. For example, on a 4-port switch, with each port running at 100 Mbps, the multiplexed bus would need to operate at 400 Mbps. An 8-port switch would require an 800 Mbps bus. The speed requirement of this technique makes it unsuitable for switching at high speeds. This problem is overcome by the parallel nature of the crossbar switch.

Control Logic

Objective 2-1

The control logic must perform several chores, including:

• Updating and searching the MAC address table

• Configuring the switching fabric

• Maintaining proper flow control through the switch fabric

Recall that the switch learns which ports are associated with specific stations by storing copies of the source MAC address from each received frame. The MAC address and port number are stored in a special high-speed memory called CAM (content addressable memory). The hardware architecture of the CAM allows its internal memory to be searched for a desired data value, such as a 48-bit MAC address. Figure 10–5 shows a simple example of a CAM being searched for the MAC address `00-C0-F0-3C-88-17`. It is important to note that all of the MAC addresses being stored in the CAM are compared with the input value, *at the same time.* For example, the MUSIC LANCAM MU9C1480 from MUSIC Semiconductor (http://www.music-ic.com) stores 1024 64-bit entries and performs comparisons in 70 nanoseconds.

FIGURE 10–5
CAM organization.

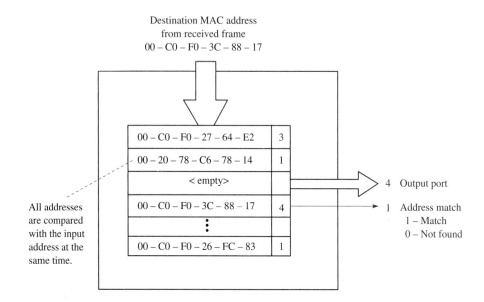

The control logic uses the lookup results from the CAM to configure the switching fabric. In the event an output port becomes unavailable due to congestion or some other problem, a flow control mechanism will prevent access to the port until it becomes available again.

■ STORE-AND-FORWARD SWITCHING

**Store-and-forward
switching**

Initially, switches handled frames using a technique called ***store-and-forward switching.*** In this technique, the entire frame is stored as it is received. If the FCS (Frame Check Sequence) is valid, the destination MAC address is used to select an output port, and the frame is forwarded to the appropriate output port via the switching fabric. If the FCS is invalid the frame is discarded as a bad frame. Because the entire frame is stored before any decisions are made, there is a delay between the time the frame is received and the time it

Latency

begins transmission on the appropriate output port. This delay is called ***latency***, and varies depending on the length of the frame. The minimum latency is obtained with a minimum size frame. For 10 Mbps Ethernet, the minimum latency is 57.6 microseconds (576 bit times at 100 nanoseconds/bit, including Preamble). Maximum-length frames have a latency just over 1.2 milliseconds.

Some applications, such as streaming audio and video, are sensitive to latency. Modern networks handle large amounts of data and store-and-forward switching is much too slow a process for many environments; however, there may be a need for using this method if your network design needs dictate checking for valid frames before transmissions take place over specific links (such as an expensive but slow WAN link). Of course, if you are experiencing a high quantity of invalid frames you have other network design issues that need to be dealt with.

■ CUT-THROUGH SWITCHING

Cut-through switching

Cut-through switching reduces the latency of a switch tremendously. In this technique, as soon as the destination MAC address of an incoming frame is received and read, the forwarding process can begin, assuming there is a free output port and the switching

Fast-forward
Fragment-free

fabric is available. This reduces the latency to just 11.2 microseconds, plus any additional time for internal switch operations. There are two forms of cut-through switching: *fast-forward* switching and *fragment-free* switching. If you have followed all the design rules of your network, such as the 5-4-3 rule for 10 Mbps networks, you should not have any significant issues with respect to invalid frames being transmitted on a network. In an Ethernet environment a minimum valid frame size is 64 bytes. The Ethernet frame contains the destination MAC address early in the frame header, well before 64 bytes of information have been transmitted. It is possible for stations to transmit a partial frame, including the destination MAC address, before detecting a collision. Fast-forward switching retransmits a frame out the destination port as soon as the destination MAC address is received and read. This means that invalid frames may be forwarded out the destination port before the collision is detected, needlessly cluttering the destination with worthless data (consuming bandwidth). Although the fast-forward is the faster of these two forwarding methods, it must be used with caution. Fragment-free switching will wait until the minimum frame size is received by the switch (64 bytes in an Ethernet environment) before it starts switching the frame out the destination port. This is a good compromise between the store-and-forward and fast-forward types of switching. Store-and-forward switching, and both versions of the cut-through switching processes, all have their place in modern network design. The decision to use store-and-forward, or either of the two cut-through switching methods, is a design decision based on the behavioral characteristics of your network.

■ SWITCHES VERSUS ROUTERS

Objective 1-6

Switches are considered layer 2 (Data-Link) devices, using MAC addresses to forward frames to their proper destination. Routers, layer 3 (Network) devices, are much more complex, using microprocessor-based circuitry to route packets between networks based on their layer 3 (e.g., IP, IPX) address. Routers provide the following services, among others:

- Route discovery
- Selection of the best route to a destination
- Adaptation to changes in the network
- Translation from one technology to another, such as Ethernet to token ring
- Packet filtering based on layer 3 address, protocol, or UDP/TCP port number
- Connection to a WAN

Because of the additional processing required for each packet, a router has a higher latency than a switch. In addition, a router requires an initial setup sequence, in which the ports are programmed and certain protocols and characteristics enabled or disabled. A switch may be simply plugged into the network, automatically learning how to forward frames as the network is used. Note that some protocols, such as NetBEUI, are non-routable. These protocols will pass through a switch but not a router.

Finally, switches are used within networks to forward local traffic intelligently. Routers are used between networks (defined by different layer 3 network IDs) to route packets between networks in the most efficient manner. The following sections examine the many different routing protocols used to enable communication between LANs.

■ ROUTING PROTOCOLS

Routing protocols communicate information about the paths between networks (what router interface do I send a packet out of to reach network X). These protocols differ from routed protocols, such as IP and IPX, that establish the layer 3 addressing scheme and have their packets transported between networks. Routing protocols are the languages that routers use to communicate between themselves. Routing protocols are not used to transport communications to end-users (PCs). Routing protocols are used to pass network path information between routers. Routing protocols operate at the Network layer (layer 3) in the OSI model. Using a device called a *router*, various types of networks are connected together to form one *logical* network or internetwork. The Internet is an example of one logical internetwork. A network is generally considered to be under the control of one administrative authority (i.e., an organization). An internet is a collection of networks (a network of networks). A router is a special-purpose computer whose primary responsibility is to move data around on the network between source and destination computers through path selection and layer 3 switching. The individual networks can be made up of different types of LAN hardware and topologies, such as Ethernet, token-ring, or ATM networks, to name just a few. The router is able to move the data between the different network types and perform any necessary translations between technologies and protocols.

When an organization chooses what type of routing protocols to use, it is a complex task based on the answers to many questions including the following:

- What is the size and complexity of the network?
- Which service provider will handle the network data?
- What is/are the network traffic level(s)?
- What are the security needs?
- What level of reliability is required?
- What are the organizational policies?

In general, each router must follow a few ground rules to process Network layer data:

- Communicate on a LAN just like any other station. For example, on an Ethernet network, a router communicates using CSMA/CD and monitors the media for their MAC address and any broadcast messages.
- Maintain tables with routing information for all reachable networks.
- Forward or block traffic based on the destination network address.
- Drop all packets to unknown destinations or pass the packets to a default path.
- Forward directed broadcasts between networks if permitted by the organization.
- Perform FCS checks on each transferred packet.

Using a router, messages are passed from one device (host computer or router) to another until the message eventually reaches the destination. Figure 10–6 shows a typical network connected to the Internet through a router. Any traffic exchanged between any of the hosts on the local network can be delivered directly without the need for a router. All traffic that is destined for the Internet must be passed on to the router.

FIGURE 10–6
A router connecting a network to the Internet.

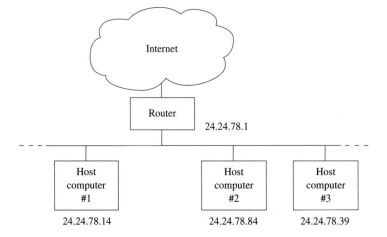

Objective 4-1

A Windows application program called NETSTAT is used to show the routes that are currently active on a personal computer running the Windows operating system. Running the NETSTAT program with the -r option produces the following output:

```
C:\WINDOWS>netstat -r

Route Table

Active Routes:

  Network Address          Netmask  Gateway Address          Interface  Metric
        0.0.0.0          0.0.0.0      24.24.78.1      24.24.78.84       1
       24.24.78.0  255.255.255.0     24.24.78.84      24.24.78.84       1
      24.24.78.84  255.255.255.255    127.0.0.1       127.0.0.1        1
   24.255.255.255  255.255.255.255   24.24.78.84      24.24.78.84       1
        127.0.0.0      255.0.0.0      127.0.0.1       127.0.0.1        1
        224.0.0.0      224.0.0.0     24.24.78.84      24.24.78.84       1
  255.255.255.255  255.255.255.255   24.24.78.84      24.24.78.84       1

Active Connections

  Proto  Local Address           Foreign Address          State
  TCP    server:1025             sbccab.cc.sunybroome.edu:139  ESTABLISHED
  TCP    server:4424             ftp-eng.cisco.com:ftp  CLOSE_WAIT
  TCP    server:4970             mail3-1.nyroc.rr.com:pop-3  TIME_WAIT
  TCP    server:4981             sunc.scit.wlv.ac.uk:80  CLOSE_WAIT
```

Objective 2-9

As you can see, NETSTAT shows the routing table and active connections for the computer. To deliver a message to a remote network, it must be transmitted from the source host to a local router (the *default gateway*). In the NETSTAT display, the default gateway has the address 24.24.78.1. Do any of the other addresses look familiar, such as the loopback address or the network masks?

After the data is sent to the default gateway router, it is passed on to another router, passed to the host computer on the destination LAN, or dropped if no path to the destination network is known. Each router implements the routing process by forwarding messages (one hop at a time) toward their final destination using information stored in a ***routing table.*** The routing table contains an entry that indicates the best path (or interface) to send the data on to the destination.

Routing table

The routing table in a router can be created and maintained using two different methods: ***statically*** or ***dynamically.*** When using purely static routes, a number of predefined routes are manually entered into the router's routing table and the router lacks the ability to discover new routes on its own. In a router with statically configured routing tables, the network administrator needs a detailed knowledge of the network topology and must take the time to manually build and update the routing table as conditions change. This involves programming all of the routes into the router's memory. Static routers can work well for small networks but do not work well in large or dynamically changing networks due to the manual effort required to maintain current routing entries. Static routers are not fault tolerant. The lifetime of a manually configured static route is indefinite. Therefore, statically configured routers do not recover from a bad link or a malfunctioning router.

Statically
Dynamically

In contrast, using dynamic routing, new routes can be discovered, and old routes can be updated as required. Dynamic routing consists of maintaining routing tables automatically using either periodic or on-demand messages through an ongoing communication between routers using the ***routing protocols***. Except for their initial configuration, dynamic routers require little ongoing maintenance. Dynamic routing is

Routing protocols

fault tolerant. Dynamic routes learned from other routers have a finite lifetime. If a router or link goes down, the routers sense the change in the network topology through the expiration of the lifetime of the learned route in the routing table. This change can then be propagated to other routers so that all the routers on the network maintain a common view of the new network topology. When changes to the network take place, and the routers have the same view of the network, we say that the network has achieved *convergence.*

The router chooses the "best" path to send the data by implementing either a *distance-vector* or a *link-state* algorithm. In the distance-vector algorithm, each router in the network contains a partial view of the complete network topology. In the link-state algorithm, each router is aware of the entire network. Distance-vector protocols receive their knowledge about the topology of the network based only on information obtained by their neighbor router. They receive the routing table of the neighbor, make adjustments to the table to include their own directly connected networks, and forward their view of the network to their neighbor router. This is sometimes referred to as *routing by rumor.* If the neighbor router has out-of-date information, the router will not have accurate information to base its own routing decisions on. Another characteristic of distance-vector routing protocols is that the updates are generally triggered by time (e.g., transmitting a routing update every 30 seconds even if no changes have taken place). Link-state routing protocols receive their knowledge of the various links of the network directly from the routers responsible for the information. Every router transmits the status of the networks that are directly connected to it to every other router on the network. Each router processes that information, independent of what any other router thinks, builds its understanding of what the network topology looks like, and builds its routing table from that information. Link-state routing protocols normally transmit link-state information (is the link up or down) when a link's status changes, versus transmitting every x amount of seconds. This makes the convergence time (when every router has the same view of the network) much faster for link-state protocols. As you study these general concepts you will note versions of how these activities take place. Some routing protocols, such as Cisco's EIGRP, are hybrids of these two basic categories.

This is a great time to review *routed* versus *routing* protocols. Routed protocols are protocols such as IP and IPX. They are layer 3 protocols. They describe such concepts as header information, addressing schema, and so on. They form the packets of information that are routed through a network. Routing protocols are the protocols used by layer 3 devices (generally routers) to talk between themselves about what layer 3 networks exist throughout the network. These protocols have nothing to do with forming packet headers. Routing protocols are designed to allow layer 3 devices to talk with each other and adjust to network changes without the intervention of a network administrator (after the initial setup of course). You do not need to have a routing protocol implemented on a network if you are using static routing.

Before we can discuss how the routing algorithms and protocols operate, it is necessary to understand where a LAN fits into the logical network as a whole. Each connected

Autonomous system   network is part of a larger network called an ***autonomous system***.

■ AUTONOMOUS SYSTEMS

Routing is based on the individual networks that are called autonomous systems, commonly abbreviated to AS. An autonomous system is a network or group of networks and routers controlled by a single administrative authority. The authority can be an institution, a corporation, or any other type of organization (e.g., the United States Army or Harvard University). An autonomous system number is associated with each autonomous system. Depending on what routing protocols are in use, your individual organization may not be assigned an autonomous system number, but someone higher up the network system (such as the ISP) has an autonomous system number assigned to them. Table 10–1 shows a brief list of autonomous system numbers. Each autonomous system has a single and clearly defined external routing policy. A new AS needs to be created if a network connects to more than one AS with a different routing policy.

TABLE 10–1
A list of autonomous system numbers.

Number	Network
3300	ATT Unisource
9744	E-Z NET Internet Service Provider
7487	Idea Net Co., Ltd.
4618	Internet Thailand Service Center
786	JANET
6453	Teleglobe Montreal
8297	Teleglobe Virginia
1849	UUnet UK

Different routing protocols are used when routing inside autonomous systems and between them. An Interior Gateway Protocol (IGP) is used inside autonomous systems. Exterior Gateway Protocols (EGPs) exchange information between different autonomous systems. Figure 10–7 illustrates how the different routing protocols are used to connect autonomous systems together.

FIGURE 10–7
Interior versus Exterior Gateway Protocols.

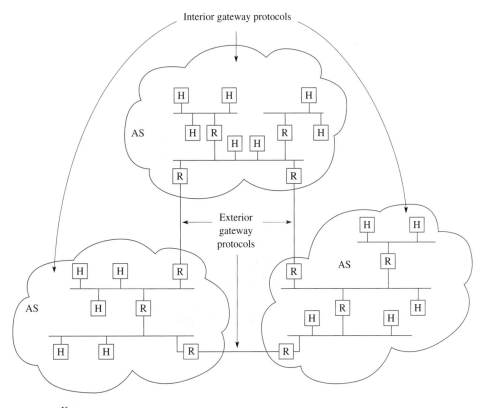

Key:
H–Host Computer
R–Router
AS–Antonomous System

Many of the protocols we will examine in this exercise are shown in Table 10–2 along with the RFC numbers that describe their operation in detail. As you will see, some of these protocols may be used as IGPs, EGPs, or both. Let us begin with a discussion of the Interior Gateway Protocols.

TABLE 10–2
RFCs associated with routing protocols.

RFC Number	Description
1058	RIP
1105	BGP
1142	OSI IS-IS Intra-Domain Routing Protocol
1247	OSPF V2
1388	RIP Version 2 Protocol Extensions
1403	BGP OSPF Interaction
1654	BGP-4
1655	Application of the Border Gateway Protocol
1656	BGP-4 Document Roadmap and Implementation Experience
1771	BGP-4 (revised)
1774	BGP-4 Protocol Analysis
2080	RIPng for IPv6
2082	RIP-II MD5 Authentication
2453	RIP Version 2

■ INTERIOR GATEWAY PROTOCOLS

Interior Gateway Protocols

Interior Gateway Protocols (IGPs) are used for communication inside autonomous systems. The following protocols are used as IGPs for IP networks:

- *Routing Information Protocol (RIP):* An RFC-based distance-vector IGP

- *Routing Information Protocol 2 (RIP-2):* An enhanced version of RIP that includes support for Classless Inter-Domain Routing (CIDR) and authentication

- *Interior Gateway Routing Protocol (IGRP):* A distance-vector IGP developed by Cisco Systems, Inc. in the 1980s. IGRP is capable of load balancing multiple network paths based on delay, bandwidth, load, and reliability of the links.

- *Enhanced Interior Gateway Routing Protocol (EIGRP):* A hybrid IGP (possessing characteristics of both distance-vector and link-state protocols) developed by Cisco Systems, Inc. EIGRP extends IGRP to support CIDR and provides several other enhancements.

- *Open Shortest Path First (OSPF):* Link-state IP protocol that is primarily used within an autonomous system but can also be used as an EGP (though this is not normally done). OSPF includes authentication and has become the IP routing protocol of choice in large environments.

- *Intermediate System to Intermediate System (IS-IS):* OSI-based connectionless link-state protocol

We will examine each of these protocols in more detail shortly.

The autonomous systems that use the IGPs are connected to other autonomous systems. The Exterior Gateway Protocols are used for the communication between the autonomous systems.

■ EXTERIOR GATEWAY PROTOCOLS

Exterior Gateway Protocols   *Exterior Gateway Protocols* (EGPs) are used between different autonomous systems. EGPs define the way that all of the networks within the AS are advertised outside the AS. Each EGP advertises the "reachability" to the networks it can connect to. Figure 10–8 shows what messages an EGP might broadcast to other EGPs.

FIGURE 10–8
EGP messages.

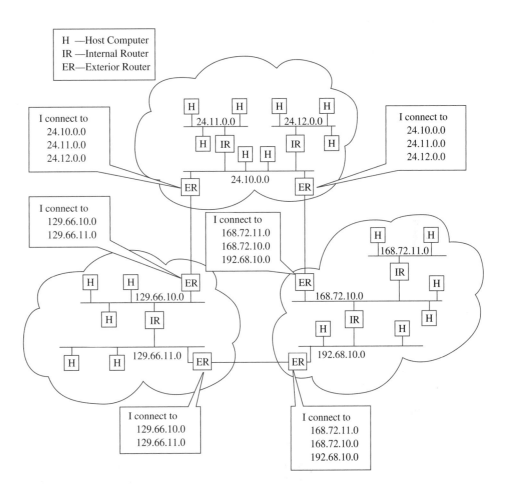

Note that the EGPs are independent of the IGPs used within the autonomous system. EGPs can facilitate the exchange of routes between autonomous systems that may use different IGPs. Many autonomous systems contain two or more EGP routers for redundancy. If one EGP router is down, the second must temporarily handle the additional load. In practice, the internal and external routers may be located within the same box, performing both internal and external routing decisions simultaneously. For example, on a Cisco router, as many as 30 different routing protocols may be operating simultaneously. The combinations are made up as follows:

- Up to 30 EGP routing processes
- Up to 30 IGRP routing processes
- Up to 30 OSPF routing processes
- One RIP routing process
- One IS-IS process
- One BGP routing process

As you might agree, this is a rather impressive list of supported combinations.

The following protocols are used for EGPs in IP networks:

- *Exterior Gateway Protocol (EGP):* An RFC-based protocol that was developed for use between ASs on the Internet. EGP is no longer used on the Internet due to its lack of support for complex, multipath environments and Classless Inter-Domain Routing (CIDR).

- *Border Gateway Protocol (BGP):* An RFC-based protocol that is currently used between ASs on the Internet. BGP overcomes the weaknesses of EGP. For example, BGP is better at detecting routing loops than EGP.

- *Open Shortest Path First (OSPF):* Link-state IP protocol. OSPF includes authentication and has become the IP routing protocol of choice in large environments. OSPF is primarily used as an IGP.

We will examine many of the details of these protocols shortly as well. First, let us examine Classless Inter-Domain Routing.

■ CLASSLESS INTER-DOMAIN ROUTING

Objective 2-8

Classless Inter-Domain Routing (CIDR) was initially developed to recover many of the unused addresses in class A and class B networks. The CIDR technique is supported by interior and exterior gateway protocols and is based on subnetting and route aggregation. CIDR is a new way of looking at IP addresses that eliminates the concept of classes (class A, class B, etc.). With CIDR, IP addresses and their *subnet* masks are written as 4 octets, separated by periods, followed by a forward slash and a 2-digit number that represents the length of the subnet mask. For example, the class B network 178.217.0.0, which is an illegal class C network address, is a legal class C address when it is represented in a CIDR environment. It is written as 178.217.0.0/24. The /24 indicates that the subnet mask consists of 24 bits (counting from the left). Therefore, 178.217.0.0/24 represents the address 178.217.0.0 with a mask of 255.255.255.0.

Route aggregation

CIDR makes it easy to aggregate or combine routes. **Route aggregation** is the process of using several different routes in such a way that a single route can be advertised, which minimizes the size of the routing tables maintained by a router. Table 10–3 shows various CIDR prefixes with the number of class C equivalent addresses.

TABLE 10–3
CIDR address prefix and number of class C addresses.

CIDR Prefix	Number of Equivalent Class C Addresses	Number of Host Addresses
/28	1/16 of one class C	16 hosts
/27	1/8 of one class C	32 hosts
/26	1/4 of one class C	64 hosts
/25	1/2 of one class C	128 hosts
/24	1 class C	256 hosts
/23	2 class Cs	512 hosts
/22	4 class Cs	1,024 hosts
/21	8 class Cs	2,048 hosts
/20	16 class Cs	4,096 hosts
/19	32 class Cs	8,192 hosts
/18	64 class Cs	16,384 hosts
/17	128 class Cs	32,768 hosts
/16	256 class Cs	65,536 hosts
/15	512 class Cs	131,072 hosts
/14	1,024 class Cs	262,144 hosts
/13	2,048 class Cs	524,288 hosts

Currently, big blocks of addresses are assigned to the large ISPs, who then reallocate portions of their address blocks to their customers. The implementation of CIDR has been critical to the continued growth of the Internet, allowing more organizations and users to take advantage of this increasingly vital global networking and information resource. The terms *supernetting* and *subnetting* are often used to depict how we use the network bits with respect to defining our network ID. When we aggregate network IDs into one larger network ID we use fewer bits to represent the new resultant network ID. This is called supernetting. When we subnet (divide) a normal network ID into smaller portions, making more network IDs but having less hosts per subnet, we are subnetting. Subnetting can also be used in a classful environment. Whether you can work in a classful environment (where you must follow the classful boundaries of the IP addressing schema) or a CIDR environment is dependent on the software, applications, and protocols in use. Most modern software (i.e., operating systems) and applications are fully capable of working in a CIDR environment. If you use routing protocols such as RIP (version 1) or IGRP you can gain some of the advantages of a CIDR environment but not all of them (such as variable length subnet masking (VLSM), which we will not cover in this book). If you implement other protocols such as RIP v.2, EIGRP, and OSPF you can use all the features of a CIDR environment.

Distance-vector routing

Link-state routing

We continue with a brief introduction to the routing algorithms. The routing algorithms are based on one of two different approaches to finding the "best" or shortest path to the destination. The first method, called ***distance-vector routing***, is based on determining the fewest number of hops to the destination. The metric (or measure) of distance is based on the number of exchanges (or hops) between routers that must be performed. The second routing method, called ***link-state routing***, is more complex and more efficient than distance-vector algorithms. First, let us examine the distance-vector routing algorithm and a few of the protocols that use it.

■ DISTANCE-VECTOR ROUTING

The distance-vector routing algorithm (also called the Bellman-Ford algorithm) is a type of routing algorithm that is based on the number of hops in a route between a source and a destination computer. The shortest path algorithm is attributed to Bellman and the distributed nature of the algorithm is attributed to Ford. Distance-vector routing algorithms call for each router to send its entire routing table to its neighbor in each update. An update is performed at specific time intervals depending on the protocol in use. The distance-vector routing algorithm is distributed between the routers on the network.

The most common measure of distance (metric) is based on the number of hops the data needs to take to reach the destination. To keep the metric value simple, the number of hops from any router to itself is 0 and a connection to a neighbor is assigned a value of 1. Figure 10–9 shows a small network containing 4 LANs, labeled A, B, C, and D.

FIGURE 10–9
Routing based on hop count.

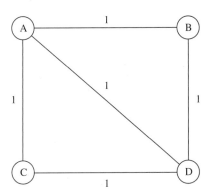

Network A is connected directly to networks B, C, and D. Network B is connected to networks A and D. Network C is connected to networks A and D. Lastly, network D, like network A, is connected to all of the other networks. Notice that the best route between hosts A and B is the direct connection between them with the cost of 1. Similarly, connections between B and C have a cost of 2. As you will see, it is possible to use other metrics as well.

Although distance-vector protocols are usually easy to implement, they have many weaknesses. For example, the distance-vector algorithm is susceptible to routing loops and cannot differentiate between the speeds of different links; and the time it takes to propagate all messages to every router in a large network is slow.

Each router that implements the distance-vector routing algorithm maintains a routing table that contains one entry for each network in the entire network. The routing table entry contains two fields: one is used to indicate the distance to the destination and the other one indicates the network interface adapter to use to get there. The distance-vector routing algorithm was chosen as the original ARPAnet routing algorithm, the predecessor to the modern Internet. A common distance-vector protocol is called the Routing Information Protocol, more commonly known as RIP.

RIP

Objective 2-3

The Routing Information Protocol (RIP) is a commonly used distance-vector routing protocol that uses the underlying UDP transport. RIP is based on a 1970s Xerox design that was ported to TCP/IP when LANs first appeared in the 1980s. RIP uses a 4-bit metric to count router hops to a destination. Due to the size of this field, a RIP network can be no larger than 15 hops between the furthest connected stations. The value 16 is used to represent infinity. If hop counts are elevated on slower or less reliable links, this can quickly become a problem.

Every 30 seconds a RIP router broadcasts its routing table of networks and subnets it can reach to its neighbor. The neighboring router in turn will pass the information on to its next neighbor and so on, until all routers within the network have the same knowledge of routing paths, a state known as network ***convergence***. RIP uses a hop count as a way to determine network distance.

Convergence

Depending on the length of the routing table, which depends on the size of the network, bandwidth usage with RIP can become excessive as the size of the routing table increases. In addition, RIP has no security features.

RIP also has several benefits. It is in widespread use, since it is the only Interior Gateway Protocol that can be counted on to run on every router platform. Configuring the RIP protocol is very easy. Finally, RIP uses an algorithm (distance-vector) that does not impose serious computation or storage requirements on hosts or routers.

Each entry in a RIP routing table contains:

- Address of the destination
- Address of the next router
- Metric value
- Recently Updated Flag
- Various timers

RIP has changed little in the past few decades and suffers from the limitations previously identified, some of which have been overcome with a newer version of the protocol called RIP-2. RIP-2 maintains compatibility with RIP-1. RIP-2 provides these additional routing features:

- Authentication
- Classless Inter-Domain Routing (CIDR)
- Next Hop
- Multicasting

The message headers for both RIP-1 and RIP-2 are shown in Figure 10–10.

FIGURE 10–10
Routing Information Protocol packets.

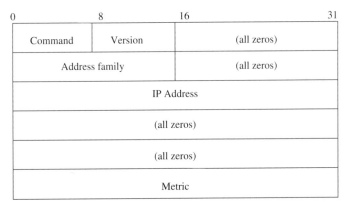

(a) RIP-1.

(b) RIP-2.

A brief description of each of the header fields is provided in Table 10–4. Note that as many as 25 routes may be broadcast inside every single RIP message.

TABLE 10–4
Routing Information Protocol header field information.

Field Name	Version	Size	Meaning
Command	1, 2	8 bits	RIP command value
Version	1, 2	8 bits	RIP version
Routing Domain	2	16 bits	Network routing domain
Address Family	1, 2	16 bits	Type of address
Route Tag	2	16 bits	Used to separate internal and external routes
IP Address	2	32 bits	IP address
Subnet Mask	2	32 bits	Subnetwork mask applied to the IP address
IP Address (next hop)	2	32 bits	Immediate IP address of the next hop
Metric	1, 2	32 bits	Hop count, etc.

Interior Gateway Routing Protocol

The Interior Gateway Routing Protocol (IGRP) is a Cisco-proprietary solution to many of the problems associated with the RIP protocol. In general, IGRP is characterized by the following properties:

• IP transport
• Updates broadcast every 90 seconds

- Hold down protocol enhancement
- New metrics
- Bandwidth
- Delay
- Load
- Reliability
- Protection against loops
- Multipath routing
- Default route handling

IGRP is an Interior Gateway Protocol (IGP). IGRP uses distance-vector routing technology. The proprietary nature of the IGRP protocol means that Cisco routers are the only routers that can use it.

The most important properties that set IGRP apart from RIP include less bandwidth consumed with broadcast updates, newer and more efficient methods to compensate for changing network conditions, additional metric parameters that can be used to allow a network administrator to provide additional measures of control as to how routes are chosen, increased prevention against routing loops, better handling of multiple paths, and the selection of a default route.

To prevent routing loops, several new features are included. These features include:

- Hold down
- Poison-reverse update
- Split horizon

A hold down feature is used to prevent the condition where a route that has become unstable is used prematurely. A poison-reverse update is used to eliminate routing loops by removing the routes from routing tables. Lastly, a split horizon is used to prevent routing information from being sent back on a link from the direction in which it was originally received.

The IGRP enhancements also include the addition of several new timer variables. These timers are:

- Flush
- Hold-time
- Invalid
- Update

The flush timer variable is used to control the lifetime of each entry in the routing table. The hold-time timer variable determines how long a route is kept in a hold down condition. The invalid timer variable determines how long a route remains valid in the absence of an update message. The update timer variable is used to determine how often update messages are distributed. The values specified for each of these timer variables allow for the most efficient use of the router processor and network bandwidth utilization.

You are encouraged to spend some additional time on your own exploring the features of IGRP and the advantages that Cisco routers provide.

Although IGRP has many advantages over RIP, a more advanced version called EIGRP provides many other capabilities.

Enhanced Inter-Gateway Routing Protocol

Cisco developed Enhanced IGRP in the early 1990s to improve the operating efficiency of IGRP. Improvements to IGRP include:

- A distributed update algorithm
- MD5 authentication (authentication of routing updates)

- Protocol Independent Routing
- Metric changes (not entire routing tables) exchanged every 90 seconds
- CIDR support

Due to the proprietary nature of the EIGRP protocol, it is only supported by Cisco routers. EIGRP is rapidly replacing implementations of IGRP.

■ LINK-STATE ROUTING

Dijkstra's algorithm

In contrast to the distance-vector algorithm, the link-state routing algorithm multicasts information about the cost of reaching each of its neighbors to all other routers in the network. This allows the link-state algorithm to create a consistent view of the network at each router. The method used to compute the shortest distance is based on *Dijkstra's algorithm*, an open shortest path algorithm. The primary difference between distance-vector routing and link-state routing is that a path with the least hops may not be chosen as the least-cost route. For example, take a look at Figure 10–11. Notice that the best path from A to B is not the single hop that directly connects the two. This could be due to the fact that the direct connection between the two of them contains a 56K link whereas all of the other links operate at T1 speed. In a large network, route computations are more complex.

FIGURE 10–11
Routing based on weighted connections.

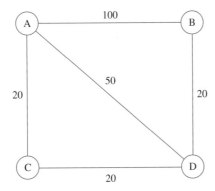

The link-state routing algorithm is not prone to routing loops or any of the other problems that are common to distance-vector routing algorithms. The problem with the link-state algorithm lies in its complexity.

A link-state router has the following characteristics:

- Automatically discovers any neighboring routers
- Shared information via multicast transmissions
- Routing tables are built using first-hand information only
- Hello packets containing route information are forwarded to all routers
- Uses metrics other than hop count
- Supports load balancing
- No assumption that routing information is accurate and has been received from a trusted source
- Computes the shortest path to every router in the network

Flooding protocol

Spanning tree

In link-state protocols, the router keeps a list of all routers that it knows in a table. In the routing table the distance to each network is specified. Routers update their routing tables periodically according to other routers' routing tables and advertise their own routing tables to other routers. Each of the routes is calculated during every link-state modification. A special *flooding protocol* is used to propagate the changes in a link's status quickly throughout the network. To reduce the amount of multicast router traffic on the network, a *spanning tree* is used to create non-looping paths between the routers in the network. Figure 10–12 illustrates a spanning tree example on a small network.

FIGURE 10–12
Choosing the best route between nodes using a spanning tree.

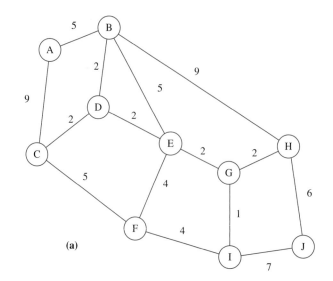

(a)

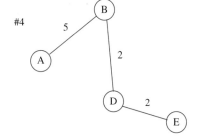

#1

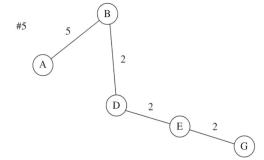

#4

#5

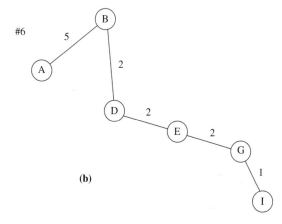

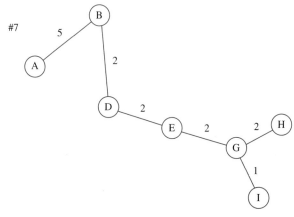

(b)

FIGURE 10–12
(b) *continued*

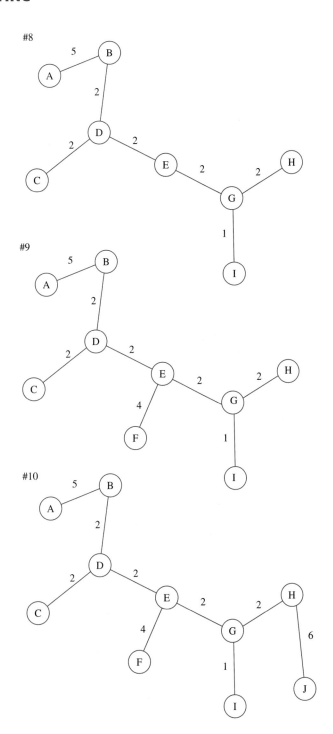

FIGURE 10–12
(continued)

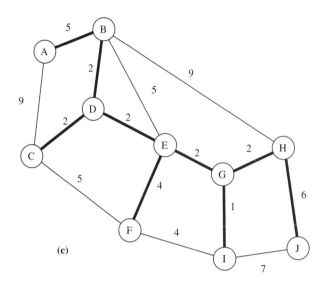

(c)

To build a spanning tree path between all of the routers in the network, we begin at router A and examine each of the paths to the other routers that are connected to A, choosing the shortest. Next, it is necessary to examine each of the remaining paths between each of the currently linked routers, again choosing the shortest link to a new router. This process continues until all routers are in the tree. Figure 10–12(b) shows each of the individual steps required to build the spanning tree between each of the routers in the small network. Figure 10–12(c) shows the complete spanning tree with the darkened lines indicating the resulting path.

Although link-state routing requires much more computation power, it is generally considered more efficient for modern networks. The advantages of link-state routing include:

• Fast, loopless convergence

• Support for multiple metrics

• Support for multiple paths

The link-state header is shown in Figure 10–13.

FIGURE 10–13
Link-state header fields.

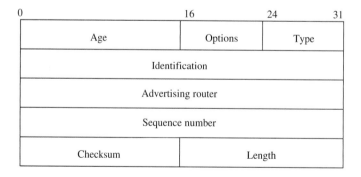

Table 10–5 describes each of the fields in the header.

Intermediate System to Intermediate System

Intermediate System to Intermediate System (IS-IS) is an OSI link-state hierarchical routing protocol that floods the network with link-state information to build a complete, consistent picture of network topology. To simplify router design and operation, IS-IS

TABLE 10–5
Link-state header field
information.

Field Name	Size	Meaning
Age	16 bits	Time in seconds since first advertisement
Options	8 bits	Description of the capabilities of the advertising router
Type	8 bits	Type of link-state connection: • External link • Network link • Router link • Summary Link (Border network) • Summary Link (IP network)
Identification	32 bits	Link Identification chosen by the advertising router
Advertising Router	32 bits	Address of the advertising router
Sequence Number	32 bits	Identifier associated with the advertisement
Checksum	16 bits	Computed checksum value
Length	16 bits	Length of the record including the 20-byte header

distinguishes between Level 1 and Level 2 ISs. Level 1 ISs communicate with other Level 1 ISs in the same area. Level 2 ISs route between Level 1 areas and form an intradomain routing backbone. Hierarchical routing simplifies backbone design because Level 1 ISs only need to know how to get to the nearest Level 2 IS. The backbone routing protocol also can change without impacting the intra-area routing protocol.

IS-IS uses a single required default metric with a maximum path value of 1,024. IS-IS uses three basic packet formats: *IS-IS hello packets, link-state packets (LSPs)*, and *sequence-number packets (SNPs)*. Each of the three IS-IS packets has a complex format with the following three different logical parts. The first part consists of an 8-byte fixed header shared by all three packet types. The second part is a packet-type–specific portion with a fixed format. The third part is also packet-type–specific but of variable length. Figure 10–14 illustrates the logical format of IS-IS packets.

FIGURE 10–14
IS-IS packet header.

0	8	16	24	31

Protocol identifier	Header length	Version	ID length
Packet type	Version	Reserved	Maximum area addresses

Table 10–6 shows the common header fields of the IS-IS packets.

TABLE 10–6
IS-IS header field descriptions.

Field Name	Description
Protocol Identifier	Identifies the IS-IS protocol and contains the constant 131.
Header Length	Contains the fixed header length. The length is always equal to 8 bytes.
Version	Contains a value of 1 in the current IS-IS specification.
ID Length	Specifies the size of the ID portion of an NSAP address. If the field contains a value between 1 and 8 inclusive, the ID portion of an NSAP address is that number of bytes. If the field contains a value of 0, the ID portion of an NSAP address is 6 bytes. If the field contains a value of 255 (all ones), the ID portion of an NSAP address is 0 bytes.
Packet Type	Specifies the type of IS-IS packet (hello, LSP, or SNP).
Version	Repeats after the Packet Type field.
Reserved	Is ignored by the receiver and is equal to 0.
Maximum Area Addresses	Specifies the number of addresses permitted in this area.

Following the common header, each packet type has a different additional fixed portion, followed by a variable-length portion. A more robust version of the protocol is called integrated IS-IS.

Integrated IS-IS

Integrated IS-IS is a routing protocol based on the OSI routing protocol, but it also supports IP and other protocols. Integrated IS-IS sends only one set of routing updates, making it more efficient than two separate implementations, formerly called the dual IS-IS routing method. Integrated IS-IS is a version of the OSI IS-IS routing protocol that uses a single routing algorithm to support connection-oriented communication also.

NetWare Link Services Protocol

Objective 2-3

The NetWare Link Services Protocol (NLSP) is a link-state routing protocol based on IS-IS. NLSP is the successor to the IPX protocol. Routers employing NLSP use incremental updates (as opposed to periodic updates) when exchanging network topology changes with their immediate neighbors. NLSP was designed to overcome some of the limitations associated with the IPX Routing Information Protocol (based on RIP) and its companion protocol, the Service Advertisement Protocol (SAP). NLSP was designed to replace RIP and SAP, Novell's original routing protocols that were designed when networks were local and relatively small.

As compared to RIP and SAP, NLSP provides improved routing, better efficiency, and scalability. In addition, NLSP-based routers are backward-compatible with RIP-based routers. NLSP-based routers use a reliable delivery protocol, so delivery is guaranteed. Furthermore, NLSP facilitates improved routing decisions because NLSP-based routers store a complete map of the network, not just next-hop information such as RIP-based routers use. Routing information is transmitted only when the topology has changed, not every 30 seconds as RIP-based routers do, regardless of whether the topology has changed. Additionally, NLSP-based routers send service-information updates only when services change, not every 60 seconds as SAP does.

In terms of scalability, NLSP can support up to 127 hops. Recall that RIP supports only 15 hops. Compared to RIP, NetWare Link Services Protocol offers the following benefits:

- Improved routing
- Reduced network overhead
- Very low WAN overhead
- Faster data transfer
- Increased reliability
- Less CPU usage
- Better scalability
- Superior manageability
- Backwards compatibility
- Support for multiple networking media
- Optional manual link-cost assignment

Border Gateway Protocol

Border Gateway Protocol

The **Border Gateway Protocol** (BGP) provides loop-free inter-domain routing between autonomous systems. BGP is often run among the networks of Internet service providers (ISPs), although BGP can be used as a protocol for both internal and external routing. The format of a BGP header is shown in Figure 10–15 and a description of the fields is provided in Table 10–7.

FIGURE 10–15
BGP header fields.

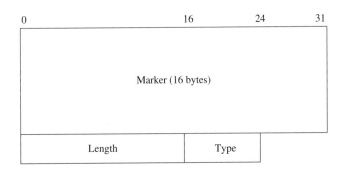

TABLE 10–7
BGP header fields.

Field Name	Size	Meaning
Marker	16 bytes	Identification number used for security purposes
Length	2 bytes	Message length in bytes
Type	1 byte	Four types are defined: • Keep Alive • Notification • Open • Update

Before BGP exchanges information with an external autonomous system it ensures that networks within the AS are reachable. This is done by a combination of internal BGP peering among routers within the AS and by redistributing BGP routing information to Interior Gateway Protocols (IGPs) that run within the AS, such as Interior Gateway Routing Protocol (IGRP), Intermediate System to Intermediate System (IS-IS), Routing Information Protocol (RIP), and ***Open Shortest Path First*** *(OSPF)*.

Open Shortest Path First

BGP uses the Transmission Control Protocol (TCP) as its transport protocol (specifically port 179). Any two routers that have opened a TCP connection to each other for the purpose of exchanging routing information are known as *peers* or *neighbors*. BGP peers initially exchange their full BGP routing tables. Thereafter, BGP peers send incremental updates only. BGP peers also exchange keep-alive messages (to ensure that the connection is up) and notification messages (in response to errors or special conditions).

When a BGP router receives updates that describe different paths to the same destination, it chooses the single best path for reaching that destination. Once the best path is chosen, BGP propagates it to its neighbors. The decision is based on the value of attributes (such as next hop, administrative weights, local preference, the origin of the route, and path length) that the update contains and other BGP-configurable factors.

The latest version of BGP, called BGP-4, has been used on the Internet since 1995. BGP-4 includes support for CIDR.

■ POLICY ROUTING

Policy-based routing

Policy-based routing refers to any type of routing that is based on factors other than the selection of the "shortest path." One of the primary uses of policy routing is to accommodate acceptable use policies of the various interconnected networks. Other considerations are also incorporated, such as:

• Contract obligations

• Quality of service (resource reservation)

• Service provider selection

One good example of the use of policy-based routing is with a network incorporating voice over IP (VOIP). VOIP uses UDP packets to reduce the overhead of the transmission of the voice packets. Additionally, if a voice packet gets dropped along the way it would be undesirable to retransmit a delayed voice packet (that would do more harm to the conversation than good). A network administrator would typically design the network to give preference to a packet containing voice transmissions over many other packets containing data such as a Web page. The voice packets are time sensitive as compared to many other types of network traffic. A delay in a voice packet disrupts a normal conversation carried on between humans, but the momentary delay of a Web page download is normally not significant.

Other types of routing algorithms are also possible, such as those based on routing IP information over ATM, for example, Multi-Protocol Label Switching and the Private Network-Network Interface.

Layer 3 Switching

Layer 3 switching

A layer 3 switch is essentially a switch and a router combined into one package. *Layer 3 switching* has become popular due to the ever-increasing demand for bandwidth, low latency, and services. Traditional routers have become bottlenecks in the campus and corporate LAN environments, due to their microprocessor-based operation and high latency. Layer 3 switches utilize ASIC (application specific integrated circuit) technology to implement the routing functions in hardware. This enables the layer 3 switch to perform router duties while forwarding frames significantly faster than an ordinary router.

Replacing the campus or corporate routers with layer 3 switches, or adding layer 3 switching to a routerless network, has many benefits:

- Fewer network components to manage (via SNMP)
- Faster forwarding (close to *wire speed*, the speed of the frames on the wire)
- Helps provide QoS (quality of service) to the LAN environment
- Compatible with existing routing protocols

There is a great deal of information about layer 3 switching available on the Web.

Figure 10–16 summarizes the layer-based networking components we have examined in this chapter, including the layer 3 switch. Let us see how these hardware components and protocols work together in an Internet service provider.

FIGURE 10–16
Network components and their associated layers.

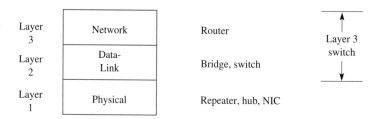

Layer 3	Network	Router	
Layer 2	Data-Link	Bridge, switch	Layer 3 switch
Layer 1	Physical	Repeater, hub, NIC	

■ INSIDE AN ISP

Figure 10–17 shows an overhead view of the networking and telecommunications room at a small ISP (Internet service provider). Along the east wall are the incoming phone lines (200 pairs), modem bank (groups of sixty-four 56K modems in a rack-mountable case), and the 44.736 Mbps T3 connection (to a higher-level ISP).

The west wall contains the routers and switches that make up the ISP topology and logical networks. The center of the room contains the server farm, where all of the servers

FIGURE 10–17
Overhead view of ISP network hardware.

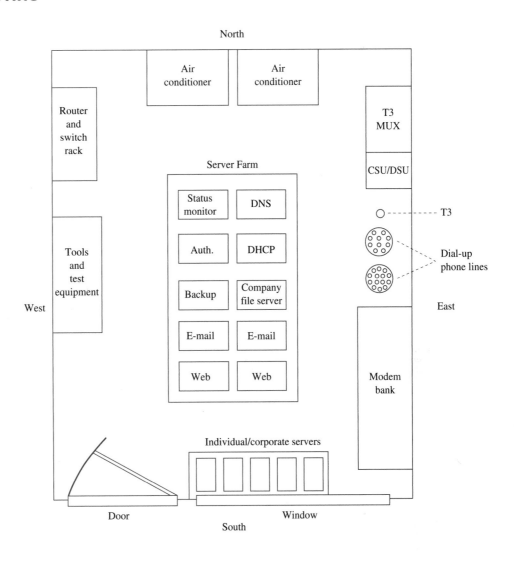

required for operation of the ISP reside. These include servers for DNS, DHCP, electronic mail, Web pages, and authentication. One machine is dedicated to monitoring the network (via SNMP) and another for performing backups.

The south wall contains server space for individual and corporate servers, which, along with the dial-up users, help generate income for the ISP.

Numerous UPS (uninterruptible power supply) units provide 30 minutes of power in the event of a main power loss.

Figure 10–18 illustrates the logical layout of the network. The T3 connection is the WAN connection to the higher-level ISP providing the actual Internet connection. Traffic in the T3 connection is filtered by the *firewall*. The I-router connects the individual subnetworks together and acts as the gateway to the Internet through the firewall. Employee computers, some of which have 100 Mbps switched service, communicate with their own file server or may tap into the server farm via the I-router. Individual and corporate servers share their own switch, as do the modems in the modem bank and the servers in the server farm. The F-router is used to lighten the load on the I-router for traffic moving between the server farm and the modem bank.

The network was designed in this fashion to allow the subnetworks to keep operating in the event that the main I-router goes down. Dial-up users can still check e-mail or work on their Web pages. Employees can continue to work as well, although without access to the Internet or the server farm.

Firewall

Objective 3-8

Objective 3-10

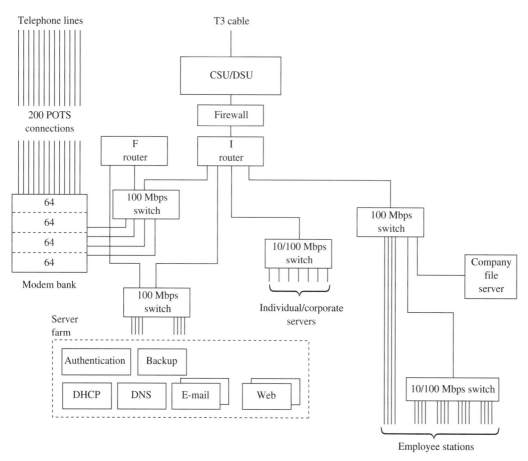

Telephone lines

T3 cable

200 POTS connections

Modem bank

Server farm

FIGURE 10–18
ISP network diagram.

■ TROUBLESHOOTING TECHNIQUES

It is good for network technicians and administrators to look at the big picture as well as concentrating on the little details. For example, a network administrator concerned with slow Internet access may first look for the cause in the local LAN. If no reason can be found in the LAN, the slowdown may be due to slow traffic over the WAN connection. Perhaps a router central to the traffic flow has failed. One interesting way to check on the status of routers all across the Internet, as well as traffic characteristics, is to use the Internet Traffic Report located at http://www.internettrafficreport.com. While this site does not necessarily provide any concrete network analysis information useful for troubleshooting specific problems, it does provide some interesting perspective on the general state of Internet-wide communications.

To discover information about the topology of the underlying networks on the Internet, visit http://www.caida.org. This site is hosted by the Cooperative Association for Internet Data Analysis. There is a great deal of information about the structure of the Internet at the CAIDA site. There are also many tools available at the site for attaining general Internet topology information.

Trouble at the ISP

Here are some actual problems encountered in ISP setups similar to the one described in Figures 10–17 and 10–18.

Objective 4-3

Problem #1: User Cannot Connect Using Modem, Part 2   A user installed a new modem and attempted to use the modem to dial in to an ISP to perform a speed test. The modem was not able to dial the ISP from a company phone line, but was able to dial from home. The user simply forgot to configure the modem to dial '9' while at work to get an outside line before dialing the ISP access number.

Objective 4-8

Problem #2: Domain Names Not Working   Several users call in to an ISP to report problems. Sample complaints include:

- "When I click on a link, my browser can't find the Web site."
- "PING doesn't work unless I use an IP address instead of a domain name."
- "I can't do anything with my e-mail program."
- "I'm entering FTP FTP.DSC.COM, just like I always do, and it just sits there."

Now, what does the IT technician make of all this? Users are having trouble with almost every network application commonly used. The one hint at the cause of the problem is the user reporting the PING problem. Since PING works with an IP address but not with a domain name, that suggests a problem with DNS. A problem with DNS would affect Web page requests, e-mail, FTP, Telnet, PING, TRACERT, browsers, and any network applications that reply on DNS to resolve domain names into IP addresses.

Once the IT technician suspected DNS as the cause of the problems, he examined the DNS server machine in the ISP server farm. It was off. A check of the DNS server revealed a faulty power supply.

Objective 4-6

Problem #3: Chat Does Not Work   A Web site hosted on an ISP provides a Java-based chat tool that has a Web interface. Some Internet users are not able to connect to the chat server.

The users that cannot connect to the chat server are all located behind firewalls that are blocking traffic through TCP port 8000, which is being used by the Java-based chat application for chat messages.

INDUSTRY TIP

When installing new networks there are a lot of choices that can be made with respect to type of equipment (hubs, switches, routers), which model to install, which features are important to the network, the budget of the customer, and so forth. When I contract for an installation job I normally have design documents indicating which products to install at what locations throughout the network. These design documents are normally developed during consultations between an individual trained in network design and the customer. Hubs are frequently used in areas such as offices where the bandwidth use is not excessive and where security is not a high concern. Hubs are much less expensive than switches and offer a cost-conscious solution for connecting many users to a common network segment. In areas that have a large number of users, you can use multiple hubs to connect groups of users and then uplink the hub connections into a switch. This provides a trade-off between an all switched network and a tight budget. Business must always be concerned with the bottom line of their balance sheet, and selling them a more expensive product than they need is a poor way to conduct business. A network of higher bandwidth usage, or with a need for increased security, is a good place to install switches instead of hubs. Switches provide dedicated bandwidth to each port, reducing the effect of collisions on common Ethernet networks. Switches also reduce the ability of network users to snoop on network traffic. As hacker tools become more common and easy to use, companies are finding out that a significant part of their security vulnerabilities are coming from inside employees. While using a switch does not eliminate all sniffing capabilities, it does place a simple and cost-effective obstacle to the casual hacker. Other network devices typically installed include routers and firewalls. Routers are normally used at the connection between a company's network and the ISP. In larger networks they are also placed in areas where the network is divided by network addressing schemes (layer 3 of the OSI model). In addition to routing traffic, routers can also provide many firewall services to help limit unwanted traffic (for security or traffic flow reasons). For more specific traffic flow control a dedicated firewall device is often installed. Advanced software firewall installations may want to use a product such as Check Point's firewall product. For a hardware-based solution to firewall needs consider using a PIX firewall from Cisco corporation. Cisco provides a large selection of firewall products to serve the needs of small businesses and large corporations.

CAREER DEVELOPMENT

When businesses install or upgrade their networks they often turn to professional network designers. These are individuals that are trained in how networks function, understand the protocols and applications used on networks, and maintain current knowledge of available solutions to meet the customer's needs. There are two network design certifications offered by the Cisco Corporation. The Cisco Certified Design Associate (CCDA) certification exam focuses on certifying individuals at a foundation or apprentice level of knowledge of design. According to the Cisco Web site: "CCDA certified professionals can design routed and switched network infrastructures involving LAN, WAN, and dial access services for businesses and organizations." At a more advanced level Cisco offers the Cisco Certified Design Professional (CCDP) certification. Individuals certified at this level possess advanced or journeyman knowledge of network design principles. According to Cisco, "With a CCDP, a network professional can design routed and switched networks involving LAN, WAN, and dial access services, applying modular design practices and making sure the whole solution responds optimally to the business and technical needs and is designed to be highly available. Content and storage application networking, voice/video applications, critical modern infrastructure services such as wireless access, and network services such as security and management, QoS, and multicast are also included." Statistics have shown that these individuals are of great value to an organization and individuals highly skilled in network design often earn high levels of pay and benefits. If you enjoy the network career field, and enjoy knowledge of how a network functions, you should consider attaining one of these respected certifications.

■ SELF-TEST

1. True or False: A hub will forward a frame to a specified port.

2. In the network represented below, Host A transmits a frame to Host D. Which of the listed devices will receive a copy of the frame?
   a. Host D
   b. Hosts C and D
   c. Hosts B, C, and D
   d. Hosts A, B, C, and D

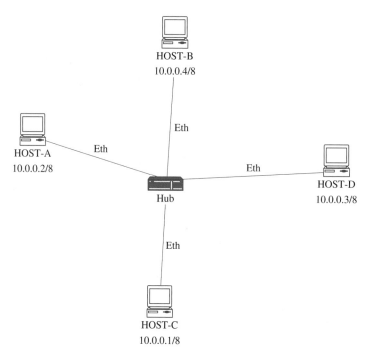

3. In the network represented below, how many collision domains exist in this portion of the network?

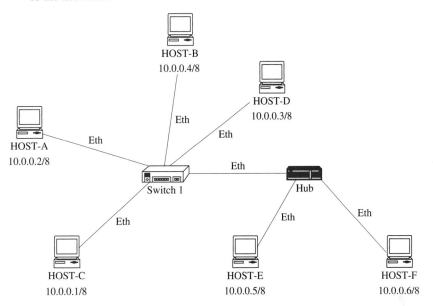

a. 2
b. 4
c. 5
d. 6

4. Which of the following is **not** a component of a switch?
a. Input port logic
b. Output port logic
c. Route port logic
d. Switching fabric
e. Control logic

5. Which switch component is responsible for updating and searching MAC address tables, configuring the switching fabric, and maintaining the flow through the switch fabric?
a. Input port logic
b. Output port logic
c. Switching fabric
d. Control logic

6. What is the high-speed memory called that stores copies of the source MAC addresses associated with each port on a switch?
a. RAM
b. CRAM
c. CAM
d. SDRAM

7. What type of switching requires only the destination address of the incoming frame before beginning the forwarding process?
a. Progressive
b. Multiplex
c. Store-and-forward
d. Cut-through

8. How many bytes of a frame must be received before the fragment-free switching method forwards the frame?
a. 32
b. 64
c. 128
d. Entire frame

9. True or False: Traffic exchanged between hosts on a local network within the same network segment requires the services of a router to exchange data locally.

10. Routers forward packets based on the information stored in the _____.
    a. CAM table
    b. routing table
    c. gateway host
    d. management workstation

11. What is the lifetime of a statically configured route?
    a. 1 day
    b. 1 month
    c. 1 year
    d. Infinite

12. Which of the following routing methods is considered fault tolerant?
    a. Static
    b. Dynamic
    c. Cut-through
    d. Store-and-forward

13. True or False: The link-state routing algorithm provides a view of the entire network.

14. _____ routing protocols converge more quickly than _____ routing protocols. (Choose two.)
    a. Distance-vector
    b. Static
    c. Link-state
    d. Autonomous

15. What command generated the output shown in the following figure?
    a. ipconfig
    b. netstat -r
    c. netstat -s
    d. netstat -S

16. A(n) _____ is defined as a network or group of networks controlled by a single administrative authority.
    a. autonomous system
    b. dynamic network
    c. internetwork
    d. interior gateway

17. _____ are used for communication inside autonomous systems.
    a. EGPs
    b. RFCs
    c. IGPs
    d. NTPs

18. What is a technique used to recover many unused IP addresses in class A and class B networks?
    a. BGP
    b. RCP
    c. CIDR
    d. IPv6

19. What is the metric advertised by distance-vector protocols to specify the shortest path to distant networks?
    a. Delay
    b. Hops
    c. Bandwidth
    d. Load

20. How often are RIP routing updates sent to a neighbor router?
    a. 5 seconds
    b. 30 seconds
    c. 60 seconds
    d. 90 seconds

21. What is a routing protocol feature used to eliminate routing loops by removing the routes from routing tables?
    a. Hold down
    b. Poison reverse
    c. Split horizon
    d. Flush

22. What is the routing protocol that provides communication between level 1 devices in the same area and between level 1 devices in different areas using level 2 intradomain backbones?
    a. IS-IS
    b. OSPF
    c. EIGRP
    d. BGP

23. _____ is a link-state routing protocol based on IS-IS and is characterized as the successor to IPX.
    a. IGP
    b. NLSP
    c. SPX
    d. OSPF

24. What does BGP use as a transport protocol to exchange routing information between neighbors?
    a. TCP
    b. UDP
    c. NCP
    d. IGP

25. Layer 3 switches utilize _____ technology to implement routing functions in hardware.
    a. QOS
    b. ASIC
    c. LMI
    d. SVC

Network Management and Security

PERFORMANCE OBJECTIVES

Upon completion of this chapter, you will be able to:

■ Discuss the various elements of network management and security.

■ Explain various encryption and authentication techniques.

■ Describe the purpose of IP masquerading and tunneling.

 ## NETWORK+ OBJECTIVES

This chapter provides information for the following Network+ objectives:

2.7 Identify the purpose of the following network services:
- DHCP/BOOTP
- DNS
- NAT/ICS
- WINS
- SNMP

2.13 Identify the following security protocols and describe their purpose and function:
- IPSec
- L2TP
- SSL
- Kerberos

3.4 Identify the main characteristics of network attached storage.

3.5 Identify the purpose and characteristics of fault tolerance.

3.6 Identify the purpose and characteristics of disaster recovery.

3.8 Identify the purpose, benefits, and characteristics of using a firewall.

3.9 Identify the purpose, benefits, and characteristics of using a proxy.

3.10 Given a scenario, predict the impact of a particular security implementation on network functionality (e.g., blocking port numbers, encryption, etc.).

4.3 Given a troubleshooting scenario involving a remote connectivity problem (e.g., authentication failure, protocol configuration, physical connectivity), identify the cause of the problem.

4.7 Given output from a diagnostic utility (e.g., TRACERT, PING, IPCONFIG, etc.), identify the utility and interpret the output.

■ INTRODUCTION

This chapter examines two important areas: network management and network security. Network management involves managing the network technologies to provide a business or organization a cost-efficient, reliable, secure computer network. Network security (a subset of network management) involves the methods used to protect the confidentiality and integrity of the organization's data while providing appropriate access for the intended users. This chapter also examines network storage management, another subset of network management.

■ NETWORK MANAGEMENT

Network management is one of the most important tasks that is performed in a networked computer environment. The network management function within a company or an organization is performed by a system administrator, network administrator, network manager, or network engineer. Planning what network topology is used, what computers are part of the network, how they participate in the network, what type of information they can access and share, how they get backed up, and how they get restored in the event of a hard drive crash or corruption are each an essential element of network management. Other important elements include how physical access to the network hardware is granted, how network printers are configured, and how other network resources can be shared. Each of the essential elements requires careful planning and record keeping to maintain a current view (or status) of the network. These items can be expanded into several different categories that must be reviewed. A partial list of these categories follows:

- System hardware and software configuration and management
- Network storage management
- Users (permissions, access times)
- Time (for applications using NTP)
- Security management
- Traffic management
- Performance management
- Hardware and software maintenance
- Disaster planning and backup management
- Consulting and outside resource management

In addition to these items, a network manager must also answer a host of questions and concerns that involve reviewing and selecting new network technology. Some of these concerns are:

- What can a new technology do for a business?
- How is the current environment affected?
- What is the cost of new technology?
- What is the learning curve associated with new technology?
- What are the risks?
- How does it compare with alternative technologies?
- How would the new technology affect business partners?
- How does the new technology impact clients and customers?
- What effect will the new technology have on employees?
- If the technology breaks, how does it affect the rest of the network?
- How easily can the technology be repaired?

- Can the technology be made fault tolerant?
- How difficult is the technology to administer and maintain?
- Can existing staff manage the new technology?
- Will retraining of staff be required? How much will it cost?
- What are the recurring costs associated with the technology?
- What is the useful life of the new technology?
- How does the technology compare with that of other companies or organizations of about the same size?
- What technologies are other companies and organizations using?

Obviously, some of these questions require an investment of time and energy to perform the necessary research and to make an informed decision.

Disaster Recovery

Objective 3-6

What types of disasters could occur in a computer lab or network operations center? A short list serves up a note of caution:

- Fire (and possibly additional water damage from the fire-fighting efforts), flood, earthquake, or other natural phenomena
- Theft
- Catastrophic power loss
- An electrical storm
- Intrusion by hackers
- Intentional damage caused by a disgruntled employee
- Viruses
- Accidents (janitor spills coffee into mainframe or trips over equipment)

Planning for disasters involves methods designed to reduce or eliminate threats, as well as knowing how to recover when a disaster occurs.

A number of safeguards can be used to help guarantee a relatively quick and painless recovery. They include the following:

- Maintain up-to-date off-site backups.
- Use an uninterruptible power supply (UPS) on critical systems.
- Maintain an inventory of spare components.
- Secure and monitor all equipment adequately.
- Restrict access to sensitive equipment.
- Use fiber for external building-to-building connections instead of copper wire.

Fault Tolerance

Objective 3-5

Joining hand-in-hand with a good disaster recovery plan should be some form of fault tolerance. Fault tolerance is the capability of a system to withstand a hardware or software fault and keep functioning. For example, losing an entire hard drive in a multidrive system would be very bad. Having a backup archive adds a degree of fault tolerance because the system can be restored to an operational state in a short period of time. Using RAID would offer even more fault tolerance, with the capability of rebuilding all the missing hard drive data.

RAID

RAID stands for Redundant Array of Inexpensive Disks. Figure 11–1 shows a RAID-based server computer.

Four hot swappable drives are shown at the lower right of the unit. A system using RAID uses two or more hard drives to implement fault tolerance. There are six levels of

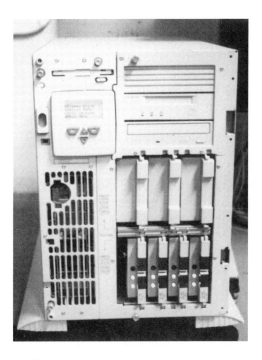

RAID and modern systems may support any or all of them. The three most common implementations of RAID in use on modern systems are listed below:

- *RAID Level 0:* Stripe Sets
- *RAID Level 1:* Disk Mirroring
- *RAID Level 5:* Stripe Sets with Parity

Let's examine the features of these technologies.

RAID Level 0: Stripe sets   In this technique, files are read/written in 64K chunks simultaneously using from 2 to 32 physical drives. The data is not duplicated. Figure 11–2 shows how two drives are used to store a large file.

FIGURE 11–2
RAID level 0: Stripe sets.

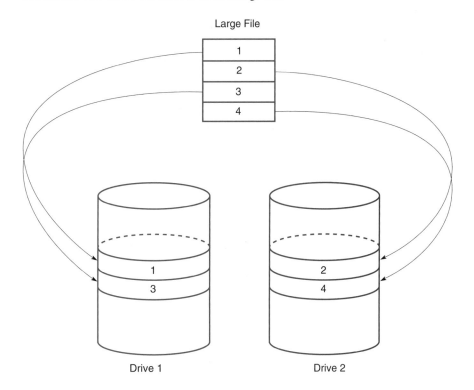

It is important to note that using a stripe set does not provide fault tolerance, since data is not duplicated on the drives. Performance is improved, however, because of the parallelism available during reads and writes. For example, the large file in Figure 11–2 requires only two reads from each disk to access the entire file. Each read brings in 128K (64K from each disk at the same time). Write operations are similarly improved. This is a big advantage in speed-conscious environments since the physical movement of the hard drive heads is the biggest speed bottleneck during read and write operations. A disadvantage to using stripe sets is that system and boot partitions may not be stored on them.

RAID Level 1: Disk Mirroring   Disk mirroring is used to make an *exact* copy of data on two drives. Data is written to both drives simultaneously. If one drive fails, the second drive still has a good copy of the data, so the system is not affected. Both system and boot partitions may be mirrored. Figure 11–3 shows how a file is mirrored.

FIGURE 11–3
RAID level 1: Disk mirroring.

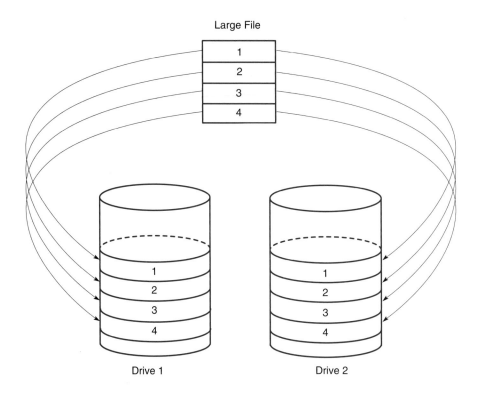

Typically, one controller is used to control both drives. A special variation of disk mirroring is *disk duplexing*, in which each drive has its own controller. This provides additional fault tolerance, since now a drive or a controller may fail without seriously affecting the system.

A disadvantage to using disk mirroring is that you get only 50% of the hard drive space you pay for. For example, using two 8 GB drives only provides 8 GB of storage capacity. Using the same drives in a stripe set would provide 16 GB of capacity (but no fault tolerance).

RAID Level 5: Stripe Sets with Parity   This technique is similar to ordinary stripe sets, except parity information is also written to each disk, as indicated in Figure 11–4. If one of the drives in the stripe set fails, the parity data stored on each drive can be used to reconstruct the missing data.

FIGURE 11–4
RAID level 5: Stripe sets with parity.

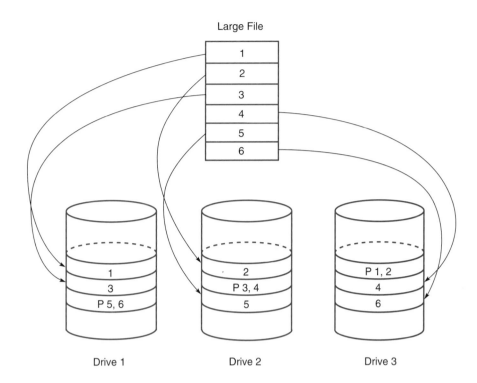

A minimum of three drives must be used to employ RAID level 5. The equivalent of one drive is used for parity information, even though parity is distributed across all drives. The available data capacity can be found by the following equation:

$$\text{Capacity} = ((\text{Drives} - 1)/\text{Drives}) \times 100\%$$

With three drives, the available storage capacity for data is 66 percent. For four drives, the capacity becomes 75 percent.

RAID can be implemented in software or hardware. When RAID is implemented in software the splitting of the file, and creation of the parity information, is performed in the main CPU and system RAM. When using software-based RAID, file servers should be equipped with enough CPU power and RAM to handle the additional workload. Implementing RAID in hardware requires the purchase of a special RAID daughterboard (an auxiliary system card that plugs into the motherboard of the server). When implementing RAID in this manner, the server's CPU will redirect the file to the RAID daughterboard, which will perform the RAID operations using the processor and RAM contained on the daughterboard. This takes the burden of the RAID process off the main server CPU and RAM but requires an initial hardware investment above the cost of the main server components. The decision between implementing RAID in software versus hardware should be based on server performance levels versus budget. If server performance is the primary issue, implement RAID in hardware. If the budget is the primary issue, implement RAID in software.

How else can servers (or even workstations) utilize fault tolerance? Redundant hardware provides many of the answers, including dual power supplies, two or more NICs in a single machine (possibly connected to parallel, but independent, networks), and even mirrored computers performing identical functions.

An institution may utilize two or more different connections to the Internet through its router to provide fault tolerance. For example, two T1 connections, each to different off-site ISPs, can be used with a load-balancing router. If one T1 goes off-line, the institution still has access to the Internet.

For networks that require high reliability, the money spent on fault tolerance is more than worth the expense.

Protocol Analyzers

Objective 4-7

The protocol analyzer is used to report the traffic type and usage on a computer network. The purpose of a protocol analyzer is to quickly identify network problems. Using the information provided by a protocol analyzer, it is easier to proactively monitor and plan for future network growth. Many different companies such as Network General Corporation, Fluke, and Cisco provide equipment and software to monitor and analyze network traffic.

Protocol analyzers connect to the network, and collect statistical information about the network performance. These statistics are usually converted into graphical real-time views that are useful to identify and isolate network problems. It must be noted that protocol analyzers analyze only the traffic of the segment on which they are connected. To monitor the whole network, one would need to attach the protocol analyzer to each segment or obtain "probes" to bring in the distant network segment. Ethereal provides a breakdown of the protocols in a small window, as shown in Figure 11–5. Notice that a small set of protocol categories are provided. These numbers are updated in real time as Ethereal monitors the network traffic. Review Appendix E for additional information on Ethereal.

FIGURE 11–5
Ethereal window showing protocol statistics.

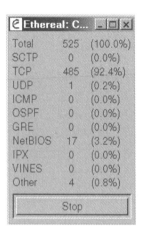

The RMON and RMON2 standards provide for support of packet capturing and protocol decoding. Using these standards, it is almost as easy to access data from remote network locations as it is to access it from the local segment of a LAN. RMON allows traffic monitoring at the MAC layer and the RMON2 standard provides access to information at higher layers in the protocol stack. RMON2 can provide access to additional information such as the protocol breakdown by the following:

• Segment
• Network address
• Traffic between different network addresses
• Application layer for a network address
• Application layer for exchanges between different network addresses

The Simple Network Management Protocol provides support for these standards.

SNMP

Objective 2-7

Unlike a protocol analyzer, the mechanism to gather the statistics on a device-by-device basis is performed using the Simple Network Management Protocol, or SNMP. Network devices that are categorized as *managed* support SNMP. These devices include hubs, switches, routers, and other network devices. SNMP has existed since 1990 and is described by various RFCs. SNMP uses *agents* to gather network statistics and *management stations* to report on the data.

SNMP has become very popular because of its usefulness and simplicity of use. Four operations involved in SNMP are shown in Table 11–1. Of these four operations, GET and GET-NEXT are used to retrieve the information from the managed device; the SET operation is used to manage (create or modify) the network object; and the TRAP operation is used to capture network events of interest.

TABLE 11–1
Fundamental simple network management protocol operations.

Operation	Description
GET	Retrieve a specific object
GET-NEXT	Retrieve a collection of objects in a MIB tree
SET	Create or modify a specific object
TRAP	Send notification of an event to a management station

To fully understand how SNMP is used, examine its three categories of communication. Together, they define the full scope of how SNMP is used.

The first category is the *SNMP protocol* itself, which specifies the format of SNMP messages and the rules on how the messages are exchanged.

The second category to consider is the rules for specifying what type of management information is collected. These rules are called the *structure of management information*, or SMI. The SMI rules are used both to name and define the individual objects that we choose to manage.

Third, how the information is organized and used should be analyzed. The *management information base*, or MIB, is a collection of the entire list of managed objects used by a device.

With this set of tools available to the network administrator, you can begin to focus your attention on the area of network security.

■ NETWORK SECURITY

Objective 3-6

Network security begins with the security measures in place on a host computer. Protection of files and limited access to resources are simple measures that can be instituted on every host. With adequate measures in place for the hosts, the network security issues can be addressed. Network security can be grouped into two categories: the methods used to secure the data and the methods used to regulate what data can be transmitted.

The methods used to secure data can go from one extreme, in which a computer should not even be connected to a network, to the other, in which all of the information on a computer can be publicly accessed. A middle-of-the-road approach is usually adequate for most businesses and organizations. Securing a host is often accomplished using a variety of virus scanning software, an encryption process, and restricting the rights and access that users have on the specific host. Access to data is normally allowed on a "need to know" basis.

The methods used to regulate the transmission of data are accomplished by placing devices (router, firewall, etc.) between the data and the users. If the transmission of the data is authorized, the transmission is allowed; otherwise, the transmission is blocked and a notification sent to the security administrator.

To gain a better understanding, it is useful to be knowledgeable about the types of threats and the types of problems that a security administrator faces on a daily basis.

Threats

The threats to a networked computer environment are many. Essentially, the goal for networked computers is to transmit information from a source location to a destination, as shown in Figure 11–6. Figure 11–6(a) shows a rather simplistic view of the exchange of information between a source and a destination location. In practice, the communication may be encrypted for added security, or IP tunneling may be employed to further restrict access to sensitive information. Figure 11–6(b) through Figure 11–6(e) show several different scenarios that are commonly associated with exchanging information between computers.

FIGURE 11–6
Typical information exchange scenarios between A and B.

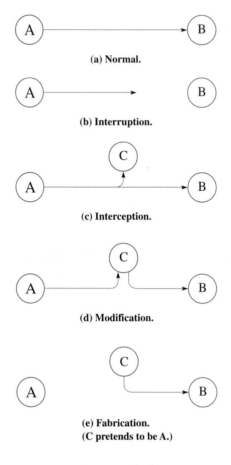

Different security measures are employed to deal with each of the problems highlighted in Figure 11–6. Table 11–2 describes the common security measures that are employed to strengthen network security.

TABLE 11–2
Different types of security measures.

Security Measure	Description
Accessibility	Allow access to information on a restricted basis
Authentication	Correctly identify the origin of an electronic message
Availability	Make sure that computer resources are available when needed
Confidentiality	Allow only authorized parties to access information
Integrity	Allow only authorized parties to update information
Nonrepudiation	Provide a mechanism to prevent the sender the ability to deny having sent an electronic transmission

One of the most commonly encountered scenarios in a computer network involves computer viruses. A computer virus can infect a corporate network, small business, or personal computer and stop or reduce regular network activity.

Viruses

Objective 3-5

Objective 3-6

A computer *virus* is a piece of software that has been written to enter a computer system and corrupt the files on the hard drive or cause other host operational problems. Some computer viruses are a nuisance, like the common cold, and others can render your computer worthless, often requiring a complete operating system and software reload. With more than 50,000 known strains, the chances that your computer will contract one at some point are high unless you employ active virus scanning procedures and keep the anti-virus software updated. A technician managing a network must consider viruses as a major threat to its stability. Some viruses generate large amounts of network traffic, thereby affecting the overall performance of the network. Others attack files, typically corrupting them beyond repair. Backup archives of all system and user files from all servers (and possibly even workstations) are thus very important, and a frequent backup plan must be in place and operational. To maintain a high level of fault tolerance, the backup archives should be stored in a separate location, within a fireproof safe or container. Some companies use an off-site storage area network to maintain high-speed access to archived data. Only with a safe copy of all critical files will an institution be able to survive a devastating virus attack on its network. Any disaster plan should pay significant attention to backup procedures and invest in up-to-date virus scanning technology.

Computer viruses are categorized into four main types: boot sector, file or program, macro, and multipartite viruses.

- **Boot sector viruses** are usually transmitted when an infected floppy disk is left in the drive and the system is rebooted. The virus is read from the infected boot sector of the floppy disk and written to the master boot record of the system's hard drive. The master boot sector is the first place your system reads from when booting up from the hard drive. Then, whenever the computer is booted up, the virus will be loaded into the system's memory.

- **Program or file viruses** are pieces of viral code that attach themselves to executable programs. Once the infected program is run, the virus is transferred to your system's memory and may replicate itself further.

- **Macro viruses** are currently the most commonly found viruses. They infect files run by applications that use macro languages, like Microsoft Word or Excel. The virus looks like a macro in the file, and when the file is opened, the virus can execute commands understood by the application's macro language.

- **Multipartite viruses** have characteristics of both boot sector viruses and file viruses. They may start out in the boot sector and spread to applications, or vice versa.

Although they are not technically viruses, other malicious programs such as worms and Trojan horses usually are included in the virus category. They typically have the same type of results as viruses and are written to wreak havoc on a system or network, or both. The latest types of viruses are called *stealth*, *polymorphic*, and *armored*.

Worm

A *worm* is a program that replicates itself, but does not necessarily infect other programs. The Melissa and ILOVEYOU e-mail viruses that caused widespread problems are good examples of worms. These worms replicated themselves using e-mail systems, making use of Microsoft Outlook address books.

Trojan horses

Trojan horses (as in Greek mythology) contain a concealed surprise. A Trojan horse program resides hidden in another seemingly harmless piece of software until some condition triggers execution.

Viruses can be written to affect almost any type of file, so it is important to be aware of this when installing software on a system. Note that there are many instances of viruses being accidentally included in licensed, shrink-wrapped software, although you are generally safe when installing legally purchased software that has been obtained through normal channels.

The process of tracking and developing methods to render a computer virus harmless is big business since viruses can affect governments, corporations, educational institutions, and individuals. As far as network and security administrators are concerned, what is important is virus prevention, virus detection, and virus elimination, in that order. With proper virus prevention safeguards, it is likely that a catastrophic event can be avoided. Unfortunately, a virus is not the only threat to a computer network.

Network Sniffers

Network sniffer

A *network sniffer* is a specific variation of the generic protocol analyzer. Using a network sniffer, it is possible for network traffic to be captured and decoded. This includes passwords, trade secrets, or other proprietary information that may be considered highly confidential. A network sniffer operates in a passive mode. The device is attached to the network and then proceeds to silently collect information. After a period of time, the contents of the data that have been collected can be reviewed and the sensitive information extracted. This is one of the worst types of security breaches due to the fact that often no one knows that network security has been compromised. Network sniffers work by making NICs function in the promiscuous mode. This means that instead of just listening to messages addressed to their MAC address, and the broadcast MAC address, they will listen to all messages sent on the media that they are attached to. Occasionally there are techniques to detect a network sniffer depending on which NIC is in use, or how the sniffer software responds to some network transmission, but it is often impossible to detect these sniffers on a network.

Plain-Text Encryption

A first line of defense in protecting network data is to prevent passwords from being exchanged on the network in plain text. It may be helpful to review the common terms associated with network security shown in Table 11–3 before continuing.

TABLE 11–3
Common terminology used in computer and network security.

Term	Description
Cipher	The method used to encrypt and decrypt data
Ciphertext	An encrypted message
Cleartext	Original data in unmodified form
Cryptography	Process to encode data to keep information secret
Cryptoanalysis	Process to break a ciphertext message without knowledge of the key
Cryptology	Branch of mathematics that studies cryptographic methods
Decryption	Retrieving a plain text message from Ciphertext
DES	Data Encryption Standard
DSS	Digital Signature Standard
Key	A secret key used to encrypt or decrypt data
NIST	National Institute of Standards and Technology
NSA	National Security Agency
Plain text	Original data in unmodified form
Private Key	A key used to decrypt a message
Public Key	A key used to encrypt a message
RSA	Rivest-Shamir-Adelman encryption algorithm

One of the methods used to prevent disclosure of sensitive information, such as a password, is to *encrypt* it. In a Windows environment, the password used to gain access to a domain must be transmitted to the server for authentication. While in transit, the packet can be intercepted and decoded. For example, examine the following decoded NetBIOS packet. Note in particular the information between addresses 0030 and 0070:

```
Destination     Source          Protocol      Summary        Size    Time Tick
----------------------------------------------------------------------------------
200.200.200.255  200.200.200.200  SMB C Transaction  UDP NETBIOS Datagram Service
268     12/13/99 13:46:41.415


Addr.   Hex. Data                                       ASCII
0000:   FF FF FF FF FF FF 00 C0 F0 25 0B 2A 08 00 45 00  .........%.*..E.
0010:   00 FE 39 00 00 00 80 11 DD 95 C8 C8 C8 C8 C8 C8  ..9.............
0020:   C8 FF 00 8A 00 8A 00 EA 9C CD 11 02 00 3E C8 C8  .............>..
0030:   C8 C8 00 8A 00 D4 00 00 20 45 45 46 43 45 50 45  ........EEFCEPE
0040:   4F 45 46 44 43 43 41 43 41 43 41 43 41 43 41 43  OEFDCCACACACACAC
0050:   41 43 41 43 41 43 41 41 41 00 20 46 43 45 42 46  ACACACAAA.FCEBF
0060:   4A 45 44 45 42 46 44 46 45 43 41 43 41 43 41 43  JEDEBFDFECACACAC
0070:   41 43 41 43 41 43 41 43 41 42 4F 00 FF 53 4D 42  ACACACACABO..SMB
0080:   25 00 00 00 00 00 00 00 00 00 00 00 00 00 00 00  %...............
0090:   00 00 00 00 00 00 00 00 00 00 00 00 11 00 00 3A  ...............:
00A0:   00 00 00 00 00 00 00 00 00 00 00 00 00 00 00 00  ................
00B0:   00 00 00 3A 00 56 00 03 00 01 00 01 00 02 00 4B  ...:.V.........K
00C0:   00 5C 4D 41 49 4C 53 4C 4F 54 5C 42 52 4F 57 53  .\MAILSLOT\BROWS
00D0:   45 00 0F 07 C0 D4 01 00 44 52 4F 4E 45 32 00 00  E.......DRONE2..
00E0:   00 00 00 00 00 00 00 04 00 03 20 45 00 15 04  ........... E...
00F0:   55 AA 76 69 64 65 6F 2F 6E 65 74 77 6F 72 6B 20  U.video/network
0100:   65 6E 67 69 6E 65 65 72 69 6E 67 00              engineering.


802.3 [0000:000D]
  0000:0005   Destination Address: FFFFFFFFFFFF (Broadcast)
  0006:000B   Source Address: 00C0F0250B2A (Kingston250B2A)
  000C:000D   Ethernet Type: DOD Internet Protocol (IP)
IP [000E:0021]
  000E:000E   Version: 4, Header Length: 20
  000F:000F   TOS, Precedence: Routine, Delay: Normal, Throughput: Normal,
             Reliability: Normal
  0010:0011   Packet Length: 254
  0012:0013   Identification: 0x3900
  0014:0014   Fragment Flag (bit 6..5): Undefined
  0014:0015   Fragment Offset: 0x0000
  0016:0016   Time to Live: 128
  0017:0017   Transport: User Datagram
  0018:0019   Header Checksum: 0xDD95
  001A:001D   Source Address: 200.200.200.200
  001E:0021   Destination Address: 200.200.200.255
UDP [0022:0029]
  0022:0023   Source Port: NETBIOS Datagram Service
  0024:0025   Destination Port: NETBIOS Datagram Service
  0026:0027   Packet Length: 234
  0028:0029   Checksum: 0x9CCD
NETBIOS [002A:007B]
  002A:002A   Type: Direct Group Datagram
  002B:002B   Flags: 0x02
  002C:002D   ID: 62
  002E:0031   Source IP: 200.200.200.200
  0032:0033   Source Port: 0x008A
  0034:0035   Length: 212
```

```
0036:0037   Packet Offset: 0
0038:0059   Source Name: DRONE2
005A:007B   Destination Name: RAYCAST
SMB [007C:009B]
007C:007F   ID: 0xFF, 'SMB'
0080:0080   Command Code: Transaction (Client Command)
0081:0081   Error Class: Success
0082:0082   Reserved: 0
0083:0084   Error Code: Success
0085:0085   Flag: 0x00
0086:0087   Flag2: 0x0000
0088:0093   Reserved: Not Used
0094:0095   Tree ID: 0x0000
0096:0097   Process ID: 0x0000
0098:0099   User ID: 0x0000
009A:009B   Multiplex ID: 0x0000
```

The plain-text encryption used by NetBIOS is plainly illustrated. The encoded text beginning at address 0039 is EEFCEPEOEFDCCACACACACACACACAAA. To decode this text string, we find the difference between each letter and A. Each pair of difference values makes an ASCII code representing the original symbol encoded. For example, the EE codes become 44 (E minus A is 4), which is the hexadecimal code for an ASCII D. The next two characters, FC, become 52, which is the hex code for an ASCII R. Figure 11–7 illustrates this process for the entire string, which encodes the NetBIOS name DRONE2. All of the CA codes represent blanks used to pad out the 15-character NetBIOS name field. Verify for yourself that the encoded text beginning at address 005B represents the name RAYCAST. Though not difficult to crack, the NetBIOS plain-text encryption provides an easy way to provide a small measure of security to your networked resources. A more reliable method to allow access is based on authentication services that are available on some operating systems.

FIGURE 11–7
Decoding NetBIOS names.

$$|\text{EE}|\text{FC}|\text{EP}|\text{EO}|\text{EF}|\text{DC}|\text{CA}|\text{CA}|\cdots|\text{CA}|\text{AA}|$$

EE becomes 44, which is an ASCII D.
FC becomes 52, which is an ASCII R.
EP becomes 4F*, which is an ASCII O.
EO becomes 4E*, which is an ASCII N.
EF becomes 45, which is an ASCII E.
DC becomes 32, which is an ASCII 2.
CA becomes 20, which is a blank.
AA becomes 00, which signifies the end of the name.

*Note that P–A = 15, which is a hexadecimal F.
O–A = 14, which is a hexadecimal E.

Kerberos

Kerberos

Objective 2-13

Kerberos is an authentication service developed at the Massachusetts Institute of Technology. Kerberos uses secret-key ciphers for encryption and authentication. Kerberos was designed to authenticate requests for network resources rather than to authenticate ownership of documents.

In a Kerberos environment, there is a designated site on each network, called the Kerberos server, that performs centralized key management and administrative functions. The server maintains a database containing the secret keys of all users, authenticates the identities of users, and distributes session keys to users and servers who want to authenticate one another. Kerberos requires trust in a third party (the Kerberos server). If the server is compromised, the integrity of the whole system is lost. Public-key cryptography was designed precisely to avoid the necessity of trusting third parties with secret information. Kerberos is generally considered adequate within an administrative domain; however, across domains the more robust functions and properties of public-key systems are preferred. There has been some developmental work to incorporate public-key cryptography into Kerberos.

SSL

Secure Sockets Layer (SSL)

Objective 2-13

The *Secure Sockets Layer (SSL)* is a protocol developed by Netscape to facilitate secure communication on the Internet. SSL uses public-key encryption to encrypt the data before it is transmitted. Both Netscape Navigator and Microsoft Internet Explorer (as well as many other Internet applications) support SSL. To enable the use of SSL transmissions, the URL specifies the https protocol rather than http.

SSL is used to create a secure channel between the client and the server over which any amount of data can be transmitted. The SSL protocol is implemented between the network protocol layer and the application layer of the TCP/IP stack as illustrated in Figure 11–8. This allows an SSL-enabled server to authenticate itself to an SSL-enabled client, allows the client to authenticate itself to the server, and allows both machines to establish an encrypted connection. To enable SSL sessions, it is necessary to get a digital certificate for the server.

The SSL protocol includes two sub-protocols: the SSL record protocol and the SSL handshake protocol. The SSL record protocol defines the format necessary to transmit data, and the SSL handshake protocol uses the SSL record protocol to ex-

FIGURE 11–8
TCP/IP protocol stack.

Applications
SSL
TCP/UDP Transport

change messages between an SSL-enabled server and an SSL-enabled client when they first establish an SSL connection. This exchange of messages is designed to facilitate the following actions:

- Authenticate the server to the client
- Allow the client and server to select the cryptographic algorithms, or ciphers, that they both support
- Optionally authenticate the client to the server
- Use public-key encryption techniques to generate shared secrets
- Establish an encrypted SSL connection

SSL comes in two strengths: 40-bit and 128-bit. This number refers to the length of the session key generated by every encrypted transaction. The longer the key, the more difficult it is to break the encryption code. Most browsers support 40-bit SSL sessions. The latest browsers provide users the ability to encrypt transactions in 128-bit key sessions. SSL has been adopted as a standard by the Internet Engineering Task Force (IETF).

Public-Key Encryption

As the name indicates, *public-key encryption* uses a public key. Public-key encryption actually uses two keys: one public key and one private key. The public key is used to encrypt the data to be transmitted. The public key cannot be used to decrypt the data. Instead, the private key is used to decrypt the data. This eliminates the problem with other encryption technologies in which the same key is used to encrypt and decrypt the data. Public-key encryption is a more convenient method to encrypt and decrypt the data, since the public key can be posted for public access. Only the private key must be guarded very carefully and protected from disclosure.

In public-key encryption, the public keys for individuals are stored on a public key ring. As messages are created, the public key ring can be accessed and the appropriate public key used to encrypt the message so that only the receiver of the message (with the corresponding private key) can decode the message and read it. This procedure is shown in Figure 11–9.

FIGURE 11–9
Information exchange using public-key encryption.

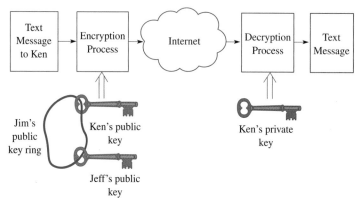

(a) Encryption.

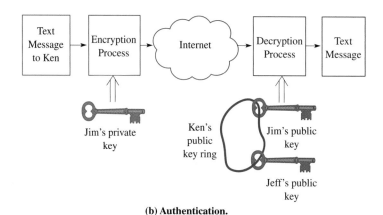

(b) Authentication.

Notice that Jim's key ring contains entries for Ken and Jeff. When a message is composed and sent to Ken, Ken's public key is used to encrypt the message. While the encrypted message is transmitted on the network, the message contents cannot be examined. Only Ken, the receiver of the message, can decrypt and read the message text.

Certificates

A *certificate* is a method used to help guarantee that the sender of an e-mail message is who they say they are. Certificates are digital verifications signifying that someone is who they claim to be. Certificates are issued by certificate authorities (CAs). Many corporations, such as Microsoft, establish their own CAs and then use their own issued certificates to verify that the software you are downloading from their Web site is valid software distributed by them. If an individual or organization wants to use a third-party CA they can contact one of the many commercial CAs such as Verisign. These third-party CAs are widely known and trusted.

Certificates are necessary because it is important to know who it is that you are communicating with. They provide an opportunity to:

- Manage Web site domain names and server certificates
- Safeguard network resources using public-key encryption
- Secure network applications such as e-mail and messaging
- Enable e-commerce applications that support online payments and purchases

Certificates of authority are a necessary element in virtual private networks, business-to-business communications, secure e-mail, Web server certificates, wireless server certificates, and application security.

PGP

PGP

Objective 3-10

PGP (Pretty Good Privacy) is a security application produced by Phil Zimmermann. PGP provides confidentiality and authentication services that can be used with electronic messages as well as file storage applications. PGP has gained significant popularity because of the following important elements:

- Uses the best cryptographic algorithms as basic building blocks, including public-key encryption and certificates of authority
- Unlimited distribution of source code and documentation
- Not controlled by a government or other standards organization

Specifically, PGP provides support mechanisms for digital signatures, message encryption, compression, and transparent compatibility with many application programs.

PGP provides an easy method to begin corresponding with a person who prefers to use encrypted messaging. The PGP freeware can be downloaded from the MIT Web server using the following address: http://web.mit.edu/network/pgp.html

After the PGP software has been downloaded and installed, it is necessary to generate the key pair (one public key and one private key), publish the keys to the PGP server, and create public and private key rings. Depending on the type of e-mail software in use, the appropriate plug-in is installed.

The PGP tools program menu is the launching pad for most PGP-related activities. Actions that can be selected directly are the PGP keys program, encrypt a file or message, sign a message, encrypt and sign a message, decrypt and verify a message, and wipe files or free information from a disk.

Spoofing

Spoofing takes on several different forms in computer networking and networking security. As a threat, or attack, spoofing can be used to enable one party to masquerade as another party.

IP spoofing is a technique used in a network or system attack in which the attacking computer assumes the identity of a computer in the internal network. The attacking computer spoofs or imitates the IP address of the internal computer either to send data as if they were on the internal network or to receive data intended for the machine being spoofed.

Firewalls

Objective 3-8

A *firewall* is a software program or hardware device that examines information packets to determine whether or not to allow the communication exchange to occur. Figure 11–10 shows how a firewall is used to protect an internal network from external access. Notice that some network traffic may be blocked from passing through the firewall in either direction, whereas other traffic passes freely.

FIGURE 11–10
Communication networks
connected to a firewall.

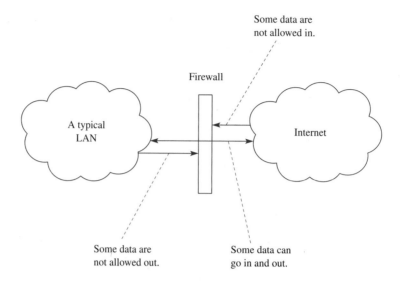

When a firewall is used within an organization, it must be placed in a strategic location to prevent access to the private information but at the same time allow access to the public. As you can see from Figure 11–11, the firewall is placed between the public and private networks and allows packets to be exchanged based on rules determined by the network/security administrator.

FIGURE 11–11
Placement of a firewall in a
networked environment.

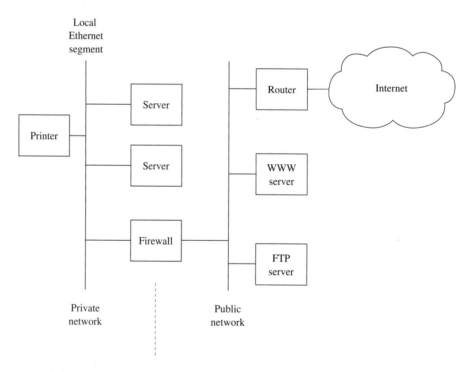

A firewall product called ZoneAlarm is available for users who want a software-based firewall. Individuals that maintain always-on broadband connections, such as Digital Subscription Line (DSL) and cable modem services, are strongly encouraged to download and install at least the free version of this product. You can find this software at www.zonelabs.com. To check a computer for some basic vulnerabilities visit Gibson Research Corporation at www.grc.com for a friendly interrogation using the Shields Up program.

Proxy Server

Objective 3-9

A proxy server is a server-type application program that is positioned between a user workstation and the Internet so that an organization can provide an additional level of administrative control, an optional caching service, and a higher level of security by providing the ability to monitor and log network activity. A proxy server is typically used in conjunction with a gateway to isolate a LAN from the Internet and to protect the network from intruders.

The proxy server receives requests from users on the LAN (such as Web pages). The proxy server looks in its local cache (assuming the caching feature is enabled) of previously downloaded Web pages and, if the page is found, it is returned to the user without the need to send the request out to the Internet. If the page is not found in the local cache, the proxy server requests the page from the remote Web server. When the page is returned, the proxy server caches the page contents and then forwards the response to the user.

From the user's point of view, the proxy server is transparent, with the exception that the proxy server's IP address must be added during configuration of the browser. One advantage of using a proxy server is that the cache can serve all the users on a LAN. Popular Web pages are likely to be stored in the proxy server's cache, which improves response time to the user.

The functions of a proxy server/caching server and a firewall may be written as separate programs or combined in a single program. These programs may be located in the same computer or different computers depending on the needs of the organization. For example, a proxy server may run on the same machine as the firewall server, or it may be located on a separate server that forwards the requests through the firewall. In either case, the proxy server can be a valuable addition, saving both time and precious network bandwidth.

IP Security

IPSec

Objective 2-13

IPSec (IP security) provides the capability to secure communications across a LAN, between public and private networks, and across the Internet. IPSec can be used to secure the transmission of data in the following situations:

- Secure branch office connectivity using the Internet
- Secure remote access to a user connected by an ISP
- Secure access to business partners

IPSec is incorporated into the TCP/IP protocol stack below the UDP and TCP transport protocols. This means that there is no need to modify the software on a system or user computer.

Tunneling

Objective 2-13

Tunneling is a security measure that uses the public network infrastructure, such as the Internet, as part of a private network. When data is transmitted on the network, it is encapsulated in such a way that the original source address, destination address, and payload data are encrypted. This is illustrated in Figure 11–12. A user who captures these encrypted packets cannot determine any information about the packet contents other than the source and destination addresses of the captured packet header, which provides no additional insight.

FIGURE 11–12
Tunnel-mode encryption and authentication.

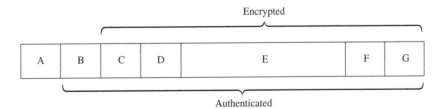

A—New IP header
B—Encapsulating Security Payload (ESP) headers
C—Original IP header
D—TCP header
E—Data
F—ESP trailer
G—ESP authentication data

L2TP

Objective 2-13

The Layer 2 Tunneling Protocol (L2TP) is a combination of the Point-to-Point Protocol (from Microsoft) and the Layer 2 Forwarding Protocol (from Cisco). L2TP is the standard tunneling protocol for VPNs, which are implemented by many ISPs. Typically, a user obtains a layer 2 connection to a Network Access Server (NAS) using one of a number of techniques (e.g., dial-up POTS, ISDN, ADSL, etc.) and then runs PPP over that connection. Figure 11–13 illustrates how an L2TP stack is implemented.

FIGURE 11–13
L2TP protocol structure.

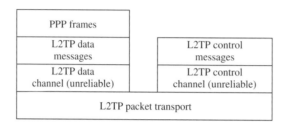

Multiple protocols can be encapsulated within the tunnel, making L2TP very versatile. Note that the network routers, or other gateway device, must support the use of L2TP. The format of the L2TP header is shown in Figure 11–14.

FIGURE 11–14
L2TP packet format.

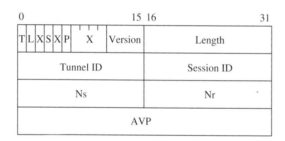

Table 11–4 contains a description of each L2TP packet field. RFC2661 provides much more information about L2TP.

Denial-of-Service Attacks

Objective 4-3

A *denial-of-service attack* is characterized by an attempt to prevent legitimate users of a service from using that service. Examples include attempts to "flood" a network, thereby preventing legitimate network traffic; attempts to disrupt connections between two machines, thereby preventing access to a service; attempts to prevent a particular individual from accessing a service; and attempts to disrupt service to a specific system or person. Illegitimate use of resources also may result in denial of service. For example, an intruder may use your anonymous FTP area as a place to store illegal copies of commercial software, consuming disk space and generating network traffic. Denial-of-service attacks can essentially disable your computer or your network. Some denial-of-service attacks can be executed with limited resources against a large, sophisticated site.

Denial-of-service attacks come in a variety of forms and aim at a variety of services. There are three basic types of attack:

• Consumption of limited resources

• Destruction or alteration of configuration files

• Physical destruction or modification of network components

TABLE 11–4
L2TP packet fields.

Packet Field	Packet Field Description
T	The T bit indicates the type of message. It is set to 0 for data messages and 1 for control messages.
L	When L is set, the Length field is present, which indicates the total length of the received packet. This bit must be set for control messages.
X	X bits are reserved for future extensions of the protocol. These bits are set to 0 on all outgoing messages. The bits are ignored on all incoming messages.
S	When the S bit is set, both the Nr and Ns fields are present. The S bit must be set for control messages.
O	When O is set, the Offset Size field is present in payload messages. This bit is always set to 0 for control messages.
P	The Priority (P) bit is used for data messages. If P is a 1, this data message receives preferential treatment in its local queuing and transmission. The P bit has a value of 0 for all control messages.
V	The value of the version bits is always 002. This indicates a version 1 L2TP message.
Length	The length field contains the overall length of the message, including header, message type, and all AVPs.
Tunnel ID	The Tunnel ID specifies the tunnel to which a control message is applied. If the Tunnel ID has not yet been set, the Tunnel ID must be set to 0. Once the Tunnel ID is received (from the peer), all further packets must be sent with Tunnel ID set to the indicated value.
Call ID	The Call ID identifies the control message in a user session within a tunnel. If a control message does not apply to a single user session within the tunnel, Call ID must be set to 0.
Nr	Nr is the sequence number expected in the next control message to be received.
Ns	Ns is the sequence number for this data or control message.
Offset size	Data field which specifies the number of bytes past the L2TP header the payload data is expected to start.
Offset padding	Bits between the offset field and the payload data.

Denial-of-service attacks can result in significant loss of time and money for many organizations. The following steps can be taken to reduce the likelihood of a denial-of-service attack:

• Implement a firewall or filters on the router traffic

• Guard against TCP SYN flooding

• Disable any unneeded or unused network services

• Establish baselines for normal activity on the network

■ STORAGE MANAGEMENT

Objective 3-4

Storage management is becoming an increasingly important aspect of network management. This is especially true for companies (or even individuals) that utilize large quantities of data.

Network Attached Storage

NAS

Network Attached Storage (*NAS*) is a technology where high-capacity file storage is directly connected to the network. Typical servers provide many services in addition to file serving such as e-mail, Web hosting, user authentication in domain environments, and print services. The operating system is thus busy doing many things that have nothing to do with file serving. A NAS device contains only files to be served and software capable of interfacing with many different operating systems. Data is typically transferred out of the NAS device at a higher rate than that of a typical OS-based file server.

Here are some characteristics of NAS devices:

- May use hard drives (EIDE, SCSI, or ATA) or CD-ROMs to store their data
- Fault tolerance is possible using RAID technology
- Communication via TCP/IP and IPX/SPX
- Support for file-sharing protocols CIFS/SMB, NFS, and NCP
- Compatible with many network operating systems (Windows, UNIX/Linux, NetWare)
- Centralized management of data

Examine two examples of how NAS is utilized.

Example 11.1 A school with several computer laboratories uses a Windows NT server to store the hard drive images for the computers in each laboratory. When a laboratory is configured, the hard drives on each computer are loaded with a copy of the image stored on the NT server. A typical image takes 40 minutes to transfer over the network.

After adding a NAS device, the image transfer time drops to 12 minutes.

Example 11.2 A printed-circuit board manufacturer has several machine floors. One consists of 10 high-speed drills. Each drill machine is loaded with a drill plan before beginning operation. The drill plan for each machine may be different, with each drill plan requiring an average of 500 MB. Examine Figure 11–15 to see how a NAS device is used to feed the drill machines. NAS drill plans are fed to the drill computers via a multiport Gigabit switch. The files are loaded into the NAS from the master server at 100 Mbps.

FIGURE 11–15
NAS drill plans.

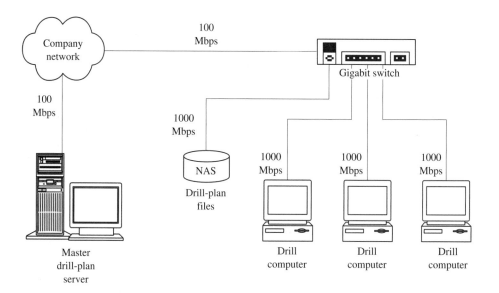

A dedicated Gigabit switch is used to connect all drill machine computers with a NAS device storing the drill plans. New drill plans are uploaded to the NAS device from a master file server at a lower speed of 100 Mbps. Rather than pumping the drill pattern files over the company network, the dedicated switch keeps the traffic localized so that total network performance does not suffer when the drill machines are being loaded.

SAN

Another type of network storage is called *SAN* (Storage Area Network). A SAN uses a special switch (typically utilizing Fiber Channel technology) to connect servers and storage devices on their own physical network. One server acts as a gateway to the SAN. This allows internal SAN traffic (backups, RAID operations) to be isolated from the main network. Clients on the main network access data on the SAN through the gateway. Figure 11–16 shows a company network connected to a SAN. Some companies use multiple SANs, mirroring the data sent to each SAN, and providing an extra level of fault tolerance to the overall network. SANs may connect to each other over wide distances using ATM or SONET.

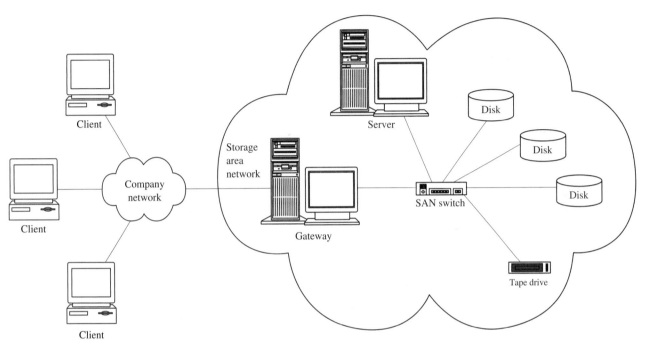

FIGURE 11–16
Company network connected to a SAN.

■ TROUBLESHOOTING TECHNIQUES

Troubleshooting a network management problem requires patience and determination. Depending on the type of problem, there may be several different possible choices to choose from. Each of the choices may provide a workable solution, but one choice may be better than the others. For some problems it may be possible to choose the cheapest solution, but other problems may require a more complete solution, one that costs more money than is available in the budget.

Troubleshooting a network security issue may involve a significant amount of research. It is best to have established a good baseline of normal system activity on which to start the investigative process. One of the most important tools available to the network/security administrator is a log of the system activities. By default, many activities are not written to a log file, but they probably should be. Examine what type of information is available, log the events to a file on a daily basis, and back up the log file information on a regular basis. Do not recycle the log file backups, because it may be necessary to review the contents of a log file long after the event originally occurred.

The Computer Emergency Response Team (CERT) provides a centralized resource to collect and disseminate information regarding security issues on the Internet. You are encouraged to visit the CERT Web site at http://www.cert.org. The CERT Coordination Center provides incident response services to sites that have been the victims of attack, publishes a variety of security alerts, researches security, and develops information to help improve network security.

INDUSTRY TIP

When securing an organization's network there are several things that need to be addressed. The primary starting point for establishing security for a network is to develop a security plan. The plan not only provides the blueprint for what security measures are to be implemented, but it becomes the authority for which all security measures are established. The security plan should be developed with the needs of all users of the network being given due consideration. It is generally considered a good practice to include a representative from each section of an organization on the security plan development committee. After the security plan is developed, and all interested parties have had an opportunity to express concerns about any portion of the plan, the final product should be signed by the senior executive of the organization (or that individual's authorized representative). That signature provides the authority to implement the security plan throughout the organization. After the security plan is approved, specifics of the plan can be implemented. A typical security plan will address items such as employee training, acceptable use of the organization's computer systems (such as whether to let employees use the system to check their private e-mail accounts), who authorizes the use of new software on the network, the network protection processes that will be used (firewalls, anti-virus, etc.), security plan change management procedures, and how network attacks will be handled. Of course these are only a few representations of the items that should be included in a security plan. Organizations that are having a lot of problems with information systems security frequently do not have (or do not follow) a well thought-out security plan. Those organizations that do have, and follow, a comprehensive security plan usually have much fewer problems with security.

CAREER DEVELOPMENT

This chapter barely touched the surface of security issues associated with modern information systems. Computer networks, by design, are developed to seamlessly exchange data in a rapid and seamless manner. The TCP/IP protocol suite is designed to process information with little regard to privacy and security of data. Though computer users and organizations have been aware of the need to protect data, that has not always been the primary focus of system and network administrators. It has only been recently that security issues have become a mainstream concern. There are many security training and certification programs that exist or are in development. SANS (www.sans.org) sponsors the Global Information Assurance Certification (GIAC) track, which tests knowledge in a variety of areas concerning practitioner level skills. For those with a technical and managerial background in information system security, International Information Systems Security Certification Consortium (www.isc2.org) manages two certifications. Their Certified Information Systems Security Professional (CISSP) is generally regarded as a premier certification within the IT security field. A newer certification offered by CompTIA is the Security+ certification. It covers a wide area of industry standard knowledge, and the target audience for that exam is a networking professional with two years of networking experience with an emphasis on security. This exam covers a wide base of foundation security knowledge and should provide a good benchmark for anyone wanting to start a career path in the security realm of the networking career. You can find more information about this certification at www.comptia.com/certification/default.asp. The Cisco corporation also has a new security certification called Cisco Certified Security Professional. Achieving this level of certification requires the candidate to pass five exams after possessing the prerequisite CCNA certification. This would be a certification to pursue after having a year or two of experience in the networking career field. The security field is challenging and a lot of great employment opportunities are available for security professionals.

■ SELF-TEST

1. Network management is concerned with providing a business with a _____, _____, and _____ computer network. (Choose three.)
   a. cost-efficient
   b. reliable
   c. secure
   d. organizationaly balanced

2. Which of the following is a part of a disaster recovery plan?
   a. Establishing user permissions on server
   b. Maintaining updated off-site backups
   c. Using SSL for Internet communication
   d. Specifying how users access network

3. Which of the following is **not** considered a network disaster?
   a. Virus
   b. Accidental disconnection of vital equipment
   c. One mirrored server fails
   d. International damage by employee

4. _____ is the ability of a system to withstand a hardware or software problem and keep functioning.
   a. Fault tolerance
   b. Disaster recovery
   c. Security management
   d. Software management

5. What does RAID stand for?
   a. Ready archive identification
   b. Reliable and inexpensive disk
   c. Redundant array of inexpensive disks
   d. Rapid archive of inexpensive disks

6. If _____ is used for a backup method and disk fails, the parity data on each drive can be used to restore the information lost on the failed disk.
   a. striping
   b. disk duplexing
   c. RAID 3
   d. RAID 5

7. Problems on a network related to wrong encapsulation type causing dropped packets may be observed in real time using a(n) _____.
   a. Time Domain Reflectometer
   b. IPconfig utility
   c. protocol analyzer
   d. frame delimiter

8. The _____ standard provides support for traffic monitoring at the layers above layer 2 of the OSI model.
   a. 802.5
   b. IEEE
   c. RMON
   d. RMON2

9. Which of the following is **not** one of the four operations of SNMP?
   a. GET
   b. GET-NEXT
   c. SET
   d. SET-NEXT
   e. TRAP

10. The transmission of data across a network is regulated through the use of _____ and _____ between users. (Choose two.)
    a. firewalls
    b. switches
    c. routers
    d. hubs

11. _____ can be used to protect data and provide security as it travels across networks.
    a. Compression
    b. Convergence
    c. MIB
    d. Encryption

12. The security measure concerned with correctly identifying the originator of a message is called _____.
    a. integrity
    b. nonrepudiation
    c. authentication
    d. accessibility

13. True or False: Program or file viruses are pieces of code that attach to executable programs and replicate when the infected program is run.

14. Which virus type (worms or Trojan horses) may start in either the boot sector or application and spread from one to the other?
    a. Macro
    b. Boot sector
    c. Multipartite
    d. File

15. True or False: Network sniffers work by causing NICs to function in the promiscuous mode.

16. _____ will protect a password or additional data from being easily captured and decoded.
    a. PAP
    b. Authentication
    c. Nonrepudiation
    d. Encryption

17. True or False: Kerberos is considered more adequate than public-key systems for authentication between domains.

18. True or False: A host uses a public key to encrypt a message intended for a remote destination. He remembers a vital part of the message that he forgot to include. He decrypts the message with his public key and adds the information he forgot. He then encrypts the message again and sends it.

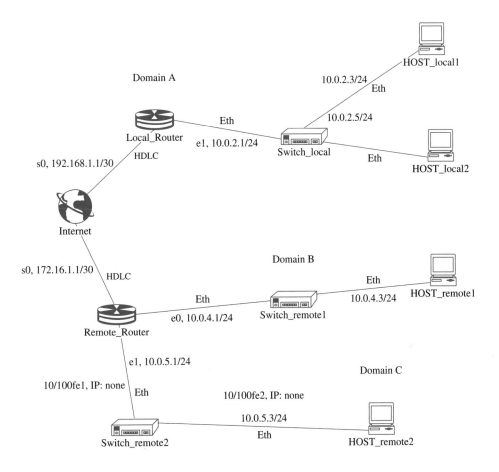

19. Each host in the network shown in the following figure is in possession of Public key 1, Public key 2, Public Key 3, and Public key 4. Private key 1 is in the possession of HOST_local1. Private key 2 is in the possession of HOST_ local2. Private key 3 is in the possession of HOST_remote1. Private key 4 is in the possession of HOST_remote2. Which key can be used by HOST_remote2 to encrypt a message?
    a. Private key1
    b. Private key 4
    c. Public key 4 only
    d. Any Public key

20. Each host in the network shown in the previous figure is in possession of Public key 1, Public key 2, Public key 3, and Public key 4 and can use any of these to encrypt a message. Private key 1 is in the possession of HOST_local1. Private key 2 is in the possession of HOST_local2. Private key 3 is in the possession of HOST_remote1. Private key 4 is in the possession of HOST_remote2. Which public key can be used by HOST_remote2 to decrypt a message from HOST_local1?
    a. Public key 1
    b. Public key 4 only
    c. Any Public key
    d. None of the above

21. True or False: PGP is freeware that provides support mechanisms for digital signatures, message encryption, compression, and transparent compatibility with many application programs.

22. Which of the following prevents access to an internal network by an external network and is implemented in hardware or software?
    a. Man in the middle
    b. DMZ
    c. Cache engine
    d. Firewall

23. The process of encapsulating data in such a way that the source and destination addresses and payload data are encrypted is called _____.
    a. proxy
    b. Kerberos
    c. tunneling
    d. IPSec

24. Which popular tunneling protocol is a combination of PPTP and L2F and is the standard tunneling protocol for VPNs?
    a. R2TP
    b. L2TP
    c. PPP
    d. NTP

25. What is the term used when an attacker attempts to "flood" a network with requests, overwhelming the network and even causing a network failure?
    a. Spoofing
    b. Masquerading
    c. Cracking
    d. DOS

Electronic Mail

CHAPTER **12**

PERFORMANCE OBJECTIVES

Upon completion of this chapter, you should be able to:

- Describe the features of e-mail communication software.

- Configure an electronic mail client.
- Send and receive electronic mail.
- Discuss the protocols SMTP, POP3, and IMAP.

NETWORK+ OBJECTIVES

This chapter provides information for the following Network+ objectives:

2.5 Define the purpose, function, and/or use of the following protocols within TCP/IP:
- IP
- TCP
- UDP
- FTP
- TFTP
- SMTP
- HTTP
- HTTPS
- POP3/IMAP4
- TELNET
- ICMP
- ARP
- NTP

2.6 Define the function of TCP/UDP ports. Identify well-known ports.

2.11 Identify the basic characteristics (e.g., speed, capacity, media) of the following WAN technologies:
- Packet switching vs. circuit switching
- ISDN
- FDDI
- ATM
- Frame Relay
- Sonet/SDH
- T1/E1
- T3/E3
- Ocx

3.7 Given a remote connectivity scenario (e.g., IP, IPX, dial-up, PPPoE, authentication, physical connectivity, etc.), configure the connection.

4.3 Given a troubleshooting scenario involving a remote connectivity problem (e.g., authentication failure, protocol configuration, physical connectivity), identify the cause of the problem.

■ INTRODUCTION

E-mail

Communications software is at the heart of the personal computer revolution. In this chapter, you explore electronic mail (commonly referred to as *e-mail*), one of the most common communication tools available. This chapter covers the basic features of electronic mail, how to configure client software, how to send and receive electronic mail, and how to organize e-mail messages on a computer that is connected to the Internet.

■ WHAT IS E-MAIL?

In the early days of computer networking, a simple electronic mail program was used to exchange plain-text messages. Since then, electronic mail has evolved into a personal communication tool that can be used to:

- Send a message to several recipients
- Send a message that contains text, graphics, and even multimedia audio and video files
- Send messages that are encrypted for security purposes

Electronic mail combines the speed of electronic communication with features similar to the postal mail service. The major difference between the postal mail service and e-mail is that a computer can transmit a message across a computer network almost instantly.

When using electronic mail, several common features are available to the computer user. For example, it is possible for every user to:

- Compose an e-mail message
- Send an e-mail message
- Receive notification that an e-mail message has arrived
- Read an e-mail message
- Forward a copy of an e-mail message
- Reply to an e-mail message

Begin your examination of e-mail by looking at the SMTP (Simple Mail Transport Protocol) to see how e-mail actually works on the Internet.

■ SIMPLE MAIL TRANSPORT PROTOCOL

Simple Mail Transport Protocol

Objective 2-5

The **Simple Mail Transport Protocol** specifies how electronic messages are exchanged between computers using the TCP (Transmission Control Protocol). Recall that using TCP provides for a reliable exchange of data on the Internet. SMTP is used to exchange messages between servers or between a client and a server. Basically, SMTP is used to deliver electronic mail messages. The messages are retrieved through the use of an e-mail client program.

For computers to use e-mail, it is necessary to install software on each system. Electronic mail uses the client-server method to allow mail to be exchanged. Client computers exchange messages with a server that is ultimately responsible for delivering the e-mail messages to the destination.

On the server computer each user is assigned a specific mailbox. Each electronic mailbox or e-mail address has a unique address. It is divided into two parts, a mailbox name and a computer host name, which are separated using an "at" sign (@) such as mailbox@ computer.xxx. Together, both of these components provide for a unique e-mail address.

The mailbox portion of the address is often made from a user's name. The host name part of the address is chosen by a network administrator. For example, Joe Tekk has the e-mail address joetekk@stny.rr.com. From the example, this indicates that joetekk is the mailbox name and stny.rr.com is the computer name. Notice that Joe Tekk's e-mail address ends in .com. The .com indicates that stny.rr is a commercial organization. You will observe that the last three characters of an e-mail address normally end with a limited number of domain name categories. These categories are shown in Table 12–1.

TABLE 12–1
Common domain names.

Domain Name	Assigned Group
com	A company or commercial organization
edu	An educational institution
gov	A government organization
mil	A military organization
net	Network service provider
org	Non-profit organization
country code	A country code, for example, .us for United States, .ca for Canada, and .jp for Japan
biz	Small business Web sites
info	Resource Web sites
aero	Air-transport industry
coop	Cooperative associations
museum	Museums
name	Individuals
pro	Credentialed professionals

E-mail messages are actually exchanged using the client-server environment illustrated in Figure 12–1. Note that both of the computers in Figure 12–1 are called e-mail servers. When the mail message is exchanged, the mail transfer program on the sending computer temporarily becomes a client and connects to the mail transfer program running as a server on the receiving computer. In this way, whether mail is being sent or received will determine if the mail transfer program acts as a client or a server.

FIGURE 12–1
How e-mail is exchanged between servers.

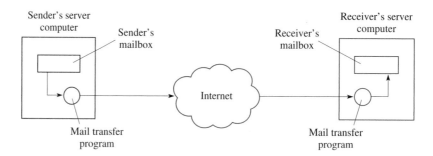

■ FORMAT OF E-MAIL MESSAGES

The format of an e-mail message exchanged between the servers is quite simple. Each message consists of ASCII text that is separated into two parts. A blank line is used as the separator between the parts. The first part of the message is called a *header*. A header consists of a keyword followed by a colon and additional information. Some of the most common header keywords are shown in Table 12–2.

The second part of the message is called the *body* and contains the actual text of the message.

Recall that the body of a mail message at first consisted of a plain-text message. In effect, the text that followed the blank line was the actual text of the message. A special scheme called **MIME** (Multipurpose Internet Mail Extensions) was developed to provide the ability to send many different file types as an attachment to an e-mail message. Information about MIME is provided later in this chapter.

MIME

TABLE 12–2
Typical e-mail header keywords.

Header Keyword	Description
To	The mail recipient's e-mail address
From	The sender's e-mail address
Cc	List of carbon copy addresses
Bcc	List of blind carbon copy addresses
Date	The date when the message was sent
Subject	The subject of the message
Reply-to	The address to which a reply should be sent

■ E-MAIL CLIENT SOFTWARE

Objective 3-7

One of the most popular client software e-mail programs is Microsoft Outlook Express. It is installed as a part of the Windows operating system. There are usually several different ways to access the Outlook Express program. For example, there may be an icon on the desktop that can be double-clicked, a small Outlook Express icon may be found on the taskbar, or it may be a program that can be selected from the Windows Start menu. In any case, after the Outlook Express program is started, the computer user is presented with a screen display similar to Figure 12–2.

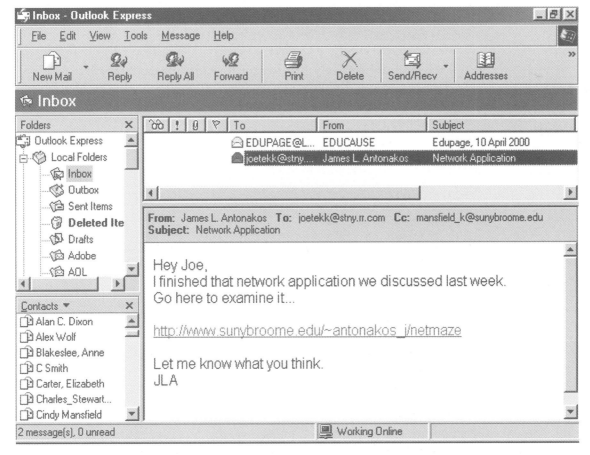

FIGURE 12–2
Microsoft Outlook Express displaying a message.

To use the Outlook Express program, it must be configured properly. This configuration consists of the following:

- Providing user information such as the user name, organization, e-mail address, and reply address. These items are located on the General Mail Properties tab, as shown in Figure 12–3.

FIGURE 12–3
Outlook Express General
E-mail Properties tab.

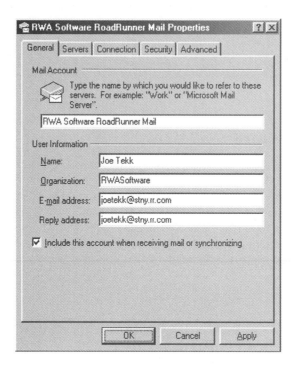

- It is also necessary to identify the server computer to which the client will connect to send and receive mail. This information is found on the Servers tab of the Mail Properties window shown in Figure 12–4. There is a server associated with both incoming and outgoing mail.

FIGURE 12–4
Outlook Express mail servers.

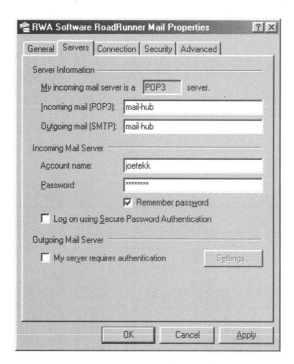

POP3

Objective 2-5

Objective 2-6

Incoming mail uses **POP3**, the Post Office Protocol, whereas the outgoing mail server uses SMTP, the Simple Mail Transport Protocol. Notice that the Servers tab is where the user enters an Incoming Mail Server account name and password. As an added convenience, it is possible for Outlook Express to save or remember the user's password for future use.

Sometimes it is necessary to change some of the mail parameters. For example, it may be necessary to change the server timeout value of the mail program or change the setting that determines if a copy of a mail message is to be left on the server computer after it has been transferred to the client. As you can see from Figure 12–5, there are several different settings that can be modified. It is always a good idea to leave the settings alone unless there is a good reason to change them, however. This is especially true for the default port numbers used by SMTP and POP3 (25 and 110, respectively).

FIGURE 12–5
Outlook Express Advanced
Mail Properties.

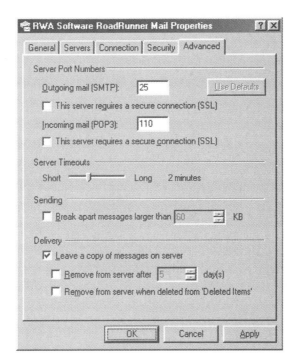

■ SENDING AN E-MAIL MESSAGE

Let us consider an example in which Joe Tekk creates the e-mail message shown in Figure 12–6. Joe uses the e-mail client to send a message to windy@alpha.com. The message is sent by Joe to the e-mail server at stny.rr.com.

The mail server at stny.rr.com forwards the message to the e-mail server at alpha.com, where the user Windy can read that message. Figure 12–7 illustrates how the e-mail message is sent using the Microsoft Outlook Express client program. Notice that the SMTP protocol is used to transfer the message everywhere except for the client connection at the destination, which uses POP3.

FIGURE 12–6
Creating a new e-mail
message.

FIGURE 12–7
Sending and receiving e-mail.

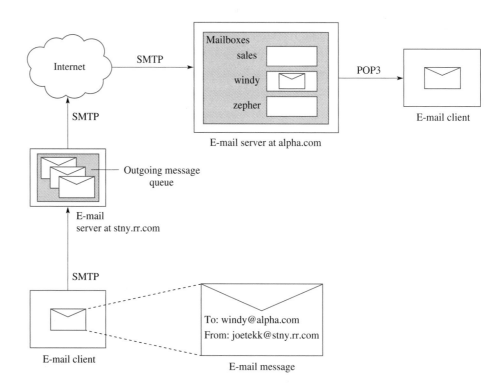

■ RECEIVING AN E-MAIL MESSAGE USING THE POST OFFICE PROTOCOL

E-mail messages are received by the server and stored in the Inbox inside a user's mailbox until they are read. For example, Figure 12–8 shows a message from the Java Developer Connection mailing list that was downloaded using the Post Office Protocol. After the message has been read, it can be deleted or saved. If a message is saved, it is normally moved

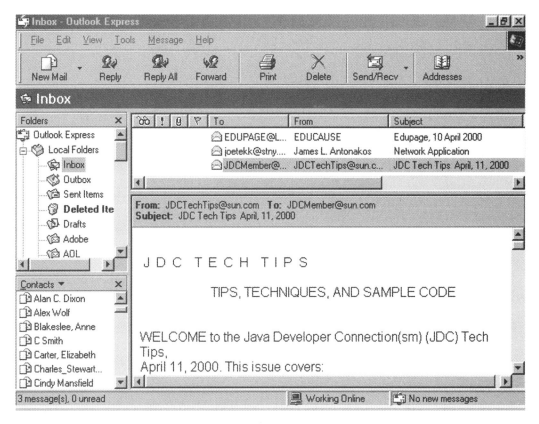

FIGURE 12–8
Reading a message in the Outlook Express Inbox.

to a folder other than the Inbox. This allows for mail to be stored in user-defined categories. To create a new folder for the Java Developer Connection message, simply right-click on the Local Folders in the folder list and select New Folder. To move the message into the folder, drag it from the Inbox message list to the appropriate folder. This provides an easy way to keep track of all related messages.

Note that Outlook Express provides the capability to store as many messages as necessary (as long as there is enough disk space available), although it is a good idea to keep the mailbox clean.

■ E-MAIL ERROR MESSAGES

There are several reasons why an error message may be generated when trying to send e-mail. Two of the most common errors stem from the user incorrectly specifying either the mailbox name or the computer name. In either case, a message will be sent back to the sender indicating what type of error has occurred. Figure 12–9 illustrates an error with the mailbox portion of the address.

Figure 12–10 indicates a problem with the computer portion. Other problems with the mail will have their own specific message, which may help to resolve the problem.

■ ACCESS TO E-MAIL USING THE WEB

Some e-mail servers allow access to the mail system using a World Wide Web browser. The browser acts the same as an e-mail client that allows a user to send and receive e-mail

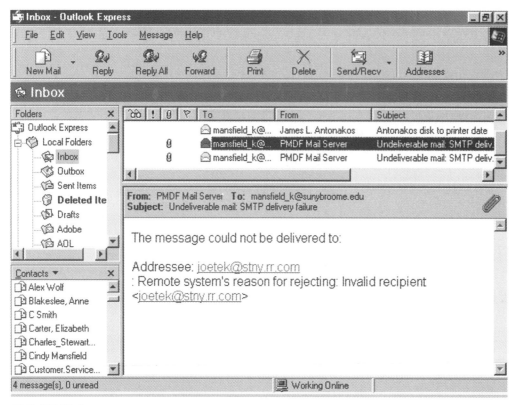

FIGURE 12–9
E-mail message indicating an invalid recipient.

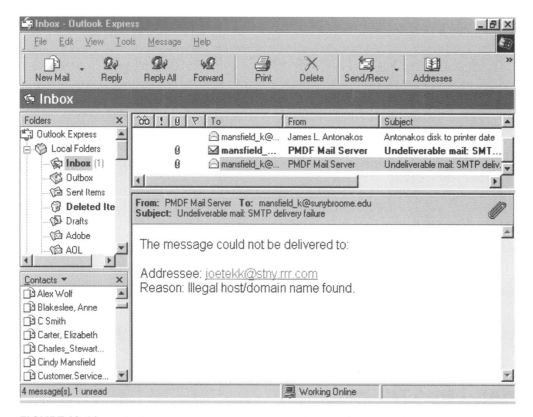

FIGURE 12–10
E-mail message indicating an invalid host-domain name.

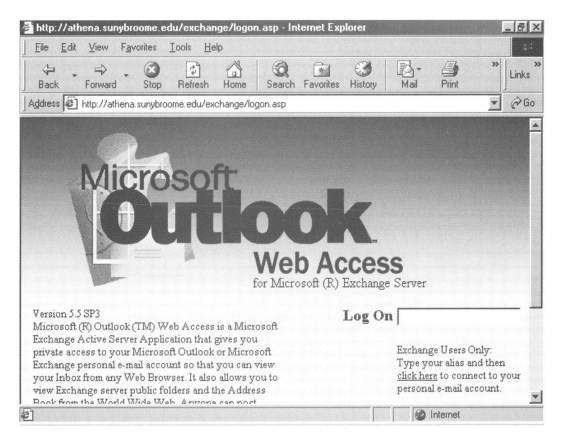

FIGURE 12–11
Accessing the e-mail server using the Web.

messages. Figure 12–11 shows the opening screen of the Microsoft Outlook Web Access program, which uses the Microsoft Exchange Server. Note that a user name and password are required in order to access any mail files.

■ MIME (MULTIPURPOSE INTERNET MAIL EXTENSIONS)

MIME

MIME provides a way for binary programs, graphical images, or other types of files to be attached to an e-mail message. Before the introduction of MIME, there were only a few methods to send electronic mail messages that contained anything other than plain ASCII text. Two of the most popular were uuencode and uudecode, available in the UNIX environment.

The MIME standard provides several important features such as the following:

- Specifications for other character sets
- Definitions for content types such as applications, images, and other multimedia file types
- A method to include several different objects within a single message
- An extended set of possible headers
- Standard encoding methods such as base64 and quote printable

Note that although MIME was designed for electronic mail, Web browsers also use MIME to specify the appropriate plug-ins to handle the specified MIME data type. Table 12–3 shows a list of some of the common MIME data types.

The MIME data type is associated to a file by the file extension. There are currently several hundred different MIME types. Additional MIME types are added as necessary.

Base64
Quote printable

The standard encoding methods used by MIME include *base64* and *quote printable*. The base64 encoding method is used primarily to transfer binary attachments.

TABLE 12–3
Common MIME data types.

MIME Type	Description
.au	Audio file
.bin	Binary file
.exe	Binary executable application file
.gif	GIF image file
.htm	HTML file
.java	Java text source file
.jpg	JPEG image file
.mid	MIDI audio file
.mime	Message/RFC822 format
.mov	QuickTime movie file
.mpg	MPEG video file
.ra	Real audio file
.rtf	Rich text file
.tif	TIFF file
.uu	Uuencoded file
.wav	WAV file
.zip	ZIP file

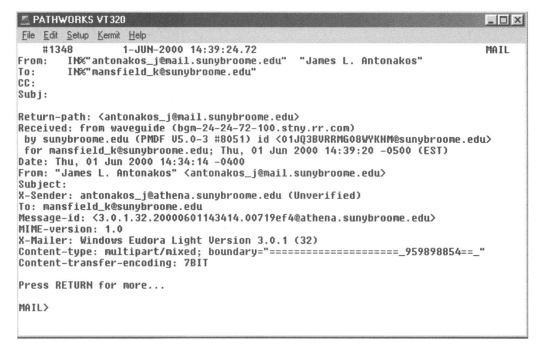

FIGURE 12–12
Text-based e-mail message with a binary attachment (header).

Figure 12–12 illustrates how an e-mail message is displayed as a text file. Figure 12–12 shows the beginning of an e-mail message that contains the address information and all of the message headers. Notice that in order to continue reading the message as a text file, it is necessary to press the Return (or Enter) key as indicated at the bottom of the display.

Examine the separator lines and Content-Type lines in the message displayed in Figure 12–13. This is where the base64 encoding method is specified for the message attachment. The string of characters that follows is the ZIP file shown in base64 encoded form.

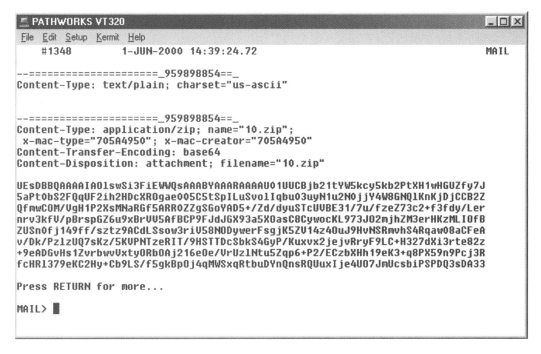

```
PATHWORKS VT320                                                         _ □ ×
File  Edit  Setup  Kermit  Help
   #1348            1-JUN-2000 14:39:24.72                               MAIL

--=====================_959898854==_
Content-Type: text/plain; charset="us-ascii"


--=====================_959898854==_
Content-Type: application/zip; name="10.zip";
 x-mac-type="705A4950"; x-mac-creator="705A4950"
Content-Transfer-Encoding: base64
Content-Disposition: attachment; filename="10.zip"

UEsDBBQAAAAIAO1swSi3FiEWWQsAAABYAAARAAAAUO1UUCBjb21tYW5kcy5kb2PtXH1wHGUZfy7J
5aPtObS2FQqUF2ih2HDcXROgaeOO5C5tSpILuSvolIqbuO3uyN1u2NOjjY4W8GNQlKnKjDjCCB2Z
QfmwCOM/UgH1P2XsMNaRGf5ARROZZgSGoYAD5+/Zd/dyuSTcUUBE31/7u/fzeZ73c2+f3fdy/Ler
nrv3kfU/pBrspGZ6u9xBrVU5AfBCP9FJdJGX93a5XOasC8CywocKL973JO2mjhZM3erHKzMLIOfB
ZUSnOfj149ff/sztz9ACdLSsow3riV58NODywerFsgjK5ZU14z40uJ9HvNSRmvhS4Rqaw08aCFeA
v/Dk/PzlzUQ7sKz/5KVPNTzeRIT/9HSTTDcSbkS4GyP/Kuxvx2jejvRryF9LC+H327dXi3rte82z
+9eADGvHs1ZvrbwvUxtyORbOAj216eOe/UrUzlNtu5Zqp6+P2/ECzbXHh19eK3+q8PX59n9Pcj3R
fcHR1379eKC2Hy+Cb9LS/f5gkBpOj4qMWSxqRtbuDYnQnsRQUuxIje4UO7JmUcsbiPSPDQ3sDA33
```

Press RETURN for more...

MAIL> █
```

**FIGURE 12–13**
Text-based e-mail message with a binary attachment (base64 encoding).

The quote printable encoding method is used to encode 8-bit text codes, such as those used in a foreign language character set, into 7-bit U.S. ASCII characters. This quote printable format creates documents that are readable even in encoded form. Note that all MIME-compliant applications are capable of working with these standard encoding methods.

## ■ INTERNET MESSAGE ACCESS PROTOCOL (IMAP)

**IMAP**

Objective 2-5

***IMAP*** is a newer protocol designed to provide access to electronic messages that are stored on a mail server. IMAP was developed at Stanford University in 1986. IMAP is designed to eliminate the typical problems that are caused by downloading the electronic messages to a client computer using the POP (Post Office Protocol). Instead, IMAP provides direct access to the messages that are stored on the server. This allows for mail messages to be managed from any computer at any time.

The current version of IMAP, IMAP4, provides full compatibility with the Internet and MIME standards. In addition, IMAP4 includes several other new features such as concurrent access to shared mailboxes, online and offline access to messages, and management from any computer.

## ■ E-MAIL PACKET CAPTURE

Using a protocol analyzer, it is possible to capture all of the activity associated with sending an electronic mail message. For example, consider sending the following text message:

```
To: mansfield_k@sunybroome.edu
From: "James L. Antonakos" <antonakos_j@mail.sunybroome.edu>
Subject: Test message
Cc:
Bcc:

Ken,
Just wanted to capture this.

JLA
```
```

Objective 2-5

As you can see from the message text, it contains less than 40 characters. Examine each of the entries in Table 12–4, which shows the sequence of exchanges between the client and the server to deliver the message.

TABLE 12–4
Electronic mail packet captures.

Message	Packet	Destination	Source	Protocol	Summary	Size	Tick (msec.)
	1	Broadcast	Waveguide	ARP	Request	60	0
	2	Waveguide	bgm-41-1.stny.rr.com	ARP	Reply	60	20
	3	sbccab.cc.sunybroome.edu	Waveguide	SMTP	TCP (SYN)	62	0
	4	Waveguide	sbccab.cc.sunybroome.edu	SMTP	TCP (ACK,SYN)	60	45
	5	sbccab.cc.sunybroome.edu	Waveguide	SMTP	TCP (ACK)	60	0
	6	Broadcast	bgm-144-1.stny.rr.com	ARP	Request	60	1910
220	7	Waveguide	sbccab.cc.sunybroome.edu	SMTP	TCP (ACK,PSH)	120	165
HELO	8	sbccab.cc.sunybroome.edu	Waveguide	SMTP	TCP (ACK,PSH)	70	5
250	9	Waveguide	sbccab.cc.sunybroome.edu	SMTP	TCP (ACK,PSH)	112	70
RSET	10	sbccab.cc.sunybroome.edu	Waveguide	SMTP	TCP (ACK,PSH)	60	15
250	11	Waveguide	sbccab.cc.sunybroome.edu	SMTP	TCP (ACK,PSH)	63	40
MAIL FROM:	12	sbccab.cc.sunybroome.edu	Waveguide	SMTP	TCP (ACK,PSH)	99	5
250	13	Waveguide	sbccab.cc.sunybroome.edu	SMTP	TCP (ACK,PSH)	71	40
RCPT TO:	14	sbccab.cc.sunybroome.edu	Waveguide	SMTP	TCP (ACK,PSH)	92	5
	15	Waveguide	sbccab.cc.sunybroome.edu	SMTP	TCP (ACK)	60	95
250	16	Waveguide	sbccab.cc.sunybroome.edu	SMTP	TCP (ACK,PSH)	87	205
DATA	17	sbccab.cc.sunybroome.edu	Waveguide	SMTP	TCP (ACK,PSH)	60	0
354	18	Waveguide	sbccab.cc.sunybroome.edu	SMTP	TCP (ACK,PSH)	94	50
<text>	19	sbccab.cc.sunybroome.edu	Waveguide	SMTP	TCP (ACK,PSH)	488	40
	20	Waveguide	sbccab.cc.sunybroome.edu	SMTP	TCP (ACK)	60	105
	21	sbccab.cc.sunybroome.edu	Waveguide	SMTP	TCP (ACK,PSH)	60	0
	22	Waveguide	sbccab.cc.sunybroome.edu	SMTP	TCP (ACK)	60	205
250	23	Waveguide	sbccab.cc.sunybroome.edu	SMTP	TCP (ACK,PSH)	63	155
QUIT	24	sbccab.cc.sunybroome.edu	Waveguide	SMTP	TCP (ACK,PSH)	60	5
221	25	Waveguide	sbccab.cc.sunybroome.edu	SMTP	TCP (ACK,PSH)	82	55
	26	sbccab.cc.sunybroome.edu	Waveguide	SMTP	TCP (ACK,FIN)	60	5
	27	Waveguide	sbccab.cc.sunybroome.edu	SMTP	TCP (ACK,FIN)	60	25
	28	sbccab.cc.sunybroome.edu	Waveguide	SMTP	TCP (ACK)	60	0
	29	Waveguide	sbccab.cc.sunybroome.edu	SMTP	TCP (ACK)	60	20
	30	Broadcast	bgm-135-1.stny.rr.com	ARP	Request	60	180

To help understand this exchange of packets, a list of the SMTP commands is shown in Table 12–5.

A list of possible server responses is provided in Table 12–6.

TABLE 12–5
SMTP commands.

Command	Parameter
HELO	<domain>
MAIL	FROM:<reverse-path>
RCPT	TO:<forward-path>
DATA	(none)
RSET	(none)
SEND	FROM:<reverse-path>
SOML	FROM:<reverse-path>
SAML	FROM:<reverse-path>
VRFY	<string>
EXPN	<string>
HELP	[<string>] (optional)
NOOP	(none)
QUIT	(none)
TURN	(none)

TABLE 12–6
SMTP reply codes.

Reply Code	Meaning
211	System status, or system help reply
214	Help message
220 <domain>	Service ready
221 <domain>	Service closing transmission channel
250	Requested mail action okay, completed
251	User not local; will forward to <forward-path>
354	Start mail input; end with <CRLF>
421 <domain>	Service not available, closing transmission channel
450	Requested mail action not taken: mailbox unavailable
451	Requested action aborted: local error in processing
452	Requested action not taken: insufficient system storage
500	Syntax error, command unrecognized
501	Syntax error in parameters or arguments
502	Command not implemented
503	Bad sequence of commands
504	Command parameter not implemented
550	Requested action not taken: mailbox unavailable
551	User not local; please try <forward-path>
552	Requested mail action aborted: exceeded storage allocation
553	Requested action not taken: mailbox name not allowed
554	Transaction failed

Three packet decodes are provided here to illustrate how a mail message is exchanged. First, let us examine the contents of packet number 8, which contains the HELO message to waveguide:

```
Packet 8

Destination Source    Protocol       Summary    Size   Time Tick
---------------------------------------------------------------------
192.203.130.2    24.94.41.254     Simple Mail Transfer Protocol TCP 70
      04/27/99 15:05:04.998

Addr.  Hex. Data                                     ASCII
0000:  08 00 3E 02 00 DD 00 60 97 2B E6 0F 08 00 45 00  ..>....'.+....E.
0010:  00 38 98 E5 40 00 80 06 DC B0 18 5E 29 FE C0 CB  .8..@......^)...
0020:  82 02 04 94 00 19 05 7C C6 43 01 A3 EC 43 50 18  .......|.C...CP.
0030:  21 3E E8 3E 00 00 48 45 4C 4F 20 77 61 76 65 67  !>.>..HELO waveg
0040:  75 69 64 65 0D 0A                                uide..


802.3 [0000:000D]
  0000:0005  Destination Address: 08003E0200DD
  0006:000B  Source Address: 0060972BE60F
  000C:000D  Ethernet Type: DOD Internet Protocol (IP)
IP [000E:0021]
  000E:000E  Version: 4, Header Length: 20
  000F:000F  TOS, Precedence: Routine, Delay: Normal, Throughput: Normal,
Reliability: Normal
  0010:0011  Packet Length: 56
  0012:0013  Identification: 0x98E5
  0014:0014  Fragment Flag (bit 6..5): Don't Fragment
  0014:0015  Fragment Offset: 0x0000
  0016:0016  Time to Live: 128
  0017:0017  Transport: Transmission Control
  0018:0019  Header Checksum: 0xDCB0
  001A:001D  Source Address: 24.94.41.254
  001E:0021  Destination Address: 192.203.130.2
TCP [0022:0035]
  0022:0023  Source Port: 0x0494
  0024:0025  Destination Port: Simple Mail Transfer Protocol
  0026:0029  Sequence Number: 92063299
  002A:002D  Acknowledgment Number: 27520067
  002E:002E  Header Length (bit 7..4): 20
  002F:002F  Control Bit - Acknowledgment; Push function;
  0030:0031  Window Size: 8510
  0032:0033  Checksum: 0xE83E
  0034:0035  Urgent Pointer: 0x0000
```

Next, packet number 12 shows the MAIL FROM: header, which identifies antonakos_j@mail.sunybroome.edu as the sender of the message.

```
Packet 12

Destination Source    Protocol       Summary    Size   Time Tick
---------------------------------------------------------------------
192.203.130.2    24.94.41.254     Simple Mail Transfer Protocol  TCP  99
      04/27/99 15:05:05.128


Addr.  Hex. Data                                     ASCII
0000:  08 00 3E 02 00 DD 00 60 97 2B E6 0F 08 00 45 00  ..>....'.+....E.
```

```
0010:   00 55 9A E5 40 00 80 06 DA 93 18 5E 29 FE C0 CB    .U..@......^)...
0020:   82 02 04 94 00 19 05 7C C6 59 01 A3 EC 86 50 18    .......|.V....P.
0030:   20 FB 9F C0 00 00 4D 41 49 4C 20 46 52 4F 4D 3A    .....MAIL FROM:
0040:   3C 61 6E 74 6F 6E 61 6B 6F 73 5F 6A 40 6D 61 69    <antonakos_j@mai
0050:   6C 2E 73 75 6E 79 62 72 6F 6F 6D 65 2E 65 64 75    l.sunybroome.edu
0060:   3E 0D 0A                                           >..
```

```
802.3 [0000:000D]
  0000:0005   Destination Address: 08003E0200DD
  0006:000B   Source Address: 0060972BE60F
  000C:000D   Ethernet Type: DOD Internet Protocol (IP)
IP [000E:0021]
  000E:000E   Version: 4, Header Length: 20
  000F:000F   TOS, Precedence: Routine, Delay: Normal, Throughput: Normal,
Reliability: Normal
  0010:0011   Packet Length: 85
  0012:0013   Identification: 0x9AE5
  0014:0014   Fragment Flag (bit 6..5): Don't Fragment
  0014:0015   Fragment Offset: 0x0000
  0016:0016   Time to Live: 128
  0017:0017   Transport: Transmission Control
  0018:0019   Header Checksum: 0xDA93
  001A:001D   Source Address: 24.94.41.254
  001E:0021   Destination Address: 192.203.130.2
TCP [0022:0035]
  0022:0023   Source Port: 0x0494
  0024:0025   Destination Port: Simple Mail Transfer Protocol
  0026:0029   Sequence Number: 92063321
  002A:002D   Acknowledgment Number: 27520134
  002E:002E   Header Length (bit 7..4): 20
  002F:002F   Control Bit - Acknowledgment; Push function;
  0030:0031   Window Size: 8443
  0032:0033   Checksum: 0x9FC0
  0034:0035   Urgent Pointer: 0x0000
```

Lastly, examine the contents of packet number 19, which shows a large block of data that contains the actual text of the original message. Notice that the message consists of the mail headers as well as the mail message body.

```
Packet 19

Destination Source        Protocol      Summary      Size  Time Tick
-------------------------------------------------------------------------
192.203.130.2    24.94.41.254           Simple Mail Transfer Protocol TCP  488
        04/27/99 15:05:05.563


Addr.  Hex. Data                                         ASCII
0000:  08 00 3E 02 00 DD 00 60 97 2B E6 0F 08 00 45 00    ..>....;.+....E.
0010:  01 DA 9D E5 40 00 80 06 D6 0E 18 5E 29 FE C0 CB    ....@......^)...
0020:  82 02 04 94 00 19 05 7C C6 B2 01 A3 EC E0 50 18    .......|......P.
0030:  20 A1 A5 BC 00 00 4D 65 73 73 61 67 65 2D 49 64    .....Message-Id
0040:  3A 20 3C 33 2E 30 2E 31 2E 33 32 2E 31 39 39 39    : <3.0.1.32.1999
0050:  30 34 32 37 31 35 30 35 30 32 2E 30 30 36 65 62    0427150502.006eb
0060:  64 33 63 40 61 74 68 65 6E 61 2E 73 75 6E 79 62    d3c@athena.sunyb
0070:  72 6F 6F 6D 65 2E 65 64 75 3E 0D 0A 58 2D 53 65    roome.edu>..X-Se
```

```
0080:   6E 64 65 72 3A 20 61 6E 74 6F 6E 61 6B 6F 73 5F    nder: antonakos_
0090:   6A 40 61 74 68 65 6E 61 2E 73 75 6E 79 62 72 6F    j@athena.sunybro
00A0:   6F 6D 65 2E 65 64 75 0D 0A 58 2D 4D 61 69 6C 65    ome.edu..X-Maile
00B0:   72 3A 20 57 69 6E 64 6F 77 73 20 45 75 64 6F 72    r: Windows Eudor
00C0:   61 20 4C 69 67 68 74 20 56 65 72 73 69 6F 6E 20    a Light Version
00D0:   33 2E 30 2E 31 20 28 33 32 29 0D 0A 44 61 74 65    3.0.1 (32)..Date
00E0:   3A 20 54 75 65 2C 20 32 37 20 41 70 72 20 31 39    : Tue, 27 Apr 19
00F0:   39 39 20 31 35 3A 30 35 3A 30 32 20 2D 30 34 30    99 15:05:02 -040
0100:   30 0D 0A 54 6F 3A 20 6D 61 6E 73 66 69 65 6C 64    0..To: mansfield
0110:   5F 6B 40 73 75 6E 79 62 72 6F 6F 6D 65 2E 65 64    _k@sunybroome.ed
0120:   75 0D 0A 46 72 6F 6D 3A 20 22 4A 61 6D 65 73 20    u..From: "James
0130:   4C 2E 20 41 6E 74 6F 6E 61 6B 6F 73 22 20 3C 61    L. Antonakos" <a
0140:   6E 74 6F 6E 61 6B 6F 73 5F 6A 40 6D 61 69 6C 2E    ntonakos_j@mail.
0150:   73 75 6E 79 62 72 6F 6F 6D 65 2E 65 64 75 3E 0D    sunybroome.edu>.
0160:   0A 53 75 62 6A 65 63 74 3A 20 54 65 73 74 20 6D    .Subject: Test m
0170:   65 73 73 61 67 65 0D 0A 4D 69 6D 65 2D 56 65 72    essage..Mime-Ver
0180:   73 69 6F 6E 3A 20 31 2E 30 0D 0A 43 6F 6E 74 65    sion: 1.0..Conte
0190:   6E 74 2D 54 79 70 65 3A 20 74 65 78 74 2F 70 6C    nt-Type: text/pl
01A0:   61 69 6E 3B 20 63 68 61 72 73 65 74 3D 22 75 73    ain; charset="us
01B0:   2D 61 73 63 69 69 22 0D 0A 0D 0A 4B 65 6E 2C 0D    -ascii"....Ken,.
01C0:   0A 4A 75 73 74 20 77 61 6E 74 65 64 20 74 6F 20    .Just wanted to
01D0:   63 61 70 74 75 72 65 20 74 68 69 73 2E 0D 0A 0D    capture this....
01E0:   0A 4A 4C 41 0D 0A 0D 0A                            .JLA....
```

802.3 [0000:000D]
  0000:0005   Destination Address: 08003E0200DD
  0006:000B   Source Address: 0060972BE60F
  000C:000D   Ethernet Type: DOD Internet Protocol (IP)
IP [000E:0021]
  000E:000E   Version: 4, Header Length: 20
  000F:000F   TOS, Precedence: Routine, Delay: Normal, Throughput: Normal,
Reliability: Normal
  0010:0011   Packet Length: 474
  0012:0013   Identification: 0x9DE5
  0014:0014   Fragment Flag (bit 6..5): Don't Fragment
  0014:0015   Fragment Offset: 0x0000
  0016:0016   Time to Live: 128
  0017:0017   Transport: Transmission Control
  0018:0019   Header Checksum: 0xD60E
  001A:001D   Source Address: 24.94.41.254
  001E:0021   Destination Address: 192.203.130.2
TCP [0022:0035]
  0022:0023   Source Port: 0x0494
  0024:0025   Destination Port: Simple Mail Transfer Protocol
  0026:0029   Sequence Number: 92063410
  002A:002D   Acknowledgment Number: 27520224
  002E:002E   Header Length (bit 7..4): 20
  002F:002F   Control Bit - Acknowledgment; Push function;
  0030:0031   Window Size: 8353
  0032:0033   Checksum: 0xA5BC
  0034:0035   Urgent Pointer: 0x0000

Recall that the original message contained less than 40 bytes of data. Consider that each of these packet exchanges is required to send the message.

You are encouraged to study all of these packets to gain a deeper appreciation and understanding of the underlying processes involved in sending an e-mail message.

■ TROUBLESHOOTING TECHNIQUES

Objective 2-5

Objective 4-3

One reason it might be helpful to know a few basic POP3 commands has to do with a real-world situation in which several e-mail messages were queued up behind an e-mail with a very large (over 4 MB) attachment. Unfortunately, a network router problem creating frequent packet losses prevented the e-mail with the attachment from being properly transferred to the recipient's e-mail client. To get at the queued-up e-mail messages, the user used Telnet to connect to the POP3 server and delete the e-mail message containing the large attachment. This allowed the remaining messages to transfer to the e-mail client. Since the messages were small, they transferred quickly, with only a slight delay introduced by the router problem.

A Telnet session to a POP3 server is accomplished by choosing the Start, Run menu, and entering a command similar to the following:

```
telnet athena.sunybroome.edu 110
```

This instructs the Telnet application to connect to port 110 on the athena.sunybroome.edu computer system. Port 110 is the location where the POP3 server is installed. An actual interaction with the POP3 server follows:

```
+OK Microsoft Exchange POP3 server version 5.5.2650.23 ready
user antonakos_j
+OK
pass
-ERR Logon failure: unknown user name or bad password.
user antonakos_j
+OK
pass ********
+OK User successfully logged on
list
+OK
1 11605
2 14542
3 28602
4 28088
5 674
6 272530
.
.
.
40 12107
41 16549
42 42543
43 15640
.
retr 43
+OK
Received: from sbccab.cc.sunybroome.edu by athena.sunybroome.edu with SMTP
(Microsoft Exchange Internet Mail Service Version 5.0.1457.7) id CLT5Z7QR;
Mon, 2 Mar 1998 08:31:48 -0500
```

```
Received: from sunybroome.edu by sunybroome.edu (PMDF V5.0-3 #8051)
 id <01IU6NDXNT1C984NDS@sunybroome.edu>; Mon, 02 Mar 1998
08:34:11 -0500 (EST)
Date: Mon, 02 Mar 1998 08:34:11 -0500 (EST)
From: "ALAN C. DIXON" <DIXON_A@sunybroome.edu>
Subject: T1 Discussion
To: BCC002407@acad.sunybroome.edu, BleeF@worldnet.att.net,
dixon_a@mail.sunybroome.edu
Message-id: <01IU6NDXPAPU984NDS@sunybroome.edu>
X-VMS-To: @EET252,@DEPT
X-VMS-Cc: DIXON_A
MIME-version: 1.0
Content-type: TEXT/PLAIN; CHARSET=US-ASCII
Content-transfer-encoding: 7BIT


The Bell System's Digital Signal Hierachy
----------------------------------------------------------------------------
        To improve signal/noise ratio on multi-line phone trunks, Bell began
converting some frequency division multiplexing (FDM) lines to time division
multiplexing (TDM) back in the 1960s.
        The digitization technique chosen was pulse code modulation (PCM), taking
8000 samples/second of the analog waveform and quantizing it to 8 bit precision with
an analog to digital (A/D) converter.  When the bits are serially shifted out, the
signal source is called a "DS0" by the phone company.
        Including several DS0 channels in one TDM bit stream requires the addition
of framing bits, so the individual channels can be identified on recovery.  A "DS1"
is composed of 24 byte-wise interleaved 8-bit samples (from 24 different DS0s) and
one framing bit.  The total bit rate is: total rate = 8000 samples/sec *
[(8 bits/sample * 24 samples) + 1 frame bit] = 1.544 Mbps


 a1 a2 a3 a4 a5 a6 a7 a8 b1 b2 b3 b4 b5 b6 b7 b8 ... x6 x7 x8 f0
 |                       |                       |           |
    sample from 1st DS0     sample from 2nd DS0 .....   frame
                                                        bit
                Sample Bit Frame


        Four DS1s can be combined into a DS2; 7 DS2s compose a DS3.  There are also
DS4s and DS5s, used for long-distance trunks often running on optical fiber.


.
del 43
-ERR Protocol Error
dele 43
+OK
stat
+OK 42 4116756


.
quit
+OK Microsoft Exchange POP3 server version 5.5.2650.23 signing off
```

It is fascinating to see that the subject of the message blocked by the large attachment is a technical description of the T1 line frame format used to multiplex 24 phone conversations. You are encouraged to connect to a POP3 server to try a few of these commands on your own.

INDUSTRY TIP*

For all the complexity of the Internet, e-mail is the one simple tool on which people most rely. Sometimes this simple tool proves to be not so simple or reliable. However, a few common practices can greatly improve the likelihood of making your e-mail successful.

There are two steps for your e-mail to be successful. One is getting your e-mail message delivered. The other is getting the recipient to read it.

Getting the e-mail delivered involves many technologies to work properly. In most cases, this is beyond your control, but there are things you can control. The most common mistake in sending e-mail is to misspell or mistype the recipient's e-mail address. Many times e-mail addresses are given to us scribbled on napkins or scraps of paper. These are often illegible, so we make our best attempt. Other times we simply press the wrong keys. A simple solution to this is to use an address book with simple name entries. After all, which is easier to type without a mistake, "mark" or "mdye@bevillcntr.org"?

Another common reason our e-mail is not delivered has to do with the attachments. We either send attachments that are too large or are in a format that is not permitted. Most e-mail servers limit attachments to less than 1 MB. We often get a bounced e-mail because the attachment exceeds this limit. You should try to limit any attachment to 1 MB or less unless you know that the recipient's e-mail server will allow larger attachments. You may send several e-mails with attachments to forward all the documents you wish.

Because of e-mail viruses and worms, many firewalls will not permit e-mail attachments that are executable. The firewall may allow the message to be delivered with the attachment stripped. Alternatively, the firewall may block the e-mail altogether. For this reason, your attachments should not be .exe, .bat, .cmd, .pif, or other executable files.

Once the e-mail has been received by the recipient's computer, you would most probably want them to read it. This is becoming less and less likely. With the constant onslaught of spam and e-mail worms, people are careful about what e-mail they open. One of the key reasons they may not open and read the e-mail is they do not recognize the sender. Often our e-mail addresses do not reflect our name. If the receiver does not know your e-mail address, they possibly will delete your message without ever opening it. One way to ensure that your name shows up in the receiver's in basket is to set up your real name in your e-mail client. Seeing a name will provide the receiver a level of comfort that your e-mail is legitimate.

Another reason that e-mail is not opened is what you put in the subject line. Always put a subject in the subject line. E-mails without subjects make their way to the trash quickly. However, be careful with the subject you put on your e-mail. Many people create e-mail filters that will look in the subject line and forward the e-mail to the trash based on certain words in the subject. If you are like me, you receive massive amounts of e-mails letting you know about ". . . . Discount . . .", ". . . Mortgage rate . . .", or ". . . Sex . . .". These are only a few of the most common items that people recognize and filter.

There are two ways that you can get a higher level of confidence that your e-mail will be delivered. One is to mark the priority of the e-mail. E-mails with priority changed, either greater or lower priority, will most probably be opened. The other is to use "Return Receipt." This allows the recipient to send a return receipt, to notify the sender that the e-mail has been opened. Neither of these methods is foolproof, but they will increase your chances. As with any other tool if these are overused, they become a part of normal e-mail procedure and are no longer effective in ensuring that important e-mail gets the desired attention.

*Mark A. Dye, CCNP, CCDP, CCAI, MCSE(W2K), MCSE(NT4), MCT, MCP+I, MCP, HTI+, NET+, BET
Technology Manager
Bevill Manufacturing Technology Center
401 Trade School Road
Gadsden, AL 35903

■ SELF-TEST

1. E-mail messages can be used to _____, _____, and _____. (Choose three.)
   a. send audio files
   b. control remote computers
   c. send encrypted messages
   d. send messages to several recipients

2. What protocol specifies how electronic messages are exchanged between computers?
   a. IP
   b. POP3
   c. SMTP
   d. IANA

3. Each e-mail address is divided into how many parts?
   a. 2
   b. 3
   c. 4
   d. 5

4. What is the computer host name portion of the following e-mail address: joe@tekk.com?
   a. joe
   b. @
   c. tekk
   d. tekk.com

5. The .com part of the e-mail address indicates that the organization that joe@tekk.com is a part of a(n) _____ organization.
   a. communications
   b. incorporated
   c. commercial
   d. company

6. College and university e-mail addresses typically end with the letters _____.
   a. .gov
   b. .com
   c. .mil
   d. .edu

7. When a mail message is exchanged, the mail transfer program on the sending computer temporarily becomes a _____ and connects to the mail transfer program running as a _____ on the receiving computer.
   a. client, server
   b. server, client
   c. host, node
   d. client, client

8. The second part of an e-mail message that contains the actual text of the message is called the _____.
   a. body
   b. trailer
   c. frame check sequence
   d. MLME

9. In the output of the e-mail message box listed in the following figure, what letter in parentheses indicates the intended recipient(s) of the e-mail? (Choose all that apply.)
   a. (A)
   b. (B)
   c. (C)
   d. (D)

10. True or False: Outlook Express limits the amount of messages stored in the inbox to 10 MB.

11. True or False: E-mail messages are received by the server and stored in the inbox of a user's mailbox until they are read and deleted.

12. What will happen if the user incorrectly specifies the mailbox name when creating an e-mail?
    a. An error message is generated.
    b. The mail is sent to the default server.
    c. The mail is sent to the inbox.
    d. The mail is sent to the outbox.

13. True or False: The Microsoft Outlook Web Access program uses the Microsoft Exchange Server.

14. _____ provides a way for binary programs, graphics, and other file types to be attached to e-mail messages.
    a. EXT
    b. MIME
    c. SMTP
    d. POP3

15. What MIME extension is used to e-mail a Quicktime movie file?
    a. .comp
    b. .zip
    c. .Qt
    d. .mov

16. What MIME extension is used to send uuencoded files?
    a. .comp
    b. .unc
    c. .au
    d. .uu

17. True or False: All MIME-compliant applications are capable of working with base64 encoding methods.

18. What version of IMAP provides full compatibility with Internet and MIME standards?
    a. IMAP4
    b. IMAPv4
    c. IMAP+
    d. IMAP3

19. The command in the output listed in the following figure could be used to connect to a(n) _____ server and delete an e-mail message.

   a. FTP
   b. SMTP
   c. Telnet
   d. POP3

20. Including several DSO channels in one TDM stream requires the addition of _____.
   a. status bits
   b. framing bits
   c. trunking bits
   d. error recovery bits

21. What is the term commonly used by network technicians to refer to a DS1?
   a. T1
   b. T3
   c. E3
   d. Drop

22. Many firewalls will not permit e-mail attachments that are _____.
   a. executable
   b. text only
   c. .zip
   d. .gif

23. True or False: The transmission of a 2 MB file to a recipient whose server only allows a 1 MB attachment cannot be done.

24. True or False: Many firewalls will not permit executable e-mail attachments because of e-mail viruses and worms.

25. What is one key reason that recipients of e-mail messages do not open them?
   a. They cannot read them because of different encoding methods.
   b. They cannot open them because of different software usage.
   c. They cannot recognize the sender of the e-mail.
   d. They cannot open e-mails less than 1 MB.

FTP and Telnet

PERFORMANCE OBJECTIVES

Upon completion of this chapter, you will be able to:

- Describe the purpose of the File Transfer and Telnet protocols.

- Explain how File Transfer Protocol clients and servers are configured.

- Discuss the various FTP and Telnet commands.

 ## NETWORK+ OBJECTIVES

This chapter provides information for the following Network+ objectives:

2.5 Define the purpose, function, and/or use of the following protocols within TCP/IP:

- IP
- TCP
- UDP
- FTP
- TFTP
- SMTP
- HTTP
- HTTPS
- POP3/IMAP4
- TELNET

- ICMP
- ARP
- NTP

2.6 Define the function of TCP/UDP ports. Identify well-known ports.

3.7 Given a remote connectivity scenario (e.g., IP, IPX, dial-up, PPPoE, authentication, physical connectivity, etc.), configure the connection.

4.11 Given a network troubleshooting scenario involving a client connectivity problem (e.g., incorrect protocol/client software/ authentication configuration, insufficient rights/permission), identify the cause of the problem.

■ INTRODUCTION

Objective 2-5

The FTP and Telnet applications presented in this chapter have many practical applications. Some of these include:

- Authors exchanging manuscript files
- A faculty member hosting class notes and files
- Using Telnet to connect to a POP3 mail server
- Using FTP to update pages on a Web server
- Transferring network configuration between network administrators
- Downloading device drivers from a manufacturer

Examine the details of each application (and associated protocols).

■ FTP CLIENTS AND SERVERS

The capability to copy a file between computers is provided by the FTP (File Transfer Protocol). FTP uses connection-oriented TCP as the underlying transport protocol, providing guaranteed reliability. FTP can transmit or receive text or binary files as described in RFC 959. The primary function of FTP is defined as transferring files efficiently and reliably among host computers and allowing the convenient use of remote file storage capabilities. Essentially, FTP is a client-server application that uses two ports on both the client and the server. One port is used to exchange FTP control or command information and the other port is used to transfer the data. This is illustrated in Figure 13–1.

FIGURE 13–1
FTP client-server interaction.

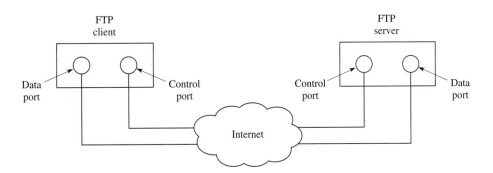

Objective 2-6

On the FTP server computer, port 20 is used for data transfer and port 21 is used for control by default. The FTP client can also use any port number greater than 1023.

FTP Commands

An FTP exchange of information consists of *requests* sent by the client and *responses* sent by the server. After the client connects, the server sends a response to the client either *accepting* or *rejecting* the connection. If the server accepts the connection, the client sends requests to the server for processing. The server sends one or more responses back to the client. The last response from the server for a specific request indicates whether the request was accepted or rejected by the server.

An FTP request consists of a command or an action to be performed. A list of FTP commands is shown in Table 13–1. Note that a command may optionally include parameters.

TABLE 13–1
File Transfer Protocol Windows
client commands.

Command	Meaning
!	Escape to a DOS shell
delete	Delete remote file
literal	Send arbitrary FTP command
prompt	Force interactive prompting on multiple command
send	Send one file
?	Print local help information
debug	Toggle debugging mode
ls	List contents of remote directory
put	Send one file
status (or stat)	Show current status
append	Append to a file
dir	List contents of remote directory
mdelete	Delete multiple files
pwd	Print working directory on remote machine
trace	Toggle packet tracing
ascii	Set ASCII transfer type
disconnect	Terminate FTP session
mdir	List contents of multiple remote directories
quit	Terminate FTP session and exit
type	Set file transfer type
bell	Beep when command completed
get	Receive file
mget	Get multiple files
quote	Send arbitrary FTP command
user	Send new user information
binary	Set binary transfer type
glob	Toggle metacharacter expansion of local file names
mkdir	Make directory on the remote machine
recv	Receive file
verbose	Toggle verbose mode
bye	Terminate FTP session and exit
hash	Toggle printing '#' for each buffer transferred
mls	List contents of multiple remote directories
remotehelp	Get help from remote server
cd	Change remote working directory
help	Print local help information
mput	Send multiple files
rename	Rename file
close	Terminate FTP session
lcd	Change local working directory
open	Connect to remote FTP
rmdir	Remove directory on the remote machine

The command and parameters are separated by one space. The FTP command STAT (short for *status*) does not require any parameters, whereas a GET command does require a parameter, the name of the file to get, such as GET TEST.DAT.

A server response from a request consists of one or more lines. The client can identify the last line of the response because it begins with three ASCII digits and a space, whereas the previous response lines do not. The three digits form a *code*. Codes between 100 and 199 indicate marks; codes between 200 and 399 indicate acceptance; and codes between 400 and 599 indicate rejection. Typical FTP response codes are shown in Table 13–2. Many other response codes are defined and may be displayed during an FTP exchange.

TABLE 13–2
Common FTP server response codes.

FTP Response Code	Response Meaning
125	Data connection already open; transfer starting
150	File status okay; about to open data connection
200	Command okay
221	Service closing control connection
220	Service ready for new user
226	Closing data connection
230	User logged in, proceed
250	Requested file action okay, completed
331	User name okay, need password
421	Service not available, closing control connection
450	Requested file action not taken
500	Syntax error, command unrecognized
501	Syntax error in parameters or arguments
550	Requested action not taken

Now that the ground rules for communication have been laid, you can examine how FTP works from both the client and server sides. We begin by looking at the client-side application program.

FTP Clients

An FTP client is provided for almost every type of hardware and operating system platform available. On a Windows computer, an FTP client is installed when the TCP/IP protocol is installed. Generally, there are two types of access to an FTP server: *anonymous* logins, and logins requiring a valid user ID and password combination.

Anonymous FTP

Anonymous FTP is a mode of operation that allows public access to files stored on an FTP server without the need for a predefined user ID and password. This type of access is useful in many different circumstances. For example, a manufacturer may provide free updates to device drivers or an easy method to distribute shareware applications.

The FTP client program can be started on a Windows computer through the Run option on the Start menu. Figure 13–2 shows the Run dialog box specifying the FTP program name and an Internet host to connect to. Note that the FTP client can also be run directly from the DOS prompt.

FIGURE 13–2
Running FTP on a Windows client.

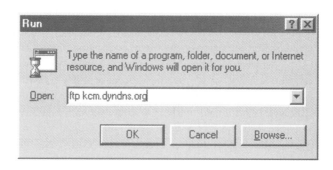

A sample anonymous FTP session run from the DOS prompt is as follows:

```
C:> ftp kcm.dyndns.org
Connected to kcm.dyndns.org.
220 server Microsoft FTP Service (Version 3.0).
User (kcm.dyndns.org:(none)): anonymous
331 Anonymous access allowed, send identity (e-mail name) as password.
Password:
230 Anonymous user logged in.
ftp> dir
200 PORT command successful.
150 Opening ASCII mode data connection for /bin/ls.
-r-xr-xr-x   1 owner     group          4487 Jul 24   1999 cgi_perl.c
-r-xr-xr-x   1 owner     group          4509 Oct  4   1997 client.c
-r-xr-xr-x   1 owner     group         62907 Nov 16   1998 cppsrc.zip
-r-xr-xr-x   1 owner     group          1287 Feb 22   5:16 getpost.pl
-r-xr-xr-x   1 owner     group      42755470 Oct 15   1999 itc.zip
-r-xr-xr-x   1 owner     group          3363 Feb  2   1:03 lab3.c
-r-xr-xr-x   1 owner     group        933851 Oct 30   1998 mgc115eq.zip
-r-xr-xr-x   1 owner     group         16452 Nov 13   1997 pdp10.jpg
-r-xr-xr-x   1 owner     group          4429 Oct  4   1997 server.c
226 Transfer complete.
ftp: 629 bytes received in 0.05Seconds 12.58Kbytes/sec.
ftp> stat
Connected to kcm.dyndns.org.
Type: ascii; Verbose: On ; Bell: Off ; Prompting: On ; Globbing: On
Debugging: Off ; Hash mark printing: Off .
ftp> binary
200 Type set to I.
ftp> get cppsrc.zip
200 PORT command successful.
150 Opening BINARY mode data connection for cppsrc.zip(62907 bytes).
226 Transfer complete.
ftp: 62907 bytes received in 3.90Seconds 16.13Kbytes/sec.
ftp> close
221 Goodbye
ftp> quit
```

In this example, the FTP server you want to connect to is running on a computer called kcm.dyndns.org. The first message shown is the connect message. Following the connect message, a message is displayed that identifies itself as a Microsoft FTP Service. The version number is typically displayed for informational or debugging purposes.

When the user is prompted to provide a user name, the word "anonymous" is entered. The following message appears from the server:

```
331 Anonymous access allowed, send identity (e-mail name) as password.
```

This message indicates that anonymous access to the server is allowed and furthermore instructs the user to enter his or her e-mail name as the password. On some systems, simply entering the word *guest* is allowed.

After the connection is established, the client can enter any of the commands from Table 13–1. In the example, the first command entered is `dir` (short for directory) and the server returns several responses. The `dir` command is not traditionally a UNIX command, but most UNIX FTP servers support this command, for the sake of DOS users, through the use of an alias that translates the `dir` command into an `ls` (UNIX) command. The first response

```
200 PORT command successful.
```

indicates that the command was accepted by the server. The server continues by opening an ASCII connection and then proceeds to list each of the files in the directory as follows:

```
150 Opening ASCII mode data connection for /bin/ls.
-r-xr-xr-x   1 owner      group               4487 Jul 24   1999 cgi_perl.c
-r-xr-xr-x   1 owner      group               4509 Oct  4   1997 client.c
-r-xr-xr-x   1 owner      group              62907 Nov 16   1998 cppsrc.zip
-r-xr-xr-x   1 owner      group               1287 Feb 22   5:16 getpost.pl
-r-xr-xr-x   1 owner      group           42755470 Oct 15   1999 itc.zip
-r-xr-xr-x   1 owner      group               3363 Feb  2   1:03 lab3.c
-r-xr-xr-x   1 owner      group             933851 Oct 30   1998 mgc115eq.zip
-r-xr-xr-x   1 owner      group              16452 Nov 13   1997 pdp10.jpg
-r-xr-xr-x   1 owner      group               4429 Oct  4   1997 server.c
```

For each file displayed, several of the file properties are shown in a UNIX-style format. From left to right, the first item is the file permissions (-r-xr-xr-x), followed by the file owner and group, the file size, the file date, and lastly, the name of the file. The format of the file permission codes is shown in Table 13–3.

TABLE 13–3
UNIX-style file permission codes.

Position Number	Permission Type	Meaning	
1	File Type	d = Directory	– = Regular file
2	Owner Read	r = Read Access	– = no Read Access
3	Owner Write	w = Write Access	– = no Write Access
4	Owner Execute	x = Execute	– = no Execute Access
5	Group Read	r = Read Access	– = no Read Access
6	Group Write	w = Write Access	– = no Write Access
7	Group Execute	x = Execute	– = no Execute Access
8	World Read	r = Read Access	– = no Read Access
9	World Write	w = Write Access	– = no Write Access
10	World Execute	x = Execute	– = no Execute Access

The file permissions determine whether or not a file can be accessed. For an anonymous login, it is necessary for the file to contain world read access. The file owner determines the file permissions. When the directory listing is complete, an informational message is displayed indicating that the transfer is complete, followed by the number of bytes transmitted and the amount of time necessary to complete the transfer.

```
226 Transfer complete.
ftp: 629 bytes received in 0.05Seconds 12.58Kbytes/sec.
```

To transfer files, it is necessary to select the appropriate type of file transfer mode. The `stat` command is used to show the status of the connection. For example,

```
ftp> stat
Connected to kcm.dyndns.org.
Type: ascii; Verbose: On ; Bell: Off ; Prompting: On ; Globbing: On
Debugging: Off ; Hash mark printing: Off .
```

indicates that a session is currently established, the current type of transfer is ASCII, the verbose flag is set to On, and so on. Of particular importance here is the "Type," which is set to ASCII. To transfer a zip file (a binary file) it is necessary to change the mode to binary. This is accomplished by entering the command

```
ftp> binary
200 Type set to I.
```

The server response indicates that the Type is now set to "I," which stands for Image, or binary. After setting the mode, the cppsrc.zip file may be transferred as follows:

```
ftp> get cppsrc.zip
200 PORT command successful.
150 Opening BINARY mode data connection for cppsrc.zip(62907 bytes).
226 Transfer complete.
ftp: 62907 bytes received in 3.90Seconds 16.13Kbytes/sec.
```

Again, notice that informational responses are sent by the server to indicate the progress of the file transfer using binary mode. When the transfer is complete, the number of bytes and transfer time are displayed.

When the FTP session is complete, the connection can be closed and the program terminated using the following commands:

```
ftp> close
221 Goodbye
ftp> quit
```

Objective 4-11

The second mode of FTP operation requires an account and password on the particular computer. In this mode of operation, access to files is restricted and not for the public. The commands used for both modes of operation are the same. A sample FTP exchange using a valid computer account follows:

```
C:\>ftp ftp.sunybroome.edu
Connected to sbccab.cc.sunybroome.edu.
220 sbccab.cc FTP Server (Version V4.1-12) Ready.
User (sbccab.cc.sunybroome.edu:(none)): mansfield_k
331 Username MANSFIELD_K requires a Password.
Password:
530 Login incorrect.
Login failed.
ftp> close
425 Session is disconnected.
ftp> open ftp.sunybroome.edu
Connected to sbccab.cc.sunybroome.edu.
220 sbccab.cc FTP Server (Version V4.1-12) Ready.
User (sbccab.cc.sunybroome.edu:(none)): mansfield_k
331 Username MANSFIELD_K requires a Password.
Password:
230 User logged in.
ftp> cd cgi
250 CWD command succesful.
```

```
ftp> put getpost.c
200 PORT command successful.
150 Opening data connection for GETPOST.C (24.24.78.124,1168)
226 Transfer complete.
ftp: 5350 bytes sent in 0.00Seconds 5350000.00Kbytes/sec.
Ftp> quit
221 Goodbye.
```

In this FTP session, the first attempt to log in was unsuccessful because an invalid password was entered. Because of this error situation, it is necessary to disconnect the current session using the close command and then open another connection using the open command as shown. Following the successful login, the private directory tree can be navigated and files transferred as necessary.

In addition to the built-in Windows FTP client program, many other clients are available. One of the most popular FTP client programs is WS_FTP, produced by Ipswitch Incorporated. WS_FTP LE (Limited Edition) is available at no charge to qualified non-business users at www.ipswitch.com. The WS_FTP program is written as a Windows application rather than as a DOS application, allowing us to use the mouse instead of the keyboard for many of the controls.

Objective 3-7

After WS_FTP is installed and run, the Session Profile window is displayed to the user, as shown in Figure 13–3. The session profile allows the FTP client to be configured for each server to which the client connects.

FIGURE 13–3
WS_FTP Session Profile window.

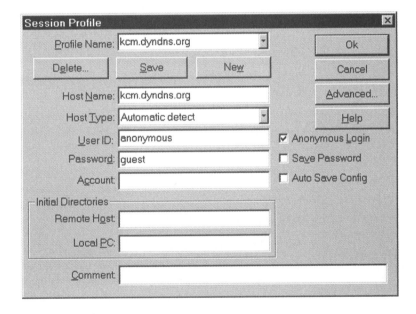

As shown in Figure 13–3, the profile name may be used to indicate the host name. For each profile, it is necessary to enter a host name and a user ID. Notice that the Anonymous Login box is checked, the user ID is set to *anonymous,* and the password is set to *guest*. This information is entered automatically by checking the Anonymous Login checkbox. After the profile information is entered, the profile should be saved by clicking on the Save button.

The FTP session is established by clicking on OK, and the user is presented with the window shown in Figure 13–4. Notice that the left side of the window displays the contents of the local system and the right side of the window displays the contents of the remote system.

For each of the systems (local and remote), the currently selected directory name is displayed as well as all of the files contained in the directory. On the local system, the wsftp32 directory contents are displayed, and the root directory "/" is displayed on the remote system.

FIGURE 13–4
WS_FTP main window.

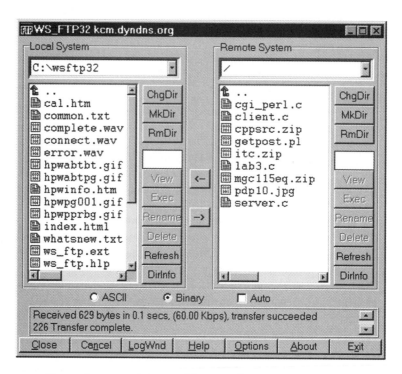

For each system, it is possible to perform the following operations by selecting the appropriate button on the display:

• Change to a different directory

• Make a new directory

• Remove a directory

• Refresh the current display

• Obtain directory information

In addition, if a file is selected in one of the windows, it is possible to

• View the file

• Execute the file

• Rename the file

• Delete the file

Between the windows, two arrows are used to indicate the direction of the transfer. Below the local and remote system windows, notice that the two file transfer options plus an Auto check box are displayed. The Auto selection determines the file type by using the file's extension. For example, an .exe or .com file will be set to binary and a file with a .txt extension would automatically be set to ASCII. The binary file type is selected by default, but the type can be set to any of the three values using one of the WS_FTP configuration screens. Below the file transfer type fields, a status window is displayed that contains a complete list of the text messages exchanged by the client and server. Lastly, along the bottom of the screen, buttons are provided to perform the following:

• Close the current session

• Cancel an operation

• Open the message log window

• Obtain online help

• Change the program options

• Review the About program information

• Exit the program

Perform the file transfer operation completed earlier with the DOS-based client using the WS_FTP program.

To duplicate the transfer in WS_FTP, it is necessary to select the file to be transferred (cppsrc.zip) and then click on the left arrow between the local and remote system windows to indicate which direction the file is being transferred. In this case the transfer is from the remote system to the local system. During the transfer, an informational window is displayed to show the progress of the exchange. This is illustrated in Figure 13–5.

FIGURE 13–5
WS_FTP file transfer status.

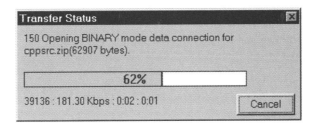

During the transfer, the cancel option may be selected and the transfer aborted if necessary. Note that it might be necessary to abort a transfer if it is taking an excessive amount of time or you notice that the wrong file or file type was selected. When the file transfer is complete, the new file is displayed in the directory listing on the local computer as shown in Figure 13–6. Now a copy of the cppsrc.zip file is located on both the local and remote computer systems.

FIGURE 13–6
WS_FTP main window after file transfer.

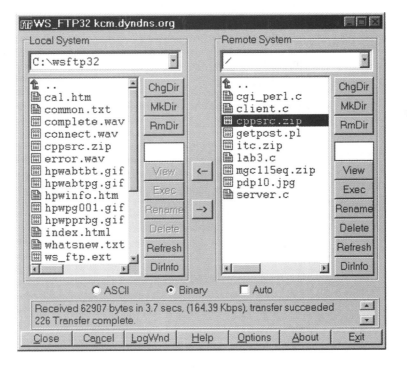

Obviously, the Windows user interface for the WS_FTP program has many advantages over the DOS-based client. It is worth mentioning that the same steps, or processing are performed by each of the clients. We can prove this by examining the contents of the WS_FTP status window (also contained in the Message Log) with the exchange of messages observed during the DOS exchange. A complete copy of the WS_FTP Message Log is shown in Figure 13–7 for comparison purposes. Do you notice any similarities or differences? You will probably find that the WS_FTP message log contains more information.

FIGURE 13–7
WS_FTP Message Log.

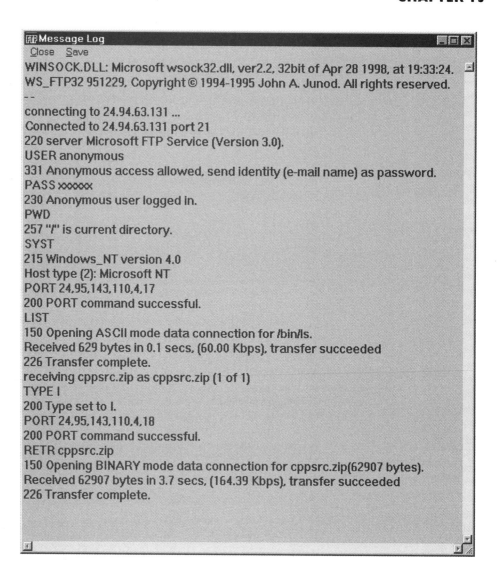

The Options button at the bottom of the WS_FTP window allows the user to customize many of the features available in WS_FTP. The Options window shown in Figure 13–8 identifies each of the categories for customization. Two of these categories, Program Options and Session Options, contain the fields that are updated most often.

FIGURE 13–8
WS_FTP Options window.

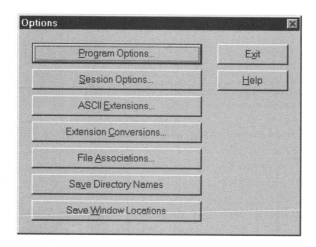

In the Program Options window, the look and feel of the WS_FTP program can be changed. For example, it is possible to display the buttons at the top of the screen instead of the bottom, change the action of double-clicking on the mouse, specify a different Log filename, and specify an e-mail address to be used during anonymous FTP, to name just a few of the options. The Program Options dialog box is shown in Figure 13–9.

FIGURE 13–9
WS_FTP Program Options
dialog box.

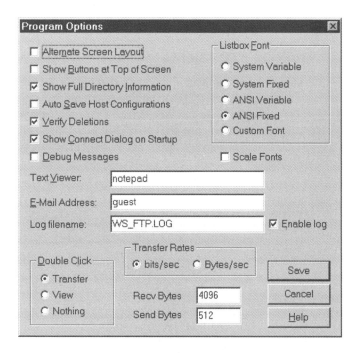

The Session Options dialog box (illustrated in Figure 13–10) provides the ability to

- Customize settings for file name differences that are commonly found between different server computers
- Control whether or not WS_FTP will use sounds to indicate successful transfers
- Set the default transfer mode shown on the main WS_FTP screen

FIGURE 13–10
WS_FTP Session Options
dialog box.

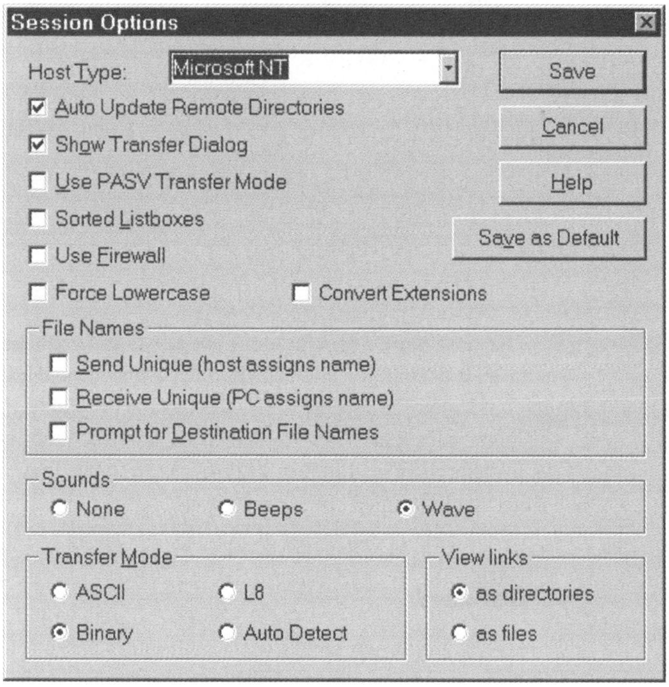

You are encouraged to explore each of the WS_FTP configuration screens. It is a good idea to make a hard copy of the default settings in case the new settings cause problems.

There are many different FTP clients to choose from. One very popular FTP client is FTP Explorer found at www.ftpx.com. This utility is easy to use, free to home and educational users, and comes in 10 languages. A search of the Web might identify a dozen or so clients that can be downloaded and installed for free or for a nominal fee.

Built-In FTP Clients

Many different application programs that use the Internet provide their own FTP capability. For example, most HTML editing programs contain a built-in FTP client to upload the HTML documents to the Web server. One such program is Softquad's HoTMetaL. For each stage of a Web page project, HTML files (or any other type of file) stored in the project can be uploaded very easily. Figure 13–11 shows a typical setup window for a specific destination.

FIGURE 13–11
HoTMetaL FTP client setup.

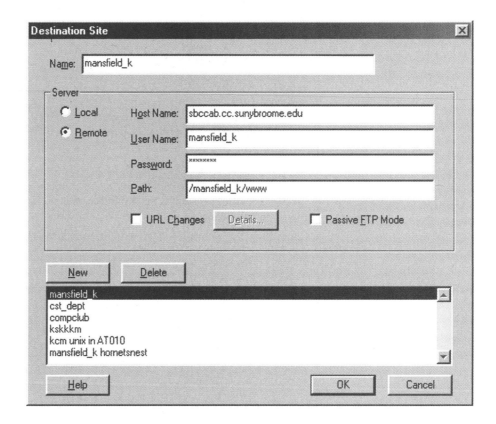

The host name, user name, password, and path provide enough parameters to perform an FTP exchange. The HTML files are published, or uploaded, to the site as needed. Figure 13–12 shows several files selected for upload to the server.

As the files are FTPed to the server, a status window is shown to indicate the progress of the transfer, as illustrated in Figure 13–13. Note that it is possible to stop the transfer at any time by clicking on the Stop button.

FTP Servers

FTP servers operate on server class computers using operating systems such as Windows NT, UNIX, and many others. FTP servers are installed as a service on ports 20 and 21 by

FIGURE 13–12
HoTMetaL selection of files to publish.

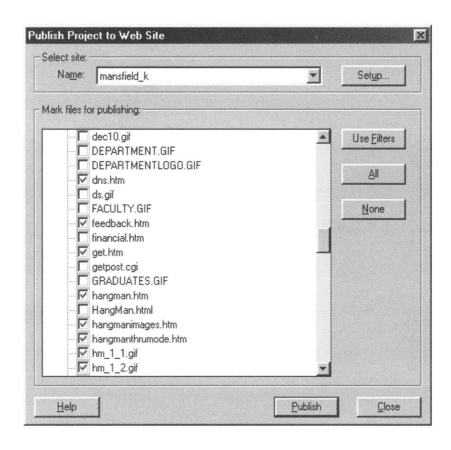

FIGURE 13–13
HoTMetaL Publishing Progress status window.

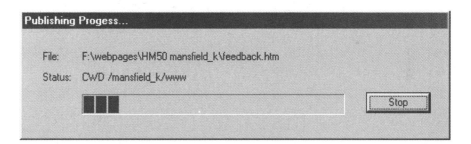

default. Port 20 is used as the channel to transfer data and port 21 is used to control the FTP session. A minimum implementation is required for all FTP servers so that each server, regardless of the underlying platform, can be used to reliably exchange information. These minimum requirements are specified in RFC 959. All hosts must operate using the standard settings specified in the RFC.

An FTP server is responsible for allowing access to the server and mechanisms are provided to authenticate users, access the server file structure, and set file transfer parameters. Authentication is accomplished by means of an account and a password. A user is permitted to transfer files only after entering a correct account name and associated password. Accessing the server file structure provides the user with the ability to navigate to a particular directory and store and/or retrieve a file.

On a Windows NT/2000 computer, the Microsoft Internet Information Server program, or IIS, provides the FTP service. During the installation of Windows NT, the system administrator is given the opportunity to install IIS. The Microsoft IIS provides three Internet services, WWW, Gopher, and FTP. Notice in Figure 13–14 that all three of the services are running. Each of the services can be controlled (stopped, paused, or started) using the buttons underneath the pull-down menus.

FIGURE 13–14
Microsoft Internet Service
Manager services.

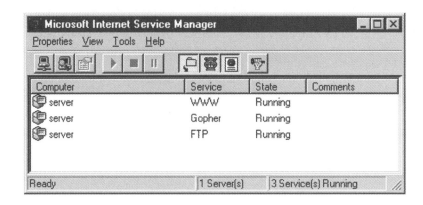

The FTP server properties can be examined by double-clicking on the FTP service or selecting the FTP service and clicking on the Properties button. Figure 13–15 shows the FTP Service Properties window.

FIGURE 13–15
Microsoft IIS FTP Service
Properties window.

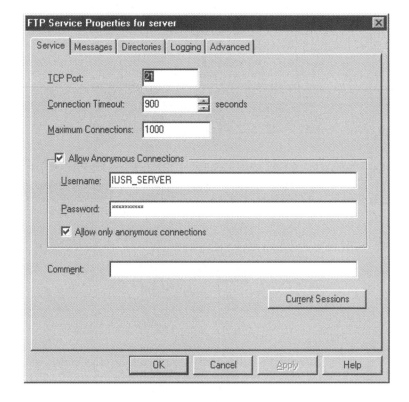

The Services tab provides access to the TCP port, which is set by default to 21. In addition, the connection time-out value and the maximum connections supported by the server can also be set. A check mark in the box for "Allow anonymous connections" indicates that anonymous connections are enabled. In fact, the second check box is set to allow only anonymous connections. This is a restriction that is useful in certain situations in which higher security is required. Notice that the current FTP sessions can be displayed by selecting the Current Sessions button. This causes the window shown in Figure 13–16 to be displayed. It is possible to disconnect any or all of the active sessions by clicking on the appropriate button on the FTP Users Display window.

The FTP Service Properties Messages tab provides the ability for the server administrator to change the default message text. This includes the greeting, the maximum connections reached, and the connection termination messages. The Directories tab provides a mechanism to create additional directories to be used by the FTP server. The server administrator may add an unlimited number of directories for use by the FTP server.

FIGURE 13–16
Microsoft IIS current FTP
sessions.

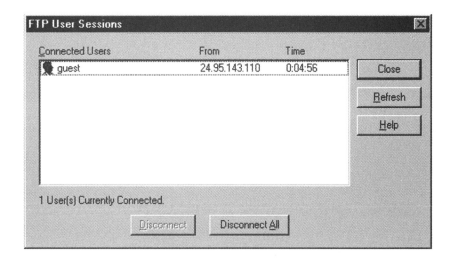

The Logging tab is used to capture the FTP activity of the server. It is possible to log the information to a file or to a database. Information stored in a log file would be useful when examining FTP server usage or instances of abuse. As indicated in Figure 13–17, it is possible to have a log file created on a daily, weekly, or monthly basis, or when the size of the log file reaches a user-specified limit. A database log would provide additional information that might be useful for a business or other organization that wants to track how the FTP server is used.

FIGURE 13–17
Microsoft IIS FTP service
logging.

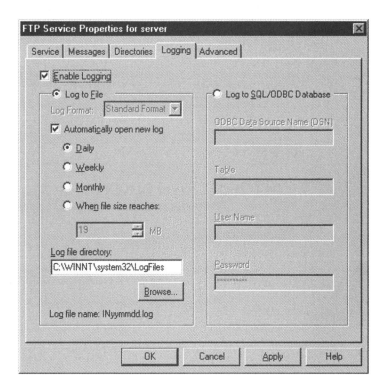

Lastly, the Advanced tab provides the ability to control who can access the FTP server. By default, all computers will be granted access to the FTP service, as shown in Figure 13–18. It is also possible to limit usage by specifying the type of access to be associated with individual IP addresses. This particular FTP server will allow access to all computers with no restrictions.

FIGURE 13–18
Microsoft IIS FTP Service
Advanced Properties.

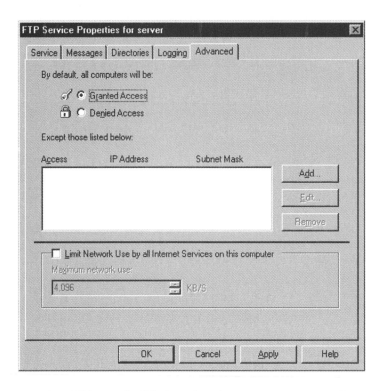

In addition to the Windows-based management screens that we have just examined, it is possible to manage the IIS services using a Web browser. The address of the management interface is http://localhost/iisadmin/default.htm. Note that `localhost` refers to the user's computer (running IIS), and not a site on the Web. `localhost` uses the loopback address available for testing purposes. The default page is displayed in Figure 13–19.

FIGURE 13–19
Microsoft IIS configuration
using a browser.

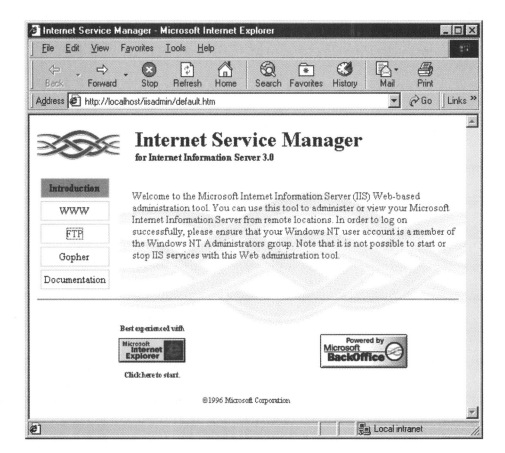

The Web management interface provides access to exactly the same information and configuration options. The main documentation for the Microsoft IIS is shown in Figure 13–20. It is well worth the time to read over all of the documentation provided.

FIGURE 13–20
Microsoft IIS Web-based help.

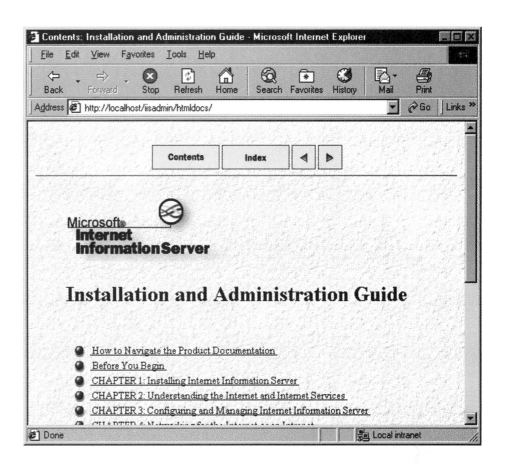

Just as there are many different FTP clients, there are also many different FTP servers. Depending on the operating system platform that is selected, an FTP server is generally available.

■ TELNET CLIENTS AND SERVERS

Objective 2-5

Telnet

The provision of remote terminal access was the very first Internet service implemented. The goal was to allow a user with an interactive terminal session attached to one mainframe computer to remotely connect to and use another mainframe computer as though it were directly connected. The *Telnet* protocol (RFC 854) provides for a bidirectional, byte-oriented service using TCP as the transport to reliably deliver messages. To provide remote terminal access, it is once again necessary to use the client-server model.

Telnet defines an NVT (Network Virtual Terminal). The NVT is an imaginary reference terminal written to a set of standards. It is necessary for Telnet to translate the characteristics of an NVT to a real terminal device and vice versa. The Telnet NVT implementation is shown in Figure 13–21.

Typically, an NVT will have fewer features than a real physical terminal. For example, a DEC VT320 terminal has many features that are not implemented in the NVT. Similarly, in an IBM environment, an IBM 3270 terminal also has features that are not implemented in the NVT. In addition, the DEC terminal and IBM terminal are not compatible. This scenario in which the systems are not compatible describes a lot of the problems that most users experience when using Telnet.

FIGURE 13–21
Telnet NVT implementation.

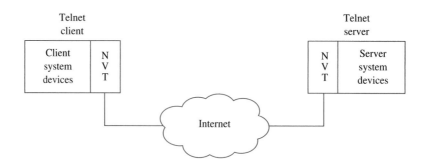

The Telnet protocol officially calls for only certain codes to be recognized and processed. The NVT defines standard control codes and nonprinting character functions. Table 13–4 shows a list of the control codes that must be recognized by Telnet clients and servers. Table 13–5 shows a list of the nonprinting characters. Due to these requirements, other manufacturer-specific codes are not supported.

TABLE 13–4
Telnet Network Virtual Terminal control codes.

Name	Code	Meaning
ABORT	238	Abort process
AO	245	Abort output
AYT	246	Are you there
BRK	243	Break
DO	253	Request support of option code
DONT	254	Request termination of option code
EC	247	Erase character
EL	248	Erase line
EOF	236	End of file
EOR	239	End of record
GA	249	Go ahead signal
IAC	255	Interpret the following octet(s) as controls
IP	244	Interrupt process
NOP	241	No operation code
SE	240	End of sub-negotiation parameters
SUSP	237	Suspend process
WILL	241	Will support option code
WONT	242	Will not support option code

TABLE 13–5
Telnet Network Virtual Terminal nonprinting characters.

Name	Code	Meaning
BEL	7	Produce a sound
BS	8	Move one character toward the left margin
CR	13	Move to left margin of current line
FF	12	Move to the top of the next page
HT	9	Move to the next horizontal tab stop
LF	10	Move to the next line
NUL	0	No operation
VT	11	Move to the next vertical tab stop

Because of the differences between manufacturers, the Telnet protocol specifies how differences are dealt with between a Telnet server and a client. This means that Telnet provides for the use of features not defined in the basic NVT using negotiated options. The negotiation process allows for the Telnet applications to either accept or reject a specific option. These options are implemented in the commands DO, DONT, WILL, and WONT. These commands are interpreted as follows:

- DO You please begin performing the option.
- DONT You please stop performing or do not begin performing the option.
- WILL I will begin performing the option.
- WONT I will stop performing or will not begin performing the option.

The first 20 NVT options that can be negotiated are shown in Table 13–6. Both Telnet servers and clients use this negotiation strategy to offer additional features to the user.

TABLE 13–6
NVT option codes.

Option	Description
0	Binary transmission
1	Echo
2	Reconnection
3	Suppress go ahead
4	Approximate message size
5	Status
6	Timing mark
7	Remote-controlled transmission and echo
8	Output line width
9	Output page size
10	Output carriage return disposition
11	Output horizontal tab stops
12	Output horizontal tab disposition
13	Output form feed disposition
14	Output vertical tab stops
15	Output vertical tab disposition
16	Output line feed disposition
17	Extended ASCII
18	Logout
19	Byte macro
20	Data entry terminal

A negotiation exchange between two NVTs is shown in Figure 13–22. In Figure 13–22(a), an offer to use an option (WILL) is sent to the remote NVT. If the remote NVT can use the option, it will respond with a DO. An offer to use an option that cannot be used is shown in Figure 13–22(b). The response to the offer to use an option is rejected with a DONT response. The local NVT acknowledges the rejection with a WONT.

Figure 13–22(c) shows a request for the other side to begin an option that can be accommodated. A WILL response is returned. Figure 13–22(d) shows a request for an option that cannot be accommodated and a WONT response is returned. The negative response is acknowledged by a DONT. A client or server NVT performs this process for every option that is requested.

FIGURE 13–22
NVT negotiations.

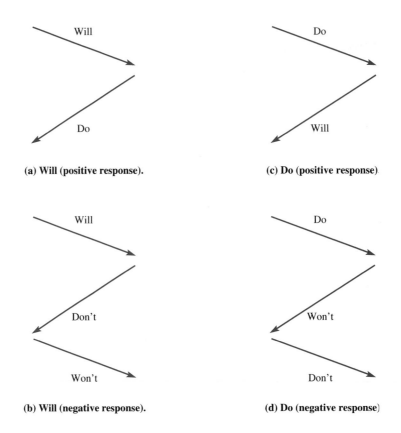

(a) **Will (positive response).**

(c) **Do (positive response)**

(b) **Will (negative response).**

(d) **Do (negative response)**

Now look at an example to illustrate how the negotiation for an ECHO option is negotiated. An IAC is sent to alert the receiving side that an option command is coming. Following the IAC, the command (WILL, WONT, DO, or DONT) is specified followed by the option number. The request to indicate an ECHO would look similar to the following because an ECHO option is number 1:

```
<IAC> WILL 1
```

The codes to represent this request are as follows:

```
<255> <251> <1>
```

In response to this request, a WILL or WONT message is expected. By default, no echoing is done over a Telnet connection.

Telnet Clients

A Telnet client is provided when the TCP/IP protocol suite is installed. On a Windows computer, the Telnet client is a DOS-based program that can be run from the DOS prompt or through the Run option on the Start menu. To begin a Telnet session, it is necessary to specify the Telnet program followed by the host to connect to. For example, the Run dialog box specifying a Telnet connection to sbccab.cc.sunybroome.edu is shown in Figure 13–23.

FIGURE 13–23
Starting a Telnet session.

Run	? ☒

🕐 Type the name of a program, folder, document, or Internet resource, and Windows will open it for you.

Open: telnet sbccab.cc.sunybroome.edu ▼

[OK] [Cancel] [Browse...]

After the Telnet program begins execution, the window shown in Figure 13–24 is displayed. The first activity to be tackled is authenticating the Telnet session. Before any interactive commands can be entered on the remote host, it is necessary for a user to enter a valid user name and password in order to gain access to the remote system. Once this is complete, the user can enter any valid operating system command on the remote computer. The computer system used in Figure 13–24 is a DEC/Compaq Alpha computer running the Open-VMS operating system.

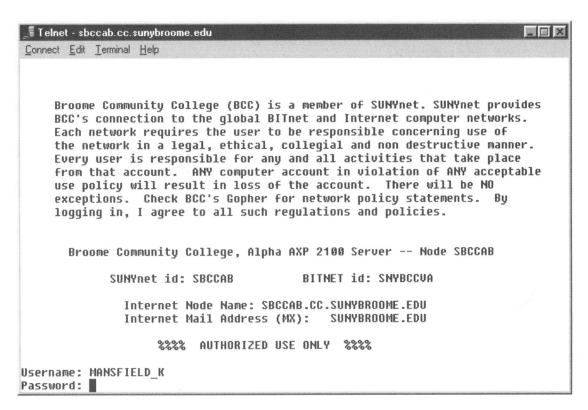

FIGURE 13–24
Authenticating a Telnet session with a username and password.

A typical terminal display window consists of 24 lines, each of which can hold 80 characters. The NVT display may be larger or smaller than the physical device. Because the screen is used for an interactive terminal session, new data is entered at the bottom of the display, and the older information scrolls off the top of the display. Because the information that scrolls off the top of the display is lost, the Telnet client offers the user an option to log the session activity to a file. Figure 13–25 shows the Open log file dialog box. The logging option is enabled on the Terminal pull-down menu.

When using the Telnet services, remember that there is a need to perform some type of remote interactive access. This may involve connecting to a mainframe computer (see Figure 13–26) to read mail, update records in a database, or update a CGI application on a Web server.

Suppose that the C source code file that was transferred to the server using the FTP protocol earlier in this chapter must be compiled and moved to a different location. The Telnet protocol may be used to accomplish this. The following Telnet dialog implements a procedure that is necessary to update a CGI application on a Web server. The Telnet client is running under the Windows operating system and the Telnet server is running under the Open-VMS operating system.

FIGURE 13–25
Specifying the filename for a
Telnet log.

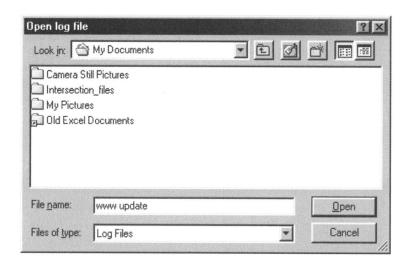

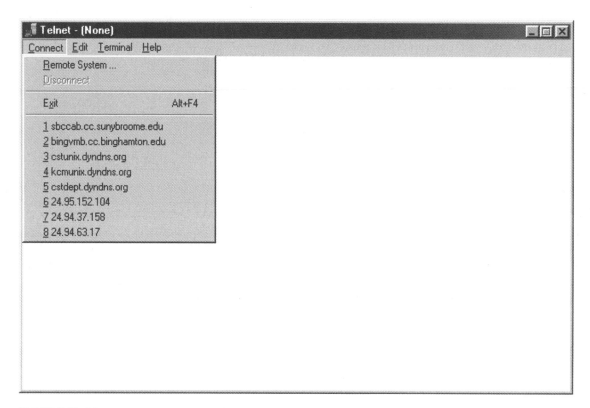

FIGURE 13–26
Windows Telnet client Connect menu.

```
Username: MANSFIELD_K
Password:

    Welcome to OpenVMS 6.2 running on a Digital Alpha-2100 Server.

    Last interactive login on Monday, 19-JUN-2000 17:11:13.67
    Last non-interactive login on Thursday, 22-JUN-2000 20:53:45.46
        2 failures since last successful login

SBCCAB>  set def [.cgi]
```

```
SBCCAB>  dir/since=today

Directory DSKB:[MANSFIELD_K.CGI]

GETPOST.C;14              11/12       22-JUN-2000 20:57:01.37   (RWED,RWED,RWE,)

Total of 1 file, 11/12 blocks.
SBCCAB>  cc getpost.c
SBCCAB>  link getpost, scriptlib, cgilib
SBCCAB>  copy getpost.exe [-.htbin]
SBCCAB>  dir [-.htbin]getpost.exe

Directory DSKB:[MANSFIELD_K.HTBIN]

GETPOST.EXE;8            58/60       22-JUN-2000 23:39:01.16   (RWED,RWED,RWE,)
GETPOST.EXE;7            57/60       12-FEB-2000 01:25:19.14   (RWED,RWED,RWE,)
GETPOST.EXE;6            56/56       12-FEB-2000 01:17:50.62   (RWED,RWED,RWE,)

Total of 3 files, 171/176 blocks.
SBCCAB>  lo
  MANSFIELD_K  logged out at 22-JUN-2000 23:40:31.98

  Accounting information:
  Buffered I/O count:              477       Peak working set size:  12048
  Direct I/O count:                304       Peak page file size:    50960
  Page faults:                    1265       Mounted volumes:            0
```

In this example, the complete session was logged to a file. The log file was closed when the session was complete.

The file GETPOST.C (FTPed to sbccab.cc.sunybroome.edu earlier) was compiled and linked into an executable image GETPOST.EXE. This file GETPOST.EXE must be copied to the proper location on the server so that the HTTP server application can find it when needed. Without the Telnet client and server applications, this process would be much more difficult to accomplish.

When a Telnet session is complete, it is necessary to disconnect it. This option is available on the Connect pull-down menu, as shown in Figure 13–26. A session is automatically disconnected if the client program is terminated.

Telnet Servers

Objective 2-6

Telnet servers are available for most hardware and operating system platforms. On a Windows computer, it is necessary to locate a third-party Telnet server because Microsoft does not provide a Telnet server program. Fortunately, there are many companies that produce Windows Telnet server application programs. Most other server class operating systems have a built-in Telnet server that is installed when the TCP/IP protocol is installed. By default, the Telnet server service is installed on port number 23.

You are encouraged to search the Web for Telnet server applications that can be run on a Windows platform. It is useful to compare the features and cost of each product.

Telnet 3270

A different version of Telnet clients and servers is required for use on most IBM mainframe computers. The Telnet 3270 protocol (commonly called TN3270) is described by RFC 1576. The architecture of the IBM operating system does not easily allow for a standard NVT to work properly. In fact, if you use a regular Telnet client to connect to an IBM mainframe, the session is not established and the server appears not to have a Telnet server application running at all. Instead, IBM provides 3270 server and client applications. The

IBM client application called Host on Demand can be used to connect to an IBM mainframe. Previously, the Host on Demand application program was distributed as a part of the Netscape Navigator product, but now it must be purchased separately.

■ TROUBLESHOOTING TECHNIQUES

Two very useful TCP/IP protocols are FTP and Telnet. We will now examine a few issues with the use of these protocols.

FTP File Types

Many of the problems experienced when using the File Transfer Protocol stem from the differences between the text and binary files that a user wants to transfer. By default, an FTP client will transfer a file using the ASCII mode. The only type of file that can be transferred without corruption in ASCII mode is an ASCII file. Any other type of file, such as an executable or a zip file, will be modified during the transfer and corrupted. Because FTP does not know what type of file a user is transferring, it requires the user to set the transfer mode accordingly. Use of an application like WS_FTP (which provides the automatic capability to determine the type of file being processed based on the file's extension) makes using the FTP program easier. You are encouraged to experiment with FTP.

Telnet Keyboard Mapping

One of the most frustrating experiences with the Telnet protocol involves keyboard mapping. The first step in solving a keyboard mapping problem is to understand what keys are supported by Telnet and then be able to locate those keys on your particular keyboard. As an example, the Backspace key on most keyboards will back up one character to the left each time the key is pressed until the beginning of the line is reached. When using a Telnet client, the Backspace key may move the cursor to the left margin on the very first press. This makes it much more difficult to correct or edit a typing mistake. A quick solution can be found by pressing a left arrow key instead of the Backspace key.

Depending on the type of computer system that is being connected to, a lot of different keyboard mapping issues arise. Approach the situation from the standpoint that some solution or compromise probably exists and then try to locate it. The Terminal Preferences option, which is also available on the Terminal pull-down menu on the Windows client, is displayed in Figure 13–27. There are very few preferences that actually can be set. The emulation mode specifies the type of physical terminal that is used. Note that a VT-100/ANSI terminal offers more features than a VT-52. Different Telnet clients may offer more or fewer preference options. You are encouraged to explore the many other features of the Telnet protocol.

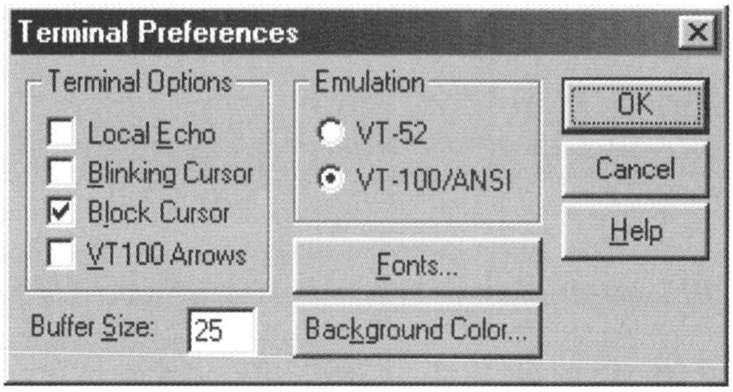

FIGURE 13–27
Telnet Terminal Preferences
dialog box.

■ SELF-TEST

1. What type of transmission is used to deliver FTP packets?
   a. Unreliable
   b. Reliable
   c. UDP
   d. DNS

2. FTP servers use port _____ to control the transfer of data between hosts by sending command information.
   a. 20
   b. 21
   c. 23
   d. 110

3. FTP requests are sent by the _____ and responses are sent by the _____.
   a. client, server
   b. server, client
   c. SAN, LAN
   d. WAN server, LAN client

4. The command and parameters in an FTP command are separated by _____.
   a. a backslash
   b. a colon
   c. one space
   d. a colon and a single space

5. What is the command used to print local help information for FTP?
   a. ?
   b. Quote
   c. Ls
   d. !

6. The three ASCII digits and a space that identify the last line of a server response form a code. Codes between 200 and 399 indicate _____.
   a. acceptance
   b. rejection
   c. marks
   d. rules

7. The FTP client program can be started on a Windows computer through the Run option on the Start menu or from the _____.
   a. programs
   b. DOS prompt
   c. Find utility
   d. File properties menu

8. When logging in as anonymous on some FTP systems, simply entering the word _____ is an accepted password.
   a. user
   b. log
   c. guest
   d. TFTP

9. Which part of the following Sample 1 FTP session dir command reveals the file permissions for the getpost.pl file?
   a. -r-xr-xr-x
   b. 1 owner
   c. group
   d. 1287

Sample 1 anonymous FTP session run from the DOS prompt

```
C:> ftp kcm.dyndns.org
Connected to kcm.dyndns.org.
220 server Microsoft FTP Service (Version 3.0).
User (kcm.dyndns.org:(none)): anonymous
331 Anonymous access allowed, send identity (e-mail name) as password.
Password:
230 Anonymous user logged in.
ftp> dir
200 PORT command successful.
150 Opening ASCII mode data connection for /bin/ls.
-r-xr-xr-x    1 owner      group             4487 Jul 24  1999 cgi_perl.c
-r-xr-xr-x    1 owner      group             4509 Oct  4  1997 client.c
-r-xr-xr-x    1 owner      group            62907 Nov 16  1998 cppsrc.zip
-r-xr-xr-x    1 owner      group             1287 Feb 22  5:16 getpost.pl
-r-xr-xr-x    1 owner      group         42755470 Oct 15  1999 itc.zip
-r-xr-xr-x    1 owner      group             3363 Feb  2  1:03 lab3.c
-r-xr-xr-x    1 owner      group           933851 Oct 30  1998 mgc115eq.zip
-r-xr-xr-x    1 owner      group            16452 Nov 13  1997 pdp10.jpg
-r-xr-xr-x    1 owner      group             4429 Oct  4  1997 server.c
226 Transfer complete.
ftp: 629 bytes received in 0.05 Second 12.8Kbytes/sec.
ftp> stat
Connected to kcm.dyndns.org.
Type: ascii; Verbose: On; Bell: Off; Prompting: On; Globbing: On
Debugging: Off; Hash mark printing: Off.
ftp> binary
200 Type set to I.
ftp> get cppsrc.zip
200 PORT command successful.
150 Opening BINARY mode data connection for cppsrc.zip(62907 bytes).
226 Transfer complete.
ftp: 62907 bytes received in 3.90Seconds 16.13Kbytes/sec.
ftp> close
221 Goodbye
ftp> quit
```

10. What determines whether or not a file can be accessed during an FTP session?
    a. Access rights
    b. Administrations
    c. Permissions
    d. Rights

11. What command must be entered before a zip file can be transferred in an FTP session?
    a. Hash
    b. Stat
    c. Binary
    d. ASCII

12. When an FTP transfer is completed, the number of bytes and _____ are displayed.
    a. connection type
    b. connection media
    c. transfer time
    d. transfer type

13. Logins to the FTP session (not anonymous) with a remote server have failed as referenced in the following Sample 2 output. Why?
    a. The word "Guest" was not entered.
    b. The wrong password was entered.
    c. A blank password, not entered.
    d. The password was not set.

Sample 2 FTP Session requiring username and password
```
C:\<ftp ftp.sunybroome.edu
Connected to sbccab.cc.sunybroome.edu.
220 sbccab.cc FTP Server (Version V4.1-12) Ready.
User (sbccab.cc.sunybroome.edu:(none)): mansfield_k
331 Username MANSFIELD_K requires a Password.
Password:
530 Login incorrect.
Login failed.
ftp> close
425 Session is disconnected.
ftp> open ftp.sunybroome.edu
Connected to sbccab.cc.sunybroome.edu.
220 sbccab.cc FTP Server (Version V4.1-12) Ready.
User (sbccab.cc.sunybroome.edu:(none)): mansfield_k
331 Username MANSFIELD_K requires a Password.
Password:
230 User logged in.
ftp> cd cgi
250 CWD command successful.
ftp> put getpost.c
200 PORT command successful.
150 Opening data connection for GETPOST.C (24.24.78.124,1168)
226 Transfer complete.
ftp: 5350 bytes sent in 0.00Seconds 5350000.00Kbytes/sec.
Ftp> quit
221 Goodbye.
```

14. The WS_FTP program is written as a Windows program instead of a _____ program.
    a. UNIX
    b. Linux
    c. DOS
    d. NETBIOS

15. FTP servers are installed as a service on port(s) _____ by default.
    a. 20 and 21
    b. 20 and 1020
    c. 19 and 20
    d. 20

16. True or False: FTP authentication is accomplished by using an account and a password.

17. True or False: ASCII mode is required to transfer a zip file.

18. True or False: An FTP user is permitted to transfer files only after entering a correct account name and an associated password.

19. What service provides the user with an interactive terminal session from one mainframe computer to remotely connect to and use another mainframe as though it were directly connected?
    a. RTP
    b. NFS
    c. Telnet
    d. TFTP

20. True or False: The DEC and IBM terminals are fully compatible in regards to Telnet.

21. True or False: The basic NVT negotiation process allows for Telnet applications to accept or reject specific options.

22. The NVT negotiated options include which of the following? (Choose four.)
    a. DO
    b. DONT
    c. CAN
    d. CANT
    e. WILL
    f. WONT

23. The negotiation exchange between two NVTs starts with an offer by the local to use an option by sending WILL to the remote NVT. The remote NVT replies with a _____ if it can use the stated option.
    a. CAN
    b. WILL
    c. CANT
    d. DO

24. A Telnet client is provided when the _____ is installed.
    a. remote service provider
    b. TCP/IP protocol suite
    c. operating system
    d. ISP connection

25. When using Telnet, it is necessary to enter a(n) _____ before gaining access to a remote system.
    a. key card
    b. username and password
    c. access code
    d. service code

26. When a Telnet session is complete, it is necessary to _____.
    a. notify the administrator
    b. log the activity
    c. authenticate
    d. disconnect

Multimedia Networking

CHAPTER 14

PERFORMANCE OBJECTIVES

Upon completion of this chapter, you will be able to:

- Explain the basic properties of .GIF and .JPG image files.

- Discuss the various sound file formats, such as .WAV, .MID, and .MP3.

- Describe MPEG, voice-over-IP, and multicasting.

NETWORK+ OBJECTIVES

This chapter provides information for the following Network+ objectives:

1.6 Identify the purpose, features, and functions of the following network components:
- Hubs
- Switches
- Bridges
- Routers
- Gateways
- CSU/DSU
- Network Interface Cards/ISDN adapters/system area network cards
- Wireless access points
- Modems

2.5 Define the purpose, function, and/or use of the following protocols within TCP/IP:

- IP
- TCP
- UDP
- FTP
- TFTP
- SMTP
- HTTP
- HTTPS
- POP3/IMAP4
- TELNET
- ICMP
- ARP
- NTP

4.8 Given a scenario, predict the impact of modifying, adding, or removing network services (e.g., DHCP, DNS, WINS, etc.) on network resources and users.

■ INTRODUCTION

Multimedia—or multiple types of media such as video, sound, and so on—has become a large part of the computing experience. Computers of the past were basically number crunchers and word processors. With the acceptance and widespread use of the Internet and the World Wide Web, multimedia has become an important form of communication. Processor and PC designers now design their products with multimedia applications in mind, to improve performance.

In this chapter we will examine several important multimedia components, including images, sound, and video.

■ IMAGE FILES

Web browsers accept two different types of image files: .GIF (Graphics Interchange Format) and .JPG or JPEG (Joint Photographic Experts Group) images.

GIF files were created by CompuServe as a method to exchange graphical information. The features of a .GIF file are as follows:

- Maximum of 256 colors
- Lossless compression using LZW (Lempel-Ziv-Welch) algorithm
- Support for animation and transparency built in

Lossless compression means that none of the original data is lost during compression. When the image data is decompressed for display purposes, an exact copy of the original data is reproduced.

Compare the properties of a .GIF file with those of a JPEG file:

- 24-bit color (16,777,216 colors)
- *Lossy* compression using the DCT (Discrete Cosine Transform) algorithm on 8-by-8 blocks of pixels
- No animation or transparency available

JPEG files are preferred for their photographic-quality color. In addition, the lossy compression provides better compression, in general, than the lossless compression used in .GIF files, with little noticeable effect on image quality. For example, consider the image shown in Figure 14–1(a).

The image contains 190 × 128, or 24,320 pixels. Without compression, a total of 24,320 bytes would be needed to store 8-bit pixel values, and 72,960 bytes would be required for 24-bit pixel values. Table 14–1 shows the results of saving the image in .GIF and JPEG formats. The JPEG compression is clearly superior to the .GIF compression. Viewing each image side by side also illustrates why JPEG is the better format for high-quality images.

To get a better feel for the differences between lossless and lossy compression, try the following experiment:

1. Create a new .GIF image using an image editor. Make the background of the image white.
2. Add a text message to the image, using black lettering.
3. Save the .GIF image.
4. Convert the .GIF image into a JPEG image and save it as well.
5. Open the .GIF image and zoom into it several times so that the pixels making up the text can be easily seen (a zoom factor of 8:1 should work fine). You should only see black pixels on a white background. This is shown in Figure 14–1(b).
6. Open the JPEG image and zoom in on the same area you examined in the .GIF image. You should notice pixels of an off-white color hovering around the text. This is the result of the lossy compression applied to the JPEG image. Figure 14–1(c) shows this

FIGURE 14–1
Sample image and the effect of compression on text.

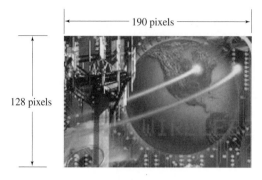

(a) Sample image.

(b) Portion of a .GIF image containing text.

(c) Portion of a JPEG image containing text.

TABLE 14–1
Comparing EARTH.JPG and EARTH.GIF files.

Property	EARTH.JPG	EARTH.GIF
Bits/pixel	24	8
Unique colors	20089	256
Possible colors	16777216	256
File size (bytes)	10097	24557

effect. Note that the off-white pixels have been changed to a darker color to make them more visible for the publishing process. In actuality, the off-white pixels are close to the color of the white background, and may not be noticeable when the image is viewed at its normal size. This is why we can get away with lossy compression in the JPEG image. Our eyes are not sensitive enough to see the effects of the lossy compression.

■ SOUND FILES

Three types of sound files are popular on the Web—.WAV, .MID, and .MP3. This section examines the features of each.

.WAV Files

.WAV

The *.WAV* file is the standard audio file format used by Windows. All the little sounds Windows makes are stored in .WAV files. The Sound Recorder found in the Entertainment folder of Accessories can be used to play, record, and even edit .WAV files. Figure 14–2 shows the Sound Recorder window with the BLAST.WAV file loaded and displayed. The waveform window is updated as the file is played.

FIGURE 14–2
Sound Recorder displaying portion of BLAST.WAV.

The Sound Recorder provides editing features such as cut, paste, and delete, and special effects, such as adding echo, reversing the audio (playing the file backwards), and adjusting the playback speed.

Figure 14–3 shows the properties of the BLAST.WAV file. The 0.30 second of audio requires 6786 bytes of sample data. Note that the audio was recorded in 8-bit stereo, at a sampling rate of 11,025 Hz (11,025 samples/second). The sampling method is *PCM*, or pulse code modulation. PCM is one of many different techniques for encoding audio into digital form.

FIGURE 14–3
BLAST.WAV properties.

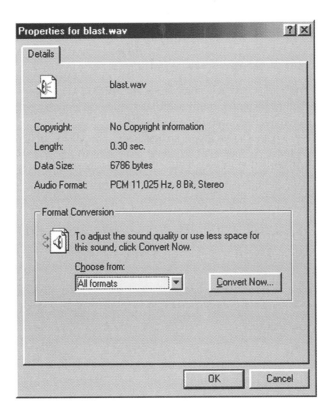

CD-quality sound

CD-quality sound is sampled at 44,100 Hz and uses 16-bit stereo samples. The Sound Recorder allows you to choose the sampling properties. Select the Recording formats entry in the "Choose from" drop-down menu in the Properties window. This will open the Sound Selection window shown in Figure 14–4. Here you are able to specify the sound quality in the Name box (CD, Radio, or Telephone), the encoding format (PCM, uLaw, ADPCM, etc.), and the sampling attributes (sampling rate, bits per channel, number of channels). The Attributes entry also indicates the data rate of the bitstream. In this case, two 16-bit channels being sampled 44,100 times per second require $2 \times 16 \times 44,100$ or 1,411,200 bits per second. Dividing by 8, we get 176,400 bytes/second (which is just over 172 kB/second).

FIGURE 14–4
Changing the sampling
properties.

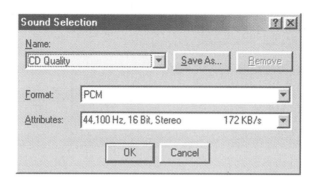

.MID Files

.MID is the file extension used on MIDI (Musical Instrument Digital Interface) files. A .MID file contains information (commands for the MIDI *sequencer*) on what notes to play and how to play them. A total of 128 pitched instruments can generate 24 notes in 16 channels. The sound card in the PC uses the MID information to reproduce the notes, using techniques such as frequency modulation and wave table synthesis. The attack, delay, sustain, and release portions of each note can be controlled.

.MID files are capable of producing very complex sounds with a small amount of data. For example, an 18 kB .MID file has a playing time of 3 minutes.

.MP3 Files

.MP3

MPEG

.MP3 files get their name from the MPEG Audio Layer 3 specification. *MPEG* (Moving Picture Experts Group) audio and video are popular encoding methods for creating high-quality, low-bit rate multimedia files.

Three audio layers are defined in the MPEG standard. Table 14–2 lists some of their features. As indicated, Layer 2 is superior to Layer 1, and Layer 3 is superior to Layer 2. Layer 3 requires the most processing power, Layer 1 the least. Layer 3 encoding did not get popular until the speed of the PC was able to support its calculations.

TABLE 14–2
MPEG audio layer differences.

MPEG Audio Layer	Encoder Complexity	Compression	Typical Bit Rate
1	Low	Low (4:1)	384 Kbps
2	Medium	Medium (8:1)	192 Kbps
3	High	High (12:1)	112 Kbps

All three layers use the same basic techniques for encoding audio and compressing the data. These techniques, called *perceptual audio coding* and *psychoacoustic compression*, utilize knowledge of how humans hear and process sounds to eliminate information that is duplicated or masked out by other sounds.

.MP3 files can be used to burn an audio CD-ROM or can be downloaded into a portable MP3 player.

■ THE DIGITAL CONVERSATION

Before examining a method for transmitting voice data over a network, take a look at how an analog voice waveform, such as one representing your voice, is sampled and converted into digital data.

Figure 14–5(a) shows the basic process of analog-to-digital (A/D) conversion. An analog waveform, such as the signal from a microphone, is sampled at regular intervals.

Each sample voltage is input to an analog-to-digital converter (ADC), which outputs an 8-bit binary number associated with the sample voltage.

FIGURE 14–5
A/D and D/A conversion.

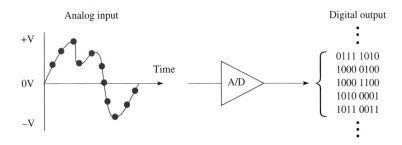

(a) Analog-to-Digital conversion.

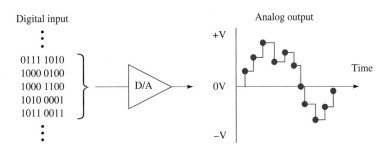

(b) Digital-to-Analog conversion.

The telephone company samples your phone conversation 8000 times each second. Using 8-bit samples gives a bit rate of 64,000 bits/second. This is a high enough bit rate to provide a reasonable amount of quality when the bitstream is converted back into an audio waveform. This process, called digital-to-analog (D/A) conversion, is shown in Figure 14–5(b). Each 8-bit sample is converted back into a corresponding voltage. The 8000 voltage samples generated by the digital-to-analog converter (DAC) each second are smoothed out using a low-pass filter.

■ TRANSMITTING DATA OVER A NETWORK

Objective 2-5

Imagine having to send each of the 8000 digital samples from the A/D converter over a network connection. At first, this would seem a reasonable thing to do. The 64,000 bits required each second is only 6.4% of the bandwidth of a 10BASE-T connection (ignoring overhead). Packing 1400 samples (the same as 1400 bytes) into a TCP message (for reliability) would require only six messages per second to support the audio stream. (The sixth message would require only 1000 bytes.) Of course, if even one message is lost, a large part of the conversation will be missing. The delay required to retransmit the missing message may affect the audio quality of the conversation.

Making the messages smaller (sending 80 bytes at a time for a total of 100 messages) would reduce the effect of a missing packet but would also require more bandwidth for transmission. Why? When only six 1400-byte messages are used, the network overhead is not significant. The network overhead consists, in this case, of the following:

- 26 bytes of Ethernet framing
- 24 bytes of IP header
- 24 bytes of TCP header

Figure 14–6 illustrates the overhead and data portions of the message in an Ethernet frame.

FIGURE 14–6

Network overhead in an Ethernet frame.

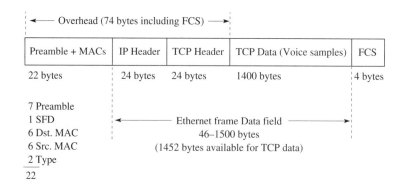

These 74 bytes of overhead are only 5.28% of the 1400 bytes of data in each message. Thus, only 5.28% more bandwidth is required to transmit the data stream. Compare this to the situation in which only 80 bytes of data are sent in a message. The 74 bytes of overhead now represent 92.5% of the 80-byte data block. This almost doubles the bandwidth required and increases the time required to transmit the data stream. So, a balance must be found between packet size and overhead. Table 14–3 provides a number of examples for comparison; the numbers suggest that a packet containing 1000 bytes of data requires the least amount of bandwidth.

TABLE 14–3

Transmitting 8000 bytes (64,000 bits) of data using multiple packets.

Data Length (Bytes)	74-Byte Overhead (%)	Number of Packets	Total Bytes	Total Bits
1400	5.28	6	8844	70752
1200	6.16	7	8918	71344
1000	7.4	8	8592	68736
500	14.8	16	9184	73472
250	29.6	32	10368	82944
150	49.33	54	12096	96768
100	74	80	13920	111360
80	92.5	100	15400	123200
64	115.62	125	17250	138000

In actual practice, UDP datagrams are preferred over TCP streams to eliminate the overhead of TCP. Reliability for UDP packets is provided by application layer protocols. Streaming audio or video packets that are lost wouldn't be useful if they were later re-sent by TCP. The message, song, or video would have already played (minus the content of the lost packet) and the re-sent packet would then be out of place in the stream and useless. The missing word or note would be useless if it were played at a later time in the stream.

Voice-over-IP

Objective 2-5

The difficulties of transmitting voice data (IP telephony) over a data network are weighed against the growing need to move all communication technologies onto a single network. Voice-over-IP (VoIP) is a method for sending voice and fax data using the IP protocol. VoIP interfaces with the public switched telephone network (PSTN) and attempts to provide the same quality of service.

Figure 14–7 shows the architecture of VoIP and its associated gateway/terminal. Several different IP protocols are used in VoIP. These are ***RTP*** (Real-Time Transfer Protocol), ***RTCP*** (Real-Time Control Protocol), and RSVP (Resources Reservation Protocol). RTP handles reliable delivery of real-time data. RTCP monitors the VoIP session to maintain the quality of service. RSVP manages network resources during the connection.

RTP
RTCP

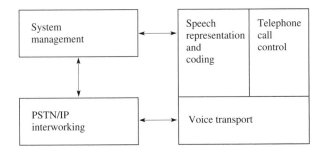

(a) Overall structure.

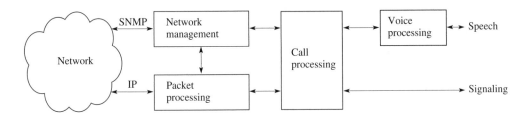

(b) VoIP gateway/terminal.

FIGURE 14–7
VoIP architecture.

The voice processing and gateway/terminal operation are specified by the H.323 standard, which also supports video over IP. VoIP is rapidly becoming an important part of corporate communication. Using VoIP corporations can communicate across the globe, using currently existing data communications networks, and save enormous cost compared to traditional voice communication channels.

VoIP requires reliable network communications to be effective. The interruption of a voice conversation, as a result of lost voice packets, is very noticeable to the human ear. To support VoIP network administrators often use quality of service (QoS) practices, thereby giving preference for bandwidth access to time-critical applications such as VoIP. In view of the knowledge and skill sets needed to support VoIP many network administrators are specializing in this discipline and obtaining certifications such as Cisco's IP Telephony specialist and CCIE Voice certification tracks.

Video

The problems associated with networked audio are increased for networked video, since greater bandwidth is required and it is easier for humans to visually spot problems with the video stream. Real-time video, both live (streaming) and through playback (from an MPEG file), requires a powerful processor and a fast network connection. As with VoIP, the RTP, RTCP, and RSVP protocols are used to manage the information stream.

It is now possible for any PC owner to purchase an inexpensive (under $100) color camera that connects to the printer port or USB port and allows real-time capture of video. Figure 14–8 shows the video camera window, showing a view of a certain author's home office.

Applications such as CU-SeeMe use live camera video to establish a video conference between two or more individuals. Windows NetMeeting provides similar features. Bear in mind that any camera connected to the printer port will require plenty of processing power to capture and frame the image. The frame rate possible with this type of interface is based on the image resolution (smaller images allow a faster frame rate).

FIGURE 14–8
Video capture using
QuickPict.

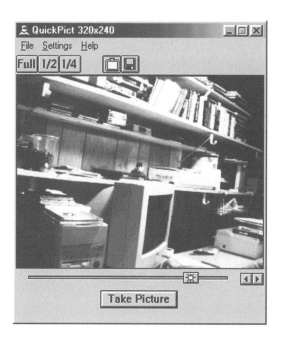

MPEG Files

As covered earlier in this exercise, the MPEG standard specifies methods used to encode CD-quality audio in a compressed format. MPEG also defines a set of digital video parameters, such as bit rate, resolution, and compression techniques. MPEG video compression is lossy, using the Discrete Cosine Transform (also found in JPEG compression). MPEG video is processed in three types of frames:

* I (Intra) frames—a stand-alone video frame
* P (Predicted) frames—frames generated using the most recent I or P frame
* B (Bidirectional) frames—frames generated based on past and future frames

   Frames are generated in a sequence similar to the following:

`. . . BPIBBPBBPBBPBBIBBP . . .`

with an I frame every 12 frames (0.4 second of time when the frame rate is 30 frames per second). Skipping through the I frames allows you to view the video in fast-forward or rewind.

   To reduce the required bandwidth, MPEG utilizes *motion vectors* that identify movement of blocks of pixels between frames. For example, suppose a 16-by-16 block of pixels in frame 10 appears in frame 11 in a slightly different position. Instead of coding the block a second time in frame 11, a motion vector is used to identify where the block has moved to in frame 11. This requires less data and helps reduce the bandwidth. A frame resolution of 352 by 240, at 30 frames per second, typically requires a 1.5 Mbps stream, although higher resolutions are possible that push the bandwidth up to 6 Mbps.

   MPEG files can be played through the Microsoft Media Player.

■ MULTICASTING

Objective 1-6

It is not difficult to imagine a network getting bogged down when multiple video streams are being transmitted to numerous clients. For example, consider Figure 14–9(a), which shows a server sending identical copies of a video packet to 30 clients. The main switch receives and forwards the 30 copies to three additional switches, each of which forwards copies to their respective clients. Clearly, the server and first switch are kept very busy.

   Figure 14–9(b) shows how multicasting eliminates a large portion of the duplicated information. The server sends one copy of the video data to a multicasting-enabled switch,

FIGURE 14–9
Unicasting versus multicasting.

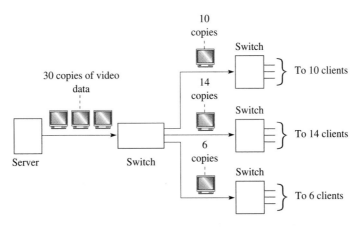

(a) Unicasting video stream to 30 clients.

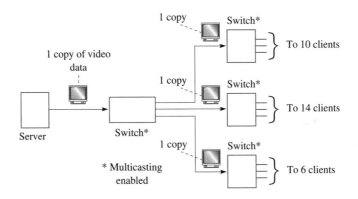

(b) Multicasting video stream to 30 clients.

which in turn forwards a single copy to each of the other three multicasting-enabled switches, which replicate the video data and forward copies to each client. The bandwidth required by the server and the first switch has been significantly reduced.

IP multicasting is possible through the use of IGMP, the Internet Group Management Protocol, which is defined in RFC 1112. Class D addresses are used for all group members.

Games

Computer games that have networking capabilities have steadily grown in popularity. Typically, one machine runs the game in server mode, with multiple game client machines connected to it at the same time. The game programmers must take many factors into account when designing the network components of the game, such as available bandwidth, communication delay, and processing speed. Care must be taken to provide each player with a real-time game environment.

Chapter 16 provides the details behind the development and operation of a two-player network game called NETMAZE. An excellent source of network game source code can be found at http://cg.cs.tu-berlin.de/~ki/engines.html. This site is the 3-D Engines List, a Web site containing 643 different game engines (at the time of this writing). Thirty-five games contain network support.

Documents

One of the biggest headaches that Web designers have is the fact that different Web browsers display Web pages differently. Even the same Web browser can display Web pages differently based on preferences set by the user. Adobe Systems Incorporated has created a document format called Portable Document Format (PDF) to help solve this issue. Using a software package called Adobe Acrobat you can produce documents in a variety of applications and then convert them into PDF files. The PDF file is read by a free downloadable reader from Adobe. Using this format, and using the Adobe Reader as an add-on to your Web browser program, documents will be displayed in the format intended by the original developer of the document. This product has become a de facto standard for delivering documents for viewing over the Internet. You can obtain the free Adobe Reader from www.adobe.com.

■ TROUBLESHOOTING TECHNIQUES

Objective 4-8

Sometimes a little math can save you a great deal of time and effort. For example, a small college wants to add an .MP3 audio server to their internal network. The administrators think that their 10BASE-T college network infrastructure is fast enough to handle the additional digital audio bandwidth, since there are only 76 employees, and in the words of one administrator, "How many employees will be listening to music at the same time?"

Well, a worst-case scenario does involve all 76 employees listening to .MP3 audio at the same time. Figure 14–10(a) shows the bandwidth calculations, assuming 12:1 compression and 15 Ethernet frames/second for each audio stream. A total of 9,612,480 bits are needed each second. Even though this is less than the 10 Mbps available with 10BASE-T, consider these important factors:

- Collisions will lower the available bandwidth.
- The college's Internet connection accounts for 22% of the total bandwidth.
- Network activity (NetBIOS sessions, printing, user authentication) accounts for 15% of the total bandwidth.
- The 9.6 microsecond interframe gap after every frame is equivalent to 96 bits of lost bandwidth.
- A network approaching 60% capacity often becomes so congested that it becomes useless.

FIGURE 14–10
Bandwidth calculations.

(a) Bits required for all streams.

	1,411,200 bps	CD-quality bit rate
÷	12	Compression factor
	117,600 bps	Compressed bit rate
+	8,880 bps	Overhead for 15 Ethernet frames
	126,480 bps	Total bits for single user
×	76	Users
	9,612,480 bps	Total bits required

(b) Number of streams possible.

	1,000,000 bits	Allocated bandwidth
÷	126,480 bps	Bit rate for one stream
	7.9	Number of streams possible

It should not be difficult to see that the 9,612,480 bps needed for the audio streams will not be available. Looking at this problem from a different perspective, suppose the administrators decide to allocate a fixed bandwidth for the digital audio equal to 1 Mbps. How many streams can be supported? As shown in Figure 14–10(b), only seven users can be supported with a 1 Mbps bandwidth allocation.

With these simple calculations, it is clear the college administration must upgrade their existing network before adding any more traffic from the audio server.

INDUSTRY TIP

One of the most exciting multimedia network applications is in the area of e-learning. Presenting instructional content in text, graphic, and interactive form can create a very compelling learning environment. Cisco Systems has developed a very sophisticated e-learning solution architecture called the Global Learning Network.

The Global Learning Network (GLN) is a Cisco AVVID-based, end-to-end, network-enhanced learning infrastructure implemented to support and scale with the continued growth of the Cisco Networking Academy Program. The GLN integrates managed services; applications for authoring, management, and assessment; and network infrastructure for global, distributed content delivery. The GLN supports the multiple learning styles of hundreds of thousands of students worldwide with efficiently delivered rich, interactive media, proficiency reporting, and personalized feedback as dynamically generated Web pages.

For more information about this application visit http://www.cisco.com/en/US/learning/le42/learning_e-learning_links_launch.html.

■ SELF-TEST

1. What type of compression is provided when using GIF files?
   a. DCT
   b. LZW
   c. L2TP
   d. Tracker

2. What type of compression is provided when using JPEG files?
   a. Lossless
   b. Lossy
   c. Lendel
   d. Tracker

3. Which image file type is preferred for its photographic-quality color?
   a. IMG
   b. JPEG
   c. MIDI
   d. GIF

4. Our eyes are not sensitive enough to see the effects of _____ compression.
   a. lossless
   b. lossy
   c. NRZ
   d. stack

5. The Windows _____ window provides editing features like cut, paste, delete, and special effects.
   a. Wave
   b. Mixer
   c. Audiotronics
   d. Sound Recorder

6. True or False: MIDI can provide a total of 128 pitched instruments generating 24 notes in 16 channels.

7. The sound card in a PC uses MID information to reproduce notes using techniques like frequency modulation and _____.
   a. time division multiplexing
   b. frequency division multiplexing

    c. wave table synthesis

    d. packet queuing

8. The attack, delay, sustain, and release portions of _____ can be controlled using MID files.

    a. video files

    b. each note

    c. video frames

    d. each packet

9. Layer _____ audio as defined in the MPEG standard provides the most superior features.

    a. 1

    b. 2

    c. 3

    d. 4

10. True or False: All the layers of the MP3 standard use the same basic techniques for encoding audio and compressing the data.

11. An analog waveform like one produced by a voice speaking into a microphone is sampled and input to a(n) _____ in order to produce digital data representing the voice.

    a. ADC

    b. AC

    c. DAC

    d. low-pass filter

12. The telephone company samples your phone conversation _____ times each second, providing reasonable sound quality.

    a. 2000

    b. 4000

    c. 8000

    d. 16000

13. Which of the following data transmission methods would provide the least amount of message loss if a single packet is lost during transmission?

    a. Sending 1400-byte TCP messages

    b. Sending 1000-byte TCP messages

    c. Sending 400-byte TCP messages

    d. Sending 80-byte TCP messages

14. True or False: UDP datagrams are preferred over TCP streams to eliminate the overhead of TCP.

15. VoIP interfaces with the _____ and attempts to provide the same quality of service.

    a. PTLN

    b. PSTN

    c. POTN

    d. OTPT

16. True or False: Using VoIP can provide tremendous cost savings for telephone services.

17. The _____ protocol is used by VoIP to manage network resources during the connection.

    a. RTP

    b. RTCP

    c. RSVP

    d. PVST+

18. True or False: Lost packets are very seldom noticed in a VoIP conversation.

19. True or False: VoIP requires reliable network communications to be effective.

20. Applications such as _____ use live camera video to produce a video conference between two or more individuals.
    a. R-U-N-There
    b. CU-SeeMe
    c. VoIP
    d. SmarTV

21. The MPEG frames that are generated using the most recent I or P frame are called _____ frames.
    a. Intra
    b. Predicted
    c. Bidirectional
    d. Directional

22. The first octet of a multicast address is in the numerical range of _____.
    a. 1–126
    b. 128–191
    c. 192–223
    d. 224–239

23. True or False: All Web browsers display a Web page in the same way.

24. Network-capable games typically have the game running on a _____ machine with multiple _____ machines connected to it at the same time.
    a. server, client
    b. client, server
    c. hub, spoke
    d. master, slave

25. Adobe created a document format called _____ to help solve the issue of Web browsers displaying the same document in different ways.
    a. PAGIT
    b. PDF
    c. MDF
    d. Read

The Internet

PERFORMANCE OBJECTIVES

Upon completion of this chapter, you will be able to:

■ Describe the basic organization of the Internet.

■ Explain the purpose of a browser and its relationship to HTML.

■ Discuss the usefulness of CGI and Java applications.

■ Identify the elements of a virtual private network.

■ List the steps involved in setting up a Web server.

NETWORK+ OBJECTIVES

This chapter provides information for the following Network+ objectives:

1.6 Identify the purpose, features, and functions of the following network components:

- ■ Hubs
- ■ Routers
- ■ Switches
- ■ Gateways
- ■ Bridges
- ■ CSU/DSU
- ■ Network Interface Cards/ISDN adapters/system area network cards
- ■ Wireless access points
- ■ Modems

2.5 Define the purpose, function, and/or use of the following protocols within TCP/IP:

- ■ IP
- ■ HTTPS
- ■ TCP
- ■ POP3/IMAP4
- ■ UDP
- ■ TELNET
- ■ FTP
- ■ ICMP
- ■ TFTP
- ■ ARP
- ■ SMTP
- ■ NTP
- ■ HTTP

2.7 Identify the purpose of the following network services:

- ■ DHCP/BOOTP
- ■ DNS
- ■ WINS
- ■ NAT/ICS
- ■ SNMP

2.13 Identify the following security protocols and describe their purpose and function:

- ■ IPSec
- ■ SSL
- ■ L2TP
- ■ Kerberos

3.3 Identify the main characteristics of VLANs.

4.2 Given a troubleshooting scenario involving a small office/home office network failure (e.g., xDSL, cable, home satellite, wireless, POTS), identify the cause of the failure.

4.6 Given a network scenario, interpret visual indicators (e.g., link lights, collision lights, etc.) to determine the nature of the problem.

4.8 Given a scenario, predict the impact of modifying, adding, or removing network services (e.g., DHCP, DNS, WINS, etc.) on network resources and users.

4.11 Given a network troubleshooting scenario involving a client connectivity problem (e.g., incorrect protocol/client software/authentication configuration, or insufficient rights/permission), identify the cause of the problem.

■ INTRODUCTION

The Internet can be defined as a worldwide communications medium providing standardized connection points for all types of computers regardless of manufacturer, size, and resources. The Internet today provides the end-user with the ability to share music, video, pictures, and voice in real time. Information related to the history of how the Internet was established can be found at http://www.darpa.mil/. Figure 15–1 shows how several networks can be connected together to form a larger network.

FIGURE 15–1
Concept of Internet connections.

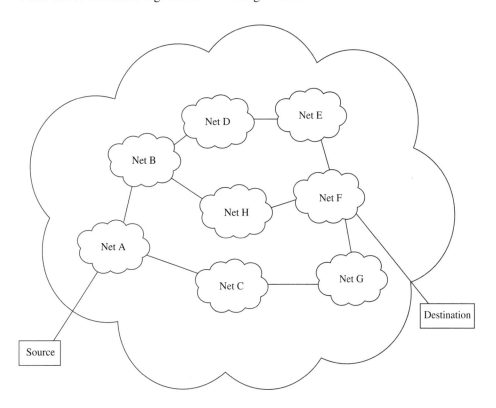

The type of connection to the Internet can take many different forms, such as a simple modem connection, a cable modem connection, a T1 line, a T3 line, or a frame relay connection. The client making the connection must be running the TCP/IP protocol suite.

■ THE ORGANIZATION OF THE INTERNET

Hosts on the Internet are reached using IP addresses. This works fine for computers, but humans do not work well with pure numerical addressing systems. This is why the Domain Naming System (DNS) was established. It is much easier to remember a Uniform Resource Locator (URL) such as www.prenhall.com than to remember an IP address such as 204.210.159.19. The DNS is broken down into several top-level domains as shown in Table 15–1. The URL of an Internet host shows the domain to which it is assigned. For example, the rwa.com domain is the name of a company, and the bcc.edu domain is an educational institution. Each domain is registered on the appropriate root server. For example, the domain rwa.com is known by the .com root server. The rwa.com URL is called a second level domain name. The .com is the first level, and when you place the rwa to the left of the .com you get a second level domain assignment. Within each second level domain, a locally administered domain name server allows for each host to be configured. If we have a URL of www.rwa.com the www portion of the URL is actually referring to a specific host with the name www. That host could be referred to by any host name that the administrator wants to use, but most organizations name their initial web site "host machine

TABLE 15–1
Common domain names.

Domain Name	Assigned Group
com	A company or commercial organization
edu	An educational institution
gov	A government organization
mil	A military organization
net	Network service provider
org	Non-profit organization
country code	A country code, for example, .us for United States, .ca for Canada, and .jp for Japan
biz	Small business Web sites
info	Resource Web sites
aero	Air-transport industry
coop	Cooperative associations
museum	Museums
name	Individuals
pro	Credentialed professionals

www" because that is what most individuals think of when going to the home web site of an organization.

Along with a domain name comes its associated IP address (which is resolved via DNS). In the past, organizations were assigned entire Class A, B, or C networks to obtain a unique IP address for each employee computer. For example, a business with 600 employees would request three Class C networks, thus having a total of 762 IP addresses available (recall that we can't use the network ID and broadcast addresses of each of those class C networks, which is why the available addresses are 762 and not 768).

Objective 2-7

As the popularity of the Internet grew, the number of available networks dropped, and soon there was a shortage. Thus began many clever methods of using a *single IP address* to share an Internet connection among multiple clients. Two of these methods are Network Address Translation (*NAT*) and Internet Connection Sharing (*ICS*). The following sections examine the operation of each method.

NAT
ICS

Network Address Translation

Network Address Translation is a technique in which the IP addresses of multiple network devices on a local network (called the *inside* network) are mapped (statically or dynamically) to IP addresses on an external network (called the *outside* network).

Internal IP addresses are mapped to a pool of external IP addresses on a rotating basis. When the number of requests exceeds the number of addresses in the pool, duplicate IP addresses from the pool are assigned with different TCP/UDP port numbers as well. A separate pool of static addresses is available for mapping critical servers on the inside network (such as e-mail and Web servers) to the outside network.

A table called the NAT table contains the known mappings and is initialized with a set of translations. A portion of the NAT entries for a Cisco NAT-enabled router are as follows:

```
ip nat pool rwasoft 217.136.48.98 217.136.48.102 netmask 255.255.255.248
ip nat inside source list 5 pool rwasoft overload
ip nat inside source static 172.4.0.5 164.32.7.5
ip nat inside source static 172.4.0.6 164.32.7.6
ip nat inside source static 172.4.1.7 164.32.7.7
ip nat inside source static 172.4.1.8 164.32.7.8
ip nat inside source static 172.4.0.251 164.32.7.251
ip nat inside source static 172.4.0.252 164.32.7.252
```

Using NAT reduces the number of outside IP addresses an institution requires to communicate over the Internet.

Internet Connection Sharing

Objective 1-6

Internet Connection Sharing is a technique used by Windows computers to share Internet access for two to twenty users over a single connection to an ISP. One computer contains a connection to the ISP as well as a second connection to the local network. This computer acts as a gateway to the ISP, managing IP addresses for the local network (such as handing out IP addresses in the Class C network 192.168.x.x) and translating all internal IP addresses to a single outgoing IP address, the one assigned by the ISP to the original connection. Static IP addresses may also be used on the local network.

An alternative solution that allows multiple computers to share a single Internet connection requires the use of a cable modem, DSL router, or similar piece of hardware. This device acts similar to a switch as well as a router, with one port connecting to the single ISP connection and the other ports providing access for local network connections. A Web-based interface is typically provided, allowing easy management of various parameters such as port forwarding, DHCP properties, and passwords, as well as viewing important status information (ISP IP address, firmware version, ARP table, etc.).

■ WINDOWS AND THE INTERNET

Objective 2-7

Organizations running the Windows operating system typically use services on the Windows NT/2000 Server operating system, such as DHCP, Remote Access Server (RAS), and Windows Internet Naming Service (WINS). WINS performs name translation in a manner similar to DNS, except WINS translates Windows computer names into IP addresses. WINS is a dynamic database of name-to-IP mappings, adjusting its entries as IP addresses are reassigned.

A Windows computer may use its own mapping table before relying on WINS. This table is contained within the LMHOSTS file located in the WINDOWS directory. The LMHOSTS entries for several name mappings are as follows:

```
172.4.0.6       web       #PRE    #DOM:RWANET
172.4.0.4       email     #PRE    #DOM:RWANET
172.4.0.5       apps      #PRE    #DOM:RWANET
172.4.0.251     ftp       #PRE    #DOM:RWANET
172.4.0.252     watcher   #PRE    #DOM:RWANET
```

where #PRE indicates that these names should be preloaded into the system's local cache, and #DOM:RWANET is the Windows RWANET domain associated with the mapped computers. Using an LMHOSTS file allows remote access to a Windows domain by providing a mapping that would otherwise be unknown to the system.

■ WORLD WIDE WEB

WWW

Objective 2-5

The World Wide Web, or **WWW** as it is commonly referred to, is actually only a portion of the services supported on the Internet and it uses the Hypertext Transport Protocol (HTTP). The HTTP protocol allows for hypermedia information to be exchanged, such as text, video, audio, animation, Java applets, images, and more. The hypertext markup language, or HTML, is used to determine how the hypermedia information is to be displayed on a WWW browser screen.

Browser

The WWW *browser* is used to navigate the Internet by selecting *links* on any WWW page or by specifying a URL to point to a specific *page* of information. There are many different WWW browsers, but one of the most popular is Microsoft Internet Explorer, or IE, shown in Figure 15–2.

FIGURE 15–2

Sample home page displayed using Internet Explorer.

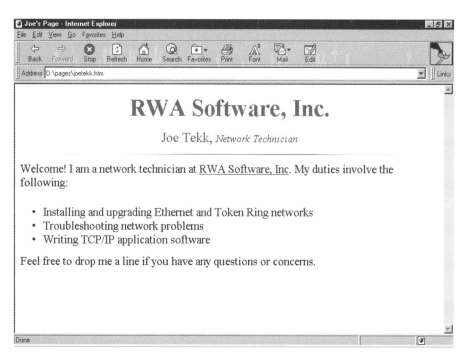

Netscape Navigator, shown in Figure 15–3, is another popular Web browser. Both IE and Netscape are available free over the Internet and contain familiar pull-down menus and graphical toolbars to access the most commonly used functions such as forward, backward, stop, print, and reload.

FIGURE 15–3

Sample home page displayed using Netscape Navigator.

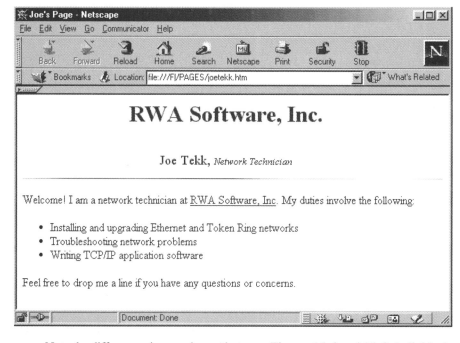

Note the differences in page layout between Figures 15–2 and 15–3. Individuals who design Web pages must take into account the different requirements of each browser so that the page looks acceptable in both browsers.

■ HTML

HTML

HTML stands for hypertext markup language. HTML is the core component of the information that composes a Web page. The HTML _source code_ for a Web page has an overall syntax and structure that contains formatting commands (called _tags_) understood by a Web browser. Following is a sample HTML source (JOETEKK.HTM). The actual Web page for this HTML code was shown in Figure 15–3.

```
<HTML>

<HEAD>
<TITLE>Joe's Page</TITLE>

<BODY BGCOLOR="#FFFF80">

<P ALIGN="CENTER"
<B><FONT SIZE="+3" COLOR="#FF0000">RWA Software, Inc.</FONT></B>
</P>

<P ALIGN="CENTER">
<FONT SIZE="+1"><FONT COLOR="#008000">Joe TekkFONT</FONT>,
<FONT SIZE="-1'><I>Network Technician</I></FONT></FONT>
</P>

<P ALIGN="CENTER">
<IMG SRC="bar.gif" ALT="Color Bar">
</P>

<P ALIGN="LEFT">
Welcome! I am a network technician at
<A HREF="http://www.rwasoftware.com">RWA Software, Inc</A>. My duties
 involve the following:
</P>

<UL>
<LI>Installing and upgrading Ethernet and Token Ring networks</LI>
<LI>Troubleshooting network problems</LI>
<LI>Writing TCP/IP application software </LI>
</UL>

<P ALIGN="LEFT">
Feel free to drop me a line if you have any questions or
concerns.
</P>

</BODY>
</HTML>
```

The HTML source consists of many different tags that instruct the browser what to do when preparing the graphical Web page. Table 15–2 shows some of the more common tags. The main portion of the Web page is contained between the BODY tags. Note that BGCOLOR= "#FFFF80" sets the background color of the Web page. The six-digit hexadecimal number contains three pairs of values for the red, green, and blue color levels desired.

Pay attention to the tags used in the HTML source and what actually appears on the Web page in the browser (Figure 15–3). The browser ignores white space (multiple blanks between words or lines of text) when it processes the HTML source. For example, the anchor for the RWA Software link begins on its own line in the source, but the actual link for the anchor is displayed on the same line as the text that comes before and after it.

WYSIWYG

Many people use HTML editors, such as HoTMetaL or Front Page, to create and maintain their Web pages. Options to display the page in HTML format or in *WYSIWYG* (what you see is what you get) are usually available, along with sample pages, image editing, and conversion tools that convert many different file types (such as a Word document) into HTML. Demo versions of these HTML editors and others can be downloaded from the Web. Figure 15–4 shows HoTMetaL's graphical page editor with Joe Tekk's page loaded.

TABLE 15–2
Assorted HTML tags.

Tag	Meaning
<P>	Begin paragraph
</P>	End paragraph
<B>	Bold
<I>	Italics
<IMG SRC. . .>	Image source
<UL>	Unordered list
<LI>	List item
<TABLE>	Table
<TR>	Table row
<TD>	Table data
<A>	Anchor

FIGURE 15–4
HoTMetaL PRO with sample
page.

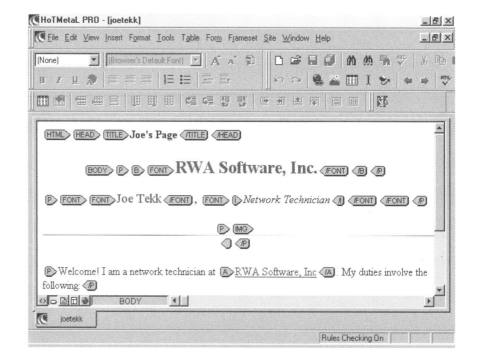

Web pages are classified into three categories: static, dynamic, and active. Static web pages are the easiest to build and involve writing HTML code. The page content is determined by what is contained in the HTML code and doesn't depend on anything other than the written code to present the page to the viewer. Dynamic Web pages contain a combination of HTML code and a "call" to a server using a Common Gateway Interface (*CGI*) application. In this scenario, information supplied by the user in an HTML form is transferred back to a host computer for processing. The host computer then returns a dynamic customized WWW page. Active pages contain a combination of HTML code and applets; therefore, the Web page is not completely specified during the HTML coding process. Instead, using a Java applet, it is specified while being displayed by the Web browser. The method used to present a Web page to the viewer through the use of a Web browser defines its category.

CGI

■ CGI

The Common Gateway Interface is a software interface that allows a small amount of interactive processing to take place with information provided on a Web page. For example, consider the Web page shown in Figure 15–5.

FIGURE 15–5
Web page with FORM element.

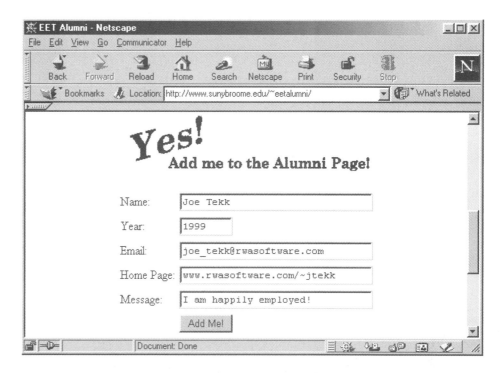

The Web page contains a FORM element, which itself can contain many different types of inputs, such as text boxes, radio buttons, lists with scroll bars, and other types of buttons and elements. The user browsing the page enters his or her information and then clicks on the Add Me! button. This begins the following chain of events:

1. The form data entered by the user is placed into a message.
2. The browser POSTs the form data (sends message to CGI server).
3. The CGI server application processes the form data.
4. The CGI server application sends the results back to the CGI client (Netscape or Internet Explorer).

The HTML code for the alumni page form looks similar to the following:

```
<FORM ACTION="/htbin/cgi-mailto/eetalumni" METHOD="POST">
<P ALIGN="CENTER"><IMG SRC="yes.gif"></P>
<CENTER>
<TABLE WIDTH="50%" ALIGN="CENTER">
<TR><TD>Name:</TT>
<TD><INPUT TYPE="TEXT" NAME="name" SIZE="32"></TD></TR>
<TR><TD>Year:</TD>
<TD><INPUT TYPE="TEXT" NAME="year" SIZE="8"></TD></TR>
<TR><TD>Email:</TD>
<TD><INPUT TYPE="TEXT" NAME="email" SIZE="32"></TD></TR>
<TR><TD>Home Page:</TD>
<TD><INPUT TYPE="TEXT" NAME="home" SIZE="32"></TD></TR>
<TR><TD>Message:</TD>
<TD><INPUT TYPE="TEXT" NAME="msg" SIZE="32"></TD></TR>
<TR><TD</TD>
<TD><INPUT TYPE="SUBMIT" VALUE="Add Me!"></TD></TR>
</TABLE>
</CENTER>
</FORM>
```

The first line of the form element specifies POST as the method used to send the form data out for processing. The CGI application that will receive the POSTed form data is the cgi-mailto program in the *htbin* directory. Specifically, cgi-mailto processes the form data and sends an e-mail message to the *eetalumni* account. The e-mail message looks similar to the following:

```
From:   SBCCVA::WWWSERVER
To:     eetalumni
CC:
Subj

REMOTE_ADDRESS: 204.210.159.19
name: Joe Tekk
year: 1998
email: joe_tekk@rwa.software.com
home: www.rwasoftware.com/~jtekk
msg: I am happily employed!
```

Note that the identifiers (name, year, e-mail, home, and msg) match the names used to identify the text input elements in the form.

Instead of e-mailing the form data, another CGI application might create a Web page on the fly containing custom information based on the form data submitted. CGI applications are written in C/C++, Visual BASIC, Java, Perl, and many other languages. The Web is full of sample forms and CGI applications available for download and inclusion in your own Web pages.

■ JAVA

The Java programming language is used to create active Web pages using Java applets. An active Web page is specified by the Java applet when the Web page is displayed rather than during the HTML coding process. A Java applet is actually a program transferred from an Internet host to the Web browser. The Web browser executes the Java applet code on a Java virtual machine (which is built into the Web browser). The Java language can be characterized by the following nonexhaustive list:

- General purpose
- High level
- Object oriented
- Dynamic
- Concurrent

Java consists of a programming language, a run-time environment, and a class library. The Java programming language resembles C++ and can be used to create conventional computer applications or applets. Only an applet is used to create an active Web page. The run-time environment provides the facilities to execute an application or applet. The class library contains prewritten code that can simply be included in the application or applet. Table 15–3 shows the Java class library functional areas.

TABLE 15–3
Java class library categories.

Class	Description
Graphics	Abstract window tool kit (AWT)
Network I/O	Socket level connnections
File I/O	Local and remote file access
Event capture	User actions (mouse, keyboard, etc.)
Run-time system calls	Access to built-in functions
Exception handling	Method to handle any type of error condition
Server interaction	Built-in code to interact with a server

The following Java program MYSW.JAVA is used to switch from one image to a second image (and back) whenever the mouse moves over the Java applet window. Furthermore, a mouse click while the mouse is over the applet window causes a new page to load.

```java
import java.awt.Graphics;
import java.awt.Image;
import java.awt.Color;
import java.awt.Event;
import java.net.URL;
import java.net.MalformedURLException;

public class myswitch extends java.applet.Applet implements Runnable
{
    Image swoffpic;
    Image swonpic;
    Image currentimg;
    Thread runner;

public void start()
{
    if (runner == null)
    {
        runner = new Thread(this);
        runner.start();
    }
}

public void stop()
{
    if (runner != null)
    {
        runner.stop();
        runner = null;
    }
}

public void run()
{
    swoffpic = getImage(getCodeBase(), "swoff.gif");
    swonpic = getImage(getCodeBase(), "swon.gif");
    currentimg = swoffpic;
    setBackground(Color.red);
    repaint();
}

public void paint(Graphics g)
{
    g.drawImage(currentimg, 8, 8, this);
}

public boolean mouseEnter(Event evt, int x, int y)
{
    currentimg = swonpic;
    repaint();
    return(true);
}
```

```
public boolean mouseExit(Event evt, int x, int y)
{
    currentimg = swoffpic;
    repaint();
    return(true);
}

public boolean mouseDown(Event evt, int x, int y)
{
    URL destURL = null;
    String url = "http://www.sunybroome.edu/~eet_dept";

    try
    {
        destURL = new URL(url);
    }
    catch(MalformedURLException e)
    {
        System.out.println("Bad destination URL: " + destURL);
    }
    if (destURL != null)
        getAppletContext().showDocument(destURL);
    return(true);
}

}
```

Programming in Java, or any other language, requires practice and skill. With its popularity still increasing, now would be a good time to experiment with Java yourself by downloading the free Java compiler and writing some applets.

■ VIRTUAL PRIVATE NETWORKS

Objective 3-3

A virtual private network (VPN) allows for remote private LANs to communicate securely through an untrusted public network such as the Internet. This technique is shown in Figure 15–6 and is in contrast to the traditional approach in which a large corporation or organization used private or leased lines to communicate between different sites in order to provide privacy of data. Using a VPN, only authorized members of the network are allowed access to the data. A VPN uses an IP tunneling protocol and security services that are transparent to the private network users.

FIGURE 15–6
RWA Software VPN (physical view).

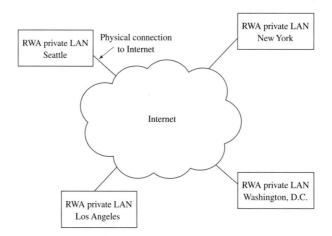

Using a VPN, a private LAN connected to the Internet can be connected to other LANs using a combination of tunneling, encryption, and authentication. *Tunneling* means that data is transferred through the public network in an encapsulated form. This is illustrated in Figure 15–7.

FIGURE 15–7
RWA Software VPN (logical view).

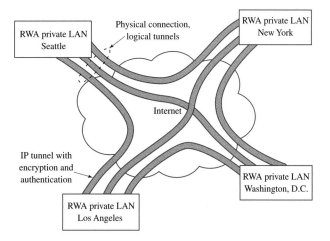

All of the data, including the addresses of the sender and destination, are enclosed within a packet. Although tunneling is sufficient to create a VPN, it does not ensure complete data security.

Complete security is accomplished when the data communication is also encrypted and authenticated. Packets that are protected by tunneling, encryption, and authentication (certified by an agreed-on certification authority such as verisign.com) offer the highest level of security. The IP Security (IPSec) standards provide a security protocol for tunneling as well as for data privacy, integrity, and authentication, creating a truly secure VPN.

Objective 2-13

IPSec is a set of protocols developed by the Internet Engineering Task Force that adds additional security solutions to TCP/IP networking. IPSec currently supports several encryption algorithms such as DES, 3DES, AES, and public-key encryption and is designed to incorporate new algorithms as they are created. IPSec offers a solution to data privacy, integrity, and authentication that is network independent, application independent, and supports all IP services such as HTTP, FTP, SNMP, and so on.

Objective 2-12

The Point to Point Tunneling Protocol was developed by the PPTP Forum. The forum consisted of Ascend Communications, Microsoft Corporation, 3Com/Primary Access, ECI Telematics, and U.S. Robotics.

By using PPTP, a corporation can use the wide-area network (Internet) as a single large LAN. It is no longer necessary to lease dedicated lines for wide-area communication. Using PPTP, a frame to be sent out on the network is encapsulated into an additional header. The additional header provides routing information so that the encapsulated payload can then be routed between tunnel endpoints over the network. The logical path that the encapsulated packets travel is called a *tunnel*. When the encapsulated frames reach their destination, the original frame data is extracted and forwarded to its final destination. The tunneling process includes encapsulation, transmission, and decapsulation of packets.

A VPN using PPTP (or L2TP) provides the following capabilities: user authentication, address management, data encryption, encryption key management, and support for multiple protocols to be delivered. In addition, the following shows several advantages of using PPTP over L2TP or IPSec:

• PPTP does not require use of digital certificates.

• PPTP can be used by all versions of Windows and many other operating systems such as UNIX/Linux, NetWare, and Mac OS X.

• PPTP clients can be located behind a NAT.

When security needs dictate the use of VPN, using the PPTP protocol can prove to be a wise choice. Additional information about PPTP can be found in RFCs 2637 and 2784.

■ INSTANT MESSAGING

One of the latest tools to communicate with on the Internet is instant messaging. Many different companies provide software to enable users to send electronic messages. Instant messaging is an application that provides the capability for a user to send and receive instant messages, which are delivered to the recipient *instantly*—even faster than electronic mail. One of the most popular instant messaging applications is AOL's Instant Messenger. This program allows for a user to send or receive instant messages.

Figure 15–8 shows the instant messaging screen for AOL's Instant Messenger program.

FIGURE 15–8
AOL Instant Message window.

Another popular way to communicate over the Internet is with Microsoft's Net-Meeting, shown in Figure 15–9. There are many additional choices available for instant

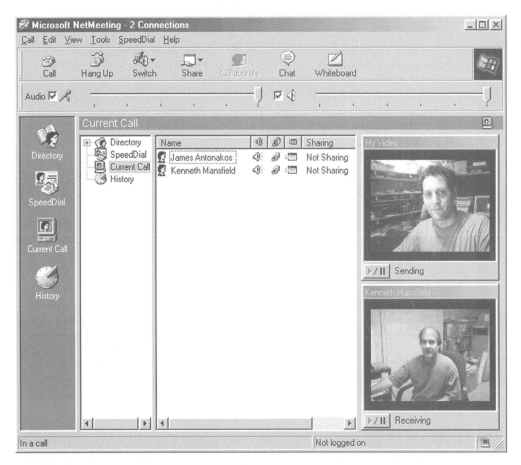

FIGURE 15–9
Microsoft NetMeeting.

messaging. You are encouraged to search for, download, and test other instant messaging applications.

■ SETTING UP A WEB SERVER

Setting up a Web server to host Web pages on the Internet is becoming a commonplace activity for business and personal use. Although a Web server is typically installed on large computer systems running UNIX or Windows NT, a Web server can also be installed on most personal computers. The first step in setting up a Web server is to choose the Web server software.

One of the most popular Web server programs is the Apache Server from the Apache Software Foundation. Two of the reasons why the Apache Server is the most popular are because it is *free* and *fully featured*. The Apache Web server is available for many operating systems, including Windows, UNIX, and many others.

The built-in features of a Web server are best explored by viewing the Apache User's Guide. From this page, all of the Apache Web server features can be explored.

Typically, after the Web server is installed, it is necessary to update the configuration file to provide a server name, e-mail contact, and several other items. When configuring the Apache Web server, it is necessary to update the httpd.conf file. This file describes:

1. Directives that control the "global" operation of the Apache Server process. Directives that are configured at the global level include
   - Server type
   - Server root
   - Scoreboard file
   - Timeout value
   - Keep-alive parameters
   - Server pool size
   - Max clients
   - Extended status settings

2. Directives that define the parameters of the main or default server. The default server responds to requests that are not handled by virtual hosts. Some of the directives defined at the default level include
   - Port number
   - Server administrator
   - Server name
   - Document root
   - Default permissions
   - Override parameters
   - Accesses file name
   - CGI script aliases
   - Cache settings

3. Settings for all virtual hosts that allow Web requests to be sent to different IP addresses or host names. The typical settings for virtual hosts include virtual host addresses, names, and directives (with similar entries used in the main or default server listed in the previous bullet point).

Each of these settings is described in detail within the httpd.conf file. All that remains after the installation is to create the HTML documents and accompanying CGI applications to be served.

■ RELATED SITES

The Internet is full of information about every aspect of the Web page development process. Many people put a tremendous amount of information on their own Web pages. You are encouraged to learn more about Web pages and Web programming. Table 15–4 shows a number of service, reference, and technology-based sites that may be of interest:

TABLE 15–4
Helpful Web links.

www.prenhall.com	Engineering and technology textbooks
www.yahoo.com	Search engine
www.internic.net	Internet authority
www.intel.com	Intel Corporation
www.microsoft.com	Microsoft Corporation
www.w3.org	World Wide Web Consortium
www.netscape.com	Netscape corporation

■ TROUBLESHOOTING TECHNIQUES

Objective 4-11

The World Wide Web is a subset of the Internet. The Internet is a physical collection of networked computers. The World Wide Web is a logical collection of information contained on many of the computers comprising the Internet. To download a file from a Web page, the two computers (client machine running a browser and server machine hosting the Web page) must exchange the file data along with other control information. If the download speed is slow, what could be the cause? A short list identifies many suspects:

- Noise in the communication channel forces retransmission of many packets.
- The path through the Internet introduces delay.
- The server is sending data at a limited rate.
- The Internet service provider has limited bandwidth.

So, before buying a new modem or upgrading your network, determine where the bottleneck is. The Internet gets more popular every day. New home pages are added, additional files are placed on FTP sites for downloading, news and entertainment services are coming online and broadcasting digitally, and more and more machines are being connected. The 10 and 100 Mbps Ethernet technology is already hard pressed to keep up with the Internet traffic. Gigabit networking is here but will provide only a short respite from the ever-increasing demands of global information exchange.

Connecting to the Internet, Scenario #1

Objective 4-11

A consultant on a business trip needed access to the Internet to join a scheduled chat session with several clients. His hotel provided free Internet access. Anyone with a laptop could simply walk up to a booth and plug the hotel's UTP cable into their NIC. The consultant connected his laptop and booted. When he opened Internet Explorer, it was not possible to view any Web pages.

The consultant ran WINIPCFG to see if his laptop had obtained a valid IP address. It had, and all other information looked valid as well (the lease period, gateway IP address, etc.); therefore, he knew that DHCP was working on the hotel's network. He opened a DOS window and tried using PING with several different domain names, but got a timeout error each time. He tried PINGing the hotel server using its IP address and got a response. Maybe DNS is not working, he thought. He tried PINGing a Web site whose IP address he knew, but the request timed out. The consultant concluded that the hotel server could not access the Internet. Maybe there was a problem with the hotel's router or ISP. When he reported the outage to the manager, he was told the hotel's IT person would not be in until the next day.

Connecting to the Internet via modem and long distance phone call was not an option, since the chat session would run for at least one hour. The consultant got in his car and drove to a public library he'd seen close to the hotel. Inside, there were several computers with Internet access. The consultant filled out a library card application, reserved a computer, and connected to his chat session with only five minutes to spare.

Connecting to the Internet, Scenario #2

Objective 4-2

A laboratory at a high school uses a cable modem for high-speed Internet access. A 4-port cable modem/router shares the Internet access among 21 computers and a networked laser printer through the use of a switch, as indicated in Figure 15–10.

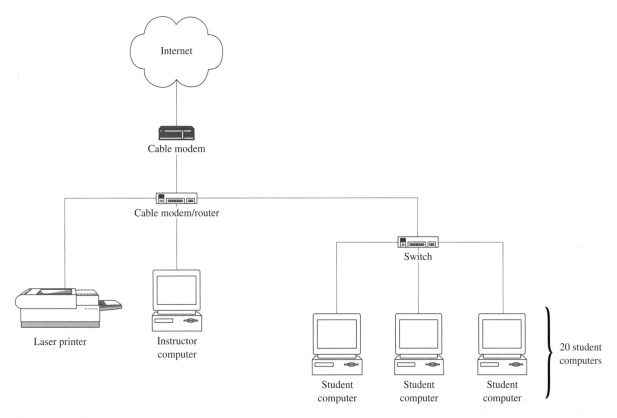

FIGURE 15–10
Network diagram of high school laboratory.

The cable modem/router acts as a DHCP server, handing out IP addresses in the network 192.168.x.x. The Instructor computer and networked laser printer have statically assigned IP addresses.

Objective 4-8

Two student computers are not able to connect to the Internet. Previously, there had been no problems with either computer. When the lab technician checks the IP address of each machine, she sees that they are set to the network addresses 200.200.200.5 and 200.200.200.6 through static assignment and not DHCP. The lab technician enables DHCP on both computers and reboots them. Internet access is restored to both computers. The lab technician later discovers that two students were experimenting with a network application and changed the IP addresses.

Connecting to the Internet, Scenario #3

Objective 4-6

The cable modem in the high school laboratory of Scenario #2 is replaced with a newer model without any noticeable changes except slightly faster download times. After a thunderstorm, the lab technician notices that the PC light on the cable modem is off. She looks at the cable modem/router. All lights are frozen on. The lab technician checks several of the computers and discovers that none of them have valid IP addresses or Internet access. She unplugs the cable modem/router power cord, waits a few seconds, and plugs it back in. All the lights come back on and are frozen again. The lab technician concludes that the cable modem/router is defective.

After replacing the cable modem/router, the student computers are still not able to access the Internet, although they can send jobs to the network printer and have valid IP addresses. The lab technician checks the manual for the cable modem and discovers that one of its new features is that it locks to the MAC address of the device connected to its Ethernet port. She then went to another lab and located the manufacturer's Web site for the new cable modem/router. A firmware upgrade was available, so she downloaded it and saved it to a floppy disk. She took the disk to the original lab and ran the upgrade program on the instructor's computer. She then connected to the cable modem/router through its Web interface and went to its MAC Cloning screen, where she entered the MAC address of

MAC Cloning

the old (and now defective) cable modem/router. The *MAC Cloning* feature allows the new cable modem/router to use the original MAC address that the new cable modem locked onto.

INDUSTRY TIP

The popularity of the Internet and the increased use of the World Wide Web have created extraordinary business opportunities for both large and small companies. Mail order giants such as Lands' End and L.L. Bean continue to do more and more business online. But the biggest beneficiaries of the growth of the Web could be small companies such as Apart creations.

After graduation from the University of New Hampshire, Tony Palleschi started to build his local Web design business. Focusing on creative design and quality development, Tony has built a successful clientele that includes companies as small as Woodbury & Morse Advertising, out of Portland, Maine, and as large as Cisco.

The Web and the business that it fosters allows technically minded creative people an exceptional business opportunity. Not only does it allow a small design company the possibility of clients of varying sizes, but it widens the physical area that the company can serve.

Tony notes that, "The Internet gives APART creations a global storefront. Before the Web, I would have been limited to my local area for potential clients and projects. But with the exposure of our Web site and the speed of communication through e-mail, it's just as easy to develop solid business relationships with groups that are two miles away as it is with ones that are 2000 miles away."

As with any worthwhile business endeavor, Web-based companies require hard work, good planning, and a solid customer service model. If these hurdles are met, a global business can be within anyone's reach.

■ SELF-TEST

1. What is the standard protocol suite used to carry information over the Internet?
   a. TCP/IP
   b. IPX
   c. DHCP
   d. ARPA

2. True or False: Computers can only be connected to the Internet through a dial-up connection, cable modem, or DSL modem.

3. Each Internet domain name is known by the appropriate _____ server.
   a. DHCP
   b. root
   c. client
   d. hostname

4. The domain name rwa.com is known as a _____ level domain assignment.
   a. first
   b. second
   c. base
   d. root

5. Network administrators may use _____ to share a single IP address among multiple clients.
   a. NAT
   b. INT
   c. NetBIOS
   d. DNS

6. True or False: When using NAT, if the number of IP address requests exceeds the number of addresses in the NAT pool, duplicate IP addresses from the pool are assigned with different default gateways.

7. NAT allows the use of _____ translations for devices that will have an IP address that must not change.
   a. dynamic
   b. static
   c. port
   d. socket

8. When using ICS, one computer acts as a _____ to the ISP managing IP addresses for the local network and translating all internal IP addresses to a single outgoing IP address.
   a. host
   b. router
   c. switch
   d. gateway

9. True or False: WINS is a dynamic database of name-to-IP mappings, adjusting its entries as IP addresses are reassigned.

10. What is used to determine how hypermedia information is displayed on a WWW browser screen?
    a. HTML
    b. HTTP
    c. IGMP
    d. IGRP

11. Which of the following is an HTML tag that sets the background color of a Web page?
    a. <BODY BGCOLOR= FFFF80
    b. <BODY BGCOLOR= "FFFF80"
    c. <BODY COLOR= "FFFF80"
    d. <BODY BGCOLOR= "GGFF80"

12. The number that contains three pairs of values for red, green, and blue colors in HTML source code is a(n) _____ number.
    a. decimal
    b. binary
    c. octal
    d. hexadecimal

13. Dynamic WWW pages contain a combination of HTML code and a "call" to a server using a(n) _____ application.
    a. ISP
    b. CGI
    c. HML
    d. WYSIWYG

14. WWW pages that are not completely specified during the HTML coding process and contain a combination of HTML code and applets are categorized as _____.
    a. static
    b. dynamic
    c. custom
    d. active

15. What type of Web page element can contain different types of inputs in order that a user who browses the page may enter information and receive interactive responses?
    a. FORM
    b. BODY
    c. HTTP
    d. WYSIWYG

16. True or False: CGI applications can be written in Java and C/C++ only.

17. True or False: A mouse click over a Java applet window (MYSW.JAVA) will cause a new page to load.

18. The Java class library category that provides user actions (mouse, keyboard, etc.) is called _____.
    a. event capture
    b. file I/O
    c. exception handling
    d. server interaction

19. What allows remote private LANs to communicate securely through an untrusted public network?
    a. VLAN version 2
    b. VPN
    c. PIX
    d. RMON

20. VPNs use an IP tunneling protocol and _____ that are transparent to the private network user.
    a. VPN switch
    b. security services
    c. IPX service
    d. IGMP services

21. True or False: VPN tunneling does not ensure complete data security.

22. Complete data security using VPNs is accomplished if the data communication is encrypted and _____.
    a. authenticated
    b. authorized
    c. accounted for
    d. protected

23. Which of the following standards provides a security protocol for tunneling as well as data privacy, integrity, and authentication?
    a. AAA
    b. FTP
    c. IPSec
    d. IDS

24. Which of the following is an application that can send and receive electronic communications in a faster mode than e-mail?
    a. Flash mail
    b. Instant messaging
    c. Text editor
    d. CGI

25. WWW pages are hosted by setting up a(n) _____ server like Apache.
    a. Web
    b. message
    c. ISP
    d. VPN

An Introduction to Networking with Windows

CHAPTER 16

PERFORMANCE OBJECTIVES

Upon completion of this chapter you will be able to:

- Identify printer resources available on a network computer.

- Create a dial-up networking connection.

 NETWORK+ OBJECTIVES

This chapter provides information for the following Network+ objectives:

2.3 Differentiate between the following network protocols in terms of routing, addressing schemes, interoperability, and naming conventions:

- TCP/IP
- NetBEUI
- IPX/SPX
- AppleTalk

2.12 Define the function of the following remote access protocols and services:

- RAS
- PPTP
- PPP
- ICA

3.1 Identify the basic capabilities (i.e., client support, interoperability, authentication, file and print services, application support, security) of the following server operating systems:

- UNIX/Linux
- Windows
- NetWare
- Macintosh

3.4 Identify the main characteristics of network attached storage.

3.7 Given a remote connectivity scenario (e.g., IP, IPX, dial-up, PPPoE, authentication, physical connectivity, etc.), configure the connection.

3.11 Given a network configuration, select the appropriate NIC and network configuration settings (DHCP, DNS, WINS, protocols, NETBIOS/host name, etc.) on network resources and users.

4.8 Given a scenario, predict the impact of modifying, adding, or removing network services (e.g., DHCP, DNS, WINS, etc.).

■ INTRODUCTION

Windows offers many different ways to connect your machine to a network and plenty of applications to assist you with your networking needs. This chapter briefly examines the basics of networking in Windows.

■ THE NETBEUI PROTOCOL

Objective 2-3

The Network BIOS Extended User Interface (NetBEUI) protocol is the backbone of Windows for Workgroups, Windows 95/98, and Windows NT networking. File and printer sharing between these network operating systems is accomplished through the use of NetBEUI.

NetBEUI provides the means to gather information about the Network Neighborhood. Table 16–1 shows the advantages and disadvantages of the NetBEUI protocol. One of the main disadvantages with NetBEUI is that it is a nonroutable protocol. This means that a NetBEUI message cannot be routed across two different networks. It was designed to support small networks (up to 200 nodes) and becomes inefficient in larger installations.

TABLE 16–1
Advantages and disadvantages of NetBEUI.

Advantages	Disadvantages
Easy to implement	Not routable
Good performance	Few support tools
Low memory requirements	Proprietary
Self-tuning efficiency	

■ THE NETWORK NEIGHBORHOOD

The Network Neighborhood is a hierarchical collection of the machines capable of communicating with each other over a Windows network. Note that systems running Windows for Workgroups, Windows 95/98, and Windows NT have the ability to connect to the network as well.

Figure 16–1 shows a typical Network Neighborhood. The three small PC icons named At213_tower, Nomad, and Waveguide all represent different machines connected to the network. Each machine is also a member of a ***workgroup***, or *domain* of computers that share a common set of properties.

Workgroup

FIGURE 16–1
Network Neighborhood window.

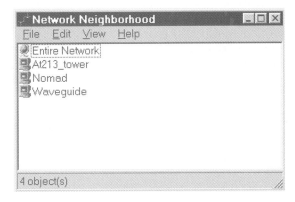

Double-clicking on Waveguide brings up the items being shared by Waveguide. As indicated in Figure 16–2, Waveguide is sharing two folders: pcx and pub.

FIGURE 16–2
Items shared by Waveguide.

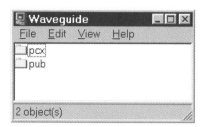

The Network Neighborhood gives you a way to graphically navigate to shared resources (files, CD-ROM drives, printers).

■ NETWORK PRINTING

Objective 3-1

A network printer is a printer that a user has decided to share. For the user's machine it is a local printer. But other users on the network can map to the network printer and use it as if it were their own printer. Figure 16–3 shows a shared printer offered by a computer named Nomad. Nomad is offering an hp 890c.

It is necessary to install the printer on your machine before you can begin using it over the network.

FIGURE 16–3
A printer shared by Nomad.

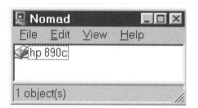

Adding a New Printer

To add a new printer, double-click the Add Printer icon in the Printers folder. This will start the Add Printer Wizard, an automated process that guides you through the installation process.

The first choice you must make is shown in Figure 16–4.

FIGURE 16–4
Choosing local/network printing.

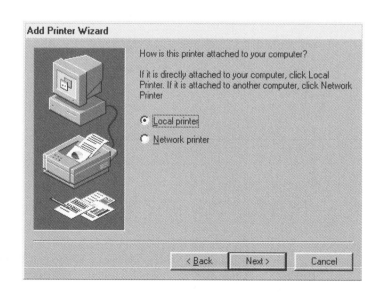

A local printer is local to your machine. A network printer can be printed to by anyone on the network who has made a connection to that printer. A network printer is also a local printer to the machine that hosts it. If you are installing a network printer, the next window will look like that shown in Figure 16–5.

FIGURE 16–5
Mapping a network printer.

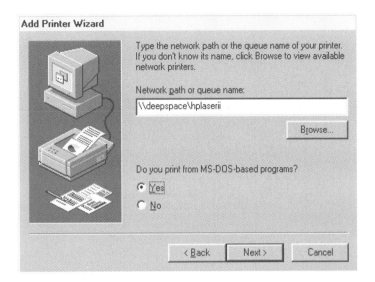

The printer being mapped is an HP LaserJet II (named "hplaserii" on the network) connected to the machine "deepspace." You can also browse the Network Neighborhood to select a network printer. DOS accessibility to the network printer is controlled from this window as well.

Next, the manufacturer and model of your printer must be chosen. Windows has a large database of printers to choose from. Figure 16–6 shows the initial set of choices. If your printer is not on the list, you must insert a disk with the appropriate drivers (usually supplied by the printer manufacturer).

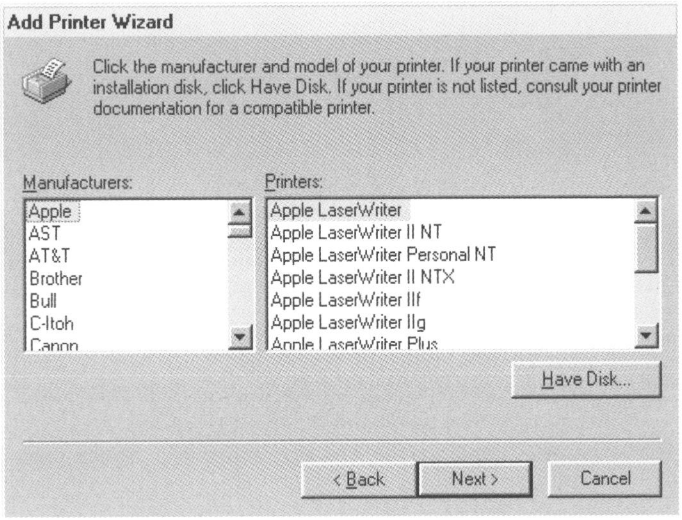

FIGURE 16–6
Choosing a printer manufacturer/model.

After the printer has been selected, the last step is to name it (as in the network printer "hplaserii").

If only one printer is installed, it is automatically the default printer for Windows. For two or more printers (including network printers), one must be set as the default. This can be done by right-clicking the printer's icon and selecting Set As Default. You can also access printer properties and change the default printer from inside the printer status window, using the Printer pull-down menu.

If the printer has been installed correctly, clicking on the Print Test Page button will cause the printer to print a test page. The test page contains a graphical Windows logo and information about the printer and its various drivers. A print dialog box appears asking whether the test page printed correctly. If the answer is no, Windows starts a printer help session. Figure 16–7 shows the initial Help window.

FIGURE 16–7
Built-in printer help.

Windows will ask several printer-related questions to help determine why the printer is not working. The causes are different for network printers, so Windows provides two different troubleshooting paths (network vs. local).

To make a shared printer on your machine available to the network, you need to double-click the Network icon in Control Panel and then click on the File and Print Sharing buttons. This opens up the window shown in Figure 16–8. The second box must be checked to allow network access to your printer.

FIGURE 16–8
Giving network access to your printer.

After a network printer connection has been established, you may use it like an ordinary local printer. Windows communicates with the network printer's host machine using NetBEUI. What this means is that jobs sent to a network printer are sent in small bursts (packets) and typically require additional time to print due to the network overhead. In a busy environment, such as an office or college laboratory, printer packets compete with all the other data traversing the network and thus take longer to transmit than data traveling over a simple parallel connection between the computer and the printer.

■ SHARING FILES OVER A NETWORK

Objective 3-4

A computer can share its disks with the network and allow remote users to map them for use as available drives on a remote computer. The first time a disk is shared and a connection is established, it may be necessary to provide a password to gain access to the data. The password is typically provided by the network administrator. Figure 16–9 shows the contents of My Computer. The small hand holding drive D: (Fireballxl5) indicates the drive is shared.

FIGURE 16–9
Indicating a shared drive.

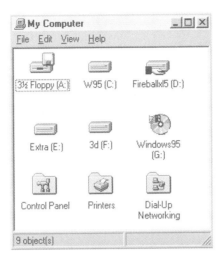

The user sharing the drive controls the access others will have to it over the network. Figure 16–10 shows the sharing properties for drive D: (right-click on the drive icon and select Properties).

FIGURE 16–10
Sharing Properties dialog box for drive D:.

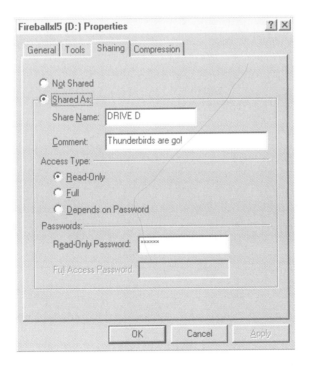

Figure 16–11 shows the E$ share properties in Windows 2000. Clearly, the user has a good deal of control over how sharing takes place.

Finding a Networked Computer

If you do not know the name of a computer that is sharing files, one way to locate it is to use the "Find...Computer" selection in the Tools menu of Windows Explorer. Figure 16–12 shows how a machine called "Waveguide" is found using this method.

FIGURE 16–11
Windows 2000 Disk Sharing
Properties dialog box.

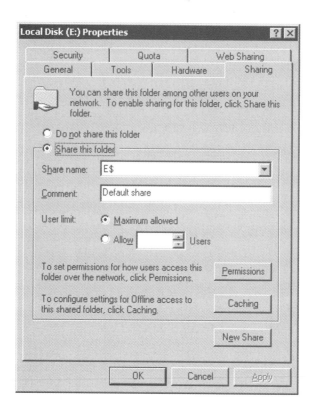

FIGURE 16–12

Searching for a computer on a
network.

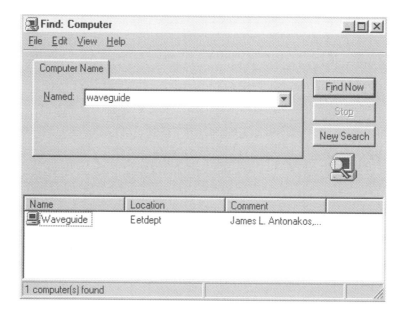

Working with Network Drives

If you have a connection to a network (dial-up PPP or network interface card), you can use Windows Explorer to *map* a network drive to your machine. This is done by selecting Map Network Drive on the Tools menu. Figure 16–13 shows the menu window used to map a network drive.

The computer automatically picks the first free drive letter (you can pick a different one) and requires a path to the network drive. In Figure 16–13 the path is \\SBCCAA\ANTONAKOS_J. The general format is \\machinename\username.

FIGURE 16–13
Mapping a network drive.

Map Network Drive

Drive: H: OK

Path: \\SBCCAA\ANTONAKOS_J   Cancel

☐ Reconnect at logon

Access to the network drive may require a password, as indicated in Figure 16–14. If an invalid password is entered, the drive is not mapped.

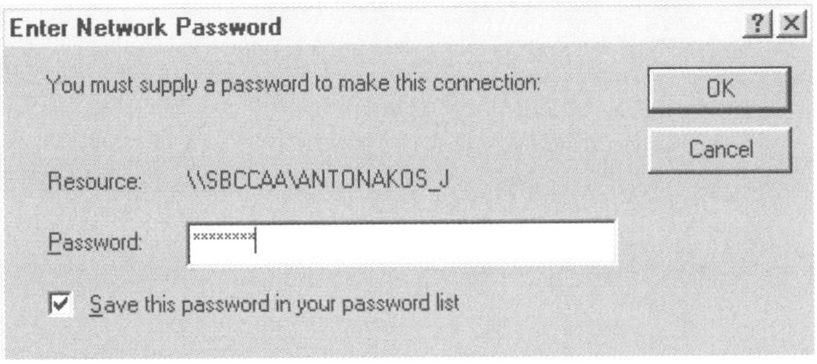

FIGURE 16–14
Supplying a network password.

Enter Network Password

You must supply a password to make this connection: OK

   Cancel

Resource: \\SBCCAA\ANTONAKOS_J

Password: xxxxxxxx

☑ Save this password in your password list

If the drive is successfully mapped, it will show up in Windows Explorer's folder display window. Figure 16–15 shows the contents of the mapped drive. Note that drive H: has a different icon from the other hard drives.

FIGURE 16–15
Contents of network drive H:.

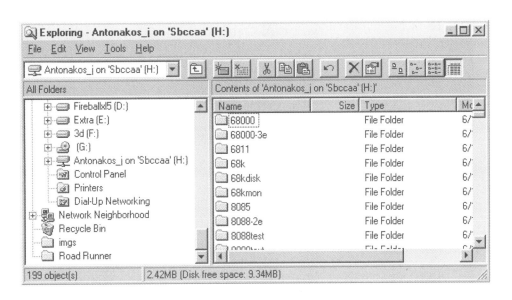

When you have finished using the network drive, you can disconnect it (via the Tools menu). This is illustrated in Figure 16–16.

FIGURE 16–16
Disconnecting a network
drive.

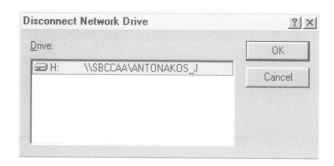

■ DIAL-UP NETWORKING

Objective 3-7

Dial-up networking is designed to provide reliable data connections using a modem and a telephone line. Figure 16–17 shows two icons in the Dial-Up Networking folder (found in Accessories on the Start menu).

FIGURE 16–17
Dial-up networking icons.

Double-clicking the Make New Connection icon will start the process to make a new connection, as shown in Figure 16–18. The name of the connection and the modem for the connection are specified.

FIGURE 16–18
Make New Connection Wizard.

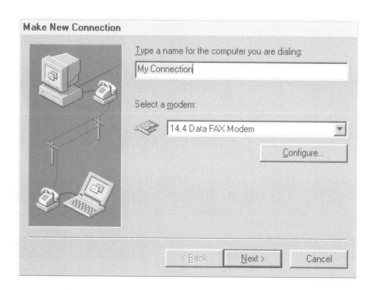

Objective 2-12

It is also necessary to provide an area code and telephone number during the configuration process. This number must be for a machine capable of supporting a PPP (point-to-point protocol) connection.

Once the connection has been created, it is activated by double-clicking it. To connect to a remote host, it is necessary to supply a user name and a password. This can be done automatically by the dial-up networking software. Figure 16–19 shows the connection window for the My Office icon.

FIGURE 16–19
Information required to access host.

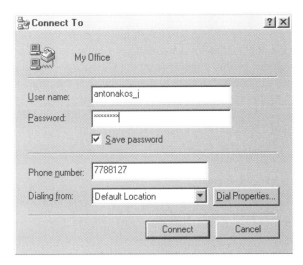

After the information has been entered, the Connect button is used to start up a connection. When the connection has been established, Windows displays a status window showing the current duration of the connection and the active protocols. Figure 16–20 shows the status for the My Office connection. Clicking on the disconnect button shuts the connection down and hangs up the modem.

FIGURE 16–20
Active dial-up networking connection.

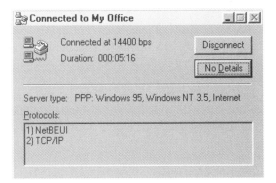

■ ICA TECHNOLOGY

ICA
Thin client

Objective 2-12

ICA (Independent Connection Architecture) is an efficient remote-access method used to connect *thin clients* to a network. A ***thin client*** is a networked device (typically a diskless workstation) that receives its software and information from a network server. No applications execute on a thin client. Instead, through ICA technology, only keystrokes, mouse clicks, and screen updates traverse the network from thin client to server. This greatly reduces the amount of network traffic required and also provides centralized control over applications that run on thin clients. Even fat clients (a real PC with lots of power) benefit from using ICA because all application processing is performed on the ICA server, and not on the client.

Developed by Citrix Systems (www.citrix.com) in 1989, ICA uses three components:

- Application server
- Network protocol
- ICA thin client software

The application server runs programs such as word processors and spreadsheets and, through ICA, communicates with one or more thin clients. It is important to understand that the application software does not run on the thin client. The ICA thin client software (which can be downloaded from the Citrix Web site) runs on the thin client and uses the network to communicate with the application running on the server.

With ICA technology in place, 32-bit high-speed processing is available to all ICA clients, regardless of their individual capabilities. Table 16–2 lists several important ICA features.

TABLE 16–2
ICA features.

ICA Feature	Description
Resources	286 or equivalent CPU, 640 kB RAM
Bandwidth	5 to 10 Kbps
Platform	DOS, Windows, UNIX, Linux, OS/2, Macintosh, Java
Protocols	TCP/IP, IPX/SPX, PPP, NetBEUI
Technologies	Modem, T1, ISDN, ATM, Internet
Security	SecureICA provides 40-, 56-, and 128-bit encryption during a session.
Load Balancing	Applications can be load balanced across multiple ICA servers in a Server Farm.

■ CONNECTING TO THE INTERNET

Besides a modem or a network interface card and the associated software, one more piece is needed to complete the networking picture: the Internet service provider (ISP). An ISP is any facility that contains its own direct connection to the Internet. For example, many schools and businesses now have their own dedicated high-speed connection (typically a T1 line, which provides data transfers of more than 1.5 Mbps).

Many users sign up with a company (such as AOL or MSN) and then dial in to these companies' computers, which themselves provide the Internet connection. The company is the ISP in this case.

Even the local cable company is an ISP now, offering high-speed cable modems that use unassigned television channels for Internet data. The cable modem is many times faster than the fastest telephone modems on the market.

After you have an ISP, the rest is up to you. You may design your own Web page (many ISPs host Web pages for their customers), use e-mail, browse the Web, Telnet to your school's mainframe and work on an assignment, or download a cool game from an ftp site.

■ TROUBLESHOOTING TECHNIQUES

Troubleshooting a network connection requires familiarity with several levels of operation. At the hardware level, the physical connection (parallel cable, modem, network interface card) must be working properly. A noisy phone line, the wrong interrupt selected during setup for the network interface card, incompatible parallel ports, and many other types of hardware glitches can prevent a good network connection.

At the software level there are two areas of concern: the network operating system software and the application software. For example, if Internet Explorer will not open any Web pages is the cause of the problem Internet Explorer or the underlying TCP/IP protocol software?

Even with all of the built-in functions Windows automatically performs, there is still a need for human intervention to get things up and running in the world of networking.

Remember that the Network menu allows you to add, modify, or remove various networking components, such as protocols (NetBEUI, TCP/IP), drivers for network interface cards, and dial-up networking utilities. You can also specify the way your machine is identified on the network, as well as various options involving file and printer sharing and protection. Figure 16–21 shows a sample network menu. Selecting any of the network components allows its properties to be examined.

FIGURE 16–21
Network menu.

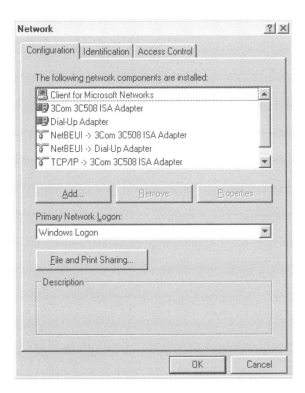

For example, typical network problems on a computer system involve the TCP/IP address settings. Figure 16–22 shows the setting that allows a Windows client computer to use a DHCP server to assign all TCP/IP network addresses (host, network mask, DNS servers, default gateway, WINS server host information).

Objective 3-11

Objective 4-8

If a problem arises with the DHCP server it may be necessary to assign the addresses manually. At a minimum (to use the Internet), this involves setting the TCP/IP address, subnet mask, default gateway, and DNS servers. Note that TCP/IP will work without a DNS server, but only IP addresses can be used, since there is no way to translate a domain name to an IP address without DNS. This would be very inconvenient for most users. A static IP address and subnet mask are entered in the IP Address tab in the TCP/IP Properties window as shown in Figure 16–23.

It is very important that the IP address be unique on the network, therefore it is necessary for the network administrator to keep track of what computer has what address. An IP address conflict prevents the client computer from accessing any of the TCP/IP network resources.

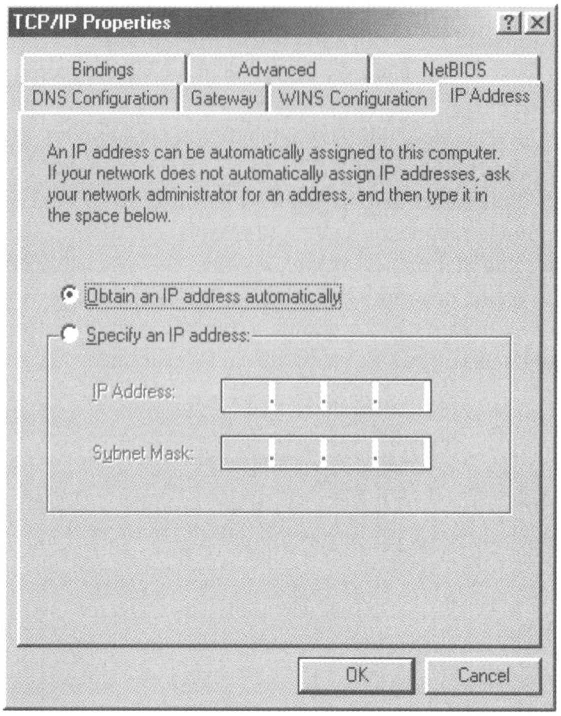

FIGURE 16–22
Using DHCP to obtain an
IP address.

FIGURE 16–23
Assigning a static IP address
along with a subnet mask.

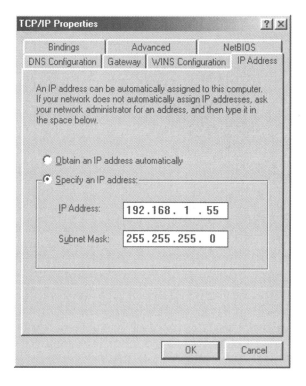

Adding a default gateway, shown in Figure 16–24, and the DNS servers, shown in Figure 16–25, provide all the information that is necessary for a client to use TCP/IP.

Note that more than one Installed Gateway and DNS Server address can be supplied, allowing a client to use the network even if some of the network resources are not available (for example, the first gateway is down). In a Windows domain setting, it may be necessary to update the WINS server address on the WINS Configuration tab to allow the computer to participate in WINS.

Considering the effort involved to manually keep track of each machine's IP address in a larger network, a DHCP server can save considerable time for a network administrator and minimize address conflicts.

FIGURE 16–24
Examining the installed
gateway configuration.

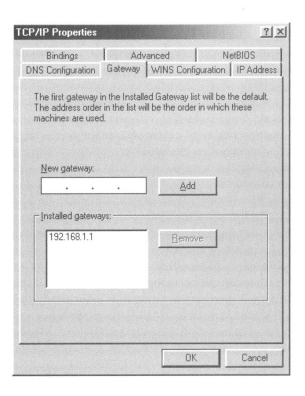

FIGURE 16–25
DNS configuration settings.

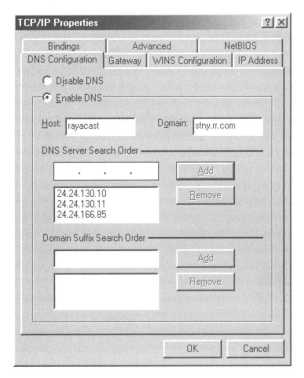

■ SELF-TEST

1. NetBEUI provides file and printer sharing for which of the following operating systems? (Choose two.)
   a. Windows 98
   b. Windows 2000
   c. Windows XP
   d. Windows NT

2. True or False: NetBEUI messages can be routed through LANs.

3. NetBEUI was designed to support networks with up to _____ nodes.
   a. 50
   b. 100
   c. 150
   d. 200

4. Double-clicking on a computer that is represented graphically by Network Neighborhood reveals what?
   a. Properties
   b. IP address
   c. Shared items
   d. Default gateway

5. If the printer that you desire to install is not on the list provided by Windows, what must be done?
   a. It cannot be installed.
   b. Uninstall the local printer
   c. Install drivers from vendor
   d. Install drivers from Windows program files

6. If only one printer is installed, it is the _____ printer.
   a. local
   b. network
   c. default
   d. shared

7. True or False: The causes for print problems are generally the same for local and networked printers.

8. Host A in the following diagram cannot print. All the other hosts on the network can print to both printers. What is the likely cause of the problem?

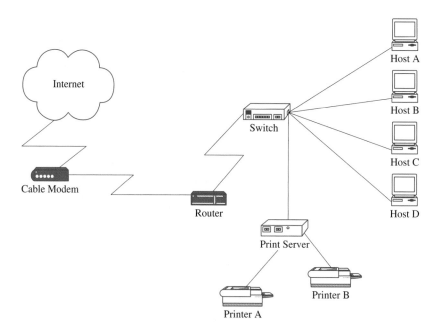

   a. Printer B is not installed on Host A.
   b. Printer A is not selected as default.
   c. The print server is down.
   d. Print drivers are not installed on Host A.

9. Jobs sent to a network printer are sent in small bursts called _____.
   a. frames
   b. bits
   c. packets
   d. segments

10. The connection between a computer and a local printer is normally a(n) _____ connection.
    a. serial
    b. parallel
    c. isochronous
    d. switched

11. What is shown when a drive is shared in Windows?
    a. Sharing is checked.
    b. Small hand over drive
    c. Small hand holding drive
    d. Different color

12. Passwords may be necessary the first time a(n) _____ is shared and a connection established.
    a. network connection
    b. disk
    c. Internet connection
    d. operating system

13. Remote users can _____ to a locally shared drive and use it as an available drive.
    a. share
    b. map
    c. link
    d. ping

14. The Find... Computer selection in the Tools menu of Windows Explorer can be used to find a computer that is _____.
    a. finding a lost file
    b. using NAT
    c. disabled
    d. sharing files

15. Explorer can be used to map a network drive to your machine if you have a _____.
    a. network server only
    b. minimum of 10 GB of free memory
    c. connection to a network
    d. connection to a printer

16. Joe Tekk is setting up a network drive to Jane Tekk's computer. His computer has a path to Jane's computer. Joe's computer has a floppy disk drive, one hard drive, and a CD-ROM. Joe's and Jane's computers have their computer names specified as Joe and Jane respectively. What is the computer name sequence shown in Windows Explorer beside the networked drive?
    a. Jane on 'Joe' (D.)
    b. Jane on 'Joe' (E.)
    c. Joe on 'Jane' (D.)
    d. Joe on 'Jane' (E.)

17. Joe Tekk is setting up a network drive to Jane Tekk's computer. His computer has a path to Jane's computer. Upon Joe's first access attempt, he is prompted for a password. What happens if he types the wrong password?
    a. The drive is mapped.
    b. The drive is not mapped.
    c. No additional attempt is allowed.
    d. The computer maps the first available drive letter.

18. When a dial-up connection is established to a remote host, which two of the following must be supplied? (Choose two.)
    a. PPTP tunnel
    b. DNS server
    c. Username
    d. Password

19. ICA is an efficient remote-access method used to connect a _____ to a network.
    a. mapped drive
    b. thin client
    c. user application
    d. fat clients

20. Which of the following is **not** a component of ICA technology?
    a. Application server
    b. Network protocol
    c. ICA fat client software
    d. ICA thin client software

21. True or False: Local cable companies can function as an ISP offering high-speed cable modems that use unassigned TV channels for Internet data transmission.

22. Which of the following is **not** a hardware glitch that can prevent adequate network connections?
    a. Noisy phone line
    b. Incompatible parallel port
    c. Network operating system
    d. Wrong interrupt used

23. Host D shown in the following illustration can contact Hosts A, B, and C but cannot access the Internet. All other hosts on the network can access the Internet. What is the likely problem?

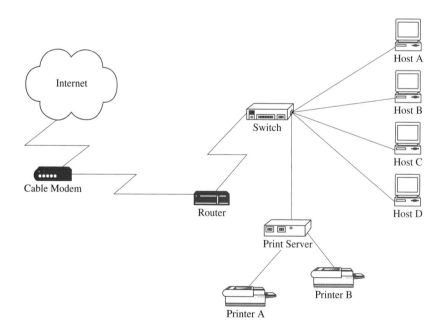

    a. The default gateway is not configured.
    b. The DHCP is not configured.
    c. The DNS server is down.
    d. Conflicting IP addresses

24. After selecting the TCP/IP network protocol as shown in the following Network dialog box, what must be done next before entering an IP address?

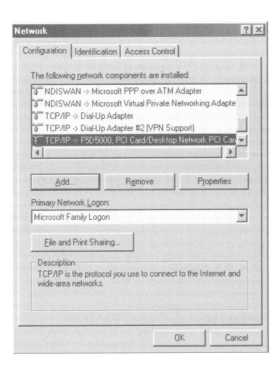

a. Right-click Properties
b. Left-click Properties
c. Click on Add
d. Click on File and Print Sharing

25. Only IP addresses can be used to connect to remote hosts if the _____ is not working.
a. DHCP server
b. DNS server
c. WINS server
d. ICA server

Windows NT/2000 Domains

CHAPTER **17**

PERFORMANCE OBJECTIVES

Upon completion of this chapter, you will be able to:

- Describe the benefits of creating a Windows NT/2000 domain.

- Explain some different types of Windows NT/2000 domains.

- Discuss the different types of clients able to join a Windows NT/2000 domain.

 ## NETWORK+ OBJECTIVES

This chapter provides information for the following Network+ objectives:

2.7 Identify the purpose of the following network services:
- DHCP/BOOTP
- DNS
- NAT/ICS
- WINS
- SNMP

2.12 Define the function of the following remote access protocols and services:
- RAS
- PPP
- PPTP
- ICA

3.1 Identify the basic capabilities (i.e., client support, interoperability, authentication, file and print services, application support, security) of the following server operating systems:
- UNIX/Linux
- NetWare
- Windows
- Macintosh

3.2 Identify the basic capabilities of client workstations (i.e., client connectivity, local security mechanisms, authentication).

3.5 Identify the purpose and characteristics of fault tolerance.

3.6 Identify the purpose and characteristics of disaster recovery.

3.11 Given a network configuration, select the appropriate NIC and network configuration settings (DHCP, DNS, WINS, protocols, NETBIOS/host name, etc.) on network resources and users.

4.1 Given a troubleshooting scenario, select the appropriate TCP/IP utility from among the following:
- TRACERT
- PING
- ARP
- NETSTAT
- NBTSTAT
- IPCONFIG/IFCONFIG
- WINIPCFG
- NSLOOKUP

4.4 Given specific parameters, configure a client to connect to the following servers:
- UNIX/Linux
- NetWare
- Windows
- Macintosh

4.11 Given a network troubleshooting scenario involving a client connectivity problem (e.g., incorrect protocol/client software/authentication configuration or insufficient rights/permission), identify the cause of the problem.

■ INTRODUCTION

Domain

Any group of personal computers can be joined together to form either a workgroup or a domain. In a workgroup, each computer is managed independently but may share some of its resources, such as printers, disks, or a scanner, with the other members of the network. Unfortunately, as the number of computers in the workgroup grows, it becomes more and more difficult to manage the network. This is exactly the situation in which a Windows domain can be used. A ***domain*** offers a centralized mechanism to relieve much of the administrative burden commonly experienced in a workgroup. A domain requires at least one computer running a Windows Server operating system (i.e., Windows NT, 2000, or later). Table 17–1 illustrates the characteristics of a workgroup and a domain. Examine the features of Windows NT/2000 before taking a detailed look at domains.

TABLE 17–1
Comparing a workgroup and a domain.

Workgroup	Domain
Small networks	Large networks
Peer-to-peer	Client–server
No central server	Central server
Low cost	Higher cost
Decentralized	Centralized

NTFS

Windows NT is an operating system developed by Microsoft. It was developed to create a large, distributed, and secure network of computers for deployment in a large organization, company, or enterprise. Windows NT actually consists of two products: Windows NT Server and Windows NT Workstation. The server product is used as the server in the client-server environment. Usually a server contains more hardware than the regular desktop-type computer, such as extra disks and memory. The workstation product is designed to run on a regular desktop computer (with an 80486 processor or better). Windows NT provides users a more stable and secure environment, offering many features not available in Windows 95/98 such as ***NTFS*** (New Technology Filing System), a more advanced file system than FAT (File Allocation Table) 16/32. A later version of Windows NT, called Windows 2000, is covered at the end of this chapter.

This chapter uses the Windows NT Server product to illustrate the user interface in the Windows NT environment. We begin by looking at the Windows NT login process.

■ WINDOWS NT OPERATING SYSTEM LOGON

One of the first things a new user will notice about the Windows NT environment is the method used to log in. The only way to initiate a logon is to press the Ctrl+Alt+Del keys simultaneously as shown in Figure 17–1. This, of course, is the method used to reboot a computer running DOS or Windows 95/98. Using Windows NT, the Ctrl+Alt+Del keys will no longer cause the computer to reboot, although it will get Windows NT's attention.

FIGURE 17–1
Windows NT Begin Logon window.

If the user is not logged on, Windows NT displays the logon screen, requesting a user name and password. During the Windows NT installation process, the Administrator account is created. If the computer is configured to run on a network, the logon screen also requests the domain information. After a valid user name, such as Administrator, and the correct password are entered, the Windows NT desktop is displayed, as shown in Figure 17–2.

FIGURE 17–2
Windows NT desktop.

■ WINDOWS NT SECURITY MENU

After a Windows NT Server or Workstation is logged in, pressing the Ctrl+Alt+Del keys simultaneously results in the Windows NT Security menu being displayed as illustrated in Figure 17–3. From the Windows NT Security menu it is possible for the operator to select from several different options, including Cancel to return to Windows NT.

FIGURE 17–3
Windows NT Security menu.

Locked

The Lock Workstation option is used to put the Windows NT Server or Workstation computer in a ***locked*** state. The locked state is usually used when the computer is left unattended, such as during lunch, dinner, nights, and weekends. When a computer is locked, the desktop is hidden and all applications continue to run. The display either enters the screen saver mode or displays a window requesting the password used to unlock the computer. The password is the same as the one used to log on.

The Logoff option is used to log off from the Windows NT computer. The logoff procedure also can be accessed from the shutdown menu by selecting the appropriate setting. The logoff procedure terminates all tasks associated with the user but continues running all system tasks. The system returns to the logon screen shown in Figure 17–1. The Shut Down option must be selected before system power can be turned off.

The Change Password option is used to change the password of the currently logged-in user.

The Task Manager option causes the Windows NT Task Manager window to be displayed. The Task Manager is responsible for running all the system applications, as indicated by Figure 17–4. Notice that individual applications may be created, selected, and ended or switched by using the appropriate buttons. It is sometimes necessary to end tasks that are not functioning properly for some reason or another. In these cases, the status of the application is usually "not responding."

FIGURE 17–4
Task Manager applications.

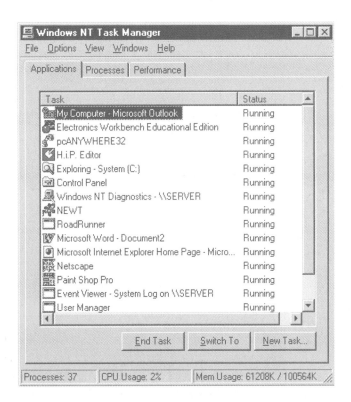

Each application controls processes that actually perform the required tasks. Figure 17–5 shows a number of processes being executed by the Task Manager. Applications may create as many processes as necessary. Extreme caution must be exercised when ending a process shown on the Processes display. The processes used to control Windows NT can also be ended, causing the computer to be left in an unknown state. If processes must be terminated, it is best to use the Applications tab.

The Task Manager can also display the system performance. Figure 17-6 shows a graphical display of current CPU and memory utilization. It also shows a numeric display of other critical information.

■ DOMAINS

Domain

Objective 3-1

Windows NT computers usually belong to a computer network called a ***domain***. The domain will collectively contain most of the resources available to members of the domain. Computers running Windows NT Server software offer their resources to the network

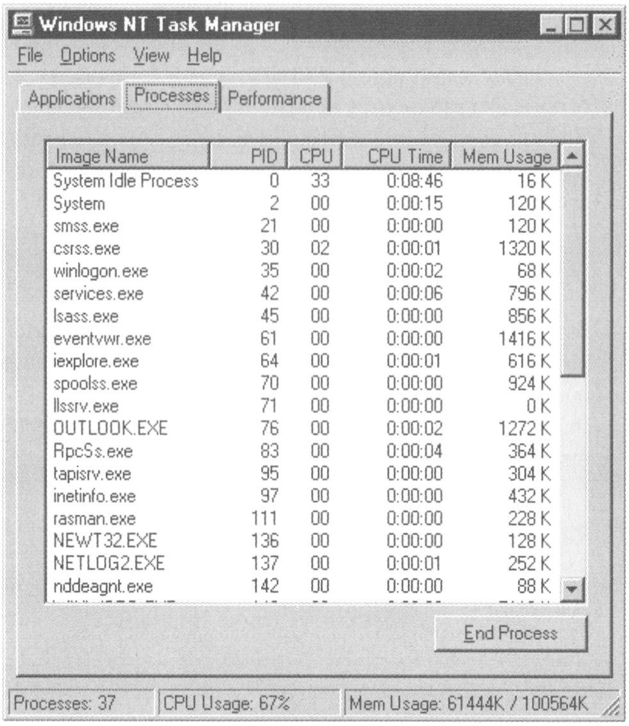

FIGURE 17–5
Windows NT processes.

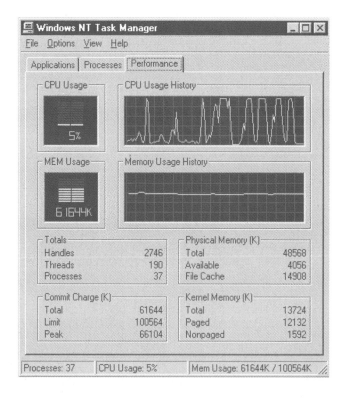

FIGURE 17–6
Task Manager Performance
display.

clients. For example, during the logon process, a Windows NT Server responsible for controlling a domain will verify the user information (a user name and password) before access to the computer is allowed. The Network Neighborhood allows access to the resources available on other computers in the domain. Figure 17–7 shows the Network menu, where network components are configured.

FIGURE 17–7
Currently installed network protocols.

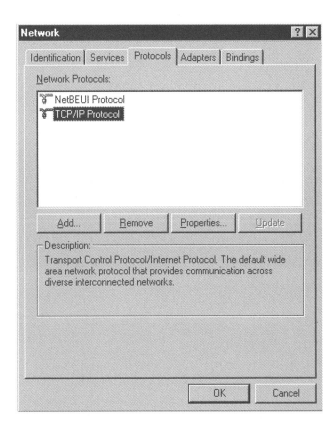

Network administrator

The *network administrator* determines how the network is set up and how each of the components is configured. It is always a good idea to know whom to contact when information about a network is required. If the setting is not correct, unpredictable events may occur on the network, creating the potential for problems.

■ WINDOWS 2000

At first glance, Windows 2000 looks similar to the older versions of Windows NT with many subtle and not-so-subtle changes. The Windows 2000 operating system consists of two general versions (similar to Windows NT 4.0), Windows 2000 Server and Windows 2000 Professional. The Windows 2000 Server product is further broken down into three products: the basic Windows 2000 Server and two additional products called Windows 2000 Advanced Server and Windows 2000 Datacenter Server. With all of these server products to choose from, a Windows 2000 Server solution is available for every size business or organization.

Windows 2000 Professional is designed for the client computers in any size business. Windows 2000 Professional extends the security, reliability, and manageability available in NT 4.0 Workstation but also includes many of the latest features and enhancements available in Windows 98. The Windows 2000 Server products are designed for file, print, application, and Web servers. Windows 2000 Server also supports the creation of domains, allowing for central administration of all Windows 2000 services. Windows 2000 Advanced Server and Windows 2000 Datacenter Server offer increased capabilities for enterprise applications and data warehousing. We will briefly examine some of the features and benefits of these new Windows operating systems.

Windows 2000 Server

Begin by looking at the desktop view of Windows 2000 Server illustrated in Figure 17–8, which shows the Administrative Tools portion of the Start menu.

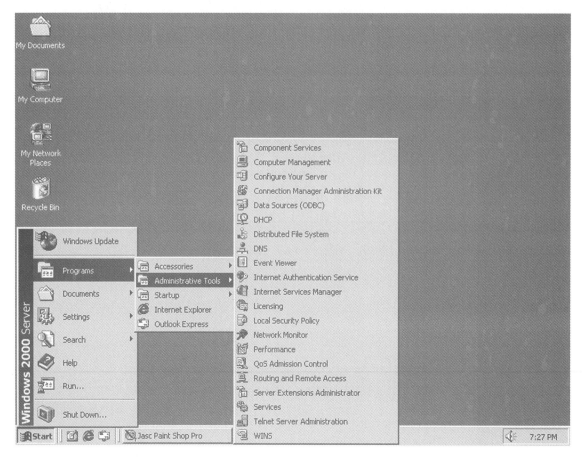

FIGURE 17–8
Windows 2000 Server desktop.

You may notice many differences in the list of Windows 2000 Administrative Tools from those available in Windows NT Server. In addition, notice that Windows NT Explorer is not listed in the Programs menu as in the previous versions of the operating system. In Windows 2000 Server, Windows NT Explorer has been renamed Windows Explorer and has been moved to the Accessories submenu. An examination of Windows Explorer shows a few more of these subtle differences, as illustrated in Figure 17–9.

Notice that the Folders list shown in the left pane of the Windows Explorer display now includes an entry for My Documents, and the Network Neighborhood has been replaced by My Network Places. Another important change is that additional help information is easily accessible on the Explorer display. Virtually every commonly used application has been enhanced in the Windows 2000 upgrade.

From a system administration point of view, Windows 2000 supports all of the existing applications such as the BackOffice application suite. In many cases, new versions of the application programs are available. There are a few major differences that help to simplify the administration of a Windows 2000 Server computer. An application called Windows 2000 Configure Your Server provides a quick method to access the most common applications, as shown in Figure 17–10.

In addition to the obvious differences between Windows 2000 and its predecessors, you will also notice changes in many application names and/or the locations where they are stored. For example, the functionality of the Disk Administrator program is now part of the Computer Management application, as shown in Figure 17–11.

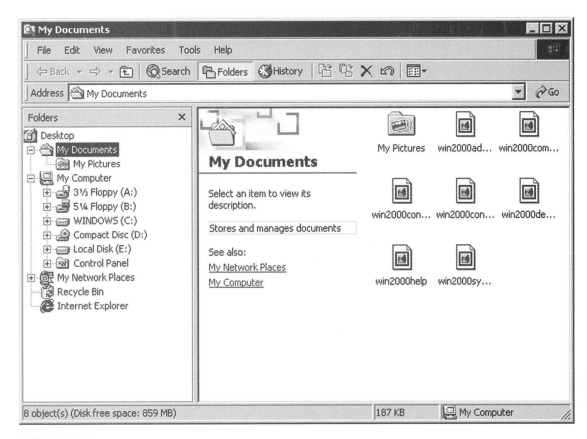

FIGURE 17–9
Windows 2000 Server Explorer.

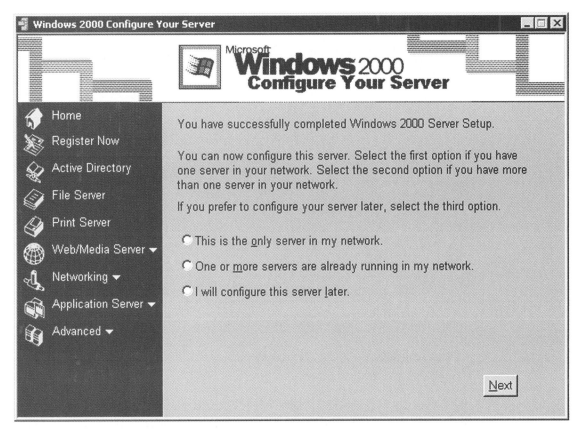

FIGURE 17–10
New Windows 2000 configuration tool.

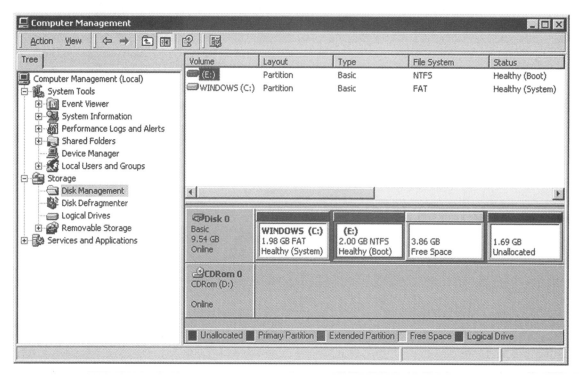

FIGURE 17–11
Windows 2000 Server Disk Management display.

Generally, all the old features of Disk Administrator are supported, but new features have also been added, such as a built-in defragmenter. Some of the most notable features of Windows 2000 Server are shown in Table 17–2.

TABLE 17–2
List of Windows 2000 Server built-in features.

Windows 2000 Features	Description
Supports the latest Windows technologies	Active directory interfaces Group policies NTFS 5.0 Plug-and-play support Resources Reservation Protocol support
Internet Server applications	Domain Name Services (DNS) Dynamic Host Configuration Protocol (DHCP) Lightweight Directory Access Protocol support Internet Printing Internet Connection sharing Network Address Translation (NAT) Streaming media server
Safe mode start-up	System Troubleshooting Tool
IntelliMirror	Windows 2000 Professional client support
File server	Folder sharing
Message queuing	Support for distributed applications
Public Key and Certificate Management	Support for Virtual Private Networks Kerberos support
Disk and File Management	Disk Quotas Distributed File System Distributed Link Training Distributed Authoring and Versioning Content Indexing Encrypting File Systems (EFS)

You are encouraged to explore these features using the updated Windows 2000 Server help system that is displayed in Figure 17–12. After a careful review, a system administrator will realize that there are many reasons to upgrade to Windows 2000 Server.

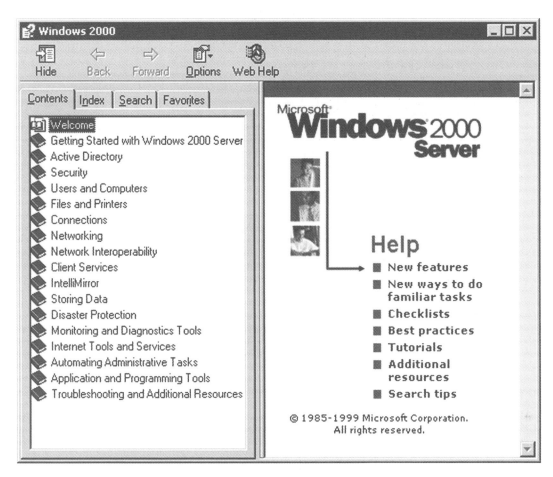

FIGURE 17–12
Windows 2000 Server Help display.

Windows 2000 Professional

The Windows 2000 Professional operating system, shown in Figure 17–13, can be used in combination with Windows 2000 Server and offers many features to the user. The Windows 2000 Professional operating system is easier to use, manage, and troubleshoot compared to Windows NT Workstation. There is additional support for adding new hardware, including an Add/Remove Hardware Wizard, plug-and-play support, and additional power-saving options. Windows 2000 Professional also provides additional support for mobile users. These features include built-in support for Virtual Private Networks, Internet Printing, and offline folders that, when used with a Synchronization Manager, are designed to keep everything current with a minimum of effort. Additional features allow for remote administration and installation.

Note that the Windows 2000 Professional operating system is not able to run any of the Windows 2000 Server applications. For example, a Windows 2000 Professional computer cannot offer Directory Services or function as a DNS, DHCP, or WINS server. If any of the server-based applications are required, it is necessary to install at least one copy of Windows 2000 Server. With these exceptions, Windows 2000 Professional shares the same user interface enhancements and many of the same general user application programs as

FIGURE 17–13
Windows 2000 Professional
desktop.

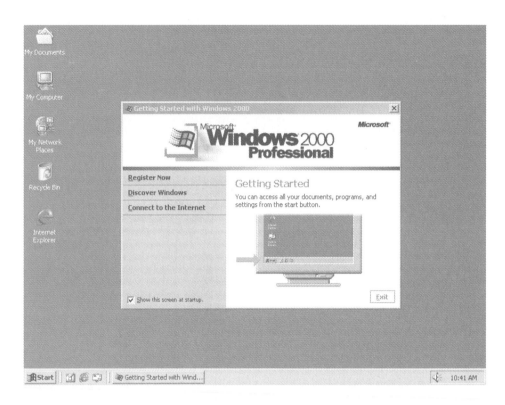

Windows 2000 Server. You are encouraged to explore the features of all the Windows 2000 operating systems.

■ WINDOWS NT DOMAINS

Objective 3-1

Each Windows NT domain can be configured independently or as a group in which all computers are members of the same domain. Figure 17–14 shows two independent domains. Each domain consists of at least one Windows NT primary domain controller (PDC) and any number of backup domain controllers (BDC). One shared directory database is used to store user account information and security settings for the entire domain.

FIGURE 17–14
Independent Windows NT
domains.

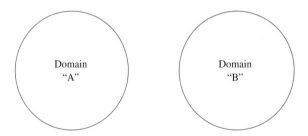

A BDC can be promoted to a PDC in the event the current PDC on the network becomes unavailable for any reason. A promotion can be initiated manually, causing the current PDC to be demoted to a backup. Figure 17–15 shows a domain containing two Windows NT Server computers. One computer is the PDC and the other computer is the BDC.

Windows NT can administer the following types of domains:

- Windows NT Server domains
- Windows NT Server and LAN Manager 2.x domains
- LAN Manager 2.x domains

FIGURE 17–15
Domain "A" configuration.

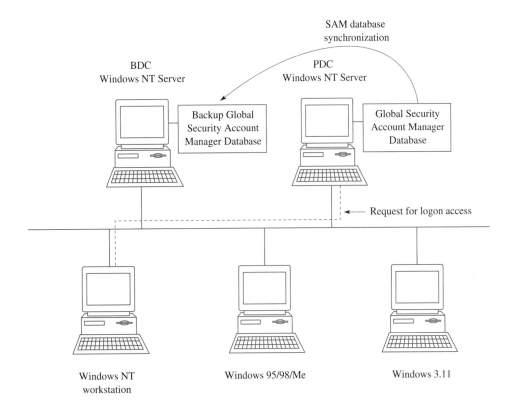

A LAN Manager 2.x domain is a previous version of Microsoft networking software used by older MS-DOS and Windows computers.

The different types of activities that can be performed on a domain include the following:

- Create a new domain
- Modify an existing domain
- Join a domain
- Add a computer to a domain
- Remove a computer from a domain
- Synchronize files in a domain
- Promote a BDC to a PDC
- Establish trust relationships

When a system is set up as a PDC, the new domain name is required in order to proceed through the Windows NT installation process. This domain name is required by all other computer users who want to join the domain. Note that each domain can contain only *one* primary domain controller. All other Windows NT Server computers can be designated as backups or ones that do not participate in the domain control process at all.

A computer can be configured to join a domain during the Windows NT installation process, using the Network icon in the system Control Panel, or by using the Server Manager tool. A computer can be removed using the Network icon in the system Control Panel or the Server Manager tool.

Synchronizing a domain involves exchanging information between a primary domain controller and any secondary or backup domain controllers as shown in Figure 17–15. The synchronization interval for a Windows NT computer is five minutes. This means that account information entered on the primary domain controller takes only five minutes to be exchanged with all secondary computers. This synchronization is performed automatically by Windows NT.

Trust relationship

Domains can also be set up to offer trust relationships. A **_trust relationship_** involves either providing or receiving services from an external domain, as shown in Figure 17–16. A trust relationship can permit users in one domain to use the resources of another domain. A trust relationship can be a one-way trust or a two-way trust, offering the ability to handle many types of requirements.

FIGURE 17–16
Domain trust relationships.

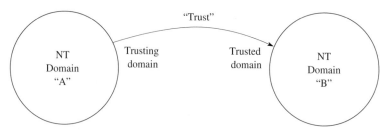

(a) One-way trust relationship.

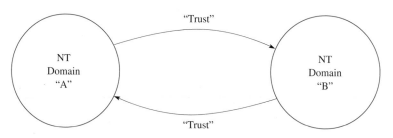

(b) Two-way trust relationship.

A one-way trust relationship as shown in Figure 17–16(a) identifies domain "B" as a trusted source for domain "A." A two-way trust, shown in Figure 17–16(b), involves two separate domains sharing their resources with each other. Each domain considers the other to be a trusted source. Extreme caution must be exercised when setting up trust relationships. If the trusted domain is really untrustworthy, valuable information can be lost using the "trusted" accounts.

■ BASIC CAPABILITIES OF WINDOWS SERVER OPERATING SYSTEMS

Objective 3-1

The basic capabilities of Windows server operating systems are classified according to the following areas:

- Client support
- Interoperability
- Authentication
- File and print services
- Application support
- Security

Let us examine the importance of each of these capabilities.

Client Support

A Windows NT domain can support many different types of clients, such as:

- Windows NT Servers
- Windows NT workstations
- Windows 95/98/Me clients

- Windows 3.11 clients
- Windows 3.1 clients
- MS-DOS clients
- OS/2 workstations
- NetWare clients
- Macintosh clients

Interoperability

Interoperability in the Windows environment is provided by a host of products. For example, Windows 2000 (Professional and Server) provides access to NFS using the Server for NFS, allowing UNIX and Linux clients the option of accessing and storing information in Windows. The UNIX Admin snap-in, which is a program designed to function similar to a UNIX device in the Windows environment, is used to manage the service. The Gateway for NFS, which runs on the Windows 2000 Server, allows non-NFS Windows clients to access NFS resources by connecting to the NFS-enabled server that acts as a gateway between the NFS (UNIX/Linux) and CIFS (Windows 2000) protocols. The Server for PCNFS provides authentication services for NFS clients to access the protected NFS files. Lastly, the server for NIS allows a Windows computer to function as an NIS master. The server for NIS must be installed on a Windows 2000 Server that is configured as a domain controller.

Microsoft Windows services for UNIX is designed to allow UNIX and Windows computers to communicate with each other. To accomplish this, Windows uses the Common Internet File System (CIFS). CIFS is an enhancement to the Server Message Block (SMB) protocol. UNIX services are integrated into Windows, allowing Windows Explorer, My Network Places, and so on to connect to NFS network resources. In addition, more than 60 command-line utilities such as *grep, tar*, and *vi* are also provided.

Likewise, additional application program tools allow for Windows to operate in Macintosh, NetWare, and many other environments, offering seamless compatibility with all major server-type operating systems.

Authentication

Authentication in a Windows server-type environment is performed by domain controllers under the supervision of the system and/or network administrator. Clients on the network gain access to network resources according to the settings maintained on the server. Proper monitoring and maintenance of user information is essential to guarantee that access is legitimate.

In addition, authentication in a domain environment is provided using trust relationships between the server systems. It is essential that a trust be granted only when it can be guaranteed that the trusting and trusted computer systems are safe. Network resources can easily be compromised if a trust relationship allows it.

File and Print Services

File and print services on a Windows server can provide capabilities to the largest organizations supporting client computer systems using virtually every type of operating system (including UNIX/Linux, NetWare, Macintosh, etc.). When properly configured with appropriate software, the client computer systems are able to participate fully in a Windows network. Figure 17–17 shows the first step in the process to allow NetWare File and Print services to be added to a Windows client.

Files can be shared, read-only, or write-accessible, depending on the user. Tracking and usage of the file accesses are maintained in the log files on the server.

Printers can also be shared network-wide with load balancing (multiple printers with the same name) for high-volume printing. Use of the printers is based on proper authentication by the network servers.

FIGURE 17–17
Built-in network services on a
Windows client.

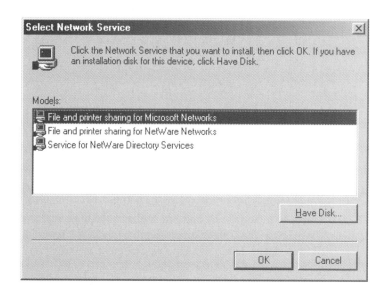

Application Support

The group of applications supported by the Windows environment is one of the most comprehensive available. Most software manufacturers support the Windows operating system. Microsoft also develops many of the applications themselves, offering a complete and comprehensive suite of office applications, word processors, spreadsheets, databases, project management programs, and many others. Although there is a cost associated with Windows-based products, many would agree that, with a high level of integration between the products, they are well worth the price.

Applications support can also be extended to the clients on the network. Network versions of software allow clients to run programs located on the server, allowing for a system and/or network administrator to manage the network much more efficiently.

Security

Security is one of the most important elements in a Windows network. When using a domain, security is the responsibility of the server with the ability to centralize the administration. All clients use a Windows server to authenticate usernames and passwords that allow access to all network resources.

Use the following checklist to offer protection against various threats:

• Perform risk assessment

• Use virus detection software

• Maintain up-to-date software

• Verify system security settings (file protections, trusts, etc.)

• Use a firewall (local computer or LAN-based)

• Use passwords that are considered strong (numbers and letters, no dictionary words, etc.)

• Perform routing security evaluation and maintenance

Note that security is only as good as the detection method. If a system is compromised and it is detected immediately, that is the best we can hope for. If the intrusion goes undetected, big problems loom on the horizon.

■ ADDING A CLIENT TO A WINDOWS NETWORK

Objective 3-11

Objective 4-4

A common activity in a network environment is adding new clients. Generally this involves adding a NIC to a stand-alone computer system or adding a new system that already contains a NIC. In either case, it is necessary to make sure that the NIC is compatible with the operating system. Each of the Windows client operating systems, such as 95/98/Me/NT Workstation, 2000 Professional, and XP Professional, has its own list of supported hardware. Windows 95/98/Me and XP have the widest choices in the selection of hardware, whereas Windows NT and 2000 have the most restrictive. Check the hardware compatibility information to be sure that the hardware is supported.

After a NIC has been installed, the operating system should automatically detect it during the boot process. If this is the case, it may be necessary to provide network settings when the system boots. Otherwise, it is necessary to follow any instructions provided by the NIC manufacturer to install the appropriate drivers.

Objective 4-11

After a NIC is installed, it must be properly configured to access the network. For example, a computer name (NETBIOS/host name) and valid IP address, network mask, default gateway, DNS server, and WINS information are needed, which can be provided by static entries or by a DHCP server. Concerning actual configuration and address information, it is typical that a DHCP server will supply the information that is required. In certain circumstances it may be necessary to assign static address information. It is important that a unique IP address be assigned to every computer in the LAN. It is best to let DHCP do all the work.

Tables 17–3 and 17–4 provide settings that may be used to configure a client on the network. Table 17–3 contains settings that can be used when a DHCP server is available on the network.

TABLE 17–3

Information needed to connect a Windows client using DHCP.

Network Configuration Parameter	Example Client Setting	Configuration Screen
Machine name	Client-1	Network Properties Identification tab
TCP/IP settings	Obtain an IP address automatically	TCP/IP Properties IP Address tab
Client for Microsoft Networks	Client for Microsoft Networks	Network Properties Primary Network Logon
Domain	RWANET	Client for Microsoft Networks Properties Domain

Table 17–4 contains settings for use when a DHCP server is not available. Obviously, use of a DHCP server makes the network administration process much simpler, allowing a network administrator more time to spend on the important issues such as security.

TABLE 17–4

Information needed to connect a Windows client without DHCP.

Network Configuration Parameter	Example Client Setting	Configuration Screen
Machine name	Client-1	Network Properties Identification tab
IP address	192.168.1.100	TCP/IP Properties IP Address tab
Subnet mask	255.255.255.0	TCP/IP Properties IP Address tab
Gateway	192.168.1.1	TCP/IP Properties Gateway tab
DNS servers	24.25.226.222 24.25.226.223	TCP/IP Properties DNS Configuration tab
WINS server	192.168.1.10	TCP/IP Properties WINS Configuration tab
Client for Microsoft Networks	Client for Microsoft Networks	Network Properties Primary Network Logon
Domain	RWANET	Client for Microsoft Networks Properties Domain. Enable check box setting for domain.

Objective 4-1

The DHCP server and default gateway IP addresses, as well as other important networking parameters, are illustrated in the following sample output from the `ipconfig` utility on a Windows 2000 computer:

```
C:> ipconfig/all

Windows 2000 IP Configuration

        Host Name . . . . . . . . . . . . : win2000s
        Primary DNS Suffix  . . . . . . . :
        Node Type . . . . . . . . . . . . : Hybrid

        IP Routing Enabled. . . . . . . . : No

        WINS Proxy Enabled. . . . . . . . : No

        DNS Suffix Search List. . . . . . : stny.rr.com

Ethernet adapter Local Area Connection:

        Connection-specific DNS Suffix  . : stny.rr.com
        Description . . . . . . . . . . . : Intel(R) PRO/100+ Management Adapter
        Physical Address. . . . . . . . . : 00-D0-B7-68-2A-15
        DHCP Enabled. . . . . . . . . . . : Yes
        Autoconfiguration Enabled . . . . : Yes
        IP Address. . . . . . . . . . . . : 192.168.1.101
        Subnet Mask . . . . . . . . . . . : 255.255.255.0
        Default Gateway . . . . . . . . . : 192.168.1.1
        DHCP Server . . . . . . . . . . . : 192.168.1.1
        DNS Servers . . . . . . . . . . . : 24.92.226.171
                                            24.92.226.172
                                            24.92.226.173
        Lease Obtained. . . . . . . . . . : Tuesday, July 30, 2002 8:41:26 PM
        Lease Expires . . . . . . . . . . : Wednesday, July 31, 2002 8:41:26 PM
```

On a computer system that participates in a NetWare network environment, it is necessary to add NetWare client capability. This is accomplished by adding the Client for NetWare Network shown in Figure 17–18.

FIGURE 17–18
Windows built-in client connectivity.

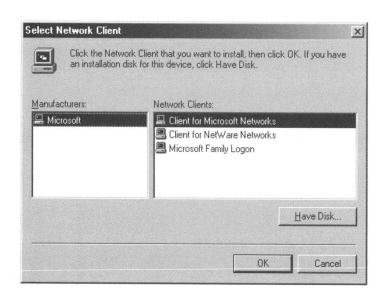

When the system is rebooted after the configuration change, NetWare resources are available provided that the client can connect to the NetWare server for authentication.

■ LOGGING ONTO A NETWORK

Objective 3-2 When a computer is configured to run in a network, each user must be authorized before access to the computer can be granted. Figure 17–19 shows a typical Windows 95/98 logon screen.

FIGURE 17–19
Windows 95/98 logon screen.

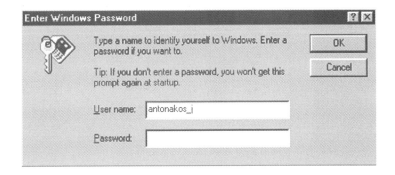

Figure 17–20 shows a typical Windows 2000 Professional logon screen. Each user must supply a valid user name and a valid password to gain access to the computer and any network resources.

FIGURE 17–20
Windows 2000 Professional login window.

In a *workgroup* setting, all password information is stored locally on each computer in PWL files. The PWL files are named using the following format: the first eight letters of the user name entered in the logon screen followed by the .PWL file extension. The PWL files contain account and password information stored in encrypted form. These files are typically stored in the Windows directory. Figure 17–21 shows the concept of a workgroup where each computer is administered independently.

In a *domain* setting, a centralized computer running Windows NT is contacted to verify the user name and password. If the information provided to the server is valid, access is granted to the local machine. If either the user name or password is invalid, access to the local computer is denied. As you might think, this method offers much more flexibility as far as the administration is concerned. This concept is illustrated in Figure 17–22.

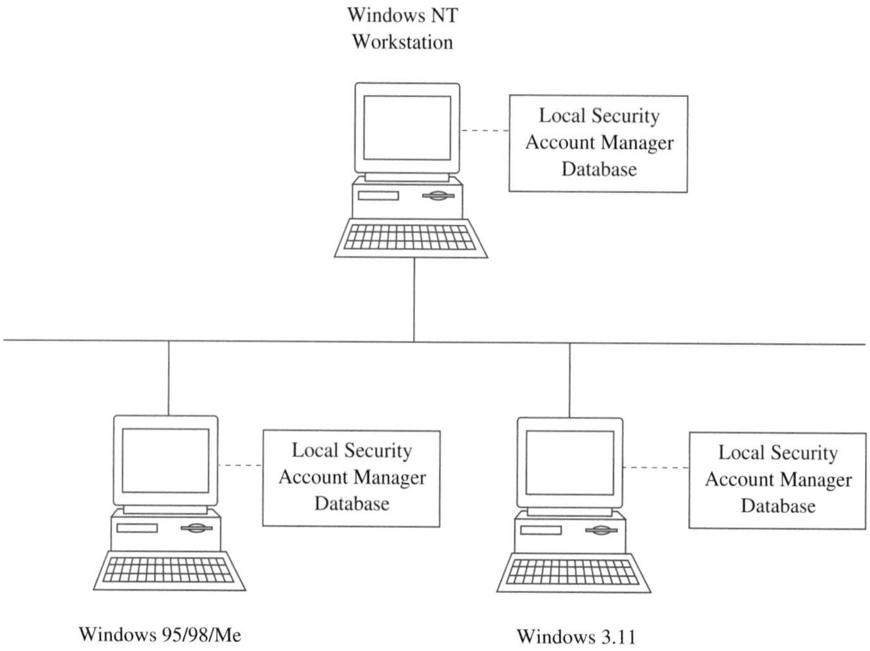

FIGURE 17–21
Workgroup concept where each computer is administered independently.

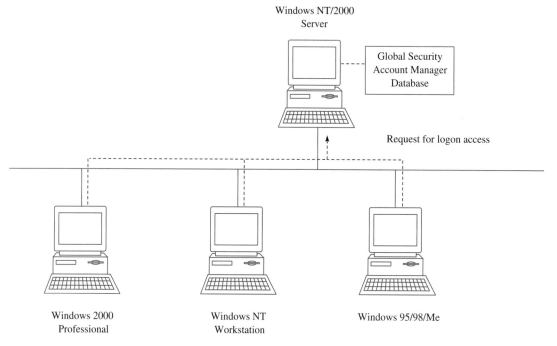

FIGURE 17–22
Domain concept.

■ RUNNING A NETWORK SERVER

Running a network server involves installing the Windows NT operating system and then configuring it to run as a primary or secondary domain controller during the installation process. After a PDC is created during the installation, the domain exists on the network. Windows NT computers can then join the domain by changing the Member of Domain as shown in Figure 17–23.

FIGURE 17–23
Configuring a Windows NT
server.

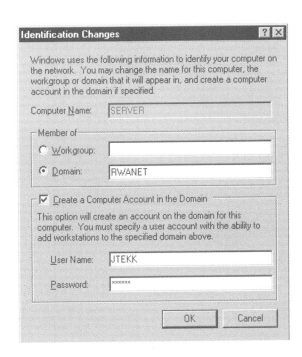

Windows computers join the domain by changing individual settings on each computer. Figure 17–24 shows the Primary Network Logon, selecting the Client for Microsoft Networks option for Windows 95/98.

FIGURE 17–24
Windows 95/98 network
settings.

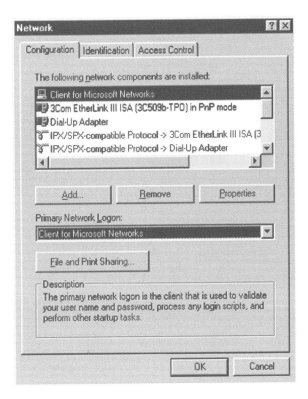

By selecting the properties for Client for Microsoft Networks, the specific domain can be identified as illustrated in Figure 17–25.

FIGURE 17–25
Configuring Windows 95/98 to
log on to a domain.

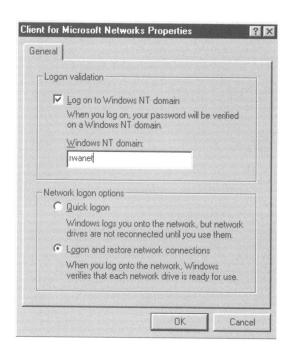

After making these changes, a system reset is necessary to make the changes active.
Figure 17–26 shows the Local Area Connection Properties screen for a Windows 2000
computer. To change the client properties, it is necessary to select "Client for Microsoft
Networks" from the list and click on the Properties button.

FIGURE 17–26
Windows 2000 network
properties.

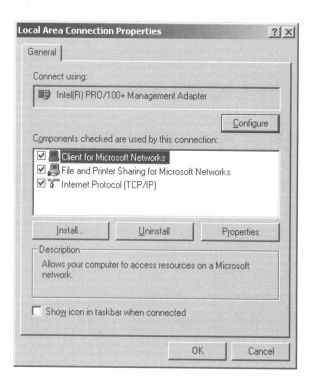

Note that on Windows 2000 computers, there are two ways for a computer to join a
domain or a workgroup depending on the environment. Figure 17–27 shows the window
that is used when the domain or workgroup may be specified directly.

FIGURE 17–27
Windows 2000 domain
configuration.

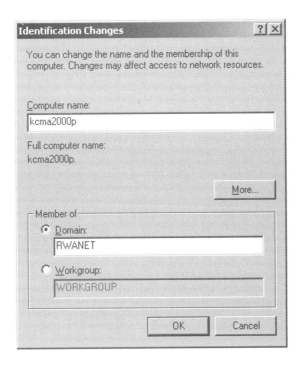

To simplify the decision-making process, Figures 17–28 and 17–29 show the first two screens of the Network Identification Wizard that will guide the user through a series of questions to determine the appropriate network settings.

FIGURE 17–28
Windows 2000 Network
Identification Wizard.

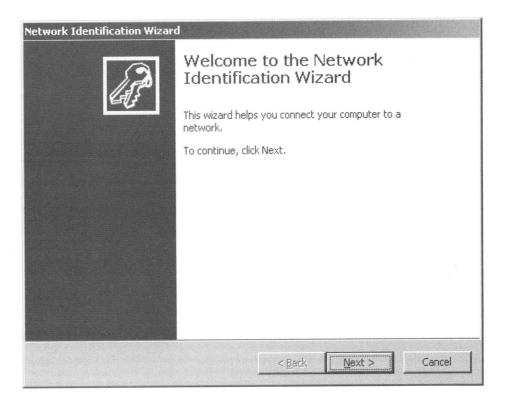

Objective 3-5

RAID

Network server computers are also assigned the task of running more applications to manage both the server and the network. For example, a Windows NT Server may be used to add fault tolerance to disks using a Redundant Array of Inexpensive Disks (**RAID**) technology. See Appendix H for more details on RAID. A server may also run the WWW server

FIGURE 17–29
Windows 2000 Network
Identification Wizard network
selection.

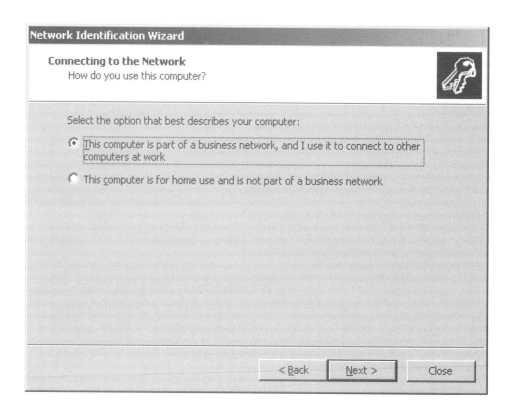

application, Windows Internet Naming System (WINS), Dynamic Host Configuration Protocol (DHCP), and Remote Access Server (RAS). These services are usually required 24 hours a day, seven days per week.

Windows NT Server computers are designed to handle the computing workload for entire organizations, corporations, or any other type of enterprise. In these cases, many servers (including a PDC and several BDCs) are made available to guarantee the availability of any required services.

We now take a closer look at two of these services—DHCP and RAS.

Dynamic Host Configuration Protocol

Objective 2-7

One nice feature of a Windows NT domain is the ability of Windows NT Server to automatically manage all the IP addresses in the domain. IP addresses may be assigned to client machines statically (by manually entering the address) or dynamically (at boot time) via DHCP.

The DHCP service is controlled by the DHCP Manager application found in Administrative Tools. Figure 17–30 shows the DHCP Manager window, indicating a DHCP server running at IP address 206.210.24.2.

FIGURE 17–30
DHCP Manager window.

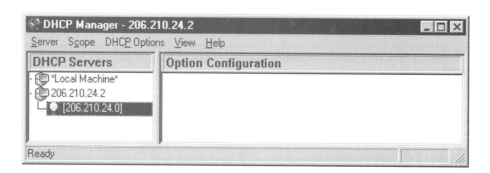

The highlighted entry (206.210.24.0) is the *scope,* or range of IP addresses managed by the DHCP server. Double-clicking the scope entry brings up the Scope Properties dialog box shown in Figure 17–31.

FIGURE 17–31
DHCP Scope Properties dialog box.

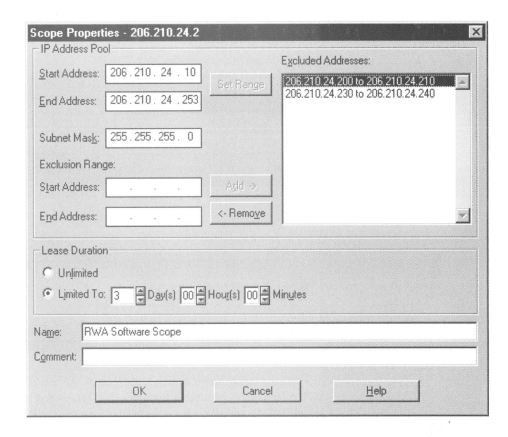

The range of IP addresses that are available for use via DHCP begins at 206.210.24.10 and ends at 206.210.24.253, with two subranges excluded. Addresses are leased for 3 days, but could also be set to unlimited duration. Clearly, the network administrator has a great deal of control over the allocation of IP addresses within the domain.

DHCP provides a time-saving, practically hands-off solution to the problem of managing IP addresses for a large number of clients.

Remote Access Service

Objective 2-12

There are many reasons why remote access to a domain, via a modem, is useful to a user. A short list includes the following:

• Employee access to company information and personal account

• Remote control of network by administrator

• Customer access

• Company used as gateway to the Internet

• System can be available 24 hours a day

RAS

Using the Windows NT operating system, a dial-in user can be granted access to the network resources using the Remote Access Service, or **RAS**. The RAS is added as a service from the Windows NT Network Services tab. After the service is added, Remote Access Services can be configured by selecting the item and clicking on the Properties button as shown in Figure 17–32.

FIGURE 17–32
Windows NT Network
services.

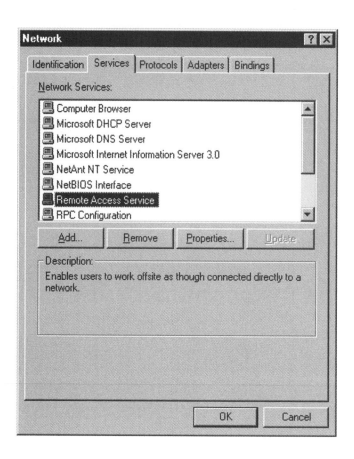

Using one or more modems, the Remote Access Service may be configured to provide each modem with up to three different types of network protocol connections: NetBEUI, TCP/IP, and IPX. This is accomplished using the Remote Access Setup program. All three protocols, and many others, are transported over the modem connection using PPP (Point-to-Point Protocol). PPP is built in to Dial-Up Networking, enabling Windows 95 and 98 clients to connect to an NT domain.

If a modem has not been installed, Remote Access Service can automatically set up and detect a modem on a specified port. A modem installed on COM2 is shown in the Remote Access Setup dialog box in Figure 17–33.

FIGURE 17–33
Remote Access Setup
dialog box.

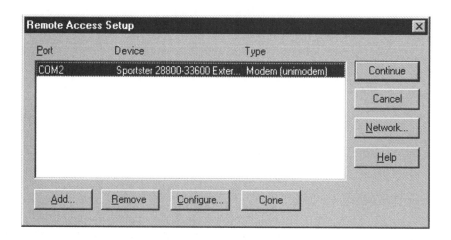

From this dialog box, it is also possible to add, remove, configure, or clone (copy) the modem ports, or set up the necessary network protocols. For example, by selecting the

Configure button, it is possible to specify how each modem port will be used (for dialing out, receiving calls, or both, as shown in Figure 17–34). Cloning a port configuration is useful when setting up a bank of modems. For security reasons, a network administrator may choose to only allow the RAS modems to receive calls.

FIGURE 17–34
Remote Access Service port
configuration.

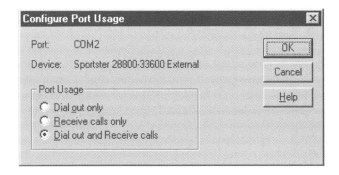

Using the Network button on the Remote Access Setup dialog box, the dial-out protocols and the server settings may be specified as shown in Figure 17–35. Protocols and settings are enabled or disabled by selecting or deselecting the appropriate check boxes. Clicking on the appropriate Configure buttons sets each of the selected server protocols. Note that several levels of security are provided by the type of authentication employed by RAS. For example, user passwords may be encrypted to help prevent detection.

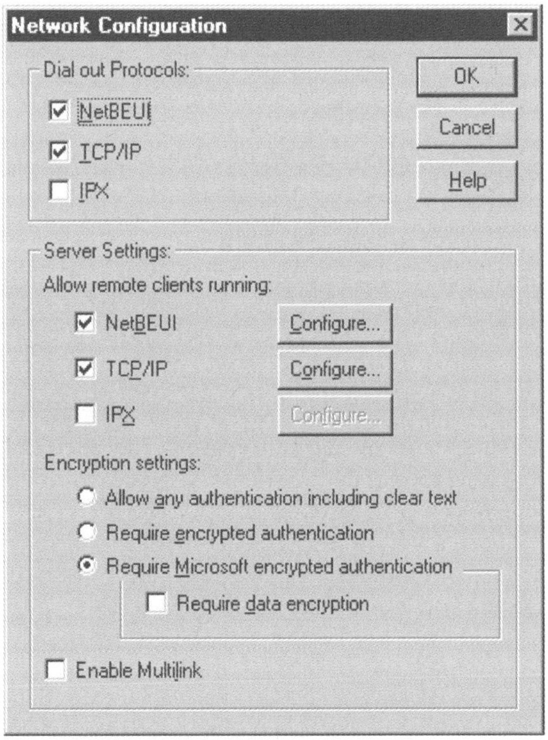

FIGURE 17–35
Remote Access Service
Network Configuration
dialog box.

The RAS Server NetBEUI Configuration is used to specify the level of access you want to grant all users who dial in to this computer using the NetBEUI protocol. This option is selected from the RAS Service NetBEUI Configuration menu, as shown in Figure 17–36. Notice that a client may be granted access to the entire network or one computer only (the NT server).

FIGURE 17–36
Configuring the NetBEUI
protocol for RAS.

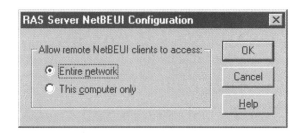

Similarly, the TCP/IP properties can be set to allow access to the entire network or this computer only. In addition, it is necessary to select a method by which IP addresses are assigned to the dial-up user. This is shown in Figure 17–37.

FIGURE 17–37
Configuring the TCP/IP protocol
for RAS.

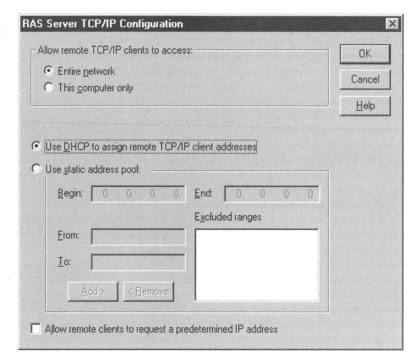

The RAS Server supports dynamic allocation and static allocation of IP addresses. You can even specify the range of static addresses available for the modem pool if DHCP is not used.

After each of the properties has been specified, the operation of the Remote Access Service can be examined as shown in Figure 17–38. At a glance it is easy to see that only one modem port is available, and it is not in use.

FIGURE 17–38
Remote Access Server Administration window.

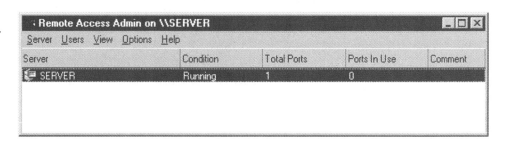

All of the RAS services within a domain may be controlled using the Remote Access Admin screen. Together with the dial-up options available to each user, RAS provides a secure way to allow remote access to the domain and its resources.

■ USER PROFILES

SAM

Objective 3-1

In a domain, the primary domain controller maintains all user profiles. This allows for centralized control of the security accounts manager (*SAM*) database. Two programs are provided to update the SAM database. One of the programs is used in a stand-alone (no domain) environment and the other is for use where a domain is specified. Otherwise the programs operate in the same way. Let's examine what is involved when setting up a user account as illustrated in Figure 17–39. Information must be specified about each user account including user name, full name, a description of the account, and the password setting. The check boxes are used to further modify the account, such as requiring a password change during the first logon, restricting changing the password, extending the life of a password, and, lastly, disabling the account.

FIGURE 17–39
New User dialog box.

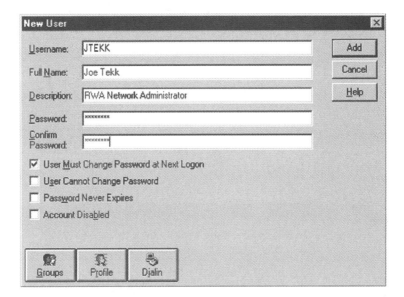

The three buttons at the bottom of the New User window (as seen in Figure 17–39) allow for each new account to be added to different *groups* as shown in Figure 17–40. It is a good idea to grant access to groups on an individual basis as certain privileges are granted by simply belonging to the group, such as administrator.

FIGURE 17–40
Group Memberships dialog box.

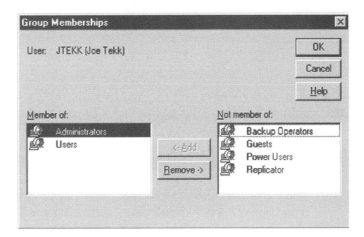

The User Environment Profile screen specifies the path to an individual profile and any required logon script name. Additionally, the home directory may be specified as shown in Figure 17–41.

FIGURE 17–41
User Environment Profile dialog box.

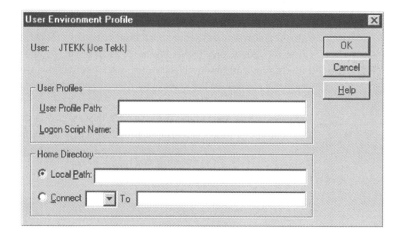

Lastly, the Dialin Information dialog box determines if a Windows NT account has access to Dial-Up Networking. The Call Back option may also be configured to require the computer to call the user back. This is an additional security feature that may be implemented if necessary. Figure 17–42 shows these settings.

FIGURE 17–42
Dialin Information dialog box.

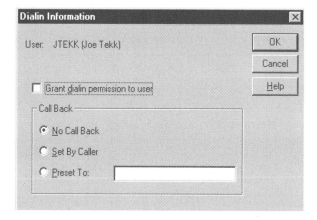

■ SECURITY

Objective 3-1

Windows NT/2000 is a C2-compliant operating system, when it is configured properly as defined by the National Computer Security Center (NCSC). C2 compliance involves properly configuring Windows NT/2000 to use the built-in safeguards. An application tool supplied with the operating system (C2CONFIG.EXE) examines the operating system setting against a recommended setting. Any exceptions are noted.

Windows NT/2000 provides security-logging features designed to track all types of system activities, such as logon attempts, file transfers, Telnet sessions, and many more. Typically, the system administrator will determine which types of events are logged by the system. Figure 17–43 shows the system log. The icons along the left margin are color coded to draw attention to more serious events. Event logs should be reviewed daily.

FIGURE 17–43
System events display.

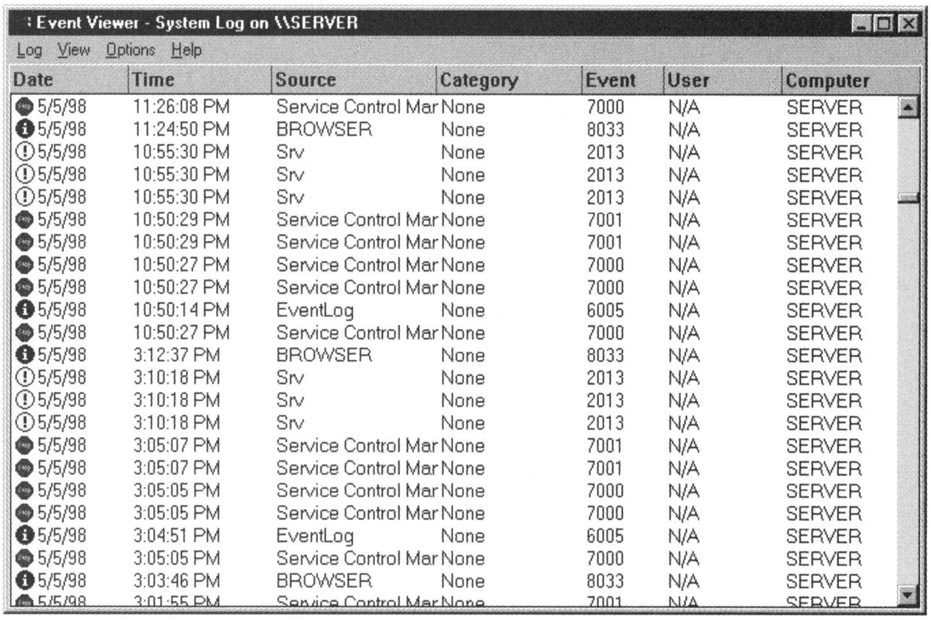

Date	Time	Source	Category	Event	User	Computer
5/5/98	11:26:08 PM	Service Control Mar	None	7000	N/A	SERVER
5/5/98	11:24:50 PM	BROWSER	None	8033	N/A	SERVER
5/5/98	10:55:30 PM	Srv	None	2013	N/A	SERVER
5/5/98	10:55:30 PM	Srv	None	2013	N/A	SERVER
5/5/98	10:55:30 PM	Srv	None	2013	N/A	SERVER
5/5/98	10:50:29 PM	Service Control Mar	None	7001	N/A	SERVER
5/5/98	10:50:29 PM	Service Control Mar	None	7001	N/A	SERVER
5/5/98	10:50:27 PM	Service Control Mar	None	7000	N/A	SERVER
5/5/98	10:50:27 PM	Service Control Mar	None	7000	N/A	SERVER
5/5/98	10:50:14 PM	EventLog	None	6005	N/A	SERVER
5/5/98	10:50:27 PM	Service Control Mar	None	7000	N/A	SERVER
5/5/98	3:12:37 PM	BROWSER	None	8033	N/A	SERVER
5/5/98	3:10:18 PM	Srv	None	2013	N/A	SERVER
5/5/98	3:10:18 PM	Srv	None	2013	N/A	SERVER
5/5/98	3:10:18 PM	Srv	None	2013	N/A	SERVER
5/5/98	3:05:07 PM	Service Control Mar	None	7001	N/A	SERVER
5/5/98	3:05:07 PM	Service Control Mar	None	7001	N/A	SERVER
5/5/98	3:05:05 PM	Service Control Mar	None	7000	N/A	SERVER
5/5/98	3:05:05 PM	Service Control Mar	None	7000	N/A	SERVER
5/5/98	3:04:51 PM	EventLog	None	6005	N/A	SERVER
5/5/98	3:05:05 PM	Service Control Mar	None	7000	N/A	SERVER
5/5/98	3:03:46 PM	BROWSER	None	8033	N/A	SERVER
5/5/98	3:01:55 PM	Service Control Mar	None	7001	N/A	SERVER

■ WINDOWS 2000 DOMAINS

Windows 2000 domains are significantly different from domains administered by a Windows NT server. The domain controller is encapsulated into a new product called the Active Directory, the features of which are outlined in Table 17–5. Note that Active Directory services can only be run on a Windows 2000 Server computer system. Active Directory is designed to support a single unified view of all objects on a Windows network.

The Active Directory installation and configuration option is the third item on the list of options used to configure a Windows 2000 Server computer system as shown in Figure 17–44.

Notice that the introductory text on the Active Directory screen dictates that, to make a Windows 2000 Server a domain controller, Active Directory must be installed on an NTFS-formatted partition. Active Directory installation is suitable for a new domain or when a server will be participating in an environment where other domain controllers are already present. When a domain already exists, the available choices are broken down into the following categories:

- Additional domain controller
- New child domain
- New domain tree
- New forest of trees

These choices allow for significant flexibility when designing a large Windows network.

Figure 17–45 shows the Domain Controller Type selection screen from inside the Active Directory Installation Wizard. Note that when a Windows 2000 server joins an existing domain, all local accounts on the system are deleted in favor of using the existing domain accounts.

TABLE 17–5
Important Active Directory features.

Feature	Description
Management	Provide better access to management activities using • Automated software distribution • Backward compatibility support for Windows NT 4.0 domains • Delegated domain administration • Enhanced group policies • Global cataloging of all Windows objects • Optimized multi-master replication between domain controllers • Single interface to manage servers, users, and clients
Security	Support for enhanced security measures including • Attribute level control for all objects • Choice of authentication mechanisms (Kerberos, X.509 certificates, etc.) • Improved Trust relationships • Secure Socket Layer (SSL) support for LDAP • Mixed environment of Active Directory and Windows NT domains • Public key infrastructure • Centralized Group management • Smart card support
Interoperability	Provides for a high level of interaction between Windows 2000 and other operating systems using • Active Directory Connectors to support Exchange and Novell Directory Services • Directory synchronization support • Native LDAP support for Internet and e-commerce • DNS naming of Windows objects • Open API function calls

FIGURE 17–44
Windows 2000 Active Directory information.

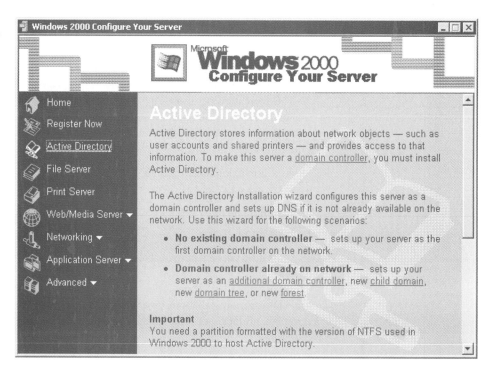

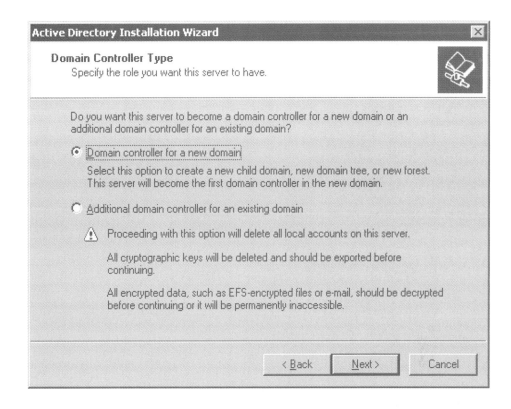

When a new child domain is created, it takes advantage of the existing domain resources. When it is necessary to create a domain that is separate from an existing domain,
the new domain tree or new forest options are available as shown in Figure 17–46.

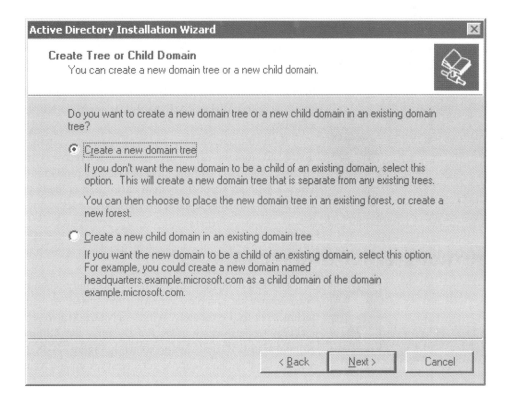

When the new domain tree option is selected, the system administrator is given the opportunity to create a new forest of domain trees or to place the tree in an existing forest as illustrated in Figure 17–47.

FIGURE 17–47
Selecting a location for the new domain.

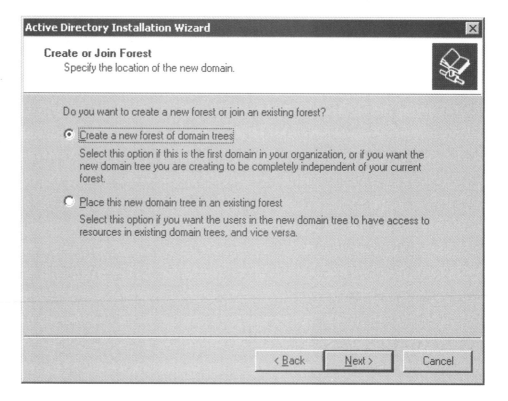

This brief introduction to Active Directory should provide a good overview of the various configuration options that are available. You are encouraged to continue to explore the features of Active Directory on your own. As you will see in the following Troubleshooting Techniques section, Windows 2000 offers a significant amount of help on this important topic.

Objective 3-5

The Windows operating system is not immune from problems; therefore, it is essential that proper attention be paid to fault tolerance and disaster recovery. Windows provides software that works seamlessly with most hardware vendors that offer fault-tolerant systems, whether implemented in hardware or software. For example, redundant power supplies, disks, RAID hardware, multiple NICs, and ECC memory are just a few of them.

Objective 3-6

Similar to any other server-type operating system, it is necessary to back up data regularly and store the copies off site to ensure recovery from a minor disk failure to a catastrophic event. Some of the most devastating problems on a Windows platform stem from viruses. Without adequate system backups, it is likely that some information will be lost, which would be unacceptable for most businesses.

■ TROUBLESHOOTING TECHNIQUES

A networked computer environment (especially when using Windows NT/2000) can become somewhat complex, requiring the system or network administrator to have many technical skills. Fortunately, Windows NT/2000 also provides many resources designed to tackle most networking tasks. For example, the Administrative Tools menu contains the Administrative Wizards option shown in Figure 17–48. Most of these wizards perform the activities that are necessary to get a network up and running.

FIGURE 17–48
Administrative Wizards window.

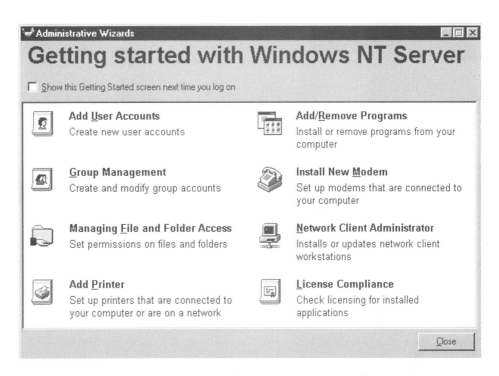

It is also a good idea to examine the online help system to get additional information, which may simplify any task. Figure 17–49 shows a Help dialog box that contains a total of 8383 topics, many of which contain information about networking.

FIGURE 17–49
Windows NT Help dialog box.

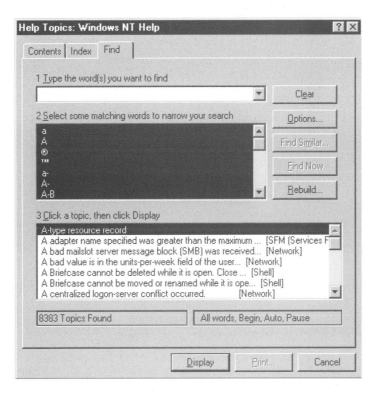

A search for information about Active Directory in a Windows 2000 server returns 245 entries as shown in Figure 17–50.

FIGURE 17–50
Windows 2000 Active Directory
Help.

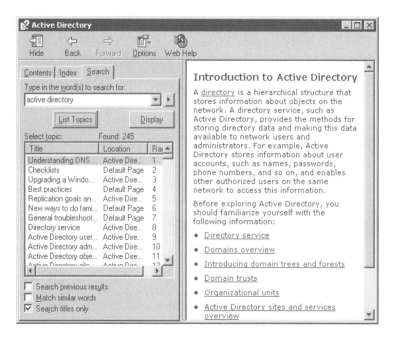

CAREER DEVELOPMENT: SERVER+

The Server+ certification tests mid- to upper-level technicians responsible for server hardware functionality. The test is focused on server issues and technology, including installation, configuration, upgrading, maintenance, troubleshooting, and disaster recovery. Many companies recommend or require this certification for their IT employees. Server+ is also required certification for IBM's warranty authorization program.

The CompTIA Server+ certification is a strong foundation that can be applied to a wide variety of careers in many industries, including:

Computer Operator, Intermediate Level

Field Support Technician, Entry Level

Hardware Installation Coordinator, Entry Level

Internet Systems Administrator, Intermediate Level

For more information on the Server+ certification visit www.comptia.org

■ SELF-TEST

1. The operation of a domain requires at least one computer _____.
   a. with administrative rights
   b. under administrative control
   c. with a server operating system
   d. running e-mail services

2. NT Workstation is designed to run on a _____ computer with an 80486 or better processor.
   a. desktop
   b. diskless
   c. thin client
   d. server

3. Pressing Ctrl+Alt+Del simultaneously is required to _____ when using Windows NT.
   a. log on
   b. delete a file
   c. interrupt the boot process
   d. delete a folder

4. True or False: Simultaneously pressing Ctrl+Alt+Del will not cause a Windows NT computer to reboot.

5. When a Windows NT computer is locked, the display screen enters the screen saver mode or displays a window requesting _____.
   a. logoff
   b. shutdown
   c. a password
   d. Task Manager

6. The Change Password option on the Windows NT Security menu is used to change the password of the _____.
   a. administrator
   b. folders
   c. currently logged-in user
   d. screen lock

7. System performance can be displayed using the _____.
   a. Applications Manager
   b. Task Manager
   c. Ctrl+Alt+Del keys
   d. Windows Explorer

8. Windows NT Task Manager can be used to display system performance displaying which two of the following? (Choose two.)
   a. Number of users
   b. CPU utilization
   c. Memory usage
   d. Available applications

9. Windows NT servers can provide services for all of the following network clients **except** _____.
   a. Windows 95
   b. Windows 98
   c. Windows for Workgroups 3.11
   d. None of the above

10. Windows 2000 Professional is designed for client computers in _____.
    a. large businesses
    b. small businesses
    c. medium businesses
    d. All of the above

11. True or False: Windows 2000 Server no longer lists Windows NT Explorer and instead uses Windows Explorer.

12. Windows 2000 Professional offers which of the following services?
    a. Directory Services
    b. DNS
    c. DHCP
    d. None of the above

13. If the Primary Domain Controller becomes unavailable for any reason the _____ Domain Controller is promoted to Primary Domain Controller.
    a. Secondary
    b. Backup
    c. Default
    d. Gateway

14. When a computer system is set up as Primary Domain Controller, the _____ is required in order to proceed through the Windows NT installation process.
    a. default users file
    b. domain name
    c. relationship
    d. synchronization

15. Computers can be configured to join a Windows NT domain using the Network icon in the system Control Panel, or through the _____.
    a. New users folder
    b. Connections folder
    c. Server Manager tool
    d. Primary Domain Controller tool

16. What is the term used to describe when information entered on the Primary Domain Controller is exchanged with all Backup Domain Controllers?
    a. Convergence
    b. Backup
    c. Synchronization
    d. Relationship

17. Which of the following are types of trust relationships between domains? (Choose two.)
    a. One-way
    b. Two-way
    c. Valued
    d. Guarded

18. In the following diagram, Domain A considers Domain B a trusted source. Domain C trusts Domain B. Which of the following statements is true?

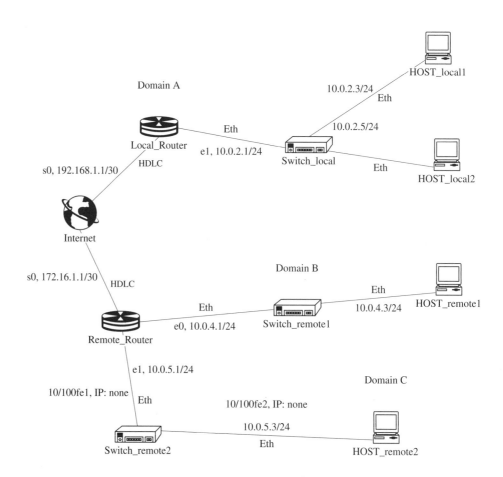

    a. Domain A trusts C.

    b. Domain B trusts A.

    c. Domain B is trusted by A and C.

    d. Domain C is trusted by A.

19. What does the term CIFS refer to?

    a. Central Internet File Server

    b. Common Internet File System

    c. Central Identity Fact Server

    d. Central Intelligence File System

20. Tracking and file accesses are maintained in the _____ on the server.

    a. user file

    b. log files

    c. sniffer files

    d. firewall

21. True or False: Network versions of software allow clients to run programs located on the server.

22. Windows computers that participate in a NetWare network require that NetWare client capability be added. How can this be done?

    a. Just add a NetWare server to the network.

    b. Add a client for the NetWare network.

    c. It cannot be done.

    d. Add a Microsoft family logon.

23. True or False: Windows 95/98, NT, and 2000 machines have this in common: They join domains using the same method.

24. True or False: The Primary Domain Controller in a domain maintains all user profiles, allowing central control of the Security Accounts Manager (SAM) database.

25. When it is necessary to create a domain separate from the existing domain, Windows 2000 Server creates _____ or _____ options. (Choose two.)

    a. two new trees

    b. forest workgroups

    c. new domain tree

    d. new forest

UNIX and Linux

CHAPTER 18

PERFORMANCE OBJECTIVES

Upon completion of this chapter, you will be able to:

- Explain the differences between the UNIX and Linux operating systems.

- Discuss the built-in Linux network applications.

- Describe the open source licensing for the Linux operating system.

NETWORK+ OBJECTIVES

This chapter provides information for the following Network+ objectives:

2.7 Identify the purpose of the following network services:
- DHCP/BOOTP
- WINS
- DNS
- SNMP
- NAT/ICS

2.13 Identify the following security protocols and describe their purpose and function:
- IPSec
- SSL
- L2TP
- Kerberos

3.1 Identify the basic capabilities (i.e., client support, interoperability, authentication, file and print services, application support, security) of the following server operating systems:
- UNIX/Linux
- Windows
- NetWare
- Macintosh

3.2 Identify the basic capabilities of client workstations (i.e., client connectivity, local security mechanisms, authentication).

3.5 Identify the purpose and characteristics of fault tolerance.

3.6 Identify the purpose and characteristics of disaster recovery.

3.11 Given a network configuration, select the appropriate NIC and network configuration settings (DHCP, DNS, WINS, protocols, NETBIOS/host name, etc.).

4.1 Given a troubleshooting scenario, select the appropriate TCP/IP utility from among the following:
- TRACERT
- PING
- ARP
- NETSTAT
- NBTSTAT
- IPCONFIG/IFCONFIG
- WINIPCFG
- NSLOOKUP

4.4 Given specific parameters, configure a client to connect to the following servers:
- UNIX/Linux
- Windows
- NetWare
- Macintosh

4.7 Given output from a diagnostic utility (e.g., TRACERT, PING, IPCONFIG, etc.), identify the utility and interpret the output.

■ INTRODUCTION

The UNIX and Linux operating systems comprise a growing segment in the operating systems market. UNIX is a trademark of The Open Group and because the source code was sold to many businesses and organizations, several different versions are available. The source code was also given to colleges and universities. One of the most popular versions of UNIX to come out of the education market was created at the University of California at Berkeley.

Linux is an operating system based on UNIX that was created by Linus Torvalds. The source code for Linux was available for free and users were encouraged to add additional features. Similar to UNIX, many different versions of the Linux operating system are available. A few of the most notable are from Red Hat, Caldera, and Corel Linux. All versions of the Linux operating system offer similar core capabilities, with the differences being various add-on features and custom services. Because the Linux operating system is so popular, many computer vendors (IBM, Dell, etc.) make their products available with Linux preinstalled.

Many times the terms UNIX and Linux are used interchangeably, but they should not be. UNIX is not Linux and Linux is not UNIX. Table 18–1 shows a comparison between the UNIX and Linux operating systems. Notice that UNIX has been around for over three decades, while Linux has been around for only one. The cost of the UNIX operating system is generally based on the type of hardware that it is running on, so a large mainframe OS configuration costs more than a mini-computer configuration. Linux is free for every type and size of hardware. The Linux OS looks like UNIX by design. When evaluating the different versions of UNIX and Linux, consider the hardware and applications that they will be running to make the best choice. This chapter examines the features of the Red Hat version of the Linux operating system.

TABLE 18–1
UNIX and Linux comparison.

Category	UNIX	Linux
Development	1969	1993
Developer	Bell Labs	Linus Torvalds
Licensing	Proprietary	Open
Availability	Purchase	Free
Clients	All popular platforms	All popular platforms
Hardware choices	Limited	Practically unlimited
Support	Purchase	Community
Reliability	High	High
Performance	High	High
Security	High	High
Compatibility	Low	High

■ RED HAT LINUX ENVIRONMENT

Objective 3-1

The Red Hat Linux operating system environment provides many features commonly found on large mainframes and mini-computers running UNIX. Some of the features found on the latest version of the Red Hat Linux operating system include:

- True multiuser, multitasking operating system
- Virtual memory

- Built-in network support
- OpenSSL with 128-bit encryption for secure communication
- Easy graphical installation with autodetection of hardware
- Software RAID support for RAID 0 through RAID 5
- USB support for mice and keyboards
- Graphical firewall configuration tool
- GUI interface
- POSIX compliant

Because of its many features, Linux is commonly used as a server on the Internet. Linux contains all of the TCP/IP network applications that are necessary to offer a full range of Internet and networking services including

- DHCP
- FTP
- Telnet
- DNS
- HTTP Server
- PING
- Traceroute
- Nslookup
- Network File System
- Network Information System
- Firewall

The software for Linux is distributed free of charge. The Linux operating system is based on the open-source software model and is distributed freely under the GNU GPL (general public license). Most operating systems based on the Linux kernel are modified versions of the GNU operating system. Under the GNU GPL, users of any type (home, education, business, or commercial) have the ability to update the source code in any way and to contribute to the ongoing development. In essence, the users are encouraged to add features that are then made available to the community at large. Many software programs are available for Linux under the open-source agreement.

Many of the programs available in UNIX and Linux can be run from the command prompt. Table 18–2 lists many of the most frequently used programs. Note that the input and output for these use only text. For example, entering the df command produces the following output:

```
# df
Filesystem          1k-blocks     Used Available Use% Mounted
/dev/hda8             256667      74168    169247  30% /
/dev/hda1              23302       2647     19452  12% /boot
/dev/hda5            3541904      15920   3346060   0% /home
/dev/hda6            3541904    1266324   2095656  38% /usr
/dev/hda7             256667      34079    209336  14% /var
#
```

The df command produces a list of the currently mounted disks. For each disk, the df command shows the file system (disk partition), how large each disk is, how much of the disk is used, a percentage of disk utilization, and the disk name under which it is

TABLE 18–2
Common commands and utility programs.

Program Name	Purpose
cat	Display file contents
cd	Change directory
chmod	Change file protection
chown	Change file owner
cp	Copy file(s)
df	Show free disk space
find	Locate files
ftp	File transfer
ifconfig	Network interface configuration
kill	Terminate process
ls	List files (directory)
man	Display online manual pages
mkdir	Create new directory
mv	Move file(s)
netstat	Display network connection status
pine	Internet news and e-mail application
ping	Test network connectivity
ps	Display current system processes
rm	Remove file(s)
shutdown	Initiate system shutdown procedure
su	Temporarily become a different user
tar	Disk backup/archival tool
telnet	Remote communication tool
traceroute	Trace route to destination
vi	Invoke text editor
who	List current system users

mounted. The names `/`, `/boot`, `/home`, `/usr`, and `/var` are typical mount points. The `df` command is useful to determine the amount of free space on each disk. Table 18–3 lists the purpose of each mounted disk, and Figure 18–1 shows the layout and structure of a typical disk.

TABLE 18–3
Common UNIX and Linux disk/directory structure.

Disk Mount Point	Purpose
/	Root disk directory
/boot	Files necessary to boot Linux
/home	User directories
/usr	Installed software directories
/var	Variable disk information such as logs and temp files

FIGURE 18–1
Typical UNIX and Linux
directory structure.

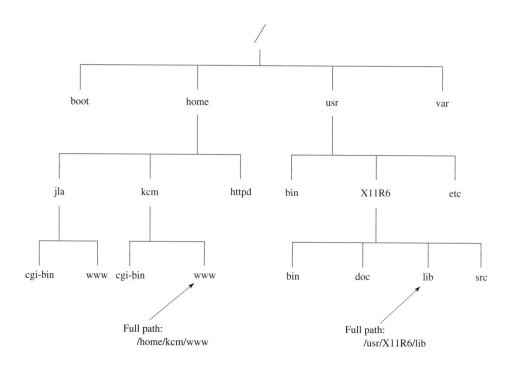

Note that although each of the programs in Table 18–2 can be run from the command prompt, most people prefer to use a graphical interface to interact with the operating system.

■ LINUX GRAPHICAL USER ENVIRONMENT

Aside from the original character-based interface, the Linux environment contains a GUI based on the X11 standard. Using X Windows, software developers have written several window manager programs. Two of the most popular are Gnome (http://www.gnome.org) and KDE (http://www.kde.org), the K Desktop Environment. Both of these window managers are available on Red Hat Linux. Basically, the window manager provides the user interface, using X Windows as the foundation.

Two of the most popular window managers are shown in Figures 18–2 and 18–3. Figure 18–2 shows a view of the Linux operating system running Gnome. The Gnome interface is provided by the GNU project. Similar to the Windows operating system, the desktop contains icons that are shortcuts to commonly used programs. At the bottom of the window, the taskbar contains the Gnome footprint that provides access to a menu system, similar to the function of the Start button in Windows. The taskbar also contains several shortcuts to open the help system, the Gnome configuration tool, a terminal emulation program, and Netscape Navigator. Next to the Netscape Navigator icon is the desktop selection tool that allows the user to select from one of four desktop views, each of which can contain any number of programs. The outline of windows inside the desktop view shows which desktops are currently active. The remainder of the taskbar is devoted to the current application list and the date and time display. Notice that the desktop being displayed contains three windows, the outlines of which are viewable in the desktop selection display. The Terminal window shown in the forefront is running the Pine program, a mail utility.

The KDE interface shown in Figure 18–3 displays the Javasoft.com home page using Netscape Navigator. Similar to the Gnome desktop, KDE provides a taskbar to allow fast access to the commonly used features, four desktop views, and a list of currently running applications that are displayed along the top of the screen. The K button operates similar to the Start button that allows access to all installed operating system and window manager features. Red Hat Linux provides a desktop switching tool to allow a user to choose between the Gnome and KDE desktops.

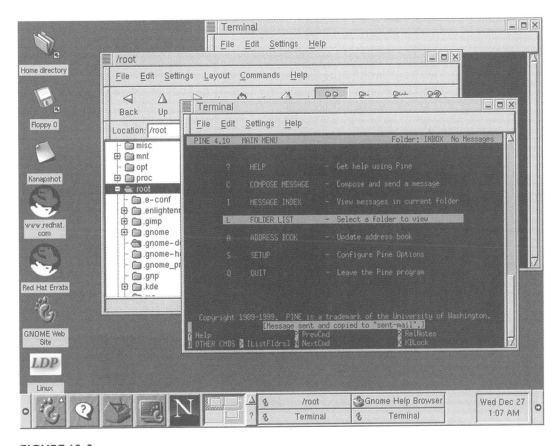

FIGURE 18–2
The Linux operating system running the Gnome desktop interface.

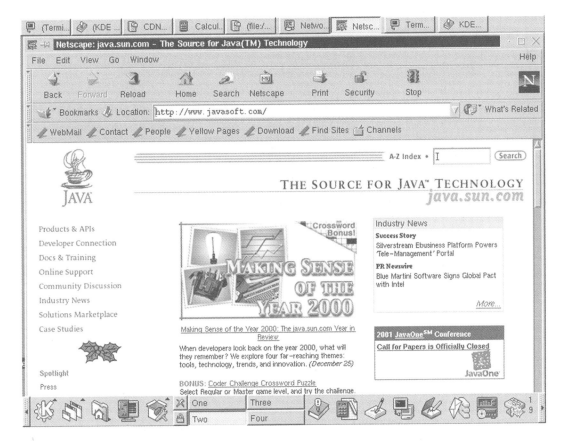

FIGURE 18–3
The Linux operating system running the KDE desktop interface.

Regarding interoperability, UNIX/Linux is one of the most interoperable operating systems available, with software to connect it to almost any other platform. Even the proprietary UNIX operating system vendors can supply (for a fee) any type of interoperability that may be required. For a Linux user, it is important to keep up to date on new software versions. Many times a security vulnerability may be fixed, and therefore it is worth the effort to install the newest versions of all software.

It is important to understand that a Linux machine is both a server and a client. Unlike Windows, which has different client and server operating systems (95/98/Me/XP for clients and NT/2000 for servers), Linux has all the client and server features built in. In this case, the type of computer running Linux may help to determine whether it is a server or client, with a powerful computer typically acting as a server.

■ INSTALLATION AND CONFIGURATION

The installation and configuration of the Linux operating system varies from manufacturer to manufacturer. The Red Hat distribution allows the system administrator to select the type of installation to perform. Figure 18–4 shows the menu that is presented during the installation process. Depending on the requirements, a user can choose a Workstation, Server, or custom installation type setting. An upgrade option is used to perform an upgrade from a previous version.

FIGURE 18–4
Red Hat Linux installation options.

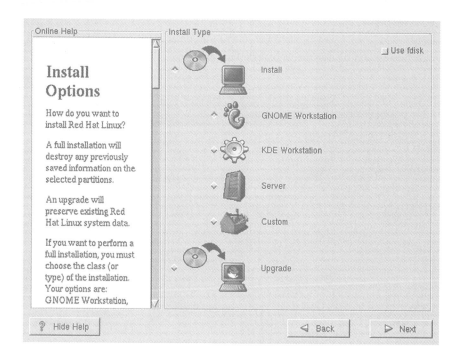

Due to the variety of hardware components available, the installation process will interrogate the system hardware to determine the correct drivers to load. After selecting the type of installation to perform, the user can also select the various packages to be installed, as shown in Figure 18–5.

After the selection of installation type and packages has been completed, the Linux installer partitions and formats the hard drive as necessary, and copies all of the files selected by the user. At the end of the operating system installation, the X Windows configuration tool, called `Xconfigurator`, is run to configure the optimum settings for the installed video card. When X Windows has been properly configured, the installation of the operating system is complete, and the system must be rebooted.

FIGURE 18–5
Red Hat Linux packages.

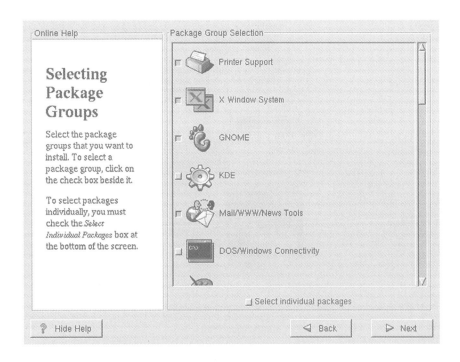

After installation, most of the system configuration that will need to be performed is done using the `linuxconf` (Linux Configuration) program. The Linux Configuration program is used to automate the process to add or maintain all of the critical system applications to keep the system running properly. You may want to visit the Linux Configuration Project home page located at http://www.solucorp.qc.ca/linuxconf/ for additional information about `linuxconf`.

Objective 3-11

Consider a situation in which you must add a Linux computer system to an Ethernet network. Similar to other operating systems, a Linux computer system must be configured with the appropriate hardware and software. The first thing to do is to select an appropriate NIC (network interface card). It is necessary that the NIC be supported by the chosen operating system. Review the specific hardware requirements of the particular operating system (Red Hat Linux, Free BSD Linux, etc.) before choosing the card to ensure that no time is wasted with a NIC that will not work. After the NIC is installed, it may not need any further attention because during the OS boot sequence, it should be detected and configured automatically using the default network protocol (TCP/IP). Note that similar to a Windows computer system, it is necessary to supply the DHCP settings and DNS settings. If DHCP is not used, an appropriate IP address and subnet mask must be supplied.

If the Linux computer system will participate in a Windows network using SAMBA (covered later in this chapter), it will also be necessary to supply the NETBIOS information so that a client connection can be performed easily.

■ APPLICATION SOFTWARE

Objective 3-1

Depending on which window manager is chosen, a variety of application software is available. For example, using the KDE interface, a mail client program (shown in Figure 18–6) allows for e-mail to be managed by the user. Similar to other mail clients, there are ways for a user to organize the mail. The system will automatically use the default folders. For example, before a new mail message is sent, it will be shown in the outbox. After it has been sent, it is moved automatically to the sent mail folder where it is stored for future reference.

FIGURE 18–6
The KDE mail client.

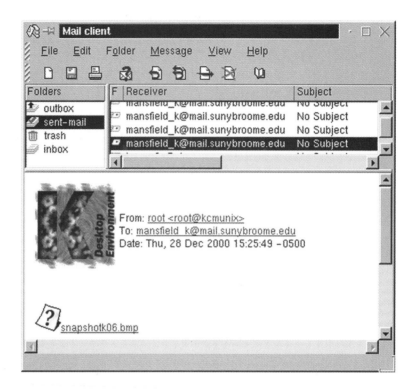

The user can also create new folders as necessary. The window shown in Figure 18–7 illustrates how easy it is to create a message that contains attachments in addition to a text message.

FIGURE 18–7
KDE mail message with attachments.

Another program from the KDE desktop environment is the network utilities program shown in Figure 18–8. It combines the functionality of PING, traceroute, host resolution (DNS), finger, and mtr in one application program. This application can be quite useful when setting up a TCP/IP-based computer network.

FIGURE 18–8
KDE network utilities program.

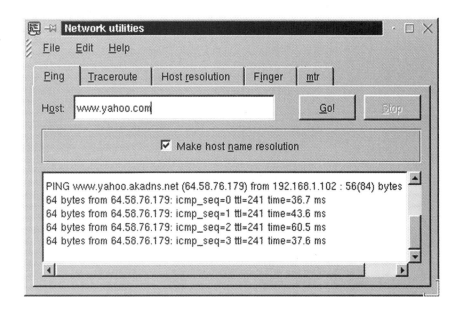

Many programs are installed during the operating system installation process. If a program is not installed, it can be installed later using the Gnome RPM (Red Hat Package Manager). Each of the installed packages can be examined and new programs can be installed. Figure 18–9 shows the Internet category of packages currently installed.

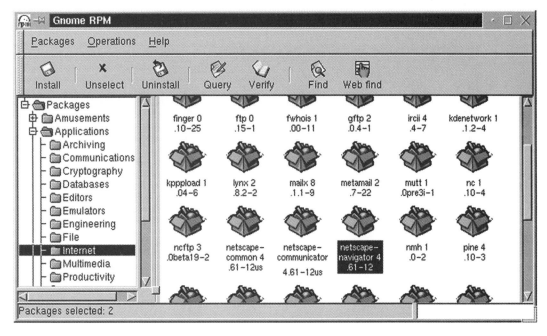

FIGURE 18–9
Gnome RPM Internet packages.

A query of the selected package (Netscape Navigator-4.61-12) shows information about the installed package, as illustrated in Figure 18–10. The size, build host, distribution, group, install date, build date, vendor, and packager are available for examination.

A description of the program and the local installation paths are also displayed. At the bottom of the Package Info screen, the application can be verified or uninstalled. If a package is not functioning properly, it may be useful to verify the installation. Figure 18–11 shows that no problems are found with the installation. The Gnome RPM program is used to download and install new packages as well. By clicking on the Web Find button, a list of additional packages is displayed. Using Gnome RPM is probably the easiest method to ensure that the latest versions of all software programs are installed. You are encouraged to explore the Gnome RPM program in detail.

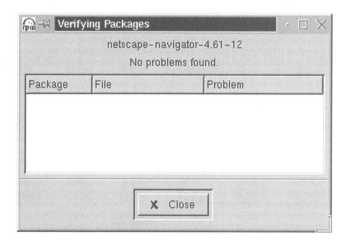

■ SYSTEM ADMINISTRATION, MANAGEMENT, AND SECURITY

Objective 3-1

Objective 3-2

The administration and management of a Linux system can be a complicated task, especially with a computer connected to the Internet. First and foremost, it is necessary for the system administrator to protect the root account. The system administrator is responsible for a wide variety of system tasks. For example, the following list of items should be reviewed regularly:

- Physical system security
- Disk backups
- Addition and removal of authorized users
- Verification of proper file permission settings
- Installation and configuration of server and client applications
- Examination and review of system resources (memory, disks, etc.)
- Setting up and maintaining printers
- Performance monitoring and tuning
- System startup and shutdown options
- System log files review

Objective 3-1

Objective 3-2

The security of a Linux system must be treated as a very important task. It is necessary to review the list of users periodically to ensure that no accounts have been added that would indicate a breach of security. For the system administrator, the management of a Linux system may be a full-time activity.

Local security on a UNIX/Linux platform involves monitoring, logging, and proper analysis of the data on the server, plus the proper software protection of the network resources. Each local and remote login and every connection to a network resource should be logged. In addition, special logging of failed attempts (login and file access failures) must be detected.

Because access to a computer system may be granted to a user who enters a username and a password found on a piece of paper in a desk drawer, security is an important issue. Access may also be granted to a public user via the Web either intentionally or unintentionally. It is very important to protect files and devices properly to prevent any unauthorized access. On a UNIX/Linux computer system, this means disabling any group and/or world access whenever possible.

Objective 2-13

Authentication in a Linux environment plays an important role in accessing data, whether stored locally or out in the network. Authenticated users are granted access to files that they own, as well as to files and resources that are granted on an individual basis and to public users. In a larger setting, Kerberos security is added to the clients and servers to allow for secure communication on the network.

Objective 3-5

No discussion about administration, management, and security would be complete without reference to fault tolerance and disaster recovery. In a fault-tolerant Linux system, special redundant hardware (disk, power supply, etc.) can be used to prevent downtime. Linux is capable of using fault-tolerant hardware such as RAID, ECC memory, multiple NICs, and so on.

Objective 3-6

In the event that a problem does occur and it is necessary to recover from a disaster of some type, it is extremely important to safeguard data by storing copies off site. In extremely sensitive situations, it is necessary to make multiple copies and store them in geographically separate locations. It is also a good idea to test the recovery process to guarantee that, when the process is actually performed, it goes smoothly.

■ TCP/IP NETWORK MANAGEMENT

Objective 4-4

The management of the TCP/IP network on a Linux system is performed using `linuxconf`. Linuxconf. Figure 18–12 shows basic host information in the `linuxconf` window. Notice that the left side of the window shows the various categories that may be configured. The right side of the display shows the current settings for each of the categories. The host name is entered during the installation of the operating system. It can be modified later using `linuxconf`. The Adaptor tabs (labeled 1–4) are used to identify each of the NIC cards that are installed.

FIGURE 18–12
Linux configuration utility
program.

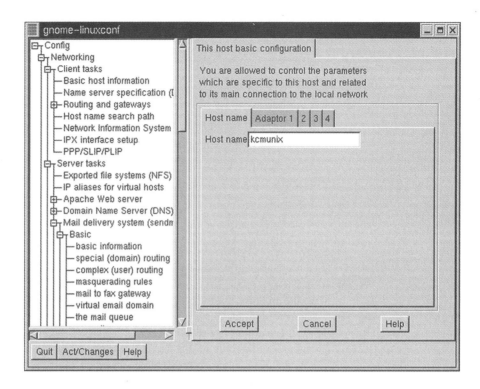

FIGURE 18–12
Linux configuration utility
program.

Figure 18–13 shows that Adaptor 1 is enabled using the DHCP configuration mode.
The network device specifies eth0 with the eepro100 kernel module or driver. By enabling
the DHCP configuration, a DHCP server must be available to assign TCP/IP network parameters when the system is booted. These are the only parameters that are necessary to get
a Linux system up on a TCP/IP network.

FIGURE 18–13
Configuration options for
Ethernet Adaptor 1.

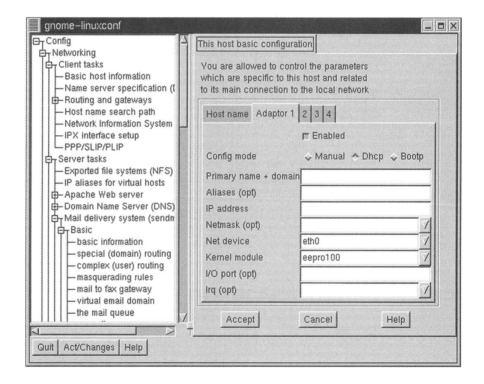

Figure 18–14 shows the name server specifications assigned to the computer. Note
that each of the name server fields has been assigned a value by the DHCP server for the

current network. If a DHCP server is not available, a valid IP address, network mask, and name server addresses must be specified.

FIGURE 18–14
Settings for the name servers assigned by DHCP.

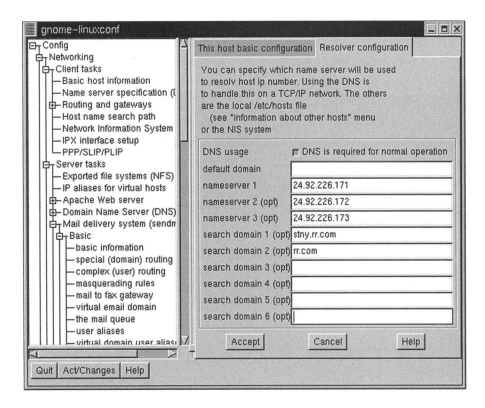

Other tools are also used in Linux to verify correct network operations. A list of built-in applications includes:

• ifconfig

• PING

• traceroute

• tcpdump

• nslookup

For example, a sample execution of the tcdump utility with the output redirected to the file TCP.TXT looks similar to the following:

```
# tcdump >> tcp.txt
Kernel filter, protocol ALL, datagram packet socket
tcpump: listening on all devices

100 packets received by filter

#
```

The tcpdump execution was terminated by pressing Ctrl + C. As noted, the contents of the TCP.TXT file consist of 100 packets. The first captured packet in the file contains:

```
13:08:51.176746 eth0 < bgm-24-95-142-58.stny.rr.com.1028 > bgm-24-
94-63160.stny.rr.com.telnet: . 4486926:4486926(0) ack 3337880229
win 65505 (DF)
```

This information may be useful when examining network traffic. You are encouraged to review the online manual pages to help examine the output from the tcpdump program.

In addition to these built-in applications, there are many other programs that can be downloaded from the Internet.

■ SAMBA

Objective 3-1

The Samba (http://www.samba.org) program allows for a Linux system to participate in a Windows network by sharing files and printers using SMB (Server Message Blocks) and CIFS (Common Internet File System) protocols.

SMB is a client-server, request-response protocol for sharing files and printers. All Windows for Workgroups, Windows 95/98, Windows NT/2000, and Windows XP systems are (or are capable of) running SMB as a client, a server, or both. CIFS is a new specification for a file access designed for the Internet. CIFS is based on the existing SMB protocol.

The `smb.conf` file located in the `/etc` directory contains the complete Samba server configuration, which is maintained by the Red Hat `linuxconf` program. The contents of a sample smb.conf file can be found at http://de.samba.org/samba/docs/man/smb.conf.5.html. Although the sample file is large, the settings provide a good starting point to add or modify any of the Samba features. It is worthwhile to review each entry to gain an appreciation for the Windows compatibility features.

The documentation on Samba is extensive, with additional material added as the product matures. It is always a good idea to refer to the Samba Web site for the most up-to-date information.

Using Samba, it is possible to connect to UNIX disks and printers from:

- LAN Manager clients
- Windows for Workgroups 3.11 clients
- Windows 95/98/Me clients
- Windows NT/2000 clients
- Linux clients
- OS/2 clients

Figure 18–15 shows the `linuxconf` windows used to configure directories to be shared using Samba.

FIGURE 18–15
Samba configuration points.

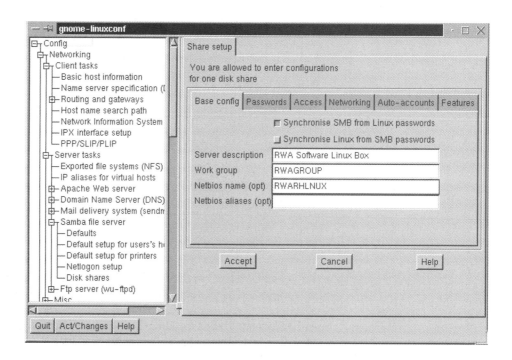

After the computer system has a suitable workgroup name and comment, it is then possible to configure the shares. For example, a network share called lbox is added in Figure 18–16.

FIGURE 18–16
Samba share settings.

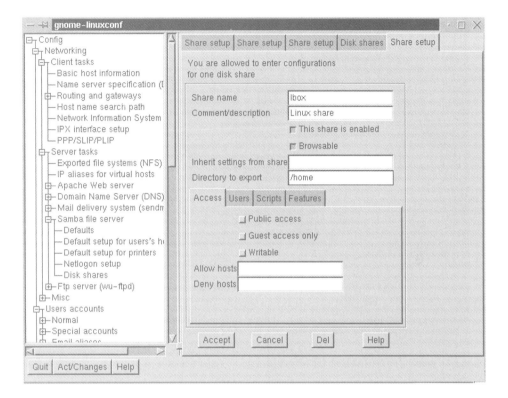

The share settings can be set to enabled and browsable (if desired), and a host of access, users, scripting, and special features can be applied as necessary. Access can be granted to the public and to guests with writable access, with additional capabilities to either allow or deny access based on host addresses. Users can be selectively enabled or disabled with scripting to allow for custom access to sensitive network resources. Features allow the maximum number of connections and additional advanced settings.

For a client to access the share, all that is necessary is to supply the share name, such as `\\rwasoft\lbox`. Access to lbox will be determined by the settings entered on the share setup screens.

Objective 2-7

What you might think of as a Windows-only service, such as the operation of a domain controller or WINS server, can be enabled using Linux as shown in Figure 18–17.

If the Linux computer system does not operate as a WINS server, the address of a WINS server computer system can be entered to allow the computer to participate.

Notice that each of the Samba configuration windows contains several different tabs, allowing the system administrator to enter many different parameters to customize the operating of Samba. Samba provides a replacement for Windows NT, Warp, NFS, or NetWare servers.

Server-type computer systems can generally run all types of software to make them compatible with any type of computing environment. This compatibility is presented as two options when connecting a client computer system to a UNIX/Linux server. The first option requires that the server computer system be configured to implement the same protocols as the client system. For example, the Linux server runs SAMBA and automatically participates in the Windows client computer network neighborhood. In this case, the client can use the resources of the server simply by mapping them.

FIGURE 18–17
Samba server networking
settings.

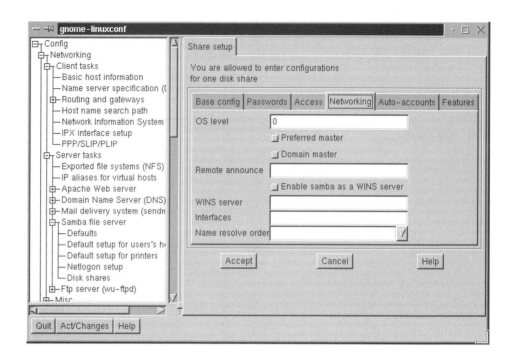

Objective 3-2

A Linux client can also participate in the Windows environment by using the SMB-CLIENT program. The SMBCLIENT program is used to communicate with the SAMBA server. Sample output from the SMBCLIENT program provides text on how to use each of the options that are available:

```
Usage: smbclient service <password> [options]
Version 2.0.5a
     -s smb.conf            pathname to smb.conf file
     -B IP addr             broadcast IP address to use
     -O socket_options      socket options to use
     -R name resolve order  use these name resolution services only
     -M host                send a winpopup message to the host
     -i scope               use this NetBIOS scope
     -N                     don't ask for a password
     -n netbios name.       Use this name as my netbios name
     -d debuglevel          set the debuglevel
     -P                     connect to service as a printer
     -p port                connect to the specified port
     -l log basename.       Basename for log/debug files
     -h                     Print this help message.
     -I dest IP             use this IP to connect to
     -E                     write messages to stderr instead of stdout
     -U username            set the network username
     -L host                get a list of shares available on a host
     -t terminal code       terminal i/o code {sjis|euc|jis7|jis8|junet|hex}
     -m max protocol        set the max protocol level
     -W workgroup           set the workgroup name
     -T<c|x>IXFqgbNan       command line tar
     -D directory           start from directory
     -c command string      execute semicolon separated commands
     -b xmit/send buffer    changes the transmit/send buffer (default: 65520)
```

As an example, a Linux client can use `smbclient` to set the NETBIOS name, username, and workgroup name as well as provide additional connectivity settings.

■ NETWORK INFORMATION SERVICES

The Network Information Service (NIS) is a method used on UNIX and Linux systems to share passwords and group file access within a computer network. NIS was created by Sun Microsystems as a part of the Sun operating systems. Originally these services were called YP (short for Yellow Pages), but due to a lawsuit the name was eventually changed to NIS.

NIS domains are created to allow servers and clients to communicate. The servers and clients must be in the same domain in order to communicate. NIS domains are supported by master NIS servers and slave NIS servers. A master NIS server contains the actual resource information to be shared on the network and the NIS clients are used to distribute the load across the network.

There is much talk about the security of NIS resources. Security and system administrators make recommendations on how the resources may be guarded to offer maximum protection. You are encouraged to read about what types of problems there are and the solutions that are available, if any.

A newer version of NIS is called NIS+, which stands for Network Information Service Plus. It was designed to replace NIS and is a default naming service for the Sun Microsystems Solaris operating system. Using YP-compatibility mode, NIS+ can provide limited support to NIS clients. One important thing to note is that there is no relation between NIS+ and NIS. NIS+ was designed from scratch and the overall structure and commands of NIS+ are different from NIS.

■ NETWORK FILE SYSTEM SERVICES

The Network File System (NFS) is the method used by UNIX and Linux systems to share disk resources. The file systems that are exported using NFS can be imported by any Linux computer within the network. A Linux computer can import and export NFS disks at the same time.

The list of directories to export is stored in the file `/etc/exports`. Each entry in the exports file contains the name of the mount point followed by a list of users or groups that are allowed to use it. This file can be edited manually to add or remove the disk resource. The file can also be maintained by `linuxconf` as shown in Figure 18–18.

FIGURE 18–18
Configuration dialog box for exported file system.

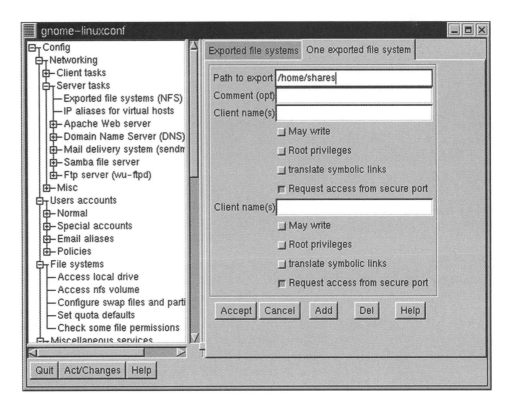

For each exported file system, the clients that may connect are given specific rights to the resource. Each client or group of clients may be given write access and root privileges, may translate symbolic links, and may request access from a secure port. The system administrator must determine what values are appropriate to use. When all of the entries have been updated, the exported file system will show up in the list of Exported file systems shown in Figure 18–19. These are the same entries that are stored in the file `/etc/exports`. The client computer systems are then able to use these resources using the mount command.

FIGURE 18–19
List of exported file systems.

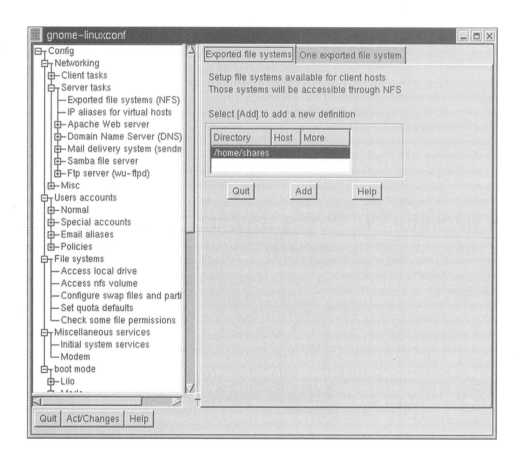

Objective 3-2

A Windows computer (and many other network operating systems) can also participate as a client in the UNIX/Linux NFS environment. It is necessary to install the NFS client on each computer that needs to use the UNIX/Linux files. Since Windows does not supply an NFS client, the appropriate client software must typically be purchased. After an NFS client is installed and the UNIX/Linux network resources are available for use on the Windows computer systems, check the Network Neighborhood and Windows Explorer to see what new network resources are available. Because a cost is associated with most of these products, technical support is also provided.

■ APACHE WEB SERVER

Objective 3-1

The Linux operating system also comes with the Apache Web server from http://www.apache.org. The Apache Server is an HTTP 1.1-compliant Web server offering the ability to use CGI scripting using Perl, Python, C/C++, plus many other compatible languages. Apache Server also provides complete Java compatibility. The Apache Server is the most popular HTTP server on the Internet, with almost 60% of the market share according to the statistics compiled at http://www.netcraft.com. The Apache Server on

Linux provides commercial-grade service with all of the bells and whistles that are required, and it's free.

The `linuxconf` program can also be used to maintain the Apache Web server. Figure 18–20 shows the Apache default settings. Notice that on the left side of the window there are several different configuration categories.

FIGURE 18–20
Apache Web server configuration options.

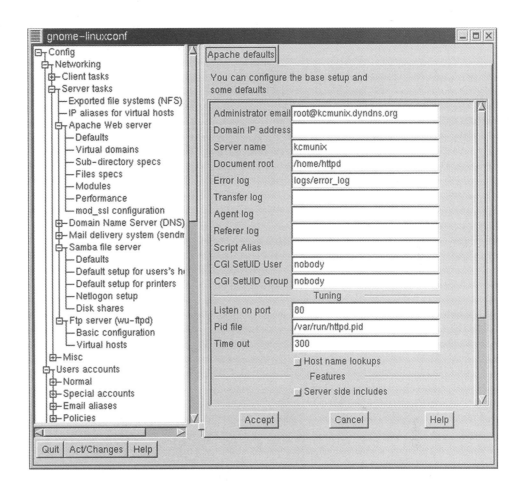

Administering a Web server is an important task. Most businesses and organizations rely on a Web presence to provide services to their customers around the clock. Using the Apache Server, there are no restrictions in what can be provided to the end-users.

■ LINUX DOCUMENTATION

When using the UNIX or Linux operating systems, it is possible to experience many different types of problems. Unfortunately there are too many problems to even list. The good news is that there are many sources of information to help solve problems that may be encountered. Figure 18–21 shows a starting point for any investigation when the Gnome interface is being used.

Figure 18–22 displays the Online Help screen when running the KDE desktop interface.

In addition to these resources, the Linux documentation project provides extensive information about most of the applications that can be installed, configured, and used on a Linux system. The Linux documentation project provides access to electronic books, FAQs, man pages, HOWTOs, plus much more. You are encouraged to visit the Linux documentation project at http://www.linuxdoc.org. All of the documentation available prepares a system administrator to maintain and enhance a Linux system with as few difficulties as possible. Don't reinvent the wheel unless it is absolutely necessary.

FIGURE 18–21
Red Hat Online Help screen for the Gnome desktop interface.

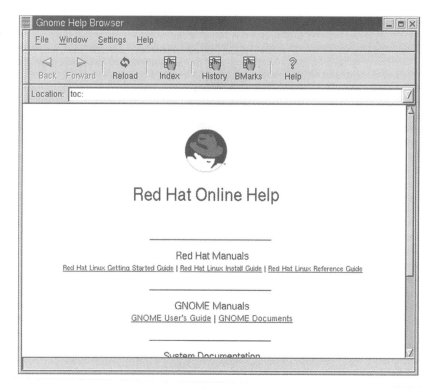

FIGURE 18–22
Red Hat Online Help screen for the KDE desktop interface.

■ TROUBLESHOOTING TECHNIQUES

Objective 4-1

When troubleshooting a Linux system, it is necessary to use all of the available tools that are provided. For example, if the network doesn't seem to be working properly, it may be necessary to make sure that the computer has a valid IP address. The `ifconfig` program is useful in this type of situation. For example, refer to Figure 18–23.

Notice that two Ethernet adapters are shown. The first, eth0, is the eepro100. The second, lo, is the loopback adapter that is useful for testing and debugging purposes. For the eth0 device the following items are listed:

- Hardware address
- Internet address

- Broadcast address
- Network mask
- Status (UP or DOWN)
- MTU
- Metric
- RX packet statistics
- TX packet statistics
- Collision statistics
- NIC hardware settings

FIGURE 18–23
Ethernet statistics shown using the ifconfig utility.

```
[root@kcmunix /root]# ifconfig
eth0        Link encap:Ethernet  HWaddr 00:D0:B7:68:2A:15
            inet addr:192.168.1.102  Bcast:192.168.1.255  Mask:255.255.255.0
            UP BROADCAST RUNNING  MTU:1500  Metric:1
            RX packets:6568 errors:1 dropped:0 overruns:0 frame:0
            TX packets:11137 errors:0 dropped:0 overruns:0 carrier:0
            collisions:0 txqueuelen:100
            Interrupt:11 Base address:0x6000

lo          Link encap:Local Loopback
            inet addr:127.0.0.1  Mask:255.0.0.0
            UP LOOPBACK RUNNING  MTU:3924  Metric:1
            RX packets:5931 errors:0 dropped:0 overruns:0 frame:0
            TX packets:5931 errors:0 dropped:0 overruns:0 carrier:0
            collisions:0 txqueuelen:0

[root@kcmunix /root]#
```

For the loopback adapter, the same information is listed, with the exception of the hardware references. By reviewing the information on this screen to make sure that a valid IP address is displayed, it is clear whether or not the network is working properly. Many other programs are also available that can be used to diagnose problems. Read all of the available Linux documentation to determine what tools are available and how to use them.

INDUSTRY TIP

Dedicated and often militant Linux users have freely and willingly supplied suggestions and new uses for this evolving operating system—a dramatic departure from closed systems such as Windows where the manufacturer controls the development process. This involvement in the development process fosters a very strong customer dedication to the current state and future of the product.

Several companies have "branded" Linux. These distributions include products by Red Hat, Debian, Caldera, Corel, and Slackware. All of these companies' products are Linux systems, but they are slightly different and appeal to personal preferences of users.

Companies that distribute Linux continually push the open source architecture. This architecture allows for future development in system and infrastructure management, configuration and application environment virtualization, distributed security, and very targeted applications. While an open source architecture is not for everyone, it does allow for a foundation upon which a wide array of user applications can be constructed. For customers or organizations that want to take advantage of these capabilities, Linux offers a secure and exciting operating system environment.

As true industry experts, technicians should gain an understanding of a variety of operating systems and how Linux can provide a technically exciting alternative to licensed operating systems.

CAREER DEVELOPMENT: LINUX+

The Linux+ certification is an international industry credential that validates the knowledge of professionals with at least six months of practical, vendor-neutral Linux experience. Professionals who want to certify their technical knowledge in basic installation, operation, and troubleshooting for the Linux operating system should consider this certification.

Earning the Linux+ designation means that the candidate can explain fundamental open source resources/licenses, demonstrate knowledge of user administration, understand file permissions/software configurations, and manage local storage devices and network protocols.

To learn more about the Linux+ certification, visit www.comptia.org.

■ SELF-TEST

1. True or False: Linux and UNIX are both basically the same operating system.

2. The GNU GPL (general public license) allows which of the following users to use the Linux software for free?
   a. Home
   b. Business
   c. Commercial
   d. All of the above

3. Which of the following commands is used to determine a list of the current users in a Linux environment?
   a. dir
   b. who
   c. df
   d. ls

4. What is the command used to locate files on a Linux machine?
   a. netstat
   b. pine
   c. ftp
   d. find

5. The purpose of a /home mount point in the Linux directory structure is _____.
   a. software directories
   b. user directories
   c. logging information
   d. boot files

6. Which of the following are the most popular window managers available with Red Hat Linux? (Choose two.)
   a. ASICS
   b. Gnome
   c. KDE
   d. REDO

7. Clicking on the Gnome footprint in the taskbar provides _____.
   a. access to the users list
   b. access to the menu system
   c. print services
   d. help services

8. True or False: UNIX/Linux is one of the most interoperable operating systems available.

9. If a compatible NIC is chosen for a Linux machine on an Ethernet network, it should be automatically detected during the OS boot sequence and configured using the default _____ protocol.
   a. IPX
   b. NETBIOS
   c. TCP/IP
   d. Samba

10. Most of the system configuration that is needed for a Linux machine will be done using the _____ program.
    a. linuxconf
    b. linusconf
    c. OS boot
    d. X Windows

11. The Linux KDE desktop environment provides a network utilities program that combines the functionality of all of the following **except** _____.
    a. PING
    b. DHCP
    c. traceroute
    d. host resolution (DNS)
    e. finger

12. The application software that is not installed during the Linux Red Hat operating system installation can be installed later using the Gnome _____.
    a. Builder
    b. Footprint
    c. RPM
    d. Instl

13. What protocol is used to provide name resolution on a Linux computer?
    a. DHCP
    b. DID
    c. Who
    d. DNS

14. RAID, ECC memory, and multiple NICs are all used to make a Linux system _____.
    a. a server
    b. fault tolerant
    c. disaster recoverable
    d. capable of being on a network

15. Management of the TCP/IP network on a Linux machine is performed using _____.
    a. linuxconf
    b. RPM
    c. NetBEUI
    d. ipconfig

16. The adapter tabs shown when viewing the linuxconf window represent _____.
    a. users connected
    b. NICs installed
    c. server connections
    d. domain used

17. How can the execution of a tcpdump utility be terminated?
    a. Ctrl+Alt+Del
    b. Ctrl+C
    c. Ctrl+Shift
    d. Ctrl+L

18. What program allows a Linux system to participate in a Windows network?
    a. Samba
    b. WINS

c. Lindows

d. linuxconf

19. Windows for Workgroups systems are able to run SMB as _____.

a. client only

b. server only

c. both client and server

d. proxy only

20. Which of the following Samba commands will tell Samba to try to resolve NetBIOS names?

a. dns proxy = yes

b. dhcp proxy = yes

c. NetBIOS = yes

d. NetBIOS = no

21. Access to a Samba share is determined by the _____ on the share setup.

a. Permissions box

b. Accounts box

c. browser settings

d. settings entered

22. True or False: A Linux computer system can act as a WINS server.

23. What is used to share disk resources on Linux machines?

a. NTP

b. NIS

c. NFS

d. L2TP

24. What Linux program is used to maintain the Apache Server?

a. linuxconf

b. RPM

c. KTH

d. LHTTP

25. Which of the following is an Ethernet adapter useful for testing and debugging Linux network connections?

a. IFLoop

b. eth0

c. loopback

d. ipconfig

Other Network Operating Systems

PERFORMANCE OBJECTIVES

Upon completion of this chapter, you will be able to:

- Compare the features of NetWare with Windows NT.

- Discuss the file organization, protocols, and security available in NetWare.

- Briefly describe the VMS and Mac OS operating systems.

NETWORK+ OBJECTIVES

This chapter provides information for the following Network+ objectives:

1.6 Identify the purpose, features, and functions of the following network components:

- Hubs
- Switches
- Bridges
- Routers
- Gateways
- CSU/DSU
- Network Interface Cards/ISDN adapters/system area network cards
- Wireless access points
- Modems

2.13 Identify the following security protocols and describe their purpose and function:

- IPSec
- SSL
- L2TP
- Kerberos

3.1 Identify the basic capabilities (i.e., client support, interoperability, authentication, file and print services, application support, security) of the following server operating systems:

- UNIX/Linux
- Windows

- NetWare
- Macintosh

3.2 Identify the basic capabilities of client workstations (i.e., client connectivity, local security mechanisms, authentication).

3.11 Given a network configuration, select the appropriate NIC and network configuration settings (DHCP, DNS, WINS, protocols, NETBIOS/host name, etc.) on network resources and users.

4.1 Given a troubleshooting scenario, select the appropriate TCP/IP utility from among the following:

- TRACERT
- PING
- ARP
- NETSTAT
- NBTSTAT
- IPCONFIG/IFCONFIG
- WINIPCFG
- NSLOOKUP

4.4 Given specific parameters, configure a client to connect to the following servers:

- UNIX/Linux
- Windows
- NetWare
- Macintosh

■ INTRODUCTION

This chapter examines several additional network operating systems, starting with a look at the features of Novell's NetWare operating system. The Mac OS X, OpenVMS, and OS/2 Warp are also presented and covered.

■ NETWARE

Objective 3-1

The NetWare operating system originated in the early days of DOS, allowing users to share information, print documents on network printers, manage a set of users, and so on. One important difference between NetWare and Windows is in the area of application software. NetWare does not provide the 32-bit preemptive multitasking environment found in Windows. Applications written for Windows will not run on NetWare. They may, however, communicate over the network using TCP/IP or NetWare's proprietary IPX/SPX protocol. The following sections describe many of the main features of NetWare.

Installing/Upgrading NetWare

Unlike Windows, the NetWare operating system runs on top of DOS (as Windows 3.x did). So before NetWare can be installed on a system, DOS must be up and running. NetWare 4.x and above provide a DOS environment as part of the installation process. Versions of NetWare older than 3.1x must be upgraded to 3.1x before they can be further upgraded to NetWare 4.x and above.

There are two ways to perform an upgrade: through *in-place migration* and through *across-the-wire migration*. In-place migration involves shutting down the NetWare server to perform the upgrade directly on the machine. Across-the-wire migration transfers all NetWare files from the current server to a new machine attached to the network. The new machine must already be running NetWare 4.x or above. This method allows the older 3.1x server to continue running during the upgrade.

The latest version of NetWare, version 6, can be downloaded from Novell's Web site (www.novell.com) as a 500+ MB Zip file. This Zip file is uncompressed to create an ISO image that is used to burn a bootable CD containing the NetWare 6 operating system. Booting a computer with this CD in the CD-ROM drive (and the appropriate BIOS and OS settings) will begin the NetWare 6 installer. The minimum requirements are a Pentium II or equivalent CPU and 192 MB of RAM. The operating system requires a 200 MB boot partition.

Objective 3-11

One note of caution: If the computer's network card is not recognized or supported, the installation will not continue. A visit to the manufacturer's Web site to determine if the network card is supported would be worthwhile in this case. There may be a new driver available for download. You may also see the NetWare icon on the box that the network card came packaged in.

If the network card is recognized, the installer will ask for the server name and IP address. Many of the following figures contain information about a NetWare 6 server called RWASOFT whose IP address is 192.168.1.25 (an internal LAN address). During the installation, TCP/IP, not the native IPX/SPX protocol suite, was chosen as the default protocol for the NetWare server. This was done for ease of use within an already established TCP/IP LAN.

NDS

The Network Directory Service (NDS) is the cornerstone of newer NetWare networks. Network administrators can manage all users and resources from one location. NDS allows users to access global resources regardless of their physical location using a single login. The NDS database organizes information on each object in the network. These objects are users, groups, printers, and disk volumes. Typically these objects are organized into a hierarchical tree that matches the internal structure of an organization. Figure 19–1 shows a typical tree structure for a small two-year college. Each major area of the organization (Administration, Academic, Student Support, and Alumni) has its own unique requirements. The requirements are applied to all the users who are associated with each specific area. Over time, as the requirements of the organization change, elements in the hierarchical tree are added, modified, or removed very easily.

FIGURE 19–1

Typical tree structure.

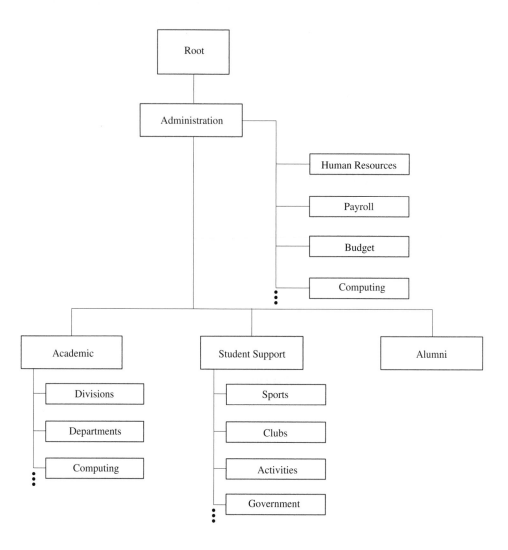

NetWare uses *data migration* to move data from one location to another to maintain effective use of available hard drive space. Large files are moved to a secondary storage system (such as a *jukebox*) and copied back (demigrated) to the hard drive when needed. Files that have been migrated still show up in directory listings.

Accurate timekeeping plays an important role in the operation of NDS. Multiple servers must agree on the network time so that file updates are performed in the correct sequence. NetWare uses several kinds of time servers to maintain an accurate Universal Coordinated Time (UCT). These servers are called *reference, primary, secondary,* and *single-reference.* Reference servers use a connection to an accurate time source (such as the U.S. Naval Observatory's Atomic Clock) to provide the network time. Primary and reference servers negotiate with each other to determine the network time. Secondary servers provide the time to NetWare clients. Single-reference time servers are designed for use on small networks where one machine has total control over the network time.

NDS add-ons are also available for Windows NT and UNIX environments, allowing those systems to fully participate in the NetWare environment.

HCSS

The High Capacity Storage System (HCSS) provided by NetWare allows for tremendously large volumes to be created that span up to 32 physical hard drives. When hard drive capacity was quite small in comparison to the sizes available today, HCSS allowed for the creation of volumes up to 32 GB in size. NetWare 5 introduced increased volume sizes up to eight terabytes (still much larger than disks typically available today). In conjunction with a configuration of RAID (Redundant Array of Inexpensive Disks), data is protected even if one of the disks in the volume fails.

 Objective 3-1

NetWare's hard drives can be mapped or shared like any other computer's drive once the appropriate client software is installed on the computer that will be accessing the NetWare server. Figure 19–2 shows Windows Explorer displaying the contents of the SYS volume on the rwasoft NetWare server. Drives N: and Z: are automatically mapped to the Windows computer when the user logs onto the NetWare server.

FIGURE 19–2
Windows Explorer window showing mapped NetWare drive icons (N: and Z:).

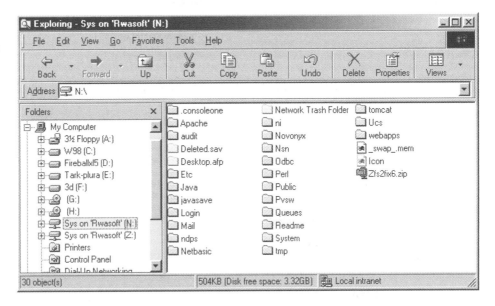

 Objective 3-2

The files and folders on the mapped drives can be cut and pasted as you would expect in a Windows environment, even though they are stored using a different file system on the NetWare server. The CIFS (Common Internet File System) protocol is used to enable the drive mapping and file sharing. CIFS is based on Microsoft's SMB (Server Message Block) protocol.

Right-clicking on the N: drive icon in Figure 19–2 brings up the context-sensitive menu shown in Figure 19–3. Notice the additional NetWare selections present in the menu. These selections are not present when the user is not logged into the NetWare server.

Selecting Properties opens the window illustrated in Figure 19–4. Note the server and object names. You can examine the properties of the mapped NetWare drive's SYS volume, such as its Object name, Name Spaces, block size, and free space. The Name Spaces DOS, MAC, NFS, and LONG indicate support for several file naming conventions. Originally, NetWare utilized DOS naming conventions (8.3 format) and later added support for other operating systems. The indicated name spaces are:

- MAC (Macintosh)
- NFS (UNIX)
- LONG (Windows 95/NT/2000/XP, OS/2)

FIGURE 19–3
Context-sensitive pop-up menu
showing NetWare entries.

FIGURE 19–4
NetWare volume information
for the SYS volume.

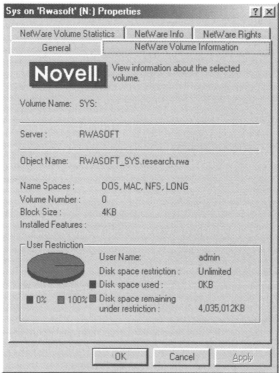

Additional details about the SYS volume are found in the NetWare Volume Statistics window shown in Figure 19–5. The disk free space and directory entry information may be useful to a user planning on saving files to the volume or to an IT manager checking on resource availability.

Objective 1-6

NetWare 6 provides Novell Cluster Services, a technique that allows up to 32 NetWare servers to operate as a cluster of shared resources, with the ability to move resources from one server to another automatically (in case of a server failure) or manually (for troubleshooting). With the wide range of supported file systems, the ability to store large quantities of information through clustering, and fault-tolerant RAID technology, the NetWare server is an ideal candidate for participation in a storage area network (SAN). The computers connect via fiber

FIGURE 19–5
NetWare volume statistics for
the SYS volume.

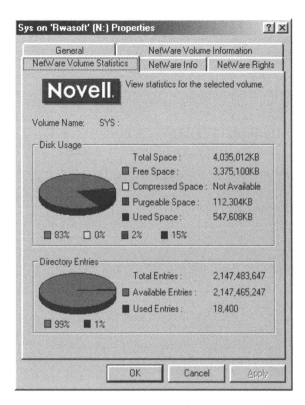

FIGURE 19–5
NetWare volume statistics for the SYS volume.

System area network cards

to a central switch, with Fibre Channel technology providing 2 Gbps data rates. To take advantage of the high speed, ordinary NICs are not used in the server computers. Instead, special *system area network cards* perform the networking chores. In an ordinary NIC, the hardware implements the Physical and Data-Link layers of the OSI model. All high-level protocol processing, such as that used in a reliable TCP session, is performed by the CPU. Thus, the processor in a typical file server is very busy during a TCP session. A system area network card implements additional ISO layers in hardware, enabling hardware-based reliable file transfers. Data is transferred directly from memory buffer to memory buffer with little processor intervention. This frees up the CPU in the server and allows a higher throughput to the network.

Clearly, NetWare provides many features not found on other network operating systems and is a valuable tool in storage-based networks.

Menus, Login Scripts, and Messaging

Several of the most important issues for the user involve the system menus, shared access to a common set of data, and electronic messaging capabilities. Access to the software located on each system is created using the menu generation program. Access to items in the menu is made available during the login process using a login script.

The login script contains a list of commands that are executed when each user logs in to the network. The commands are typically used to establish connections to network resources such as mapping of network drives. A login script is a property of a container, Profile, or User object. If a login script is defined for each of these objects, all associated login scripts will execute when a user logs in, allowing for a great deal of control over each user's environment.

Electronic messaging is provided for all users using information available through NDS. Each user's specific information is centrally maintained in the NDS database. The Message Handling Service (MHS) provides access to the X.400 standard implementation for e-mail. FirstMail client software is provided with Novell NetWare 4.1 and above, which is used to access the X.400 messaging services. Add-on products such as GroupWise offer more sophisticated support for electronic messaging. GroupWise also provides document management, calendaring, scheduling, task management, workflow, and imaging.

When a Windows computer with an installed NetWare client boots, its time and date are set to those of the NetWare server. If the NetWare server is not running, the time and date are not adjusted.

Objective 3-2

Logging onto a NetWare server is illustrated in the following figures. Figure 19–6 shows the user admin trying to connect to the rwasoft server. The user may easily select a different Tree, Context, or Server and choose the appropriate script processing during login.

FIGURE 19–6
NDS parameters for the Novell Login client.

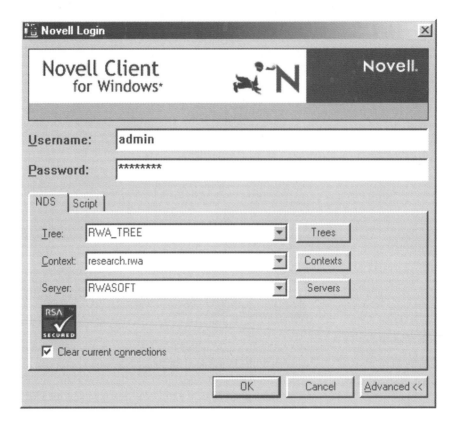

Figure 19–7 shows the results of the login attempt. Local disk drives and the mapped NetWare volume are displayed. There are two error messages at the top of the Results window, indicating two unsuccessful login attempts. The failed attempts occurred because the user tried to log in to the NetWare server before it finished booting up.

FIGURE 19–7
Results window after a successful NetWare login.

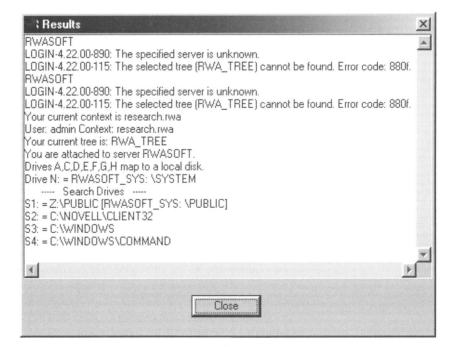

When the NetWare server is shut down, it sends a message to each connected station, as indicated in Figure 19–8. The message window pops up whenever a message is received. The NetWare server sends the shutdown message prior to unmounting its file systems, which must be done before power can be turned off.

FIGURE 19–8
Message sent from the NetWare server RWASOFT.

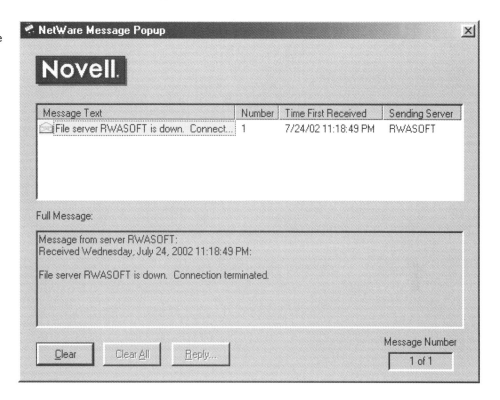

Security

The security features of the NetWare operating system offer the system and/or network administrator the ability to monitor all aspects of the system operation from a single location. There are two types of security: file system security and NDS security.

File System Security

Table 19–1 shows the various types of rights that may be assigned to a NetWare user. Note that similar rights are available under Windows NT. Rights are inherited and/or modified via filters or masks that designate permissible operations.

TABLE 19–1
NetWare rights.

Rights Name	Rights Description
Access Control	May control the rights of other users to access files and directories
Create	May create new file or subdirectory
Erase	May delete existing files or directories
File Scan	May list the contents of a directory
Modify	May rename and change file attributes
Write	May write data into an existing file

Figure 19–9 shows the NetWare Info properties window for the netbook2 directory stored on the rwasoft NetWare server. This directory was initially located on a Windows 98 computer and copied to the NetWare server. The user who copied the directory was admin, as indicated in the admin.research.rwa Owner name. The Name Space is LONG, indicating a Windows file naming system. Note that although the admin user has an unlimited Space

Restriction, a user's disk space may be limited by NetWare (in multiples of 4 KB), a nice feature when managing disk resources among multiple users.

FIGURE 19–9
NetWare Info window showing details of the netbook2 directory.

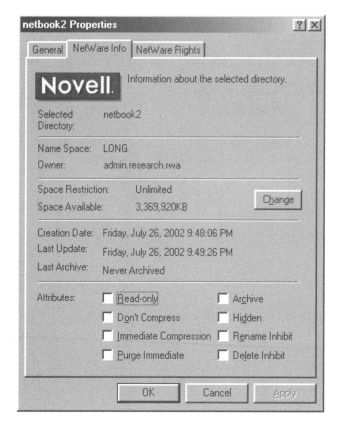

Figure 19–10 shows the NetWare Rights properties for the netbook2 directory.

FIGURE 19–10
NetWare Rights window showing effective rights of the netbook2 directory.

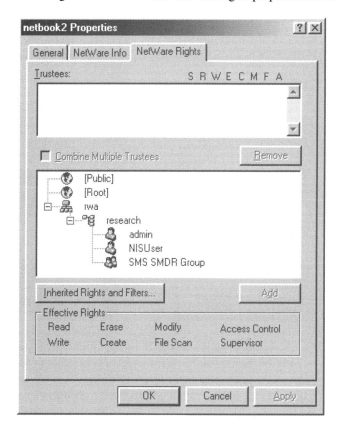

NDS Security

Objective 3-1

In addition to encryption of login passwords, NDS security provides auditing features that allow one user to monitor events caused by other users (changes to the file system, resource utilization).

Even connecting to the NetWare server through HTTP is monitored from a security standpoint, as indicated in Figure 19–11. Here the user is given a choice of proceeding with a connection to an untrusted site. Therefore, as in Windows NT/2000 server, it is necessary to establish trust relationships with all the entities accessing the NetWare server. NetWare is able to create, issue, and manage digital certificates.

FIGURE 19–11
Security Alert window opened in response to an attempted connection to a NetWare server.

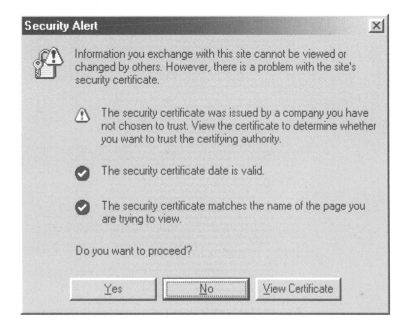

Management

Management of any network involves many different activities to ensure quality control. Some of these items include:

- Monitor network traffic to develop a baseline from which to make network-related decisions
- Monitoring unusual activities such as successive login failures, or file creation or file write errors
- Disk resource utilization issues
- Software and hardware installation and upgrades
- Backup scheduling
- Help desk support for problem resolution
- Short-range and long-range planning

Many other important items can be added to this list, depending on the organization. Some of these issues will be explored in the problems located at the end of this chapter.

NetWare 6 provides a rich Web-based environment for using, configuring, and managing the NetWare server. Figure 19–12 shows the main Web page returned by the rwasoft NetWare server located at IP address 192.168.1.25. Note the Remote Manager and Net-Storage items.

FIGURE 19–12
NetWare 6 main Web page.

FIGURE 19–12
NetWare 6 main Web page.

Objective 3-1

NetWare 6 provides many features, including:

- iFolder, Internet-based file storage and management
- Web Access, a method of accessing network resources via Web browser
- iPrint, Internet-based document printing
- Remote Manager, Web-based secure server management
- Apache Web server and Tomcat Java servlet applications
- NetStorage, Internet-based access to a NetWare storage network
- iManage, Internet-based management of eDirectory users, trees, and licenses, as well as print and DHCP servers. eDirectory is a platform-independent directory structure based on LDAP that allows creation and management of millions of objects, such as users, applications, and devices. LDAP is the Lightweight Directory Access Protocol, a protocol designed to provide access to directory services via the Internet. LDAP is part of Microsoft's Active Directory.
- Web Search, a powerful Web searching utility
- Enterprise Web Server, a powerful Web server with eDirectory features built in

The Remote Manager feature provides a way to administer and manage a NetWare server from a remote location on the Internet. Figure 19–13 shows the Remote Manager Web interface with the Disk/LAN Adapters option selected. Access to the Remote Manager is password protected. After connected, you can shut down or restart the NetWare server, manage eDirectory objects, send messages to clients, view and adjust all system parameters, and view memory and network statistics.

Figure 19–14 shows some of the protocol statistics maintained by the NetWare server.

Figure 19–15 shows the initial lines of the configuration report for the RWASOFT NetWare server. Clicking on Run Config Report in the Diagnose Server group gives you a choice of viewing the report or having a copy e-mailed to an address you supply. The e-mail feature is a handy way of sharing configuration information across widely dispersed sites.

FIGURE 19-13
Disk/LAN Adapter information for the RWASOFT NetWare server.

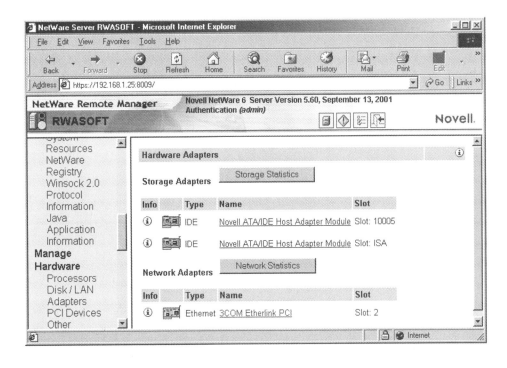

FIGURE 19-14
Protocol information for the RWASOFT NetWare server.

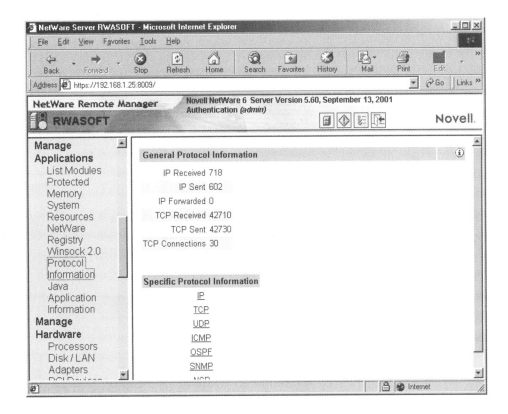

Print Services

A core component of NetWare consists of the services available for managing and using printers. Print jobs are first sent to a printer queue, where they are temporarily stored until the assigned printer is available. Printers may be attached to workstations, print servers, or even directly connected to the network.

FIGURE 19–15
Configuration report for the RWASOFT NetWare server.

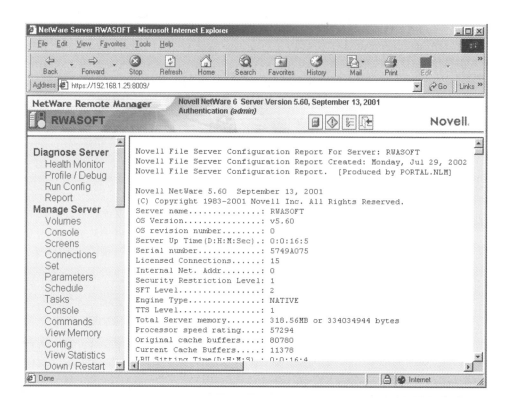

NetWare 5 expands print services to allow for notification of print job completion or status, enhanced communication between printers and clients (printer features are shared), and support for multiple operating systems. An online database of printer drivers is also provided to assist with new printer installations.

NetWare Client Software

Objective 4-4

In addition to one or more NetWare servers, there will be many NetWare clients on the network taking advantage of the services provided. Windows users can install NetWare client software and have access to the power of NetWare while still being part of a Windows network environment.

Figure 19–16 shows the new items found in the Network Neighborhood window after the NetWare client software has been installed. NetWare's icons exist side by side with Windows 98's icon for the Waveguide machine.

FIGURE 19–16
Network Neighborhood window showing NetWare entries Rwa_tree, research, and Rwasoft.

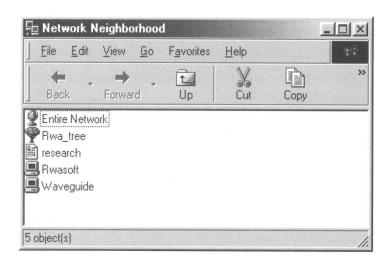

Clicking on Entire Network shows additional NetWare items, as illustrated in Figure 19–17. The NetWare Servers folder contains icons for NetWare servers running on the LAN, while the Novell Directory Services folder contains the installed directory services available.

FIGURE 19–17
Contents of Entire Network window showing NetWare folders.

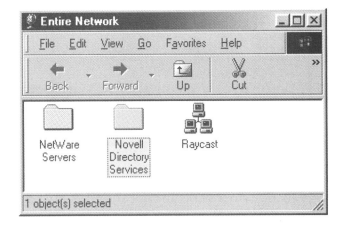

Clicking on the NetWare Servers folder opens the window shown in Figure 19–18, which indicates a single NetWare server (Rwasoft) on the network.

FIGURE 19–18
Contents of the NetWare Servers folder.

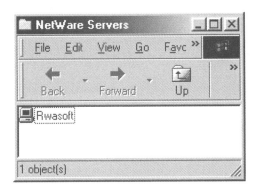

Right-clicking on the Rwasoft computer and selecting Properties generates the window shown in Figure 19–19. Notice all the interesting and useful connection information provided, such as the server name and version, IP address and port number, and client name.

FIGURE 19–19
NetWare Connection Information window.

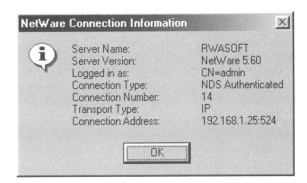

Clicking on the rwasoft icon brings up the window shown in Figure 19–20. Here you see that the NetWare server is sharing two folders and network printing capabilities. As with ordinary Windows folders, clicking on either folder will show its contents.

FIGURE 19–20
Content of the Rwasoft machine
(the NetWare server).

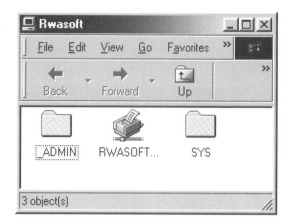

The high level of interoperability between NetWare and Windows is apparent, since the NetWare server and its files appear and operate in a fashion identical to those of a Windows computer. Software clients for Windows are available for download from Novell's Web site. You may also install NetWare network services using the Network applet in Control Panel. The NetWare network services available in Windows are illustrated in Figure 19–21.

FIGURE 19–21
Choosing a NetWare network
service to install.

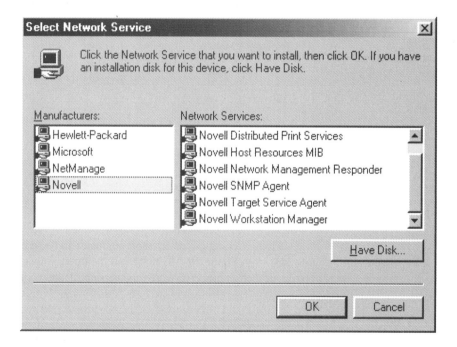

Objective 3-2

Note that clients for other network operating systems, such as UNIX, Linux, and the Macintosh, are also available. The same services are not available on all operating systems, with Windows and Linux being more heavily supported.

Figure 19–22 shows the context-sensitive menu that appears after right-clicking on the NetWare icon (N) in the system tray. Note all the different features accessible from the menu. Other NetWare properties can be examined and/or modified by selecting Novell NetWare Client properties in the Network window under Control Panel.

Adding a NetWare Server to a LAN

Objective 3-1

Adding a NetWare server to a LAN is a simple matter of selecting the network protocol to use with the server (IPX/SPX or TCP/IP), obtaining a static network address for the

FIGURE 19-22
NetWare client controls.

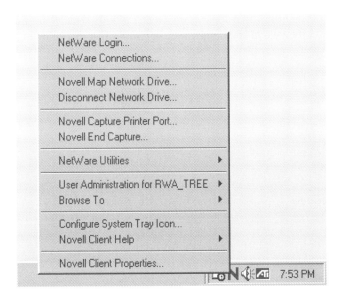

NetWare server from the LAN administrator, and entering the server address during installation. Because NetWare supports CIFS, NFS, and AFP, the NetWare server is ready for use by Windows, UNIX/Linux, and Macintosh computers as soon as the server is connected and booted up.

Connecting to a NetWare Server

Objective 3-2

A workstation connecting to a NetWare server may do so by installing the appropriate client software and using the NetWare logon screen or by accessing the NetWare server through an Internet connection. The client software network parameters are accessible through the Network applet in Control Panel. During installation, the user is asked to enter a preferred NetWare server. The server's address or name can be entered, or no NetWare server can be specified. The logon client will search for NetWare servers to connect to and offer a list of choices.

■ OPENVMS

The OpenVMS operating system was originally designed for VAX and Alpha computer systems manufactured by Digital Equipment Corporation (DEC). The OpenVMS operating system is still a popular choice for many customers such as universities and businesses. Network services provided by OpenVMS include the capability to connect computers together to form clusters of computers that act as one computer. This allows for computers to be added and removed from the cluster without affecting the overall operation of the system.

The native network in a DEC environment is called DECnet. In a DECnet network, computers are assigned a node number and an area number. Node numbers can be in the range between 1 and 1023. Area numbers range between 1 and 63. A total of almost 65,000 nodes can participate in a DECnet network. A node can be of two types, a router or an end node. A router accepts and forwards messages from the end nodes and other routers to their destinations.

Objective 4-1

Most OpenVMS computer systems run the TCP/IP network protocols in addition to DECnet. Many different TCP/IP stacks are available for the OpenVMS operating system. Each provides the capability to connect OpenVMS to the Internet. These packages generally include SMTP, FTP, and Telnet TCP/IP protocol application programs. Basic connectivity programs like PING, TRACERT, and NSLOOKUP are provided as well. A sample execution of nslookup on OpenVMS to review the MX type DNS records for suny-broome.edu and binghamton.edu looks like the following:

```
$ nslookup
Default Server:  ins1.milw.twtelecom.net
Address:  216.136.95.3

> set query=mx
> sunybroome.edu
Server:  ins1.milw.twtelecom.net
Address:  216.136.95.3

sunybroome.edu   preference = 30, mail exchanger = mail.iplt.twtelecom.net
sunybroome.edu   preference = 10, mail exchanger = sbccab.cc.sunybroome.edu
sunybroome.edu   preference = 20, mail exchanger = mail.milw.twtelecom.net
sunybroome.edu   nameserver = ins1.milw.twtelecom.net
sunybroome.edu   nameserver = ins1.iplt.twtelecom.net
mail.iplt.twtelecom.net inet address = 216.136.95.20
sbccab.cc.sunybroome.edu        inet address = 172.16.0.2
mail.milw.twtelecom.net inet address = 216.136.95.4
ins1.milw.twtelecom.net inet address = 216.136.95.3
ins1.iplt.twtelecom.net inet address = 216.136.95.19

> binghamton.edu
Server:  ins1.milw.twtelecom.net
Address:  216.136.95.3

binghamton.edu   preference = 0, mail exchanger = mail.binghamton.edu
binghamton.edu   nameserver = bingnet1.cc.binghamton.edu
binghamton.edu   nameserver = bingnet2.cc.binghamton.edu
mail.binghamton.edu     inet address = 128.226.1.18
bingnet1.cc.binghamton.edu       inet address = 128.226.1.11
bingnet2.cc.binghamton.edu       inet address = 128.226.1.18

> exit
```

In addition to the built-in TCP/IP applications like NSLOOKUP, both commercial and freeware Web servers are available for OpenVMS, allowing these computers to provide stable and reliable Web services. You may be surprised to find that many popular Web servers run the OpenVMS operating system.

■ MACINTOSH OS (MAC OS X)

Objective 3-1

The operating system for Apple Computers' Macintosh line of personal computers was first released in 1984. Mac OS X (version 10) came out in 2000. Initially based on the Motorola 680x0 series microprocessors, Mac OS has evolved to exploit the Power PC CPU.

Mac OS supports the use of multiple protocols, such as TCP/IP (through software called Open Transport) and Apple's own AppleTalk protocol, which enables Macintosh computers to share files and printers. AppleTalk running over Ethernet is called EtherTalk. A version of AppleTalk that operates over the serial port is called LocalTalk. Multiple Macintosh computers are daisy-chained through their serial ports when using LocalTalk.

Wireless networking is supported by Mac OS and is handled by a device called the AirPort. The AirPort is based on the IEEE 802.11 Direct Sequence Spread Spectrum standard and provides simultaneous connection for up to 10 users in a 150-foot radius from the AirPort. The maximum available bandwidth is 11 Mbps, with each channel having a 1 Mbps capacity.

The Web site http://www.threemacs.com provides an excellent networking tutorial for the Macintosh.

Mac OS X Details

Objective 3-1

Objective 3-2

The Mac OS X operating system is a powerful network operating system with features such as preemptive multitasking (interrupting one application to run another), protected and virtual memory, and symmetric multiprocessing (utilizing two or more CPUs). The Macintosh operating system has evolved over time from the initial 68,000 microprocessor-oriented System 1 (black and white graphics) to the most recent version of the Mac OS X that contains four layers, whose names and functions are as follows:

- **Foundation Layer:** Contains Darwin, the core component of the operating system
- **Graphics Layer:** Contains Quartz (2D graphics), OpenGL (3D graphics), and Quick-Time (for multimedia)
- **Application Layer:** Contains Classic (where Classic applications for OS 9.1 and earlier execute), Carbon (OS 8 and 9 applications), and Cocoa (for new OS X applications)
- **User Interface Layer:** Contains Aqua (the user interface, or desktop)

The Aqua user interface contains many new features compared to earlier interfaces, such as improved color, animation, and the Dock. At the heart of the OS X operating system is a product called Darwin. The Darwin product is an open-source version of BSD UNIX. Darwin is composed of the following components:

- Mach microkernel
- BSD UNIX subsystem
- File systems
- Networking
- I/O Kit

The Mach microkernel is based on Carnegie-Mellon University's Mach 3.0 that manages processor resources, scheduling, and memory, with a messaging-centered infrastructure. Darwin uses a customized version of 4.4 BSD-Lite2 kernel and Mach. It includes many POSIX APIs designed to provide the file system and network capabilities. BSD UNIX also provides the processing model, security elements, and support for multithreaded operation. Darwin uses a Virtual File System (VFS) that supports many different file systems, including:

- UNIX file system (UFS)
- Hierarchical File System (HFS)
- Universal Disk Format (UDF) for DVD drives
- ISO 9660 for CD-ROMs

VFS file names may be up to 255 characters long. Network access to the VFS is provided by the Apple File Sharing Protocol (AFP) and the Network File Service (NFS) protocol.

Darwin uses TCP/IP as the primary network infrastructure while still supporting AppleTalk. Darwin's I/O component is an object-oriented framework for developing SMP and real-time preemptive device drivers, including plug-and-play support for external devices such as digital video cameras, scanners, and secondary storage devices. Visit the Darwin Web site at http://www.opendarwin.org for more information about Darwin.

Interoperability

The Mac OS X operating system, as well as earlier versions, contains support for other network operating systems to enable file and print sharing over a TCP/IP network. Figure 19–23 shows a small LAN with each major type of computer and network operating system connected. A NetWare server manages file systems for the Macintosh, Windows, and UNIX/Linux clients.

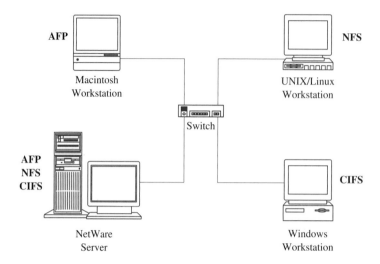

AFP AppleTalk Filing Protocol
CIFS Common Internet File System
NFS Network File System

The Macintosh uses the AppleTalk Filing Protocol (AFP) to share resources on a network. AFP provides a method to create files and directories; read, write, rename, and delete files; and access other file-related information. NetWare supports AFP, as well as CIFS and NFS for compatibility with Windows and UNIX/Linux clients. Microsoft provides AFP on Windows NT/2000 servers. Mac OS X Server 10.2 provides Open Directory, a network directory management feature based on LDAP, similar to the eDirectory of NetWare. The CIFS, AFP, and NFS protocols allow sharing with Windows, NetWare, and UNIX/Linux clients.

Installing OS X

Proof that the internal network interface and TCP/IP stack is working is given during installation of OS X. The user is asked to choose the method in which their computer connects to the Internet. The choices are:

• Telephone modem

• Local area network

• Cable modem

• DSL

• AirPort wireless

Some choices may not be available due to lack of installed hardware. For example, if there is no AirPort device connected, its choice will not be enabled. Mac OS X tests the connection once it is specified by the user. If the user has selected LAN, the installer indicates that the computer has received an IP address via DHCP. The user can choose to use the assigned address or enter a different one. Once the user has entered all registration information, the system uses the Internet to upload the information to Apple.

Figure 19–24 shows the Mac OS X desktop. At left is the Dock, an easily accessible starting point for many typical applications. The Dock can be moved to suit individual preferences.

FIGURE 19–24
Mac OS X desktop showing
built-in Ethernet network
settings.

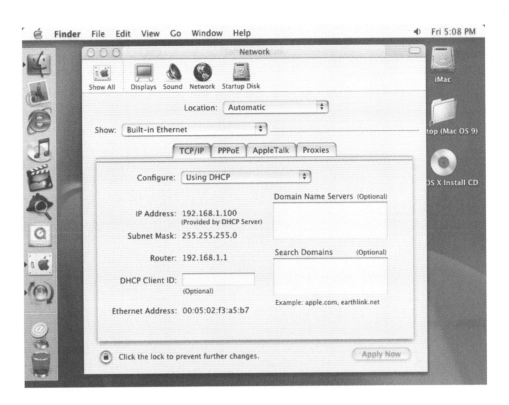

Macintosh Networking

Objective 4-4

In OS X, the parameters associated with networking are located in the Network window. Click on the Apple icon in the upper left corner of the desktop and select System Preferences from the drop-down menu. In the System Preferences window, click on the Network icon in the Internet & Network section. The Network window allows TCP/IP, PPPoE, AppleTalk, and Proxies to be configured for a specific type of Internet connection. From the Show menu, select the appropriate Internet connection (internal modem, Ethernet, AirPort, etc.). For TCP/IP, static and dynamic IP address assignment is possible. There are four options in the TCP/IP Configure menu: Manually, Manually using DHCP Router, Using DHCP, and Using BOOTP. The Manually option requires the user to enter the IP address, subnet mask, and router (default gateway) IP address. The Manually using DHCP Router option only requires the user to enter an IP address, since the computer gets the subnet mask and router IP address automatically via DHCP. The Using DHCP and Using BOOTP options do not require the user to enter any information.

The TCP/IP parameters for the internal modem provide only two configuration choices: Manually and Using PPP. The Manually option requires the user to enter an IP address. The Using PPP option does not require any input from the user. When the internal modem is selected, two additional selections, PPP and Modem, are available. The PPP option allows the user to enter the ISP telephone number, account name, and password. The Modem option is used to configure the internal modem (tone or pulse dialing, sound on or off, compression-enabled) and even select a different modem from a list.

The PPPoE option available in the Ethernet interface requires the user to enter the PPPoE ISP account name and password.

AppleTalk configuration settings are illustrated in Figure 19–25.

Note that AppleTalk settings are not available when the internal modem is selected. After AppleTalk is made active by the user, the AppleTalk Zone is selected and the computer's Node and Network IDs are configured manually or automatically.

Proxy servers are services positioned between a user and the Internet to provide additional security and administrative control. Several proxy services are offered by Mac OS X. Proxies are configured using the screen shown in Figure 19–26.

FIGURE 19–25
AppleTalk configuration settings.

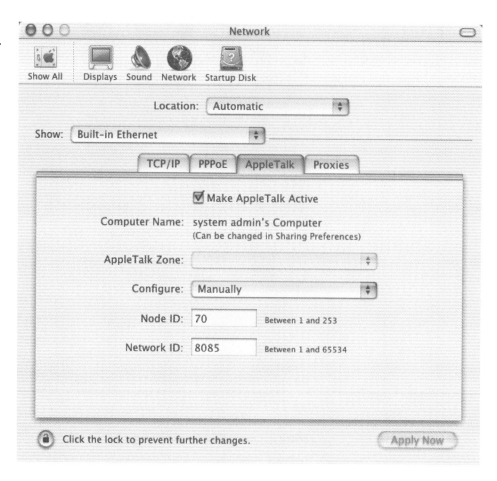

FIGURE 19–26
An interface used to adjust proxy settings.

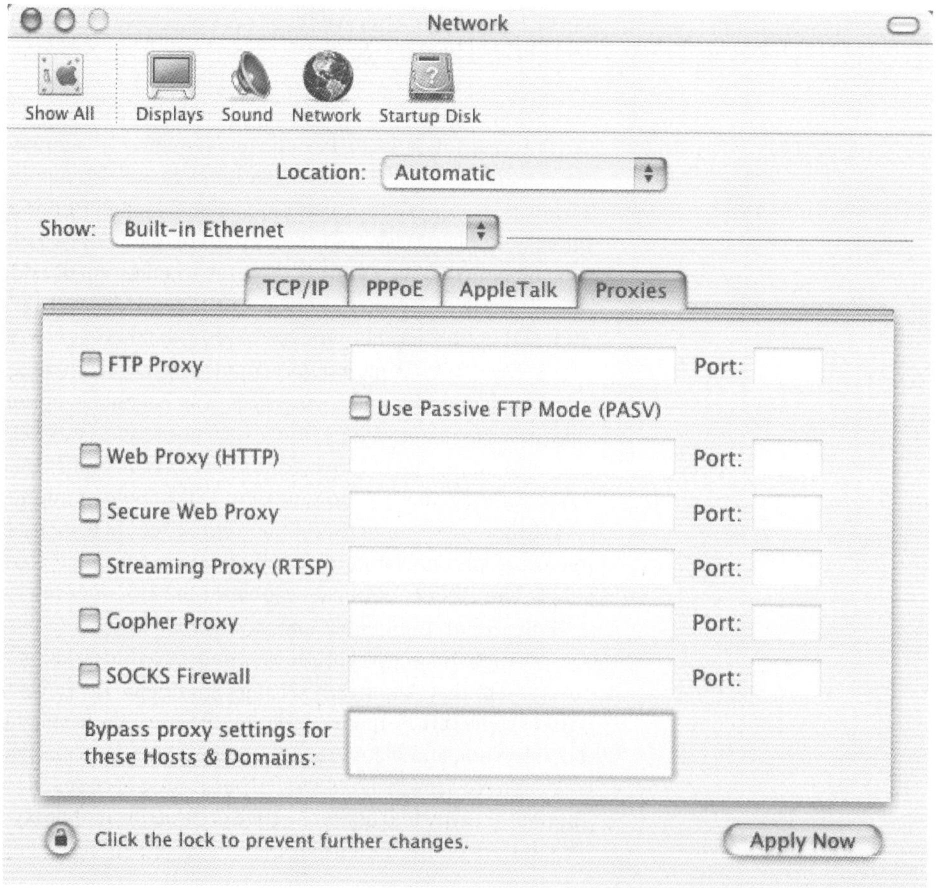

Active network ports available on a Macintosh computer are shown in the Network window illustrated in Figure 19–27.

FIGURE 19–27
Viewing the active network ports.

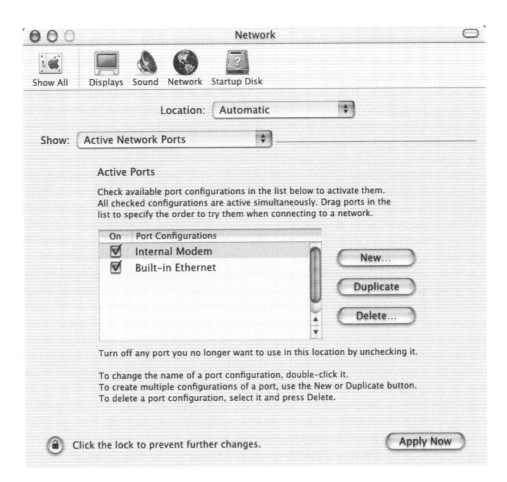

Open Transport

In older versions of the Mac OS, the Open Transport Communications Architecture was used to enable networking. Based on industry-wide standards, Open Transport integrates three key standards: the X/Open Transport Interface (XTI) and Data Link Provider Interface (DLPI) APIs from the X/Open Group, and STREAMS from UNIX System V. XTI is the POSIX- and XPG3-compliant API used to create network-enabled applications. In addition, the XTI API provides an extended version of the API that integrates support for object-oriented development using C++. Open Transport includes a direct port of UNIX Streams, providing an easy method to port code from UNIX to the Mac.

Open Transport includes the AppleTalk and TCP/IP control panels that replace the Network and MacTCP control panels used in previous versions of the Macintosh operating system. Open Transport can be used on any Macintosh computer that uses a PowerPC processor, or a 68030 or higher processor. Note that Open Transport is required on Macintosh computers that use the PCI bus.

A few of the most important benefits of using the Open Transport Communications Architecture begin with compatibility with existing network-based applications. A new user interface makes it easy to configure networking components and allows for reconfiguration and restarting of networking services without restarting the computer. In addition, Open Transport integrates serial communications and modems (to incorporate remote or dial-up networking). With Open Transport software installed on a computer, users can use more than one network protocol simultaneously. For example, AppleTalk can be used to communicate with network printers and TCP/IP can be used to connect to the Internet.

File Systems

When installing Mac OS X, the user is given a choice of using the Mac OS Extended file system or the UNIX file system. These two file systems are not the same, and their differences may affect how the computer behaves in a network where files are shared.

The Mac OS Extended file system (also called HFS Plus) allows file names up to 255 characters. A colon (:) may not be used in the file name, as it is reserved to indicate a file folder. In addition, although the period is accepted as a valid file name symbol, by convention a period is used to begin the name of a driver file. File names do not require extensions, as DOS, Windows, and UNIX/Linux files do. Instead, a signature stored with the file keeps track of the creator and format of the file using two 4-letter codes. The creator code is used to launch the application associated with the file, while the format code identifies the format of the file.

Files consist of two parts: a data fork and a resource fork. The data fork contains the data used by the file (such as the ASCII codes for a block of text) and the resource fork specifies resources used by the file (such as fonts). Two file formats, MacBinary and Bin-Hex, may be used to transfer Macintosh files to other file systems.

The case of the characters in a file name is preserved, but the names are not case sensitive. Thus, the two files "net stuff" and "Net Stuff" may not be stored in the same folder. Compare this with the UNIX file system, which is case sensitive and will treat "net stuff" and "Net Stuff" as different files and allow both to be stored in the same folder.

Some specific parameters of the OS Extended file system include:

- Maximum number of volumes: 20
- Maximum volume and data fork size: 2 terabytes
- Maximum resource fork size: 16 MB
- Maximum number of files: 2 billion
- Maximum number of files and/or folders in a folder: 32,767

To access the Macintosh file system over the network, file sharing must be enabled. To enable file sharing, go to System Preferences and click on the Sharing folder in the Internet & Network section. You can then enable file and Web sharing, remote access, and FTP. The AppleTalk computer name for your system can be entered in the Sharing folder as well. Click on Go and then select Connect to Server to locate a file server to connect to. Max OS X will search the local network for servers or allow you to enter the server name or IP address.

Print Services

Mac OS X offers built-in support for USB and network-based printers. The system automatically configures the printer when Print is chosen from within an application. Mac OS X Server uses native printing protocols: LPR for Mac OS X and other UNIX clients, SMB (Samba) for Windows operating system clients, and AppleTalk for older Mac OS 8 and Mac OS 9 systems.

Shared printers can also be added to an LDAP directory service to make it easy for Mac OS X systems to find network printers. The workgroup manager utility allows for printers to be set up throughout an organization, with controls to define which printers are available to which users, groups, and computers.

The Mac OS X print server has the following capabilities:

- Support for AppleTalk LaserWriter printers
- Support for PostScript printers supporting the LaserWriter printer driver 8.0 or later
- Support for LPR/LPD-compatible printers
- Support for LPR/LPD protocol for TCP/IP printing using port 515

Limitations of the print server include the following:

- Maximum number of attached printers: 30
- Maximum number of print queues: 10
- Maximum number of concurrent printer connections: 32

- Maximum number of jobs in queue: 500
- Maximum log file size: 64K

Using the Print Monitor utility, print queues can be monitored remotely across an entire network. The Print Monitor provides a quick method to get information about each printer, such as the number of jobs currently in the queue, printer status, and the enabled network protocols. Print queues can also be added, put on hold, and modified very quickly and easily.

Information about the jobs in an individual print queue can be examined using the Queue Monitor utility. The Queue Monitor displays information about all current print jobs including the status of the current print job, the user name who submitted it, and the number of pages in each print job. These print services are an important feature of the Mac OS X operating system.

Security

Objective 2-13

Security on the Mac OS X operating system is provided by Darwin. Darwin offers Kerberos authentication, Secure Shell (OpenSSH), secure Web transactions using OpenSSL, and file security with UNIX BSD-style permissions. Apple treats security issues very seriously and encourages security-related issues to be reported directly to Apple Security, CERT® Coordination Center (CERT/CC), or the Forum of Incident Response and Security Teams (FIRST).

To increase user security, Apple has introduced a secure key chain. The secure key chain is used to manage a user's list of all user names and passwords. The key chain stores all user information necessary to log onto file servers, Web servers, and FTP servers. When a user logs into the Mac OS X, the system automatically opens the key chain. Using the key chain, the user does not have to enter user names and passwords to access sensitive data. Mac OS X can also be set to lock the key chain when the system is inactive for a time or sleeping. When this occurs, the system will prompt the user for a password the next time that secure data is accessed. Other users who share the same system cannot use key chains or any of the data contained inside.

For high-security environments, users can encrypt part of the hard disk through use of a disk image. The disk image can be used by anyone who knows the password. To enable an encrypted disk, it is necessary to open the Disk Copy utility, create a new image file, and then set the encryption. The image then shows up as a volume on the desktop. When the key chain is locked or when a disk image is sent to another user, the image is secure. When your key chain is unlocked, files can be created, modified, and deleted just like any normal hard disk.

The following are several additional items to note about the security of a Mac OS X system:

- Apple products are configured for the security-conscious by turning off certain services by default. These services that are not enabled by default are Remote Login, File Sharing, and FTP.

- It is always in the best interest of the user to run the latest version of system software. Apple periodically releases security updates, which OS X will detect automatically and download from Apple to implement. Using the latest releases of the system software typically improves system security.

- It is recommended that users increase the security of systems by using firewall and virus protection software.

Emulation

In addition to support for original 680x0-based code for Classic applications, the Macintosh is able to emulate many versions of Windows and other operating systems. Some popular emulator applications are:

- Virtual PC (www.connectix.com) emulates DOS, Windows 95, 98, Me, NT, 2000, XP, and Linux in their own windows. Virtual PC emulates an MMX-equipped Pentium, Sound Blaster, VGA graphics, and other hardware components of a PC.

• Real PC (www.fwb.com) emulates DOS and allows installation of Windows 95 and 98. Real PC emulates an MMX-equipped Pentium.

Emulation of code, by nature, is slower than execution on the actual machine. So, plan on having a fast CPU (400 MHz or faster) and lots of RAM (256 MB or more) to get decent speed during emulation.

With all of the features just described, it is clear that the Mac OS X is a network operating system as full-featured as any other, including Windows and Linux. For updates and other information on Mac OS X, visit www.apple.com/macosx and www.apple.com/server.

■ OS/2 WARP

IBM came out with the OS/2 operating system about the same time that early versions of Windows were available. The latest version of OS/2 is called OS/2 Warp and provides for a stable 32-bit multitasking operation on Intel-based computers. OS/2 Warp contains a built-in TCP/IP stack and Microsoft LAN Manager capability. OS/2 Warp provides the ability to communicate with several other network operating systems including:

• Microsoft Windows

• Banyan Vines

• IBM LAN Server

• OS/2 Warp Server

• DECnet

OS/2 provides a stable scalable platform on which any business network can be built.

■ ADDITIONAL NETWORK OPERATING SYSTEMS

Table 19–2 lists several additional network operating systems and architectures. You are encouraged to discover more features through your own research.

TABLE 19–2

Features of additional network operating systems and architectures.

Operating System	Manufacturer	Features
BeOS	Be	• Enhanced for multimedia applications • Multiple file systems supported • Journaling to prevent loss of data
LANtastic	Artisoft	• Runs on most Windows platforms, OS/2, and DOS • Logs network resource accesses
SNA	IBM	• Systems Network Architecture • Enables different devices (mainframe, terminal, printer) to communicate with each other • Advanced Peer-to-Peer Networking (APPN) • Advanced Program-to-Program Computing (APPC)
Solaris	Sun Microsystems	• UNIX-based environment • Runs on Sun systems and x86 machines
VINES	Banyan Systems	• Virtual Network System, based on UNIX • Uses a global naming system called StreetTalk. Example: joetekk@helpdesk@rwasoftware • Communicates with SNA, TCP/IP, and AppleTalk networks
XNS	Xerox	• Xerox Network Services • Five-layer protocol

■ TROUBLESHOOTING TECHNIQUES

Selecting a network operating system is based on many factors, including the features provided and the complexity of the installation and management procedures. Is the operating system centralized or distributed? Will the network be strictly TCP/IP or should multiple protocols be supported? What file system properties are desired?

Whatever the answers are, the end result is an operating system that will require specific troubleshooting methods to diagnose and repair problems.

■ SELF-TEST

1. The NetWare operating system runs on top of what operating system?
   a. DOS
   b. 3DES
   c. OS X
   d. Windows 3.1

2. NetWare's proprietary routing protocol is called _____.
   a. UDP
   b. IPX
   c. IP
   d. NWP

3. The NetWare server must be shut down to perform the type of upgrade called _____.
   a. partial migration
   b. across-the-wire migration
   c. in-place migration
   d. full migration

4. What will happen if during the NetWare 6 installation process it is discovered that the NIC is not supported?
   a. The installation will complete.
   b. The NIC will be upgraded automatically.
   c. The installation will not continue.
   d. The NDS will take over.

5. NetWare uses _____ to allow users to access global resources regardless of their physical location.
   a. WINS
   b. NIS
   c. NDS
   d. NFS

6. NetWare uses _____ to move data from one location to another and maintain effective use of hard drive space.
   a. partial migration
   b. data migration
   c. full migration
   d. data miners

7. What type of NetWare servers provide the correct time to NetWare clients?
   a. Reference
   b. Primary
   c. Secondary
   d. Single-reference

8. A Windows client computer maps a network drive to a NetWare server and participates in file sharing through the use of the _____ protocol.
   a. NIS
   b. CIFS

   c. SMB

   d. SYS

9. NetWare servers participate in a SAN using special system area network cards that implement the _____ and _____ layers of the OSI model. (Choose two.)

   a. Physical

   b. Data Link

   c. Network

   d. Transport

10. True or False: When a NetWare server is shut down it sends a message to each connected station.

11. Which of the following is **not** an assignable NetWare user right on a NetWare file system?

   a. Erase

   b. Access Control

   c. Modify

   d. Concatenate

12 True or False: NDS security provides encryption of login passwords.

13. NDS trees can be browsed by a Windows 98 machine if either _____ or _____ software is configured. (Choose two.)

   a. Novell client for Windows

   b. Microsoft client for IPX

   c. Microsoft client for Novell NetWare

   d. IP for NetWare

14. Internet management of eDirectory users, trees, licenses, and print/DHCP servers is accomplished by the NetWare 6 _____ feature.

   a. iPrint

   b. iFolder

   c. iManage

   d. iDirect

15. The NetWare icon in the system tray appears as a(n) _____.

   a. N

   b. hand

   c. hand on computer

   d. bird

16. True or False: Windows and NetWare computer system files and operating methods make sharing and connecting between these two systems difficult at best.

17. True or False: OpenVMS operating systems provide the ability to connect computers together to form clusters of computers that act as one computer.

18. MAC OS supports the use of multiple protocols like TCP/IP through the use of software called _____.

   a. Open Transport

   b. Apple Transport

   c. Core

   d. Peel

19. The maximum available bandwidth of Mac OS wireless networking is _____.

   a. 1.544 Mbps

   b. 4 Mbps

   c. 11 Mbps

   d. 14 Mbps

20. The Mac OS X desktop contains the _____, which is an easily accessible starting point for many typical applications.

   a. Core

   b. Dock

    c. Taskbar

    d. Skin

21. An OS X user is making choices for the method by which he will connect to the Internet. The TCP/IP stack is working properly. His preferred method is LAN. Why is his preferred method not included in the available Internet connection choices?

    a. LocalTalk is down.

    b. The Internet gateway is down.

    c. The hardware is not installed.

    d. The IPX address is not entered.

22. Open Transport can be used on any Macintosh computer that uses a(n) _____ processor.

    a. PowerMac

    b. ATI

    c. PC1

    d. PowerPC

23. Which of the following are file system choices given to the Mac OS X user? (Choose two.)

    a. UNIX

    b. NTFS

    c. FAT

    d. MAC OS Extended

24. True or False: The Mac OS Extended file system preserves the case of file names, but the names of files are not case sensitive.

25. Match the printing protocol that Mac OS X uses for each of the following operating system clients:

Operating Systems	Printing Protocols
a. Mac OS X	1. AppleTalk
b. UNIX	2. SMB
c. Windows	3. LPR
d. Mac OS 8, OS 9	

Glossary

5-4-3 Rule.   An Ethernet LAN rule that stands for 5 segments, 4 repeaters, and 3 segments with nodes allowed in a single collision domain.

AO/DI.   Always On Dynamic ISDN. A technique used to help lower connection charges on an ISDN line.

ARP.   Address Resolution Protocol. A protocol used to discover the MAC address of a station based on its IP address.

ASCII.   American Standard Code for Information Interchange. A 7-bit code representing all alphanumeric and special codes required for text-based communication.

Autonomous System.   A single network or group of networks that is controlled by a single administrative authority.

Backbone Cable.   Main cable used to distribute network signals.

Baseband System.   A communication system in which a single carrier is used to exchange information. Ethernet is a baseband system.

BGP.   Border Gateway Protocol. An RFC-based exterior gateway protocol.

Bridge.   Essentially a two-port switch connecting two LANs that allows limited traffic in both directions.

Broadband System.   A communication system in which multiple carrier signals are used to exchange information. Cable television is an example of a broadband system.

Broadcast Storm.   An out-of-control flooding of the network with packets.

Broadcasting.   Transmitting a frame that is meant to be received by all stations on a network, not one specific station.

Browser.   An application capable of displaying Web pages in WYSIWYG format.

Bus Network.   A network where all stations share the same media.

Cable Modem.   A high-speed modem that provides the interface between television cable and a NIC.

Cable Tester.   A device that physically (and electronically) tests a cable for continuity, impedance, frequency response, or crosstalk.

Carrier Extension.   Technique used in Gigabit Ethernet to extend the minimum length of an Ethernet frame.

CD-Quality Sound.   CD-quality sound provides 44,100 samples per second. Each sample represents two channels (left and right) at 16 bits each.

CIDR.   Classless Inter-Domain Routing. A routing protocol that extends IP addressing by using a variable length network mask.

CGI.   Common Gateway Interface. A method for exchanging data between clients and servers over the World Wide Web.

Client.   A network station that requests services from a network server.

Cloud.   A graphic symbol used to describe a network without specifying the details of the internal connections.

Collision.   Two or more stations transmitting at the same time within the same collision domain.

Collision Domain.   A portion of a network where two or more stations transmitting at the same time will interfere with each other.

Combo Card.   A NIC that contains both 10BASE2 and 10BASE-T connections.

Congestion.   Too much traffic on a network, causing packets to be lost.

Convergence.   The amount of time required for changes in a network topology to be propagated to all routers.

CRC.   Cyclic redundancy check. An error detection scheme able to detect bit errors in streams of bits of varying length.

CSMA/CA.   Carrier Sense Multiple Access with Collision Avoidance. An IEEE 802.11 standard access method for wireless Ethernet.

CSMA/CD.   Carrier Sense Multiple Access with Collision Detection. An IEEE 802.3 standard access method used to share bandwidth among a maximum of 1024 stations. Two or more stations transmitting at a time will cause a collision, forcing random waiting periods before retransmission is attempted.

Cut-Through Switching.   A switching technique in which retransmission of a received packet begins as soon as the destination MAC address is received. Faster than store-and-forward switching.

Datagram.   A routable packet of data used in connectionless communication.

DHCP.   Dynamic Host Configuration Protocol. A protocol used to allocate IP addresses dynamically.

Diameter.   The total distance allowed in a collision domain.

Digital Certificate.   A digital identifier issued by a certification authority, consisting of a name, serial number, expiration dates, and public key of the certificate holder, which is used to establish a unique network identity.

Dijkstra's Algorithm.   An algorithm, developed by Edsger Dijkstra, which is used to compute the shortest paths in a graph. It or a variation of it is used by most link-state routing algorithms.

Distance-Vector Routing.   A routing algorithm used to compute the optimal route to a destination. Each router sends its complete routing table to each of its neighbors during each 30-second update period.

DNS.   Domain Name System. Protocol used to resolve a domain name, such as www.rwasoftware.com, into an IP address.

Domain.   A collection of networked computers managed by a central server.

Domain-Based Priority Access.   The access method used by 100VG-AnyLAN to poll stations in a round-robin fashion.

Dotted Decimal Notation.   This is another way to refer to an IP address.

EGP.   Exterior Gateway Protocol. A routing protocol used between autonomous systems.

E-Mail.   Electronic mail. Method used to exchange mail (including attachments) over a network.

Encoding.   A method of converting digital data into a different representation for transmission. Methods include Manchester, 8B6T, 4B5B, NRZI, PAM5x5, and 8B10B.

Ethernet.   LAN technology employing CSMA/CD to share access to the available bandwidth.

Fast Ethernet.   This is the term used for 100 Mbps Ethernet.

Fast Link Pulse.   Beginning with Fast Ethernet, fast link pulses are used to perform autonegotiation on a hardware link (such as a UTP cable).

FCS.   Frame check sequence. A 32-bit CRC value used to check the validity of a received frame.

FDDI.   Fiber-distributed data interface. A fiber-optic, 100 Mbps ring technology with a range of 200 kilometers (124 miles).

Fiber.   A communication media that uses two different types of plastic or glass to carry a beam of light modulated with information.

Firewall.   A program designed to control/limit the traffic into and out of a LAN.

Flooding Protocol.   The method used by many link-state routers to propagate information between routers.

FOIRL.   Fiber-optic inter-repeater link. The original specification for Ethernet communication over fiber.

Frame.   Structure used to transport data over a network. Contains source and destination addresses, data, and a 32-bit frame check sequence.

Frame Bursting.   Technique used in Gigabit Ethernet to send multiple frames in a small window of time.

FTP.   File Transfer Protocol. A protocol designed to enable reliable transfer of files between stations.

Fully Connected Network.   This network contains a link from each station to every other station.

GIF.   Graphics Interchange Format. A lossless image compression format allowing 256 colors.

Gigabit Ethernet.   This is the term used for 1000 Mbps Ethernet.

Hierarchy.   The number of levels in a network. Switches and routers add hierarchy to a network, hubs and repeaters do not.

HTML.   Hypertext markup language. A specific set of tags and syntax rules for describing a Web page in WYSIWYG format.

HTTP.   Hypertext Transport Protocol. The protocol used to exchange hypermedia (text, audio, video, images) over the Internet.

HTTPS.   A secure version of HTTP that incorporates SSL encryption technology.

Hub.   A multiport device that broadcasts frames received on one port to all other ports. All ports are in the same collision domain.

ICA.   Independent Connection Architecture. A low-bandwidth method of connecting thin clients to a network for centralized application processing.

ICMP.   Internet Control Message Protocol. A protocol used to report errors over the Internet.

ICS.   Internet Connection Sharing. A technique that allows multiple computers to share a single Internet connection.

IGP.   Interior Gateway Protocol. A routing protocol used within an autonomous system.

IMAP.   Internet Message Access Protocol. Another method for retrieving e-mail from a server.

Interframe Gap.   A deliberate gap of 96 bit times between successive Ethernet frames.

Internet.   A global collection of computer networks that allows any station to communicate with any other station.

IP.   Internet Protocol. This is the base protocol for TCP/IP. It is used to carry TCP, UDP, and many other higher-level protocols.

IP Address.   A 32-bit logical address of a station (host) on the network. An example IP address is 192.168.1.105.

IPSec.   IP Security. A set of protocols used to establish security in a TCP/IP environment.

ISDN.   Integrated Services Data Network. A telecommunications technology that provides two 64-Kbps full-duplex channels for data/voice in its basic-rate service.

ISO/OSI Network Model.   A standard seven-layer networking model that specifies the operations of each layer. The seven layers are 1. Physical, 2. Data-Link, 3. Network, 4. Transport, 5. Session, 6. Presentation, 7. Application.

ISP.   Internet service provider. A facility/organization that enables multiple users to connect to the Internet.

Jabber.   An out-of-control station transmitting garbage.

Jam Sequence.   A 32-bit sequence generated when a collision is detected, to guarantee all stations are notified of the collision.

JPEG.   Joint Photographic Experts Group. A lossy image compression format allowing 24-bit color.

Kerberos.   An authentication service that uses secret-key ciphers.

LAN.   Local area network. A collection of computers in a small geographical area.

Latency.   The delay between reception and retransmission of a packet that is associated with switches and routers.

Layer 3 Switching.   A special, high-speed switching/routing combination used on a LAN.

Link-State Routing.   A routing algorithm used to compute the optimal route to a destination. Each router broadcasts information about the cost of reaching each of its neighbors to all routers in the network.

LLC.   Logical Link Control. IEEE 802.2 standard for providing connectionless and connection-oriented sessions between two stations. LLC is the first sublayer in the Data-Link layer.

Logical Topology.   Describes the way logical addresses are allocated on a physical network and the routes used to transport information.

MAC Address.   Media access control address. A 48-bit physical address associated with every network interface. An example MAC address is 00-C0-F0-27-64-E2.

MAC Cloning.   A feature available on some cable-modem/routers that allows a user-supplied MAC address to be supplied by the router's upstream Ethernet interface instead of the MAC address provided by the manufacturer.

Manchester Encoding.   Technique used to encode 0s and 1s so that a signal transition occurs during every bit time. A 0 is represented by a low-to-high transition and a 1 is represented by a high-to-low transition.

MAU.   Multistation access unit. Device used to connect multiple stations to the same network.

Mbone.   Multicasting Backbone. A method for performing multicasting over the Internet.

MIME.   Multipurpose Internet Mail Extensions. Standard method for attaching many different types of media to an e-mail message.

Minifile.   A minimal file system used to read FAT or NTFS files during the boot process.

Modes.   The paths taken by each beam of light in a fiber. Multimode fiber allows multiple modes, whereas single-mode fiber allows only a single mode to pass through its core.

MPEG.   Moving Picture Experts Group. Standard encoding method for audio and video.

MP3.   MPEG Audio Layer 3. Encoding method allowing high-quality, low-bit-rate audio encoding.

MTU.   Maximum transmission unit. The maximum size of a frame on the network.

Multicasting. A method in which a single server stream is duplicated by routers and switches to multiple clients.

NAP. Network Access Point. A connection to the main Internet backbone.

NAS. Network Attached Storage. A high-capacity file storage device connected to a LAN and interoperable with most major network operating systems.

NAT. Network Address Translation. A technique where multiple inside network addresses are translated into one or more outside network addresses.

NBTSTAT. Utility program used to examine and modify the NetBEUI over TCP/IP protocol statistics.

NetBEUI. NetBIOS Extended User Interface. Protocol used to transport NetBIOS messages.

NetBIOS. Network Basic Input Output System. Low-level networking operations that enable network activities such as file and printer sharing.

NETSTAT. Utility program used to examine protocol statistics and display current TCP/IP network connections.

Network Diameter. The distance between the two farthest nodes in a LAN.

NIC. Network interface card. Electronic circuit used to connect a computer to the network.

Node. An individual device connected to a network.

NT1 Device. An ISDN Network Termination device used to electrically connect S/T interfaces with U interfaces.

NTFS. Windows NT File System. A file system used to efficiently and reliably process file transactions.

NTP. Network Time Protocol. A TCP/IP protocol used to synchronize the time between computers.

OSPF. Open Shortest Path First. An RFC-based link-state routing algorithm used by Interior and Exterior Gateways.

Parity. A bit indicating that the number of 1s contained in a block of data is even or odd. Used for error detection.

Peering Agreement. An agreement between two Internet providers that allows them to exchange traffic.

PGP. Pretty Good Privacy. A cryptographic utility that provides security to e-mail and files.

Physical Topology. Describes the actual hardware connections that make up the network.

Policy-Based Routing. Any type of routing that is based on factors other than the minimum number of hops or the shortest path.

POP. Point-of-presence. The location of an actual Internet connection.

POP3. Post Office Protocol. Used to receive e-mail from a mail server.

Port. A 16-bit number associated with a TCP or UDP application. Used to demultiplex the incoming packet stream.

PPP. Point-to-Point Protocol. A more advanced protocol than SLIP for serial connections.

Protocol. The rules for exchanging information between two objects (network devices, application programs).

Protocol Stack. A suite of protocols, such as TCP/IP.

PUSH. A TCP flag that initiates the delivery of all data in the pipeline between the client and the server.

RAID. Redundant Array of Inexpensive Disks. A technique for using multiple hard drives to implement fast, reliable data transfers.

RARP.   Reverse Address Resolution Protocol. A protocol used to determine the IP address of a station based on its MAC address.

RAS.   Remote Access Server. Dial-up server function provided by Windows NT/2000.

Realization.   The point in time at which a router is aware of the complete network topology.

RFC.   Request for Comments. Official standards for the Internet.

Ring Network.   A network in which all stations are connected in a circular ring (each station has exactly two connections).

RIP.   Routing Information Protocol. An RFC-based routing protocol based on a distance-vector algorithm.

Route Aggregation.   The method used by CIDR to extend the IP addressing scheme. Several routes are arranged in such a way that a single route is advertised by a router.

Router.   A multiport device that forwards packets between ports based on their IP address. Each port connects to a different LAN, and possibly even different LAN technologies.

Routing Table.   A table stored in the memory of a router that indicates the best route to use to forward a packet of data to the destination.

Runt.   A frame that is smaller than the minimum frame size.

SAM.   Security Accounts Manager. Used to administer security in a Windows NT domain environment.

SAN.   Storage Area Network. A network dedicated to data storage, independent of the network accessing the data.

Segment.   A portion of a network that may or may not contain nodes. Ethernet allows up to five segments to be connected in series.

Server.   A network station that provides services to clients.

SLIP.   Serial Line Interface Protocol. A protocol for exchanging TCP/IP over a serial connection such as a telephone modem.

Slot Time.   The time required to transmit 512 bits of data.

SMB.   Server Message Block. Main portion of a NetBIOS message.

SMTP.   Simple Mail Transport Protocol. Method used to reliably exchange electronic mail between networks.

SNMP.   Simple Network Management Protocol. A protocol used to manage network components.

Socket.   A networking port connection asociated with a TCP/IP application.

Spanning Tree.   An algorithm used to create nonlooping paths between bridges, switches, and routers on a network.

SSL.   Secure Socket Layer. An encryption technique that was developed by Netscape to facilitate secure communication between clients and servers on the Internet.

S/T Interface.   Four-wire interface that connects an ISDN device to an NT1 device.

Stackable.   Refers to a hub or switch that can be connected with other hubs or switches to make a device with more network ports.

Star Network.   A network in which all stations connect to one or more central hubs.

Store-and-Forward Switching.   A switching technique in which the entire frame is received and stored before it is retransmitted. Slower than cut-through switching.

Subnet.   A small portion of a larger network.

Supernetting.   A route made available through the use of CIDR.

Switch.   A multiport device that forwards frames to a specific port based on their destination MAC address. Each port is in its own collision domain.

System Area Network Card.   A special network adapter (also called a host bus adapter) used in SANs to enable high-speed data transfers.

Tap. Used to make a connection with coaxial cable. The tap may be a BNC T-connector or a vampire tap.

TCP. Transmission Control Protocol. Connection (session or stream)-oriented communication. Reliable exchange of data.

TCP/IP. Suite of protocols that enable communication over LANs and WANs.

Telnet. A protocol used to emulate a network virtual terminal.

Thicknet. RG-11 coaxial cable used in 10BASE5 networks.

Thin Client. A workstation (typically diskless) that receives software downloaded from a network server (operating system and applications).

Thinnet. RG-58 coaxial cable used in 10BASE2 networks.

TLS. Transport Layer Security. A protocol designed to enhance the capabilities of current SSL encryption technology.

Token Ring. An IEEE 802.5 standard LAN technology in which information circulates in a closed ring of stations.

Topology. The manner in which network components are connected.

Transceiver. A device capable of transmitting and receiving data.

Trust Relationship. Agreement between two or more Windows NT/2000 servers that determines the allowable interaction between servers regarding resources and users.

Tunnel. A logical connection between two nodes in a virtual private network.

U Interface. Two-wire ISDN interface found on wall jacks in the U.S. Connects to an NT1 device.

UDP. User Datagram Protocol. Connectionless communication; unreliable exchange of data.

URL. Uniform resource locator. A path to a specific station on the Internet, such as http://www.rwasoftware.com.

UTP. Unshielded twisted pair. Cable used in 10BASE-T Ethernet, as well as Fast and Gigabit Ethernet.

Virtual Circuit. A prearranged path through a network that is used for a single session.

VLAN. Virtual LAN. A logical network consisting of a subset of the devices connected to a LAN.

VPN. Virtual private network. A network that uses public networking facilities to carry private data. The data is encrypted before transmission.

WAN. Wide area network. A collection of LANs connected via routers over a large geographical area.

WAV. Wave file. Windows standard audio encoding file format.

Windows Socket. Networking API for the Windows operating system.

WINS. Windows Internet Naming Service. A dynamic database that maps Windows machine names (e.g., \\waveguide) to IP addresses.

Wireless Network. An IEEE 802.11 standard network using high-frequency radio signals or infrared lasers instead of wires. Typically, multiple mobile stations communicate with a single base station.

Workgroup. A set of workstations that exist as peers on the network with the capability to share local resources (disks, printers, etc.) with other users.

WWW. World Wide Web. A logical collection of computers on the Internet supported by HTTP.

WYSIWYG. What You See Is What You Get.

Appendix A:

Technical
BULLETIN

Belden

The impact of typical installation stresses on cable performance

TB-66

Unlike traditional

unbonded-pair cables

which degrade in

performance when

put through the

rigors of installation,

tests show that

Belden's patented

Bonded-Pair cables

perform to the same

high standards

whether just off the

reel or installed in

the wall.

When looking at the guaranteed performance on a cable's data sheet, it is expected that the cable will deliver that same performance after it has been installed in the wall. Ultimately, this is the only performance that matters; Category 5e cable that yields 5e performance on the reel but provides only Category 5 performance after installation is of little value.

Installation can alter cable performance. When cables are installed, they are bent around corners, pulled on, and can kink when coming off the reel. All of these installation factors change the physical properties of the cable, which in turn most often degrade the cables' electrical performance. Belden has found that many unbonded-pair cables

that pass their respective performance standards on the reel will fail those standards after a typical installation.

Test Setup

In order to demonstrate the effects a typical installation can have on an unbonded-pair cable, Belden selected several industry-leading Category 5e and Category 6 cables and subjected them to the Installation Stress Test described below. Additionally, Belden conducted identical tests on its DataTwist® 350, MediaTwist®, and DataTwist 600e Bonded-Pair cables.

Initially, 328-foot samples of each cable were tested directly off the reel, without being subjected to any stress. These tests represented the laboratory, or "on-the-reel," performance of the

cable. To simulate pulling the cable through and around cable trays, conduit, office furniture, ceilings, and walls, each cable was then run through a series of controlled bends and twists. This replicated routing the cable from the closet to the workstation outlet. Then, a 10-foot length of the cable was loosely coiled into a 12-inch service loop at the workstation end. At this point, the end of the cable was placed into a standard single-gang outlet box. The cables were tested again to identify any changes in the performance of the cable. The cables were handled without violating the installation guidelines specified in TIA/EIA 568-B.

Simulated Bends   Service Loop   Outlet Box

Courtesy of Belden Electronics Division. Reprinted with permission.

The Results

The graphs here show the striking results of Belden's tests. All of the cables tested performed within industry specifications when initially pulled off the reel; however, when the unbonded-pair cables were subjected to the installation stress test, the performance of these cables degraded sharply. In many cases, the unbonded-pair cables performed below specifications and actually failed the cable requirements.

On the other hand, the Belden Bonded-Pair cables exhibited the same high degree of performance whether just off the reel or installed in the wall. It is the type of performance one should expect from cables in actual use—and positive proof that Belden cables are durable and created to meet a higher standard of excellence day in and day out.

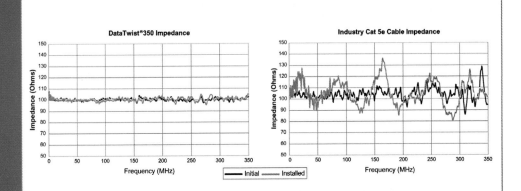

Impedance: Much has been made about "tuned" cabling systems where all of the components in the channel are "matched" to 100 ohms. Optimally, the impedance of a cable should be centered at 100 ohms.

As the charts indicate, after installation the impedance of the unbonded-pair cables quickly deviates from 100 ohms. In some instances, impedance in the unbonded-pair cables deviated as much as 35 ohms after installation. Fluctuations in a cable's impedance are directly related to decreased Return Loss performance.

In contrast to the unbonded-pair cables, the impedance of Belden's Bonded-Pair cables remained stable around 100 ohms before and after installation.

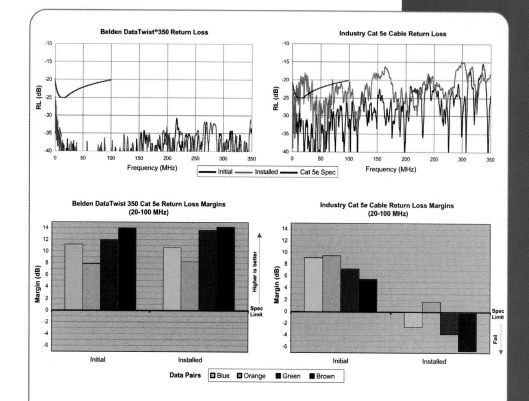

Return Loss: With full-duplex protocols such as Gigabit Ethernet, Return Loss is a critical electrical characteristic because both ends of a pair transmit and receive signals simultaneously. A cable with poor Return Loss values can significantly impact the performance of an active network, reduce network efficiency, and lead to excessive bit error rates.

Belden's tests found that, in many cases, the unbonded-pair cables that initially passed industry requirements for Return Loss "off-the-reel" failed after installation. For example, in the chart above, the unbonded-pair cable's Return Loss values degraded by more than 12 dB—Return Loss performance more than 15 times worse than prior to installation.

Unlike the unbonded-pair cables, Belden's Bonded-Pair cables exhibited little change in Return Loss performance.

NEXT & PSNEXT: As the conductors of a pair are separated due to installation stresses such as bending, pulling, and coiling, the pair takes on the characteristics of an antenna, both radiating and receiving signals. When one pair in a cable receives the emitted signal from another pair, it is referred to as crosstalk. The NEXT & PSNEXT performance of a cable are important due to their negative impact upon multiple pair protocols.

In Belden's testing, crosstalk values were found to change as much as 6 dB, almost four times, in unbonded-pair cables. In contrast, Belden's Bonded-Pair cables demonstrated marginal change in crosstalk performance from "off-the-reel" to after installation.

Technical BULLETIN

Belden

TB-66

Why Bonded-Pairs are Better

The ideal UTP cable should be structurally stable—especially during installation. Topping the list of construction features that provide desired cable consistency and stability are uniform conductor-to-conductor spacing and twisting of the pairs. When the conductors of a twisted pair become separated, impedance mismatches, Return Loss, and crosstalk problems arise. In order to prevent this separation from occurring and to provide structural stability, Belden developed its patented Bonded-Pair technology. As the picture illustrates, even when a Bonded-Pair cable is bent, its conductor-to-conductor spacing remains stable. The benefits of bonded pairs and their immunity to everyday installation stresses such as bending, coiling, and pulling are demonstrated in the illustrations.

Buyer Beware

A user specifies a certain performance level for the components of a network based upon that network's needs and demands. If the networking infrastructure dictates the need for a physical layer that performs at Category 6 levels, the user must be able to ensure that after the installation, all of the components are performing at that level. When the performance of a component in the network is compromised, overall system performance can be jeopardized.

Based on Belden's studies, if a user specifies an unbonded-pair Category 6 cable, in many cases the cable will not yield Category 6 performance after installation. In other words, the user would be specifying a component for the networking infrastructure that may not meet the network's requirements. Only Belden's

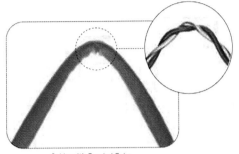

Cable with Bonded-Pairs

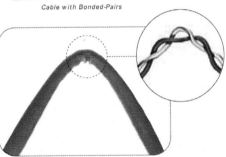

Cable without Bonded-Pairs

Bonded-Pair cables provide this level of assurance.

These studies reinforce the need for a cable to be able to maintain its performance level in order to compensate for unseen factors that can inhibit the performance of a cabling system (i.e. substandard patch cords and NICs, non-compliant installation practices, and environmental noise factors like EMI and RFI). Choosing a cable that provides the performance needed after installation, not just "off-the-reel", also protects the end user's technology investment for the future. It helps ensure that the cable does not quickly become obsolete — a very real possibility given the rapidly evolving nature of information systems.

For More Information:

Belden Electronics Division
Technical Support
1-800-Belden1 or 1-800-Belden3
www.belden.com

© Copyright 2001, Belden Inc.

Appendix B:
Web Resources

URL	Company Name	Description of Site
www.internet2.edu		Consortium of 205 universities partnered with business and industry
www.100vg.com		Web site promoting VG-anyLAN
www.10gea.org/Tech-whitepapers.htm		Site devoted to the 10 Gigabit Ethernet Alliance
www.protocols.com		Site with information about network protocols
www.whatis.techtarget.com		Definitions of networking term
www.grc.com	Gibson Research Corporation	Site containing links to virus and other security issues
www.ietf.org/rfc.html	Internet Engineering Task Force	Links to RFCs
www.mplsrc.com	Multiprotocol Label Switching	Label switching information
www.ietf.org/ids.by.wg/mpls.html		IETF Web site about Multiprotocol Label Switching
www.internettrafficreport.com		Internet Traffic Report monitors data flow around the world
www.caida.org	Cooperative Association for Internet Data Analysis	Provides tools and analysis promoting a robust global Internet infrastructure
web.mit.edu/network/pgp.html		Web site for downloading PGP (Pretty Good Privacy) software
www.zonelabs.com		Software firewalls company
www.cert.org		Internet security issues and reporting method
www.ipswitch.com		Company offering FTP and network monitoring software
www.intel.com		Site related to Intel processors
www.microsoft.com		Popular operating system site
www.internic.net		Information regarding domain name registration services
www.apache.org		Support for Apache software
www.quantum.com		Scalable storage data solutions
www.comptia.org		Site devoted to network certification
www.ethereal.com		Free Protocol Analyzer site

URL	Company Name	Description of Site
www.cisco.com		Leading network equipment and training site
www.threemacs.com		Web site explaining MacIntosh networking
www.samba.org		Samba open source information and resources
http://www.tldp.org/		Linux operating systems
www.techfest.com/networking/prot.htm		Network protocol information
www.vig.prenhall.com		Link to publisher's web site
www.yahoo.com		Popular Web search engine
www.news.netcraft.com		Internet services company
www.netscape.com		Popular Web browser
www.gnome.org		Link to popular Linux desktop environment site
www.kde.org		Link to popular Linux desktop environment site
www.fwb.com		RAID toolkit
www.apple.com/macosx		Mac OS X site
www.apple.com/server		Apple Server product line
www.Javasoft.com		Java tips and instruction
www.citrix.com		Secure access to applications or information over the Internet

Appendix C: Extended ASCII Character Set

DECIMAL VALUE →	0	16	32	48	64	80	96	112	128	144	160	176	192	208	224	240
↓ HEXADECIMAL VALUE	0	1	2	3	4	5	6	7	8	9	A	B	C	D	E	F
0 / 0	BLANK (NULL)	►	BLANK (SPACE)	0	@	P	`	p	Ⱡ	É	á	░	└	┴	∝	≡
1 / 1	☺	◄	!	1	A	Q	a	q	ü	Æ	í	▒	┴	┬	β	±
2 / 2	☻	↕	"	2	B	R	b	r	é	FE	ó	▓	┬	├	γ	≥
3 / 3	♥	‼	#	3	C	S	c	s	â	ô	ú	│	├	└	π	≤
4 / 4	♦	¶	$	4	D	T	d	t	ä	ö	ñ	┤	─	┴	Σ	∫
5 / 5	♣	§	%	5	E	U	e	u	à	ò	Ñ	╡	┼	┌	σ	∫
6 / 6	♠	▬	&	6	F	V	f	v	å	û	ª	╢	├	┌	µ	÷
7 / 7	•	↨	'	7	G	W	g	w	ç	ù	º	╖	├	┤	τ	≈
8 / 8	◘	↑	(	8	H	X	h	x	ê	ÿ	¿	╕	╚	┘	Φ	°
9 / 9	○	↓	)	9	I	Y	i	y	ë	Ö	⌐	╣	╔	┐	Θ	•
10 / A	◙	→	*	:	J	Z	j	z	è	Ü	¬	║	╩	┌	Ω	·
11 / B	♂	←	+	;	K	[	k	{	ï	¢	½	╗	╦	█	δ	√
12 / C	♀	∟	,	<	L	\	l	|	î	£	¼	╝	╠	█	∞	η
13 / D	♪	↔	-	=	M	]	m	}	ì	¥	¡	╜	═	▌	Ø	²
14 / E	♫	▲	.	>	N	^	n	~	Ä	Pts	«	╛	╬	▐	∈	■
15 / F	☼	▼	/	?	O	_	o	△	Å	ƒ	»	┐	╧	█	∩	BLANK 'FF'

Appendix D: Modems

 NETWORK+ OBJECTIVES

This appendix provides information for the following Network+ objectives:

1.6 Identify the purpose, features, and functions of the following network components:
- Hubs
- Switches
- Bridges
- Routers
- Gateways
- CSU/DSU
- Network Interface Cards/ISDN adapters/system area network cards
- Wireless access points
- Modems

2.11 Identify the basic characteristics (e.g., speed, capacity, media) of the following WAN technologies:
- Packet switching vs. circuit switching
- ISDN
- FDDI
- ATM
- Frame Relay
- Sonet/SDH
- T1/E1
- T3/E3
- Ocx

3.7 Given a remote connectivity scenario (e.g., IP, IPX, dial-up, PPPoE, authentication, physical connectivity, etc.), configure the connection.

4.12 Given a network troubleshooting scenario involving a wiring/infrastructure problem, identify the cause of the problem (e.g., bad media, interference, network hardware).

■ INTRODUCTION

Objective 1-6

For computers to communicate, four things must be in place—a communication (or message) to be sent, communications hardware such as a CSU/DSU or modem, communications software, and a link between the computers. The most convenient link to use is the already established telephone system lines. Using these lines and a properly equipped computer allows communications between any two computers that have access to a telephone line. This is a convenient and inexpensive method of communicating between computers.

Telephone lines were designed for the transmission of the human voice, not for the transmission of digital data. Telephone lines can be used to transmit computer data. Computers use binary code to represent information. Each bit is represented as a 1 (ON) or a 0 (OFF) that when grouped together as a byte of information means something to the user. It takes 8 bits (1 byte) of information to represent one character of the alphabet using ASCII. The ONs and OFFs that represent the computer's data must first be converted to an analog signal, sent over the telephone line, and reconverted from analog back to the ONs and OFFs that the computer understands, as shown in Figure D–1. The most common method of converting these ONs and OFFs is with a modem.

FIGURE D–1
The basics of using telephone lines in computer communications.

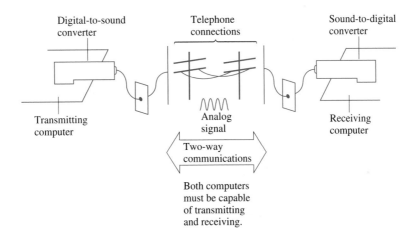

■ THE MODEM

The word *modulate* means to change; an electronic circuit that changes digital data into analog data is called a *modulator*. The word *demodulate* can be thought of as meaning to reverse a change or restore to an original condition. Any electronic circuit that converts the analog signal used to represent the digital signals back to the ONs and OFFs understood by a computer, therefore, is called a *demodulator*. Because each computer must be capable of both transmission and reception, each computer must contain an electrical circuit that can modulate as well as demodulate. Such a circuit is commonly called a *mo*dulator/*dem*odulator, or *modem*.

For personal computers, a modem may be an internal or an external circuit—both perform identical functions.

Telephone Modem Setup

Objective 3-7

The most common problem with telephone modems is the correct setting of the software. There are essentially six distinct areas to which you must pay attention when using a telephone modem:

- Port to be used
- Baud rate

- Parity
- Number of data bits
- Number of stop bits
- Local echo ON or OFF

Most telephone modems have a default setting for each of these areas. However, as a user you should understand what each of these areas means. You will have to consult the specific documentation that comes with the modem to see how to change any of these settings.

Ports

The most commonly used ports are COM1 and COM2. Other possible ports are COM3 and COM4. The port you select from the communications software depends on the port to which you have the modem connected. For most communications software, after you set the correct port number, you do not need to set it again.

Baud Rate

Typical values for the baud rate are between 9600 and 56K. Again, these values can be selected from the communications software menu. It is important that both computers be set at the same baud rate.

Parity

Parity is a way of having the data checked. Normally, parity is not used. Depending on your software, there can be up to five options for the parity bit:

- **Space:** Parity bit is always a 0.
- **Odd:** Parity bit is 0 if there is an odd number of 1s in the transmission and is a 1 if there is an even number of 1s in the transmission.
- **Even:** Parity bit is a 1 if there is an odd number of 1s in the transmission and is a 0 if there is an even number of 1s in the transmission.
- **Mark:** Parity bit is always a 1.
- **None:** No parity bit is transmitted.

Again, both the sending and receiving units should be set up to agree on the status of the parity bit.

Data Bits

The number of data bits is usually set at 8. There are options that allow the number of data bits to be set at 7, but it's important that both computers expect the same number of data bits.

Stop Bits

The number of stop bits used is normally one; however, depending on the system, the number of stop bits may be two. Stop bits are used to mark the end of each character transmitted. Both computers must have their communications software set to agree on the number of stop bits used.

Windows Modem Software

Windows has built-in modem software, accessed through the Control Panel. Clicking on the Modem icon displays the Modems Properties dialog box shown in Figure D–2.

FIGURE D–2
Modems Properties dialog box.

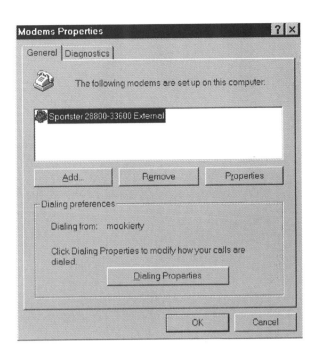

Notice that the dialog box in Figure D–2 indicates the presence of an external Sportster modem. To test the modem, click on the Diagnostics tab, shown in Figure D–3.

FIGURE D–3
Modems Properties
Diagnostics tab.

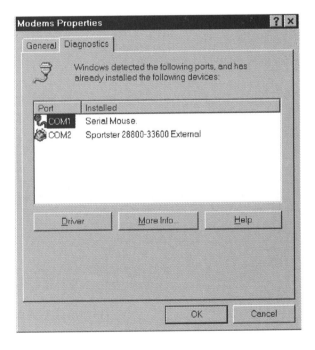

Select COM2 (the Sportster modem) and then click on More Info for Windows to interrogate the modem. The results display in a new window, shown in Figure D–4.

Specific information about the modem port is displayed, along with the responses to several AT commands. The *AT command set* is a standard set of commands that can be sent to the modem to configure, test, and control it. Table D–1 lists the typical *Hayes compatible* commands (first used by Hayes in its modem products). An example of an AT command is

```
ATDT 778 8108
```

which stands for AT (attention) DT (dial using tones). This AT command causes the modem to touch-tone dial the indicated phone number. Many modems require an initial AT command

FIGURE D–4
Modem diagnostics information.

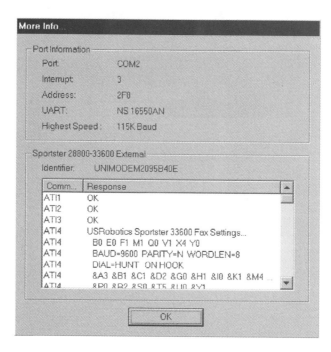

Table D–1
Selected AT commands.

Command	Function	Command	Function
A/	Repeat last command	Xn	Result code type
A	Answer	Yn	Long space disconnect
Bn	Select CCITT or Bell	Zn	Recall stored profile
Cn	Carrier control option	&Cn	DCD option
D	Dial command	&Dn	DTR option
En	Command echo	&F	Load factory defaults
Fn	Online echo	&Gn	Guard tone option
Hn	Switch hook control	&Jn	Auxiliary relay control
In	Identification/checksum	&M0	Communication mode option
Kn	SRAM buffer control	&Pn	Dial pulse ratio
Ln	Speaker volume control	&Q0	Communication mode option
Mn	Speaker control	&Sn	DSR option
Nn	Connection data rate control	&Tn	Self-test commands
On	Go online	&Vn	View active and stored configuration
P	Select pulse dialing	&Un	Disable Trellis coding
Qn	Result code display control	&Wn	Stored active profile
Sn	Select an S-register	&Yn	Select stored profile on power-on
Sn=x	Write to an S-register	&Zn=x	Store telephone number
Sn?	Read from an S-register	%En	Auto-retrain control
?	Read last accessed S-register	%G0	Rate renegotiation
T	Select DTMF dialing	%Q	Line signal quality
Vn	Result code form	-Cn	Generate data modem calling tone

string to be properly initialized. This string is automatically output to the modem when a modem application is executed.

■ TELEPHONE MODEM TERMINOLOGY

In using technical documentation concerning a telephone modem, you will encounter some specialized terminology. Figure D–5 illustrates some of the ideas behind some basic communication methods. As you can see from the figure, *simplex* is a term that refers to a communications channel in which information flows in one direction only. An example of this is a radio or a television station.

FIGURE D–5
Basic communications methods.

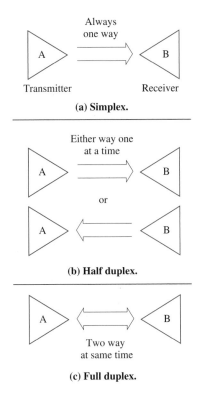

(a) **Simplex.**

(b) **Half duplex.**

(c) **Full duplex.**

Duplex

The *duplex* mode refers to two-way communication between two systems. This term is further refined as follows: *Full duplex* describes a communication link that can pass data in two directions at the same time. This mode is analogous to an everyday conversation between two people either face to face or over the telephone. The other mode, which is not commonly available with telephone modems, is the *multiplex* mode. Multiplex refers to a communications link in which multiple transmissions are possible.

Echo

The terminology used here has to do with how the characters you send to the other terminal are displayed on your monitor screen. The term *echo* refers to the method used to display characters on the monitor screen. *Local echo* means that the sending modem immediately returns or echoes each character back to the screen as it is entered into the keyboard. This mode is required before transmission so that you can see what instructions you are giving to the communications software. *Remote echo* means that during the communications between two computers, the remote computer (the one being transmitted to) sends back the character it is receiving. The character that then appears on your screen is the result of a transmission from the remote unit. This is a method of verifying what you are sending. To use the remote echo mode, you must be in the full duplex mode. The concept of echo modes is illustrated in Figure D–6.

FIGURE D–6
Echo modes.

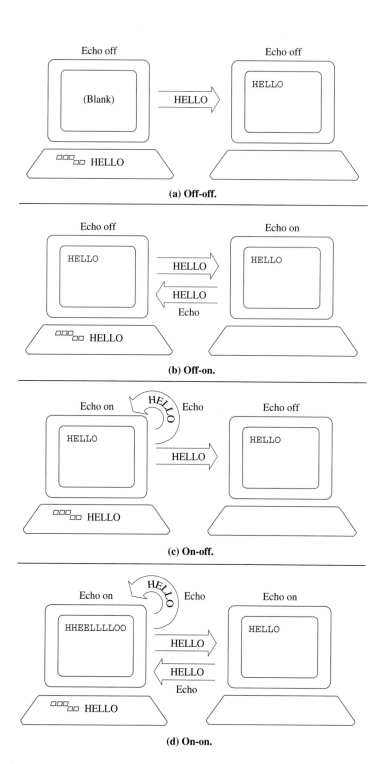

Modulation Methods

Many different techniques are used to encode digital data into analog form (for use by the modem). These techniques include

- AM (amplitude modulation)
- FSK (frequency shift keying)
- Phase modulation

These techniques are shown in Figure D–7.

FIGURE D–7
Modulation techniques.

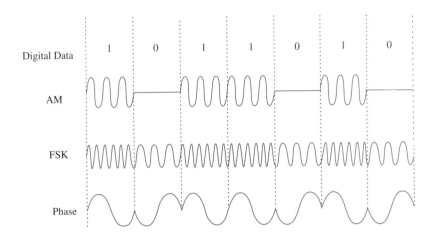

To get a high data rate (in bits per second) over ordinary telephone lines, another technique called group coding is used. In this method, one cycle of the transmitted signal encodes two or more bits of data. For example, using *quadrature modulation,* the binary patterns 00, 01, 10, and 11 encode one of four different phase shifts for the current output signal. Thus, a signal that changes at a rate of 2400 baud actually represents 9600 bps.

Another technique, called *Trellis modulation,* combines two or more other techniques, such as AM and quadrature modulation, to increase the data rate.

■ COMMON TELEPHONE MODEM PROBLEMS

Objective 4-12

Most common telephone modem problems are software related; however, other problems encountered involve very simple hardware considerations. Table D–2 lists some of the most common problems encountered with telephone modems.

Table D–2
Common telephone modem problems.

Symptom	Possible Cause(s)
Can't connect	Usually this means that your baud rates or numbers of data bits are not matched. This is especially true if you see garbage on the screen, especially the { character.
Can't see input	You are typing in information but it doesn't appear on the screen. However, if the person on the other side can see what you are typing, it means that you need to turn your local echo on. In this way, what you type will be echoed back to you, and you will see it on your screen.
Get double characters	Here you are typing information and getting double characters. This means that if you type HELLO, you get HHEELLLLOO; at the same time, what the other computer is getting appears normal. This means that you need to turn your local echo off. In this way, you will not be echoing back the extra character. With some systems *half duplex* refers to local echo on, whereas *full duplex* refers to local echo off.

Telephone modems usually come with two separate telephone line connectors. The purpose of the phone input is to connect a telephone, not the output line from the modem, to the telephone wall jack. The phone input is simply a convenience. It allows the telephone to be used without having to disconnect a telephone line from the computer to the wall telephone jack. If you mistakenly connect the line from the wall telephone jack to the phone input, you will be able to dial out from your communications software, but your system will hang up on you. Make sure that the telephone line that goes to the telephone wall jack comes from the *line output* and not the *phone output* jack of your modem.

Another common hardware problem is a problem in your telephone line. This can be quickly checked by simply using your phone to get through to the other party. If you can't do this, then neither can your computer.

A problem that is frequently encountered in an office or school building involves the phone system used within the building. You may have to issue extra commands on your software in order to get your call out of the building. In this case you need to check with your telecommunications manager or the local phone company.

Sometimes your problem is simply a noisy line. This may have to do with your communications provider or it may have to do with how your telephone line is installed. You may have to switch to a long-distance telephone company that can provide service over more reliable communication lines. Or you may have to physically trace where your telephone line goes from the wall telephone jack. If this is an old installation, your telephone line could be running in the wall right next to the AC power lines. If this is the case, you need to reroute the phone line.

■ ISDN MODEMS

ISDN

Objective 1-6

Objective 2-11

ISDN (Integrated Services Digital Network) is a special connection available from the telephone company that provides 64 Kbps digital service. An ISDN modem will typically connect to a *basic rate ISDN* (BRI) line, which contains two full-duplex 64 Kbps B channels (for voice/data) and a 16 Kbps D channel (for control). This allows up to 128 Kbps communication. ISDN modems are more expensive than ordinary modems and require you to have an ISDN line installed before you can use them. Figure D–8 shows the ISDN BRI line wiring organization and connector details.

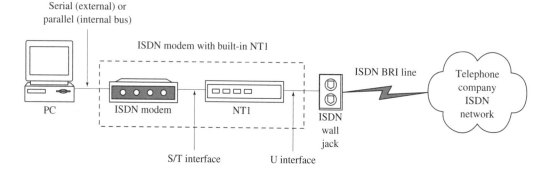

RJ-45 Pin Number	Signal	RJ-45 Pin Number	Signal
1	—	1	—
2	—	2	—
3	Tx A	3	—
4	Rx A	4	U-interface Tip
5	Rx B	5	U-interface Ring
6	Tx B	6	—
7	—	7	—
8	—	8	—
S/T interface		U interface	

FIGURE D–8
ISDN wiring and connector details.

An ISDN PRI (Primary Rate Interface) line contains up to twenty-three 64 Kbps channels, plus a 64 Kbps D channel, for a total bandwidth of 1.544 Mbps (includes some physical layer encapsulation bits). Bandwidth from each channel may be assigned individually or combined into fewer, high-bandwidth channels.

NT1

The signals from an ISDN device must pass through the S/T interface to an *NT1* (Network Termination device 1) unit, which connects to the wall jack. The NT1 unit provides the wiring interface between the phone company network and the user's ISDN equipment, assists with troubleshooting, and centralizes connections for multiple ISDN devices. Note that an ISDN modem typically has the NT1 terminating hardware built into its components, and thus can connect directly to the wall jack. Wall jacks are *U interfaces* in the U.S. and *S/T interfaces* in Europe. ISDN connectors may be RJ-11, RJ-45, or RJ-48 types. Each ISDN channel may have a Directory Number associated with it, the number dialed to access the ISDN channel. A Service Profile Identifier number (SPID) will be assigned by the ISP for each directory number. The SPID is required to configure the network connection for the channel.

U interfaces
S/T interfaces

AO/DI

ISDN users pay two types of charges: their installed line charge and a by-connection charge. Users who require an ISDN line that is always on (always connected) could pay high connection costs. A feature called Always On Dynamic ISDN (*AO/DI*) helps reduce connection charges for users whose connections are always on by utilizing bandwidth on demand. The user's ISP must provide the AO/DI feature for it to work.

ISDN modems do not modulate and demodulate an analog carrier as ordinary phone line modems do. Instead, they convert the digital ISDN signal into a communication method suitable for the PC, such as serial for a COM1 connection (with an external ISDN modem) or parallel for an ISA or PCI adapter card. Thus, the term *ISDN terminal adapter* is used interchangeably with ISDN modem.

Some ISDN modems provide additional connection features and services. For example, the Diva LAN ISDN modem, from Eicon Networks (www.eicon.com), contains the following features:

- Two POTS lines (one for a phone and the second for a FAX)
- LAN access via four 10BASE-T ports
- Tariff management to help reduce line charges
- NAT and support for up to 50 simultaneous users via Multi-Link PPP (MLPPP)
- Firewall security protection
- VPN support for Windows users via PPTP
- Connections for ISDN jack (U interface) and NT1 unit (S/T interface)

Clearly, ISDN is a good choice for users who require dedicated bandwidth at a modest expense.

■ CABLE MODEMS

One of the most inexpensive, high-speed connections available today is the cable modem. A cable modem connects between the television cable supplying your home and a network interface card in your computer. Two unused cable channels are used to provide data rates in the hundreds of thousands of bits per second. For example, downloading a 6 MB file over a cable modem takes less than 20 seconds (during several tests of a new cable modem installation). That corresponds to 2,400,000 bps. Of course, the actual data rate available depends on many factors, such as the speed the data is transmitted from the other end and any communication delays. But unlike all other modems, the cable modem has the capability to be staggeringly fast, due to the high bandwidth available on the cable. In addition, a cable modem is typically part of the entire package from the cable company and is returned when you terminate service. The cost is roughly the same as the cost of basic cable service.

■ PROTOCOLS

A *protocol* is a prearranged communication procedure that two or more parties agree on. When two modems are communicating over telephone lines (during a file transfer from a computer bulletin board or an America Online session), each modem has to agree on the technique used for transmission and reception of data. Table D–3 shows some of the more common protocols. The modem software that is supplied with a new modem usually allows the user to specify a particular protocol.

Table D–3
Modem communication protocols.

Protocol	Operation
Xmodem	Blocks of 128 bytes are transmitted. A checksum byte is used to validate received data. Bad data is retransmitted.
Xmodem CRC	Xmodem using Cyclic Redundancy Check to detect errors.
Xmodem-1K	Essentially Xmodem CRC with 1024-byte blocks.
Ymodem	Similar to Xmodem-1K. Multiple files may be transferred with one command.
Zmodem	Uses 512-byte blocks and CRC for error detection. Can resume an interrupted transmission from where it left off.
Kermit	Transmits data in packets whose sizes are adjusted to fit the needs of the other machine's protocol.

■ THE TIA-232-F STANDARD

The TIA (Telecommunications Industry Association) has published the TIA *Standard Interface Between Data Terminal Equipment Employing Serial Binary Data Interchange*—specifically, TIA-232-F. This is a standard defining 25 conductors that may be used in interfacing *data terminal equipment* (DTE, such as your computer) and *data communications equipment* (DCE, such as a modem) hardware. The standard specifies the function of each conductor, but it does not state the physical connector that is to be used. This standard exists so that different manufacturers of communications equipment can communicate with each other. In other words, the TIA-232-F standard is an example of an interface, essentially an agreement among equipment manufacturers on how to allow their equipment to communicate.

The RS-232 standard is designed to allow DTEs to communicate with DCEs. The TIA-232-F uses a DB-25 connector; the male DB-25 goes on the DTEs and the female goes on the DCEs. The TIA-232-F standard signals are shown in Figure D–9.

FIGURE D–9
The TIA-232-F standard signals.

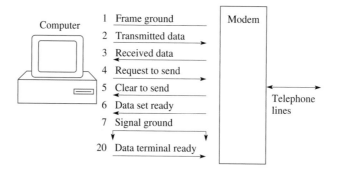

The TIA-232-F is a digital interface designed to operate at no more than 50 feet with a 20,000 bps bit rate. The *baud* actually indicates the number of *discrete* signal changes per second. In the transmission of binary values, one such change represents a single bit. What this means is that the popular usage of the term baud has become the same as bits per second (bps). Table D–4 shows the standard set of baud rates.

Table D–4
Standard baud rates.

Low Speed	High Speed
300	
600	14,400
1200	19,200
2400	28,800
4800	33,600
9600	56K

MNP Standards

MNP (Microcom Networking Protocol) is a set of protocols used to provide error detection and correction, as well as compression, to the modem data stream. Table D–5 lists the MNP classes and their characteristics.

Table D–5
MNP standards.

Class	Feature
1	Asynchronous, half duplex, byte oriented
2	Asynchronous, full duplex, byte oriented
3	Synchronous, full duplex, byte oriented
4	Error correction, packet oriented
5	Data compression
6	Negotiation
7	Huffman data compression
9	Improved error correction
10	Line monitoring

Note: There is no MNP-8 standard.

MNP classes 4 and above are used with newer, high-speed modems. When two modems initially connect, they negotiate the best type of connection possible, based on line properties and the features and capabilities of each modem. The CCITT standards supported by the modem are also part of the negotiation.

CCITT Standards

CCITT (French abbreviation for International Telegraph and Telephone Consultive Committee) standards define the maximum operating speed (as well as other features) available in a modem, which is a function of the modulation techniques used. Table D–6 lists the CCITT standards.

Table D–6
CCITT standards.

Standard	Data Rate (bps)
V.22	1200
V.22 bis	2400
V.32	9600
V.32 bis	14,400
V.32 terbo	19,200
V.34	28,800/33,600
V.90	56K

Other Standards

Earlier, low-speed standards include the Bell 103 (300 bps using FSK) and Bell 212A (1200 bps using quadrature modulation). V.22 is similar in operation to Bell 212A and is more widely accepted outside the United States.

The V.90 standard, finalized in early 1998, outlines the details of modem communication at 56 Kbps, currently the fastest speed available for regular modems. Fax modems have their own set of standards.

Appendix E:
The Ethereal
Protocol Analyzer

 NETWORK+ OBJECTIVES

This appendix provides information for the following Network+ objectives:

4.7 Given output from a diagnostic utility (e.g., TRACERT, PING, IPCONFIG, etc.), identify the utility and interpret the output.

■ INTRODUCTION

Objective 4-7

It is often necessary for a network engineer to troubleshoot problems that arise on the network by using a protocol analyzer. The Ethereal protocol analyzer is a free program distributed under the GNU Open Source License. Ethereal contains many functions that a network administrator or technician will find handy.

A protocol analyzer is a dangerous tool in the wrong hands, however. When using a protocol analyzer, the NIC in a computer is put into promiscuous mode, allowing it to see all of the traffic that is transmitted on the local network. This potentially causes a network security risk because it is possible to capture data that is considered to be private, such as passwords, social security numbers, salaries, and so on; therefore, extreme caution and good judgment should be exercised when using a protocol analyzer.

Typically, a protocol analyzer is used to collect baseline network traffic data. Using a baseline, it is possible to determine several possible situations. Examples include identification of a network trend that will allow for a network engineer to plan for future allocation of network resources or possibly identify a piece of network equipment that is malfunctioning. In general, the process to investigate a network begins by monitoring all of the network traffic.

As you work through this appendix, spend some time reviewing the contents of the Ethereal menus. Selectively display captured data, perform user-supplied decodes, navigate through the captured data, mark selected frames for later analysis or printing, and enable or disable specific protocols for decoding. Most of these options are available on the Edit menu. Experiment with these options on your own.

For additional information on Ethereal, visit the Ethereal Web site located at http://www.ethereal.com.

■ PACKET CAPTURE

When Ethereal first starts, the Ethereal Network Analyzer window shown in Figure E–1 is displayed. Note the format of the Ethereal display.

FIGURE E–1
The Ethereal Network Analyzer window.

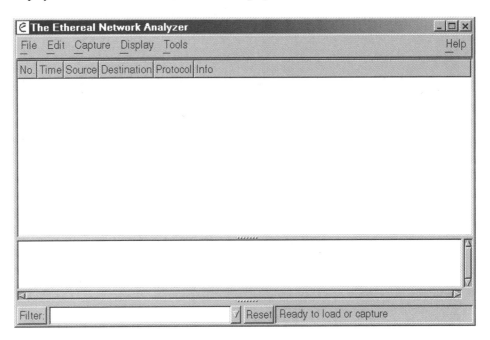

To begin monitoring the network, it is necessary to select Start from the Capture menu. This causes the Ethereal Capture Preferences window to be displayed as illustrated in Figure E–2.

FIGURE E–2
Ethereal Capture Preferences
dialog box.

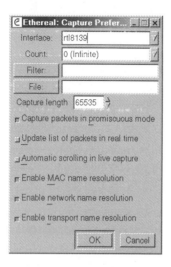

On the Ethereal Capture Preferences display, it is necessary to identify the default network adapter. This tells Ethereal which network card in a computer it will be using to capture network traffic. Since there is usually only one network card in a personal computer, there is often only one choice available, but there may be more. If two network cards or a modem is installed, more than one item will be available and one of them must be selected to begin monitoring the network.

Notice that it is possible to select many different Ethereal preference settings, including filters, real-time update, and various name resolution options. Note that all of the options are selected with the exception of the real-time update and automatic scrolling. These two options can be enabled by pressing the buttons next to each of the options. You are encouraged to experiment with both of these setting options to see how Ethereal processes network data. After selecting the various capture preferences and clicking on OK, the Ethereal Capture window shown in Figure E–3 is displayed.

FIGURE E–3
Ethereal Capture window.

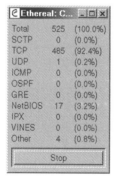

Ethereal counts the total number of frames captured as well as each type of frame. If the real-time capture and scroll preference options are selected, the Ethereal display is updated as the capture continues. When the stop button is clicked or the selected count on the preference window has been satisfied, Ethereal loads the captured data as indicated in Figure E–4.

FIGURE E–4
Loading captured network
data.

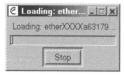

Depending on how many packets are captured and the speed of the computer system, there will be a slight delay as the packets are processed. When the processing is complete, Ethereal displays the first screen of captured data.

PACKET DISPLAY

The Ethereal initial data display, shown in Figure E–5, is divided into three areas. At the top half of the screen, Ethereal displays the list of captured packets. For each packet, the packet number, the time relative to the first packet, the packet source and destination, the protocol, and summary information are displayed. The middle portion of the Ethereal display contains each of the protocols encapsulated in the frame. The first packet highlighted in Figure E–5 includes an IEEE 802.3 Ethernet frame containing Logical Link Control and a NetBIOS message. At the bottom of the Ethereal display is the raw data contained in the frame.

FIGURE E–5
Ethereal captured data display.

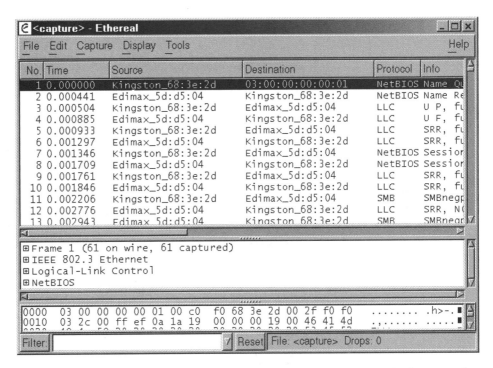

Figure E–6 displays the contents of frame number 188. Notice that the frame consists of an Ethernet II, IP, and TCP data. As the scroll bar indicates, there is more information that is not displayed. Using the scroll bars, all of the various data elements may be examined.

FIGURE E–6
Frame 188 decoded.

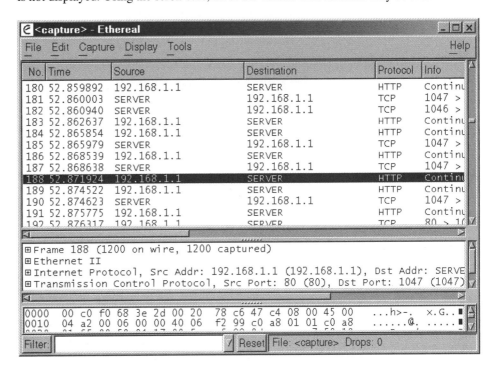

Selecting the TCP line in the frame display, as shown in Figure E–7, highlights the raw data shown at the bottom of the display.

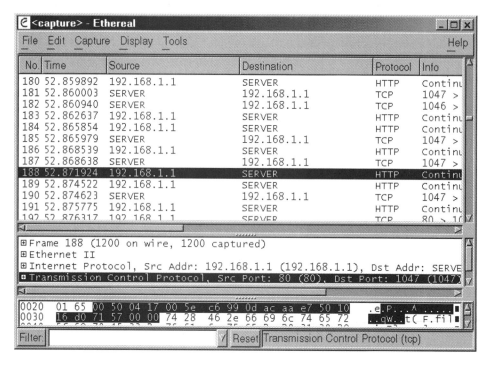

Each of the packets captured by Ethereal can be examined thoroughly.

A summary of the Ethereal traffic capture is available by selecting the Summary option from the Tools pull-down menu as shown in Figure E–8.

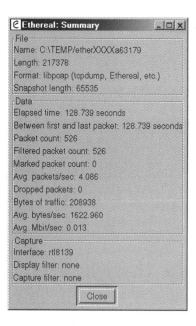

The actual summary screen shown in Figure E–8 contains the file name, length, and file format. The data is summarized to contain the elapsed time to perform the capture, the packet count, and various statistics that were identified. The bottom summary display indicates the interface on which the data was collected and any display or capture filters that were in effect at the time of the capture.

In addition to the summary, the Protocol Hierarchy Statistics shown in Figure E–9 show the hierarchy of the captured data. Notice how the Ethernet data is broken down into

Logical Link Control, Address Resolution Protocol, and Internet Protocol categories. Each of these collected items can be very important when developing a baseline of activity for a network or when performing troubleshooting.

FIGURE E–9
Ethereal Protocol Hierarchy Statistics summary.

PRINTING PACKET CAPTURE DECODES

Ethereal can print copies of the captured data to a file for later examination. To enable Ethereal to print to a file, it is necessary to modify the Ethereal preferences. This is accomplished by selecting the Preferences option in the Edit menu.

The first item on the Preferences display is associated with printing. To enable Ethereal to print to a file, it is necessary to select the Print to: File option as shown in Figure E–10. The default file name that is written to is called ethereal.out. As you can see, there are several other preferences that may be modified. You are encouraged to experiment with these on your own. After all of the preferences have been set, click on OK to activate them.

FIGURE E–10
Modified Ethereal printing preferences.

Figure E–11 shows the Print Packet option being selected from the File menu. Note the highlighted packet shown in the background of the Ethereal display.

FIGURE E–11
Printing Ethereal packets to a file.

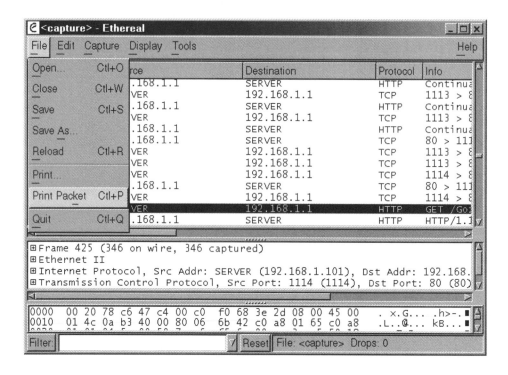

The following text was written to the file ethereal.out:

```
Frame 425 (346 on wire, 346 captured)
    Arrival Time: Nov 11, 2001 17:52:59.986015000
    Time delta from previous packet: 0.002763000 seconds
    Time relative to first packet: 14.919580000 seconds
    Frame Number: 425
    Packet Length: 346 bytes
    Capture Length: 346 bytes
Ethernet II
    Destination: 00:20:78:c6:47:c4 (Runtop_c6:47:c4)
    Source: 00:c0:f0:68:3e:2d (SERVER)
    Type: IP (0x0800)
Internet Protocol, Src Addr: SERVER (192.168.1.101), Dst Addr: 192.168.1.1
(192.168.1.1)
    Version: 4
    Header length: 20 bytes
    Differentiated Services Field: 0x00 (DSCP 0x00: Default; ECN: 0x00)
        0000 00.. = Differentiated Services Codepoint: Default (0x00)
        .... ..0. = ECN-Capable Transport (ECT): 0
        .... ...0 = ECN-CE: 0
    Total Length: 332
    Identification: 0x0ab3
    Flags: 0x04
        .1.. = Don't fragment: Set
        ..0. = More fragments: Not set
    Fragment offset: 0
    Time to live: 128
    Protocol: TCP (0x06)
    Header checksum: 0x6b42 (correct)
```

```
    Source: SERVER (192.168.1.101)
    Destination: 192.168.1.1 (192.168.1.1)
Transmission Control Protocol, Src Port: 1114 (1114), Dst Port: 80 (80), Seq:
2057762158, Ack: 13515941
    Source port: 1114 (1114)
    Destination port: 80 (80)
    Sequence number: 2057762158
    Next sequence number: 2057762450
    Acknowledgement number: 13515941
    Header length: 20 bytes
    Flags: 0x0018 (PSH, ACK)
        0... .... = Congestion Window Reduced (CWR): Not set
        .0.. .... = ECN-Echo: Not set
        ..0. .... = Urgent: Not set
        ...1 .... = Acknowledgment: Set
        .... 1... = Push: Set
        .... .0.. = Reset: Not set
        .... ..0. = Syn: Not set
        .... ...0 = Fin: Not set
    Window size: 65535
    Checksum: 0xaee2 (correct)
Hypertext Transfer Protocol
    GET /Gozila.js HTTP/1.1
    Accept: */*
    Referer: http://192.168.1.1/RouteStatic.htm
    Accept-Language: en-us
    Accept-Encoding: gzip, deflate
    User-Agent: Mozilla/4.0 (compatible; MSIE 5.5; Windows 98; Win 9x 4.90)
    Host: 192.168.1.1
    Connection: Keep-Alive
    Authorization: Basic Omtlbm55aWlp
```

You should thoroughly examine this block of text to fully understand the contents of the packet.

■ PACKET CAPTURE FILTERS

When monitoring or troubleshooting a network, it is often necessary to monitor a small portion of the data being transmitted. For example, Ethereal can be used to look for network traffic from a specific host computer or to look for a specific type of protocol. This is accomplished by setting up a packet capture filter.

By using a filter, much of the networking traffic is eliminated from the buffer, therefore saving only the traffic that is desired. This makes investigating network problems much easier by isolating the information. Once again, you are encouraged to experiment with filters to gain a better understanding of how to use the Ethereal Network Analyzer tool.

Appendix F:
Network Certification

The rapid and continual growth of communication technology has created an ongoing need for skilled network technicians and administrators. In addition to a technical degree of some kind, employers are now also looking for further proof of an individual's competence in networking. This need has spawned a number of different network certifications such as

- CompTIA Network+
- Cisco CCIE
- Microsoft MCSE

Let us examine the requirements of each certification.

■ COMPTIA NETWORK+

The CompTIA (Computing Technology Industry Association) Network+ certification is for network technicians who have accumulated 18 to 24 months of experience in their field. One test is used to certify that an individual has the necessary skills for the information technology industry. Visit www.comptia.org/certification/networkplus/index.htm for more information.

■ CISCO CCNA

The Cisco CCNA (Cisco Certified Network Associate) certification exam is designed to test individuals at the apprentice level of a network professional. To obtain this certification you must pass a minimum of one exam. Cisco has just released a new testing process for this certification, which allows you another option of taking two tests that cover specific areas of the overall knowledge. Both of these tests, combined, cover the same knowledge base that the single CCNA test covers.

■ CISCO CCNP

The CCNP (Cisco Certified Network Professional) certification program tests the networking professional's knowledge required to support medium to large organizations. Currently you must pass four exams to obtain this certification.

■ CISCO CCIE

The Cisco CCIE (Cisco Certified Internetworking Expert) allows one to choose from several tracks (such as Routing and Switching, WAN Switching, and Design). The certification involves a written exam and a hands-on lab exam. Visit www.cisco.com for more information.

■ MICROSOFT MCSE

The Microsoft MCSE (Microsoft Certified Systems Engineer) is one of several certifications offered by Microsoft. The MCSE certification involves taking five core exams and two elective exams. The core exams are strongly based in the Windows 2000/XP area. Visit www.microsoft.com and search for MCSE for additional information.

■ SAMPLE NETWORK CERTIFICATION TEST QUESTION

Bill and Mary have to assemble a small network of four computers for a demonstration. Three computers run Windows 95 and the fourth runs Windows 98. During the demonstration the computers will need to share files.

Bill connects each machine to a 10BASE-T hub with UTP cables he pulls out of a box. Mary adjusts the network properties of each computer, setting each one the same way. When they are finished, three of the computers can share files, but the fourth one (a Windows 95 machine) is not even visible under Network Neighborhood.

Bill examines the UTP cable from the fourth machine and discovers it is a crossover cable. He replaces it with a straight-through cable and reboots the fourth computer. What effect does this have on the problem?

a. It solves it completely.
b. It only allows files less than 32K to be shared.
c. It has no effect; the problem still exists.

Appendix G: Telecommunication Technologies

 NETWORK+ OBJECTIVES

This appendix provides information for the following Network+ objectives:

1.2 Specify the main features of 802.2 (LLC), 802.3 (Ethernet), 802.5 (token ring), 802.11b (wireless), and FDDI networking technologies, including

- Speed
- Access
- Method
- Topology
- Media

2.11 Identify the basic characteristics (e.g., speed, capacity, media) of the following WAN technologies:

- Packet switching vs. circuit switching
- ISDN
- FDDI
- ATM
- Frame Relay
- Sonet/SDH
- T1/E1
- T3/E3
- Ocx

The world of telecommunications is getting both larger and smaller at the same time. From a hardware standpoint, more equipment is being installed every day, connecting more and more people, businesses, and organizations. At the same time, the pervasiveness of the World Wide Web has made it easy to communicate with someone practically anywhere on the planet. The world does not seem as large as it once did.

This appendix examines the many different telecommunication technologies available and presents the parts they play in everyday communication.

■ TDM

Objective 2-1

Time-division multiplexing, or TDM, is a technique used by the telephone company to combine multiple digitized voice channels over a single wire. Telephone conversations are digitized into 8-bit PCM (pulse code modulation) samples and sampled 8000 times per second. This gives 64,000 bps for a single conversation. Using a multiplexer, if you rapidly switch from one channel to another, it is possible to transmit the 8-bit samples for 24 different conversations over a single wire. All that is required is a fast bit rate on the single wire. Figure G–1 shows a timing diagram for the TDM scheme on a basic carrier called a *T1 carrier*. The T1 provides 1.544 Mbps multiplexed data for twenty-four 64,000 bps channels. The 8 bits for each channel (192 bits total) plus a framing bit (a total of 193 bits) are transmitted 8000 times per second.

FIGURE G–1
Time-division multiplexing.

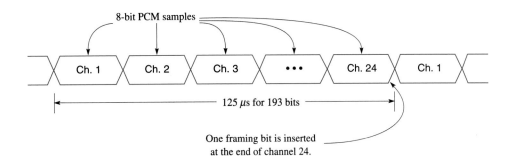

Table G–1 shows the different levels of T-carrier service available. Note that each T signal has a corresponding Digital Signal (DS) number.

Table G–1
T-carrier services.

Level	Number of Voice Channels	Data Rate (Mbps)
T1/DS1	24	1.544
T2/DS2	96 (4 T1s)	6.312
T3/DS3	672 (28 T1s)	44.736
T4/DS4	4032 (6 T3s)	274.176

The T1 hierarchy of signals are used in North America and Japan. An alternate TDM scheme is used in Europe and is standardized by the ITU-T (International Telecommunication Union, formerly the CCITT). This scheme is based on an E1 carrier that multiplexes thirty 8-bit channels, plus two additional channels for control and synchronization, for a total of 2.048 Mbps. Table G–2 lists the various E-carriers.

Table G–2
E-carrier services.

Level	Number of Voice Channels	Data Rate (Mbps)
E1	30	2.048
E2	120 (4 E1s)	8.448
E3	480 (16 E1s)	34.368
E4	1920 (64 E1s)	139.264
E5	7680 (256 E1s)	565.148

Objective 1-6

T-carrier signals are exchanged over two pairs of wires (transmit-pair and receive-pair). The electrical signals on each pair are converted to and from binary using a device called a CSU/DSU (Channel Service Unit/Data Service Unit). The CSU drives and terminates the T1 signals on the wire pairs, plus provides loopback testing for the T1 line as well as lightning protection. The DSU connects digital terminal equipment (DTE), such as a router's V.35 interface, to the CSU, and converts between binary data and the +/−3-volt AMI or B8ZS TDM encoding levels used on the T1 pairs. Figure G–2 shows the use of a CSU/DSU in a network interface.

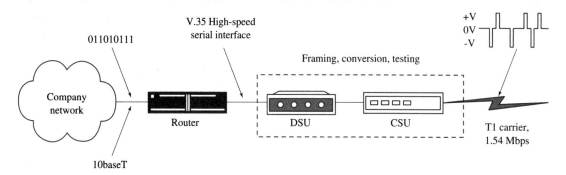

FIGURE G–2
A CSU/DSU provides the interface between the T1 carrier and the router.

■ CIRCUIT SWITCHING

Objective 2-11

In the early days of the telephone system, large rotary switches were used to switch communication lines and make the necessary connections to allow end-to-end communication. The switches completed a circuit, hence the name *circuit switching.*

Eventually these slow, mechanical switches were replaced with fast, electronic switches. Also called an *interconnection network,* a switch is used to direct a signal to a specific output (such as the telephone you are calling).

Figure G–3 shows one way to switch a set of eight signals. This type of switch is called a *crossbar switch.* Connections between input and output signals are made by closing switches at specific intersections within the 8-by-8 grid of switches. Only one switch is turned on in any row or column (unless we are broadcasting). Since each intersection contains a switch that may be open or closed, one control bit is required to represent the position of each switch. The pattern for the first row of switches in Figure G–3 is 01000000. The pattern for the second row is 00000100. A total of 64 control bits are required. A nice feature of the crossbar switch is that any mapping between input and output is possible.

FIGURE G–3

Eight-signal crossbar switch.

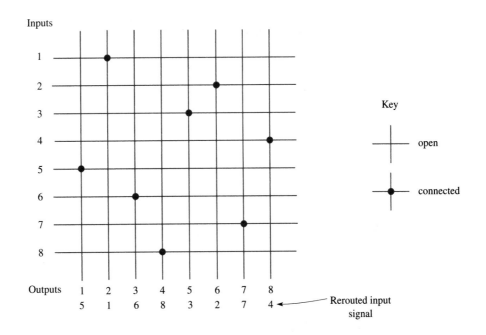

If the cost of 64 switches is too much for your communication budget, a different type of switch can be used to switch eight signals, but with less than half the number of switches. Called a *multistage switch,* it relies on several stages of smaller switches connected in complex ways. Figure G–4 shows a sample three-stage switch capable of switching eight signals. Each smaller switch can be configured as a straight-through or crossover switch, with a single control bit specifying the mode. Now, with only 12 smaller switches, the control information has shrunk from 64 bits in the crossbar switch to only 12 bits. The number of switches is 24 (one switch for straight-through, one switch for crossover, times 12), which is less than half of the 64 required in the crossbar switch.

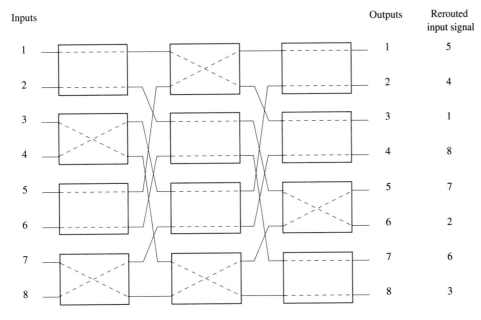

FIGURE G–4

Eight-signal multistage switch.

The price we pay for the simplified hardware in the multistage switch is a smaller number of switching possibilities. For example, in Figure G–4, is it possible to set up the 12 smaller switches so that the output maps to 87654321? The answer is no, indicating that the multistage switch may block some signals from getting to the correct output. This problem is usually temporary because memory buffers are typically used to store data that cannot be transmitted right away.

■ PACKET SWITCHING

Figure G–5 shows a simple WAN connecting four networks (A, B, C, and D). Suppose that a machine on network A wants to send a large chunk of data to a machine on network D. Using packet switching, the large chunk of data is broken down into smaller blocks and transmitted as a series of packets.

FIGURE G–5
Sample WAN.

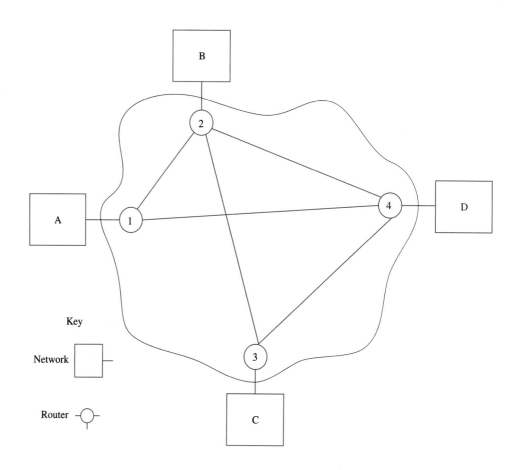

Due to the nature of traffic on shared networks, some packets may go directly from router 1 to router 4 (one hop), whereas others may go from router 1 to router 2, then to router 4 (two hops). A three-hop route is also possible. Thus, it is likely that packets arrive at network D out of order. This is a characteristic of packet switching. Packets can be reassembled in the correct order by including a sequence number within the packet. Even so, this characteristic makes packet switching unsuitable for digitized phone conversations, which, unlike an e-mail message, cannot wait for gaps to be filled in at some unknown later time. These features provide a means for choosing between circuit switching and packet switching.

■ FRAME RELAY

Objective 2-11

Packet switching was designed during a time when digital communication channels were not very reliable. To compensate for errors in a channel, a handshaking arrangement of send-and-acknowledge packets was used to guarantee reliable data transfers. This error protocol added time-consuming overhead to the packet switching network, with transmitting stations constantly waiting for acknowledgments before continuing.

Frame relay takes advantage of the improvement in communication technology (fiber links, for example, have a very low error rate compared with copper links) and relies on fewer acknowledgments during a transfer. Only the receiving station needs to send an acknowledgment.

With fewer acknowledgments and a lower error rate, frame relay provides a significant improvement in communications technology.

■ ATM

Objective 2-11

Asynchronous transfer mode (ATM), also called *cell relay,* uses fixed-size cells of data and supports voice, data, or video at either 155.52 Mbps or 622.08 Mbps. Cells are 53 bytes each, with 5 bytes reserved for a header and the remaining 48 for data, as indicated in Figure G–6. The reason for using fixed-size cells is to simplify routing decisions at intermediate nodes in the ATM system.

FIGURE G–6
An ATM cell.

5-Byte Header	48-Byte Payload

ATM uses communication connections called *virtual channel* connections. A virtual channel is set up between the end-to-end stations on the network and fixed-size cells are sent back and forth. Decisions concerning routing are resolved using information supplied in the ATM header, which is shown in Figure G–7. Notice the entries for virtual path and virtual channel identifiers.

■ ISDN

Objective 2-11

The simplest Integrated Services Data Network (ISDN) connection is called a *basic rate interface,* and consists of two 64 Kbps B channels (for data) and one 16 Kbps D channel (for signaling). The design of ISDN supports circuit-switching, packet-switching, and frame operation. When ISDN is carried over a T1 line (1.544 Mbps), twenty-three 64 Kbps B channels and one 64 Kbps D channel are possible.

■ SONET

Objective 2-11

The Synchronous Optical Network (SONET) technology was designed to take advantage of the high speed of a fiber connection between networks. An equivalent specification is

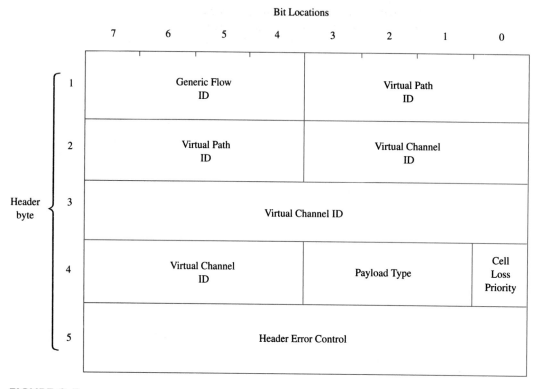

FIGURE G–7
ATM header fields.

called SDH (Synchronous Digital Hierarchy). As Table G–3 indicates, the lowest-speed SONET signal level (STS-1) runs at 51.84 Mbps. That is equivalent to more than nine hundred 56 Kbps modems running simultaneously (minus a few for overhead). STS-48 has 48 times the bandwidth of STS-1, so you can imagine how many telephone calls can be carried over a single STS-48 fiber link.

Table G–3
SONET signal hierarchy.

SONET level	SDH level	Data Rate (Mbps)
STS*-1/OC†-1	x	51.84
STS-3/OC-3	STM‡-1	155.52
STS-9/OC-9	STM-3	466.56
STS-12/OC-12	STM-4	622.08
STS-18/OC-18	STM-6	933.12
STS-24/OC-24	STM-8	1244.16
STS-36/OC-36	STM-12	1866.24
STS-48/OC-48	STM-16	2488.32

*STS (Synchronous Transport Signal)

†OC (Optical Carrier)

‡STM (Synchronous Transport Module)

The STS designations have an equivalent set of optical carrier (OC) designations. There are additional benefits to using fiber: It is not susceptible to electrical noise, it can be run farther distances than copper wire before requiring a repeater to extend the signal, and it is easier to repair. SONET uses a dual-ring topology, with the second ring acting as a backup.

Figure G–8 shows the format of a SONET STS-1 frame. A total of 810 bytes are transmitted in a 125-microsecond time slot. Several bytes from each row of the frame are used for control/status information, such as several 64 Kbps user channels, 192 Kbps and 576 Kbps control, maintenance, and status channels, and several additional signaling items. Note that multiplying 810 bytes/frame by 8000 frames/sec gives 6.48 million bytes/sec, which equals 51.84 Mbps.

FIGURE G–8
SONET STS-1 frame format.

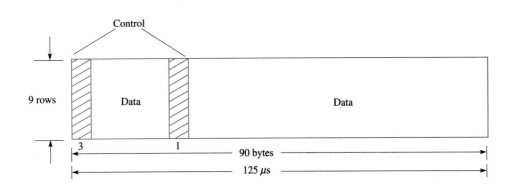

■ FDDI

Objective 1-2

Objective 2-11

The Fiber Distributed Data Network (FDDI) was developed to provide 100 Mbps connections between LANs over a wide geographical area. Dual fiber rings are used, with the second ring serving as a backup for the first ring, called the *primary* ring. A token-passing scheme similar to token-ring technology is used to allow access to the ring.

The use of fiber allows longer distances between stations (or LANs). The FDDI physical layer allows for up to 100 fiber repeaters in the ring, with a spacing of 2 kilometers between repeaters. Thus, the size of the FDDI ring covers a perimeter of 200 kilometers (more than 124 miles). This is an attractive technology for long–distance communication.

■ DENSE WAVE DIVISION MULTIPLEXING (DWDM)

The demands of network users and their applications have pushed even the speed limits of the available fiber-based SONET and FDDI technologies. To provide relief, technology was developed to allow *multiple* channels of light to coexist on the same fiber (by carefully varying the wavelength of the optical carrier, hence the terms *dense* and *division*). Thus, instead of a single OC-48 optical stream (2.4 Gbps), there may be as many as 40 different OC-48 streams, giving a total of 100 Gbps bandwidth. Even more than 40 optical channels will be possible in the future, with 128 channels already being discussed.

Additional benefits of DWDM are

• Easy mixing of different optical carriers

• Longer fiber segments (800 kilometers or more)

• Good for long-haul, point-to-point connections

With fiber optics as the fastest communication medium currently available, DWDM provides one way to keep up with the ever-increasing demand for bandwidth.

■ MOBILE COMMUNICATION

Objective 1-2

Almost by definition, mobile communication implies the use of wireless technologies. The traditional cellular technologies are quickly migrating from analog to digital signals that offer additional features and significantly enhanced security benefits. Older geosynchronous satellite communication systems are being replaced by low earth orbit satellite communication systems that can provide wireless coverage for the entire planet.

Wireless technology is based on the concept of having transmitters and receivers. The transmission of wireless signals falls into two categories: omnidirectional and directional. Omnidirectional signals propagate from the transmitter in all directions, similar to the transmitter used for an AM or FM radio station. A directional signal is focused at the receiver. Using a combination of these two types of signals, many different applications of the technology are possible. Some of these applications are shown in Table G–4.

Table G–4
Wireless technologies applications.

Wireless Technology	Application
Digital Cellular	Voice, Data
Wireless LAN	Voice, Data, Video
Personal Communication System	Voice, Data, Video, Fax, Global Positioning

To accompany the new wireless technologies, the IEEE 802.11 specifications provide a software framework on which to build. A new protocol, DFWMAC (Distributed Foundation Wireless MAC), was created to work in the MAC layer of the OSI network model. A modified version of Ethernet called CSMA/CA (Collision Sense Multiple Access/Collision Avoidance) is used to transmit data in the network.

■ INFRARED NETWORKING

Objective 1-2

Infrared networking takes place between two infrared-compliant devices in a line-of-sight fashion. For example, a user may walk up to a network printer that has an infrared port, point the portable computer's infrared port at the printer, and send a print job to the printer after a connection is automatically established. Two infrared devices will connect to each other just by pointing them at each other (assuming both devices are enabled and within the correct distance). Both devices must be IrDA compliant, the accepted standard for infrared devices. IrDA (Infrared Data Association) is now at version 2.0. If a computer contains an installed infrared port, there will be an entry in the Ports section of Device Manager. The infrared port may use IRQ 3, I/O port 2F8, or DMA channel 3. The infrared port must be enabled in the BIOS setup program. Infrared ports typically use COM4 for serial communication and LPT3 for printing. Infrared ports work best at distances within one or two meters. SIR (serial infrared) operates at 115 Kbps. FIR (fast infrared) operates at speeds up to 4 Mbps. IrDA uses two protocols to establish and maintain an infrared connection. They are IrLAP (IrDA link access protocol) and IrLMP (IrDA link management protocol). IrLAP is used to discover an infrared device and provide a reliable connection between two devices. IrLMP is used to maintain multiple channels over the infrared connection.

■ TELECOMMUNICATION CAREERS

The sophistication of the wide variety of telecommunication equipment requires expertise that is typically beyond that obtained in an ordinary electronics or engineering technology program. Fully developed telecommunication degree programs are now available that train the student in all aspects of the field, using state-of-the-art equipment, such as optical time domain reflectometers, network analyzers, and digital sampling oscilloscopes. Becoming a telecommunication technician or engineer would be a challenging and rewarding pursuit.

Appendix H:
Windows NT/2000
Fault Tolerance

 NETWORK+ OBJECTIVES

This appendix provides information for the following Network+ objectives:

3.1 Identify the basic capabilities (i.e., client support, interoperability, authentication, file and print services, application support, security) of the following server operating systems:

- UNIX/Linux
- NetWare
- Windows
- Macintosh

3.5 Identify the purpose and characteristics of fault tolerance.

4.6 Given a network scenario, interpret visual indicators (e.g., link lights, collision lights, etc.) to determine the nature of the problem.

The Windows NT, 2000, XP, and 2003 operating systems' internal architectures are much more complex than the Windows 95/98 architecture because of the internal modifications necessary to achieve a more stable, reliable, and secure environment. There are basic differences in the way these operating systems provide fault tolerance. These Windows operating systems can accommodate any type and size of organization.

Figure H–1 illustrates all the various components in both the *user* and *kernel* modes of Windows NT.

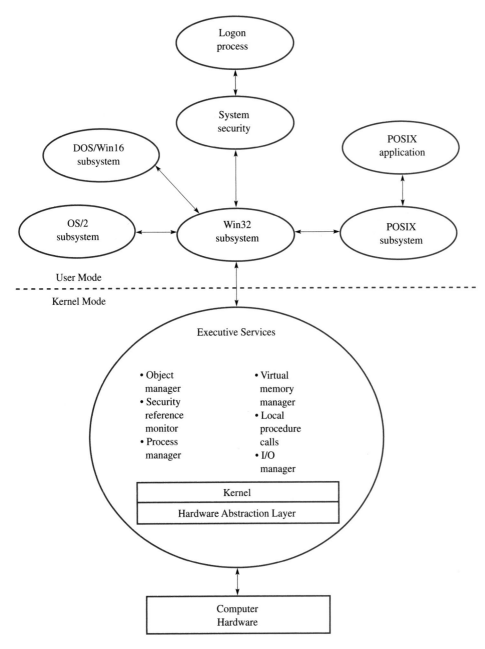

FIGURE H–1
Windows NT system architecture.

■ WINDOWS NT ARCHITECTURE

Notice from Figure H–1 that only the kernel mode has access to the physical hardware, thereby offering a high level of system protection. The executive services provided by the kernel are the foundation on which all other processing activities are performed in user mode. Table H–1 shows a brief description for each of the components in each mode.

Table H–1
Windows NT components.

Component	Description
DOS, Win16, and OS/2 subsystems	Support for applications written for earlier operating systems.
POSIX subsystem	Portable operating system interface for computing environments (POSIX) support.
Win32 subsystem	32-bit API support between application and operating system. Also manages keyboard, mouse, and display I/O for all subsystems.
Object manager	Responsible for creating, naming, protecting, and monitoring objects (operating system resources).
Security reference monitor	Manages security (access to objects).
Process manager	Manages processes and threads.
Virtual memory manager	Implements and manages virtual memory. All processes are allocated a 4 GB virtual address space.
Local procedure calls	Message-passing facility providing communication between client and server processes.
I/O manager	Interfaces with I/O drivers to provide all operating system I/O functions.
Kernel	Schedules tasks (processes of one or more threads) among multiple processors. Manages dispatcher objects and control objects.
Hardware abstraction layer	Provides a machine-independent interface by "virtualizing" the actual hardware of the base system.

■ WINDOWS 2000 ARCHITECTURE

Refinements and enhancements provide even greater system reliability with access to the latest hardware devices. Depending on the size of a particular organization, the Windows 2000 family of operating systems provides many different capabilities to the system administrator. Table H–2 shows the capabilities for the different versions of Windows 2000 that are available. As the size of an organization grows, an appropriate version of Windows 2000 is available.

Table H–2
Windows 2000 family capabilities.

Windows 2000 Product	Number of Supported Processors	Total Physical Memory (GB)	Number of Concurrent Client Connections
Professional	2	4	10
Server	4	4	Unlimited
Advanced Server	8	8	Unlimited
Data Center Product	32	64	Unlimited

Within this larger framework, each version of Windows 2000 performs a similar set of functions to support the operation of the system. Similar to its predecessors, Windows 2000 provides a layer of software (called the Kernel) between the computer hardware and the application programs. The Kernel protects the hardware from a rogue user process by preventing any direct contact with the hardware. At the heart of Windows 2000 is a core group of components that run in Kernel mode and ultimately direct all of a system's activities. Figure H–2 shows a simplified diagram of the interaction between user mode and Kernel mode architecture.

FIGURE H–2
Windows 2000 architecture.

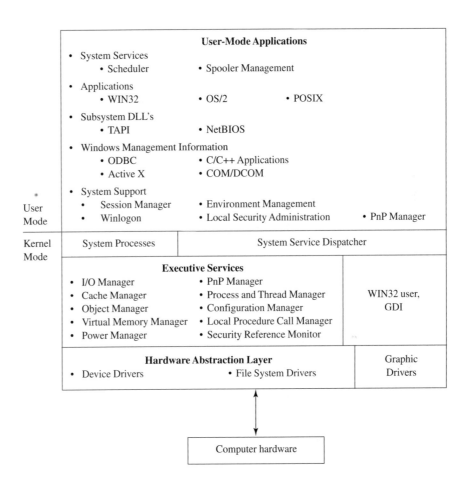

Note that the protection ring security mechanism used in Windows 95/98 is still used in Windows 2000 with ring 0 reserved for Kernel mode processing and ring 3 for User-mode processing (with ring 0 having a higher privilege level than ring 3). In addition, note that there are many new components that are used to make Windows 2000 significantly better than Windows NT. Table H–3 lists the primary Windows 2000 components along with their respective features.

To bring all of these elements together, the system Registry is used to store all of the static and dynamic system information.

When comparing the Windows operating systems to each other, one thing becomes quite clear: An even higher level of control over the allocation of resources will be possible. The price for the increased level of control is complexity. You will want to develop a list of references that you can count on to provide access to the latest information available about new computer and operating system technology. Consult these references frequently to stay abreast of the latest news and information.

Table H–3
Windows 2000 components.

Component	Feature
Cache Manager	Provides efficient services for local and network file systems.
DLL components	Provide access to callable subroutines that are dynamically loaded.
Environment subsystem	Provides support for Win32, OS/2, and POSIX environments.
I/O manager	Performs device-independent I/O.
Kernel routines	Support Windows 2000 operating system functions.
LPC (Local Procedure Call)	Passes messages between client and server processes on the same computer.
LSASS (Local Security Authority Sub System)	A user mode process that manages local security authentication, policies, and access/permissions.
Object Manager	Manipulates Windows 2000 executive objects.
PnP Manager	Assigns appropriate I/O ports, IRQs, DMA channels, and memory to Plug-and-Play devices.
Power Manager	Monitors and reacts to changes in system usage.
Process and Thread Manager	Support execution of programs, threads.
SAM service	Processes local group and user information.
Security Reference Monitor	Logs system events and user-defined auditable activities.
Subsystem DLLs	Support user access to system resources.
System Services	Support process management, spooler management, etc.
System Processes	Required system processes found on every Windows 2000 system.
Virtual Memory Manager	Manages virtual memory system based on a flat 32-bit address space.
Win32	Access to Win32 API.
Windows Management Information	Support for user-mode access to network-based devices.

Objective 3-1

■ WINDOWS XP ARCHITECTURE

Windows XP is built on the same software core code that was used in the NT and 2000 operating systems. XP provides preemptive multitasking, fault tolerance, and system memory protection. These features work to help prevent and solve problems. The reason for all these features is to keep your computer system running smoothly. Windows XP provides the ability to recover your work even if the application crashes before your work is saved. Memory protection works to prevent poorly written software from causing operating system instability. Software can often be installed without rebooting the operating system as required by earlier Windows operating systems.

■ WINDOWS 2003 ARCHITECTURE

Windows 2003 uses RAID and clustering technologies to provide fault-tolerant storage. Windows 2003 is designed to meet the needs of organizations that cannot tolerate downtime.

■ FAULT TOLERANCE IN WINDOWS

Objective 3-5

Fault tolerance is the ability to tolerate failures in system hardware. Consider a networked environment in which many users access files on a shared server. What would happen if the server loses a hard drive, or even just one or more files? The impact on the network could be substantial. Windows NT, 2000, and 2003 use a technology called *RAID* that can help prevent this type of hardware failure.

RAID stands for Redundant Array of Inexpensive Disks. Figure H–3 shows a RAID-based server computer. Four hot-swappable drives are shown at the bottom right of the unit. A system using RAID uses two or more hard drives to implement fault tolerance.

FIGURE H–3
Server computer containing 4-drive RAID storage.

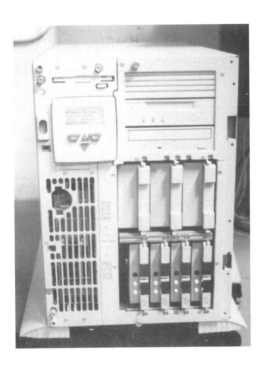

Windows NT supports three levels of RAID technology:

- *RAID Level 0:* Stripe Sets
- *RAID Level 1:* Disk Mirroring
- *RAID Level 5:* Stripe Sets with Parity

The features of these technologies include:

- **RAID Level 0: Stripe Sets**   In this technique, files are read/written in 64K chunks simultaneously using from 2 to 32 physical drives. The data is not duplicated. Figure H–4 shows how two drives are used to store a large file.

  It is important to note that using a stripe set does not provide fault tolerance, since data is not duplicated on the drives. Performance is improved, however, because of the parallelism available during reads and writes. For example, the large file in Figure H–3 requires only two reads from each disk to access the entire file. Each read brings in 128K (64K from each disk at the same time). Write operations are similarly improved.

  A disadvantage to using stripe sets is that system and boot partitions may not be stored on them.

- **RAID Level 1: Disk Mirroring**   Disk mirroring is used to make an exact copy of data on two drives. Data is written to both drives simultaneously. If one drive fails, the second drive still has a good copy of the data, so the system is not affected. Both system and boot partitions may be mirrored. Figure H–5 shows how a file is mirrored.

  Typically, one controller is used to control both drives. A special variation of disk mirroring is disk duplexing, in which each drive has its own controller. This provides additional fault tolerance, since now a drive or a controller may fail without affecting the system.

  A disadvantage to using disk mirroring is that you get only 50% of the hard drive space you pay for. For example, using two 8 GB drives provides only 8 GB of storage capacity. Using the same drives in a stripe set would provide 16 GB of capacity (but no fault tolerance).

FIGURE H–4
RAID level 0: Stripe sets.

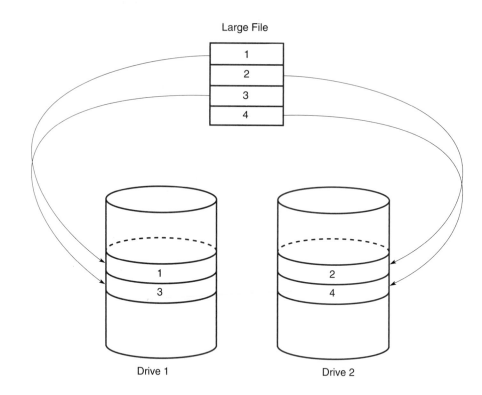

FIGURE H–5
RAID level 1: Disk mirroring.

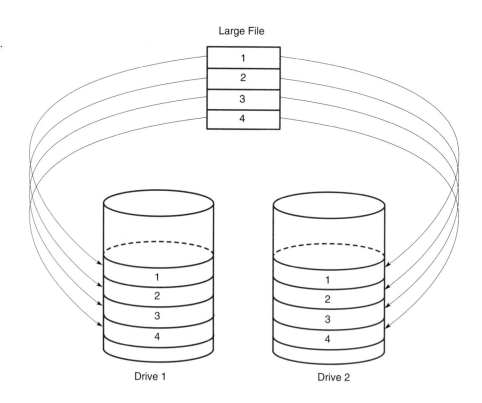

- **RAID Level 5: Stripe Sets with Parity** This technique is similar to ordinary stripe sets, except that parity information is also written to each disk, as indicated in Figure H–6. If one of the drives in the stripe set fails, the parity data stored on each drive can be used to reconstruct the missing data.

FIGURE H–6
RAID level 5: Stripe sets with parity.

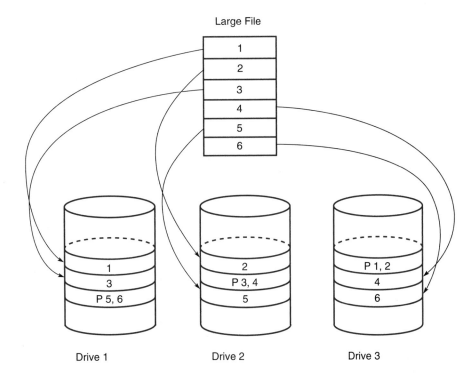

A minimum of three drives must be used to employ RAID level 5. A maximum of 32 drives is allowed. The equivalent of one drive is used for parity information, even though parity is distributed across all drives. The available data capacity can be found by the following equation:

$$\text{Capacity} = \frac{\text{Drives} - 1}{\text{Drives}} \times 100\%$$

Therefore, with three drives, the available storage capacity for data is 66%. For four drives, the capacity becomes 75%.

A disadvantage to using stripe sets with parity is that extra system memory is required for the parity calculations. File servers should be equipped with enough RAM to handle the additional workload.

Appendix I:
Setting Up a
Networking
Repair Shop

▬◯▶ NETWORK+ OBJECTIVES

This appendix provides information for the following Network+ objectives:

1.4 Recognize the following media connectors and/or describe their uses:
- RJ-11
- RJ-45
- AUI
- BNC
- ST
- SC

1.5 Choose the appropriate media type and connectors to add a client to an existing network.

4.5 Given a wiring task, select the appropriate tool (e.g., wire crimper, media tester/certifier, punch-down tool, tone generator, optical tester, etc.).

This appendix covers some of the items necessary to begin repairing computer networks. It is not the author's intention that you start your own business after reading this appendix, or even after having read this entire book. Rather, this appendix provides a starting point for your own investigation into what is required in a network repair shop.

■ TOOLS

You need tools to perform repairs and upgrades to your customers' computers. You may need to replace or install disk drives, motherboards, power supplies, network adapter cards, coprocessors, and/or RAM. You should plan to include the following tools in your toolkit:

- Screwdriver assortment (flat-blade and Phillips)
- Plier assortment (large and long-nose)
- Wrench assortment
- Nut drivers
- Wire cutter strippers
- IC extractor
- Soldering iron
- Files
- Magnifying glass

The wire cutter stripper and the soldering iron are used to fix worn or broken cables. It is not recommended that you use a soldering iron to remove or replace any nonsocketed ICs.

■ GENERAL HAND TOOLS

Hand tools are instruments used with the hands to extend the hands' working capabilities. During a repair job, hand tools are used to aid in the disassembly and reassembly of microcomputer equipment and parts. They are not intended to serve as any kind of electrical testing devices; attempting to use them in this manner is very dangerous.

Figure I–1 illustrates the hand tools that will be used in this appendix.

All the hand tools shown in Figure I–1 are made of metal. Because metal is a good conductor of electricity, such tools present a potential shock hazard when used in working with electrical equipment. Properly made hand tools for working on electrical equipment have metal handles that are insulated with a rubber coating or cast in an insulating plastic. This is illustrated in Figure I–2.

Note from Figure I–2 that when using hand tools on electrical equipment, you do not touch the metal part of the hand tool with any part of your body. By grasping the tool only on the insulating material, you reduce your chance of electrical shock. Recall that an insulator is not a good conductor of electricity. Hand tools on which the insulation is frayed or has been removed should not be used; it is best to discard such tools for a new set.

Diagonal Cutters

Figure I–3 illustrates a typical set of diagonal cutters and the correct way to use them. As illustrated, diagonal cutters can be damaged by cutting thick material close to the ends of the cutting tips.

FIGURE I–I
Hand tools for microcomputer repair.

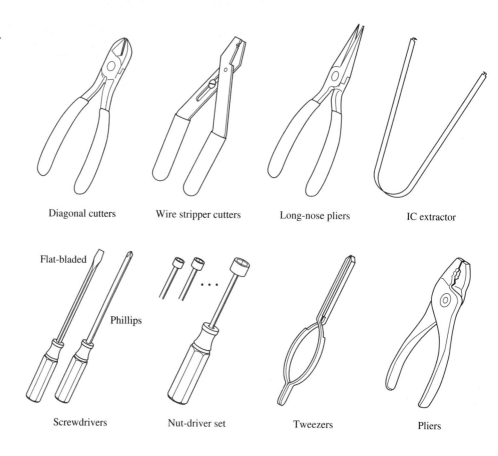

Diagonal cutters Wire stripper cutters Long-nose pliers IC extractor

Flat-bladed Phillips

Screwdrivers Nut-driver set Tweezers Pliers

FIGURE I–2
Insulated hand tools.

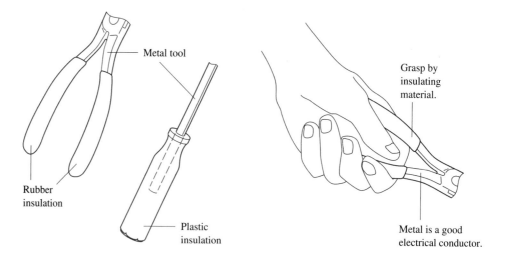

Metal tool

Rubber insulation

Plastic insulation

Grasp by insulating material.

Metal is a good electrical conductor.

FIGURE I–3
Diagonal cutters.

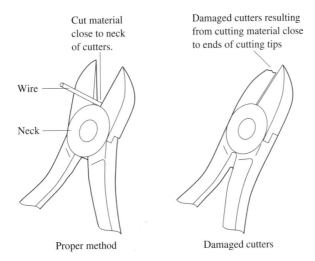

Wire Stripper Cutters

Figure I–4 illustrates a typical set of wire stripper cutters. As shown in the figure, these instruments are used to strip the insulation from wire to prepare the wire for use in an electrical connection.

FIGURE I–4
Wire stripper cutters.

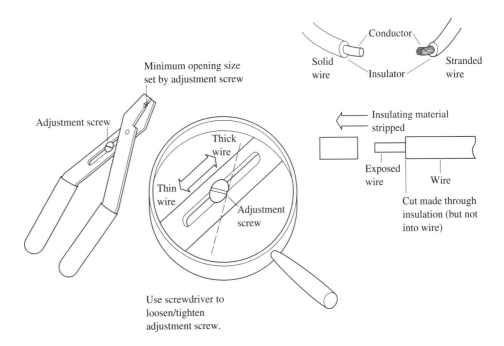

Notice from Figure I–4 that the minimum size of the wire stripper opening must be small enough to cut through the insulation of the wire completely, but not so small as to cut or nick the wire itself.

Long-Nose Pliers

Figure I–5 shows a typical set of long-nose (sometimes called needlenose) pliers. As shown in the figure, these pliers are not intended for use in removing hardware such as nuts and bolts. Such misuse can result in permanent damage to these tools.

FIGURE I–5
Long-nose pliers.

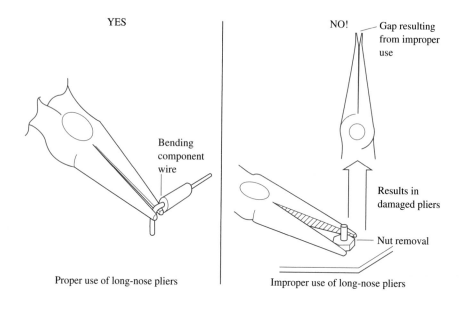

Long-nose pliers come in various sizes. Keep in mind that these are delicate instruments intended for delicate work, not for removing nuts and bolts.

Flat-Blade and Phillips Screwdrivers

A typical set of flat-blade and Phillips screwdrivers is shown in Figure I–6. These screwdrivers come in various sizes and may use a carbide tip for strength. They are intended to be used for the insertion and removal of screws. Remember to use a screwdriver of the right size for the job at hand.

FIGURE I–6
Flat-blade and Phillips screwdrivers.

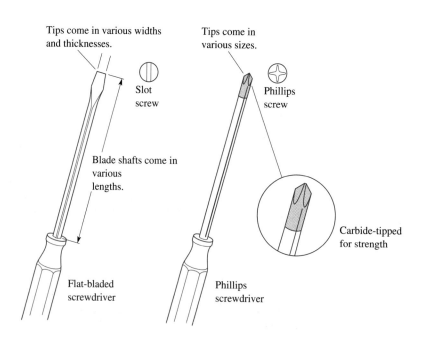

IC Extractors

Figure I–7 shows typical IC (integrated circuit) extractors. As shown in the figure, these instruments are intended for the removal of IC packages. It's important that all power be disconnected from the system before an IC is removed.

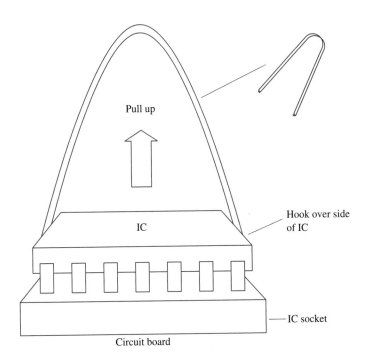

(a) DIP (Dual Inline Package) extractor.

(b) PLCC (Plastic-Leaded Chip Carrier) extra

FIGURE I–7
IC extractors.

Antistatic Wrist Strap

Static electricity can damage many types of integrated circuits, including CPU and memory devices. To avoid static damage during handling, it is common to wear an antistatic wrist strap. A typical strap is shown in Figure I–8(a). The strap wraps around your wrist and connects to a ground terminal via an attached cable, as indicated in Figure I–8(b). The cable provides a path to ground for any static electricity encountered. A resistor built into the cable is typically used to reduce the current flow during a discharge.

Antistatic mats or pads may also be used. These are placed on top of the workbench and provide a safe surface for equipment and electronics.

Tweezers

A typical pair of tweezers used in microcomputer repair is shown in Figure I–9. Tweezers may also be used as a soldering aid. Be careful of static problems introduced by tweezers.

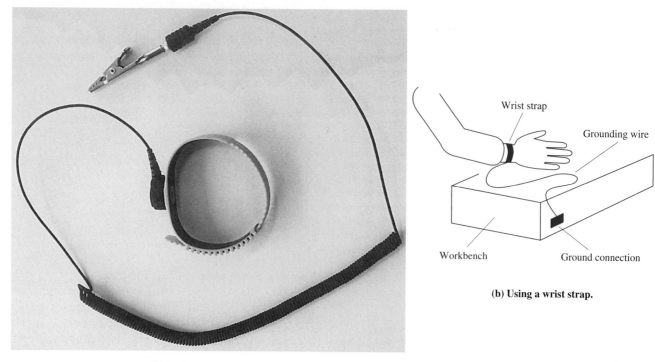

(a) Antistatic wrist strap.

(b) Using a wrist strap.

FIGURE I–8
Protection against static.

FIGURE I–9
Tweezers.

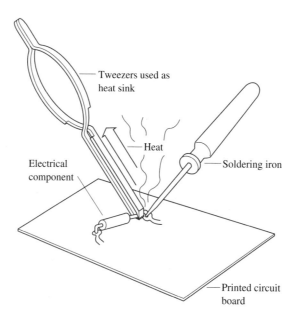

Nut Drivers

Figure I–10 illustrates a typical nut driver. As shown in the figure, nut drivers are not adjustable and therefore come in various sizes to accommodate different-sized nuts. Note that these instruments present a small surface area, thus causing minimum marring of computer surfaces. Nut drivers are always the preferred instruments for loosening or tightening of nuts.

FIGURE I–10
Nut driver.

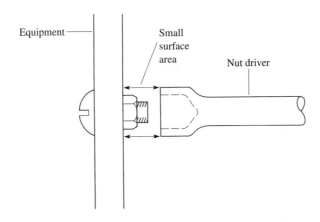

Digital Multimeter

The Digital MultiMeter (DMM) shown in Figure I–11 is used to measure voltage, current, and resistance. Buttons are used to select the quantity being measured and the scale for the measure value. The DMM can be used to easily verify the correct power supply voltages or the continuity of a signal cable. To measure voltage (such as the 5 V output from a power supply) place the black probe on ground and place the red probe on the voltage connector.

FIGURE I–11
Digital multimeter and probes.

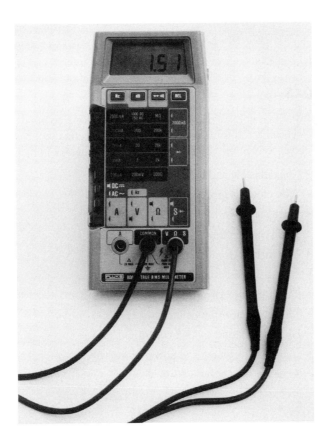

A wise man once said, "Let the tool do the work for you." That is good advice. Using the wrong tool can result in a damaged tool or piece of equipment and increase the risk of physical injury. It is well worth the investment to purchase a complete set of tools so that you will always have the right tool for the job. Figure I–12 shows a tool set designed for electronic repairs.

FIGURE I–12
Assortment of tools for
electronic repair.

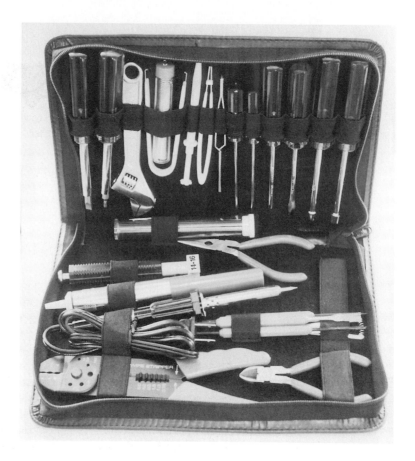

■ NETWORKING TOOLS

Objective 4-5

Installing, upgrading, and repairing networking components (cards, cables, hubs) requires a special set of tools, possibly kept in a separate tool case so that network jobs and computer jobs can be easily prepared for. This set should include the following tools:

• Coaxial cable and UTP cable crimpers
• Wire cutter strippers
• Spare cable (with and without connectors)
• Spare connectors (BNC, RJ-45)
• T-connector (for tapping into coax)
• 10BASE2-to-10BASE-T transceiver
• Cable tester or DMM
• Tone generator (phone line)
• Punch-down tool (phone wiring)
• Optical light source and power meter (fiber)
• Spare hub and several NICs
• Protocol analyzer (hardware, software, or both)

■ TELEPHONE WIRING TOOLS

Installing, repairing, and testing telephone wiring is accomplished with the tools and wiring blocks shown in Figures I–13, I–14, and I–15. Figure I–13 shows two punch-down tools that are used to push insulated telephone wire down into a thin slot in the metal connector of the wiring block.

FIGURE I–13

Punch-down tools used in telephone wiring.

The wiring block, called a type-66 punch-down block, is shown in Figure I–14. There are 50 rows of connectors, with four columns to each row. This provides for 12 four-pair phone lines, or 25 two-pair phone lines. Columns 1 and 2 (the incoming signal columns) are connected in each row, as are columns 3 and 4 (the outgoing signal columns). The incoming signals come from the telephone. The outgoing signals connect the punch-down block to the local PBX or outgoing phone lines. A small metal jumper can be placed between columns 2 and 3 to make a straight-through connection.

FIGURE I–14

Using a punch-down tool to connect telephone wire to a type-66 punch-down block.

A similar punch-down block, called a type-110 punch-down block, is used for network patch panels and contains impedance matching, which is critical for high-speed digital communications (such as 100 Mbps Ethernet).

Figure I–15 shows an audio tone generator/continuity tester and audio amplifier (for listening to the generated tone on the wires). These tools are especially helpful when trying to trace a pair of conductors through a maze of wiring. The tone generator leads clip onto a pair of wires, and an audio tone is output onto the wires. The tone plays through the audio amplifier when the probe is near the correct pair of wires.

FIGURE I–15
Telephone wire tone/continuity tester and amplifier.

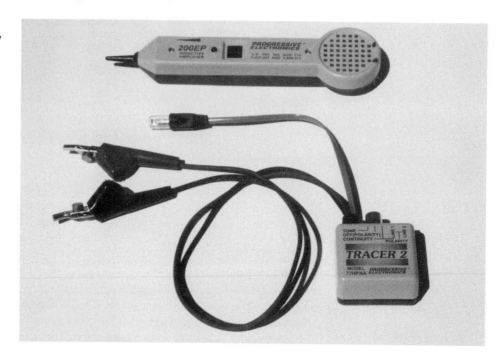

Coaxial Cable Crimper

Figure I–16 shows a coaxial cable crimper. After stripping off the outer jacket of a coaxial cable and inserting a BNC connector, the crimper is used to forcibly compress the metal casing of the connector, firmly connecting it with the ground shield mesh of the coaxial cable.

FIGURE I–16
Coaxial cable crimper.

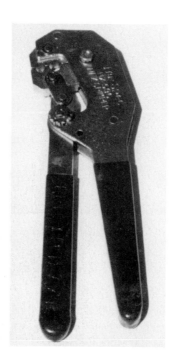

■ UTP CABLE TOOLS

Figure I–17 shows the tool used to strip the jacket off a UTP cable prior to mounting a new RJ-45 connector on it. The jacket stripper is clamped over the cable approximately one inch from the end and slowly rotated around the cable. A sharp metal edge scores the jacket, allowing you to pull it off, exposing the twisted pairs inside.

FIGURE I–17
Jacket stripper for UTP cable.

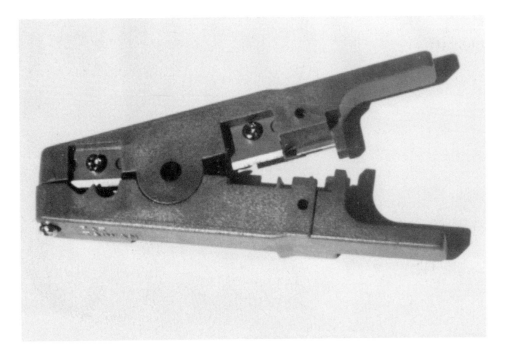

After the ends are untwisted, color-aligned, trimmed to the correct length, and inserted into the new RJ-45 connector, the crimping tool illustrated in Figure I–18 is used to mate the connector to the cable. The newly attached RJ-45 connector is inserted into the crimper, and pressure is applied to the connector to establish connections between the insulated UTP cable wires and the metal pins in the connector.

FIGURE I–18
RJ-45 crimping tool.

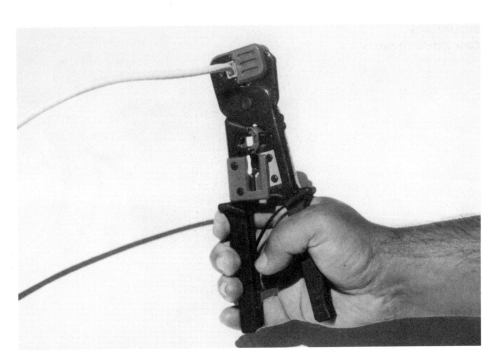

Compare the ends of the UTP cable shown in Figure I–19. The end on the left side of the figure is a factory termination, and the end on the right a termination performed by a technician. Note that there are no untwisted wires protruding from the RJ-45 connector. With only a little practice, mounting a new RJ-45 connector becomes an easy task.

FIGURE I–19
Ends of the UTP cable.

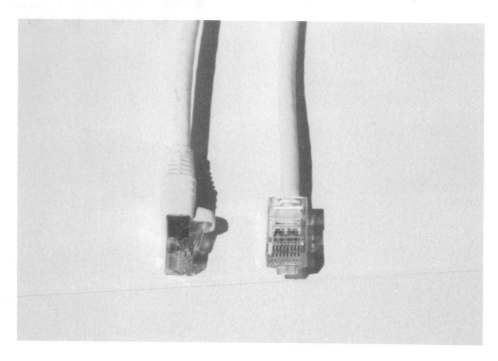

■ FIBER-OPTIC CABLE TOOLS

Before and after installing a new section of fiber-optic cable, or whenever the end of a fiber is re-terminated with a new connector, the power loss of the cable should be measured. Power loss in a fiber-optic cable is due to scattering of light within the cable and can be measured using a fiber-optic light source and power meter, such as those shown in Figure I–20. The cabling shown in the figure is 62.5/125-micrometer duplex multimode fiber with ST connectors.

FIGURE I–20
Fiber-optic light source and power meter.

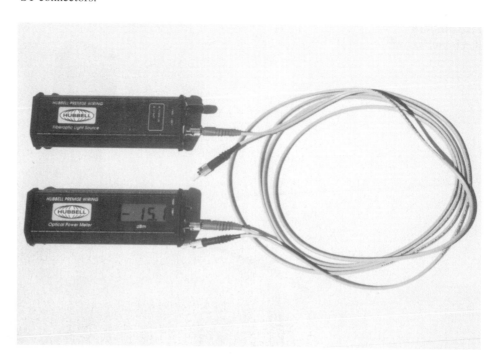

The light source outputs a known quantity of power, and the power meter reads the power arriving at the end of the fiber being tested.

Locating a fault in a long fiber-optic cable (hundreds or thousands of feet) is accomplished with the use of an OTDR (Optical Time Domain Reflectometer). Figure I–21 shows the front panel of an OTDR, which graphically displays the reflection profile of an optical fiber. Changes in the profile are used to determine the distance to the fault in the cable.

FIGURE I–21
Optical time domain reflectometer used to measure distance to a fault, such as an open cable, in a fiber-optic cable.

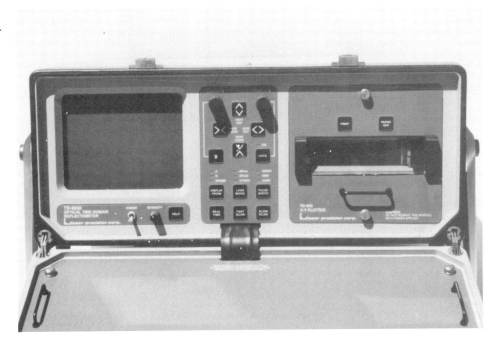

■ LEGACY NETWORK COMPONENTS

Objective 1-4

Legacy devices can be defined as devices that no longer meet the current standards relating to speed and ability. Think back to the days when a 100-megabyte hard drive was thought to be all any user could ever need. Although it is rare to find old coaxial Ethernet segments or heavy use of AUI cables to connect network devices, it is a good idea to keep an older, but still functioning, network component handy, such as the Ethernet hub shown in Figure I–22. A look at the back panel shows three different 10 Mbps Ethernet connectors: BNC (10BASE2), AUI, and RJ-45 (10BASE-T). One piece of legacy equipment provides the capability to work with three different networking technologies. It should be noted that legacy hardware may not provide the speed and functionality required of new networking hardware.

FIGURE I–22
Ethernet hub containing BNC, AUI, and RJ-45 connectors.

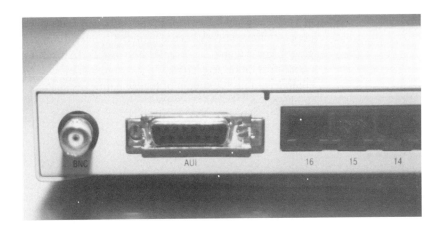

Spare Parts

Sometimes a seemingly unrelated problem interferes with network operation in a computer. If you find a bad or broken part in a machine, you will save a great deal of time and effort if you have a replacement handy. Driving to a hardware store or a computer store to get a replacement will cost you more in the long run by virtue of lost repair or installation time.

Spare parts for a typical microcomputer system are numerous. Some of the most important ones include:

- Nut, washer, and screw assortment
- Metal and insulated standoffs
- Power cords
- Printer cables
- Null-modem cable
- SIMMs, DIMMs, and RIMMs
- Cache RAM
- Resistors and capacitors
- Common semiconductor devices (diodes, transistors)
- I/O connectors (9- and 25-pin male and female)
- I/O adapter cables (male-male, female-female, male-female)
- Ribbon cable with crimp-on connectors
- Power splitter adapter cable
- LEDs (for front panel indicators)
- Push buttons (for RESET and TURBO buttons)
- Metal slot guards
- Fuses
- Plastic face plates
- Muffin fans
- Processor fans
- Processors
- Motherboards
- Floppy drives
- IDE and SCSI hard drives
- An assortment of adapter cards
- Printer cartridge and paper
- Blank disks

Objective 1-5

The size of your spare parts inventory will determine what kind of service you can provide to your customers. Remember that although Ethernet networks are considered the most popular, other networks in use by individuals and companies will also require repairs or upgrades. For example, a customer who installed a token-ring network years ago and is happy with its operation sees no reason to spend money switching over to Ethernet. But what if a component fails? A supply of legacy hardware, such as the token-ring components shown in Figure I–23, is also suggested.

■ EQUIPMENT

Although you will encourage your customers to bring their entire systems in for repair or upgrading, you will need equipment of your own to handle some jobs. The most important piece of equipment your repair shop should contain is one or more computer

FIGURE I–23
Token-ring MAU, STP cable, and NIC.

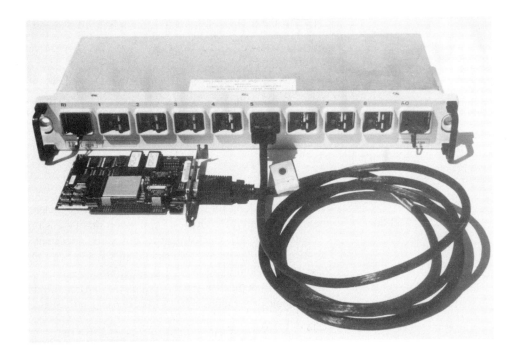

systems, complete with mouse, sound card, CD-ROM, lots of RAM, and the most current processor. This will allow you to test both hardware and software from a customer's system in your own system (as a last resort). The systems should all be networked together, with all types of network media and components. Figure I–24 shows the networking rack in a small networking laboratory. Note the many different cabling types and networking components.

FIGURE I–24
Networking rack containing hubs, switches, a cable modem, 100 Mbps fiber-optic transceiver, and UTP patch panels.

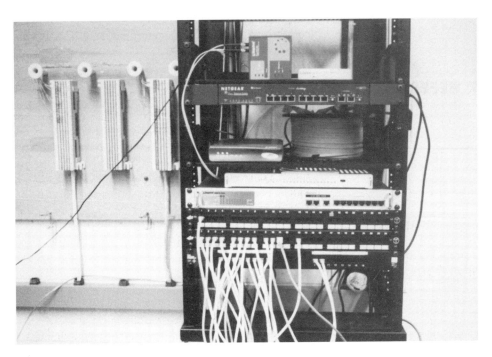

In addition, the following equipment may also come in handy:

- Multimeter
- Logic probe/analyzer
- Oscilloscope

The multimeter allows you to find broken wires in cables and missing power supply voltages. The logic probe/analyzer and the oscilloscope enable you to monitor the activity of a signal or a pin on an IC, with the scope providing much more information than the logic probe.

Software

It would be asking for trouble for you to run a customer's software on your own machine before checking it for viruses. Or, if a portion of a customer's Windows directory was accidentally deleted, what happens if the customer does not have the installation disks? These are two examples of why you should also maintain a software library in your repair shop. The library should be strictly for repairing damaged software, and not for doing free installations of popular programs (unless they are shareware).

Some of the more useful software packages to have in your library might include the following:

- Virus scanner
- DOS (versions 3.0 and up)
- Windows, Linux, Macintosh, and NetWare (all versions)
- CD-ROMs (for testing CD-ROM installations/problems)
- Typical DOS and Windows applications
- 3.5- and 5.25-inch system disks
- Modem software
- Network protocol analyzer (Ethereal)
- Data exchange software (such as FastLynx)
- Specialized diagnostic software (such as Norton Disk Doctor)
- Hard drive software (such as Partition Magic)

Making changes to a computer's network configuration may require the original OS installation CD (particularly true for Windows computers), so OS installation software is considered an important component of the software library.

■ REFERENCES

Eventually, even the best network technician reaches a dead end and requires an external source of information to help solve a problem. Most bookstores now have entire sections filled with books on practically every networking subject, from building your own network to advanced security applications. You may benefit greatly from owning one or more references. At the very least, you will pick up valuable information by just reading the books. The following are a few easy-to-find types of references:

- PC network hardware references
- PC network software references
- Manuals for printers, modems, hard drives, and other hardware devices
- BIOS and DOS references
- PC interrupt reference
- TCP/IP reference
- Cabling reference

■ THE BUSINESS ASPECT

Just having the technical skills to diagnose and repair computer networks is not enough to open your own business. There are many aspects of running a business that must be examined and provided for. Some of the required office supplies include:

- Office space (and the associated rent and utilities)
- Office supplies (paper, pens, etc.)
- Fax machine
- Postal supplies
- Cash register and credit card reader

In addition, someone will need to "do the books," keep track of sales and expenses, fill out tax forms, manage the business account at the bank, and generally do everything associated with running a business except for the repair part. If your interest in repairing networks does not include the business aspects, you have already grown to a business of two people, since you will need to hire an office manager.

The alternative to all of this is running the business out of your own home, which reduces or eliminates many of the costs. Then you simply may use an accountant to help with the business end of things.

Clearly, starting your own business is a major step and must be considered and planned very carefully.

■ PROBLEM/SOLUTION JOURNAL

Whether or not you open your own repair shop, as a user of computers you will eventually find yourself staring at an error message that you have never seen before, and you will have to figure out what to do. It would be a good idea to write down the problem and its eventual solution in a problem/solution journal. Keep track of all the strange network problems that you encounter. Often, a problem comes back again, and you may not remember exactly what you did to fix it. Windows problems are especially notorious in this regard and also difficult to diagnose. Keeping a journal of your repair (and installation) efforts will be rewarding in the long run.

■ TROUBLESHOOTING TECHNIQUES

When you begin a new repair job, it is important to ask yourself a few questions. Did the computer or network ever work? If it was working, your job should require less effort to repair than a system that never worked. For example, if a customer's laser printer suddenly quits, there are several obvious things to check, such as cabling, fuses, the power cord, toner level, and network/printer drivers. If, however, a customer complains that the 32-node network they just installed themselves does not work, your job is much different. It is possible that the network may never work, no matter what you do. Or the problem could be as simple as bad crimps on the connectors.

In general, it pays to think about these things before you even begin a repair job. You may save yourself time and effort.

Answers to Self-Test Questions

Chapter 1—Self-Test Answers

1. C   2. A   3. D   4. C   5. B   6. C   7. False   8. B
9. B   10. C   11. A, D   12. A, B, D   13. B   14. A
15. C   16. B   17. D   18. D   19. B   20. D   21. C
22. C   23. D   24. C   25. B

Chapter 2—Self-Test Answers

1. False   2. A, B   3. B   4. D   5. A   6. B   7. C
8. B   9. D   10. C   11. False   12. B   13. B   14. B
15. B   16. A   17. D   18. C   19. B   20. B   21. A
22. B   23. A   24. B   25. A

Chapter 3—Self-Test Answers

1. B   2. B   3. B   4. A   5. B   6. A   7. D
8. B, E, D   9. C   10. C   11. C   12. B   13. C   14. B
15. True   16. C   17. False   18. D   19. False   20. B
21. True   22. True   23. D   24. False   25. False   26. C
27. A   28. D

Chapter 4—Self-Test Answers

1. False   2. B   3. False   4. D   5. C   6. False   7. B
8. True   9. B   10. False   11. B   12. A, D   13. True
14. C   15. C   16. B   17. True   18. B   19. C   20. False
21. D   22. B   23. A   24. A   25. False   26. B   27. B
28. B

Chapter 5—Self-Test Answers

1. A   2. D   3. C   4. D   5. A   6. False   7. B   8. C
9. B   10. C   11. A   12. True   13. False   14. A
15. True   16. B, C   17. False   18. D   19. True   20. B
21. B   22. D   23. C   24. A   25. False   26. A

Chapter 6—Self-Test Answers

1. C   2. B   3. True   4. C   5. C   6. D   7. A, C
8. A, D   9. C   10. D   11. True   12. C   13. B   14. B
15. D   16. A   17. B   18. False   19. C   20. True   21. B
22. D   23. A   24. C   25. C

Chapter 7—Self-Test Answers

1. D   2. True   3. A   4. C   5. D   6. False   7. C
8. A   9. D   10. A   11. B   12. D   13. D   14. False
15. D   16. A   17. D   18. D   19. B   20. C   21. A
22. B   23. C   24. False   25. True

Chapter 8—Self-Test Answers

1. B 2. C 3. C 4. D 5. D 6. B 7. A 8. A
9. D 10. B 11. A, B 12. D 13. C 14. C 15. D
16. B 17. A 18. B 19. D 20. A 21. B 22. B
23. C 24. A 25. C

Chapter 9—Self-Test Answers

1. A 2. C 3. C 4. A 5. C 6. C 7. B 8. A
9. C 10. C 11. D 12. B 13. A 14. D 15. B
16. C 17. D 18. B 19. C 20. C 21. A 22. False
23. B 24. A 25. True

Chapter 10—Self-Test Answers

1. False 2. C 3. C 4. C 5. D 6. C 7. D 8. B
9. False 10. B 11. D 12. B 13. True 14. C, A
15. B 16. A 17. C 18. C 19. B 20. B 21. B
22. A 23. B 24. A 25. B

Chapter 11—Self-Test Answers

1. A, B, C 2. B 3. C 4. A 5. C 6. D 7. C
8. D 9. D 10. A, C 11. D 12. C 13. True 14. C
15. True 16. D 17. False 18. False 19. D 20. D
21. True 22. D 23. C 24. B 25. D

Chapter 12—Self-Test Answers

1. A, C, D 2. C 3. A 4. D 5. C 6. D 7. A
8. A 9. A, B 10. False 11. True 12. A 13. True
14. B 15. D 16. D 17. True 18. A 19. D 20. B
21. A 22. A 23. False 24. True 25. C

Chapter 13—Self-Test Answers

1. B 2. B 3. A 4. C 5. A 6. A 7. B 8. C
9. A 10. C 11. C 12. C 13. B 14. C 15. A
16. True 17. False 18. True 19. C 20. False 21. True
22. A, B, E, F 23. D 24. B 25. B 26. D

Chapter 14—Self-Test Answers

1. B 2. B 3. B 4. B 5. D 6. True 7. C 8. B
9. C 10. True 11. A 12. C 13. D 14. True 15. B
16. True 17. C 18. False 19. True 20. B 21. B 22. D
23. False 24. A 25. B

Chapter 15—Self-Test Answers

1. A 2. False 3. B 4. A 5. A 6. False 7. B 8. D
9. True 10. A 11. B 12. D 13. B 14. D 15. A
16. False 17. True 18. A 19. B 20. B 21. True
22. A 23. C 24. B 25. A

Chapter 16—Self-Test Answers

1. A, D 2. False 3. D 4. C 5. C 6. C 7. False
8. D 9. C 10. B 11. C 12. B 13. B 14. D
15. C 16. D 17. B 18. C, D 19. B 20. C 21. True
22. C 23. A 24. B 25. B

Chapter 17—Self-Test Answers

1. C	2. A	3. A	4. True	5. C	6. C	7. B	8. B, C
9. D	10. D	11. True	12. D	13. B	14. B	15. C	
16. C	17. A, B	18. C	19. B	20. B	21. True	22. B	
23. False	24. True	25. C, D					

Chapter 18—Self-Test Answers

1. False	2. D	3. B	4. D	5. B	6. B, C	7. B
8. True	9. C	10. A	11. B	12. C	13. D	14. B
15. A	16. B	17. B	18. A	19. C	20. A	21. D
22. True	23. C	24. A	25. C			

Chapter 19—Self-Test Answers

1. A	2. B	3. C	4. C	5. C	6. B	7. C	8. B
9. A, B	10. True	11. D	12. True	13. A, C	14. C		
15. A	16. False	17. True	18. A	19. C	20. B	21. C	
22. D	23. A, D	24. True	25. A = 3, B = 3, C = 2, D = 1				

INDEX